# Mastering Palo Alto Networks

Deploy and manage industry-leading PAN-OS 10.x solutions to secure your users and infrastructure

**Tom Piens**

**Packt>**

BIRMINGHAM—MUMBAI

# Mastering Palo Alto Networks

**Commissioning Editor**: Vijin Boricha
**Acquisition Editor**: Paulson Philip
**Senior Editor**: Shazeen Iqbal
**Content Development Editor**: Ronn Kurien
**Technical Editor**: Sarvesh Jaywant
**Copy Editor**: Safis Editing
**Project Coordinator**: Neil Dmello
**Proofreader**: Safis Editing
**Indexer**: Rekha Nair
**Production Designer**: Alishon Mendonca

First published: September 2020

Production reference: 1060820

Published by Packt Publishing Ltd.
Livery Place
35 Livery Street
Birmingham
B3 2PB, UK.

ISBN 978-1-78995-637-5

www.packt.com

# Packt>

# Contributors

## About the author

**Tom Piens**, PCNSE, CISSP, and founder of PANgurus, has nearly 10 years of experience working with Palo Alto Networks customers. Tom has been at the forefront of engaging with customers, responding to questions, and analyzing unique needs to apply the best possible solutions or workarounds. He has authored a great many articles on the Palo Alto Networks knowledge base and discussion forum solutions, including the popular Getting Started series. Also known as "reaper" on the PANgurus and LIVEcommunity forums, and @PANWreaper on Twitter, Tom has been recognized by Palo Alto Networks user groups and community members, and by countless thankful customers.

*I am extremely lucky to have a loving and supporting wife and son that helped me stay inspired working long hours into the night writing this book.*

*Special mentions to Kim Wens and Ron Cowen for making sure my content is accurate, and Kris "Ndx" for sharing his insights.*

*I am very grateful to Gail Wilson and Ronn Kurien for their editorial insights and Gina Hancher for her mentorship.*

*Special thanks to Andrea Simon for always being there.*

# About the reviewers

**Kim Wens** has been an IT network and IT security enthusiast for over 23 years. All these years of experience have molded Kim into a solution-minded security engineer with a take-action mentality. Kim also loves to share his acquired knowledge through discussion forums, technical writings, and educational videos. Kim has worked together with the author for over 20 years for different companies.

**Ron Cowen** has been in the network security industry for over a decade, spanning roles at AT&T, Juniper Networks, and his current position as a security architect for Palo Alto Networks. He is based in Seattle, WA.

*I'd like to acknowledge and thank all of those who have supported, and those who continue to support, my growth as a network security professional, as well as my wife and our two daughters.*

# Packt is searching for authors like you

If you're interested in becoming an author for Packt, please visit `authors.packtpub.com` and apply today. We have worked with thousands of developers and tech professionals, just like you, to help them share their insight with the global tech community. You can make a general application, apply for a specific hot topic that we are recruiting an author for, or submit your own idea.

# Table of Contents

# Section 2: Advanced Configuration and Putting the Features to Work

## 3

## Building Strong Policies

## 4

## Taking Control of Sessions

# 5

# Services and Operational Modes

# 6

# Identifying Users and Controlling  Access

# 7

# Managing Firewalls through Panorama

# Section 3: Maintenance and Troubleshooting

# 8

## Upgrading Firewalls and Panorama

# 9

## Logging and Reporting

# 10
# VPN and Advanced Protection

# 11
# Troubleshooting Common Session Issues

# 12
# A Deep Dive into Troubleshooting

# 13
## Supporting Tools

## Other Books You May Enjoy

## Index

# Preface

*Mastering Palo Alto Networks* covers all aspects of configuring and maintaining Palo Alto Networks firewalls and Panorama management systems. We start with setting up a new system from the factory default settings and learning how the technology works, and move on to building advanced configurations and leveraging next-generation features to safeguard the network and its users. Plenty of tricks, gotchas, and advanced commands are revealed to help administrators gain a firm hold on their deployments.

## Who this book is for

This book is for admins at any level of expertise. Anyone who is new to Palo Alto Networks will find their way around the basic configurations and will be able to set up a complex configuration after finishing this book. Expert admins will pick up solid tips and tricks to make their config and methodologies even better.

## What this book covers

*Chapter 1, Understanding the Core Technologies*, introduces PAN-OS functions and explains the core next-generation firewall features.

*Chapter 2, Setting Up a New Device*, provides everything that's needed to get a fresh device or VM up and running.

*Chapter 3, Building Strong Policies*, explains how to create and optimize rules to their maximum potential.

*Chapter 4, Taking Control of Sessions*, demonstrates how shaping and redirecting sessions over alternate links can optimize bandwidth usage. It also covers how to apply decryption to inspect encrypted sessions.

*Chapter 5, Services and Operational Modes*, covers configuring supportive services such as DHCP and DNS proxy and explains how to increase resilience with logical instances and high availability.

*Chapter 6, Identifying Users and Controlling Access*, explains how to leverage User-ID to control user access regardless of their IP address and physical location.

*Chapter 7, Managing Firewalls through Panorama*, demonstrates setting up the Panorama central management system, building shared policies, and system configuration.

*Chapter 8, Upgrading Firewalls and Panorama*, provides a straightforward and complete process to upgrade any system.

*Chapter 9, Logging and Reporting*, demonstrates how to configure log collectors and log forwarding, and explains how to customize and schedule reports

*Chapter 10, VPN and Advanced Protection*, shows how to set up site-to-site and user VPNs, as well as how to configure DDoS protection and custom signatures.

*Chapter 11, Troubleshooting Common Session Issues*, guides you through basic troubleshooting steps and session details.

*Chapter 12, A Deep Dive into Troubleshooting*, explains advanced troubleshooting techniques, leveraging flow analysis and global counters.

*Chapter 13, Supporting Tools*, discusses integrating with third-party tools to gain advanced visibility and control.

# To get the most out of this book

To follow all the topics we will be covering, it will be helpful if you have access to an up-to-date firewall and Panorama in a lab environment. Being able to spin up test devices that can serve as domain controllers, authentication servers, clients, Docker hosts, and generic web servers will be helpful with some of the more involved chapters. It will also allow you to test your new skills before implementing them in a production environment. Basic networking and system administration skills are needed.

| Software/Hardware covered in the book | OS Requirements |
| --- | --- |
| PAN-OS, all chassis and VM versions | Any OS capable of supporting a web browser and SSH client |

You will need an SSH- and TTY-capable client such as PuTTY or Terminal to access the command line and console interfaces.

**If you are using the digital version of this book, we advise you to type the code yourself or access the code via the GitHub repository (link available in the next section). Doing so will help you avoid any potential errors related to the copy/pasting of code.**

# Download the example code files

You can download the example code files for this book from your account at www. packt.com. If you purchased this book elsewhere, you can visit www.packtpub.com/ support and register to have the files emailed directly to you.

You can download the code files by following these steps:

1. Log in or register at www.packt.com.
2. Select the **Support** tab.
3. Click on **Code Downloads**.
4. Enter the name of the book in the **Search** box and follow the onscreen instructions.

Once the file is downloaded, please make sure that you unzip or extract the folder using the latest version of:

- WinRAR/7-Zip for Windows
- Zipeg/iZip/UnRarX for Mac
- 7-Zip/PeaZip for Linux

The code bundle for the book is also hosted on GitHub at https://github.com/ PacktPublishing/Mastering-Palo-Alto-Networks. In case there's an update to the code, it will be updated on the existing GitHub repository.

We also have other code bundles from our rich catalog of books and videos available at https://github.com/PacktPublishing/. Check them out!

# Code in Action

Code in Action videos for this book can be viewed at https://bit.ly/2DhrTBp

# Download the color images

We also provide a PDF file that has color images of the screenshots/diagrams used in this book. You can download it here: http://www.packtpub.com/sites/default/ files/downloads/9781789956375_ColorImages.pdf

# Conventions used

There are a number of text conventions used throughout this book.

`Code in text`: Indicates code words in text, database table names, folder names, filenames, file extensions, pathnames, dummy URLs, user input, and Twitter handles. Here is an example: "Before you can create a VWire interface, you first need to set two interfaces to the `Virtual Wire` type and assign each of them a different zone."

Any command-line input or output is written as follows:

```
configure
set deviceconfig system type static
set deviceconfig system ip-address <IP>
set deviceconfig system netmask <x.x.x.x>
set deviceconfig system default-gateway <IP>
set deviceconfig system dns-setting servers primary <IP>
set deviceconfig system dns-setting servers secondary <IP>
commit
```

**Bold**: Indicates a new term, an important word, or words that you see onscreen. For example, words in menus or dialog boxes appear in the text like this. Here is an example: "If you already have an account, log in and click on **Register a Device** from the home page"

---

**Tips or important notes**
Appear like this.

---

# Get in touch

Feedback from our readers is always welcome.

**General feedback**: If you have questions about any aspect of this book, mention the book title in the subject of your message and email us at customercare@packtpub.com.

**Errata**: Although we have taken every care to ensure the accuracy of our content, mistakes do happen. If you have found a mistake in this book, we would be grateful if you would report this to us. Please visit www.packtpub.com/support/errata, selecting your book, clicking on the Errata Submission Form link, and entering the details.

**Piracy**: If you come across any illegal copies of our works in any form on the Internet, we would be grateful if you would provide us with the location address or website name. Please contact us at copyright@packt.com with a link to the material.

**If you are interested in becoming an author**: If there is a topic that you have expertise in and you are interested in either writing or contributing to a book, please visit authors.packtpub.com.

# Reviews

Please leave a review. Once you have read and used this book, why not leave a review on the site that you purchased it from? Potential readers can then see and use your unbiased opinion to make purchase decisions, we at Packt can understand what you think about our products, and our authors can see your feedback on their book. Thank you!

For more information about Packt, please visit packt.com.

# Section 1: First Steps and Basic Configuration

In this section, you'll learn about the core technologies that make up the Palo Alto Networks next-generation firewall, and how to connect to a freshly booted firewall appliance or virtual machine. You'll also learn how to apply the basic configuration for you to get up and running.

This section comprises the following chapters:

- *Chapter 1, Understanding the Core Technologies*
- *Chapter 2, Setting Up a New Device*

# 1
# Understanding the Core Technologies

In this chapter, we're going to examine the core technologies that make up the Palo Alto Networks firewall.

We are going to take a closer look at how security zones control how security, **Network Address Translation (NAT)**, and routing verdicts are made. We will review the mechanics behind App-ID and Content-ID so you get a deeper understanding of how packets are processed and security decisions are made by the firewall, and we will review how User-ID contributes to a more robust security stance by applying group-based or user-based access control.

This chapter will cover the following topics:

- Understanding the zone-based firewall
- Understanding App-ID and Content-ID
- The management and data plane
- Authenticating users with User-ID

# Technical requirements

For this chapter, no physical installation is required; the technology is only explained. It is helpful if you've already worked with Palo Alto Networks firewalls, but it is not required. Some experience with firewalls or web proxies in general is recommended, as this will make the subject matter more tangible.

# Understanding the zone-based firewall

Traditionally, when considering the firewall as an element of your network, most likely you will imagine a network design like the one in the following image, with two to four areas surrounding a box. Most of the time, whatever is placed in the north is considered dangerous, east and west are somewhat grey areas, and the south is the happy place where users do their daily tasks. The box in the middle is the firewall.

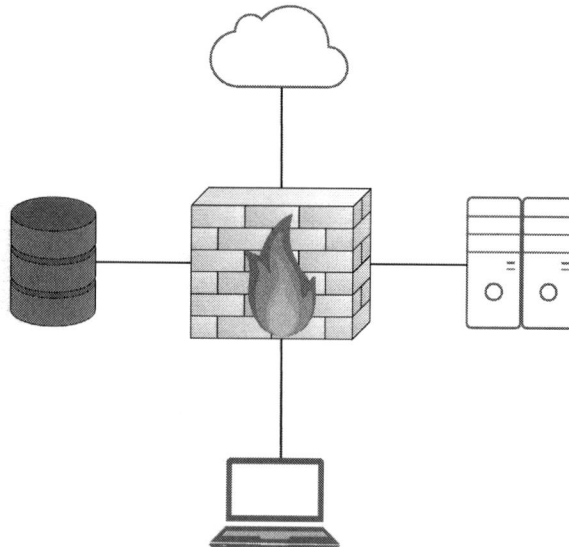

Figure 1.1 – Basic network topology

In reality, a network design may look a lot more complex due to network segregation, segmentation, remote offices being connected to the headquarters via all sorts of different technologies, and the adoption of cloud vendors.

In a route-based firewall, zones are simply an architectural or topological concept that helps identify which areas comprise the global network that is used by the company and are usually represented by tags that can be attached to a subnet object. They hold no bearing in any of the security decisions made by the system when processing security policies.

The zone-based firewall, on the other hand, will use zones as a means to internally classify the source and destination in its state table. When a packet is first received, a source zone lookup is performed. If the source zone has a protection profile associated with it, the packet is evaluated against the profile configuration. If the first packet is a TCP packet, it will also be evaluated against TCP state where the first packet needs to be a SYN packet, and a SYN-cookie is triggered if the protection profile threshold is reached. Then, a destination zone is determined by checking the **Policy-Based Forwarding (PBF)** rules and if no results are found, the routing table is consulted. Lastly, the NAT policy is evaluated as the destination IP may be changed by a NAT rule action, thereby changing the destination interface and zone in the routing table. This would require a secondary forwarding lookup to determine the post-NAT egress interface and zone:

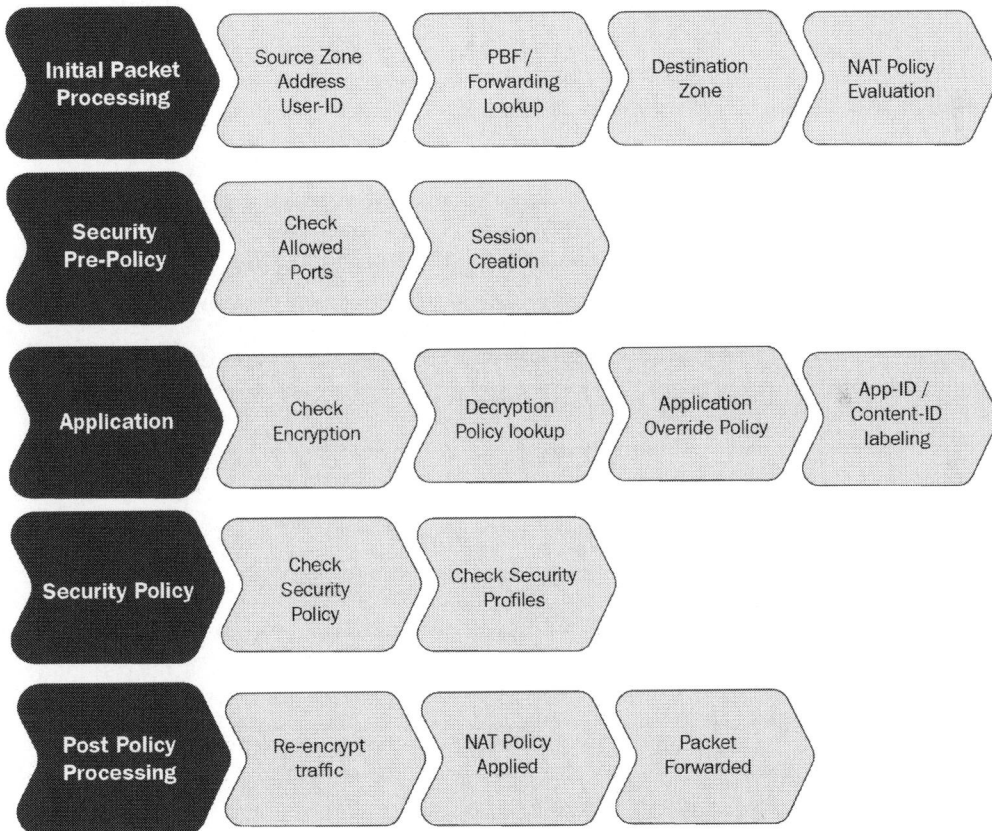

| Initial Packet Processing | Source Zone Address User-ID | PBF / Forwarding Lookup | Destination Zone | NAT Policy Evaluation |
| Security Pre-Policy | Check Allowed Ports | Session Creation | | |
| Application | Check Encryption | Decryption Policy lookup | Application Override Policy | App-ID / Content-ID labeling |
| Security Policy | Check Security Policy | Check Security Profiles | | |
| Post Policy Processing | Re-encrypt traffic | NAT Policy Applied | Packet Forwarded | |

Figure 1.2 – Phases of packet processing

After these zone lookups have been performed, the firewall will continue to the security policy evaluation.

The policy evaluation then uses the 'six tuple' (6-Tuple) to match establishing sessions to security rules:

1. Source IP
2. Source Port
3. Destination IP
4. Destination Port
5. Source Zone
6. Protocol

Zones are attached to a physical, virtual, or sub interface. Each interface can only be part of one single zone. Zones can be created to suit any naming convention and can be very descriptive in their purpose (**untrust**, **dmz**, **lan**, and so on), which ensures that from an administrative standpoint, each area is easily identifiable.

It is best practice to use zones in all security rules and leveraging a clear naming convention prevents misconfiguration and makes security rules very readable. Networks that are physically separated for whatever reason but are supposed to be connected topologically (for example, users spread over two buildings that come into the firewall on two separate interfaces) can be combined into the same zone, which simplifies policies.

It is important to note that there are implied rules that influence intra- or interzone sessions. These rules can be found at the bottom of the security policy:

- Default intrazone connections: Packets flowing from and to the same zone will be implicitly allowed.
- Default interzone connections: Packets flowing from one zone to a different zone are implicitly blocked.

Security rules can also be set to only accept traffic within the same zone, between different zones only, or both. This way, an administrator could set a specific rule for the intrazone setting and allow all applications without inadvertently allowing this full access to be open to a different network. Adding a second zone to that same rule would allow the same access inside the new zone, but there would not be any access granted between the zones; that would require a new interzone or universal rule:

| | NAME | TYPE | Source | | Destination | | APPLICATION | SERVICE | ACTION | PROFILE | OPTIONS |
|---|---|---|---|---|---|---|---|---|---|---|---|
| | | | ZONE | ADDRESS | ZONE | ADDRESS | | | | | |
| 1 | intrazone | intrazone | dmz<br>lan | any | (intrazone) | any | allowed web apps | application-default | Allow | | |
| 2 | interzone | interzone | dmz<br>lan | any | dmz<br>lan | any | allowed web apps | application-default | Allow | | |
| 3 | universal | universal | dmz<br>lan | any | dmz<br>lan | any | allowed web apps | application-default | Allow | | |
| 9 | intrazone-default | intrazone | any | any | (intrazone) | any | any | any | Allow | none | none |
| 10 | interzone-default | interzone | any | any | any | any | any | any | Deny | none | none |

Figure 1.3 – Different security rule types and default rules

Let's now look at the expected behavior when determining zones.

# Expected behavior when determining zones

When a packet arrives on an interface, the PBF policy or routing table will be consulted to determine the destination zone based on the original IP address in the packet header.

Let's consider the following routing table:

```
> show routing route
flags: A:active, ?:loose, C:connect, H:host, S:static,
~:internal, R:rip, O:ospf, B:bgp,

        Oi:ospf intra-area, Oo:ospf inter-area, O1:ospf
ext-type-1, O2:ospf ext-type-2, E:ecmp, M:multicast


VIRTUAL ROUTER: default (id 1)
    ==========
destination         nexthop         metric flags  interface
0.0.0.0/0           198.51.100.1    10      A S    ethernet1/1
198.51.100.0/24     198.51.100.2    0       A C    ethernet1/1
198.51.100.2/32     0.0.0.0         0       A H
192.168.0.0/24      192.168.0.1     0       A C    ethernet1/2
192.168.0.1/32      0.0.0.0         0       A H
172.16.0.0/24       172.16.0.1      0       A C    ethernet1/3
172.16.0.1/32       0.0.0.0         0       A H
total routes shown: 7
```

Let's assume ethernet1/1 is the external interface with IP address 198.51.100.2 set to zone **external**, ethernet1/2 is the DMZ interface with IP address 192.168.0.1 set to zone **dmz**, and ethernet1/3 is the LAN interface with IP 172.16.0.1 and set to zone **lan**. The default route is going out of interface ethernet1/1 to 198.51.100.1 as next-hop. There are a few scenarios that will influence how the zone is determined:

- **Scenario 1**: A packet is received from client PC 172.16.0.5 with destination IP 1.1.1.1.

  The firewall quickly determines the source zone is **lan** and a route lookup determines the destination IP is not a connected network, so the default route needs to be followed to the internet. The destination zone must be **external** because the egress interface is ethernet1/1.

- **Scenario 2**: A packet is received from client PC 172.16.0.5 with destination IP 1.1.1.1 but a PBF rule exists that forces all traffic for 1.1.1.1 to the next-hop IP 192.168.0.25. As PBF overrides the routing table, the destination zone will become **dmz** as the egress interface is now ethernet1/2.

- **Scenario 3**: A packet is received from internet IP 203.0.113.1 with destination IP 198.51.100.2. This is a typical example of what NAT looks like to the firewall: It receives a packet with its external IP address as the destination. From the perspective of the NAT policy, the source zone will be **external** as the IP is not from a connected network and no static route exists, and the destination zone will also be **external** as the IP is connected to that interface. From a security aspect, however, once NAT is applied, the destination zone will change to whatever NAT action is applied.

> **Important note**
> Remember that NAT policy evaluation happens after the initial zones have been determined, but before the security policy is evaluated.

# Understanding App-ID and Content-ID

App-ID and Content-ID are two technologies that go hand in hand and make up the core inspection mechanism. They ensure applications are identified and act as expected, threats are intercepted and action is applied based on a configurable policy, and data exfiltration is prevented.

# How App-ID gives more control

Determining which application is contained within a specific data flow is the cornerstone of any next-generation firewall. It can no longer be assumed that any sessions using TCP port 80 and 443 are simply plaintext or encrypted web browsing, as today's applications predominantly use these ports as their base transport and many malware developers have leveraged this convergence to well-known ports in an attempt to masquerade their malware as legitimate web traffic while exfiltrating sensitive information or downloading more malicious payloads into an infected host:

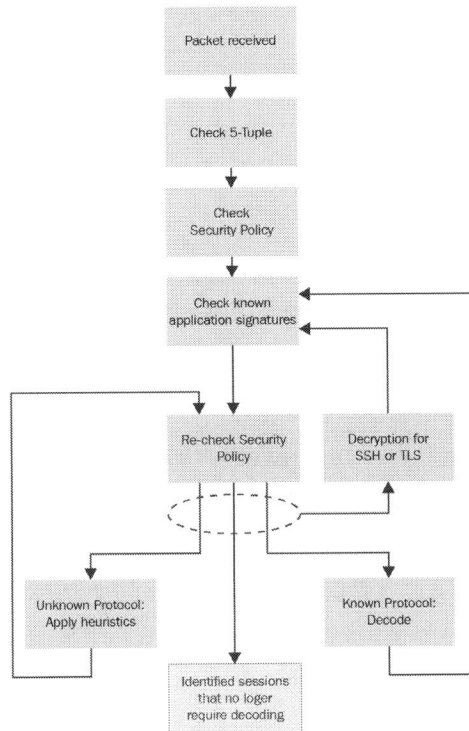

Figure 1.4 – How App-ID classifies applications

When a packet is received, App-ID will go through several stages to identify just what something is. First, the **6-Tuple** is checked against the security policy to verify whether a certain source, destination, protocol, and port combination is allowed or not. This will take care of low-hanging fruit if all the unnecessary ports have been closed off and *unusual* destination ports can already be rejected. Next, the packets will be checked against known application signatures and the app cache to see if the session can be rapidly identified, followed by a second security policy check against the application, now adding App-ID to the required set of identifiers for the security policy to allow the session through.

If at this time or in future policy checks, it is determined that the application is SSH, TLS, or SSL, a secondary policy check is performed to verify whether decryption needs to be applied. If a decryption policy exists, the session will go through decryption and will then be checked again for a known application signature, as the session encapsulated inside TLS or SSH may be something entirely different.

If in this step, the application has not been identified (a maximum of 4 packets after the handshake, or 2,000 bytes), App-ID will use the base protocol to determine which decoder to use to analyze the packets more deeply. If the protocol is known, the decoder will go ahead and decode the protocol, then run the payload against the known application signatures again. The outcome could either be a known application, or an unknown generic application, like unknown-tcp. The session is then again re-matched against the security policy to determine whether it is allowed to pass or needs to be rejected or dropped.

If the protocol is unknown, App-ID will apply heuristics to try and determine which protocol is used in the session. Once it is determined which protocol is used, another security policy check is performed. Once the application has been identified or all options have been exhausted, App-ID will stop processing the packets for identification. Throughout the life of a session, the identified application may change several times as more information is learned from the session through inspecting packet after packet. A TCP session may be identified as SSL, which is the HTTPS application as the firewall detects an SSL handshake. The decryption engine and protocol decoders will then be initiated to decrypt the session and identify what is contained inside the encrypted session. Next, it may detect application web-browsing as the decoder identifies typical browsing behavior such as an HTTP GET. App-ID can then apply known application signatures to identify flickr. Each time the application context changes, the firewall will quickly check whether this particular application is allowed in its security rule base.

If at this point flickr is allowed, the same session may later switch contexts again as the user tries to upload a photo, which will trigger another security policy check. The session that was previously allowed may now get blocked by the firewall as the sub-application flickr-uploading may not be allowed.

Once the App-ID process has settled on an application, the application decoder will continuously scan the session for expected and deviant behavior, in case the application changes to a sub-application or a malicious actor is trying to tunnel a different application or protocol over the existing session.

# How Content-ID makes things safe

Meanwhile, if the appropriate security profiles have been enabled in the security rules, the Content-ID engine will apply the URL filtering policy and will continuously, and in parallel, scan the session for threats like vulnerability exploits, virus or worm infections, suspicious DNS queries, **command and control (C&C or C2)** signatures, DoS attacks, port scans, malformed protocols, or data patterns matching sensitive data exfiltration. TCP reassembly and IP defragmentation are performed to prevent packet-level evasion techniques:

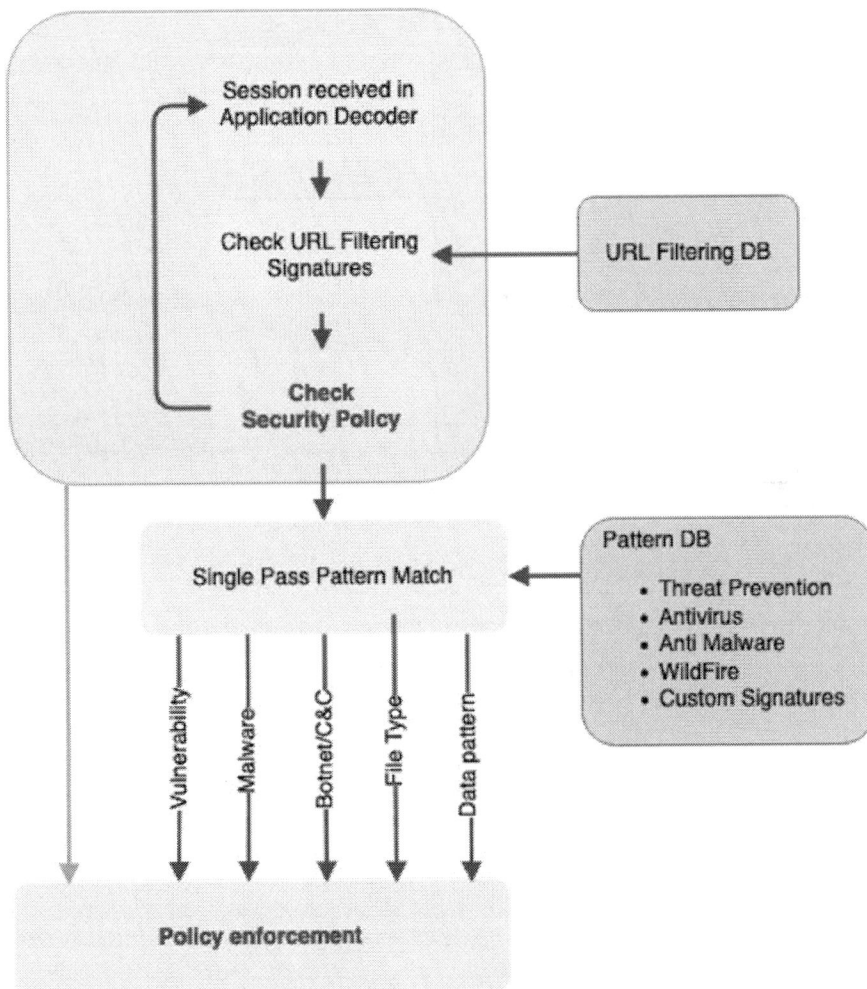

Figure 1.5 – How Content-ID scans packets

All of this happens in parallel because the hardware and software were designed so that each packet is simultaneously processed by an App-ID decoder and a Content-ID stream-based engine, each in a dedicated chip on the chassis or through a dedicated process in a **Virtual Machine** (**VM**). This design reduces latency versus serial processing, which means that enabling more security profiles does not come at an exponential cost to performance as is the case with other firewall and IPS solutions.

Hardware and VM design is centered on enabling the best performance for parallel processing while still performing tasks that cost processing power that could impede the speed at which flows are able to pass through the system. For this reason, each platform is split up into so-called *planes*, which we'll learn about in the next section.

# The management and data plane

There are two main **planes** that make up a firewall, the **data plane** and the **management** plane, which are physical or logical boards that perform specific functions. All platforms have a management plane. Larger platforms like the PA-5200 come with 2 to 3 data planes and the largest platforms have replaceable hardware blades (line cards) that have up to 3 data plane equivalents per line card and can hold up to 10 line cards. The smaller platforms like the PA-220 only have the one hardware board that virtually splits up responsibilities among its CPU cores.

The **management plane** is where all administrative tasks happen. It serves the web interfaces used by the system to allow configuration, provide URL filtering block pages, and serve the client VPN portal. It performs cloud lookups for URL filtering and DNS security, and downloads and installs content updates onto the data plane. It also performs the logic part of routing and communicates with dynamic routing peers and neighbors. Authentication, User-ID, logging, and many other supporting functions that are not directly related to processing packets.

The **data plane** is responsible for processing flows and performs all the security features associated with the next-generation firewall. It scans sessions for patterns and heuristics. It maintains IPSec VPN connections and has hardware offloading to provide wire-speed throughputs. Due to its architecture and the use of interconnected specialty chips, all types of scanning can happen in parallel as each chip processes packets simultaneously and reports its findings.

A switch fabric enables communication between planes so the data plane can send lookup requests to the management plane, and the management plane can send configuration updates and content updates.

Another important feature is the ability to identify users and apply different security policies based on identity or group membership.

# Authenticating users with User-ID

Frequently neglected but very powerful when set up properly is a standard feature called User-ID. Through several mechanisms, the firewall can learn who is initiating which sessions, regardless of their device, operating system, or source IP. Additionally, security policies can be set so users are granted access or restricted in their capabilities based on their individual ID or group membership.

User-ID expands functionality with granular control of who is accessing certain resources and provides customizable reporting capabilities for forensic or managerial reporting.

Users can be identified through several different methods:

- Server monitoring:

    --Microsoft Active Directory security log reading for log-on events

    --Microsoft Exchange Server log-on events

    --Novell eDirectory log-on events

- The interception of **X-Forward-For** (**XFF**) headers, forwarded by a downstream proxy server

- Client probing using Netbios and WMI probes

- Direct user authentication

    -- The Captive Portal to intercept web requests and serve a user authentication form or transparently authenticate using Kerberos

    -- GlobalProtect VPN client integration

- Port mapping on a multiuser platform such as Citrix or Microsoft Terminal Server where multiple users will originate from the same source IP

- The XML API

- A syslog listener to receive forwarded logs from external authentication systems

# Summary

You should now understand which basic technologies make up the security ecosystem on the Palo Alto Networks firewall. It's okay if this seems a bit vague as we will see more practical applications, and implications, in the next two chapters. We will be taking a closer look at how security and NAT rules behave once you start playing with zones, and how to anticipate expected behavior by simply glancing at the rules.

# 2
# Setting Up a New Device

In this chapter, we will cover how you can gain access to the console and web interface of a fresh-out-of-the-box firewall appliance or a cleanly staged **Virtual Machine (VM)**. You will learn how to license, update, and upgrade the firewall so that the latest features are available when you start building your security policy, and the latest signatures are always loaded onto the device to protect your users and infrastructure from malware and vulnerability exploits.

We are going to harden your management configuration to ensure a rigid security stance, and we will also look at the different types of network interface modes—aggregated interfaces and routing.

In this chapter, we're going to cover the following main topics:

- Gaining access to the user interface
- Adding licenses and setting up dynamic updates
- Upgrading the firewall
- Hardening the management interface
- Understanding the interface types

# Technical requirements

For this chapter, a basic understanding of network appliances is required as we will be looking at physically connecting to a device, configuring the management environment, and choosing the data plane interface's deployment mode. Basic knowledge of standing up a virtual appliance in a virtual environment, including connecting it to virtual switches or virtual interfaces and providing it with network access on a hypervisor, is also required.

# Gaining access to the user interface

If you are deploying your firewall on a cloud provider, you can skip this step and go directly to the *Connecting to the web interface and CLI* section.

When taking a new device out of the box or setting up a VM on a local hypervisor, such as VMware ESXi, Fusion, NSX, Hyper-V, and KVM, one of the first things you may need to do is to connect a console cable to gain access to the **Command-Line Interface (CLI)**. You will need a standard DB9 to RJ45 console cable with the following pinout:

```
1 - Empty - Data Carrier Detect (DCD)
2 - 3 - Receive Data (RXD)
3 - 6 - Transmit Data - (TXD)
4 - 7 - Data Terminal Ready (DTR)
5 - 4 - Ground (GND)
6 - 2 - Data Set Ready (DSR)
7 - 8 - Request To Send (RTS)
8 - 1 - Clear to Send - (CTS)
9 - Empty - Ringing Indicator (RI)
```

Here is an example of an RJ45 to DB9 console cable:

Figure 2.1 – RJ45 to DB9 console cable

Some models also come with a micro USB port, which allows a console connection to be made using a standard USB-A to micro USB cable, as in the following diagram:

Figure 2.2 – PA-220 RJ45 and the micro USB console ports

In all cases, you will need to find which COM or TTY port is being used on your computer's operating system.

On a Windows machine, you can access the Control Panel and access **Devices and Printers**. For a micro USB connection, double-click on the **MCP2221 USB** device and remember the COM port it uses. For the DB9 to RJ45 cable, find **Ports (COM & LPT)** to see which ports are in use. If you are using a USB to DB9 dongle, find the USB device and double-click it to see which COM ports are assigned.

On Windows, you will need a terminal emulation client to connect to the console. You can use a free client for this, such as PuTTY from https://www.putty.org. Besides the COM port, you may need to provide more settings to be able to connect. If asked, use these settings:

```
Bits per second  : 9600
Data Bits        : 8
Parity           : none
Stop bits        : 1
Flow control     : none
```

On macOS X and Linux, a USB serial connection will usually create a new **tty** (**TeleTYpewriter**) entry in the /dev/ directory; a USB to DB9 dongle may create a **Call-Up** (**CU**) entry in the /dev/ directory.

Find the proper device by searching with either of these commands:

```
ls /dev/tty.*
```

```
ls /dev/cu.*
```

You will find /dev/cu.usbserialxxxxx or /dev/tty.usbmodemxxxxx, where xxxxx is the serial device name.

Once you determine the appropriate device, you can connect to the console port by using the `screen` command set to `9600` bits per second:

```
screen /dev/tty.usbmodemxxxxx 9600
```

Now, go ahead and connect the console cable or micro USB to your laptop and appliance. If you have a port free on your management network, go ahead and connect the firewall's MGT port to the switch. If you don't have a management connection available yet, you will need to connect your laptop directly to the MGT port for easier access once the IP is set up on the management interface. Lastly, plug in the power cable

If the firewall is loaded in a VM or cloud entity, hit the **Start** button to boot up the virtual appliance.

Once you've logged on to the console, you will see the operating system boot up, and if the firewall is already connected to a DHCP-enabled management network, you will see something similar to the following, where the DHCP address is already listed for your convenience:

Figure 2.3 – PA-VM post-boot DHCP information

If you missed this information, you can log on and use the following command to see the DHCP information:

```
admin@PA-220> show system info

hostname: PA-220
ip-address: 192.168.27.116
public-ip-address: unknown
netmask: 255.255.255.0
default-gateway: 192.168.27.1
ip-assignment: dhcp
```

> **Important note**
>
> The default username and password for a factory settings appliance or VM are as follows:
>
> Username: admin
>
> Password: admin

If, for some reason, you have not received a DHCP address yet from your DHCP server, you can initiate a renew action from the CLI by using a > request dhcp client management-interface renew command.

If your network does not have a DHCP server, or you connected the firewall directly to your laptop, you will need to set an IP address manually. Copy and paste the following sheet into a text file and alter the <IP> entries with the appropriate IP for your management interface, the default gateway it will use to reach out to the internet, and the DNS servers it will use to resolve the domain names. Type the netmask in quad decimals, *not* in CIDR (slash notation subnet, such as /16 and /24):

```
configure
set deviceconfig system type static
set deviceconfig system ip-address <IP>
set deviceconfig system netmask <x.x.x.x>
set deviceconfig system default-gateway <IP>
set deviceconfig system dns-setting servers primary <IP>
set deviceconfig system dns-setting servers secondary <IP>
commit
```

You can chain set commands that belong in the same path and class so that you do not need to set each attribute in each set command; instead, you can add all the desired settings all at once. In the next example, I went into the configuration mode, switched the management interface from DHCP to static configuration, and then combined all the configuration parameters for the management interface into one set command. Start by changing the default password to a new one, and then add the interface configuration:

```
admin@PA-220> set password
Enter old password :
Enter new password :
Confirm password    :

Password changed
```

```
admin@PA-220> configure
Entering configuration mode
[edit]
admin@PA-220# set deviceconfig system type static

[edit]
admin@PA-220# set deviceconfig system ip-address 192.168.27.5
netmask 255.255.255.0 default-gateway 192.168.27.1 dns-setting
servers primary 1.1.1.1 secondary 1.0.0.1

[edit]
admin@PA-220# commit

Commit job 2 is in progress. Use Ctrl+C to return to command
prompt
.............................................55%....75%.....98%..
...................100%
Configuration committed successfully

[edit]
admin@PA-220#
```

You may need to log back in after running the commit statement as the admin password
was changed.

---

**Important note**

The > prompt in username@hostname> indicates that you are in
operational mode and can execute runtime commands. The # prompt in
username@hostname# indicates that you are in configuration mode and
can add configuration parameters.

Operational commands can be run from config mode by prefixing run to a
command—for example, user@host# run show clock.

---

Once the commit job finishes, you will be able to connect to the web interface through
https://<IP> or by using an SSH client, such as PuTTY, or the ssh command in
Linux or macOS.

# Connecting to the web interface and CLI

Now that your device has an IP address, you can connect to its web interface via any browser using `https://<IP>`.

You will be met with an unfriendly error message, as in the following screenshots. This is due to the web interface using a self-signed certificate that has not been validated by any authority. For now, this can be safely ignored:

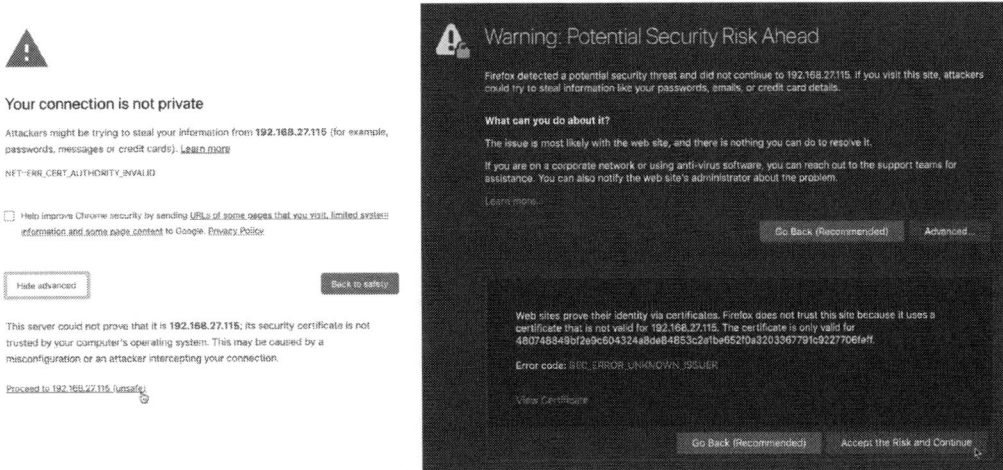

Figure 2.4 – Certificate warnings in Chrome and Firefox

An SSH client will provide you with a slightly friendlier question:

```
tom$ ssh -l admin 192.168.27.115
The authenticity of host '192.168.27.115 (192.168.27.115)'
can't be established.
RSA key fingerprint is SHA256:Qmre8VyePwwGlaDmm6JTYtjou42d1i/
Ru6xZmmEk8Yc.

Are you sure you want to continue connecting (yes/no)?
```

The SSH connection will provide you with mostly the same user experience as the console connection, but SSH is more responsive and secure, and you can now access your device from anywhere on the management network.

The web interface provides you with a whole new user experience. When prompted for your username and password, input the default `admin/admin` combination or the username and password you created on the cloud provider.

Once your are logged in, the first screen you will see is the dashboard, which contains some general information about the health of your system, config changes, and which admins are logged on. The dashboard can be customized and additional widgets can be added from a list of prepared widgets, or widgets can be removed if they are not relevant. For now, the **General Information** widget contains the most important information as you will need the serial number of the physical device, or the **CPU ID** and **UUID** on a virtual device, as shown:

| General Information | |
|---|---|
| Device Name | Reaper-PA-220 |
| MGT IP Address | 192.168.27.115 |
| MGT Netmask | 255.255.255.0 |
| MGT Default Gateway | 192.168.27.1 |
| MGT IPv6 Address | unknown |
| MGT IPv6 Link Local Address | unknown |
| MGT IPv6 Default Gateway | |
| MGT MAC Address | 08:30:6b:7b:6e:00 |
| Model | PA-220 |
| Serial # | 0 |
| Software Version | 10.0 |
| GlobalProtect Agent | 5.1.3 |
| Application Version | 8284-6141 (06/17/20) |
| Threat Version | 8284-6141 (06/17/20) |
| Antivirus Version | 3386-3897 (06/21/20) |
| Device Dictionary Version | 1-202 |
| WildFire Version | 464843-467778 (06/21/20) |
| URL Filtering Version | 20200621.20331 |
| GlobalProtect Clientless VPN Version | 86-182 (04/23/20) |
| Time | Mon Jun 22 00:04:06 2020 |
| Uptime | 5 days, 22:39:44 |
| Device Certificate Status | None |

| General Information | |
|---|---|
| Device Name | 9dot2 |
| MGT IP Address | 192.168.27.14 |
| MGT Netmask | 255.255.255.0 |
| MGT Default Gateway | 192.168.27.1 |
| MGT IPv6 Address | unknown |
| MGT IPv6 Link Local Address | fe80::: |
| MGT IPv6 Default Gateway | |
| MGT MAC Address | 00:0c: |
| Model | PA-VM |
| Serial # | 0 |
| CPU ID | ESX: |
| UUID | 564 8531 |
| VM License | VM-50 |
| VM Mode | VMware ESXi |
| Software Version | 10.0 |
| GlobalProtect Agent | 0.0.0 |
| Application Version | 8250-6008 |
| Device-ID Version | 1-202 |
| URL Filtering Version | 0000.00.00.000 |
| GlobalProtect Clientless VPN Version | 0 |
| Time | Mon Jun 22 00:07:46 2020 |
| Uptime | 0 days, 0:04:37 |
| Plugin VM series | vm_series-2.0.0-c36 |
| Device Certificate Status | None |

Figure 2.5 – On the left is a PA-220 device, and on the right is a PA-VM device

We will now look at licenses and updates.

# Adding licenses and setting up dynamic updates

Before we can start adding licenses, the device needs to be registered. You will need to note down the device's serial number or, if you do not have a support portal account, the sales order number to create a new account.

Open a new tab or browser and navigate to `https://support.paloaltonetworks.com`

If you do not have an account yet, create a new one.

## Creating a new account

When creating a new account, you will be asked for an email address and whether you want to register using a serial number or an **Authorization** (**auth**) code, as in the following screenshot. The serial number is needed when registering a hardware appliance; the auth code is used when registering a VM device:

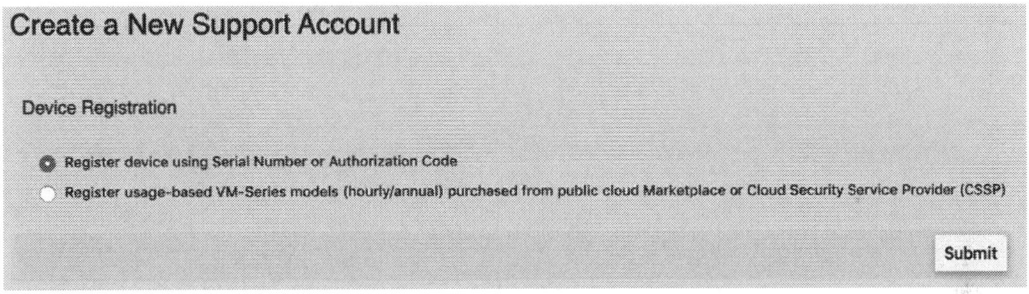

**Create a New Support Account**

Device Registration

- ● Register device using Serial Number or Authorization Code
- ○ Register usage-based VM-Series models (hourly/annual) purchased from public cloud Marketplace or Cloud Security Service Provider (CSSP)

Submit

Figure 2.6 – Serial or authorization code device registration

Alternatively, if you have set up a virtual appliance on one of the cloud providers, you can pick which provider your device is running on (such as Amazon Web Services, Azure, and Google Cloud Platform).

You then need to provide some basic details, such as the address, password, the device's serial number, the auth code, and the sales order number or customer ID, if your company already has an account:

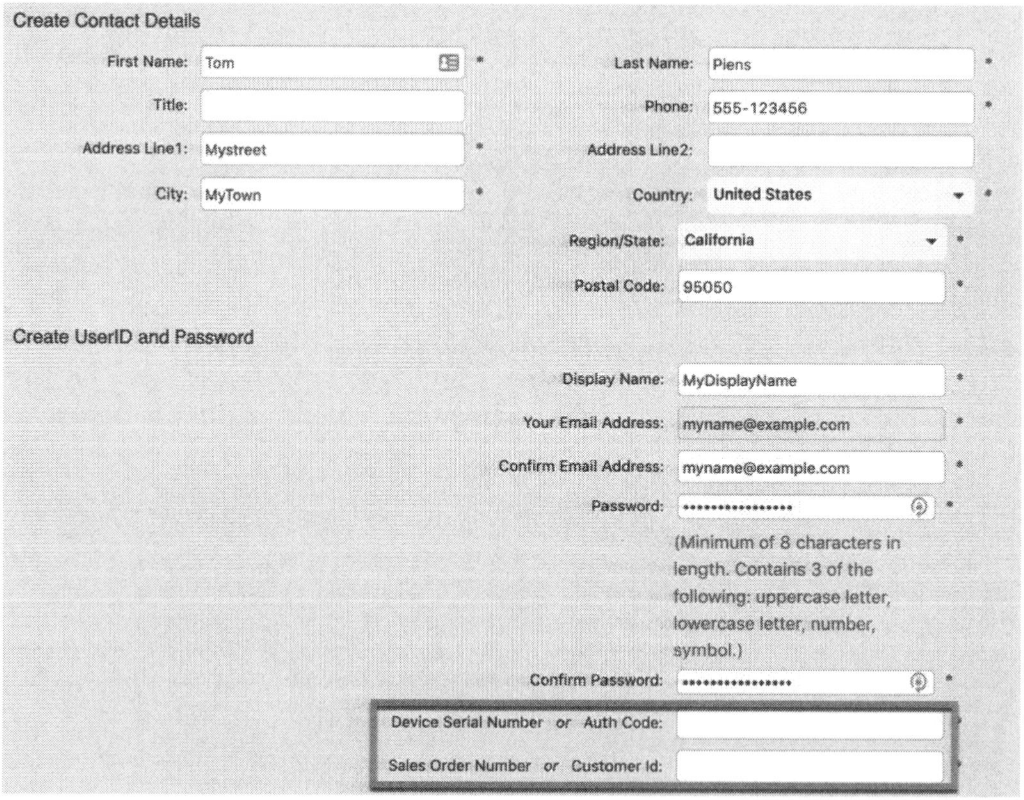

Figure 2.7 – General information and device and sales order details

After creating your `Support Portal` account, you can go ahead and register your devices.

# Registering a new device

If you already have an account, log in and click on **Register a Device** from the home page:

Figure 2.8 – Register a Device from the support portal home page

You will be presented with the option to register using a serial number or an auth code. The serial number is needed when registering a hardware appliance and the auth code is used when registering a VM device:

Select Device Type

⦿ Register device using Serial Number or Authorization Code

◯ Register usage-based VM-Series models (hourly/annual) purchased from public cloud Marketplace or Cloud Security Service Provider (CSSP)

Figure 2.9 – Serial or auth code device registration

**Register Device using Serial Number or Authorization Code** will ask you for the serial number, a friendly device name, and a tag if you have several "pools" of devices in your account already. It will also request address details as to where the device will be deployed for RMA purposes.

If you deployed a cloud instance, you can choose to register usage-based VM series models. You'll be asked for the serial number, CPUID, and UUID:

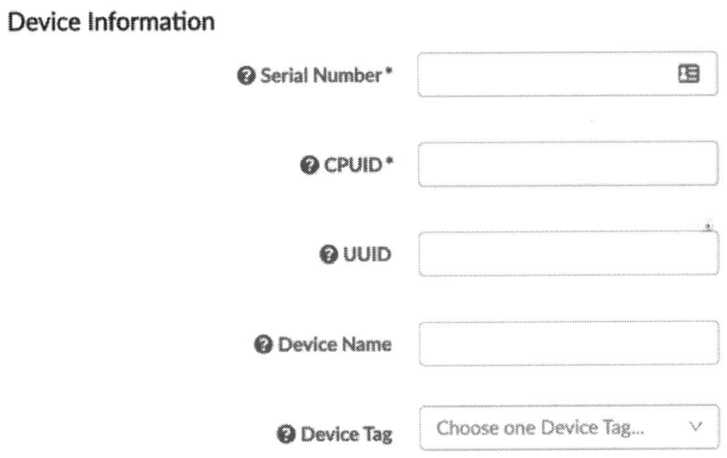

Device Information

❷ Serial Number *

❷ CPUID *

❷ UUID

❷ Device Name

❷ Device Tag     Choose one Device Tag...     ⌄

Figure 2.10 – Adding a cloud instance to the assets

Now that the devices are registered, it is time to activate the feature and support licenses.

# Activating licenses

Once the device is registered, you can add the licenses. You will have received one (a bundle) or several auth codes that you need to enter on the portal or via the **device licenses** tab to activate the license and start using the feature on your device.

Some of the most common licenses include the following:

- Support: Platinum, premium, standard, or partner-enabled.
- Threat prevention: Antivirus, anti-spyware, threat prevention, and daily updates.
- PAN-DB URL filtering.
- GlobalProtect portal: Enables mobile applications on Android, iOS, Win10 UWP, Chrome OS, and Linux. It enables **Host Information Profile (HIP)** checks and agentless VPNs.
- DNS security: Dynamic DNS signature lookups.
- WildFire: Threat signature feed and updates every minute
- Decryption port mirroring: Allows decrypted sessions to be copied to a different device

More features are being added as Palo Alto Networks announces new products.

## Activating licenses via the customer support portal

In the **Customer Support Portal (CSP)**, you can find your registered devices under the **Assets** tab as a device. There's a pencil icon that allows you to activate auth codes:

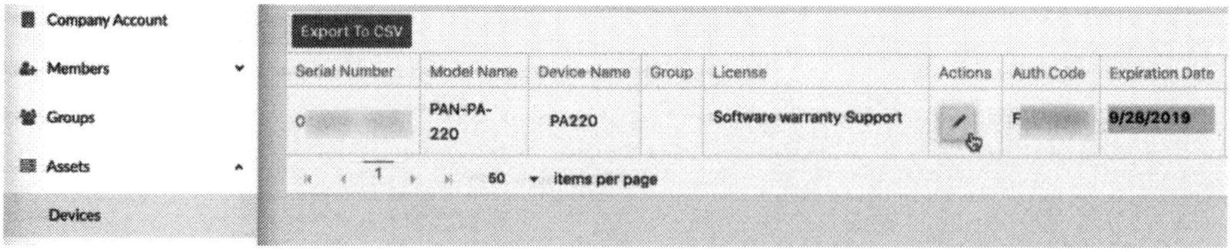

Figure 2.11 – The Devices page in the CSP

You will notice there is already a software warranty support license active for a limited amount of time. This is a temporary support license that allows a **Return Merchandise Authorization (RMA)** to be started if your device arrives broken in the box. To add the actual support license and any feature licenses, click on the pencil icon:

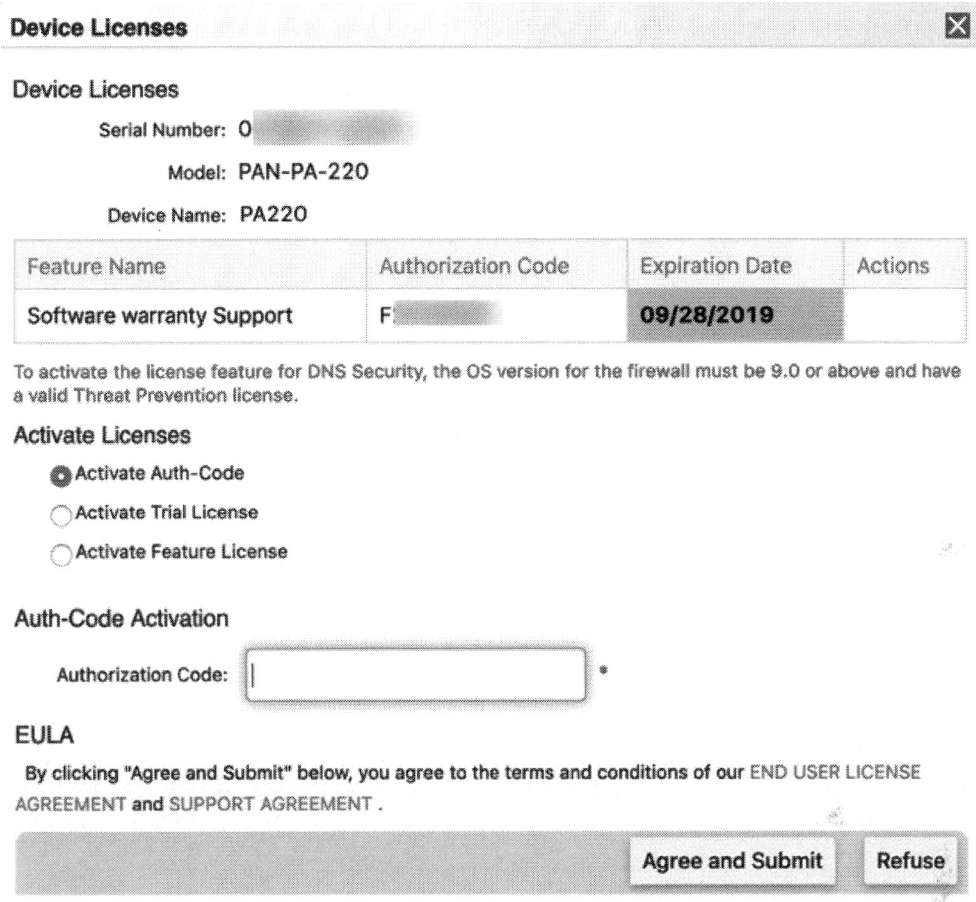

**Device Licenses**    ☒

**Device Licenses**

Serial Number:  O▓▓▓▓▓▓▓▓

Model:  PAN-PA-220

Device Name:  PA220

| Feature Name | Authorization Code | Expiration Date | Actions |
|---|---|---|---|
| **Software warranty Support** | F▓▓▓▓▓▓ | **09/28/2019** | |

To activate the license feature for DNS Security, the OS version for the firewall must be 9.0 or above and have a valid Threat Prevention license.

**Activate Licenses**

⦿ Activate Auth-Code

◯ Activate Trial License

◯ Activate Feature License

**Auth-Code Activation**

Authorization Code: |                              | •

**EULA**

By clicking "Agree and Submit" below, you agree to the terms and conditions of our END USER LICENSE AGREEMENT **and** SUPPORT AGREEMENT .

| | Agree and Submit | Refuse |
|---|---|---|

Figure 2.12 – Adding auth codes to activate services

Once you've added all your licenses, the device should look something like this:

| | PAN-PA-3260 | PERIM 01 | Threat Prevention ⚊ | | 4▓▓▓▓ | 4/23/2023 |
|---|---|---|---|---|---|---|
| ▓▓▓▓▓▓ | | | PAN-DB URL Filtering ⚊ | | 8▓▓▓▓ | 4/23/2023 |
| | | | GlobalProtect Portal ⚊ | ✎ | 2▓▓▓▓ | 11/11/2023 |
| | | | Premium Partner Support ⚊ | | 6▓▓▓▓ | 4/23/2023 |
| | | | WildFire License ⚊ | | 9▓▓▓▓ | 4/23/2023 |

Figure 2.13 – A fully licensed device

> **Important note**
>
> The little download icons next to each license allow you to download the license key file so that you can upload the key onto the firewall. This is required if you intend to run the firewall without an internet connection and want to be able to upload signature files and enforce security profiles.

Besides activating licenses via the support portal, they can also be activated directly from the firewall interface.

## Activating licenses via the web interface

You can also activate licenses by navigating to **Device | Licenses**.

If you activated the licenses in the CSP and then proceeded to download the license key files, you can click on **Manually upload license key**.

If you activated the licenses on the CSP and want to fetch the licenses, click **Retrieve license keys from license server**. Make sure the firewall has been set up with a functional default gateway and DNS servers.

If you want to activate new licenses with an auth code, click on **Activate feature using authorization code** and you will see a popup where you can enter each auth code individually:

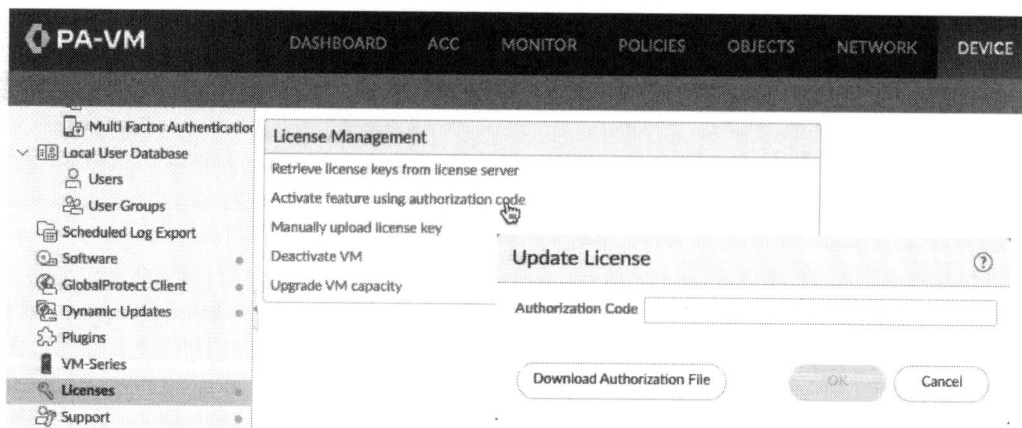

Figure 2.14 – Activating a license using an auth code

With each added license, a section will be added containing the license information:

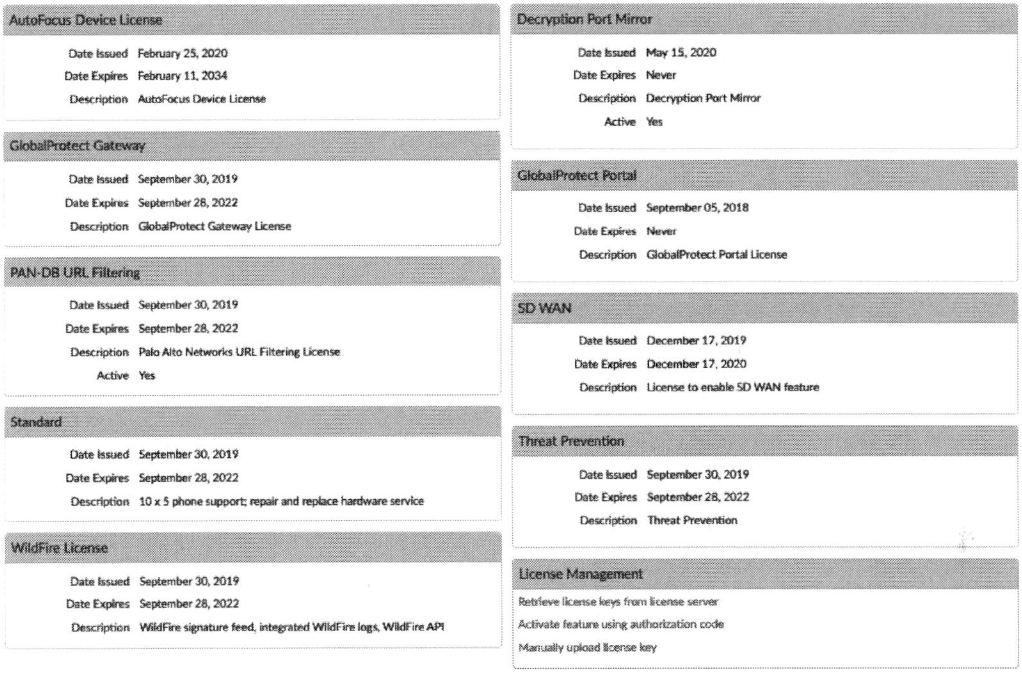

Figure 2.15 – Active licenses on the device

To activate the support license, you may need to activate the auth key through the **Support** menu item:

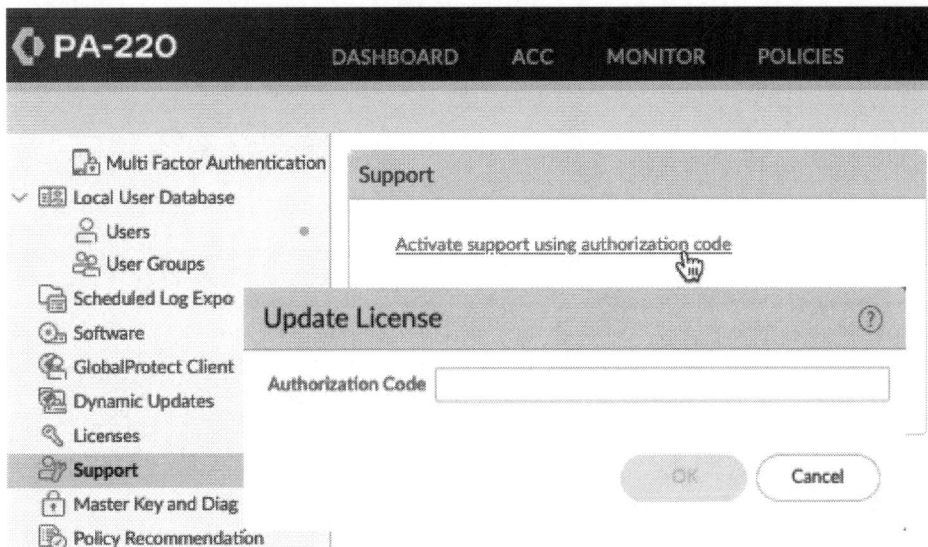

Figure 2.16 – Activate support using an authorization code

> **Important note**
>
> The support license is more like a contract than a license required for a feature to work; a support person will take your call if something goes wrong, a replacement device will be sent if your unit is broken, and so on. This is the only license that does not need to be on the device necessarily.

After all licenses are activated on the device, the next step is to start downloading and scheduling updates to the different databases.

# Downloading and scheduling dynamic updates

Now that all the licenses are active, you can set up dynamic updates and start downloading all the content packages.

Navigate to the **Dynamic Updates** menu under the **Device** tab, where you can manually download content packages and set up schedules and installation preferences. The first time you visit this menu, it may look a bit off as the available content has not been loaded onto the device yet. Click the **Check Now** button to connect to the updates server and fetch the available packages for your system, as shown:

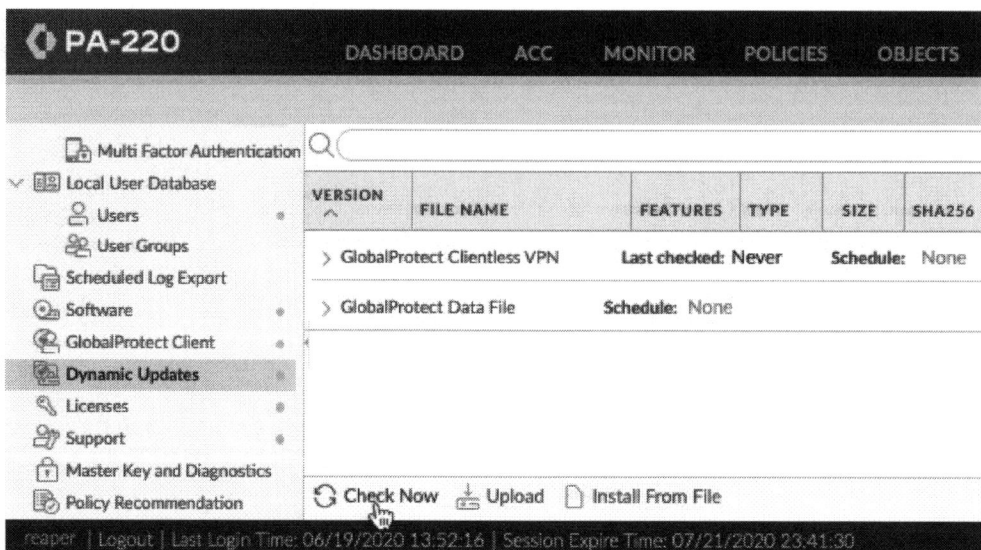

Figure 2.17 – The initial Dynamic Updates view

Once the updates have been fetched, you may still notice that some antivirus packages are missing. This is because the device first needs to be brought up to date with all the app ID and content ID application and decoder updates before further packages can be loaded onto the system. Go ahead and download the latest **Applications and Threats** package:

> **Important note**
> If no threat prevention license has been activated, there will only be an
> **Applications** package available for download.

| VERSION ∧ | FILE NAME | | FEATURES | TYPE | SIZE | RELEASE DATE | DOW... | CURR... INST... | ACTION | DOCUMENTATION |
|---|---|---|---|---|---|---|---|---|---|---|
| ∨ Applications and Threats | Last checked: 2020/06/22 00:03:11 CEST | Schedule: Every Wednesday at 01:02 (Download only) | | | | | | | | |
| 8276-6104 | panupv2-all-contents-8276-6104 | | Apps, Threats | Full | 50 MB | 2020/05/22 04:59:18 CEST | | | Download | Release Notes |
| 8277-6107 | panupv2-all-contents-8277-6107 | | Apps, Threats | Full | 50 MB | 2020/05/23 03:11:27 CEST | | | Download | Release Notes |
| 8278-6109 | panupv2-all-contents-8278-6109 | | Apps, Threats | Full | 50 MB | 2020/05/28 02:51:13 CEST | | | Download | Release Notes |
| 8279-6115 | panupv2-all-contents-8279-6115 | | Apps, Threats | Full | 50 MB | 2020/06/03 01:06:06 CEST | | | Download | Release Notes |
| 8280-6121 | panupv2-all-contents-8280-6121 | | Apps, Threats | Full | 50 MB | 2020/06/05 00:14:35 CEST | | | Download | Release Notes |
| 8281-6129 | panupv2-all-contents-8281-6129 | | Apps, Threats | Full | 50 MB | 2020/06/09 19:08:18 CEST | | | Download | Release Notes |
| 8282-6133 | panupv2-all-contents-8282-6133 | | Apps, Threats | Full | 50 MB | 2020/06/12 00:53:26 CEST | | | Download | Release Notes |

Figure 2.18 – Downloading the first Applications and Threats package

Once the package has been downloaded, click **Install**. Once the installation has
completed, click **Check Now** again, and the antivirus will become available. Go ahead
and download and install the latest package of antivirus updates.

> **Important note**
> URL filtering and DNS security do not have update packages because URLs are
> looked up against the cloud service and then stored in the local cache.

You can now start building schedules by clicking on the blue **None** option after **Schedule**:

| VERSION ∧ | FILE NAME | | FEATURES | TYPE | SIZE | RELEASE DATE | DOW... | CURR... INST... |
|---|---|---|---|---|---|---|---|---|
| > Antivirus | Last checked: 2020/06/22 00:03:11 CEST | Schedule: None (Manual) | | | | | | |
| > Applications and Threats | Last checked: 2020/06/22 00:03:11 CEST | Schedule: Every Wednesday at 01:02 (Download only) | | | | | | |
| > GlobalProtect Clientless VPN | Last checked: 2020/06/21 02:00:23 CEST | Schedule: None (Manual) | | | | | | |
| > GlobalProtect Data File | Schedule: None (Manual) | | | | | | | |
| > WildFire | Last checked: 2020/06/22 00:30:10 CEST | Schedule: None (Manual) | | | | | | |

**Antivirus Update Schedule** ⑦     **WildFire Update Schedule** ⑦

Recurrence | Hourly ∨     Recurrence | Real-time ∨
Minutes Past Hour | 15
Action | download-and-install ∨     Delete Schedule   OK   Cancel
Threshold (hours) | 5
A content update must be at least this many hours old for the
action to be taken.

Delete Schedule   OK   Cancel

Figure 2.19 – The antivirus and WildFire schedules

The antivirus and WildFire schedules look very similar.

**Recurrence** tells the firewall how regularly it needs to check for updates. The update interval options for **Antivirus** are **Weekly**, **Daily**, **Hourly**, or **Manual**. The update interval options for **WildFire** are **Real-time**, **Every minute**, **15 minutes**, **30 minutes**, **1 hour**, or **Never**. When **Recurrence** is set to any value higher than 1 minute, you can additionally set at which minute within the frame the actual check should take place. This helps prevent conflicting update connections to the update server in cases where the outgoing internet bandwidth is restricted. The action can be set to simply download or to download and install. If the action is set to download, manual installation is required.

**Threshold** is a feature that the antivirus update shares with **Applications and Threats**:

## Applications and Threats Update Schedule

Recurrence | Hourly
Minutes Past Hour | 34
Action | download-and-install
☐ Disable new apps in content update
Threshold (hours) | 5

A content update must be at least this many hours old for the action to be taken.

**Allow Extra Time to Review New App-IDs**

Set the amount of time the firewall waits before installing content updates that contain new App-IDs. You can use this wait period to assess and adjust your security policy based on the new App-IDs.

New App-ID Threshold (hours) | 24

Delete Schedule          OK          Cancel

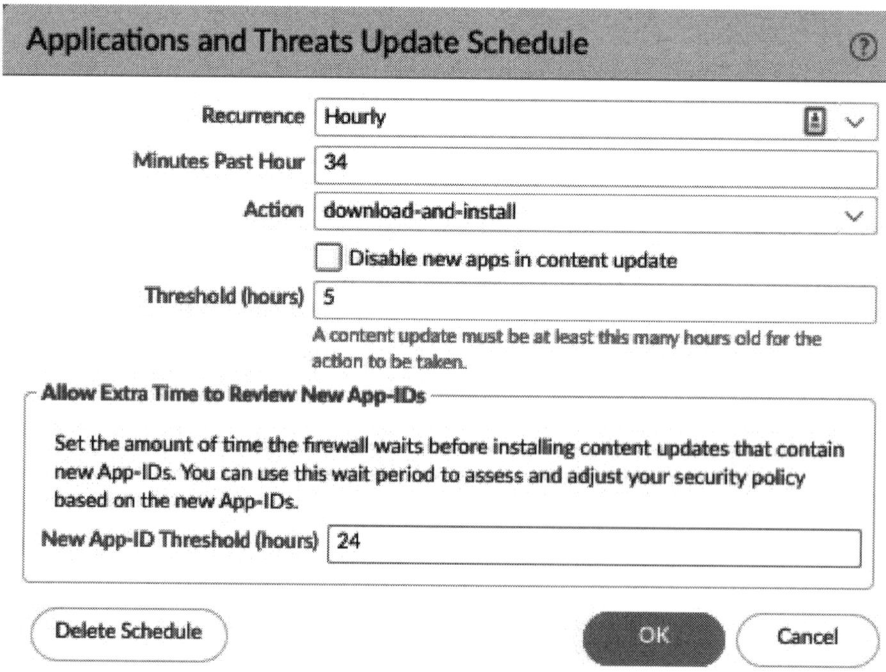

Figure 2.20 – Antivirus and WildFire schedules

**Threshold** is a setting that delays the installation of a content package for a set amount of hours. At the time that this threshold expires, the firewall checks for a new update package. If a new package is found, the new package is downloaded and **Threshold** is reset for one more attempt. If yet another update package is found after the first reset, the schedule will reset until the next full occurrence. If no new packages are detected, the package will be installed as defined by **Threshold**.

> **Important note**
>
> The threshold delay is a mechanism to prevent installing faulty packages; A delay is set in hours which allows other accounts to experience any faults and report the content issue back to the support teams. If the content package is rolled back before the threshold expires, the package is not installed. This thresholding option correlates a company's tolerance for the risk of vendor errors and the balance of new emerging threats to the organization.

The **Application** content package also has an option to completely disable all new app IDs or enable a separate threshold on the app IDs only. The reasoning here is that what is identified as web browsing today may change into a unique application after installing the **Application** content package tomorrow. If the security policy has been set up to only allow previously known applications, this could potentially cause issues with users who suddenly can't access that specific application.

The **Threshold** setting allows you to schedule a review period to see whether any applications need to be accounted for in the security policy before they become active. If no action is needed, the applications will become active automatically. The **Disable new apps in content update** option will not activate any new applications until you manually review and activate all new applications.

> **Important note**
>
> At the time of writing, the release schedule for new applications is every third Thursday of each month. Regular threat package updates happen on Tuesdays, but urgent updates are sent our immediately.

The following section provides a quick set of recommendations for scheduling Dynamic Updates on.

## Dynamic Updates cheat sheet

1. Click on **Check Now**.

2. Download and install the latest `panupv2-all-contents` or `panupv2-all-apps` package.

3. Click **Check Now**.

4. Download and install the latest `panup-all-antivirus` package.

5. Set an **Antivirus** update schedule:

   --**Hourly recurrence**

   --**15 minutes after the hour**

--**Download and install**

--**5 hour threshold**

6.  Set a **WildFire** update schedule:

--**Every minute**

--**Download and install**

7.  Set an **Applications and Threats** update schedule:

--**Hourly recurrence**

--**34 minutes past the hour**

--**Download and Install**

--**5 hour threshold**

--**24 hour threshold (or more) on new App-ID if the security team wishes to review new applications before they are activated.**

Let's now have a look at the steps needed to upgrade your firewall.

# Upgrading the firewall

In this section, you will learn how to upgrade your firewall and what steps need to be taken to ensure a smooth process. We will review important information to keep in mind when preparing your maintenance window and providing for a contingency plan.

## Understanding the partitions

Before we start the upgrade procedure, there's an important bit of information you need to know. Like most Linux systems, the hard disk has been partitioned into specific segments. These segments serve a specific purpose.

A few important ones are as follows:

*   / is the root partition, which is where the operating system is installed.
*   /opt/pancfg is where the configuration files and dynamic update files are kept.
*   /opt/panrepo is the repository for downloaded operating system (PAN-OS) images.
*   /opt/panlogs is the partition where logdatabase is stored.

The disk space usage can be viewed with the following command:

```
admin@PA-220> show system disk-space
Filesystem          Size  Used Avail Use% Mounted on
/dev/root           3.8G  1.7G  1.9G  48% /
none                2.0G   60K  2.0G   1% /dev
/dev/mmcblk0p5       12G  3.3G  7.5G  31% /opt/pancfg
/dev/mmcblk0p6      3.8G  2.2G  1.5G  59% /opt/panrepo
tmpfs               2.0G  247M  1.8G  13% /dev/shm
cgroup_root         2.0G     0  2.0G   0% /cgroup
/dev/mmcblk0p8      4.6G  3.5G  942M  79% /opt/panlogs
/dev/loop0          111M  5.6M  100M   6% /opt/panlogs/wildfire/
tmpfile
tmpfs                12M     0   12M   0% /opt/pancfg/mgmt/lcaas/
ssl/private
None
```

The cool thing about the / root partition is that it is actually one of two `sysroot` partitions. The system has actually been partitioned with two operating system-specific partitions, of which just one is mounted at a time. The upgrade procedure actually installs the new PAN-OS onto the inactive partition. This allows inline upgrades without interrupting the production. Once the new operating system has been installed, the GRUB bootloader is configured to load the other `sysroot` partition at the next boot, causing the new PAN-OS to become active:

```
admin@PA-220> debug swm status
Partition           State             Version
-------------------------------------------------
sysroot0            REVERTABLE         9.0.3
sysroot1            RUNNING-ACTIVE     9.0.5
maint               EMPTY              None
```

This mechanism also allows a smooth rollback in case an upgrade fails and it is decided you need to go back to the previous situation. You can trigger the > `debug swm revert` debug command to tell the bootloader to switch the toggle again to the previous `sysroot` partition and reboot the system via > `request restart system`, and after the device has rebooted, you are back on the previous PAN-OS with the pre-upgrade configuration loaded.

# Upgrade considerations

When upgrading, you will need to map out where you are, where you need to go, and how you need to get there. Finding where you are can be achieved by looking at the dashboard's **General Information** section and looking for the software version. Deciding where you need to go may require some research and consideration:

- **Which features are required?** Determining which features are contained in each PAN-OS version requires the most research. You can open `https://docs.paloaltonetworks.com` and search `Feature Guide`, which will return all the new feature guides for the major PAN-OS versions.

- **Is the code train "mature?"** Maturity can be estimated by looking at the maintenance release version. All PAN-OS versions are made up of three numbers: PAN-OS X.Y.Z (for example, 9.0.5):

  --X is the number of the major software release.

  --Y is the number of the feature version release.

  --Z is the number of the maintenance release.

  X will change when a new major software version is released containing new functionality and usually containing some changes in its expected behavior and possibly a new look and feel.

  Each new software release is usually followed by a new feature version around 6 to 9 months after its release, mostly containing some new features. Maintenance release versions are released for all code trains anywhere between 5 to 9 weeks and mostly contain bug fixes.

  There will occasionally be PAN-OS version names that end in -hx, which denotes a hotfix. This is a maintenance release that was published ahead of schedule and usually only contains one or a few critical hotfixes (for example, 9.0.2-h1).

  A code train will reach a reliable maturity around the x.x.4 or x.x.5 maintenance release version when it is somewhat safe to assume most critical bugs have been found and addressed.

  Check the release notes for any known issues so that you can appropriately prepare if there are any caveats: `https://docs.paloaltonetworks.com/pan-os/9-1/pan-os-release-notes.html`

  Are there outstanding advisories that trump the required features? Advisories regarding which maintenance release versions to choose or to avoid can be found at `https://securityadvisories.paloaltonetworks.com/` and `https://live.paloaltonetworks.com/t5/Customer-Resources/`.

- **Required and optional versions**: Each major version has a base image, usually the x.x.0 version, which contains all the vital parts of the PAN-OS image. This allows the following maintenance versions to be smaller in size, containing only critical updates. The base image needs to be downloaded onto the system before a maintenance version can be installed. It is not required for the base image to be installed in order to be able to install the maintenance version when upgrading from a lower major version. It is also not required to install any intermediate maintenance versions unless the release notes explicitly mention that there is an issue that requires a step in between.

Say, for example, that your firewall is currently on PAN-OS 8.1.4 and you need to get to PAN-OS 9.0.5. You can download a PAN-OS 9.0.0 base image, followed by PAN-OS 9.0.5, and then directly install and reboot PAN-OS 9.0.5. Your system will be directly upgraded from 8.1.4 to 9.0.5.

If your firewall is currently on PAN-OS 8.0.10 and you want to go to PAN-OS 9.0.5, you do need to download, install, and reboot to a PAN-OS 8.1.0 base image before you can install PAN-OS 9.0.5

> **Important note**
>
> In the latter case, it is recommended, but not mandatory, to download and install the preferred maintenance release (see the previous *Customer Resources URL*) in the PAN-OS 8.1 code train to prevent running into bugs that could halt the upgrade process.

## Upgrading via the CLI

You first need to retrieve the available software images that can be installed on your system. You won't be able to download any images before the list is retrieved:

```
admin@PA-220> request system software check


Version            Size            Released on Downloaded

---------------------------------------------------------------

9.0.5              349MB 2019/11/14  00:54:41           no

9.0.4              304MB 2019/09/26  11:22:07           no

9.0.3              301MB 2019/07/12  10:29:30           no

9.0.3-h3           301MB 2019/08/20  20:30:53           no

9.0.3-h2           301MB 2019/08/08  13:11:19           no

9.0.2              295MB 2019/05/09  07:33:51           no
```

```
9.0.2-h4              302MB 2019/06/27  11:45:18        no
9.0.1                 287MB 2019/03/28  00:43:23        no
9.0.0                 472MB 2019/02/06  00:34:51        yes
```

Next, you can download the desired PAN-OS version:

```
admin@PA-220> request system software download version 9.0.5
Download job enqueued with jobid 31
```

You can track the download status with the following command:

```
admin@PA-220> show jobs id 31


Enqueued             Dequeued ID Type    Status Result Completed
----------------------------------------------------------------
2019/12/17 23:24:15 23:24:15 31 Downld FIN     OK      23:25:31
Warnings:
Details:Successfully downloaded
Preloading into software manager
Successfully loaded into software manager
```

When the software is successfully downloaded, you can commence installing it onto the system. You will be prompted that a reboot is required to complete the installation and to confirm whether you are sure that you want to continue. Type *Y* to proceed with the installation:

```
admin@PA-220> request system software install version 9.0.5
Executing this command will install a new version of software.
It will not take effect until system is restarted. Do you want
to continue? (y or n)
Software install job enqueued with jobid 32. Run 'show jobs id
32' to monitor its status. Please reboot the device after the
installation is done.
```

You can track the installation progress through the show jobs command:

```
admin@PA-220> show jobs id 32
Enqueued              Dequeued ID Type    Status Result Completed
-------------------------------------------------------------
2019/12/17 23:35:28 23:35:28 32 SWInstall FIN OK       23:38:59
Warnings:
Details:Software installation successfully completed. Please
reboot to switch to the new version.
```

To complete the installation, reboot the firewall. Type *Y* into the dialog if you are certain that you want to go ahead with the reboot. Rebooting will cause all sessions to be interrupted and no new sessions to be accepted until the firewall has completed the autocommit job:

```
admin@PA-200> request restart system
Executing this command will disconnect the current session. Do
you want to continue? (y or n)
```

The autocommit job runs right after a reboot and serves to load the configuration onto the data plane. After a software upgrade, this process can take a while:

```
admin@PA-200> show jobs all
Enqueued              Dequeued ID Type    Status Result Completed
-------------------------------------------------------------
2019/12/17 15:06:27 15:06:27 1  AutoCom FIN    OK       15:07:36
```

Next, we will upgrade the firewall via the web interface.

## Upgrading via the web interface

Software images can be downloaded and installed from the **Device | Software** menu. The first time you access this page, you will be presented with an error message because no repository has been loaded yet:

Figure 2.21 – Error message on the first visit to the software page

You can ignore this warning; click **Close** and then click **Check Now**. Once the repository has loaded, you will see all the available software images:

| VERSION ⌄ | SIZE | RELEASE DATE | AVAILABLE | CURRENTLY INSTALLED | ACTION | |
|---|---|---|---|---|---|---|
| 9.1.2-h1 | 277 MB | 2020/04/29 08:01:29 | | | Download | Release Notes |
| 9.1.2 | 277 MB | 2020/04/08 10:49:11 | | | Download | Release Notes |
| 9.1.1 | 277 MB | 2020/02/10 14:10:23 | | | Download | Release Notes |
| 9.1.0 | 421 MB | 2019/12/13 12:51:48 | Downloaded | | Install | Release Notes |
| 9.0.8 | 358 MB | 2020/04/16 13:29:06 | | | Download | Release Notes |
| 9.0.7 | 356 MB | 2020/03/17 13:50:11 | | | Download | Release Notes |
| 9.0.6 | 356 MB | 2020/01/27 14:28:15 | | | Download | Release Notes |

Figure 2.22 – Software management page

Click the download link next to the PAN-OS version you want to upgrade to and wait for the download dialog to complete.

Once the new PAN-OS package is downloaded, it will be listed as such on the **Software** page, as shown. Click the **Install** link next to the image to start the installation:

| VERSION ⌄ | SIZE | RELEASE DATE | AVAILABLE | CURRENTLY INSTALLED | ACTION | | |
|---|---|---|---|---|---|---|---|
| 9.1.2-h1 | 277 MB | 2020/04/29 08:01:29 | Downloaded | | Install | Release Notes | ☒ |
| 9.1.2 | 277 MB | 2020/04/08 10:49:11 | | | Download | Release Notes | |
| 9.1.1 | 277 MB | 2020/02/10 14:10:23 | | | Download | Release Notes | |
| 9.1.0 | 421 MB | 2019/12/13 12:51:48 | Downloaded | | Install | Release Notes | ☒ |
| 9.0.8 | 358 MB | 2020/04/16 13:29:06 | | | Download | Release Notes | |
| 9.0.7 | 356 MB | 2020/03/17 13:50:11 | | | Download | Release Notes | |
| 9.0.6 | 356 MB | 2020/01/27 14:28:15 | | | Download | Release Notes | |

Figure 2.23 – Image downloaded and ready to install

At the end of the installation, you will be prompted to reboot. You can skip the reboot if you want to postpone the actual upgrade to a later time. Otherwise, click **Yes**, as shown:

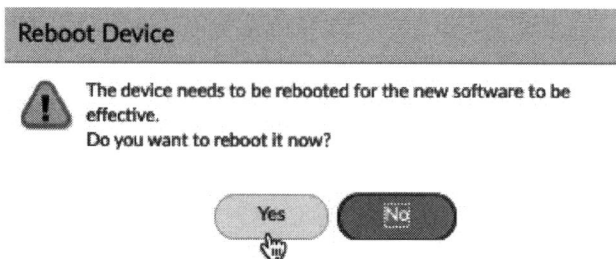

**Reboot Device**

The device needs to be rebooted for the new software to be effective.
Do you want to reboot it now?

Yes        No

Figure 2.24 – Post-installation reboot dialog

We will now check the upgrade cheat sheet.

## Upgrade cheat sheet

The next steps outline a solid methodology to get to a stable PAN-OS version before placing the firewall in production:

1. Go to `https://live.paloaltonetworks.com/t5/Customer-Resources/` for release recommendations.

2. In *Device | Software* , click on **Check Now** to load the latest list of available PAN-OS images.

3. Download and install the recommended image of your **current** release.

4. When the installation completes, a dialog window will ask if you want to reboot the device. Click **Yes**.

5. Wait for the unit to boot up again and download the base image for the next major version.

6. Download and install the recommended maintenance release for the next major version.

7. When the dialog asks you to reboot the device, click **Yes**.

8. Repeat steps 5 through 7 until you're on the version you need to reach.

Remember that for an HA cluster or panorama environment, you need to do the following:

- Disable preemption in the High Availability configuration before you start and re-enable it after the upgrade is completed on both members.

- Check both members for functionality before you start.

- The upgraded device will become non-functional until the lowest member has caught up (the cluster favors the lowest software member).

- Upgrade the panorama centralized management first.

Once the devices are upgraded to the appropriate version, it is time to complete the management configuration.

# Hardening the management interface

It is paramount that the management interface is kept secure and access is limited to only those administrators that need access. It is recommended to place the physical management interface in an **Out-of-Band** (**oob**) network, which limits exposure to the broader network. If access is needed to the management server from a different network, it is best to set up a dual-homes bastion host that mediates the connection, either through only allowing admins to log into it and use services from there, or having it set as a (transparent) proxy with a log of all sessions and limiting the source users and IP subnets as much as possible.

## Limiting access via an access List

The management interface local access list can be edited by navigating to **Device | Setup | Interfaces** and clicking on the **Management Interface**:

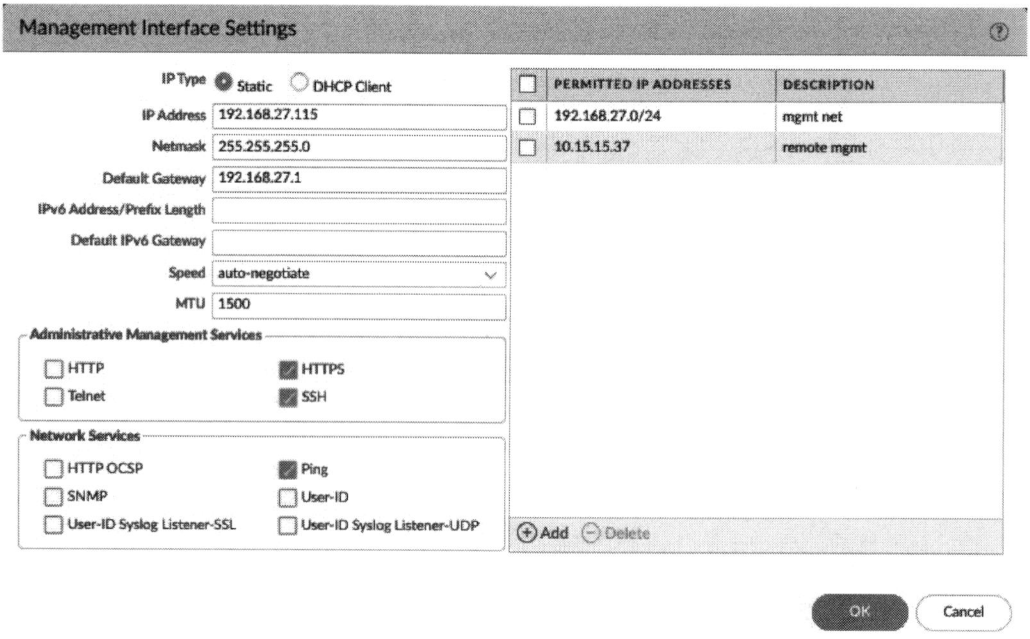

Figure 2.25 – Management interface access list

The associated CLI `configure` mode command is as follows:

```
admin@PA-220>configure
admin@PA-220#set deviceconfig system permitted-ip
192.168.27.0/24 description "management net"
```

You can also attach an interface management profile (seen in the following screenshot) to an interface, which enables the selected services (SSH and HTTPS, usually) on the IP address of the assigned data plane interface. This is not recommended as it introduces significant risk if not implemented properly:

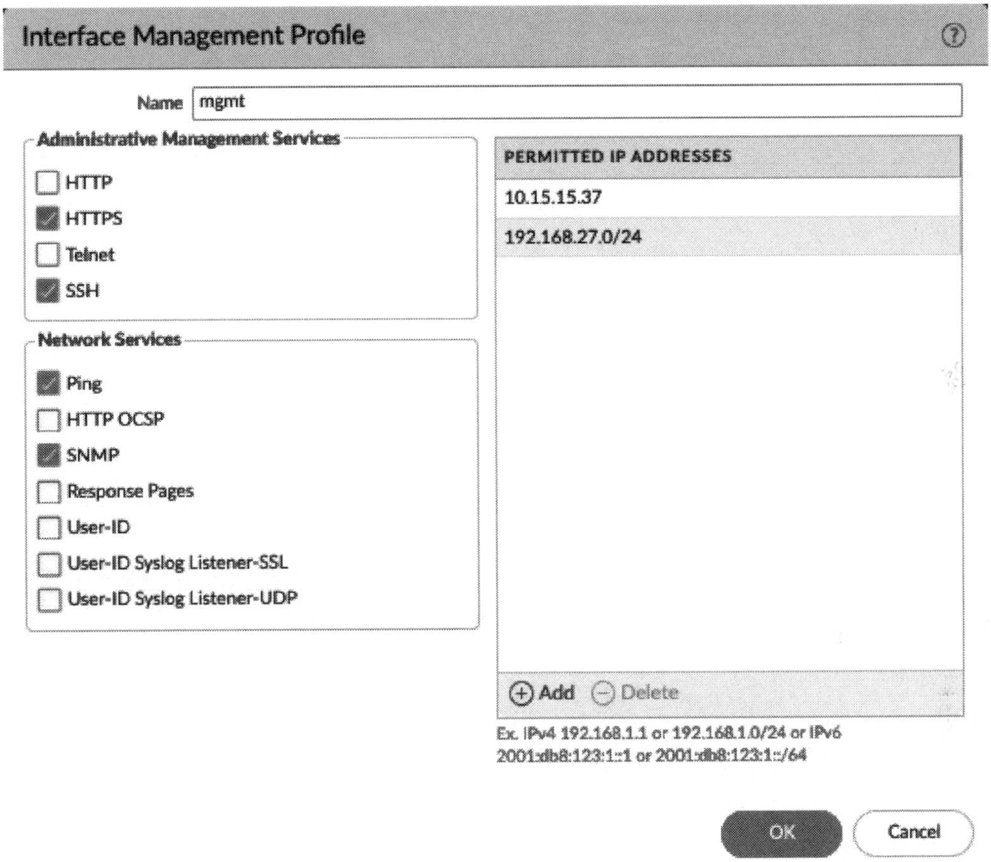

Figure 2.26 – Interface Management Profile

If you must enable this profile, make sure it is on a sufficiently shielded interface, preferably a loopback interface, that has security policies associated with gaining access to the management services. As a secondary measure, also enable an access list on the profile. These profiles can be configured in **Network | Network Profiles | Interface Management Profile** and then attached to an interface in **Network | Interfaces** under the **Advanced** tab of the selected interface:

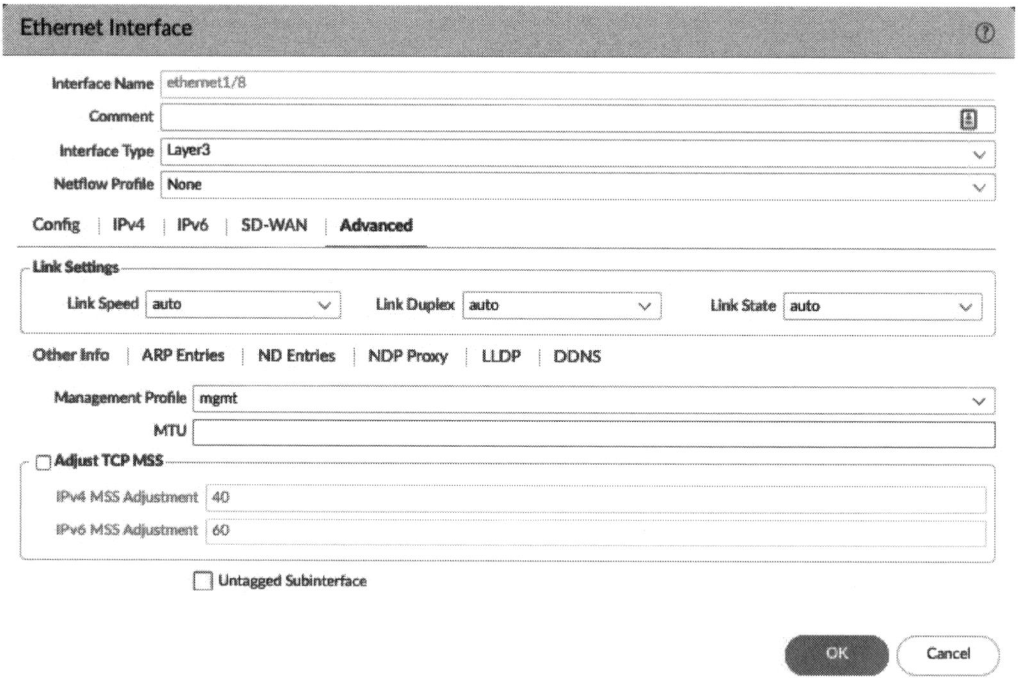

Figure 2.27 – An interface management profile attached to an interface

The CLI command to create an interface management profile, sets its services to HTTPS and SSH, and adds an ACL as follows:

```
# set network profiles interface-management-profile mgmt https
yes ssh yes permitted-ip 10.15.15.37
```

The subsequent ACL items can be set via the following command:

```
# set network profiles interface-management-profile mgmt
permitted-ip 192.168.0.5
```

Now that access to the management interface has been set, let's look at access from the management interface.

# Accessing internet resources from offline management

If the management interface does not have access to the internet, this can create interesting challenges as it will not be able to retrieve updates or perform cloud lookups. A workaround is to enable service routes that route specific applications, services, or protocols via the backplane onto a designated data plane interface, allowing the management plane to reach out to the internet while its physical interface does not have access outside of its management LAN.

Service routes can be configured from the **Device | Setup | Services** menu, where you can click on **Service Route Configuration** to get the following dialog:

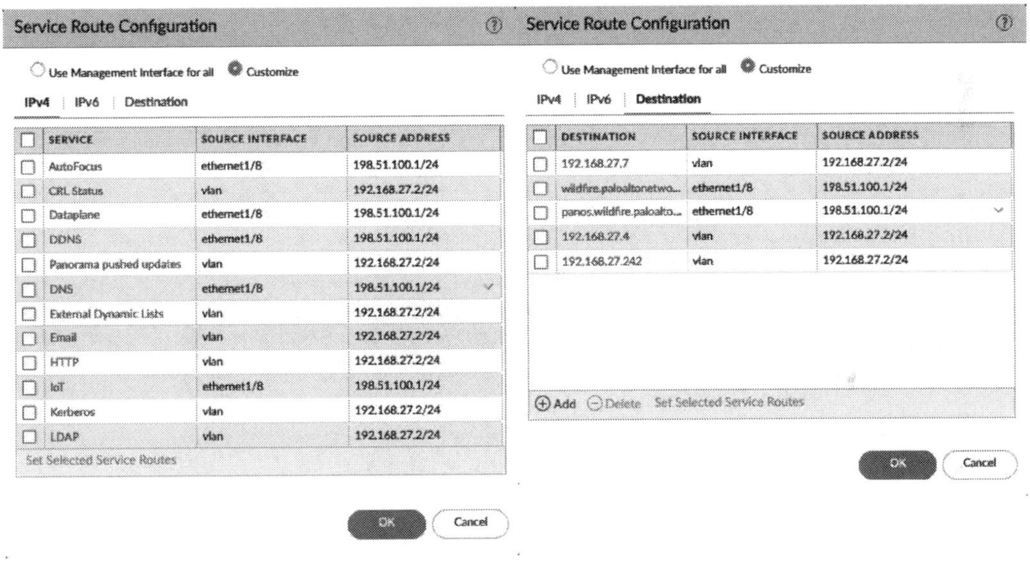

Figure 2.28 – Service Route Configuration

Once you set the radio button from the **Use Management Interface for all** to **Customize**, you will be able to select which source interface will be used for each service. From the **Destination** tab, you can also add specific IP addresses or entire subnets that need to be routed out of a specific interface. The routing table used by the target interface will be used to determine how the session is routed to the destination.

The associated CLI configuration command to set a service route is as follows:

```
#set deviceconfig system route service dns source interface
  ethernet1/8
```

> **Important note**
> If you want to see a full list of all the available services, hit the *Tab* key after
> typing `service:`

```
#set deviceconfig system route service <Tab>
  autofocus                          AutoFocus Cloud
  crl-status                         CRL servers
  ddns                               DDNS server(s)
  ...
```

This will enable access to resources that are normally not accessible through the
management network. In the next section, we'll prepare administrator accounts and
provide access as needed.

## Admin accounts

'Admin' accounts are probably one of the most abused accounts in internet history, so
your next task is to get rid of it.

There are two types of admin accounts: dynamic and role-based:

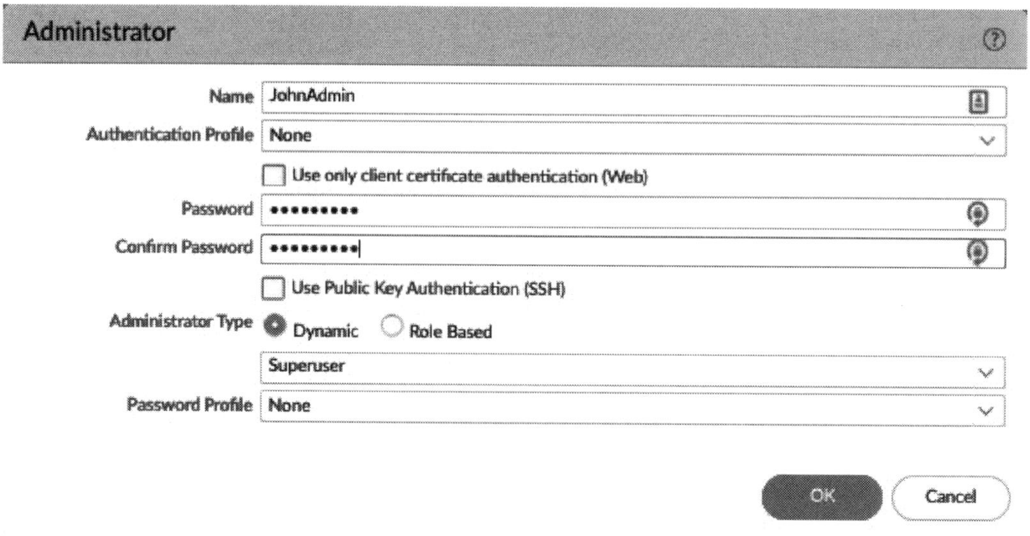

Figure 2.29 – Creating a new admin account

## Dynamic accounts

Dynamic accounts are comprised of **superusers**, who can do everything, and **device administrators**, who can do everything besides create new users or virtual systems. Virtual system-capable devices also have **virtual system administrators**, who are also device administrators and are restricted to one or several specific virtual systems. There are also read-only flavors of both that can view everything but not make changes.

Your first account will need to be a new superuser to replace the default admin account.

## Password security

You will need to add a password profile by going to **Device | Password Profiles** to ensure that the password is changed on a regular basis:

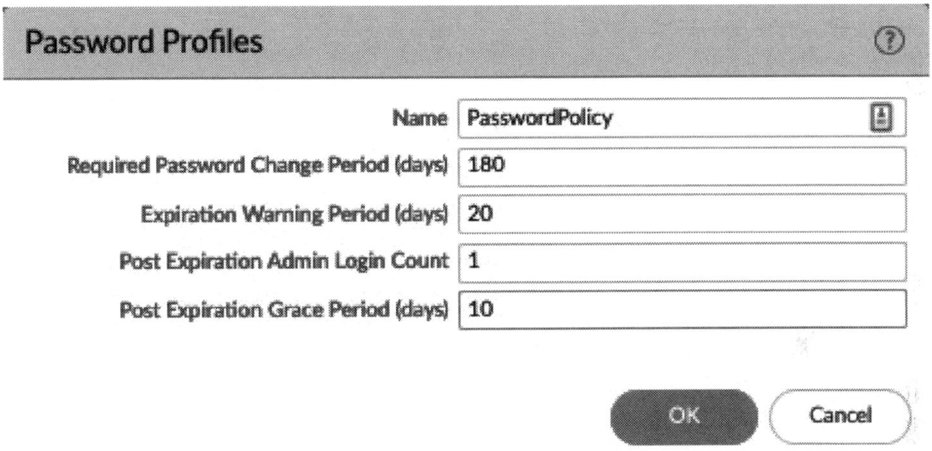

Figure 2.30 – Password Profiles

These are the configurable settings in the **Password Profile:**

- The change period indicates how long a password is valid.

- The expiration warning pops up a warning when an admin logs on if their password is about to expire.

- The post-expiration login feature allows the admin to log on a certain number of times, even after their password has expired.

- The post-expiration grace period indicates how long an admin will be able to log on after their account has expired before it is locked permanently and will require intervention from a different admin.

Additionally, you should enforce a minimum password complexity for local accounts to ensure no weak passwords are used by administrators via **Device | Setup | Management | Minimum Password Complexity**:

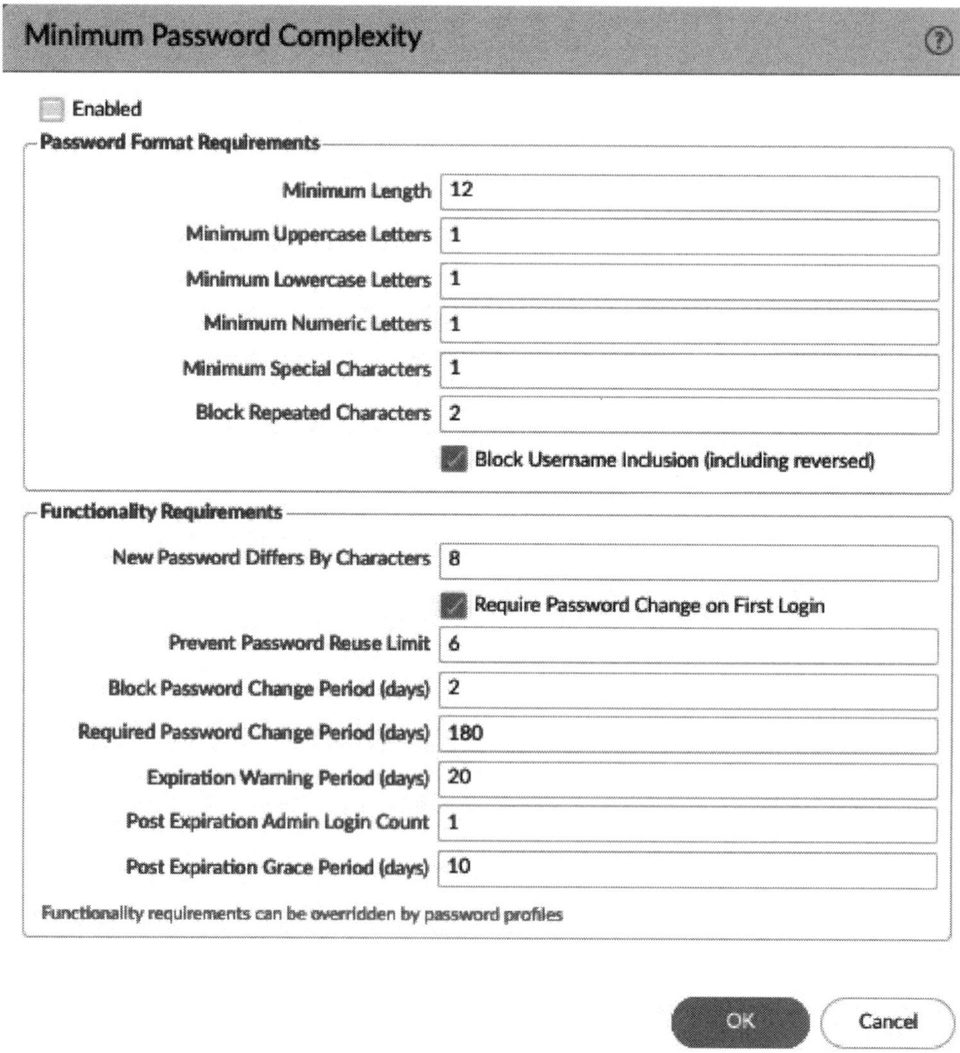

Figure 2.31 – Minimum Password Complexity

NIST has an extensive guideline on authentication and life cycle management that can be found at `https://pages.nist.gov/800-63-3/sp800-63b.html`.

## Role-based administrators

Once all the required superusers and device administrators are created, additional role-based administrators can be added for teams that only require limited functionality.

Role-based administrators can be customized down to individual menu items so that they can do anything or have read-only or no access.

The roles can be configured through the **Device | Admin Roles** menu:

Figure 2.32 – Admin Role Profile

Set each topic to one of the following options by clicking the icon to cycle to the option you need:

- A red cross indicates that these administrators will not see the menu item.

- A lock indicates that the admin will be able to see objects or menu items, but not make any changes.

- A green checkmark indicates that the admin has full access to this menu item and can make changes to objects or configuration within it.

In the **XML API/REST API** tabs, each role can be granted or denied access to certain API calls:

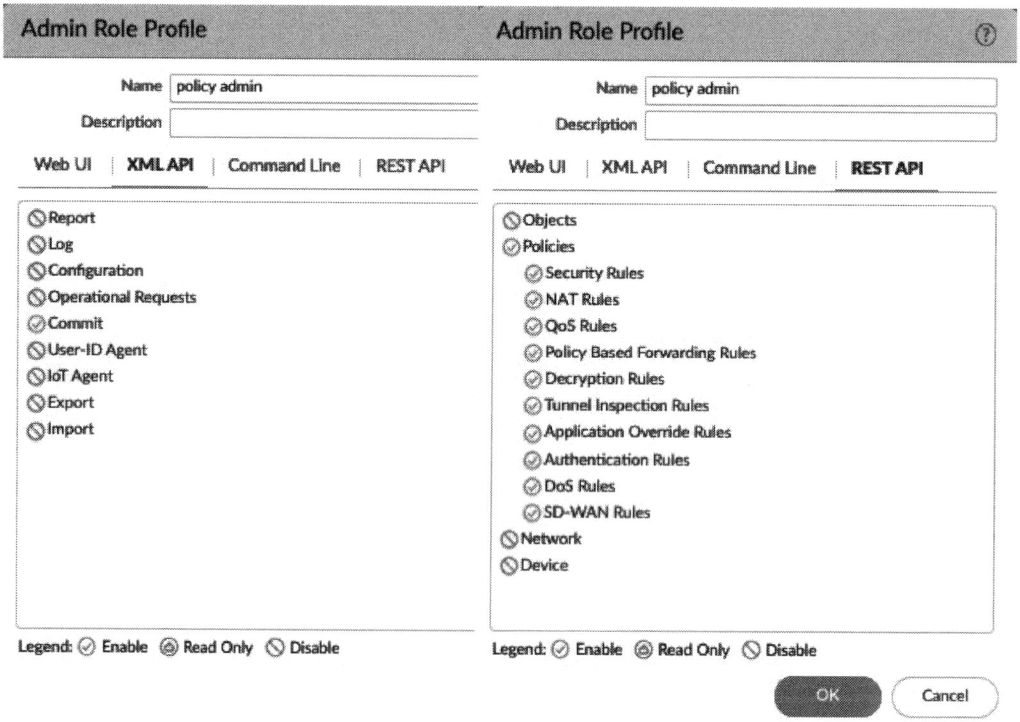

Figure 2.33 – XML API/REST API

In the **Command Line** tab, each role can be granted a certain level of access or denied access altogether:

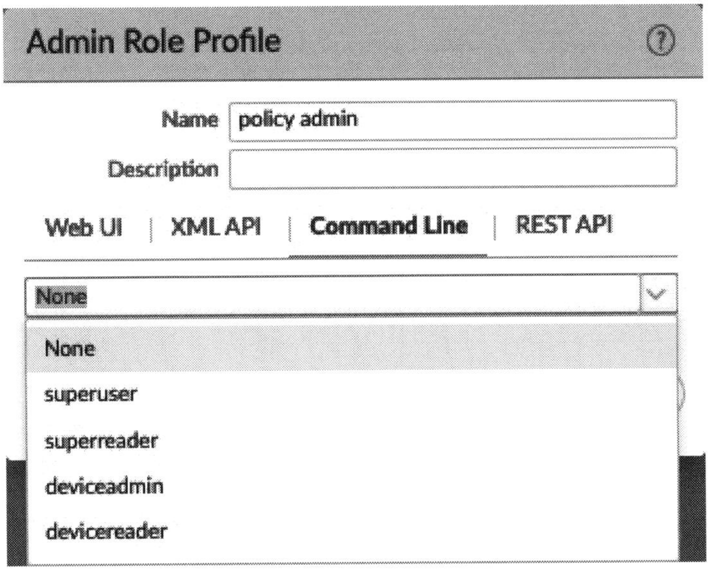

Figure 2.34 – The Command Line permissions

Let's now look at the external authentication factors.

## External authentication

It is best to use external authentication factors, such as Kerberos, LDAP, RADIUS, or SAML, to keep control over credentials in a centralized system, which enables admins to only change passwords once for multiple devices or to be locked out of all critical infrastructure at once if they leave the organization.

You first need to create a server profile from the **Device | Server Profiles** menu. Each server type has its own configuration parameters.

## The TACACS+ server profile

TACACS+ requires you to choose between **Password Authentication Protocol (PAP)** and **Challenge-Handshake Authentication Protocol (CHAP)** and set the secret associated with connecting to the TACACS+ authentication server. Optionally, you can set the profile so that it can only be used for administrator authentication, and set the profile to use a single session for all authentication events, rather than a new session per authentication event:

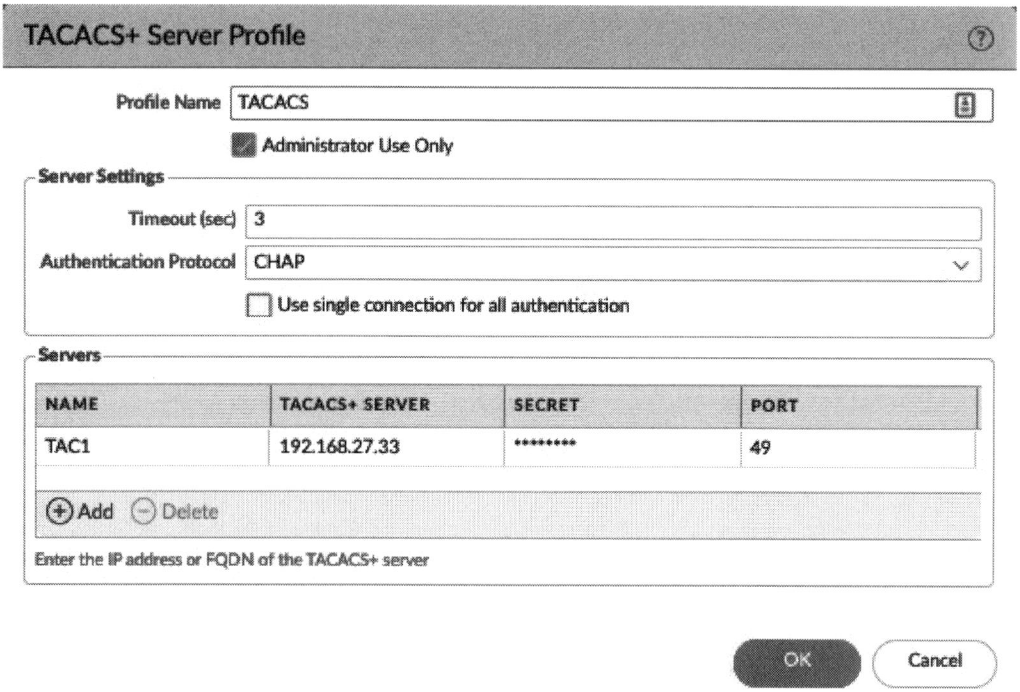

Figure 2.35 – TACACS+ Server Profile

While TACACS+ is somewhat rare, LDAP authentication is very common:

## The LDAP server profile

For an LDAP profile, you need to provide the type of the LDAP server, which can be **active-directory**, **E-directory**, **sun**, or **other**.

One thing to remember is that when you configure the server IPs and you have **Require SSL/TLS secured connection enabled**, the default port for LDAP is 636, rather than 389.

You need to provide a **Base DN** value, which is the domain name (or the distinguished name) of the LDAP tree. The **Bind DN** field is for the user account that will be used to connect to the LDAP server and perform the request and its password. **Bind DN** can be fully qualified, as shown in the following screenshot, or be a user principal name (`user@domain`):

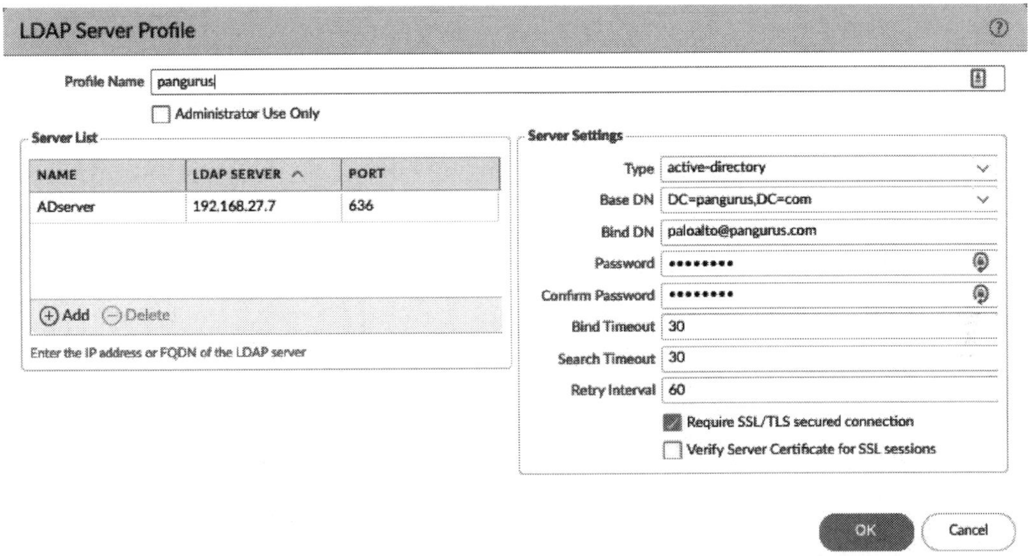

Figure 2.36 – LDAP Server Profile

If your LDAP server has an externally signed certificate, enable **Verify Server Certificate for SSL sessions** to ensure the authenticity of your server. For the certificate check to work, the LDAP server root and intermediary certificates need to be in the device certificate store in **Device | Certificate Management | Certificates | Device Certificates**. The server name in the profile must match the **Fully Qualified Domain Name (FQDN)** certificate and `Subject AltName` attribute for this check to pass.

## The RADIUS server profile

RADIUS is one of the more popular authentication methods and supports the following authentication protocols:

- PEAP-MSCHAPv2: Protected **Extensible Authentication Protocol (PEAP)** with Microsoft CHAP v2 provides improved security over PAP or CHAP by transmitting both the username and password in an encrypted tunnel.

- PEAP with **Generic Token Card (GTC)**: PEAP with **GTC** enables the use of one-time tokens in an encrypted tunnel.

- EAP-TTLS with PAP: **EAP** with **Tunneled Transport Layer Security (TTLS)** and PAP is used to transport plain text credentials for PAP in an encrypted tunnel.

- CHAP: Used if the RADIUS server does not support EAP or PAP or is not configured for it.

- PAP: Used if the RADIUS server does not support EAP or CHAP or is not configured for it.

- Palo Alto Networks uses vendor code 25461.

Like the other profiles, RADIUS can be set so that it is only used for administrator authentication. The **Allow users to change password after expiry** option is limited to GlobalProtect users if the profile is also used to authenticate GlobalProtect inbound connections. The **Make Outer Identity Anonymous** option ensures the admin username is not visible for anyone sniffing the authentication sessions if PEAP-MSCHAPv2, PEAP with GTC, or EAP-TTLS are used and the server supports this:

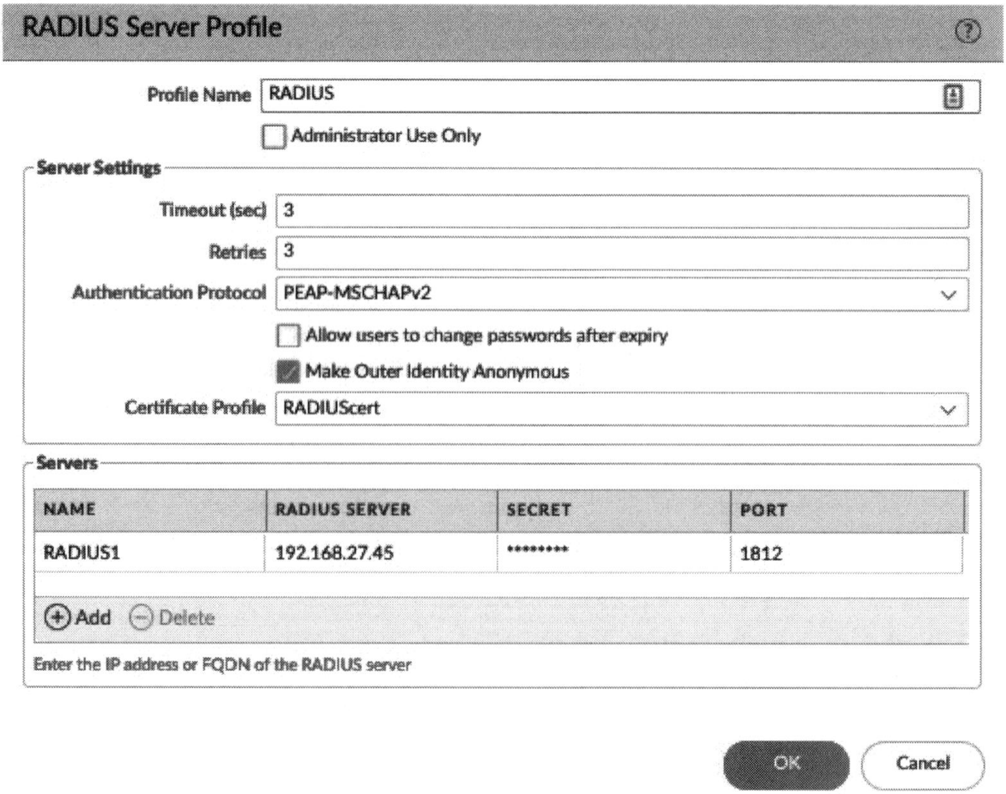

Figure 2.37 – RADIUS Server Profile

The certificate verification for RADIUS server profiles requires a certificate profile that allows more checks to be performed than just having the root certificate in the trusted certificate store compared to TACACS+. Several mechanisms can be used to verify server validity and actions can be taken if particular conditions are met with the certificate check, such as opting to allow or block a session if the certificate is valid but has expired:

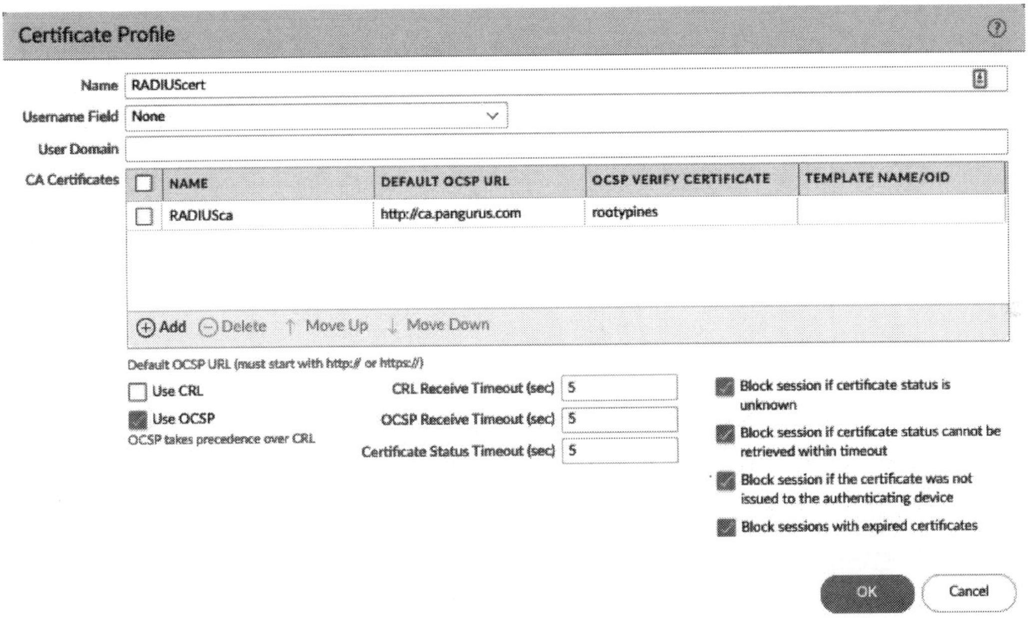

Figure 2.38 – Certificate Profile

Next, we will have a look at the Kerberos server profile.

## The Kerberos server profile

The Kerberos server profile is very simple to configure as it only requires an IP or FQDN and a port number, but it does require a few specific configuration settings:

- The firewall needs to have the domain set from **Device | Setup | Management | General Settings**.
- The firewall is synced to an NTP server from **Device | Setup | Services** so that its clock is in sync with the local `ActiveDirectory` server.
- Its DNS servers need to be set to internal DNS servers that are joined to the domain, rather than external DNS servers.

With Single Sign-On adoption on the rise and many authentication services making a move to the cloud, so is the popularity of SAML authentication increasing:

## The SAML server profile

The SAML profile enables authentication against an external **Single Sign-On (SSO)** provider (such as PingID and Okta).

Your **Identity Provider (IdP)** should provide you with the following:

- An identifier so that it can certify whether the authentication session originates from you.
- The root and intermediary certificates, which you can load to **Device | Certificate Management | Device Certificates** to verify the identity of the SSO and **Single Log Out (SLO)** sites
- An SSO URL
- An SLO URL

SAML HTTP binding provides an option to post, which sends a Base64-encoded HTML form to the IdP, or redirect, in which case the firewall will send Base64-encoded and URL-encoded SSO messages within the URL parameters.

You can sign SAML messages to the IdP with `Certificate for Signing Requests`, which can be configured in the authentication profile:

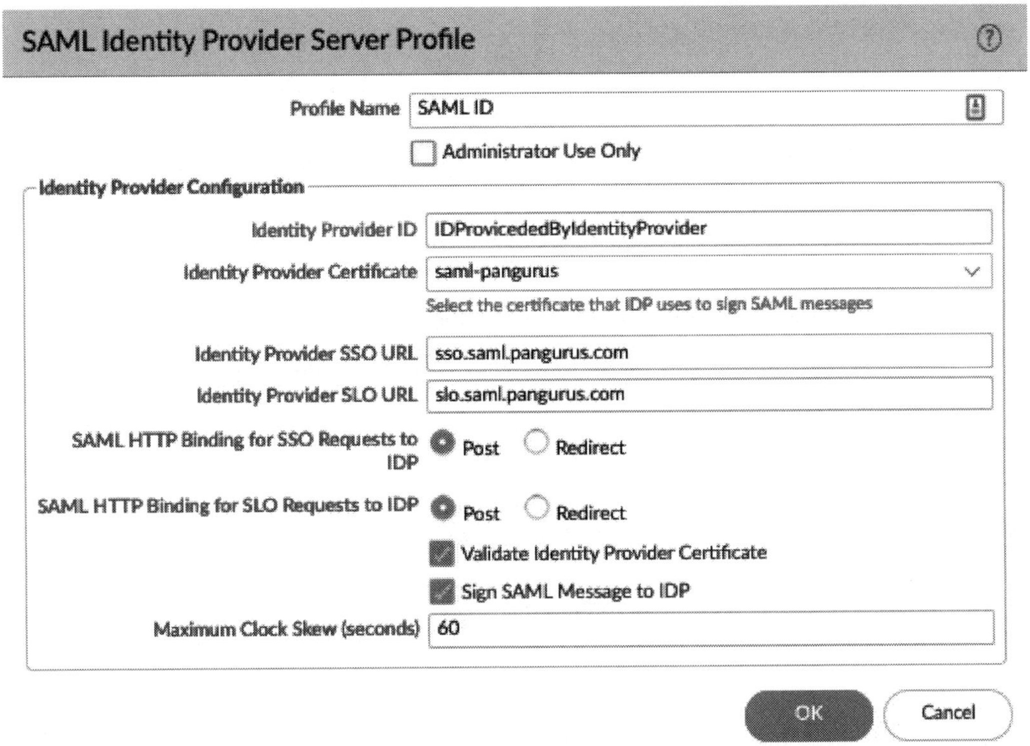

## SAML Identity Provider Server Profile    ⑦

Profile Name   SAML ID

☐ Administrator Use Only

**Identity Provider Configuration**

Identity Provider ID   IDProvicededByIdentityProvider

Identity Provider Certificate   saml-pangurus    ⌄

Select the certificate that IDP uses to sign SAML messages

Identity Provider SSO URL   sso.saml.pangurus.com

Identity Provider SLO URL   slo.saml.pangurus.com

SAML HTTP Binding for SSO Requests to IDP   ● Post   ○ Redirect

SAML HTTP Binding for SLO Requests to IDP   ● Post   ○ Redirect

☑ Validate Identity Provider Certificate

☑ Sign SAML Message to IDP

Maximum Clock Skew (seconds)   60

OK      Cancel

Figure 2.39 – SAML Identity Provider Server Profile

It is highly recommended to add Multi-Factor authentication as regular passwords require good hygiene from each administrator and could be inadvertently shared, stolen, or guessed.

## The multi-factor authentication profile

Currently, four **Multi-Factor Authentication (MFA)** providers are supported: Duo, Okta, RSA, and PingID. To configure this profile, you will need some parameters from the provider. Settings such as the API host may depend on your geolocation and keys and secrets will be unique identifiers to your account:

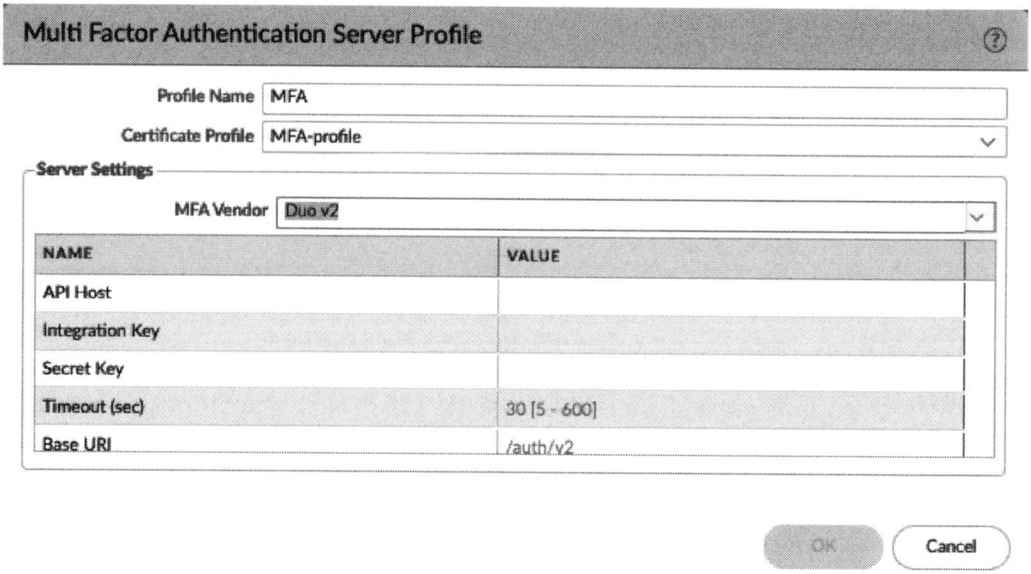

| Multi Factor Authentication Server Profile | | ⑦ |
|---|---|---|
| Profile Name | MFA | |
| Certificate Profile | MFA-profile | ⌄ |

**Server Settings**

| MFA Vendor | Duo v2 | ⌄ |
|---|---|---|

| NAME | VALUE |
|---|---|
| API Host | |
| Integration Key | |
| Secret Key | |
| Timeout (sec) | 30 [5 - 600] |
| Base URI | /auth/v2 |

OK    Cancel

Figure 2.40 – Multi Factor Authentication Server Profile

Once the appropriate server profiles have been set up, they need to be added to an authentication profile.

## Authentication profile

Now that the appropriate server profile has been configured for your environment, we can go ahead and set up an authentication profile, which will set the stage for the administrators to sign in. Go to **Device | Authentication Profile** and create a new authentication profile.

The **Authentication** tab lets you choose the type of authentication you want to use for this profile; this will match the server profile you configured in one of the previous steps. You can then add additional parameters, such as setting `sAMAccountName` or `userPrincipalName` for LDAP. **Username Modifier** lets you control how the username that the end user enters is translated and sent to the authentication server. This allows you to simply forward what the user inputs or add the user domain in **User Principal Name (UPN)** format (`user@domain`) or traditional `domain\user` backslash format:

- `%USERINPUT%`

- `%USERDOMAIN%\%USERINPUT%`

- `%USERINPUT%@%USERDOMAIN%`

This may be necessary in a multi-forest domain environment:

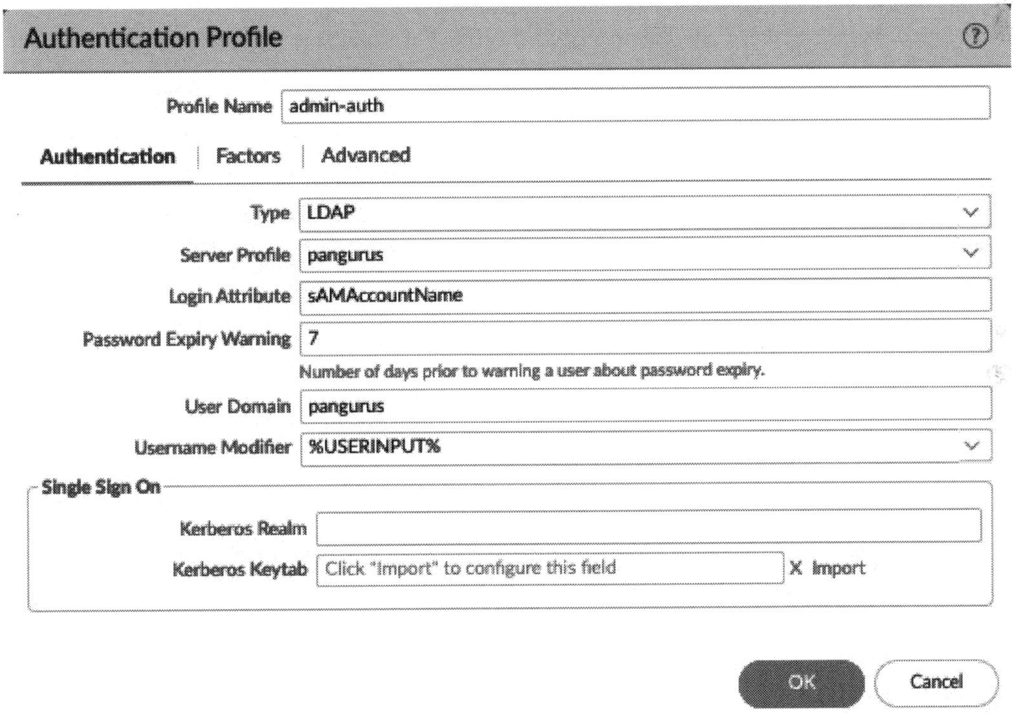

Figure 2.41 – Authentication profile LDAP example

In the **Factors** tab, you can add a profile for an MFA policy that will trigger the secondary authentication once an administrator logs in:

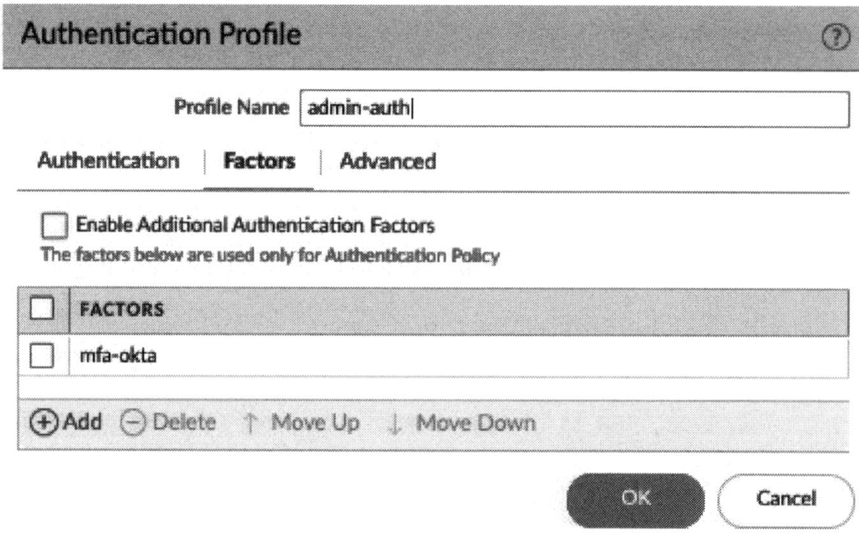

Figure 2.42 – Authentication profile MFA

The **Advanced** tab creates a bit of a chicken-and-egg situation as it requires you to tell the firewall which usernames are allowed to attempt authentication, but the list of users is only populated after you have properly set up the user ID. If you have not set up a user ID yet, set the user to **all** until you can return and narrow down the list to the actual admins.

For security purposes, you should configure a lockout policy that prevents logins for an amount of time after several failed attempts to log in:

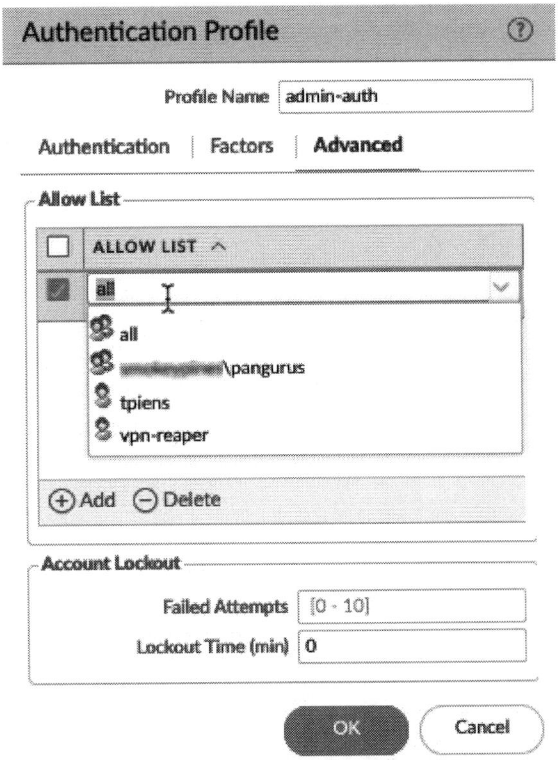

Figure 2.43 – Authentication Profile allowed users

When the profile is created, you can use it instead of a static password when creating administrator accounts. This will replace the static password for the administrator with remote authentication:

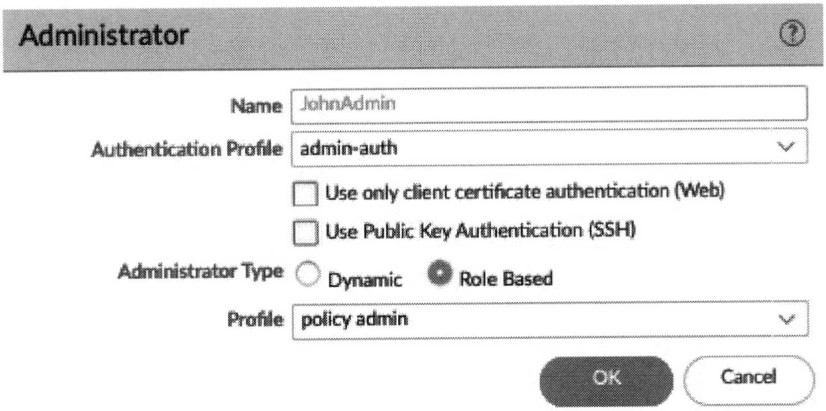

Figure 2.44 – Admin account with an authentication profile

In the next section, we will learn about the different types of interfaces.

# Understanding the interface types

When you open the **Network | Interfaces** menu, you will see an assortment of physical interfaces.

There are four basic interface types that determine how an interface will behave, which we will discuss in this section:

- Virtual Wire (**VWire**)
- Layer 3
- Layer 2
- Tap

Let's discuss them in more detail.

## VWire

Just as the name suggests, VWire is intended to be a "bump in the wire." VWire always consists of two physical interfaces—no more and no less. There is no low-level interference with VLAN tags and there are no routing options; packets are inspected in flow.

Using a VWire interface can be an easy way to "drop in a firewall" without needing to interfere with an existing routing or switching environment. It easily plugs in in front of an ISP router or can be placed in between a Honeypot and the network to add a layer of detection.

Before you can create a VWire interface, you first need to set two interfaces to the Virtual Wire type and assign each of them a different zone:

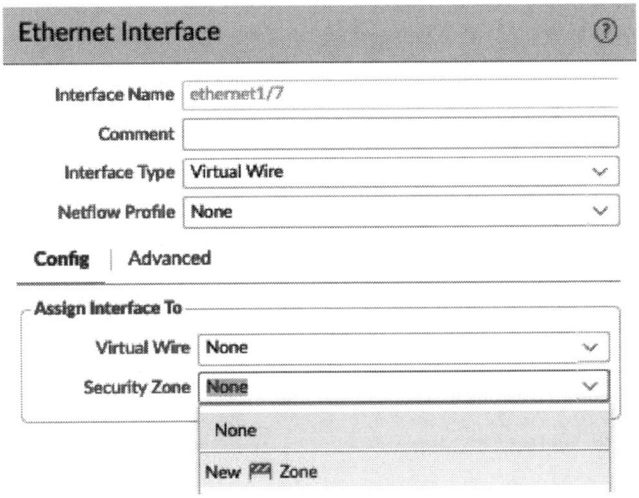

Figure 2.45 – VWire interface

You can now create a new VWire interface by going to **Network | Virtual Wires**.

You will need to select the two interfaces that you will connect over VWire. If the VWire interface is placed over a trunked link (one that contains the VLAN/802.1Q tags), you need to indicate which ones are allowed. If you want to allow all tags, set 0-4094. If you want to add single tags or ranges, you can add integers or ranges, separated by commas (for example, 5,15,30-70,100-110,4000). Multicast firewalling needs to be checked if you want to be able to block or otherwise apply security policies to multicast traffic. If unchecked, multicast is forwarded across VWire.

**Link State Pass Through** brings the opposite interface down if one side loses its connection. This ensures that both the client and server sides see the link go down and respond accordingly:

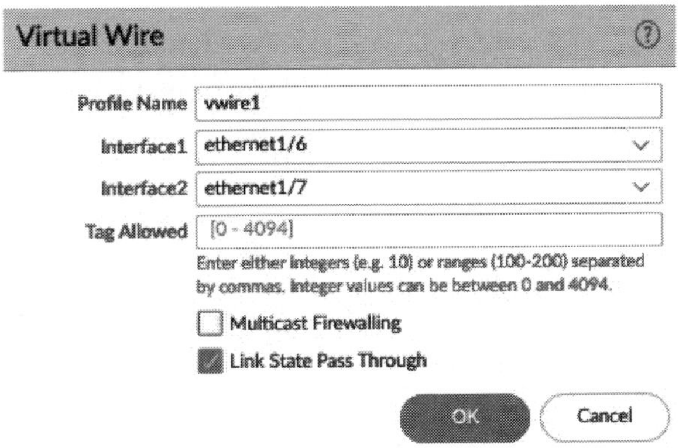

Figure 2.46 – VWire configuration

Next, let's look at the Layer 3 interface.

## The Layer 3 interface

A Layer 3 interface is a routed interface. This means it has an IP address and can be used as a default gateway for clients on the inside connected to it. On the outside, it can communicate with ISP routers and forward traffic out to the internet.

In the **Config** tab of the interface, you need to assign a **Virtual Router** (**VR**) and a security zone. This zone will represent the subnet(s) connected to it when traffic needs to flow from one interface to another:

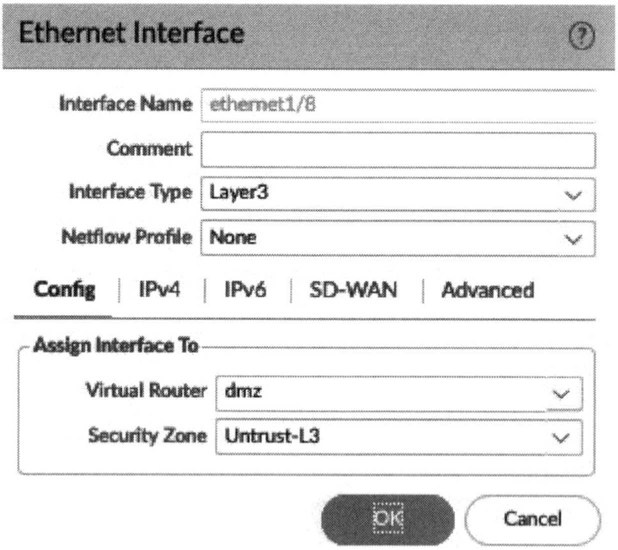

Figure 2.47 – Layer 3 interface configuration

The IP configuration can be statically configured as an IP/subnet. If needed, multiple IP/subnets can be added to represent additional networks that are directly connected to the interface. Remotely connected networks (located behind a router) can be configured in the **VR** field:

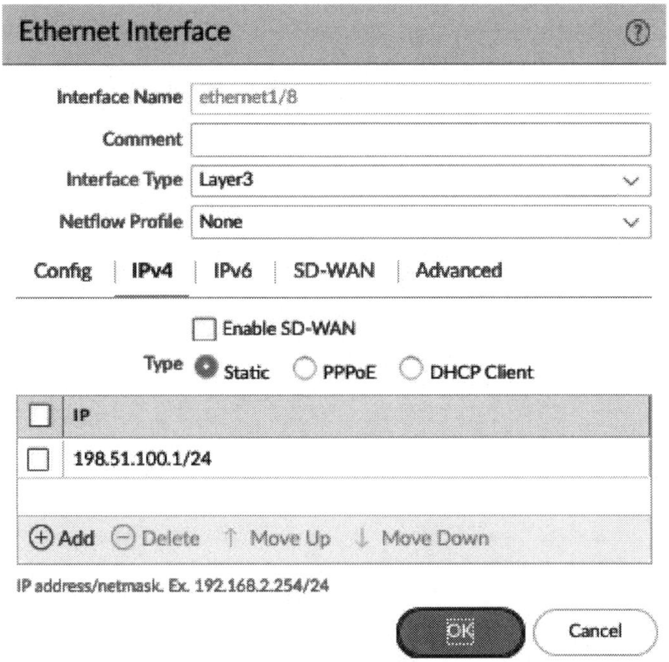

## Ethernet Interface                                                ⑦

| | |
|---|---|
| Interface Name | ethernet1/8 |
| Comment | |
| Interface Type | Layer3 ⌄ |
| Netflow Profile | None ⌄ |

Config | **IPv4** | IPv6 | SD-WAN | Advanced

☐ Enable SD-WAN

Type ⦿ Static  ◯ PPPoE  ◯ DHCP Client

| ☐ | IP |
|---|---|
| ☐ | 198.51.100.1/24 |
| | |

⊕ **Add**  ⊖ Delete  ↑ Move Up  ↓ Move Down

IP address/netmask. Ex. 192.168.2.254/24

**OK**    Cancel

Figure 2.48 – Layer 3 interface IP

A Layer 3 interface can also be set as a **Point-to-Point Protocol over Ethernet (PPPoE)** client if the upstream connection is provided by a broadband ISP over cable or DSL. In the **General** tab, the ISP authentication username and password can be configured:

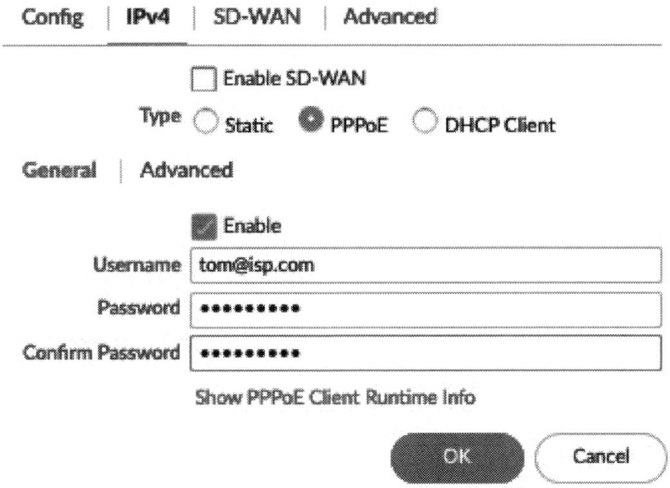

Config | **IPv4** | SD-WAN | Advanced

☐ Enable SD-WAN

Type ◯ Static  ⦿ PPPoE  ◯ DHCP Client

**General** | Advanced

☑ Enable

| | |
|---|---|
| Username | tom@isp.com |
| Password | •••••••••• |
| Confirm Password | •••••••••• |

Show PPPoE Client Runtime Info

OK    Cancel

Figure 2.49 – Layer 3 PPPoE

In the **Advanced** tab, you set the authentication protocol to **PAP**, **CHAP**, **auto**, or **none**. If the ISP has provided you with a static IP, you can configure it here and you can add an access concentrator and service string if the ISP requires them to be able to connect. If required, you can disable adding the default route received by the ISP to the routing table. Some ISPs require PPPoE clients to be in a passive state as they initiate the connection. You can enable this here:

Figure 2.50 – Layer 3 PPPoE advanced options

Once you've configured the interface and have committed the change, click on **Show PPPoE Client Runtime Info** to return information on the connection. From the CLI, you can issue the following command to see the same output:

```
admin@PA-220> show pppoe interface <interface>
```

For the layer 3 subnets and IP addresses to be reachable across interfaces, they need to be added to a routing table; this is accomplished in the virtual router.

# Virtual router

A VR is the routing element of the firewall, but, as the name suggests, it is not made up of a single engine, but rather a routing set that an interface is subscribed to. Each Layer 3, loopback, and VLAN interface needs to be associated with a VR, but multiple VRs can be used on a system. Not all interfaces need to be associated with the same VR. You can configure the default VR or add new VRs from the **Network | Virtual Routers** menu.

In the **Router Settings** tab of a VR, you can see and add interfaces associated with this VR, and adjust the administrative distances if needed. An administrative distance associates a priority with a routing protocol. By default, static routes have a higher priority (lower administrative distance) than **OSPF (Open Shortest Path First)**, but you can change this priority if you want OSPF routes to have priority and only use static routes if OSPF becomes unavailable. Routes within the same routing protocol can be assigned a metric to give them a higher (lower metric) or lower (higher metric) priority. Routes with the same metric are prioritized based on the size of their subnet. A smaller subnet (for example, /32) will have priority over a larger subnet (for example, /16):

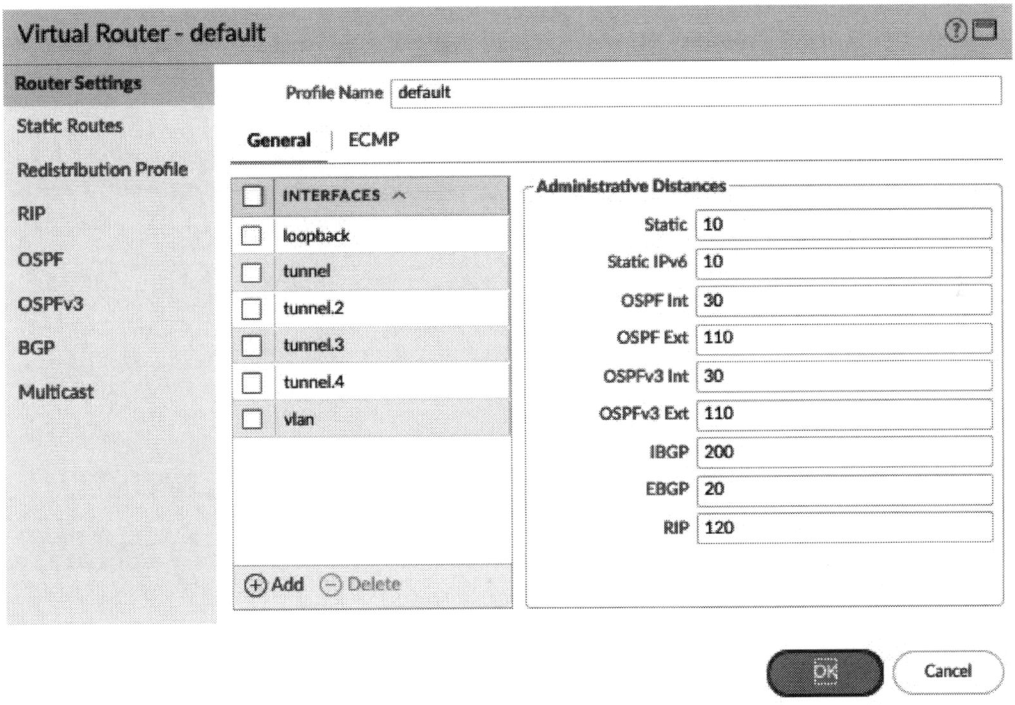

Figure 2.51 – VR settings

In the **Static Routes** tab, you can add destination routes as needed. By default, the firewall loads all the connected (configured on a Layer 3, loopback, or VLAN interface) networks in the routing table; adding static routes makes remote networks available from a routing perspective.

One of the first routes you may need to configure is the "default route," which allows clients to connect to the internet.

The destination for the default route is 0.0.0.0/0. A regular route could have a smaller subnet, such as 172.16.0.0/24.

The **Interface** option indicates what the egress interface will be. If the route is pointing to the internet, the interface will be the one where the ISP router is connected.

**Next Hop** has several options:

- **IP Address**: The IP of the upstream router to forward packets to.
- **Next VR**: Whether the packet needs to be handed over to a different VR on the same device.
- **FQDN**: If the upstream router has a dynamic IP, it could be useful to use an FQDN that is dynamically updated.
- **Discard**: Routes can be set to "black hole" certain subnets. This can be used to prevent any packets from reaching a connected out-of-band network, even if a security policy were to allow this.
- **None**: Routes may not have a next hop, such as packets routed into a VPN tunnel.

The **Admin Distance** and **Metric** settings can be changed for each route if necessary.

**Route Table** is used to add routes to regular unicast routing, to multicast routing, or to both.

You can, if you have redundancy available, use **Path Monitoring** to send a heartbeat ping over the route. If the ping fails a configured amount of times, the route will be disabled. The routing table will be re-evaluated for matching packets and the next best match will be used to route packets (that is, a route with a higher metric or larger subnet):

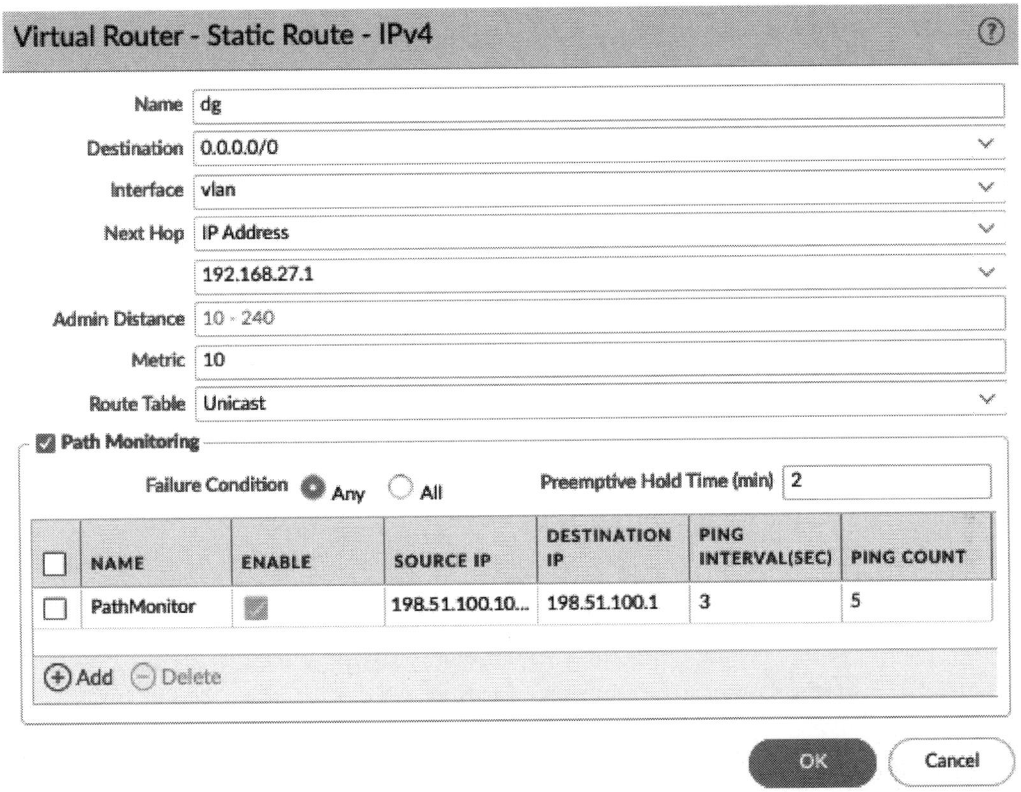

**Virtual Router - Static Route - IPv4**    ⑦

| | |
|---|---|
| Name | dg |
| Destination | 0.0.0.0/0 ⌄ |
| Interface | vlan ⌄ |
| Next Hop | IP Address ⌄ |
| | 192.168.27.1 ⌄ |
| Admin Distance | 10 - 240 |
| Metric | 10 |
| Route Table | Unicast ⌄ |

☑ **Path Monitoring**

Failure Condition  ● Any  ○ All        Preemptive Hold Time (min)  2

| ☐ | NAME | ENABLE | SOURCE IP | DESTINATION IP | PING INTERVAL(SEC) | PING COUNT |
|---|---|---|---|---|---|---|
| ☐ | PathMonitor | ☑ | 198.51.100.10... | 198.51.100.1 | 3 | 5 |

⊕ Add  ⊖ Delete

OK    Cancel

Figure 2.52 – VR default route

# The Layer 2 interface and VLANs

Setting interfaces to the Layer 2 type enables the firewall to function in a similar way to placing a switch in the network. Each interface acts as the equivalent of an access port (if you need trunk functionality, refer to the *Subinterfaces* topic) on a switch, and you can add as many interfaces as you need.

Each interface should use a different zone so that security policy can be leveraged to control traffic between the interfaces. Interfaces set to the same zone will, by default, exchange traffic without inspection and require a catch-all security policy to enable inspection.

To group the interfaces into a logical "switch," you need to create a VLAN object by going to **Networks | VLANs** and adding the interfaces you previously set to Layer 2 and want to be connected:

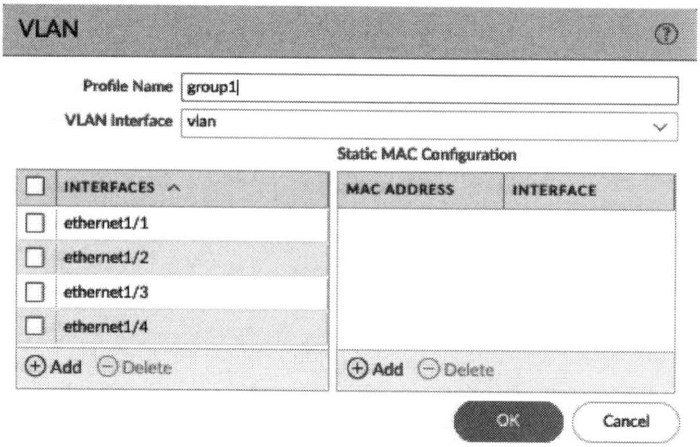

Figure 2.53 – VLAN group

The **VLAN Interface** option adds routing functionality to the group as a logical Layer 3 interface. This can be useful if you have an upstream ISP router or a different subnet connected to a Layer 3 interface that you need to interact with.

You can configure the VLAN Interface by going to **Network | Interfaces | VLAN**. Assign it to the VLAN group you created, fill in the **Virtual Router** field, and assign it a zone. This zone will represent Layer 2 interfaces when interacting with Layer 3 interfaces for security policies:

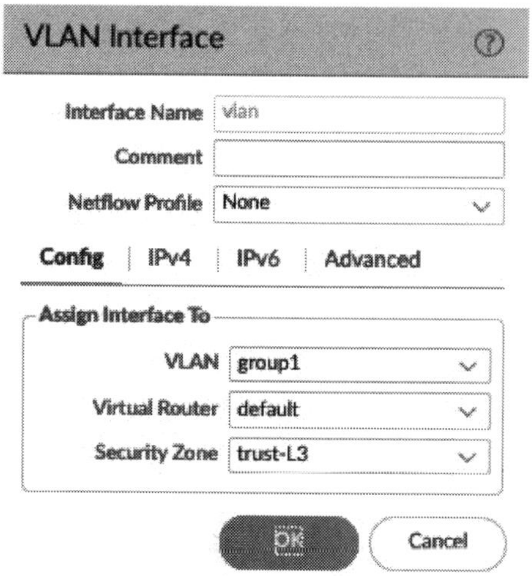

Figure 2.54 – VLAN Interface configuration

You will also need to assign the VLAN interface an IP address that the clients on Layer 2 interfaces can use as a default gateway or routing next hop. Make sure it is in the same subnet as your clients on the Layer 2 interfaces:

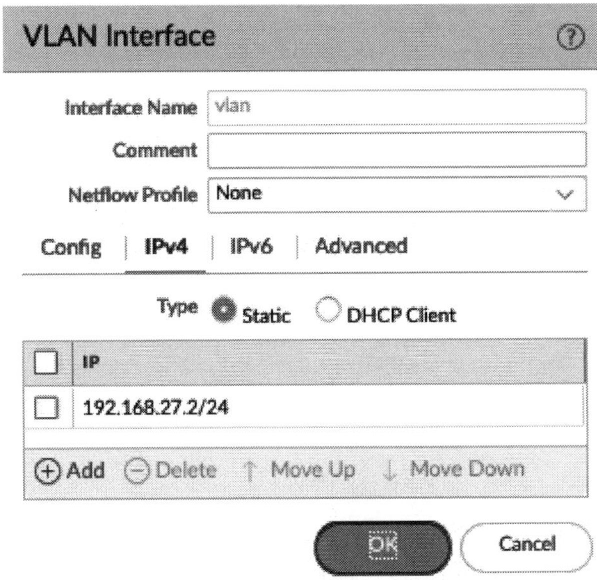

Figure 2.55 – VLAN Interface IP address

Besides Ethernet interfaces, there are also three different logical interfaces:

- Loopback
- Tunnel
- VLAN

We covered VLAN interfaces in the Layer 2 topic, so let's now take a look at the Swiss army knife of interfaces, the loopback.

# The loopback interface

A loopback interface is a logical Layer 3 interface that can serve many purposes. It needs to be configured with an IP address (only a single IP per loopback interface is supported) and a security zone and it needs to be associated with a VR.

It can be set to a new IP address in the same subnet and zone as one of the Layer 3 interfaces, so services such as **Management Profile**, **Captive Portal**, and **GlobalProtect** can be hosted on a different IP than the main IP of the physical interface.

To add extra security, it can also be set to a different zone so that a matching security rule is needed for clients to be able to connect to the loopback interface:

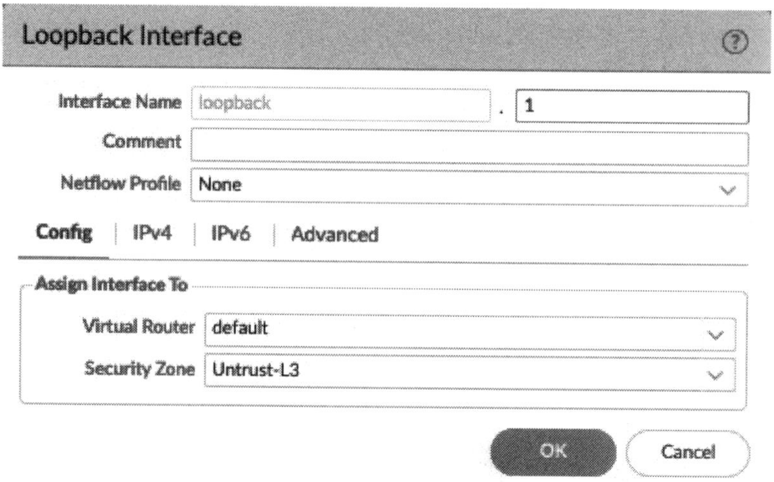

Figure 2.56 – Loopback interface

The number next to **Interface Name** is an identification number for the logical interface.

# The tunnel interface

Tunnel interfaces are logical interfaces that serve as the ingress and egress point of tunneled traffic, both site-to-site VPN and GlobalProtect SSL and IPSec. The physical tunnel is terminated on a Layer 3 or loopback interface, but the packets that need to be encrypted should be routed to the tunnel interface:

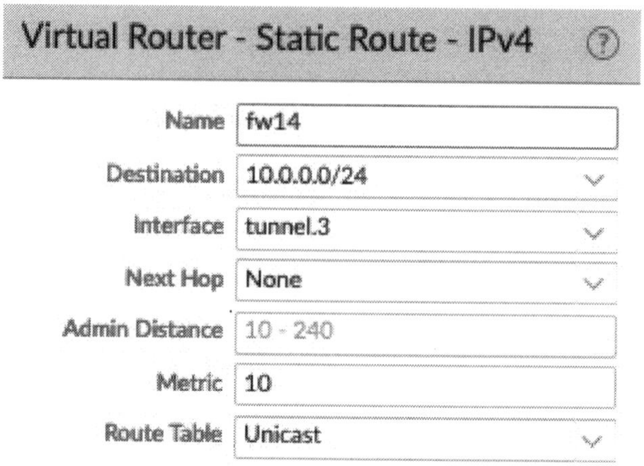

Figure 2.57 – Static route for a VPN tunnel

This interface needs to be associated with a VR and a security zone, as you can see in the following screenshot:

> **Important note**
> For a strong security posture, set a separate zone for individual VPN connections, even for known locations. Treating each zone and remote network as "trust but verify" ensures adequate visibility and control. A remote office could be exposed to malware (think WannaCry) and infect other offices if the VPN tunnel is set to the same zone for all remote offices. The default `intrazone` security rule allows all sessions to run and does not apply scanning.

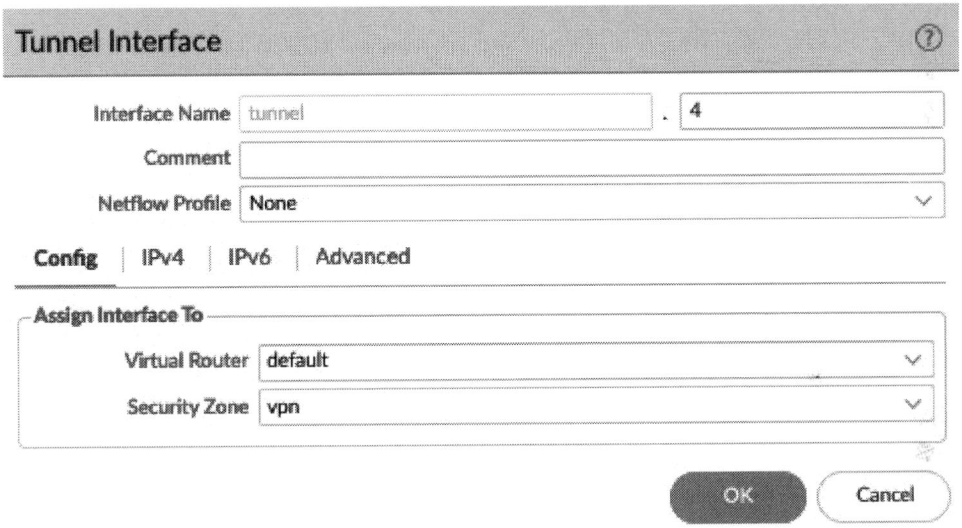

**Tunnel Interface** ⑦

| | | |
|---|---|---|
| Interface Name | tunnel | . 4 |
| Comment | | |
| Netflow Profile | None | ⌄ |

**Config** | IPv4 | IPv6 | Advanced

─ Assign Interface To ────────────────
| Virtual Router | default | ⌄ |
| Security Zone | vpn | ⌄ |

OK    Cancel

Figure 2.58 – Tunnel Interface

The number next to **Interface Name** is an identification number for the logical interface.

There are also several "special" interface types that provide a specific functionality:

- Subinterfaces
- **High Availability (HA)**
- **Aggregate Ethernet (AE)**
- The tap interface
- Decryption Port Mirror

When a switch uplink needs to contain multiple 802.1q VLAN tags, it can be configured as a trunk and, on the firewall, subinterfaces can be created to correspond to each VLAN tag.

## Subinterfaces

All physical (that is, **Layer2**, **Layer3**, **VWire**, and **Aggregate**) interfaces can have subinterfaces. You can create these by selecting the desired physical interface and clicking on **Add Subinterface**:

| INTERFACE | INTERFACE TYPE | LINK STATE | IP ADDRESS | MAC ADDRESS | VIRTUAL ROUTER | SECURITY ZONE |
|---|---|---|---|---|---|---|
| ethernet1/3 | Layer3 | | none | 00:1b:17:00:32:12 | none | none |
| ethernet1/3.10 | Layer3 | | 172.16.0.1/24 | | default | finance |
| ethernet1/3.20 | Layer3 | | 192.168.27.1/... | | default | trust-L3 |

Figure 2.59 – Creating a subinterface

A subinterface is used when the physical interface is connected to a trunked link containing VLAN (802.1Q) tagged packets. The physical interface is not able to interpret the tags, but subinterfaces are. For each VLAN carried by the trunk, you can create a subinterface to represent the virtual network coming from the switch. The advantage of using subinterfaces is that each VLAN can be associated with its own security zone.

The subinterface will mimic all the configuration specifics of its parent physical interface, but interface types cannot be different from the physical interface type (for example, a Layer 3 physical interface cannot host a Layer 2 subinterface).

## HA interfaces

**HA** interfaces are required when setting up a cluster of two firewalls. Some chassis will have built-in dedicated HA interfaces, in which case you may not need to create any HA interfaces yourself. If no onboard HA interfaces are available, or additional interfaces are required to serve as back-up HA links, data plane interfaces can be selected to fulfill this role and are connected to the HA peer.

# AE interfaces

To increase available bandwidth above the physical limitations of the interfaces, interfaces can be bundled into an AE group using the 802.1AX protocol. Up to eight interfaces can be combined into a logical bundle.

A new group can be created by clicking on **Add Aggregate Group** under **Network | Interfaces | Ethernet**.

You first need to set the type to **Layer 2, Layer 3, VWire, or HA**, which will require the same configuration as the physical interface equivalent (that is, security zone, VR, or VLAN or VWire).

Additionally, you can configure the **Link Aggregation Control Protocol (LACP)** to improve interface failure detection. LACP enables link failure detection on the physical and data link layer, while the default protocol only detects physical link failure.

You can set whether the firewall is in **Active** or **Passive** mode. This configuration setting needs to be reviewed with the LACP peer (typically the switch) as only one peer can be configured as **Active**, but LACP will not work if both are set to **Passive**.

The transmission rate will have an impact on the responsiveness of link failure detection, but it will also have an overhead. Slow transmission means every 30 seconds, while fast transmission means every second.

**Fast Failover** will fail to an operational interface within 1 second when an interface goes down. Traditional failover happens after 3 seconds.

**System Priority** determines which peer determines port priorities.

**Maximum Interfaces** determines how many interfaces can be active at the same time within the aggregate group. This number should not exceed the number of physical interfaces you assign to the group, but can be leveraged to limit total available bandwidth while keeping hot interfaces in reserve in case of failure (for example, if a total bandwidth of 4 gigabits is needed for an aggregate group, but you also do not want to exceed this bandwidth to preserve system resources, you can assign five or more interfaces to the aggregate group, and set **Maximum Interfaces** to 4. Only when an interface fails will another one be activated to pick up the work):

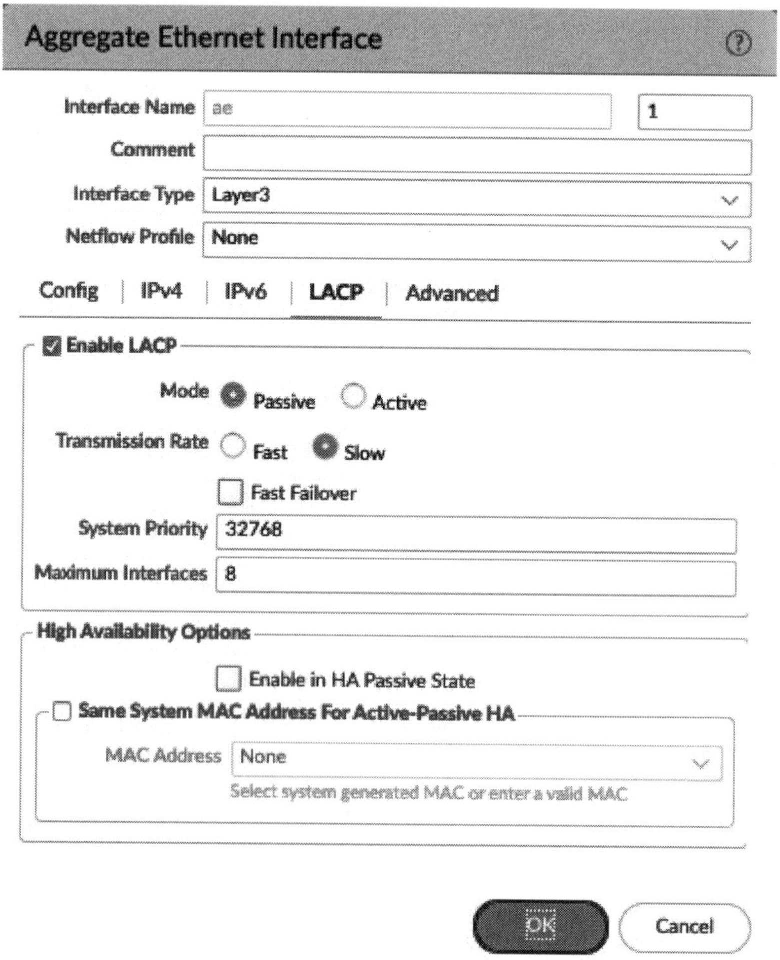

Figure 2.60 – Link Aggregation Control Protocol

When the Aggregate Group is created, you can add the interfaces by setting the **Interface Type** to Aggregate Ethernet and selecting the desired **Aggregate Group**:

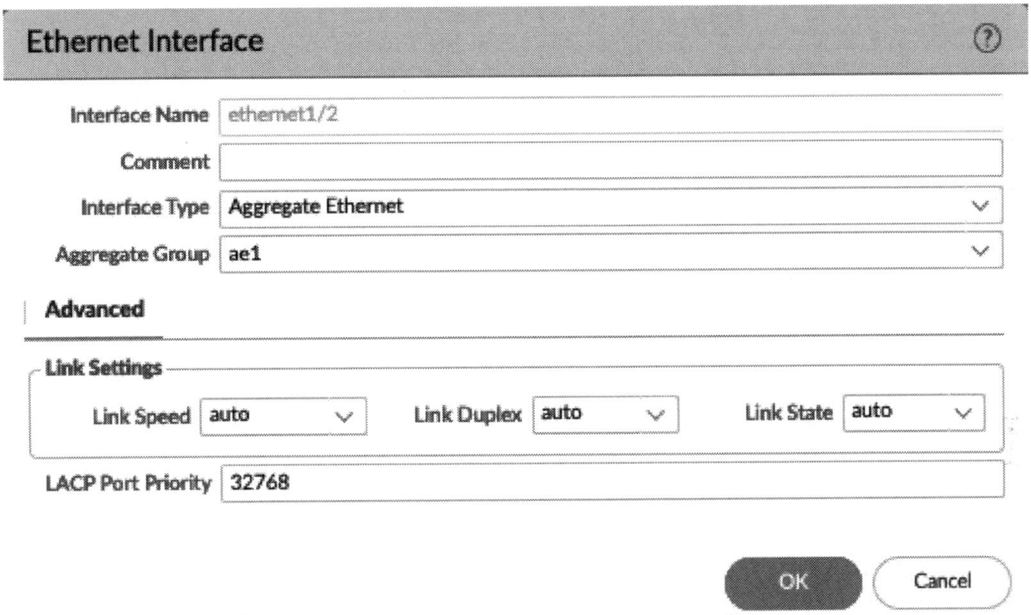

| Ethernet Interface | ? |
| --- | --- |

| Interface Name | ethernet1/2 |
| --- | --- |
| Comment | |
| Interface Type | Aggregate Ethernet ⌄ |
| Aggregate Group | ae1 ⌄ |

**Advanced**

Link Settings

| Link Speed | auto ⌄ | Link Duplex | auto ⌄ | Link State | auto ⌄ |
| --- | --- | --- | --- | --- | --- |

| LACP Port Priority | 32768 |
| --- | --- |

OK      Cancel

Figure 2.61 – A physical interface in an aggregate group

In some cases, you may need to be able to connect to a port mirror on a switch and just listen without participating. For such instances, you can configure a TAP interface.

# Tap interfaces

Tap interfaces can be used as a passive sniffing port. If a different network device is set up with portmirroring, its egress port can be connected to the tap interface to intercept all packets and apply the app ID and content ID. As long as the tap interface is sent all packets of a session, it will be able to inspect the traffic as if it is flowing through the firewall. There are, however, a few limitations:

- As the firewall is not actively participating in the processing of packets, it cannot take action if it detects a threat; it can only report it.

- SSL decryption can only be applied to inbound connections if the server certificate can be loaded onto the firewall with its private key.

The tap interface only needs to be configured with a security zone:

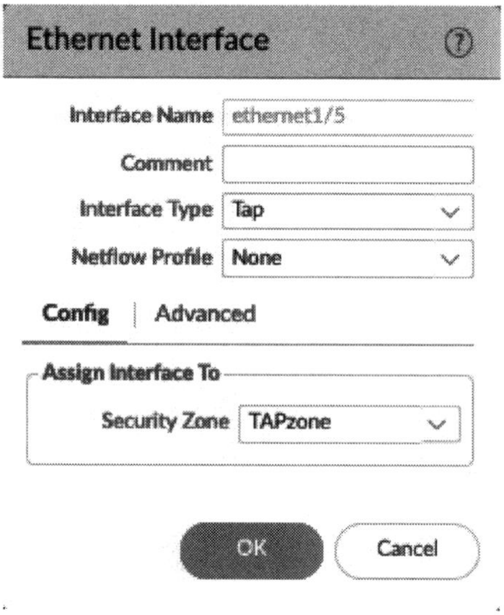
Ethernet Interface
Interface Name
ethernet1/5
Comment
Interface Type
Tap
Netflow Profile
None
Config
Advanced
Assign Interface To
Security Zone
TAPzone
OK
Cancel

Figure 2.62 – The tap interface

To optimally benefit from the tap functionality, a security rule will need to be created that allows all operations, or a specific subset, if you want to limit the scope. The firewall will discard all packets in the background, but setting the security rule to **drop** would discard the packets before inspection:

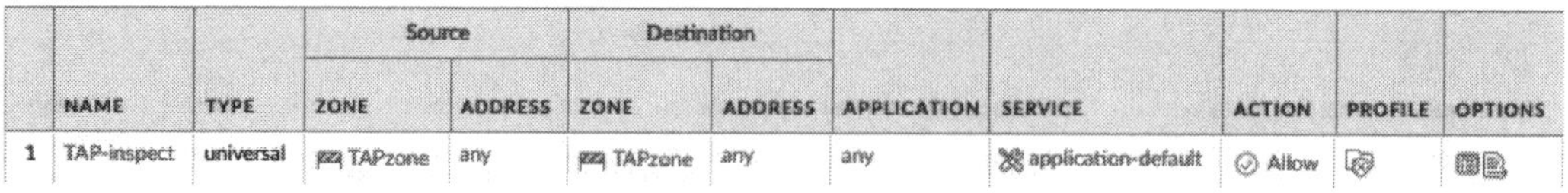
Source
Destination
NAME
TYPE
ZONE
ADDRESS
ZONE
ADDRESS
APPLICATION
SERVICE
ACTION
PROFILE
OPTIONS
1
TAP-inspect
universal
TAPzone
any
TAPzone
any
any
application-default
Allow

Figure 2.63 – The tap security rule

Similar to listening in on a port mirror, the firewall can send all unencrypted session data to a third-party **DLP** (**Data Loss Prevention**) or threat intelligence device. It can do so via a **Decryption port mirror** interface.

## The Decryption Port Mirror interface

The Decryption Port Mirror interface allows the forwarding of decrypted packets to an external device for further inspection. This can be useful for data loss prevention, for example. The license can be activated for free via the support portal by browsing to `https://support.paloaltonetworks.com` and then going to **Assets | Devices**. There, you can find your firewall and click the **actions** button. If you choose to activate a feature license, you will be able to activate **Decryption Port Mirror**:

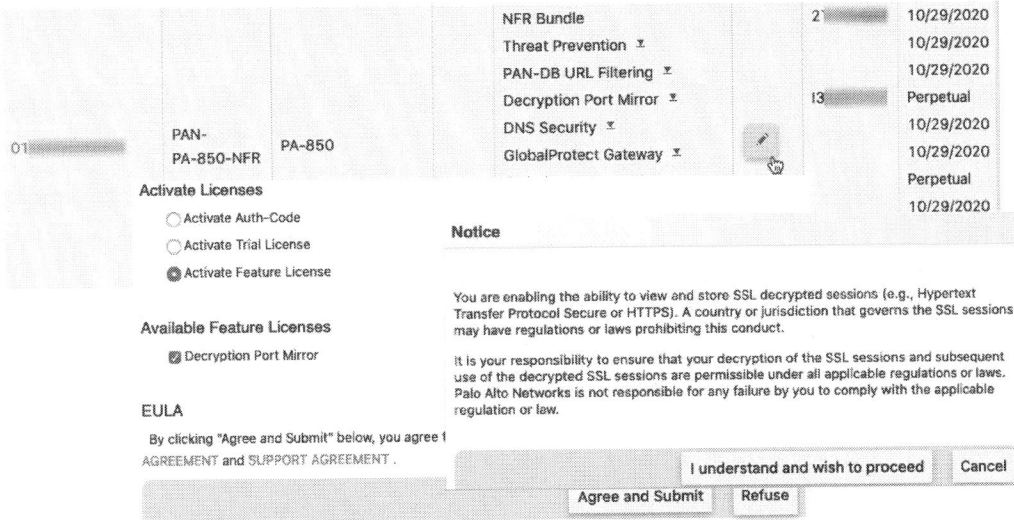

Figure 2.64 – Activating a Decryption Port Mirror license

To activate the license on the firewall, follow these steps:

1. From **Device | Licenses**, select **Retrieve license keys from license server**.

2. In **Device | Setup | Content ID | Content-ID settings**, enable **Allow forwarding of decrypted content**.

3. In **Network | Interfaces | Ethernet**, set an interface to the **Decrypt Mirror** type.

4. In **Objects | Decryption | Decryption Profiles**, open the decryption profile and add the interface to **Decryption Mirroring**.

5. In **Policies | Decryption**, create decryption rules that use the decryption profile.

6. Save the changes and connect the **Decryption Port Mirror** interface.

You are now able to set up the interfaces you need in order to connect your firewall to any environment.

# Summary

In this chapter, you learned how to create a support account, register a new device, and add licenses. You can now upgrade and update a device so that its firmware is up to date and the latest application and threat signatures are loaded to protect the network. You learned how to protect the management interface so that only legitimate users can connect, and you can now assign different accesses and privileges to administrators. You should understand what all the physical and logical interfaces are for and how to leverage them in your network.

In the next chapter, we will start building robust security policies and learn how to set a strong security posture for network traffic.

# Section 2: Advanced Configuration and Putting the Features to Work

In this section, we will start to build a more advanced configuration. You will learn how to create strong security policies and build security profiles that will enforce a strong security posture automatically.

This section comprises the following chapters:

- *Chapter 3, Building Strong Policies*
- *Chapter 4, Taking Control of Sessions*
- *Chapter 5, Services and Operational Modes*
- *Chapter 6, Identifying Users and Controlling Access*
- *Chapter 7, Managing Firewalls through Panorama*

# 3
# Building Strong Policies

In this chapter, you will get comfortable with configuring security profiles, building rule bases for security, and **Network Address Translation (NAT)**. We will learn what each setting does, what its expected behavior is, and how it can be leveraged to lead to the desired outcome. Taking full control over all of the features available in the different rule bases will enable you to adopt a strong security stance.

In this chapter, we're going to cover the following main topics:

- Understanding and preparing security profiles
- Understanding and building security rules
- Setting up NAT in all possible directions

## Technical requirements

Before you get started, your firewall must have connectivity between at least two networks, with one preferably being your **Internet Service Provider (ISP)**, to fully benefit from the information provided in this chapter.

# Understanding and preparing security profiles

Before you can start building a solid security rule base, you need to create at least one set of security profiles to use in all of your security rules.

> **Important note**
>
> Security profiles are evaluated by the first security rule that a session is matched against. If a six-tuple is matched against a security rule with no or limited security profiles, no scanning can take place until there is an application shift and the security policy is re-evaluated. It is important for *all* security rules to have security profiles.

## The Antivirus profile

The Antivirus profile has three sections that depend on different licenses and dynamic update settings. The actions under **ACTION** rely on the threat prevention license and antivirus updates, **WILDFIRE ACTION** relies on the WildFire license and the WildFire updates that are set to periodical updates (1 minute or longer intervals), and **DYNAMIC CLASSIFICATION ACTION** relies on WildFire set to real time. If any of these licenses are missing from your system, the actions listed in their columns will not be applied. **Application Exception** allows you to change the action associated with a decoder for individual applications as needed. The actions that can be set for both threat prevention and WildFire antivirus actions are as follows:

- **allow**: Allows matching signatures *without* logging
- **drop**: Drops matching signatures and writes an entry in the threat log
- **alert**: Allows matching signatures to pass but writes an entry in the threat log
- **reset-client**: Drops matching packets, sends a TCP RST to the client, and writes an entry in the threat log
- **reset-server**: Drops matching packets, sends a TCP RST to the server, and writes an entry in the threat log
- **reset-both**: Drops matching packets, sends a TCP RST to the client and server, and writes an entry in the threat log

Packet captures can be enabled for further analysis by the security team or as forensic evidence. They are attached to the threat log and are limited to packets containing matched signatures.

Create a new Antivirus profile by going to **Objects | Security Profiles | Antivirus**.

As the following screenshot shows, we will use all the default settings:

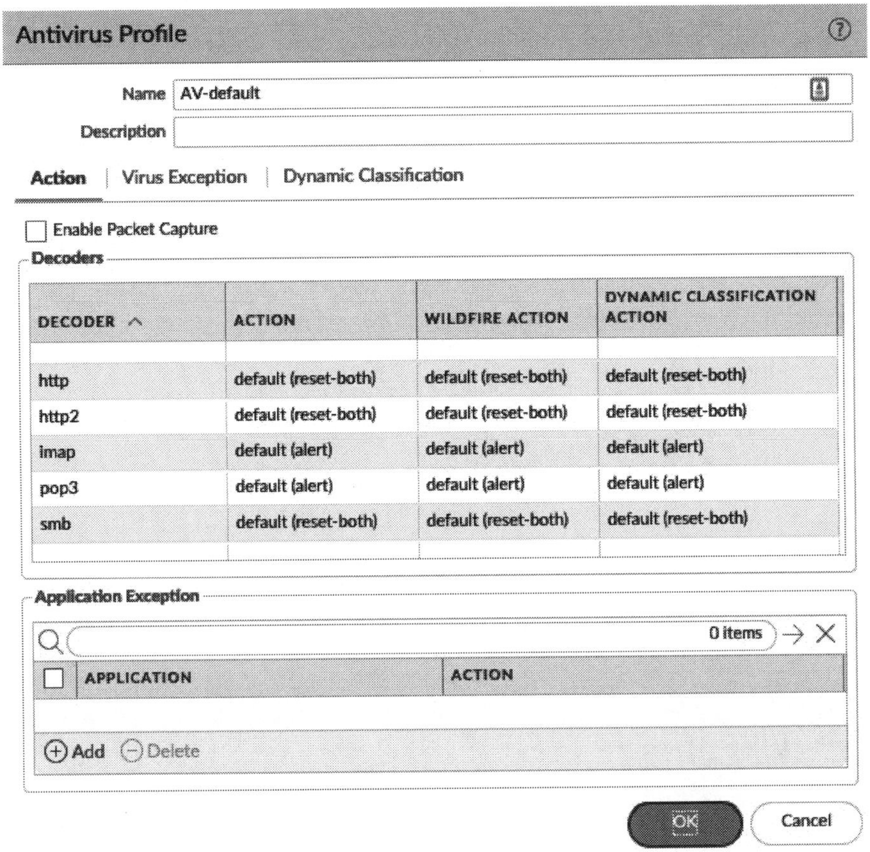

**Antivirus Profile**                                                          ⑦

| | |
|---|---|
| Name | AV-default |
| Description | |

**Action**  |  Virus Exception  |  Dynamic Classification

☐ Enable Packet Capture

**Decoders**

| DECODER ⌃ | ACTION | WILDFIRE ACTION | DYNAMIC CLASSIFICATION ACTION |
|---|---|---|---|
| http | default (reset-both) | default (reset-both) | default (reset-both) |
| http2 | default (reset-both) | default (reset-both) | default (reset-both) |
| imap | default (alert) | default (alert) | default (alert) |
| pop3 | default (alert) | default (alert) | default (alert) |
| smb | default (reset-both) | default (reset-both) | default (reset-both) |

**Application Exception**

🔍 _____  0 items  → ✕

| ☐ APPLICATION | ACTION |
|---|---|
| | |

⊕ Add  ⊖ Delete

OK      Cancel

Figure 3.1 – Antivirus Profile

We will now have a look at the Anti-Spyware profile.

# The Anti-Spyware profile

The Anti-Spyware profile is extremely customizable and is built by a set of rules within the profile. These rules serve to change the default actions associated with each threat; so, if no rules are created at all, the profile will simply apply the default action for a specific signature when it is detected.

Anti-Spyware supports the same actions as Antivirus (**allow**, **drop**, **alert**, **reset-client**, **reset-server**, and **reset-both**), as well as **block-ip**:

- **block-ip** can track by source or source-destination pair and will block the offending IP for a duration of 1-3600 seconds. Tracking by source will block all connections from the client for the duration of the block, while tracking by source-destination will only block connections from the client to the target destination and will not block the same client from connecting to other destinations.

The **Packet capture** options include none, single-packet, and extended-capture. While single-packet only captures the packet containing the payload matching a signature, extended-capture enables the capture of multiple packets to help analyze a threat. The number of packets captured by extended-capture can be configured via **Device | Setup | Content-ID**. The default is 5.

> **Important note**
> Enabling packet capture on all threats does require some CPU cycles. The impact will not be very large, but if the system is already very taxed, some caution is advised.

**Severity** indicates the severity level of the threat that applies to this rule.

Create a new Anti-Spyware profile, as in the following screenshot, and add the following rules:

- **POLICY NAME**: simple-critical

  --**SEVERITY**: critical

  --**ACTION**: block-ip (source, 120)

  --**PACKET CAPTURE**: single-packet
- **POLICY NAME**: simple-high

  --**SEVERITY**: high

  --**ACTION**: reset-both

  --**PACKET CAPTURE**: single-packet

- **POLICY NAME**: simple-medium

  --**SEVERITY**: medium

  --**ACTION**: reset-both

  --**PACKET CAPTURE**: single-packet

- **POLICY NAME**: simple-low-info

  --**SEVERITY**: low, informational

  --**ACTION**: default

  --**PACKET CAPTURE**: disable

Your profile will now look like this:

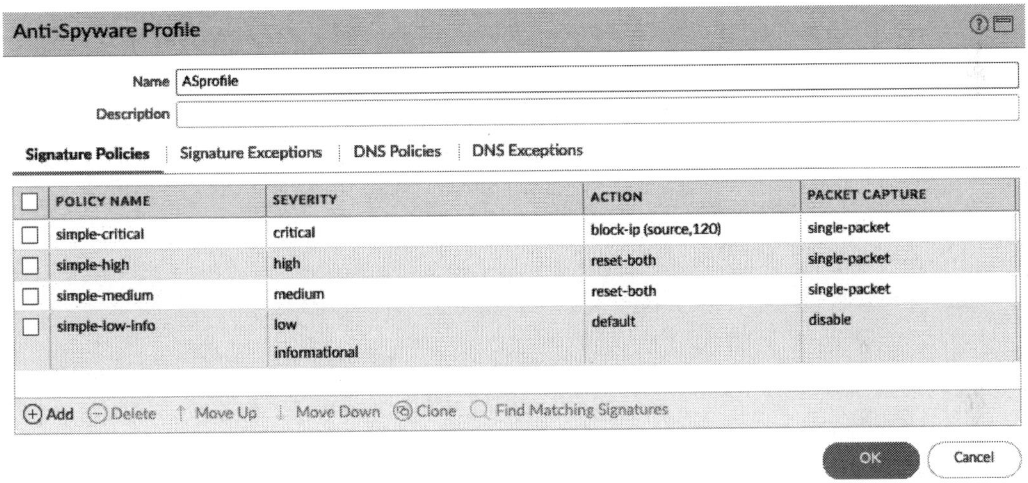

**Anti-Spyware Profile**                                                           ⑦▭

Name  ASprofile

Description

**Signature Policies**   Signature Exceptions   DNS Policies   DNS Exceptions

| | POLICY NAME | SEVERITY | ACTION | PACKET CAPTURE |
|---|---|---|---|---|
| ☐ | simple-critical | critical | block-ip (source,120) | single-packet |
| ☐ | simple-high | high | reset-both | single-packet |
| ☐ | simple-medium | medium | reset-both | single-packet |
| ☐ | simple-low-info | low<br>informational | default | disable |

⊕ **Add**  ⊖ Delete   ↑ Move Up   ↓ Move Down  ⊚ Clone  ◯ Find Matching Signatures

OK          Cancel

Figure 3.2 – Anti-Spyware Profile

As you can see in the following screenshot, we need to make sure we review **Category** as this allows a fine-grained approach to each specific type of threat if granularity and individualized actions are needed at a later stage:

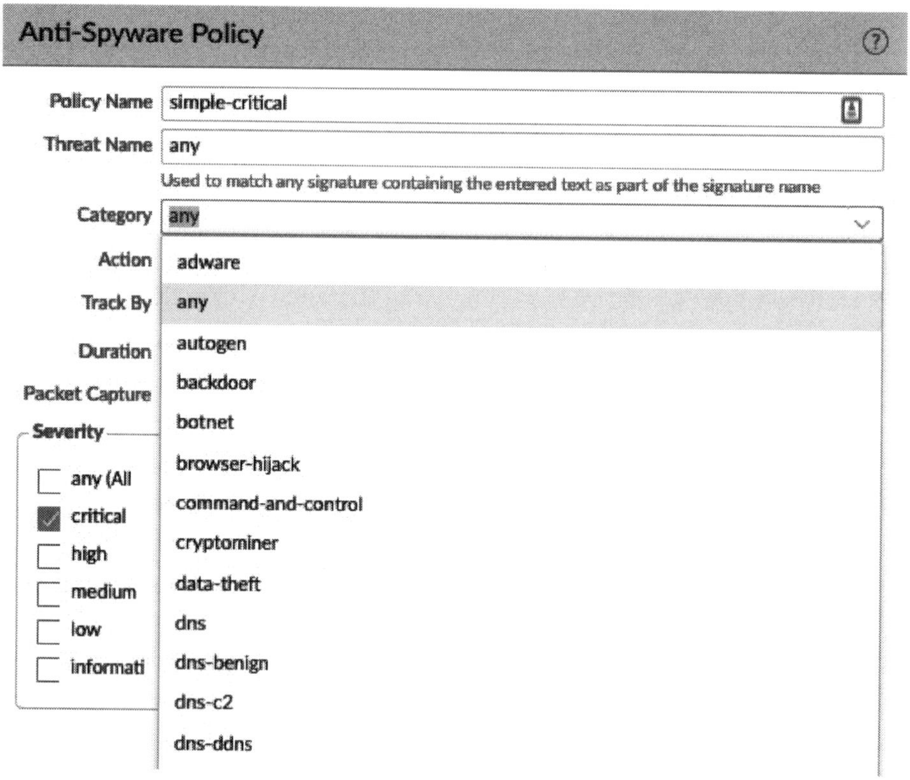

Figure 3.3 – Anti-Spyware categories

The Anti-Spyware profile also contains DNS signatures, which are split into two databases for the subscription services.

The content DNS signatures are downloaded with the threat prevention dynamic updates. The DNS Security database uses dynamic cloud lookups.

The elements in each database can be set to **Alert**, **Allow**, **Block**, or **Sinkhole**. **Sinkhole** uses a DNS poisoning technique that replaces the IP in the DNS reply packet, so the client does get a valid DNS reply, but with an altered destination IP. This ensures that infected endpoints can easily be found by filtering traffic logs for sessions going to the sinkhole IP. You can keep using the Palo Alto Networks default sinkhole, `sinkhole.paloaltonetworks.com`, or use your preferred IP.

The way that the DNS sinkhole works is illustrated by the following steps and diagram:

1. The client sends a DNS query to resolve a malicious domain to the internal DNS server.

2. The internal DNS relays the DNS lookup to an internet DNS server.

3. The firewall forges a poisoned reply to the DNS query and replies to the internal DNS server with a record pointing to the sinkhole IP.

4. The DNS reply is forwarded to the client.

5. The client makes an outbound connection to the sinkhole IP, instead of the malicious server. The admin immediately knows which host is potentially infected and is trying to set up **Command and Control (C2)** connections:

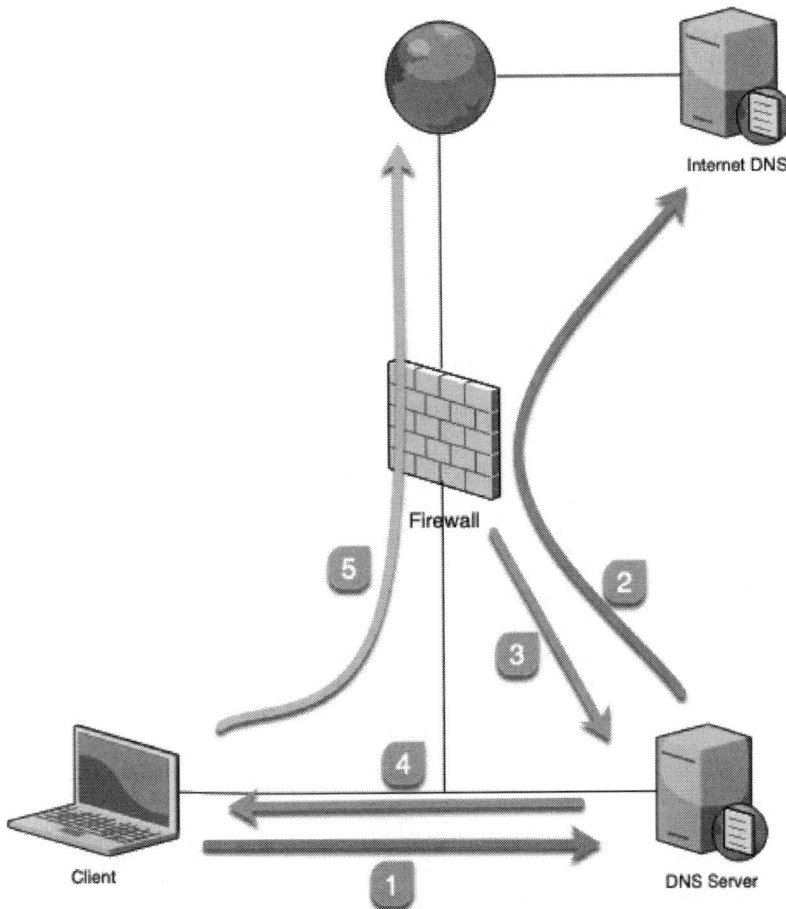

Figure 3.4 – How a DNS sinkhole works

Blocking instead of sinkholing these DNS queries would implicate the internal DNS server as requests are relayed through it. *Make sure you set the DNS Security action to sinkhole if you have the subscription license.*

The default action for the **Command and Control** and **Malware** domains is to block and change them to sinkholes, as shown. For research purposes, you can enable packet capture:

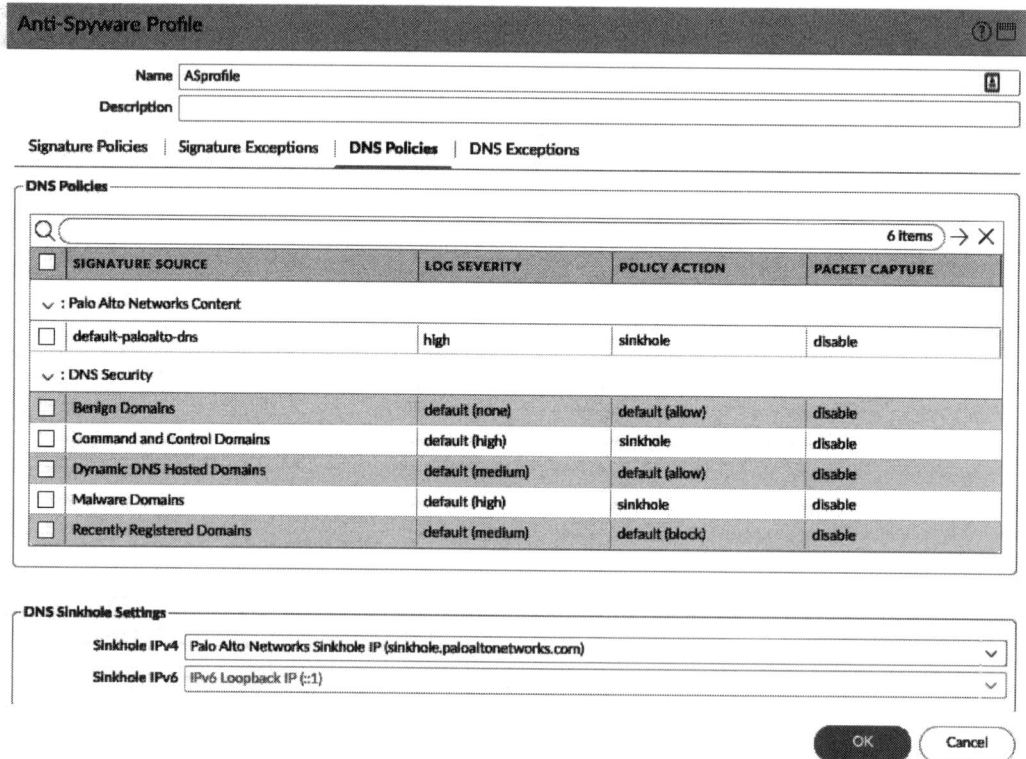

**Anti-Spyware Profile**

| Name | ASprofile |
| Description | |

Signature Policies | Signature Exceptions | **DNS Policies** | DNS Exceptions

**DNS Policies**

6 Items

| SIGNATURE SOURCE | LOG SEVERITY | POLICY ACTION | PACKET CAPTURE |
| --- | --- | --- | --- |
| ∨ : Palo Alto Networks Content | | | |
| default-paloalto-dns | high | sinkhole | disable |
| ∨ : DNS Security | | | |
| Benign Domains | default (none) | default (allow) | disable |
| Command and Control Domains | default (high) | sinkhole | disable |
| Dynamic DNS Hosted Domains | default (medium) | default (allow) | disable |
| Malware Domains | default (high) | sinkhole | disable |
| Recently Registered Domains | default (medium) | default (block) | disable |

**DNS Sinkhole Settings**

| Sinkhole IPv4 | Palo Alto Networks Sinkhole IP (sinkhole.paloaltonetworks.com) |
| Sinkhole IPv6 | IPv6 Loopback IP (::1) |

OK    Cancel

Figure 3.5 – Anti-Spyware DNS signatures

Let's now look at the Vulnerability Protection profile.

# The Vulnerability Protection profile

The Vulnerability Protection profile also uses rules to control how certain network-based attacks are handled. **ACTION** contains the same options as Anti-Spyware: **allow, drop, alert, reset-client, reset-server, reset-both,** and **block-ip**. The reset actions send TCP RST packets. **block-ip** blocks all packets coming from a source and can be set to **monitor source** to block everything, or a source destination, to only block packets to a specific destination for an amount of time.

**Host Type** helps determine whether the rule applies to a threat originating from a client (upload), server (download), or either.

Make sure you review **Category**, as in the following screenshot, as this allows a fine-grained approach to each specific type of threat if granularity and individualized actions are needed at a later stage:

Figure 3.6 – The Vulnerability Protection profile categories

Create the following rules:

- **Rule Name:** `simple-client-critical`

  --**Host Type:** `client`

  --**Severity:** `critical`

  --**Action:** `block-ip (source, 120)`

  --**Packet Capture:** `single-packet`
- **Rule Name:** `simple-client-high`

  --**Host Type:** `client`

  --**Severity:** `high`

  --**Action:** `reset-both`

  --**Packet Capture:** `single-packet`
- **Rule Name:** `simple-client-medium`

  --**Host Type:** `client`

  --**Severity:** `medium`

  --**Action:** `reset-both`

  --**Packet Capture:** `single-packet`
- **Rule Name:** `simple-server-critical`

  --**Host Type:** `server`

  --**Severity:** `critical`

  --**Action:** `block-ip (source, 120)`

  --**Packet Capture:** `single-packet`
- **Rule Name:** `simple-server-high`

  --**Host Type:** `server`

  --**Severity:** `high`

  --**Action:** `reset-both`

  --**Packet Capture:** `single-packet`
- **Rule Name:** `simple-server-medium`

  --**Host Type:** `server`

  --**Severity:** `medium`

--**Action:** `reset-both`

--**Packet Capture:** `single-packet`

- **Rule Name:** `simple-low-info`

--**Host Type:** `any`

--**Severity:** `low, informational`

--**Action:** `default`

--**Packet Capture:** `disable`

Your profile should now look like this:

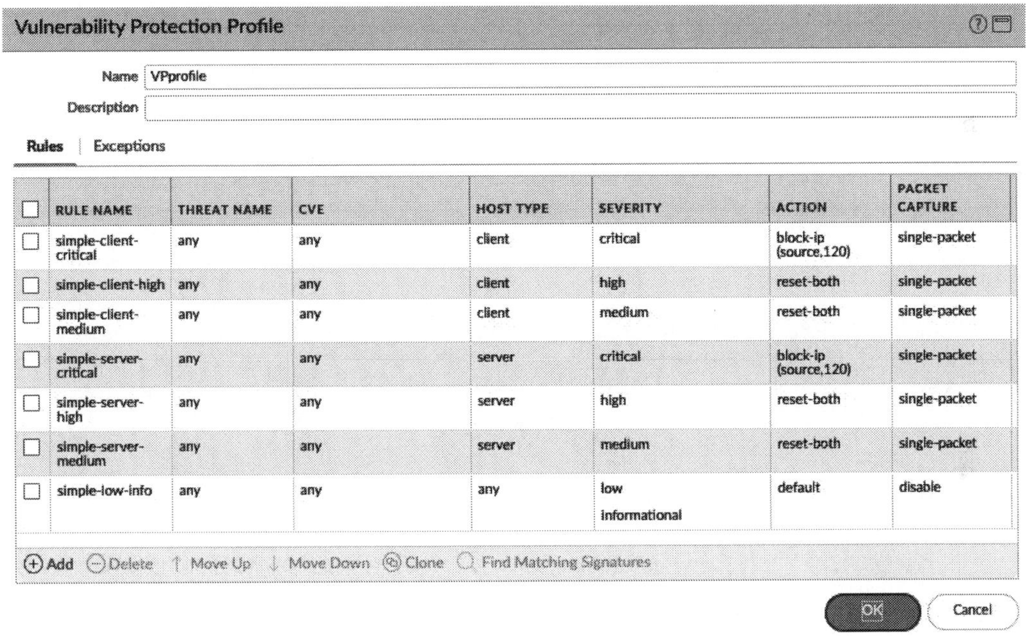

| | RULE NAME | THREAT NAME | CVE | HOST TYPE | SEVERITY | ACTION | PACKET CAPTURE |
|---|---|---|---|---|---|---|---|
| ☐ | simple-client-critical | any | any | client | critical | block-ip (source,120) | single-packet |
| ☐ | simple-client-high | any | any | client | high | reset-both | single-packet |
| ☐ | simple-client-medium | any | any | client | medium | reset-both | single-packet |
| ☐ | simple-server-critical | any | any | server | critical | block-ip (source,120) | single-packet |
| ☐ | simple-server-high | any | any | server | high | reset-both | single-packet |
| ☐ | simple-server-medium | any | any | server | medium | reset-both | single-packet |
| ☐ | simple-low-info | any | any | any | low informational | default | disable |

**Vulnerability Protection Profile**

Name  VPprofile
Description

**Rules** | Exceptions

⊕ Add ⊖ Delete ↑ Move Up ↓ Move Down ⊛ Clone ◯ Find Matching Signatures

OK    Cancel

Figure: 3.7 – Vulnerability Protection Profile

In the next subsection, we will learn about URL filtering and its categories.

# URL filtering

URL filtering leverages URL categories to determine what action to take for each category.

There are two groups of categories: custom URL categories and the dynamic categories provided by the URL filtering license.

## Custom URL categories

Custom URL categories do not require a license, so you can create these objects and apply URL filtering even without access to the URL filtering license.

Go to **Objects | Custom Objects | URL Category** to create a new custom category and add websites. It takes a light form of **Regular Expression (RegEx)** matched against the address, so neither `http://` nor `https://` are required to match.

The string used in a custom URL category is divided up into substrings, or tokens, by separators. The `./?&=;+` characters are considered separators, so `www.example.com` has three tokens and two separators. Each token can be replaced by a wildcard (`*`) to match subdomains or entire **Top-Level Domains (TLDs)**. Wildcards cannot be used as part of a token; for example, `www.ex*.com` is an illegal wildcard. Each string can be closed by a forward slash (`/`) or be left open by not adding an end slash. Not ending a string could have consequences if the string is very short or very common as it could match unintended longer addresses. For example, the `*.com` string could match `www.communicationexample.org`, so adding an ending slash would prevent this.

## URL filtering profile

When configuring the URL filtering profile, you need to select which action to apply.

Some possible actions are as follows:

- **Allow**: Allows a category without logging.
- **Alert**: Allows a category and logs the access in the URL filtering log.
- **Block**: Blocks the request, injecting an `HTTP 503` error and a redirect to a page hosted on the firewall explaining to the user their access was declined and the action logged.
- **Continue**: Injects an interactive web page informing the user that they are about to access a restricted website and provides a **Continue** button for them to acknowledge the risk associated with accessing the site.
- **Override**: Injects an interactive web page that allows the user to continue if they are able to provide a password to continue. This password can be set in **Device | Setup | Content-ID | URL Admin Override**. An **Interface Management** profile (**Network | Network Profiles | Interface Mgmt**) needs to be created, with the **Response pages** service enabled and added to the interface where users connect to for this page to work, as follows:

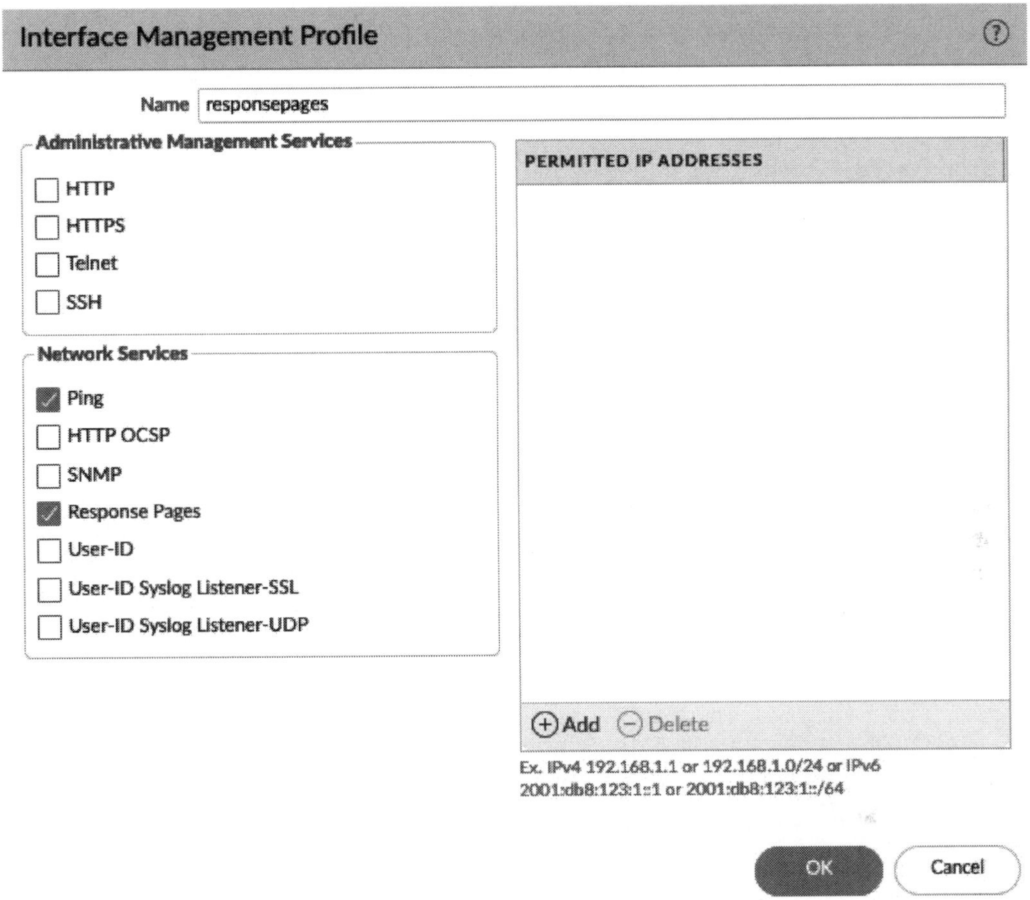

## Interface Management Profile

Name  responsepages

**Administrative Management Services**

☐ HTTP

☐ HTTPS

☐ Telnet

☐ SSH

**Network Services**

☑ Ping

☐ HTTP OCSP

☐ SNMP

☑ Response Pages

☐ User-ID

☐ User-ID Syslog Listener-SSL

☐ User-ID Syslog Listener-UDP

**PERMITTED IP ADDRESSES**

⊕ Add  ⊖ Delete

Ex. IPv4 192.168.1.1 or 192.168.1.0/24 or IPv6
2001:db8:123:1::1 or 2001:db8:123:1::/64

OK    Cancel

Figure 3.8 – Interface Management Profile

As you can see in the following screenshot, the URL filtering profile requires each **CATEGORY** field to be set to an action individually for site access, and if **USER CREDENTIAL SUBMISSION** is enabled, additional filtering can be applied to decide whether a user is allowed to submit corporate credentials to a certain category. This helps prevent phishing attacks:

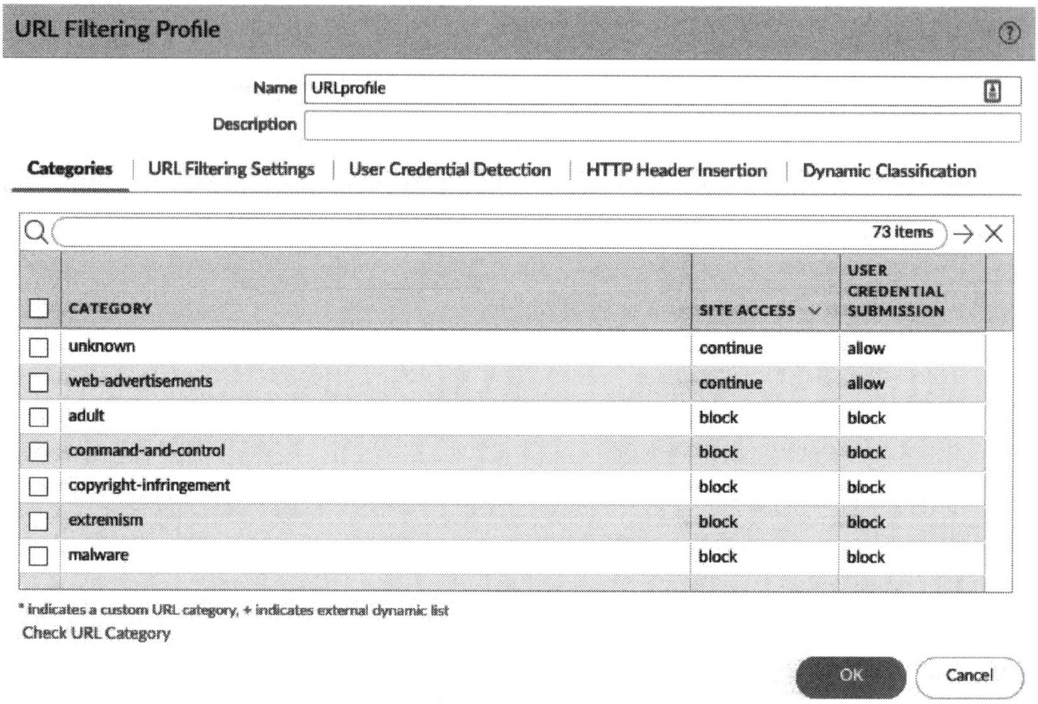

Figure 3.9 – URL Filtering Profile

As you can see in the following screenshot, if you want to change a lot (or all) of the actions at once, there's a shortcut to help you. If you hover your mouse over **SITE ACCESS** or **USER CREDENTIAL SUBMISSION**, there will be a little arrow that lets you select **Set All Actions** or **Set Selected Actions**:

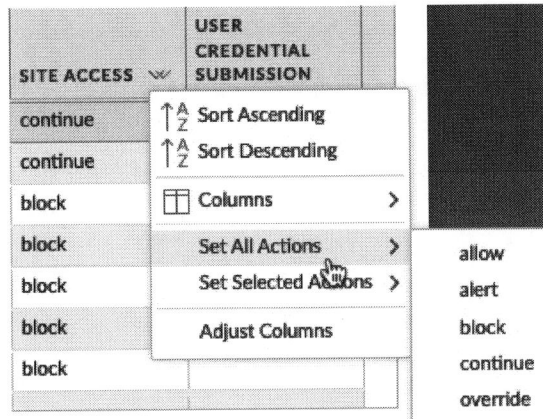

Figure 3.10 – Set All Actions in URL Filtering Profile

A good baseline URL filtering policy can be set up as follows:

1. Set all of the categories to `Alert`. This will ensure that all of the URL categories are logged.

2. Set **Adult, Command and Control, Copyright Infringement, Extremism, Malware, Peer-to-Peer,** and **Phishing and Proxy Avoidance and Anonymizers** to `Block`.

3. Set **Dating, Gambling, Games, Hacking, Insufficient Content, Not-Resolved, Parked, Questionable, Unknown,** and **Web Advertisements** to `Continue`.

4. Tweak the settings in accordance with your company policy or local laws and regulations (some URL categories cannot be logged by law, for example).

The **Categories** set to **Continue** are commonly on the fringes of acceptance, but may still need to be accessed for legitimate purposes. The **Continue** action gives the user the opportunity to ensure that they are intending to go to this URL before actually opening the web page.

The URL filtering settings contain several logging options that may come in handy depending on your needs:

- **Log container page only**: This setting only logs the actual access a user is requesting and will suppress related web links, such as embedded advertisements and content links on the page that the user is visiting, reducing the log volume.

- **Safe Search Enforcement**: This blocks access to search providers if strict safe search is not enabled on the client side. Currently, Google, Bing, Yahoo, Yandex, and YouTube are supported.

Additional logging can also be enabled:

- **User-Agent**: This is the web browser that the user is using to access a web page.

- **Referer**: This is the web page that links to the resource that is being accessed (for example, Google or CNN linking to a resource page).

- **x-forward-for**: If a downstream proxy is being used by users, this masks their original source. If the downstream proxy supports enabling the **x-forward-for** feature, it will add the client's original IP in the c header, allowing the identification of the original user.

The following steps and screenshot show you how to enable these settings in your URL filtering profile:

1. Enable **Log container page only** to provide some privacy to your users and prevent the logging of embedded ad pages.

2. Enable **Safe Search Enforcement**.

3. Enable additional logging for **User-Agent** and **Referer**:

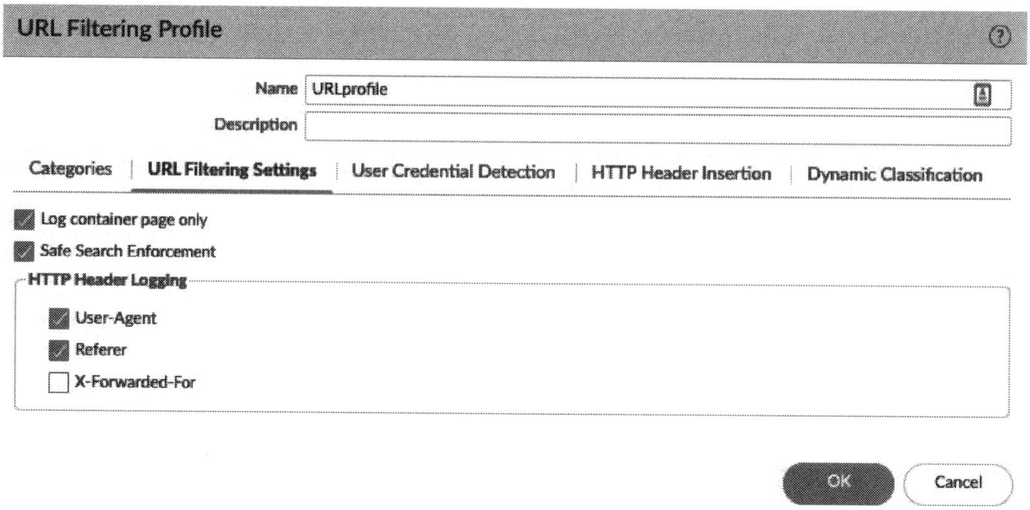

Figure 3.11 – URL filtering settings

The **User Credential Detection** tab allows you to enable credential detection (see *Chapter 6, Identifying Users and Controlling Access* for more details).

**HTTP Header Insertion** lets you control web application access by inserting HTTP headers into the `HTTP/1.x` requests to application providers. As you can see in the following example, this can help you control which team IDs can be accessed in Dropbox, which tenants and content can be accessed in Office 365 and Google app-allowed domains. You can create any URL that needs to have a certain header inserted to ensure users are accessing the appropriate instance:

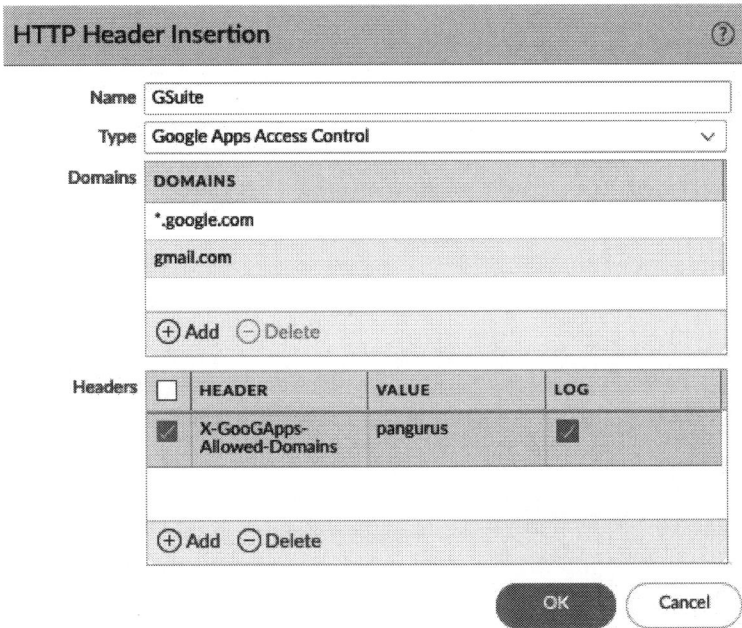

Figure 3.12 – HTTP Header Insertion

Now, let's look at the file blocking profile.

# The file blocking profile

The default strict file blocking profile contains all the file types that are commonly blocked and serves as a good template to start from. Select the strict profile and click on the **clone** action, as in the following screenshot, to create a new profile based on this one. If any file types do need to be allowed in your organization, remove them from the block action:

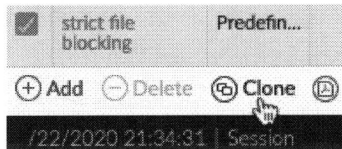

Figure: 3.13 File blocking profile clone

The direction lets you determine whether you want to only block uploads or downloads or both directions for a specific file type, as well as groups of file types. File blocking profiles also use rules so that file types can be grouped with their own directions and actions. The default action is `Allow`, so any file type not included will be allowed to pass through (but will be scanned if an appropriate security profile is attached to the security policy). The available actions are **Alert**, **Block**, and **Continue**, which works similarly to the URL filtering **Continue** option if the file is being downloaded from a web page that supports the HTTP redirect to serve the user a warning page before continuing with the download or upload.

Review all the file types and set the ones you want to block. Any file types that you are not sure about and would like to get a chance to review first can be set to the **Alert** action so that you can keep track of occurrences under **monitor | logs | data filtering**.

As you can see in the following screenshot, we can create sets of file types by clicking on the **Add** button and selecting the file type, and then setting the action:

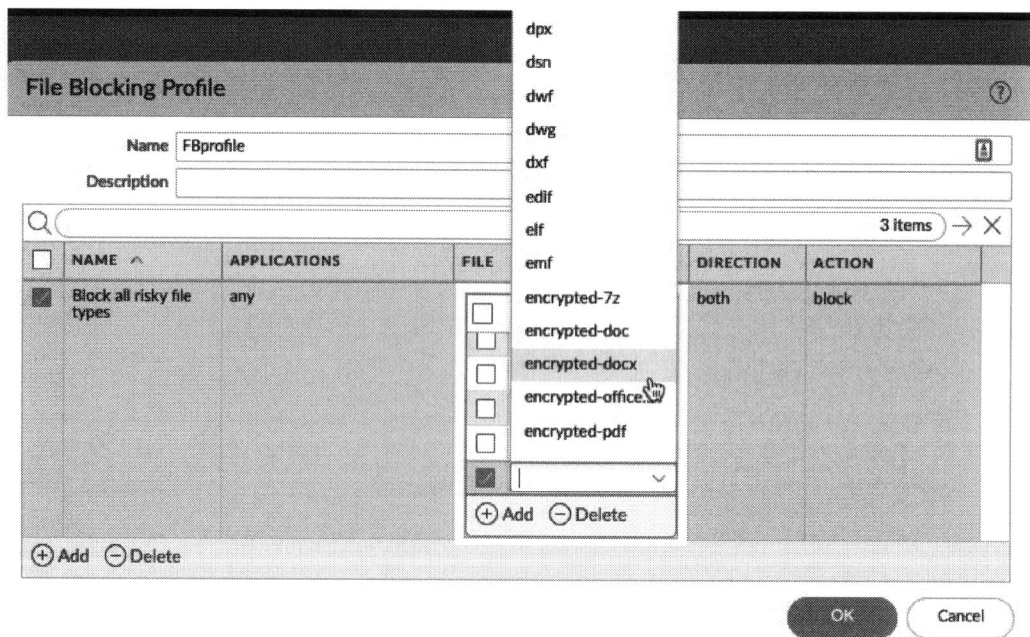

Figure: 3.14 File Blocking Profile

We will now have a look at the WildFire Analysis profile.

# The WildFire Analysis profile

The WildFire Analysis profile controls which files are uploaded to WildFire for analysis in a sandbox and which ones are sent to a private instance of WildFire (for example, the WF-500 appliance). Clone the default profile to upload all files to WildFire, or create a new profile if you want to limit which files are forwarded or need to redirect files to a private cloud. If no WildFire license is available, only **Portable Executables (PEs)** are forwarded to WildFire.

If all file types can be uploaded for inspection, simply set a rule for any application and any file type. If exceptions exist, either create a rule to divert specific files to a private cloud, if you have a WildFire appliance in your data center, or specify which files *can* be uploaded, as shown:

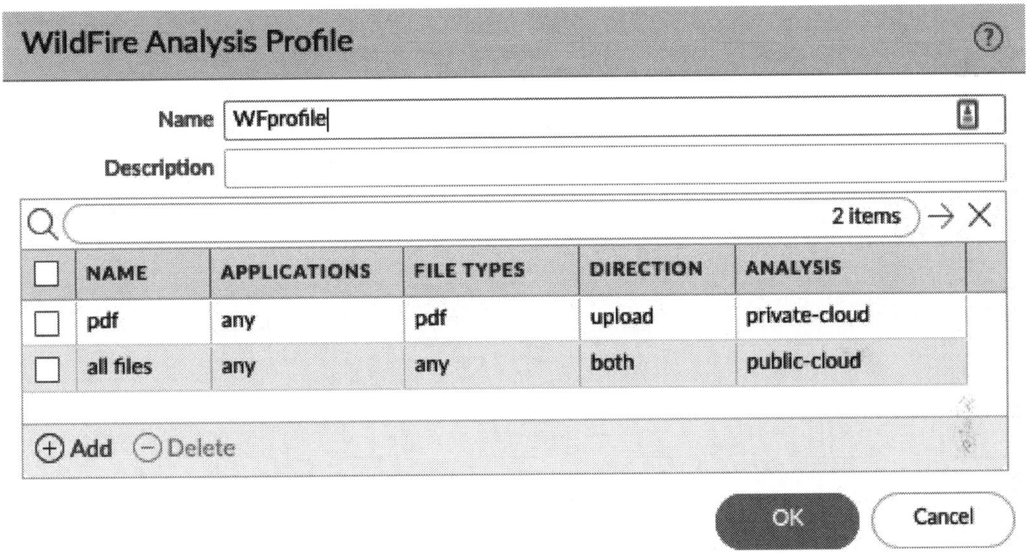

| | NAME | APPLICATIONS | FILE TYPES | DIRECTION | ANALYSIS | |
|---|---|---|---|---|---|---|
| ☐ | pdf | any | pdf | upload | private-cloud | |
| ☐ | all files | any | any | both | public-cloud | |

Figure 3.15 – WildFire Analysis Profile

Next, let's learn about custom objects.

# Custom objects

Some security profiles support custom objects. We have already looked at custom URL categories, but the other custom objects are explained in the following sections.

## The Custom Spyware/Vulnerability objects

You can create your own signatures using RegEx to detect spyware phone-home/C2 or network vulnerabilities. The **Configuration** page, as shown in the following screenshots, requires basic information, such as an ID number that is between 15.000-18.000 for spyware and 41.000-45.000 for vulnerabilities, a name, a severity value, a direction, and any additional information that may be useful later on. The direction and affected client help the Content-ID engine identify which direction packets that match this signature can be expected:

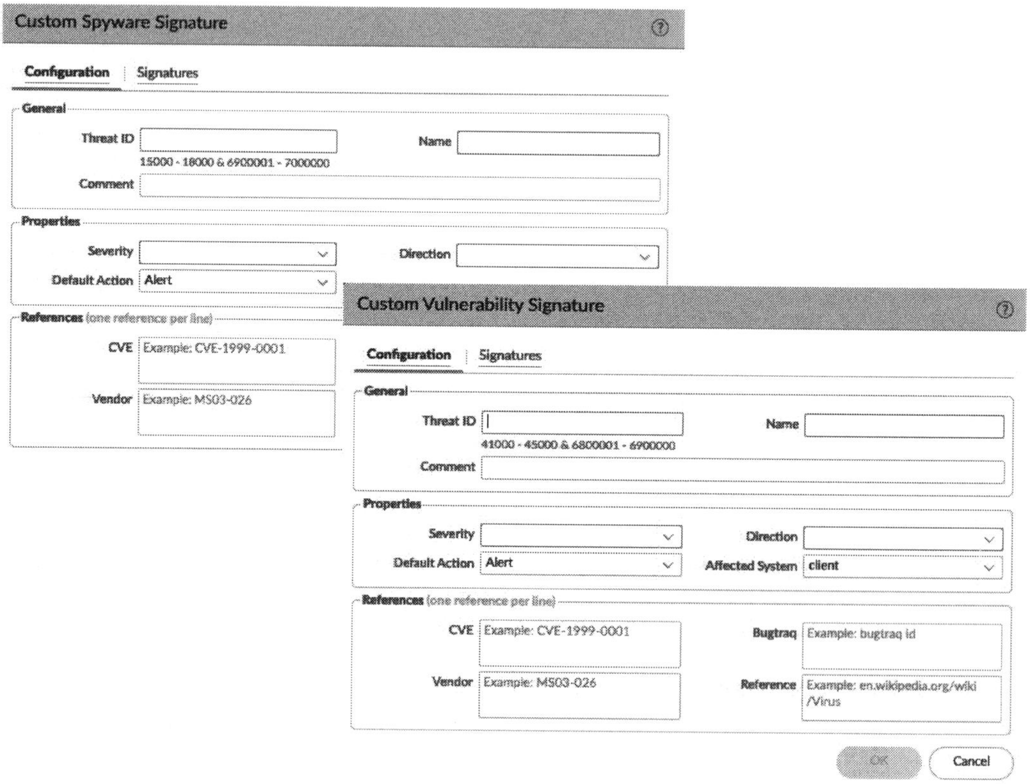

Figure 3.16 – The Custom Spyware and Vulnerability objects

Under **Signatures**, you have two main modes of adding signatures, as you can see in the following screenshot:

- **Standard**: This adds one or more signatures, combined through logical AND or OR statements.

- **Combination**: This combines predefined (dynamic update) signatures with a timing component requiring $n$ number of hits over $x$ amount of time, aggregated for source, destination, or source-destination:

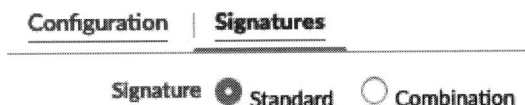

Figure 3.17 – The Standard or Combination signatures

Let's focus on standard signatures. From the main screen, you can add sets of signatures, which are all separated by a logical OR statement.

Once you start building a set, you need to decide on the scope. The transaction matches a signature in a single packet and the session spans all the packets in the session. If the signature you are adding to identify a threat always occurs in a single packet's payload, you should set a transaction. This will allow the Content-ID engine to stop scanning at once. If you are adding multiple strings, you can enable **Ordered Condition Match**, which requires the signatures to match from top to bottom in an ordered way. If this option is turned off, the last signature may be detected before the first. If you add multiple strings, you can link them by adding an AND condition.

A signature consists of the following:

- **An operator**, which is either a pattern, or a greater, equal, or smaller operator. Greater, equal, and smaller operators allow you to target a header, payload, payload lengths, and more. A pattern lets you match an exact string found anywhere in a packet or a series of packets.

- **A context**, which is where, in any of the available protocols, the signature may be found (for example, if you look for a string in `http-req-host-header`, that same string will not be matched if it is seen in the payload). Many contexts will be self-explanatory, as you can see in the following screenshot, but for a full list, there's a good online resource describing all the contexts at `https://knowledgebase.paloaltonetworks.com/KCSArticleDetail?id=kA10g000000ClOFCA0`:

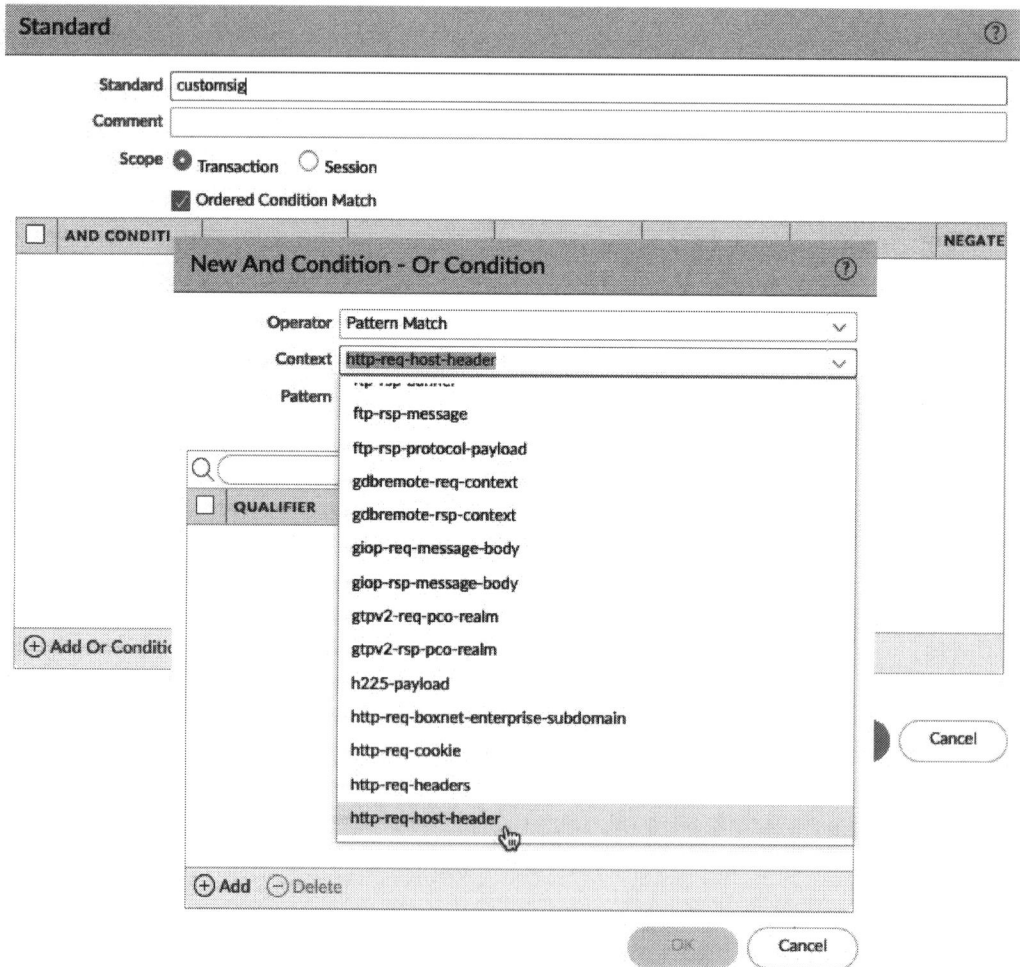

Figure: 3.18 – Creating signatures

- **A pattern or value**: If you want to, for example, match a hostname in an `http` request header, you would use the `domain\.tld` RegEx, where the backslash indicates that the dot following it is an exact match for a dot and not a RegEx wildcard.

The available RegEx wildcard characters include the following:

| . | 1.3 | matches a single character (e.g. 123, 133) |
|---|---|---|
| ? | dots? | matches string with or without last character (e.g. dot, dots) |
| * | dots* | matches string with or without last character, and multiple repeats of last character (e.g. dot, dots, dotssss) |
| + | dots+ | matches single or multiple repetitions of the preceding letter (e.g. dots, dotssss) |
| \| | ((exe)\|(msi)) | OR function to match multiple possible strings (e.g. dot.exe, dot.msi) |
| [] | x[abc] | matches preceding string followed by any character between squared brackets (e.g. xa, xb, xc) |
| - | x[a-z] | matches any character in a range (e.g. xa,xm) |
| ^ | x[^AB] | matches any character except the ones listed (e.g. xC, x5) |
| {} | x{1,3} | matches anything after x as long as it is 1 to 3 bytes in length (e.g. x1, x123) |
| \ | x\.y | Escape character to exactly match a special character (e.g. www\.pangurus\.com) |
| &amp | | used to match & in a string |

Figure 3.19 – Supported RegEx wildcard characters

- **A qualifier** can further limit in which stage of a transaction a pattern can be matched, either in method or type. Using a qualifier is optional:

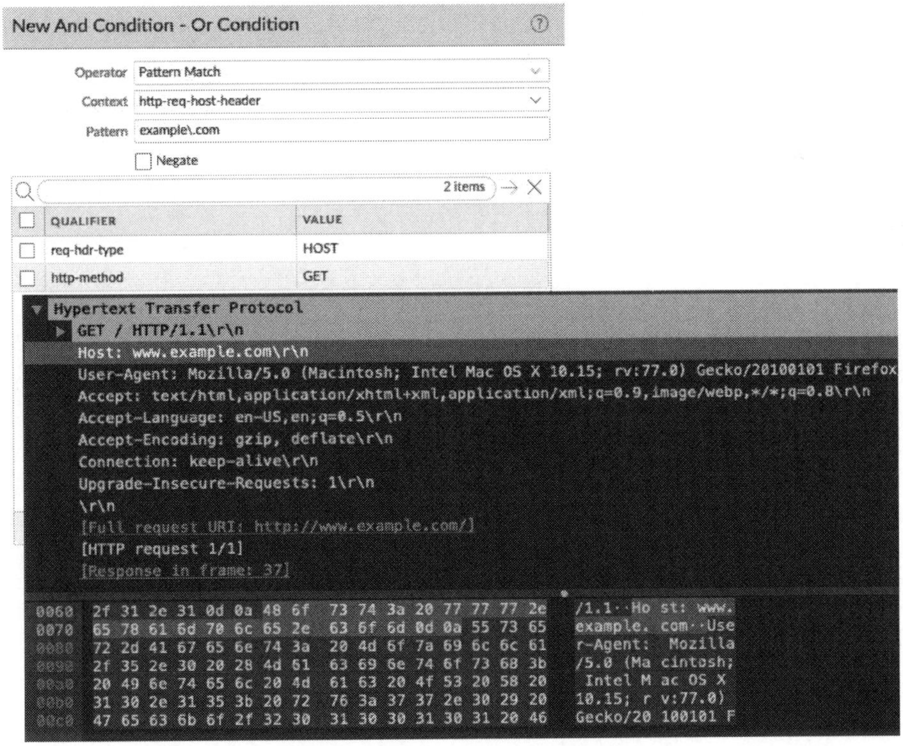

Figure 3.20 – Host Header pattern

With the above custom objects you are able to identify sessions behaving in a specific way, but this process can also be applied to identify information and keywords inside a session.

## The custom data pattern

In the custom data pattern, you can add strings of sensitive information or indicators of sensitive information being transmitted. There is a set of predefined patterns, including social security numbers, credit card numbers, and several other identification numbers. You can use regular expressions to match exact strings in documents or leverage file properties. Once the appropriate parameters have been chosen, you can add these custom data patterns to a data filtering profile and, as you can see in the following screenshot, assign weights. These weights determine how many times a certain marker can be hit in a session before an alert is generated in the form of a log entry and when a session should be blocked for suspicious behavior (for example, it might be acceptable for an email to go out containing one social security number, but not multiple):

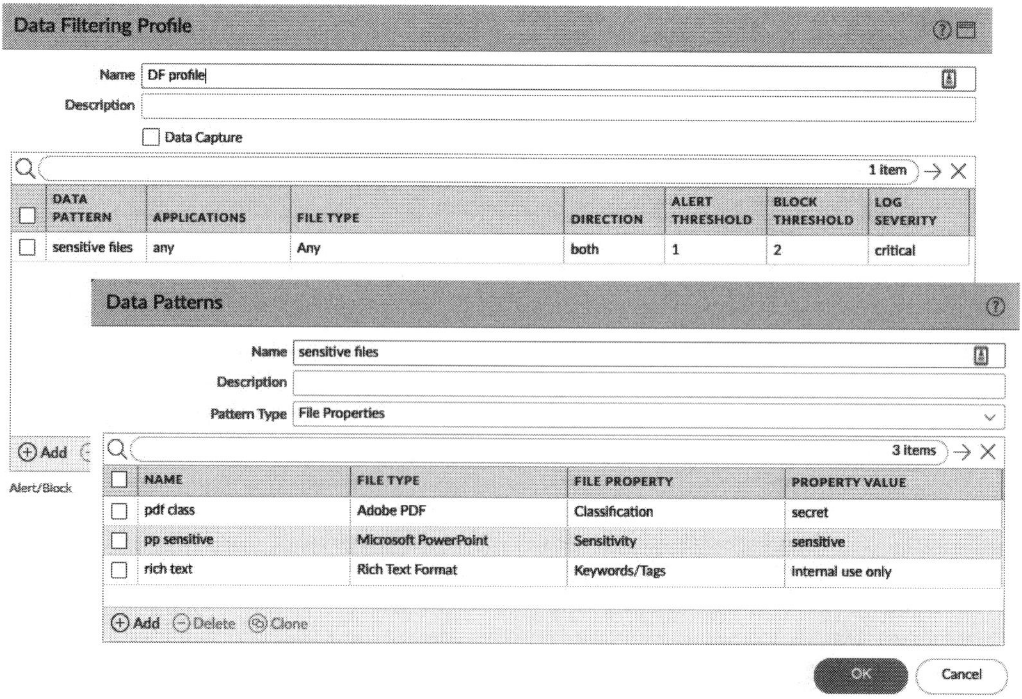

### Data Filtering Profile

| | DATA PATTERN | APPLICATIONS | FILE TYPE | | DIRECTION | ALERT THRESHOLD | BLOCK THRESHOLD | LOG SEVERITY |
|---|---|---|---|---|---|---|---|---|
| | sensitive files | any | Any | | both | 1 | 2 | critical |

**Name** DF profile

**Description**

☐ Data Capture

1 item

#### Data Patterns

**Name** sensitive files

**Description**

**Pattern Type** File Properties

3 items

| | NAME | FILE TYPE | FILE PROPERTY | PROPERTY VALUE |
|---|---|---|---|---|
| | pdf class | Adobe PDF | Classification | secret |
| | pp sensitive | Microsoft PowerPoint | Sensitivity | sensitive |
| | rich text | Rich Text Format | Keywords/Tags | internal use only |

⊕ Add ⊖ Delete ⊚ Clone

OK    Cancel

Figure 3.21 – Data filtering

Now that you've had a chance to review and configure all the available security profiles, the easiest way to apply them to security rules is by using **Security Profile Groups**.

## Security profile groups

Now that you've prepared all of these security profiles, create a new security profile group, as in the following screenshot, and call it `default`. This will ensure that the group will automatically be added to every security rule you create:

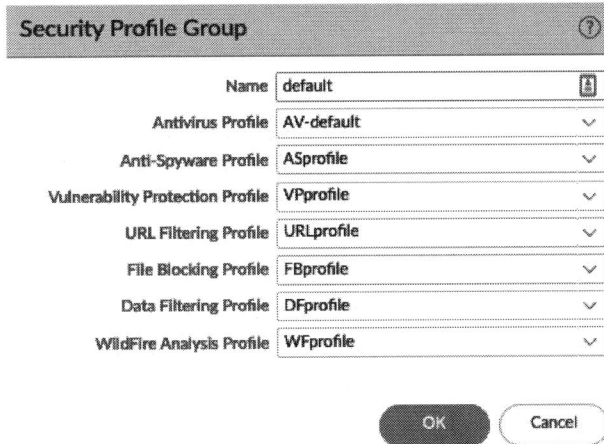

Figure 3.22 – The default security profile group

> **Important note**
> It is not harmful to add *all* of the security policies to a security rule as Content-ID will intelligently only apply appropriate signatures and heuristics to applications detected in the session (for example, `http` signatures will not be matched with `ftp` sessions).

Also, create a **Log Forwarding** profile called `default`, but you can leave the actual profile empty for now.

# Understanding and building security rules

We now need to build some security rules to allow or deny traffic in and out of the network. The default rules will only allow intrazone traffic and will block everything else, as you can see here:

| | NAME | TYPE | Source | | Destination | | APPLICATION | SERVICE | ACTION | PROFILE | OPTIONS |
|---|---|---|---|---|---|---|---|---|---|---|---|
| | | | ZONE | ADDRESS | ZONE | ADDRESS | | | | | |
| 10 | Intrazone-default | intrazone | any | any | (intrazone) | any | any | any | ⊘ Allow | none | none |
| 11 | Interzone-default | interzone | any | any | any | any | any | any | ⊘ Deny | none | none |

Figure 3.23 – Default security rules

We will first make sure "bad" traffic is dropped by creating two new rules—one for inbound and one for outbound traffic.

## Dropping "bad" traffic

The inbound rule will have the external zone as a source and the three **External Dynamic Lists** (**EDLs**) containing known malicious addresses. These lists are updated via the threat prevention dynamic updates. The **Source** tab should look similar to the following:

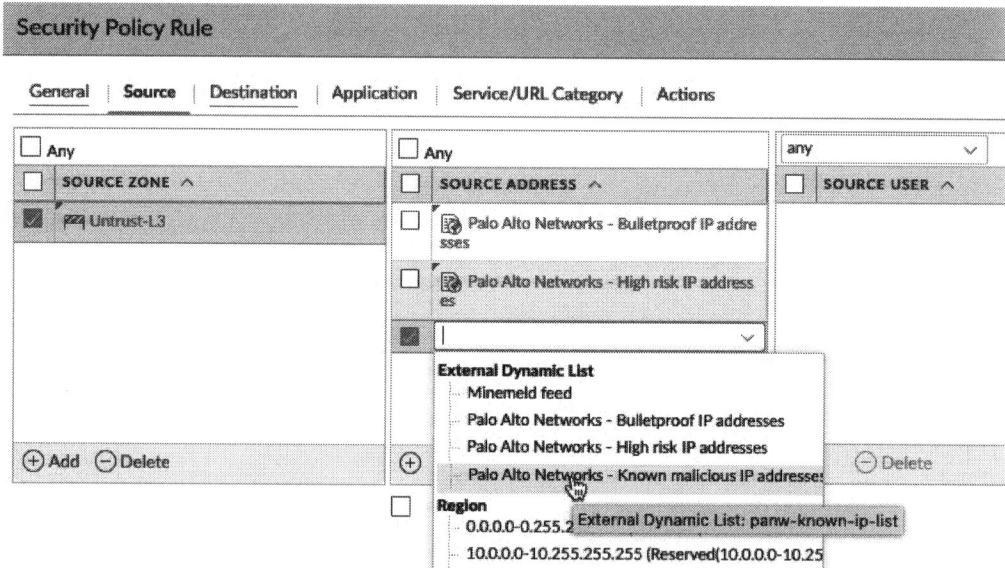

Figure 3.24 – Reconfigured external dynamic lists

In the **Destination** tab, set the destination zones to both the external zone and any zone where you intend to host internal servers that you will allow inbound NAT to (for example, corporate mail or web servers) and set the destination addresses to Any, as in the following screenshot:

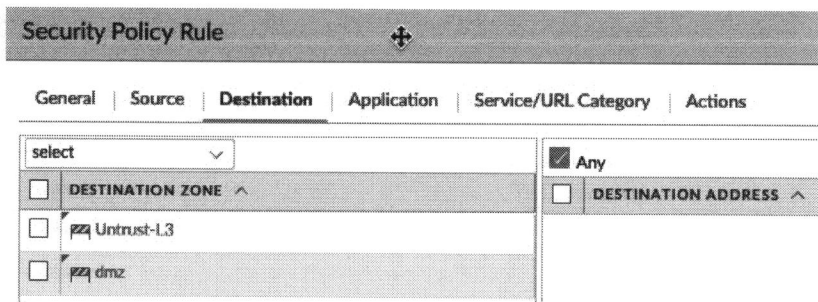

Figure: 3.25 – Security rule destination zones

In the **Actions** tab, set the action to Drop. This will silently discard any inbound packets:

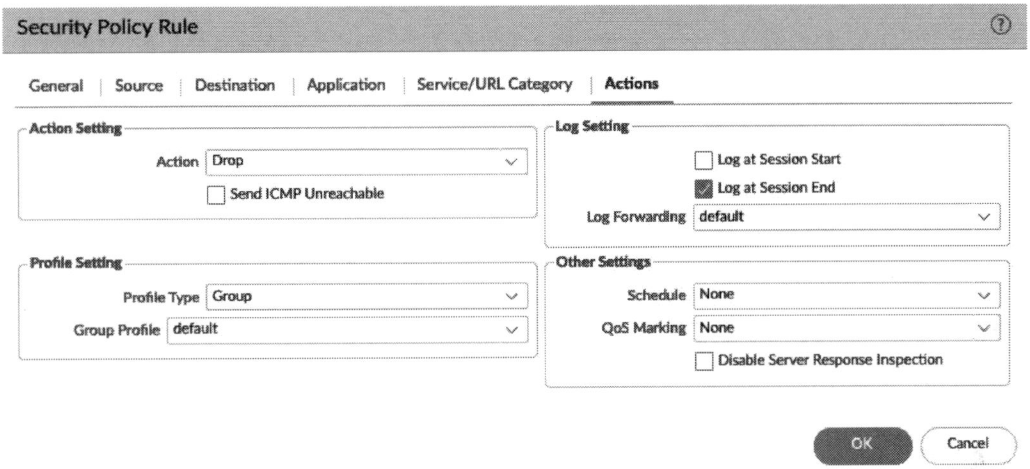

Figure 3.26 – Security rule actions

Follow the next steps to create this rule:

1. Create a new security rule and give it a descriptive name.

2. Set the source zone to any zone that is connected to the internet (for example, **Untrust**).

3. Set the source addresses to the three predefined EDLs.

4. Set the destination zones to your internal zones that will accept inbound connections from the internet (for example, DMZ), also including the external zones.

5. Set the action to **Drop**.

> **Important note**
> You may have noticed that the **Profile Setting** fields and **Log Forwarding** are filled out with the **default** profiles that you created in the previous step. In all rules where sessions are blocked, content scanning will not take place, so having these profiles will not cause overhead.

Click **OK**, and then make the reverse rule, as in the following screenshot, setting the source zones to your internal zones, the destination to the external zone, and the predefined EDL as addresses. If you changed the DNS sinkhole IP address to one of your choosing, add this IP here as well:

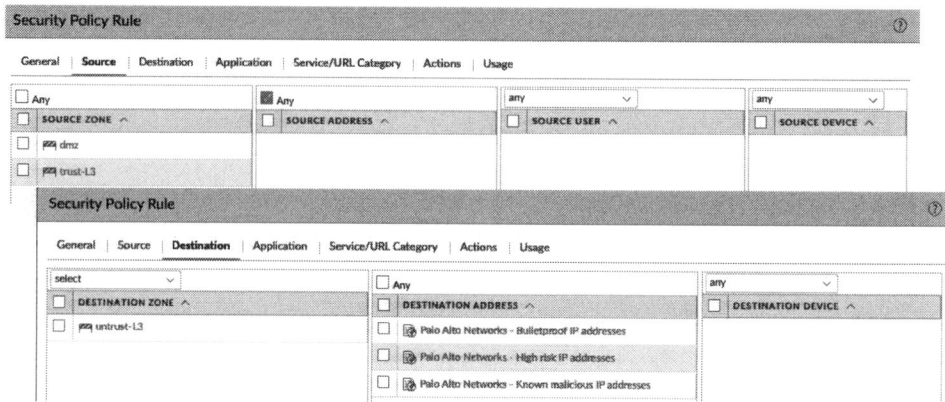

Figure 3.27 – Outbound drop rules

Follow these steps to create the above rule:

1. Create a new security rule and give it a descriptive name.

2. Set the source zone to your internal zones.

3. Set the destination zone to any zone leading out to the internet (for example, **Untrust**).

4. Set three destination addresses and for each one, select one of the predefined EDLs.

5. Set **Action** to Drop.

A good practice is to add some catch all rules to the end of your rule base, as in the following screenshot, once all the required policies have been added to any catch connections that are not allowed. One catch all rule should be set to application-default and one to any; this will help identify standard applications that are not hitting a security policy and (more suspicious) non-standard applications that are not using a normal port (see the *Allowing applications* section to learn about the application-default service):

| 12 | catchall | universal | any | any | any | any | any | application-default | Drop | | |
| 13 | catchall-any | universal | any | any | any | any | any | any | Drop | | |
| 14 | intrazone-default | intrazone | any | any | (intrazone) | any | any | any | Allow | none | none |
| 15 | interzone-default | interzone | any | any | any | any | any | any | Deny | none | none |

Figure 3.28 – The catch all rules at the end of the rule base

You now have some rules actively dropping connections you do not want to get past the firewall, but there are more options available than to just silently discard packets. We'll review the other options next.

## Action options

There are multiple actions that handle inbound connections, some of which are stealthy and some of which are noisy and informative, depending on your needs:

- **Deny**: This action will drop the session and enforce the default **Deny** action associated with an application. Some applications may silently drop while others send an RST packet.
- **Allow**: This allows the session to go through.
- **Drop**: This silently discards packets.
- **Reset Client**: This sends a TCP RST to the client.
- **Reset Server**: This sends a TCP RST to the server.
- **Reset Both**: This sends a TCP RST to both the client and the server.

If you check the **Send ICMP Unreachable** checkbox and the ingress interface is Layer 3, an **ICMP Unreachable** packet is sent to the client for all of the dropped TCP or UDP sessions.

# Allowing applications

There are generally two approaches to determining which applications you want to allow:

- Creating a group of known applications
- Creating an application filter to sort applications by their behavior

From **Objects | Application Groups**, you can create groups of known applications that can be used in security policies, as shown:

> **Important note**
> The security rule base is evaluated from top to bottom and the evaluation is stopped once a match is found, then the matching security rule is enforced. This means blocking rules need to be placed *above* the allowing rule if there could be an overlap.

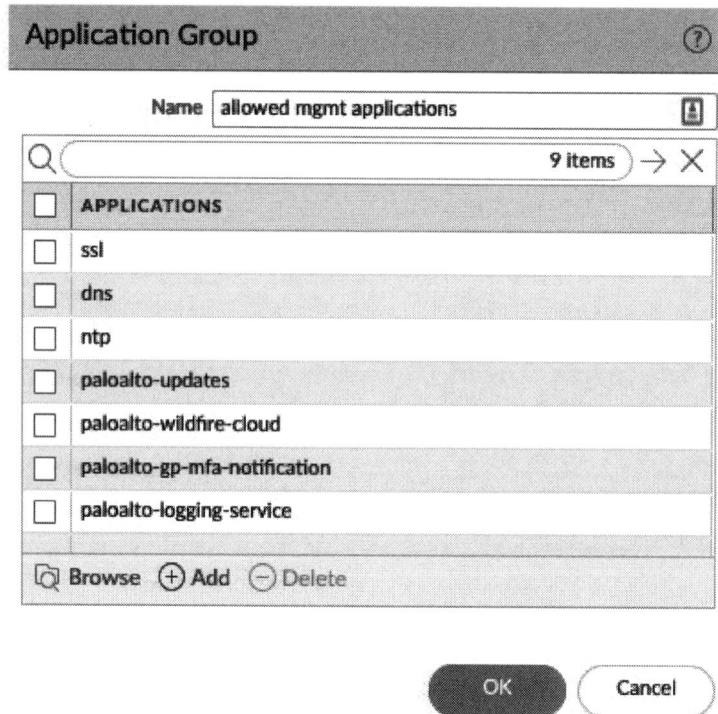

Figure 3.29 – Application Group

With the widespread adoption of cloud-based hosting and cheap SaaS solutions, more traditional programs are turning into web-based applications that are accessible over a web browser. This makes it harder for an administrator to easily determine which applications need to be allowed as the needs of the business change quickly. Application filters created in **Objects | Application Filters** let you create a dynamic application group that adds applications by their attributes, rather than adding them one by one. These attributes can be selected for both "good" properties to be added to allow rules (as you can see in the following screenshot) or "bad" properties to drop rules:

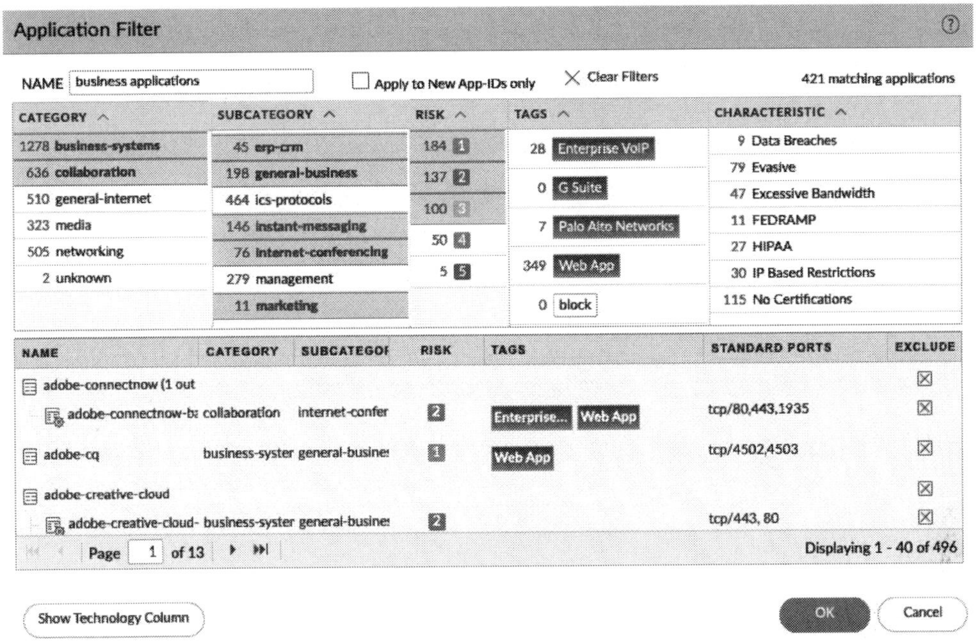

Figure 3.30 – Application Filter with basic attributes

Alternatively, the filter can be based on the predefined and custom tags assigned to applications, as follows:

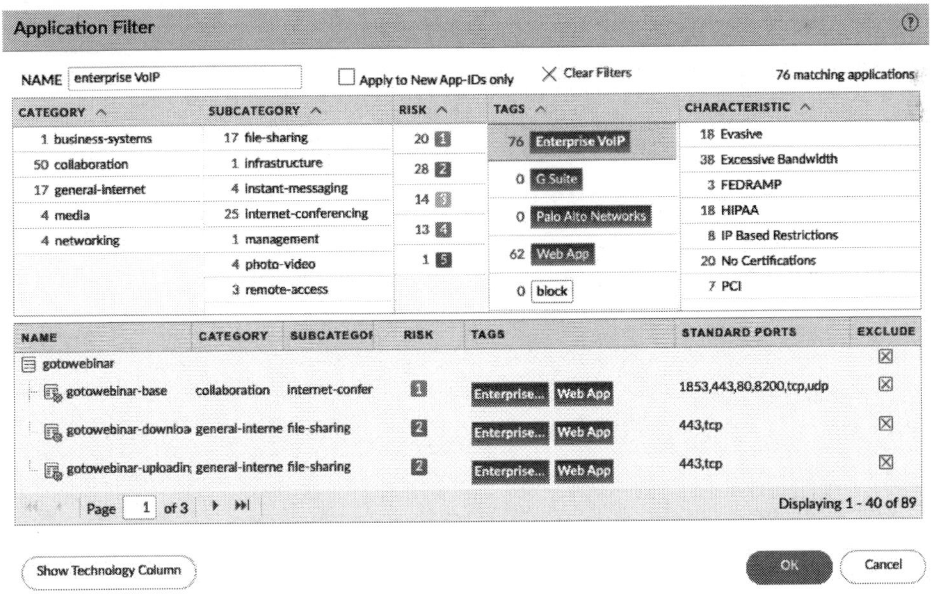

Figure 3.31 – Application Filter with tags

You can mix and match application groups and filters to build further security rules by adding them to the **APPLICATIONS** tab, as you can see here:

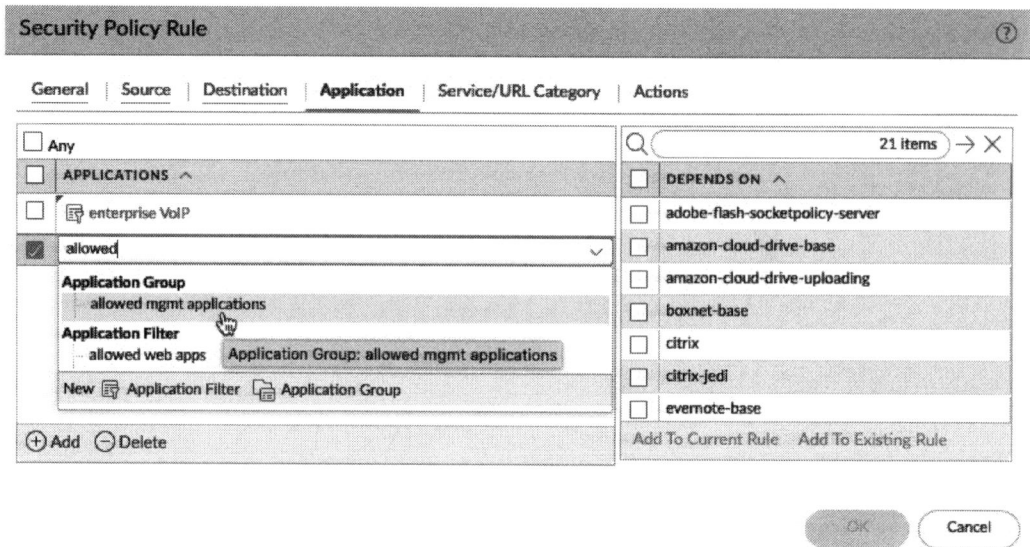

Figure: 3.32 – The APPLICATIONS tab

To create a new **Allow** rule using an application filter, do the following:

1.  Create a new security rule and add a descriptive name.

2.  Set the source zone to the internal zones that will connect to the internet.

3.  Set the destination zone to `external zone`.

4.  In **APPLICATIONS**, add a new line and select **Application Filter**.

5.  Click on all of the desired attributes and review some of the applications at the bottom. Add a descriptive name and click **OK** on the filter, and again on the security rule.

You now have an **allow** rule based on an application filter!

## Application dependencies

As you may have noticed in the previous screenshot, when you start adding applications to a security rule, there may be applications that have dependencies. These applications rely on an underlying protocol or build on an existing more basic application that needs to be added and allowed in the security rule base for this sub application to work. They do not necessarily need to be added to the same security policy.

Starting from PAN-OS 9.1, these dependencies are displayed in the security rule. As you can see in the following screenshot, they appear when you are adding new applications and can immediately be added to the same security rule or to a different one in the security rule base. In older PAN-OS versions, users will only be warned about these dependencies once the configuration is committed. You can review application dependencies for individual applications via **Objects | APPLICATIONS**, too:

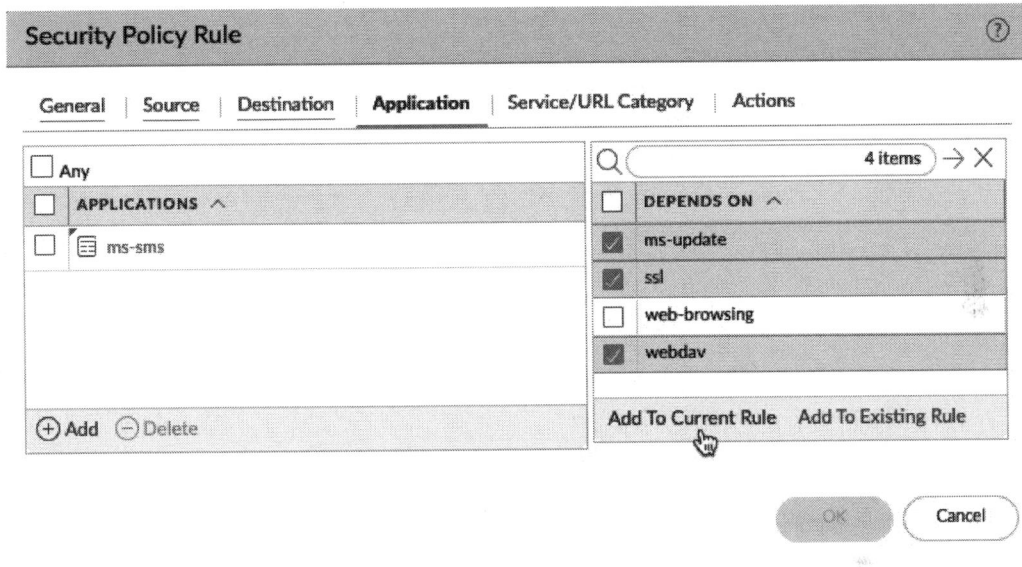

Figure: 3.33 – Application dependencies

Now that the applications have been set, let's look at how service ports are controlled.

## Application-default versus manual service ports

Each application will use a certain service port to establish a connection. By default, each service is set to `application-default`, which forces each application to use its default ports (for example, web-browsing uses ports `80` (unsecured) and `443` (SSL) secured, FTP uses ports `21` (unsecured plaintext) and `990` (secured), and so on).

> **Important note**
>
> Protocols that use pinholing, such as FTP, are automatically taken care of via the **Application Layer Gateway** (**ALG**), which is a part of the content decoder that is specific to this protocol.

If an application needs a custom port, you can add a manual service object, but this would prevent the use of `application-default`. So, any exceptions should preferably be made in individual rules to prevent applications from "escaping" via an unusual port:

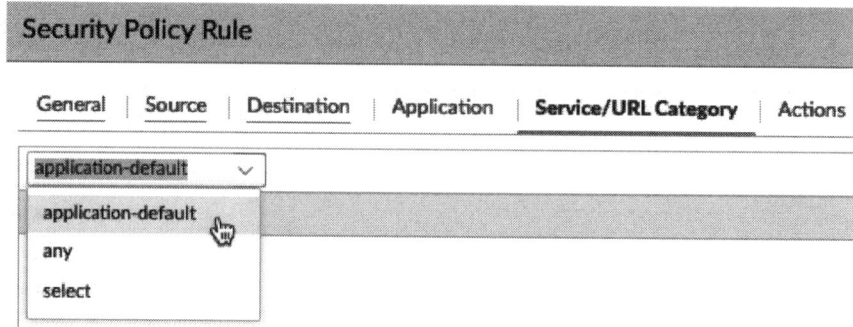

Figure 3.34 – Service ports

Adding a URL category can be used to allow or block URL categories at the TCP layer. For **drop** or **deny** actions, this will mean that the session is dropped, rather than returning a friendly blocked page to the user.

## Controlling logging and schedules

By default, each security rule is set to **Log at Session End**. This means that a log is only written to the traffic log once a session is broken down. For some sessions, it may be interesting to log more interactions, and so **Log at Session Start** could be enabled. This does cause quite a lot of overhead, however, as there will be a log for each new stage of a session when the SYN packet is received and for every application switch. So, there could be two to five additional log entries for a single session.

Other applications that are very chatty or less relevant may not need to be logged at all, such as DNS.

> **Important note**
>
> Even with both start or end log disabled in the security rule action tab, any threats detected in a session will still be logged to the threat log.

Log forwarding can be used to forward logs to Panorama or a syslog server or to send out an email. As you can see in the following screenshot, if you call one of the log forwarding profiles `default`, it will be used in all the new rules, so logs are automatically forwarded:

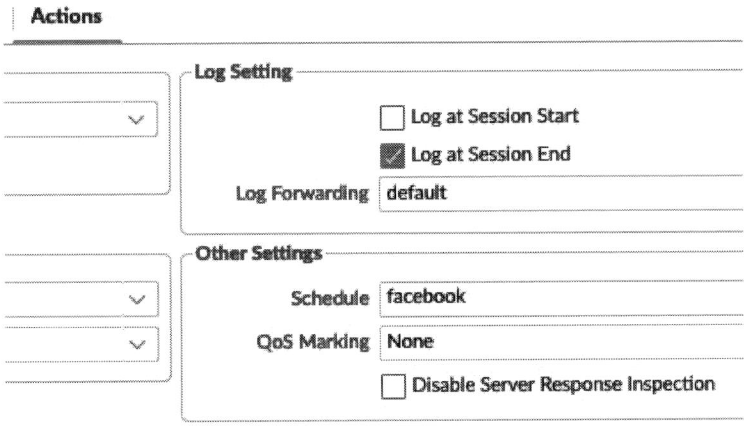

Figure 3.35 – Log options and schedules

**Schedule** can be used to create timeframes when this security rule will be active if certain applications are only allowed at specific times of the day (for example, Facebook can be allowed during lunch and after hours):

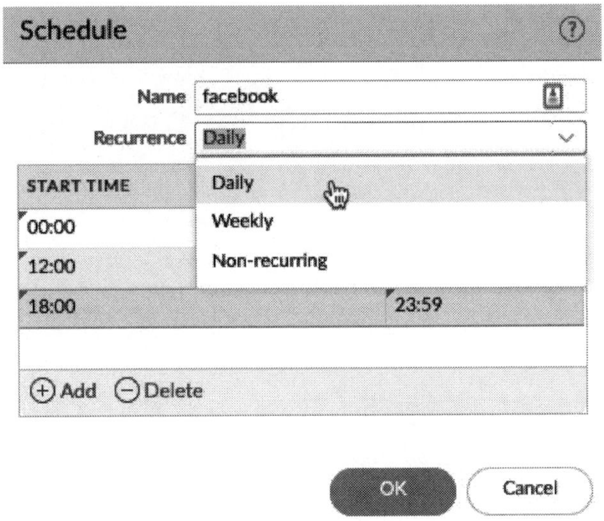

Figure 3.36 – Schedules

Before you continue putting this new knowledge to work and start creating more rules, let's review how you can prepare address objects.

# Address objects

To make managing destinations in your security and NAT policy a little easier, you can create address objects by going to **Objects | Addresses**. When you create a new object here, you can reuse the same object in different rules, and if something changes, you only need to change the address object for all the security and NAT rules to be automatically updated:

1. Click on **Add** and provide a descriptive name for the address. It is good practice to set up a naming convention so that you can repeat this process for all other address objects. A good example is to prefix all server names with S_ and all networks with N_ so that they're easily identifiable.

2. Set a description if needed.

3. Select the type of object that this will be.

   --**IP Netmask** lets you set an IP with a subnet mask down to /32 or /64 for a single IPv4 or Ipv6 address (no need to add /32).

   --**IP Range** lets you define a range that includes all the IP addresses between the first and last IP set in the range, separated with a dash (-).

   --**IP Wildcard Mask** lets you set a subnet masking that covers binary matches, where a zero bit requires an exact match in the IP bit, and 1 is a wildcard. So, for example, a wildcard subnet of 0.0.0.254 translates to 000000000.0000000.0 000000.11111110. the first three bytes are set and in the last byte, all but the first bit are wildcards. This means that if the associated IP address is set to 10.0.0.2 (00001010.0000000.000000.00000010), all of the IPs in the subnet that end in 0 will be matched (that is, all of the even IP addresses). If the IP is set to 10.0.0.1, all of the odd IPs would match. This type of object can only be used in security rules.

   --**FQDN** lets you set a domain name that the firewall will periodically resolve according to the **Time To Live (TTL)** and cache. Up to 10 A or AAAA records are supported for each FQDN object. Use the **Resolve** link to verify that the domain can be resolved.

4. Add a tag to easily identify and filter policies for this object.

5. Click **OK**.

Once you have sets of objects that are similar, you can also create groups by going to **Objects | Address Groups**. These groups can be used to bundle objects for usc in security or other policies.

# Tags

Tags can be leveraged to group, filter, or easily identify many other objects. Security zones, policy rules, or address objects can all be tagged with up to 64 tags per object. By going to **Objects | Tags**, you can create new tags:

1. Click on **Add** and create a descriptive and preferably short name for the tag (up to 127 characters). You can also use the dropdown to select one of the already-created security zones, which will cause the tags to be automatically assigned to this zone.

2. Select a color or leave it as None.

3. Add a comment.

4. Click **OK.**

As you can see in the following screenshot, tags can then be used to visually enhance your rule base or to filter for specific types of rules:

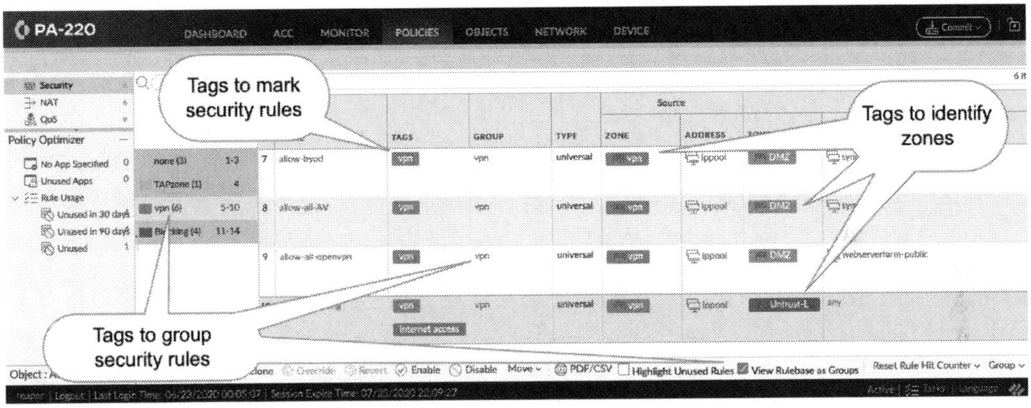

Figure: 3.37 – Tags in the security policy

> **Important note**
> While building security rules, objects (such as addresses, applications, services, and so on) can be clicked and dragged from the object browser on the left into any rule, and from one rule to another. There is no need to open a rule and navigate to the appropriate tab to add objects.

While you're on the **Security policy** tab, there's a tool called **Policy Optimizer** on the bottom left-hand side that can help improve your security rules by keeping track of rule usage.

# Policy Optimizer

After a while, you will want to review the security rule base you've built to make sure you haven't missed any applications, left rules too open, or have any duplicates that leave rules unused. Policy Optimizer records statistics relating to your rules and can report the following:

- Rules that have been unused for 30 days, 90 days, or for all time so that you can delete them

- Rules that are set up with no applications defined and the applications that were accepted by those rules

- Rules that have applications that are not being used so that you can remove these excess applications

Now that you are able to build a complete security rule base, there may need to be Network Address Translation for sessions coming in from the internet.

# Creating NAT rules

Unless you are one of the lucky few organizations that were able to get their very own A (/8) or B (/16) class subnets, your internal network segments will most likely be made up of one or several of the well-known RFC1918 private IP address allocations: 10.0.0.0/8, 172.16.0.0/12, or 192.168.0.0/16. NAT is needed for your hosts to be able to reach the internet and your customers and partners to reach publicly available resources hosted in your data center. NAT rules can be configured through **Policies | NAT**.

For this section, keep the following interface setup in mind:

| INTERFACE | INTERFACE TYPE | MANAGEMENT PROFILE | LINK STATE | IP ADDRESS | VIRTUAL ROUTER | SECURITY ZONE |
|---|---|---|---|---|---|---|
| ethernet1/1 | Layer3 | | | 198.51.100.2/24 | default | Untrust-L3 |
| ethernet1/2 | Layer3 | | | 192.168.27.1/24 | default | Trust-L3 |
| ethernet1/3 | Layer3 | | | 10.0.0.1/24 | default | DMZ-L3 |

Figure 3.38 – Interface zone and IP configuration

Address translation comes in different flavors depending on the direction and purpose, each with its own nuances. Let's first review Inbound NAT.

# Inbound NAT

For Inbound NAT, it is important to remember that the firewall is zone-based and the source and destination zone are determined *before* the NAT policy is evaluated:

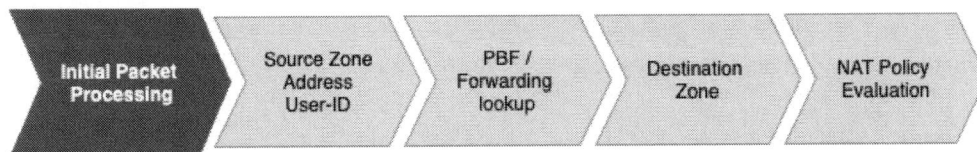

Figure 3.39 – Packet flow stages

This means that for inbound NAT, the source and destination zone will be identical. The routing table will determine the source zone based on the default route and the destination zone based on the connected network, which is configured on the external interface.

For example, if the 203.0.113.1 internet IP is connecting to the 198.51.100.2 firewall IP to reach the 10.0.0.5 server, the firewall will look up 203.0.113.5 in its routing table and find that it only matches the default route, 0.0.0.0/0, which points out of the ethernet1/1 interface, which is in the Untrust-L3 zone. It will then look up 198.51.100.2 (the original destination IP in the packet header) and find it in the 198.51.100.0/24 connected network on the ethernet1/1 interface, which is in the Untrust-L3 zone.

The **Original Packet** tab needs to have the following:

- The same source and destination zones.

- **Source Address** can be **Any** for generic internet sources, specific IP addresses, or subnets if the source is known.

- **Destination Interface** indicates which interface the packet is headed to. This can be important in cases where there are multiple interfaces with overlapping routes.

- **Service** can be used to restrict which destination port is allowed in the received packets. This will help in cases where the IP space is restricted and **Port Address Translation** (**PAT**) is required to host different services on the same external IP and will prevent over-exposing an internal host.

- **DESTINATION ADDRESS** needs to be a single IP for a one-to-one destination NAT (don't add a subnet). Having a subnet-based destination NAT is possible, but only for **Session Distribution**:

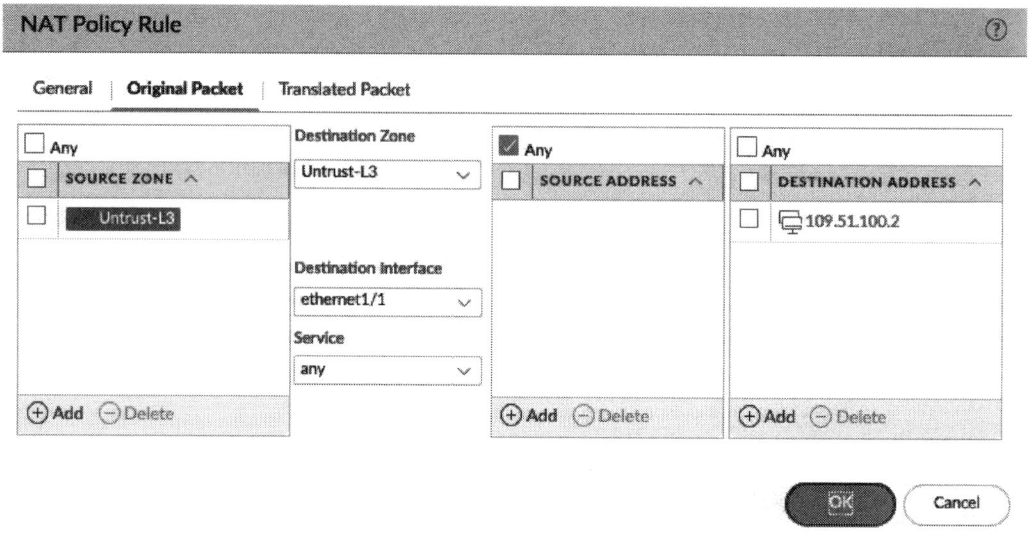

Figure 3.40 – Original Packet NAT translation

In the **Translated Packet** tab, you can set what needs to be changed for the external client to be able to reach the internal server:

- **Source Address Translation** will usually be set to None, but it can be set to match an internal interface subnet or loopback interface if required. This would let the server receive a packet sourced from an internal IP, rather than the original internet IP.

- Destination translation to a static IP, also known as one-to-one NAT, changes the destination IP to a single internal server.

- **Translated Port** can be used if the internal service runs on a different port than the externally advertised one. For example, externally, a web server could be reachable on default SSL port 443, while on the server itself, the service is enabled on 8443:

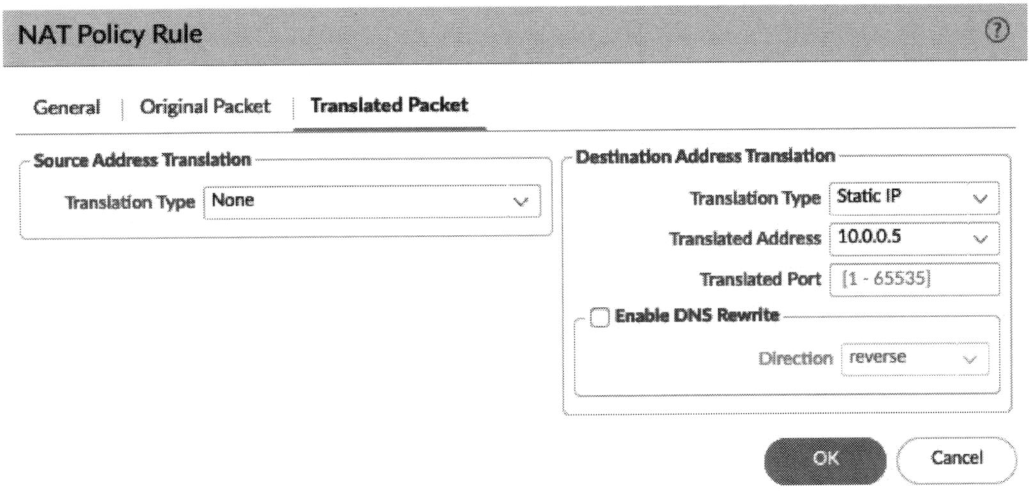

**NAT Policy Rule**

General  |  Original Packet  |  **Translated Packet**

**Source Address Translation**

Translation Type  None

**Destination Address Translation**

Translation Type  Static IP

Translated Address  10.0.0.5

Translated Port  [1 - 65535]

☐ Enable DNS Rewrite

Direction  reverse

OK    Cancel

Figure 3.41 – Translated Packet NAT translation

Next, let's take a look at address translation in the opposite direction.

# Outbound NAT

Outbound NAT rewrites the source IP addresses of internal clients to the interface associated with a different zone. This could be an internet-facing zone or one connecting to a partner, VPN, or WAN, as in the following screenshot:

- The source zone will reflect the interface that the clients are connected to.
- The destination zone and destination interface will reflect the egress interface that a routing lookup determines based on the original packet:

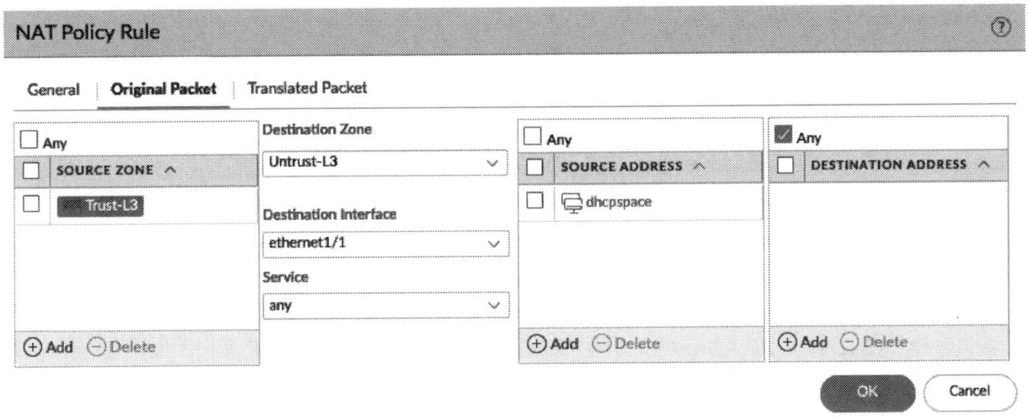

**NAT Policy Rule**

General  |  **Original Packet**  |  Translated Packet

☐ Any

☐ SOURCE ZONE ⌃

☐ Trust-L3

⊕ Add  ⊖ Delete

Destination Zone

Untrust-L3

Destination Interface

ethernet1/1

Service

any

☐ Any

☐ SOURCE ADDRESS ⌃

☐ 🖥 dhcpspace

⊕ Add  ⊖ Delete

☑ Any

☐ DESTINATION ADDRESS ⌃

⊕ Add  ⊖ Delete

OK    Cancel

Figure 3.42 – Outbound NAT Original Packet

> **Important note**
>
> When using an IP pool for source translation, the firewall will use proxy ARP to gain ownership of IP addresses. This means that you don't need to physically configure all of the IP addresses on an interface, but it is recommended that you have at least the subnet configured on an interface so that the firewall knows which interface is used to broadcast the proxy ARP packets. If the subnet does not exist on an interface, proxy ARP will be broadcast out of all the interfaces.

## Hide NAT or one-to-many NAT

The most common implementation of outbound NAT is the infamous *hide NAT*, or many-to-one, which changes the source IP addresses of all internal clients to the external IP(s) of the firewall. It is best to place this rule near the bottom of the rule base as it will catch any non-specific sessions and rewrite the source IP to that of the firewall.

The best option for this type of NAT is **Dynamic IP and Port (DIPP)**. DIPP rewrites the source IP to that of a selected interface or a manually entered IP, IP-range, or subnet, and assigns a random source port to the session on egress, as you can see here:

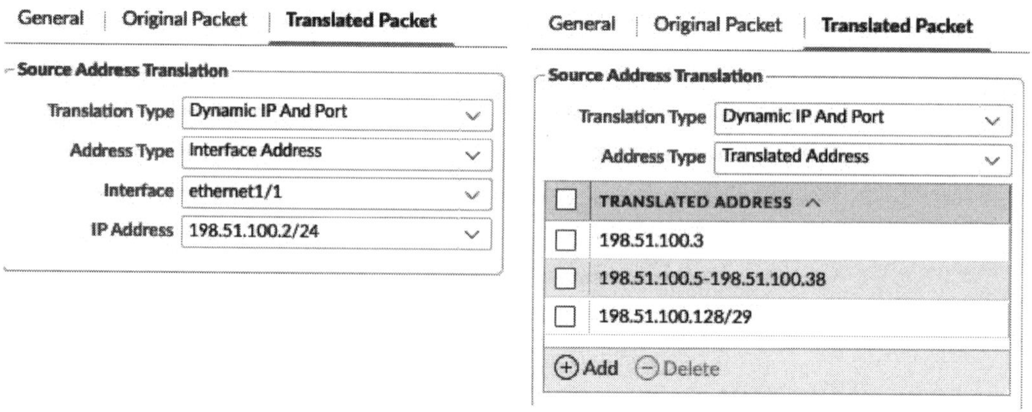

Figure 3.43 – DIPP to an interface IP or manual selection

DIPP supports around 64.000 concurrent sessions per available source IP, multiplied by the oversubscription factor supported by the platform you are deploying these rules on. As a rule of thumb, smaller platforms commonly support 2x oversubscription, larger platforms support 4x, and extra-large platforms up to 8x. When multiple IPs are available, DIPP assigns a rewrite IP based on a hash of the source IP so that the same source always gets the same translation address. Once the concurrent allowance for a given translation address is depleted, new sessions will be blocked until existing sessions are freed up.

You can check the current oversubscription ratio by using the following command:

```
admin@PA-220> show running nat-rule-ippool rule <rule name>

VSYS 1 Rule <rule name>:
Rule: <rule name>, Pool index: 1, memory usage: 20344
------------------------------------------------
Oversubscription Ratio:            2
Number of Allocates:               0
Last Allocated Index:              0
```

If more than `64.000 x oversubscription ratio` concurrent sessions per source are needed, or source ports need to be maintained, you can opt to use Dynamic IP instead of DIPP. Dynamic IP will simply "hop" to the next available IP in its assigned translation addresses for a given source IP while maintaining the source port. As a fallback, if the available IP pool does get depleted because Dynamic IP does not support oversubscription, you can enable DIPP. The IP used in the fallback should not overlap with any of the main IP pools:

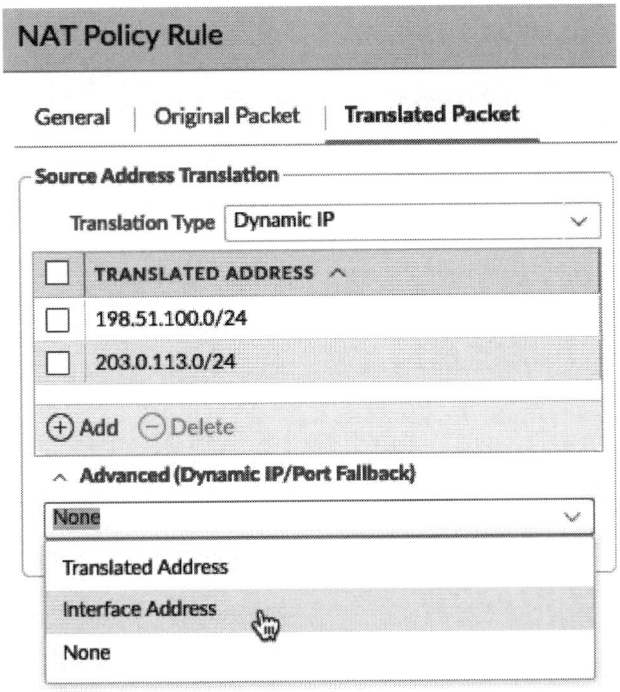

Figure 3.44 – Dynamic IP with two subnets and DIPP fallback

In some cases a server or host on the network will need to "own" its own IP address, which can be achieved with one-to-one NAT rules.

## One-to-one NAT

Static IP will always translate a source into the same translation IP and maintain the source port. An IP range can be set, in which case the source IPs will be sequentially matched to the translated IPs, but it is important that the source range and translation range are identical in size; for example, `10.0.0.5-10.0.0.15` translates to `203.0.113.5-203.0.113.115`.

The bi-directional option creates an *implied* inbound NAT rule to allow inbound translation for the same source/translated-source pairs. This implied rule reuses the destination zone set in the rule and `any` as the new source zone. The 'Translated source' address of the configured rule will be used as the 'Original destination' address, and the 'Original Source' of the configured rule will be used as the 'Translated destination' of the implied rule.

For the outbound rule, as you can see in the following screenshot, you have the following:

- **Source**: `Trust-L3`
- **Destination**: `Untrust-L3`
- **Original source**: `serverfarm`
- **Translated source**: `serverfarm-public`

For rules that have bi-directional set, the following implied NAT rule will be created:

- **Source**: `any`
- **Destination**: `Untrust-L3`
- **Original destination**: `serverfarm-public`
- **Translated destination**: `serverfarm`

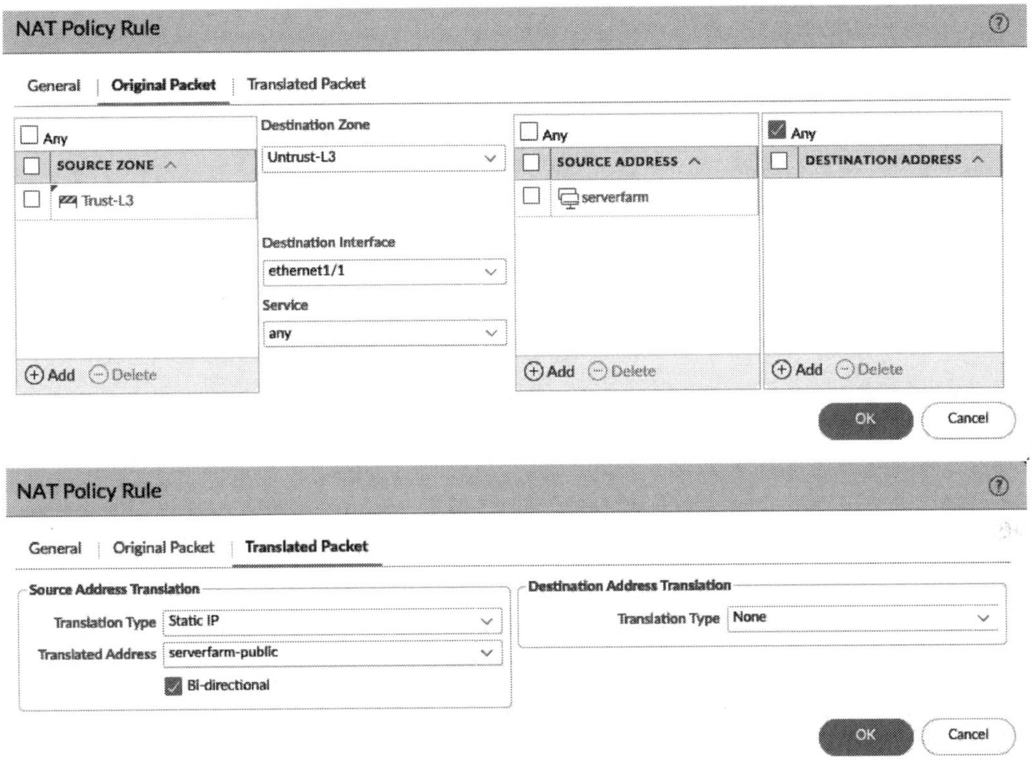

Figure 3.45 – Static IP NAT with the Bi-directional option

In some cases "double NAT" needs to be applied to sessions that need to take an unusual route due to NAT. These types of NAT rules are called U-turn or hairpin NAT rules.

## U-turn or hairpin NAT

If an internal host needs to connect to another internal host by using its public IP address, a unique problem presents itself.

For each session, only one NAT rule can be matched. When the client connects to the public IP, the routing table will want to send the packet out to the internet, which will trigger the hide NAT rule, which translates the source IP. The packet should then go back inside as the destination IP is also owned by the firewall, but a second NAT action can't be triggered, so the packet is discarded.

> **Important note**
>
> If the hide NAT IP is identical to the destination IP, which is common in environments with few public IP addresses, the packet will be registered as a land attack:

```
admin@PA-220> show counter global | match land

Global counters:
Elapsed time since last sampling: 26.05  seconds

name       value   rate severity category  aspect   description
-----------------------------------------------------------------
Flow_parse_land 1 1    drop        flow        parse     Packets
dropped: land attack
```

A workaround to this problem, if changing the internal DNS record or adding an entry to the host file of the client is not possible, is to configure a U-turn or hairpin NAT.

> **Important note**
>
> If you are using PAN-OS 9.0.2 or later, refer to the following *Enable DNS Rewrite* section.

This type of NAT combines the destination and source NAT and must be placed at the top of the rule base to prevent the hide NAT rule from catching these outbound sessions. The reason the source NAT is required is to make the session stick to the firewall so that no asymmetric routes are created.

If you were to configure the destination NAT to rewrite the public IP for the internal IP without translating the source, the server would receive a packet with the original source IP intact and reply directly to the client, bypassing the firewall. The next packet from the client would be sent to the firewall, which would try to perform TCP session sanity checks and determine whether the TCP session was broken, discarding the client packet. Adding source translation would force the server to reply to the firewall, which would then forward the translated packet back to the client:

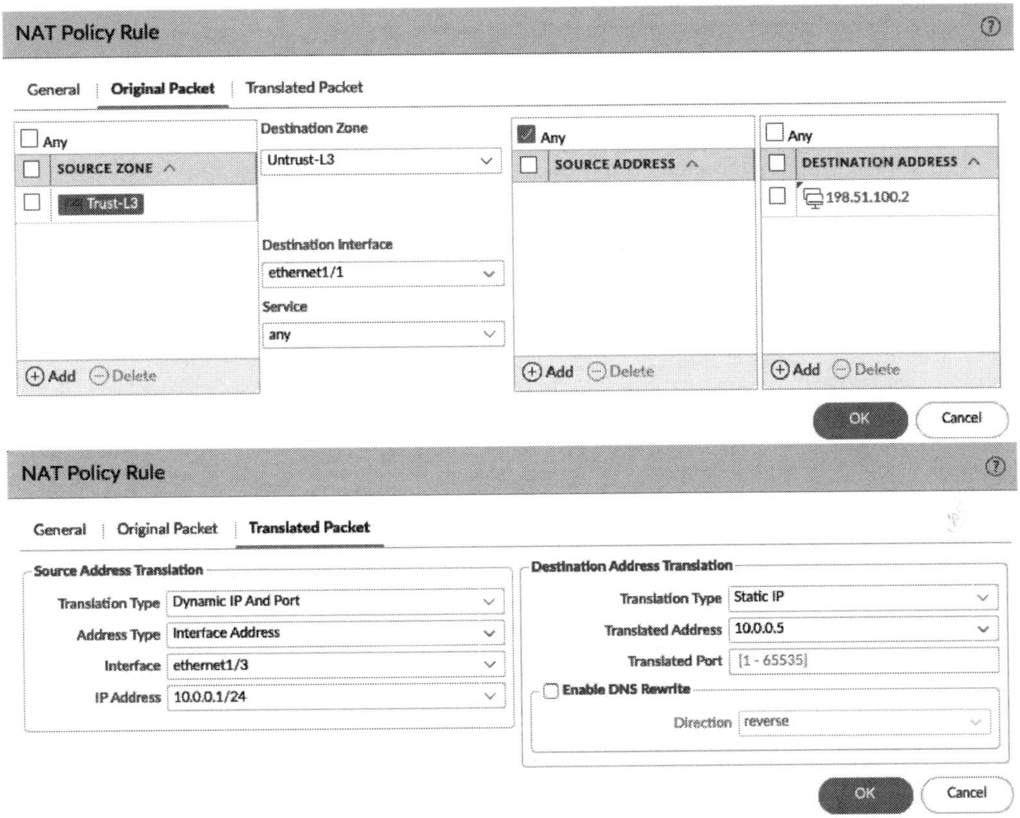

## NAT Policy Rule

General | **Original Packet** | Translated Packet

| ☐ Any | Destination Zone | ☑ Any | ☐ Any |
|---|---|---|---|
| ☐ SOURCE ZONE ∧ | Untrust-L3 ∨ | ☐ SOURCE ADDRESS ∧ | ☐ DESTINATION ADDRESS ∧ |
| ☐ Trust-L3 | | | ☐ 198.51.100.2 |
| | Destination Interface | | |
| | ethernet1/1 ∨ | | |
| | Service | | |
| | any ∨ | | |
| ⊕ Add ⊖ Delete | | ⊕ Add ⊖ Delete | ⊕ Add ⊖ Delete |

OK    Cancel

## NAT Policy Rule

General | Original Packet | **Translated Packet**

**Source Address Translation**

| Translation Type | Dynamic IP And Port ∨ |
|---|---|
| Address Type | Interface Address ∨ |
| Interface | ethernet1/3 ∨ |
| IP Address | 10.0.0.1/24 ∨ |

**Destination Address Translation**

| Translation Type | Static IP ∨ |
|---|---|
| Translated Address | 10.0.0.5 ∨ |
| Translated Port | [1 - 65535] |
| ☐ Enable DNS Rewrite | |
| Direction | reverse ∨ |

OK    Cancel

Figure 3.46 – U-turn NAT

This type of complication can also be addressed by changing the DNS query to the internal IP of the final destination.

## Enable DNS Rewrite

**Enable DNS Rewrite** was introduced in PAN-OS 9.0.2 and later and enables the NAT policy to be applied inside DNS response packets:

- It reverse translates the DNS response that matches the *translated* destination address in the rule. If the NAT rule rewrites `198.51.100.2` to `10.0.0.5`, the reverse rewrite will change the DNS response of `10.0.0.5` to `198.51.100.2`.

- It forward translates the DNS response that matches the *original* destination address in the rule. The forward DNS rewrite changes the DNS response of `198.51.100.2` to `10.0.0.5`.

This could be useful in a scenario where internal hosts need to query a DNS server in the DMZ for an FQDN of a server also hosted in a DMZ where they receive the external IP in the DNS response. This could lead to odd routing issues (see the *U-turn or hairpin NAT* section) as the destination IP will match the external zone, but both the client and server are on internal zones:

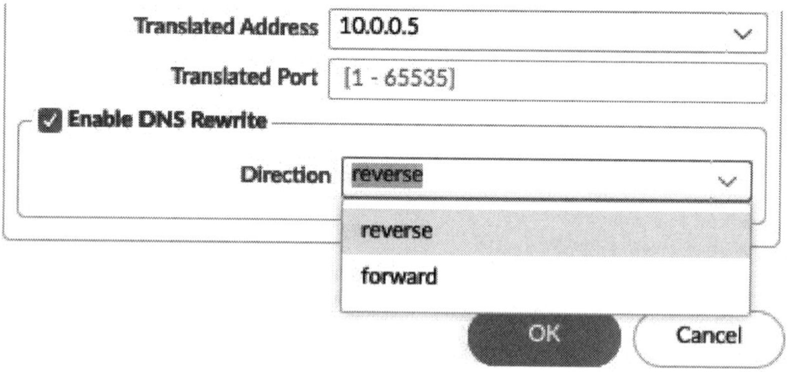

Figure 3.47 – Enable DNS Rewrite

If a service is hosted on several physical servers (the original destination is an FQDN that returns several IP addresses), the destination translation settings can be set to **Dynamic IP (with session distribution)**. The firewall will rewrite the destination IP according to the chosen method:

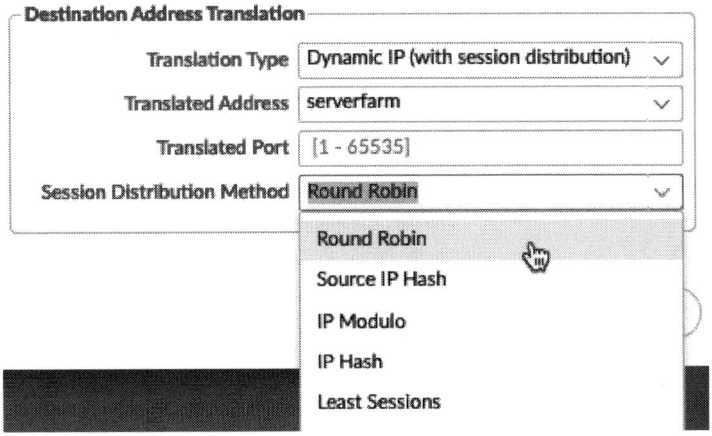

Figure 3.48 – Dynamic IP (with session distribution)

With this information you will now be able to resolve any Network Address Translation challenges you may face.

# Summary

In this chapter, you learned how to create security profiles and how to build a set of profiles that influence how your firewall processes threats. You learned how to create a default security profile group so that your security rule base starts off with a strong baseline of protection, as well as how to create solid security rules. You can now make complex NAT policies that cater to the needs of your inbound and outbound connections.

In the next chapter, we will see how to take even more control of your sessions by leveraging policy-based routing to segregate business-critical sessions from the general internet, limit bandwidth-hogging applications with quality of service, and look inside encrypted sessions with SSL decryption.

# 4
# Taking Control of Sessions

In this chapter, you will see how you can ensure critical applications do not run out of bandwidth and less important applications are prevented from consuming too much bandwidth. You will learn how to bypass the routing table and make exceptions for certain sessions, as well as how to decrypt encrypted sessions and look within them to determine actual applications and stop threats.

In this chapter, we're going to cover the following main topics:

- Controlling the bandwidth with quality of service policies
- Leveraging SSL decryption to break open encrypted sessions
- Redirecting sessions over different paths using policy-based forwarding

## Technical requirements

This chapter requires a working knowledge of measuring network bandwidth and available resources. You should understand the implications of sending packets over different interfaces, rather than where routes are pointing to, and you should have a good understanding of certificate chains.

# Controlling the bandwidth with quality of service policies

**Quality of Service (QoS)** is the collective name for several technologies that can help improve the quality of applications and the data flows that they are applied to by prioritizing them over other flows or reserving bandwidth to ensure adequate throughput and acceptable latency. In this section, you will learn how QoS marking can be applied to a firewall to interact with network devices downstream.

There are two ways for a firewall to participate in applying **QoS** to network traffic:

- **Differentiated Services Code Point (DSCP)** and **Type of Service (ToS)** headers
- QoS enforcement through built-in capabilities

Let's review external headers first.

## DSCP and ToS headers

DSCP headers allow the firewall to let upstream and downstream devices know that certain sessions have a certain priority. These headers can be set in the security policies under the **Actions** tab, as in the following screenshot:

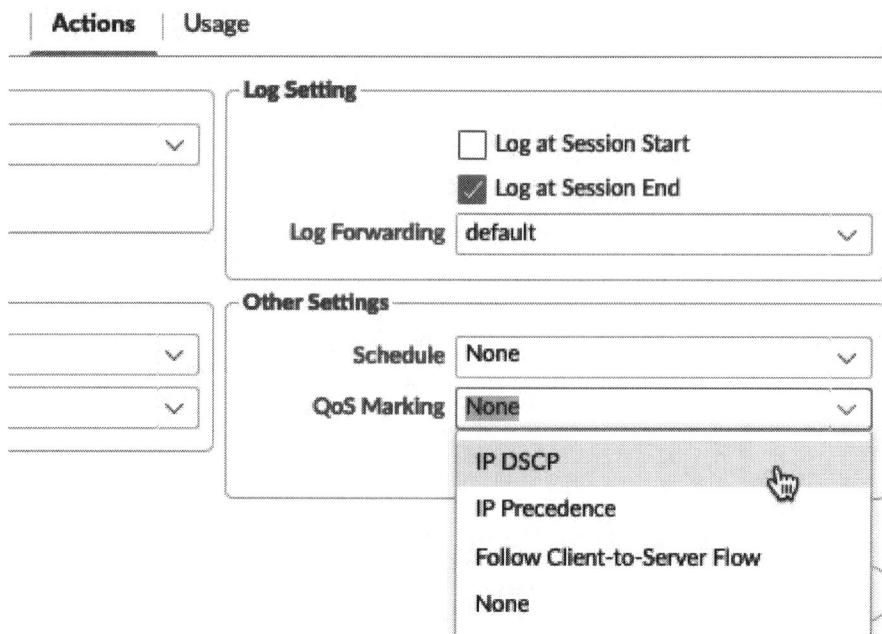

Figure 4.1 – IP DSCP headers in a security policy

In DSCP, you can set **Assured Forwarding (AF)**, **Expedited Forwarding (EF)**, or **Class Selector (CS)** code points. The **IP Precedence** ToS can be used when communicating with legacy network devices and **Follow Client-to-Server Flow** can be used to apply inbound DSCP marking to a returning outbound flow.

In the next section, we will cover controlling flows directly in the firewall.

## QoS enforcement in the firewall

The firewall can also enforce bandwidth restrictions or guarantees, and that's what we will focus on here. The Palo Alto Networks firewall uses a system of eight classes combined with policies.

Each interface is set up with a QoS profile that mandates how each class is treated, and then policies are created to identify sessions as belonging to a certain class. The default class is class4, so anything that is not caught by a QoS rule will automatically become class4 and be subject to the restrictions for that class.

We'll use the following topology to build an example QoS policy:

- An internet link on eth1/1 with a download bandwidth of 200 Mbps per second and an upload bandwidth of 50 Mbps.

- A DMZ network containing some servers on eth1/2 connected to a 1 Gbps interface.

- A LAN where the users sit on eth1/3 connected to a 1 Gbps interface.

- Users need 20 Mbps of guaranteed upload and download bandwidth for their enterprise **Voice over Internet Protocol (VoIP)**, but some internet downloads need to be limited to 50 Mbps.

- File share traffic between users and servers needs to be limited to 300 Mbps.

- Site-to-site VPN connections need a 20 Mbps guarantee for business-critical applications.

This topology is illustrated as follows:

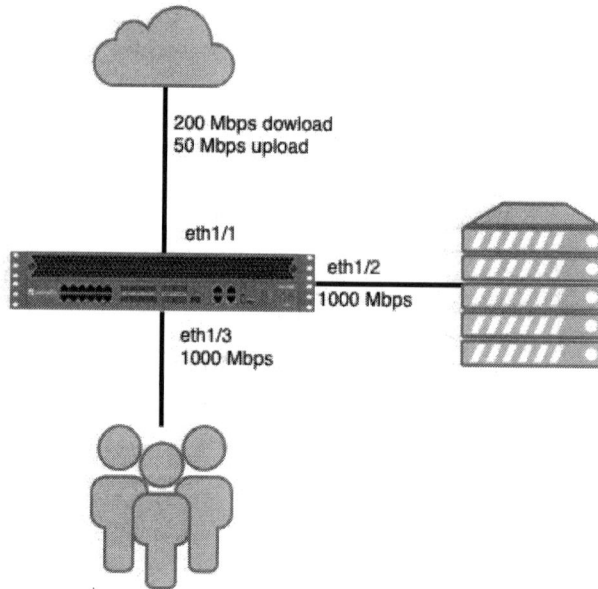

Figure 4.2 – Example topology

Next, we will start laying down the groundwork for what will eventually become QoS enforcement.

## Creating QoS profiles

Go to **Network | Network Profiles | QoS Profile**; you need to create at least one new profile to get started. The classes themselves do not carry any weight, so class1 could be your most important class, but also your lowest, depending on how you configure its parameters.

The **priority** setting does require special consideration; the **real-time** priority has its own queue in packet processing, making sure that any packets that end up in the queue (due to bandwidth congestion) go out first. All the lower priorities (high to low) share the main queue, with the lowest priority packets being discarded first if packets need to be let go in favor of higher priority sessions.

**Egress Max** at the top of the profile is the total of the maximum and reserved bandwidths for the whole profile, while **Egress Max** next to the class indicates how much bandwidth all of the sessions in that class get to share.

Let's build a few profiles first:

1. Create a profile called `internet-upload`.

2. Set the profile's **Egress Max** value to 50 Mbps to limit the total bandwidth usable by the profile to 50 Mbps. This tells the QoS engine that it needs to use its queuing mechanism and prioritize packets once it reaches the maximum limit.

3. Create `class1`, set it to **real-time**, and set a guarantee of 20 Mbps.

   This profile can also be created with the following commands in the **Command-Line Interface (CLI)**:

```
reaper@pa-220# set network qos profile internet-upload
aggregate-bandwidth egress-max 50
```

```
reaper@pa-220# set network qos profile internet-upload
class-bandwidth-type mbps class class1 priority real-time
class-bandwidth egress-guaranteed 20
```

4. Create a profile called `internet-download`.

5. Set the profile's **Egress Max** value to 200 Mbps.

6. Create `class1`, set **Priority** to **real-time**, and set its guarantee to 20 Mbps.

7. Create `class5` and set the **Egress Max** value to 50.

   This profile can also be created with the following commands:

```
reaper@pa-220# set network qos profile internet-download
aggregate-bandwidth egress-max 200
```

```
reaper@pa-220# set network qos profile internet-download
class-bandwidth-type mbps class class5 priority medium
class-bandwidth egress-max 50
```

```
reaper@pa-220# set network qos profile internet-download
class-bandwidth-type mbps class class1 priority real-time
class-bandwidth egress-guaranteed 20
```

8. Create a profile called `internal`.

9. Do not set this profile's **Egress Max** value; we will be mixing this profile with the internet one, so we will let the interface maximum egress determine the maximum for this profile.

10. Create `class8`, set it to **low** priority, and set **Egress Max** to `300`.

    `internal` can also be created in the CLI, as follows:

    ```
    reaper@pa-220# set network qos profile internal class-
    bandwidth-type mbps class class8 priority low class-
    bandwidth egress-max 300
    ```

11. Create a profile called `vpn`.

12. Create `class4` and set it to guarantee `20` Mbps and to **real-time** priority; for this profile, we will let IPSec connections default to `class4`.

    `vpn` can be created in the CLI, as follows:

    ```
    reaper@pa-220# set network qos profile vpn class-
    bandwidth-type mbps class class4 priority medium class-
    bandwidth egress-guaranteed 20
    ```

    The QoS profiles should look as follows:

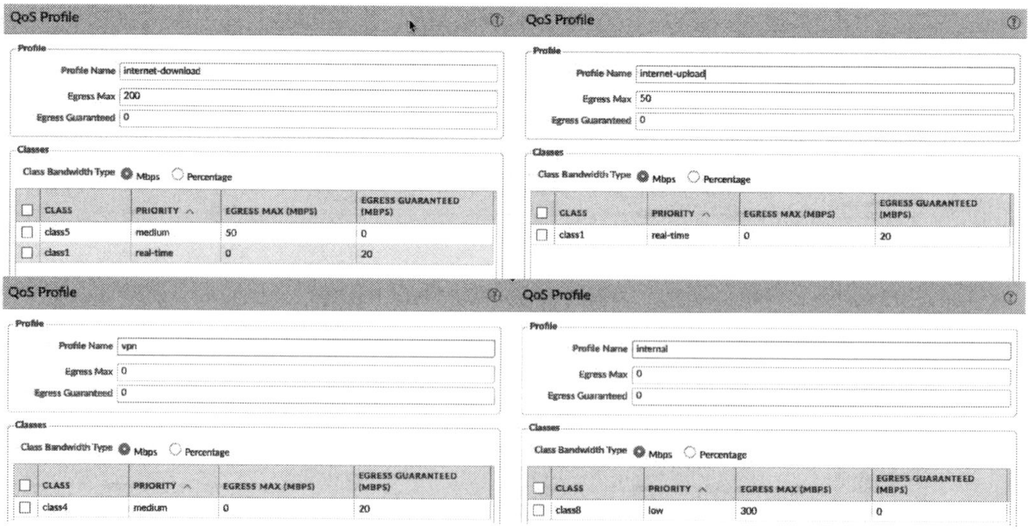

Figure 4.3 – QoS profiles

Next, the interfaces need to be set to enforce QoS. In **Network | QoS**, add all the interfaces. Then, for `ethernet1/1`, the internet-facing interface, do the following:

1. Check the **Turn on QoS feature on this interface** box as illustrated in the following screenshot, or execute the following CLI command:

   ```
   reaper@pa-220# set network qos interface ethernet1/1
   enabled yes
   ```

2.  Set the interface **Egress Max** value to 50 Mbps to limit uploads to the internet:

```
reaper@pa-220# set network qos interface ethernet1/1
interface-bandwidth egress-max 50
```

3.  Set the `internet-upload` profile as a **Clear Text** profile so that classes can be applied:

```
reaper@pa-220# set network qos interface ethernet1/1
regular-traffic default-group qos-profile internet-upload
```

4.  Set the vpn profile as the **Tunnel Interface** profile (as in the following screenshot):

```
reaper@pa-220# set network qos interface ethernet1/1
tunnel-traffic default-group per-tunnel-qos-profile vpn
```

This applies QoS to any site-to-site VPN connections sourced from the firewall to a remote peer (on a local tunnel interface):

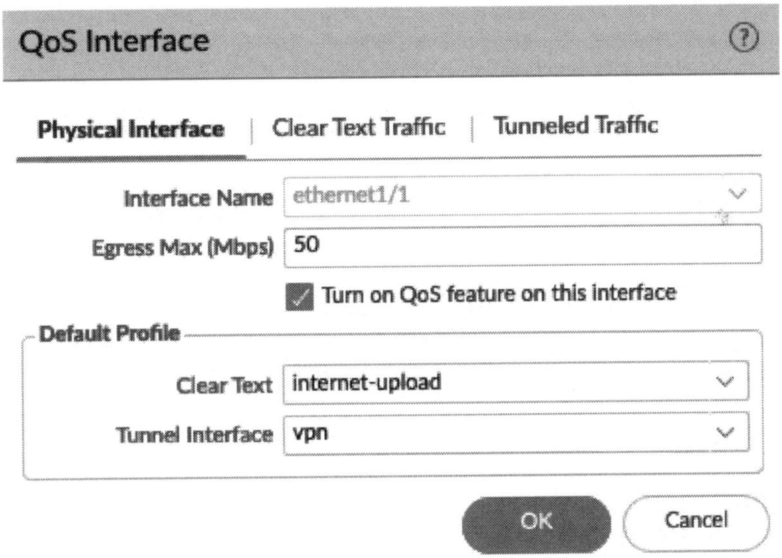

Figure 4.4 – eth1/1 QoS configuration

For `ethernet1/2`, the DMZ-facing interface, do the following:

1.  Check the **Turn on QoS feature on this interface** box as illustrated in the following screenshot, or use the following CLI command:

    ```
    reaper@pa-220# set network qos interface ethernet1/2
    enabled yes
    ```

2.  Set the interface **Egress Max** value to `1000` Mbps, but leave **Clear Text** as `default` and **Tunnel Interface** as `none`:

    ```
    reaper@pa-220# set network qos interface ethernet1/2
    interface-bandwidth egress-max 1000
    ```
    ```
    reaper@pa-220# set network qos interface ethernet1/2
    regular-traffic default-group qos-profile default
    ```

3.  In the **Clear Text** tab, set the **Egress Max** value to `1000` Mbps:

    ```
    reaper@pa-220# set network qos interface ethernet1/2
    regular-traffic bandwidth egress-max 1000
    ```

4.  Add a new profile line:

    --Call it `userupload`.

    --Assign the `internal` QoS profile.

    --Set the source interface to `ethernet1/3`:

    ```
    reaper@pa-220# set network qos interface ethernet1/2
    regular-traffic groups regular-traffic-group members
    userupload match local-address address any
    ```
    ```
    reaper@pa-220# set network qos interface ethernet1/2
    regular-traffic groups regular-traffic-group members
    userupload match local-address interface ethernet1/3
    ```
    ```
    reaper@pa-220# set network qos interface ethernet1/2
    regular-traffic groups regular-traffic-group members
    userupload qos-profile internal
    ```

5.  Add a second profile line:

    --Call it `internet`.

    --Assign the `internet-download` profile.

--Set the source interface to `ethernet1/1`:

```
reaper@pa-220# set network qos interface ethernet1/2
regular-traffic groups regular-traffic-group members
internet match local-address address any
```

```
reaper@pa-220# set network qos interface ethernet1/2
regular-traffic groups regular-traffic-group members
internet match local-address interface ethernet1/1
```

```
reaper@pa-220# set network qos interface ethernet1/2
regular-traffic groups regular-traffic-group members
internet qos-profile internet-download
```

These settings allow different profiles to be applied, as you can see in the following screenshot, depending on where the packets originate from. Downloads from the internet will be limited to 200 Mbps in total, and `class5` can be applied to limit sessions to 50 Mbps as needed, while sessions from the user's LAN can use up to 1000 Mbps and limit the bandwidth to 300 Mbps uploads for the `class8` sessions:

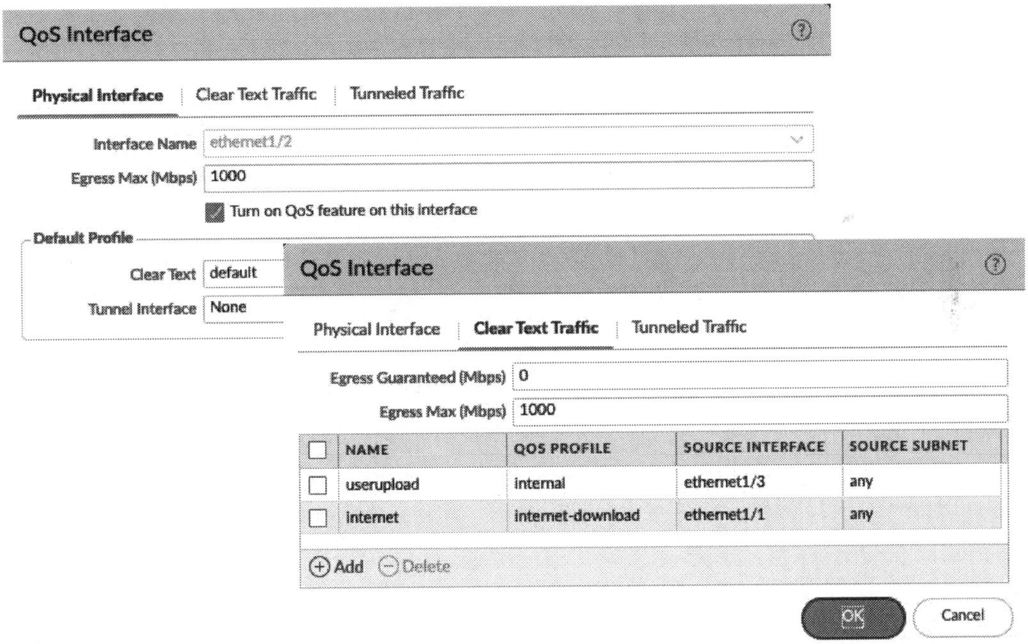

Figure 4.5 – eth1/2 QoS configuration

For `ethernet1/3`, the user-facing interface, do the following:

1.  Check the **Turn on QoS feature on this interface** box as illustrated in the following screenshot, or execute the following CLI command:

    ```
    reaper@pa-220# set network qos interface ethernet1/3
    enabled yes
    ```

2.  Set the interface's **Egress Max** value to `1000` Mbps, but leave **Clear Text** as `default` and **Tunnel Interface** as none:

    ```
    reaper@pa-220# set network qos interface ethernet1/3
    interface-bandwidth egress-max 1000
    ```

3.  In the **Clear Text** tab, set **Egress Max** to `1000` Mbps:

    ```
    reaper@pa-220# set network qos interface ethernet1/3
    regular-traffic bandwidth egress-max 1000
    ```

4.  Add a new profile line:

    --Call it `userdownload`.

    --Assign the `internal` QoS profile.

    --Set the source interface to `ethernet1/2`:

    ```
    reaper@pa-220# set network qos interface ethernet1/3
    regular-traffic groups regular-traffic-group members
    userdownload match local-address address any
    ```

    ```
    reaper@pa-220# set network qos interface ethernet1/3
    regular-traffic groups regular-traffic-group members
    userdownload match local-address interface ethernet1/2
    ```

    ```
    reaper@pa-220# set network qos interface ethernet1/3
    regular-traffic groups regular-traffic-group members
    userdownload qos-profile internal
    ```

5.  Add a second profile line:

    --Call it `internetdownload`.

    --Assign the `internet-download` profile.

    --Set the source interface to `ethernet1/1`:

    ```
    reaper@pa-220# set network qos interface ethernet1/3
    regular-traffic groups regular-traffic-group members
    internetdownload match local-address address any
    ```

```
reaper@pa-220# set network qos interface ethernet1/3
regular-traffic groups regular-traffic-group members
internetdownload match local-address interface
ethernet1/1
```

```
reaper@pa-220# set network qos interface ethernet1/3
regular-traffic groups regular-traffic-group members
internetdownload qos-profile internet-download
```

These settings will limit the maximum Mbps when downloading (or streaming) things from the internet while guaranteeing that the class1 sessions are not deprived of bandwidth and that the bandwidth from the DMZ server is also maximized for all of the sessions to 1 Gbps, except class8, which is limited to 300 Mbps downloads. This should look as follows:

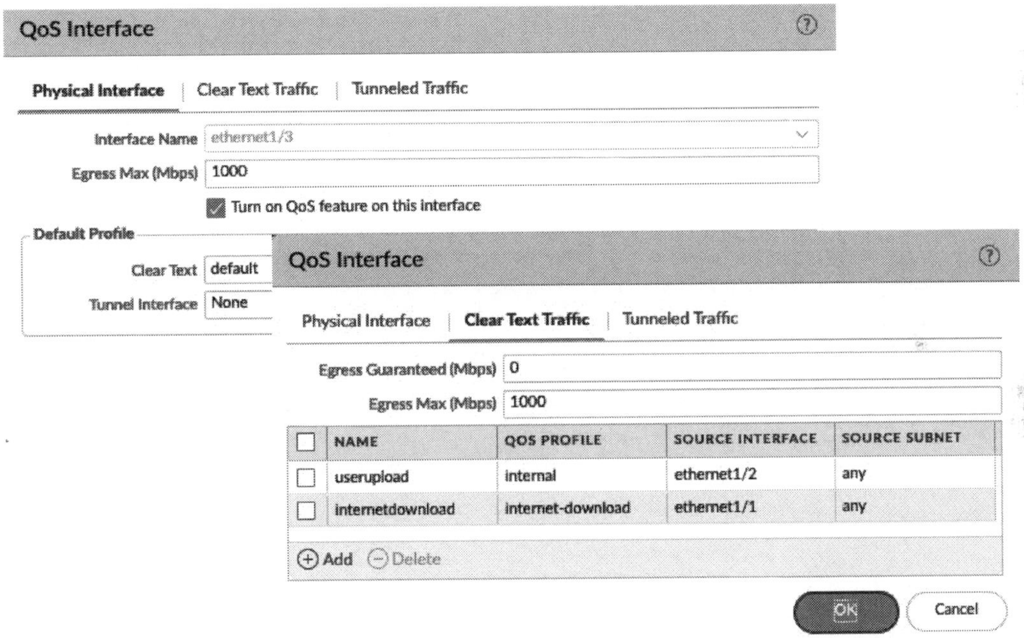

Figure 4.6 – eth1/3 QoS configuration

We have now created a framework that can apply traffic shaping to sessions. Next, we will define which applications are classified and how that is done.

## Creating QoS policies

Without any QoS rules, only `class4` will be enforced, which in the previous case will only set **Egress Max** to the maximum internet speed, but with no guarantees. The first policy we need to set will define **enterprise VoIP** as `class1` so that we can guarantee 20 Mbps downloads over the internet link:

1. Create a new rule by going to **Policies | QoS**.

2. Call the rule `enterprise voip`.

3. Set the zone(s) to the `trust-L3` and `dmz-L3` zones so that outbound calls are classified as `class1`.

4. Set the destination zone where the sessions will egress the firewall.

5. Set the class to `class1`:

```
reaper@pa-220# set rulebase qos rules "enterprise
voip" from [ dmz-L3 trust-L3 ] to Untrust-L3 source any
destination any category any application any action class
1
```

Your policy should look similar to the following:

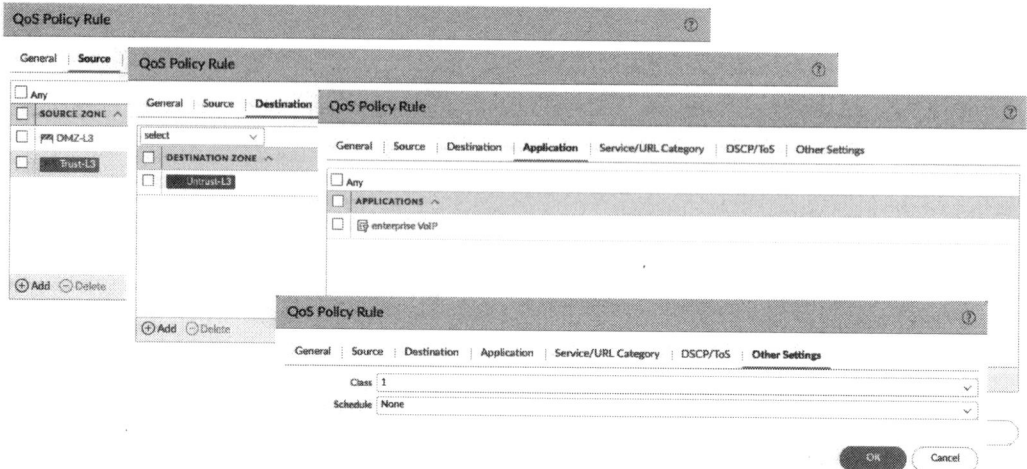

Figure 4.7 – Setting VoIP to class1 outbound

The second rule sets the same guarantee, but for sessions that are started from the internet (such as an inbound SIP call). Follow these steps to create an inbound rule (if inbound sessions are not allowed by the security policy, you can skip this rule):

1.  Create a rule and call it `enterprise voip in`.

2.  Set the source zone to the `Untrust-L3` zone.

3.  Set the destination zone to the internal zones where calls can be accepted (the internal client or DMZ gateway).

4.  Set the class to `class1`:

```
reaper@pa-220# set rulebase qos rules "enterprise
voip" to [ dmz-L3 trust-L3 ] from Untrust-L3 source any
destination any category any application any action class
1
```

The inbound rule will look as follows:

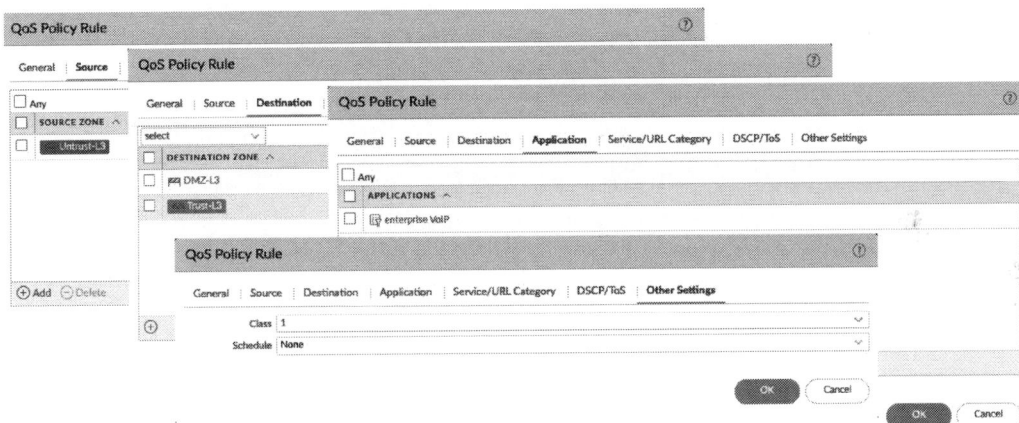

Figure 4.8 – Setting VoIP to class1 inbound

We will also need to limit certain sessions between the user's LAN and DMZ networks. Assuming the security policy only allows users to connect to the DMZ and no sessions to be allowed from the DMZ to the user network, only one QoS rule will be needed as QoS classes are assigned to all packets in a session, regardless of their direction (so, `class8` will be applied in both directions even if you only have your QoS rule set in one direction). Follow these steps to create an internal QoS rule:

1.  Create a new QoS rule and call it `fileshares`.

2.  Set the source zone to the `Trust-L3` network.

3. Set the destination zone to the DMZ network.

4. Add the appropriate filesharing applications.

5. Set the class to `class8`:

```
reaper@pa-220# set rulebase qos rules fileshares from
trust-L3 to dmz-L3 source any destination any application
[ ftp ms-ds-smb scps ] service application-default action
class 8
```

6. Save the changes.

Your internal rule will look as follows:

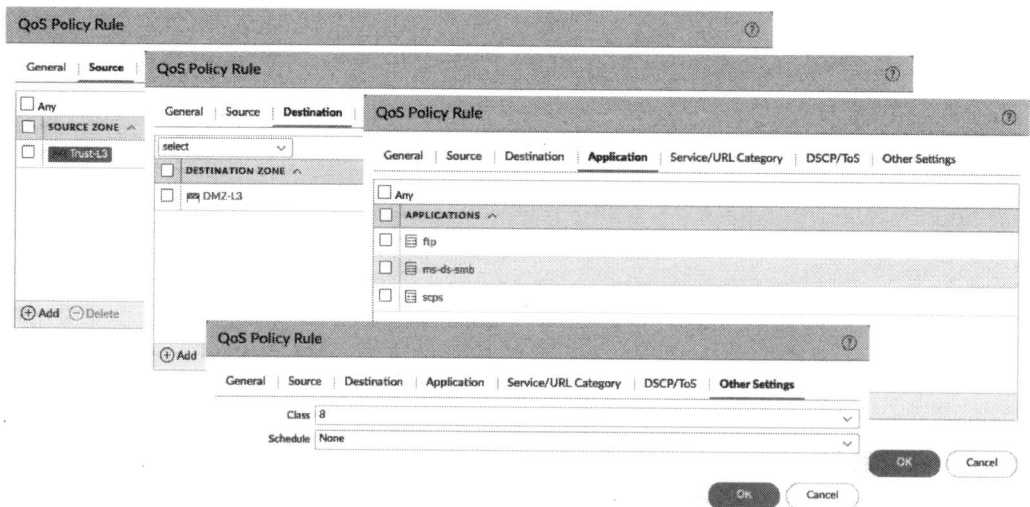

Figure 4.9 – Setting file transfer applications to class8

To quickly check whether the limitations and guarantees are being enforced properly, you can access a live graph next to each enabled interface from **Network | QoS | Statistics**:

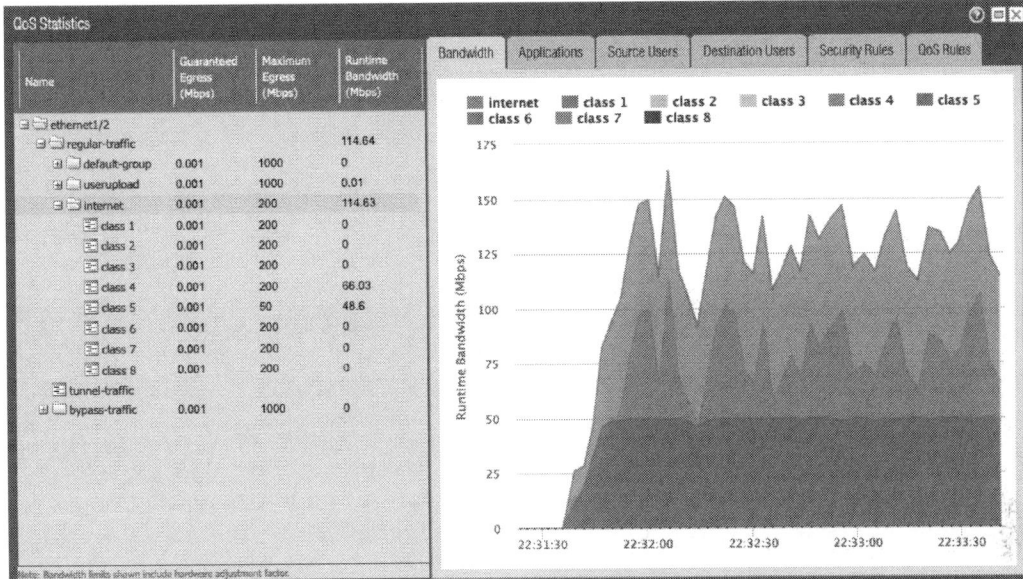

Figure 4.10 – class 5 is limited to 50 Mbps

To recap, we have learned the following:

- QoS is applied to the egress interface.
- Bandwidth restrictions and guarantees are shared within a class, not per session.
- Real-time priority has its own queue; the others share a queue.
- **Egress Guaranteed** or **Egress Max** cannot exceed the interface maximum.
- `Class4` is the default class.
- Classes may have different guarantees or limitations, depending on the direction of the packet.
- If a guarantee in a class is not filled, other classes may consume more bandwidth (without exceeding their max) until the guarantee is required.

You can now create QoS profiles and understand the implications of priorities, guarantees, and the egress maximum. You can apply these profiles to interfaces and define different profiles depending on the source interface. You can also create rule sets that classify applications so that they can be shaped according to your profiles.

In the next section, we will see how encrypted sessions can be decrypted and inspected and how applications within an SSL session can be determined and threats stopped.

# Leveraging SSL decryption to break open encrypted sessions

SSL/TLS and SSH decryption perform a man-in-the-middle attack but for good instead of evil—an encrypted session is intercepted, then through the use of trusted certificates, the session is deciphered and the payload is made visible for content inspection and App-ID to take a look at. There are three modes of SSL decryption currently available:

- SSH proxy
- SSL forward proxy
- SSL inbound inspection

Let's look at each of them in detail.

## SSH proxy

SSH proxy allows the interception of SSH sessions. It requires a decryption profile that contains a trusted root signing certificate, a **Certificate Authority (CA)**, and allows you to control tunneling over an SSH session by setting a security policy for `ssh-tunnel`.

## SSL forward proxy

SSL forward proxy is used for all outbound sessions. There are two distinct directions, and the outbound option is proxied because of how certificates are used to sign a website's SSL/TLS certificate. In the world of certificates, a handful of trusted organizations hold "trusted root signing certificates," which are regarded with the same authority as a notary with regard to signing documents. They sign off on a subset of subordinate or intermediary certificates, which are then used to sign off on server certificates, which represent domain names such as `google.com` or `packtpub.com`. This chain of trust needs to be resistant to attack so that "bad actors" can't set up a fake website and dupe visitors into trusting them, which makes legitimate interception difficult. For more details, refer to `https://en.wikipedia.org/wiki/Public_key_certificate`.

When accessing a website on the internet, the root and intermediary certificates can be any of the dozens of available options, so the only way to get the internal client to trust an intercepted connection is to replace the entire chain and make the client trust the root signing certificate. This can be accomplished in several ways, the most straightforward method being a manual import, but this may be more difficult to accomplish in a large environment. You can also leverage Microsoft **Group Policy Objects** (**GPOs**) and several other deployment methods, toolkits, scripts, and software packages; but whatever you do, don't let your users get used to ignoring a browser certificate warning—that is a dangerous habit to get into! Put in the time to install your organization's root signing authority and intermediary, or your self-signed root certificate and intermediary into the trusted root signing certificate store of all your clients' computers (and Firefox, as it uses its own certificate store). It will pay off in the long run, I promise.

If your organization already has a CA set up, you can simply have it create a new, easily identifiable intermediary that can be used for decryption. Export it with its private key and export the root certificate without a private key. Go to **Device | Certificate Management | Certificates** and import both, starting with the root.

If you do not have a CA available or you want to test the waters before you take a dive, we'll set SSL decryption up with a self-signed certificate for you to play with.

Go to **Device | Certificate Management | Certificates** and generate a root signing certificate by checking the **Certificate Authority** box and calling it `root signing certificate`. Then, create a subordinate certificate by setting **Signed By** as the root signing certificate and checking the **Certificate Authority** box and calling it `decryption subordinate`. Finally, make a third certificate that is not signed by the root signing certificate, set it as a CA, and name it `untrusted cert`.

You will need one certificate that your users will trust to decrypt websites. You also need an untrusted certificate because during decryption, the entire certificate structure is replaced with your own. If the real certificate has any problems, the firewall will keep decrypting but will use the untrusted certificate instead, so the user gets a certificate warning in their browser, making them halt and think about continuing.

These are the steps to create all the certificates you need:

1. Create a new certificate and call it `root signing cert`.
2. Set the CA flag.
3. Fill out the attributes and click **Generate**.
4. Create a new certificate and call it `decryption`.
5. Set the CA flag.

6. Set the **Signed By** field to the root certificate.

7. Fill out the attributes and click **Generate**.

8. Create a third certificate and name it `untrusted cert`.

9. Set the CA flag.

10. Make sure you do not set this one as signed by the root.

11. As a minimum, set the **Email** attribute. This will help savvy users that investigate why they received a certificate warning find the relevant contact details.

Your certificates should look similar to the following:

Figure 4.11 – The root, decryption, and untrusted certificates

When you click on the certificates, you can select three different options:

- **Forward Trust Certificate**
- **Forward Untrust Certificate**
- **Trusted Root CA**

**Forward Trust Certificate** is used for decryption and **Forward Untrust Certificate** is used if there is a problem with the upstream certificate and a warning should go out to users (if an upstream certificate is problematic or suspicious, using a trusted certificate would not prompt the user that there is something up as the firewall takes the responsibility of interacting with the endpoint). **Trusted Root CA** can be set so that the firewall itself trusts the root CA, which comes in handy if the dynamic update sessions go through the firewall and are decrypted.

Set each of the three certificates to their appropriate roles:

- Set the root signing certificate as **Trusted Root CA.**
- Set the decryption subordinate certificate as **Forward Trust Certificate.**
- Set the untrusted certificate as **Forward Untrust Certificate.**

You will now need to select the root signing certificate and export it to your computer. When asked whether you want to include the key, select **No** as you do not need it on your endpoints.

As the following screenshot shows, check the box in front of the certificate and click **Export Certificate** at the bottom:

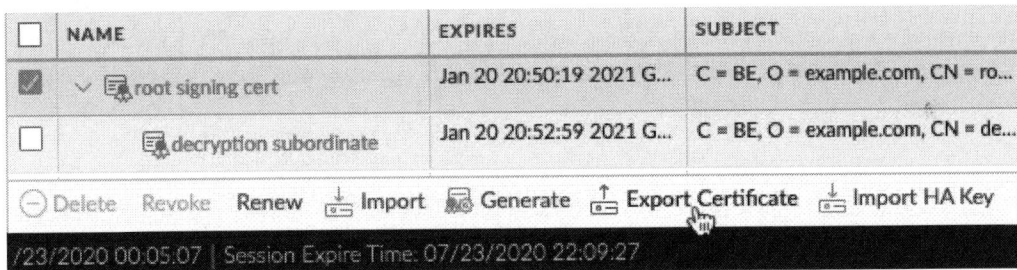

| | NAME | EXPIRES | SUBJECT |
|---|---|---|---|
| ☑ | ∨ 📑 root signing cert | Jan 20 20:50:19 2021 G... | C = BE, O = example.com, CN = ro... |
| ☐ | 📑 decryption subordinate | Jan 20 20:52:59 2021 G... | C = BE, O = example.com, CN = de... |

⊖ Delete    Revoke    Renew    ⬆ Import    📑 Generate    ⬆ Export Certificate    ⬇ Import HA Key

/23/2020 00:05:07 | Session Expire Time: 07/23/2020 22:09:27

Figure 4.12 – Exporting the root signing certificate

Once exported, you need to import the certificate onto your test machine's **trusted root certificate store**. If you intend to use Firefox, remember to add it to Firefox separately as Firefox doesn't use the machine certificate store (Internet Explorer, Edge, Chrome, and Safari do use the machine store).

Next, you need to create a decryption profile by going to **Objects | Decryption | Decryption profiles**. The default one is a bit weak and we want to ensure that certificate enforcement is a bit more robust:

1. Create a new SSL decryption profile and give it a useful name.

2. In the **SSL forward proxy** and **SSL inbound inspection** tabs, enable all of the options unless you want to allow exceptions (maybe you need to allow unsupported versions because a partner has not updated their infrastructure just yet).

3. In **SSL Protocol sessions**, disable 3DES, RC4, and SHA and set the minimum version to TLS1.2.

4. In the **No Decryption** tab, set the flags to block expired and untrusted certificates.

5. Finally, set all the flags on the **SSH Proxy** tab.

6. Click **OK**.

Now that the certificates are loaded and the decryption profile is created, you can go ahead and create the decryption rules by going to **Policy | Decryption**.

Building a decryption rule is pretty much the same as building a security rule. There's a source zone and network, a destination zone and network, and a service or URL category (no applications here). However, the options are a little different here. You can choose to perform **No Decrypt**, which comes in handy if you need to account for privacy-sensitive topics, such as online banking or religion.

> **Important note**
> You will need to build a policy where you need to carefully balance work and private life, which is usually a mixture of local law and company policy. Consider whether your organization will allow certain URL categories to be accessed from company equipment or on the company's network. Also, consider whether decryption should be applied to some personal categories as it may be prohibited by law to inspect certain sessions.

Commonly, some categories are allowed to be accessed but are not decrypted for privacy reasons. These categories should be added to a **No Decrypt** rule and placed at the top of the decrypt rule base.

For everything else, create an SSL **Forward Proxy** rule.

These are the steps to set up your basic decryption policy:

1. Create a new rule and call it `no-decrypt`.

2. Set the source zone to `Trust-L3`.

3. Set the destination zone to `Untrust-L3`.

4. Set the URL categories to `financial-services` or any category that is accessible but should be treated as private.

5. For the options, set the action to `no-decrypt`, type `SSL Forward Proxy`, and set the decryption profile:

```
reaper@pa-220# set rulebase decryption rules no-decrypt
from trust-L3 to Untrust-L3 category financial-services
profile "decryption profile" action no-decrypt type
ssl-forward-proxy
```

6. Create a second rule and call it `decryption`.

7. Set the source zone to the `Trust-L3` zone.

8. Set the destination to the `Untrust-L3` zone.

9. Leave the URL categories as any.

10. Set the action to `decrypt`, type `SSL Forward Proxy`, and set the decryption profile:

```
reaper@pa-220# set rulebase decryption rules decrypt from
trust-L3 to Untrust-L3 category any profile "decryption
profile" action decrypt type ssl-forward-proxy
```

11. Save the changes.

When you open a web page now, you should see that the root signing certificate has replaced the original CA:

Figure 4.13 – Decryption certificate chain versus the original certificate chain

You're now able to set up the certificates needed for SSL decryption and build a decryption policy. In the next section, we'll set up inbound decryption for sites hosted in your environment.

## SSL Inbound Inspection

SSL Inbound Inspection is used when the website is hosted locally and you have access to the server certificate and its private key.

You will need to import the server certificate, including its private key, the provider's intermediary, and the root certificate (you don't need the private keys of these last two; they simply serve to complete the chain). As the following screenshot shows, you need to import the certificate and the private key files:

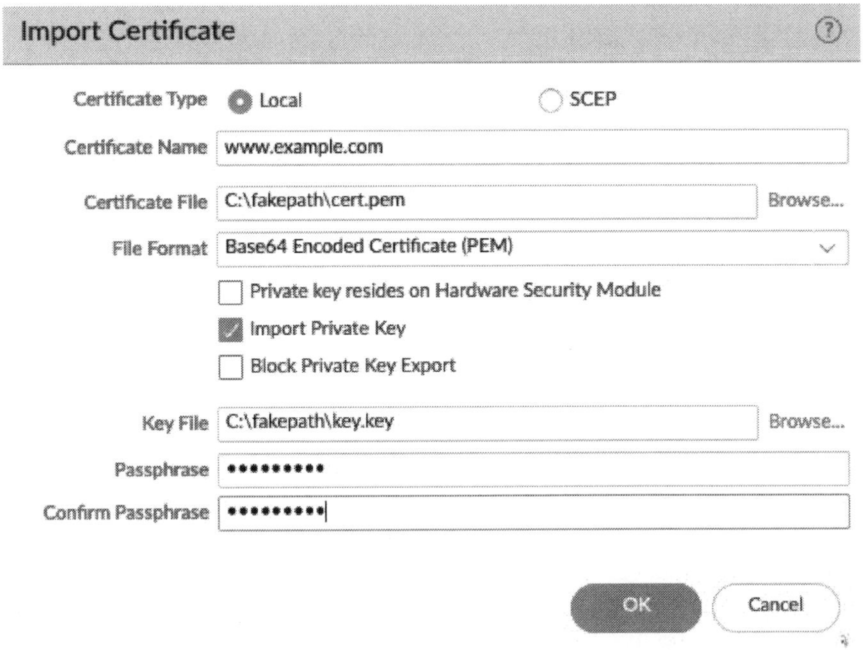

**Import Certificate**

| | | |
|---|---|---|
| Certificate Type | ● Local | ○ SCEP |

Certificate Name  `www.example.com`

Certificate File  `C:\fakepath\cert.pem`    Browse...

File Format  `Base64 Encoded Certificate (PEM)`  ⌄

☐ Private key resides on Hardware Security Module
☑ Import Private Key
☐ Block Private Key Export

Key File  `C:\fakepath\key.key`    Browse...

Passphrase  ●●●●●●●●●

Confirm Passphrase  ●●●●●●●●●

OK    Cancel

Figure 4.14 – Importing a server certificate with a private key

When the chain has been imported, your certificate page should look something similar to this:

| | | | |
|---|---|---|---|
| ▼ DigiCert Global Root CA | CN = DigiCert Global Root CA | CN = DigiCert Global Root CA | ☑ ☐ |
| ▼ DigiCert SHA2 Secure Server CA | CN = DigiCert SHA2 Secure Server CA | CN = DigiCert Global Root CA | ☑ ☐ |
| www.example.com | CN = www.example.com | CN = DigiCert SHA2 Secure Server CA | ☐ ☑ |

Figure 4.15 – Full certificate chain for your server certificate

Once you have imported the certificate chain, you can create the following policy:

1. Create a new decrypt rule and name it after your domain name or server.

2. Set the source zone to `Untrust-L3`.

3. Set the destination zone to `Dmz-L3` and the destination IP to your server `public` (pre-NAT) IP.

4. If you run multiple sites, you can create a custom URL category containing your website. Leave this as **any** for now.

5. Set the action to `decrypt`, type in `SSL Inbound Inspection`, set the certificate to your server certificate, and enable the decryption profile:

```
reaper@pa-220# set rulebase decryption rules examplecom
from Untrust-L3 to dmz-L3 destination 198.51.100.5
category any profile "decryption profile"  action decrypt
type ssl-inbound-inspection exampledotcom
```

Because the firewall has the server certificate, it can decrypt in real time; no proxying is required.

You can now set up SSL decryption for both your users and your hosted environment and choose which categories to exclude or include. In the next section, we'll learn about changing how sessions are sent from the firewall.

# Redirecting sessions over different paths using policy-based forwarding

**Policy-Based Forwarding** (**PBF**) allows you to set up rules that let certain sessions bypass routing entirely. In the first stage of packet processing, a session can be sent over a different interface than what the routing table would normally dictate. This could be handy if you want to send certain sessions over a secondary ISP link (or leased line) or if you need to ensure packets go out on a specific VLAN, tunnel, or SD-WAN interface.

## Redirecting critical traffic

A common scenario is a small office with a cheap but unreliable DSL or cable uplink with high bandwidth for internet traffic and a reliable but expensive link for business-critical applications. While the default route in the virtual router directs all traffic out of the DSL or cable model, a PBF rule could redirect critical protocols, such as SAP, SQL, and so on, over your leased line:

1. Go to **Policies | Policy Based Forwarding** to create a new rule, and call it `redirect critical apps to ISP2`.

2. For the source, set your `Trust-L3` network and subnet.

3. For the destination, set the destination address/subnet or the FQDN that hosts critical applications. Don't set applications if you don't have to; use service ports if appropriate.

4. From **Forwarding**, select the new egress interface and the next hop. The next hop could be a router IP, or none if you simply want to put traffic onto a VLAN or into a tunnel interface. If you are adding a next hop, add a monitoring profile and set it to **failover**, then check **disable this rule if nexthop/monitor IP is unreachable** so that your critical applications are routed over the regular link if your dedicated line goes down.

5. The resulting rule will look like the following screenshot:

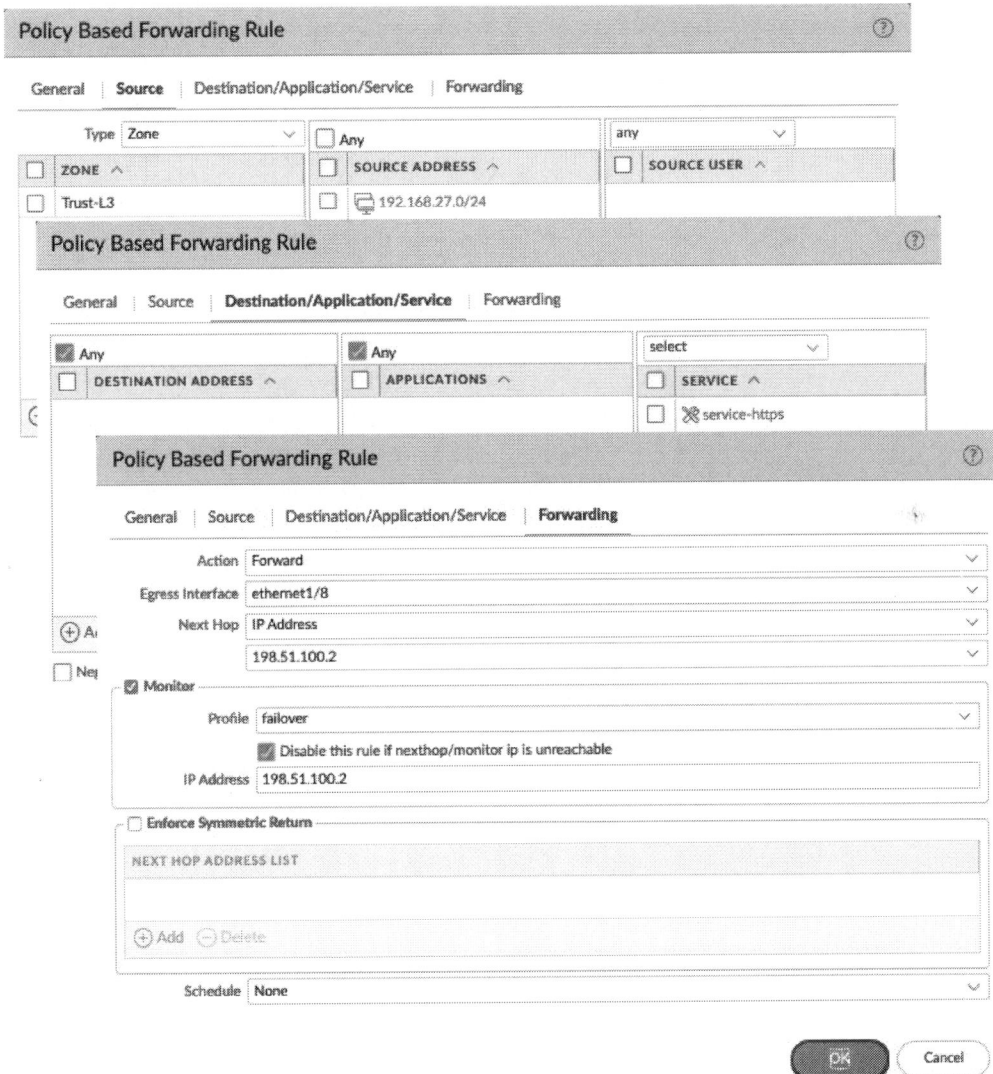

Figure 4.16 Policy Based Forwarding Rule

The rule can also be created using the following CLI commands:

```
reaper@pa-220# set network profiles monitor-profile
failover action fail-over interval 2 threshold 3
```

```
reaper@pa-220# set rulebase pbf rules "redirect critical
apps to ISP2" from zone Trust-L3
```

```
reaper@pa-220# set rulebase pbf rules "redirect critical
apps to ISP2" source 192.168.27.0/24 destination any
service service-https action forward monitor profile
failover disable-if-unreachable yes ip-address
198.51.100.2
```

```
reaper@pa-220# set rulebase pbf rules "redirect critical
apps to ISP2" action forward egress-interface ethernet1/8
nexthop ip-address 198.51.100.2
```

> **Important note**
>
> It is preferable to *not set an application* in the **Destination/Application/Service** tabs for uncommon sessions (for example, web browsing to different destinations). Stick to service ports and destination IPs instead as identifying an application takes a few packets; the first few packets cannot go through an app-based PBF rule and will take the routing table route. Recurring connections will be stored in the app's cache and can hit the PBF on the first packet. The caveat here is that the first session must be able to go through regular routing before the App-ID and associated tuples can be cached in `app-cache`.

You can now redirect important outbound sessions out of a different interface than the default route. In the next section, we will learn how to leverage multiple uplinks for inbound connections.

# Load balancing

Another common scenario is when there are two or more uplinks and both are used to provide services (such as an internally hosted website or email server) to internet users. The default route could cause return packets to leave out of a different interface than the packets that they came in through, causing asymmetric routing and failed sessions for the client. PBF can be used to enforce symmetric return, redirecting reply packets to the original interface they came in through, even if the routing table would have sent them elsewhere. These are the steps to set this up:

1.  Set the source zone to the ISP sessions that they come in from.

2.  Set the destination IP to your server and the appropriate application and service port.

3.  The Forward **Action** sends packets out of the DMZ interface directly to the mail server, which is what regular routing would achieve. However, **Enforce Symmetric Return** sends reply packets out to the secondary ISP's router instead of using the default route (to ISP1):

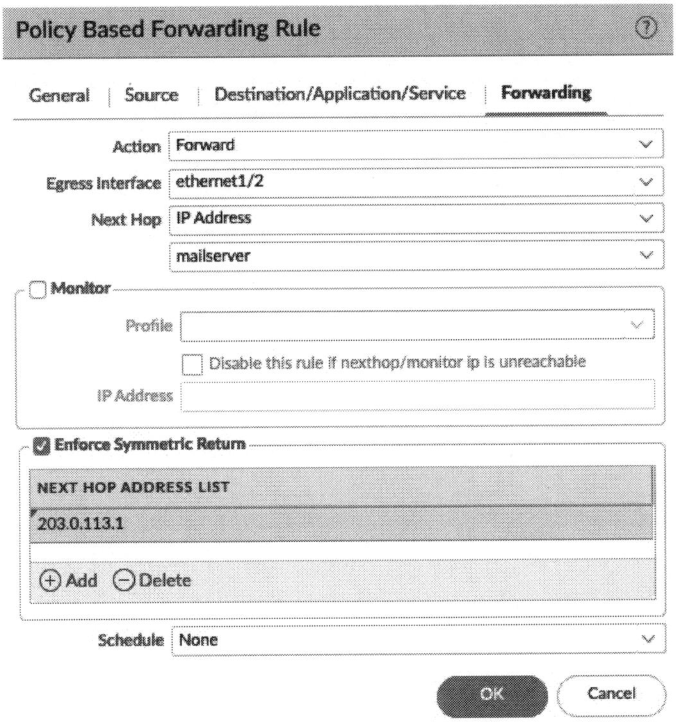

Figure 4.17 – PBF rule set for Enforce Symmetric Return

**Important note**

Since the app's cache creates entries based on the destination IP address, destination port, and protocol ID, inbound PBF sessions to the same server are easily identified by their application in app-cache.

A common use case is to set up two virtual routers and connect a different ISP to each one. Then, configure a VPN tunnel on each virtual router so that there are two simultaneous uplinks to the remote site. PBF can then be used to route user sessions to the remote end over the primary link, and if this ISP were to fail, you can revert to the default route and use the backup link, as illustrated in the following diagram:

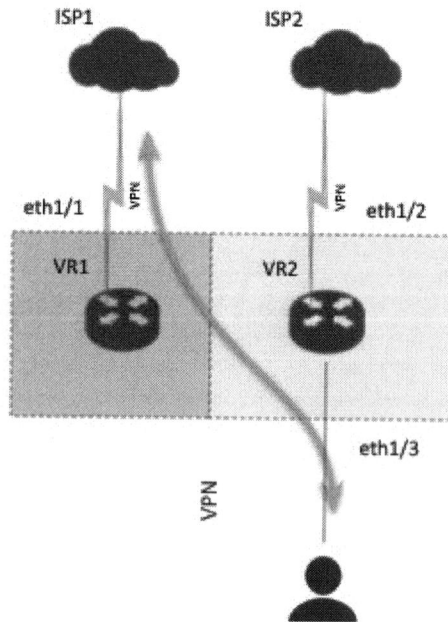

Figure 4.18 – VPN redundancy using PBF

You can now receive inbound connections on an interface that does not have (the dominant) default route and ensure return packets flow back through the original interface. In some cases, the fancy way is not always the best way. We will take a look at simplified link balancing in the next section.

## Equal-cost multipath as an alternative

As an alternative to the previous scenario, **Equal Cost Multi-Path (ECMP)** routing can be enabled on the virtual router where the ISPs are connected. ECMP enables link balancing over multiple paths so that you can combine several smaller-bandwidth ISP connections for increased performance. Where PBF requires rules to direct specific sessions, ECMP simply spreads sessions over multiple links.

ECMP supports up to four paths:

1. Enable ECMP by going to **Network | Virtual Routers | VR**, which holds your ISP uplinks.

2. Set **Symmetric return** if you want packets to go back out through the same interface that they came in through. This is useful if you host services on one or both ISP subnets.

3. Enabling **Strict Source Path** ensures firewall-sourced traffic (IKE/IPSec) is not subject to ECMP and will use regular routing to determine the route path. This setting should only be enabled if you require sticky VPN connections.

4. **Max Path** tells ECMP how many interfaces can participate. This number should correspond to the number of uplinks you intend to balance over.

5. As you can see in the following screenshot, there are several methods that you can choose from. Pick a method that best suits your needs:

    -- **IP Modulo** uses a hash of the source and destination IP to determine which ECMP route to take.

    -- **IP Hash** uses the source IP or source IP destination port to calculate which ECMP route to take.

    -- **Weighted Round Robin** lets you decide which interface gets more or fewer sessions assigned to it based on a weight; a higher weight assigns a higher preference, as shown.

--**Balanced Round Robin** balances ECMP sessions equally across all uplinks:

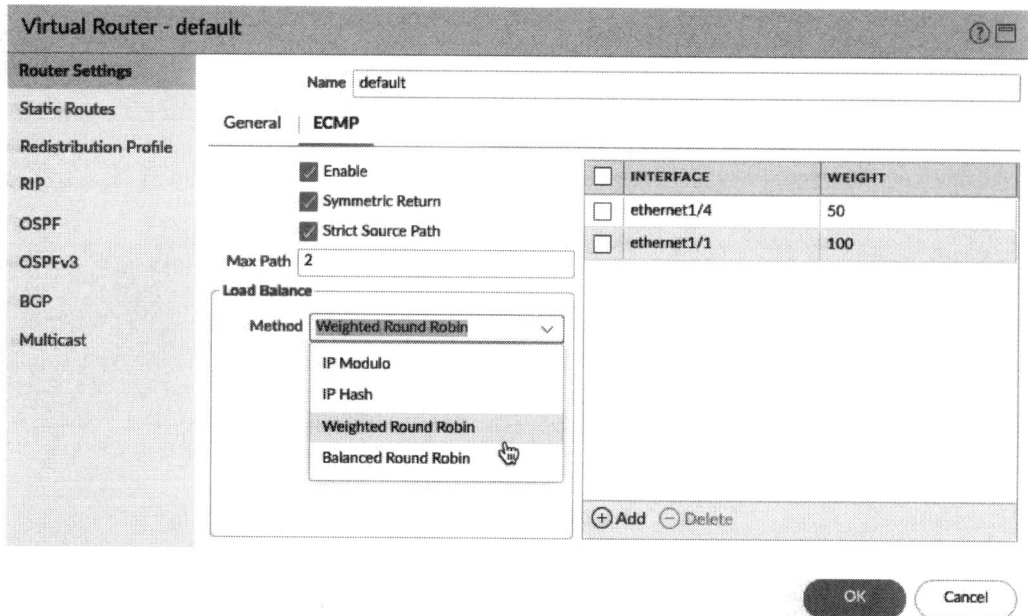

Figure 4.19 – ECMP routing

In this section, you learned how to use PBF and symmetric return to manipulate how sessions are egressed out of the firewall, as well as how ECMP can help bundle ISP uplinks.

# Summary

In this chapter, you learned how to shape sessions to prevent your internet uplink from getting flooded while guaranteeing business-critical applications always have bandwidth available. You can now implement decryption so that TLS sessions can be inspected for App-ID and threats, and you can leverage PBF and ECMP to control how sessions flow, regardless of routing.

In the next chapter, we will enable services on the firewall that are traditionally hosted on servers in the network and we will learn about setting the firewall in high-availability mode and adding virtual systems.

# 5
# Services and Operational Modes

Most networks have some supporting services to ensure users don't need to configure their laptop, mobile, or workstation to get access to corporate resources or the internet. **Dynamic Host Configuration Protocol (DHCP)** helps users connect to a network by assigning them an IP address and several other settings. The **Domain Name System (DNS)** allows them to visit websites with a friendly name. Rather than needing to stand up a server at each location, we will be configuring the firewall to provide these services.

High-availability clustering and virtualization make deployments more resilient to failure and assure businesses can go on, even if something breaks. We will be setting up high availability and reviewing implications for using both Active/Passive mode, and Active/Active mode. We will also take a deeper look at using virtual systems on a chassis to logically split up network segments.

In this chapter, we're going to cover the following main topics:

- Applying a DHCP client and DHCP server
- Configuring a DNS proxy
- Setting up high availability
- Enabling virtual systems
- Managing certificates

# Technical requirements

This chapter covers basic networking protocols like DHCP and DNS, and you should be comfortable configuring these in an enterprise environment. Prior experience with clustering and multi-tenant systems is recommended.

# Applying a DHCP client and DHCP server

In most offices, DHCP is the norm when it comes to setting clients up on the network, but for smaller offices, it can be difficult or expensive to set up a dedicated server to provide IP addresses, or your local ISP may require you to connect a DHCP client to their network before they're able to assign you an IP address and let you on the internet. Luckily, the firewall can also perform these duties. We will start by setting up the firewall as a DHCP client to a dynamic ISP.

## DHCP client

To set a data plane interface up as a DHCP client, follow the same steps as you would to configure a regular Layer 3 interface, but set the IPv4 to **DHCP Client**:

1. Edit the interface.
2. Set the mode to **Layer3**.
3. Select an appropriate zone and virtual router.
4. Set the IPv4 to **DHCP Client**.

You can choose to accept the default route from the ISP, or set your own in the virtual router, and if you want, to send a hostname upstream (some ISPs may require you to set a specific hostname, which you can set here without changing the actual system hostname):

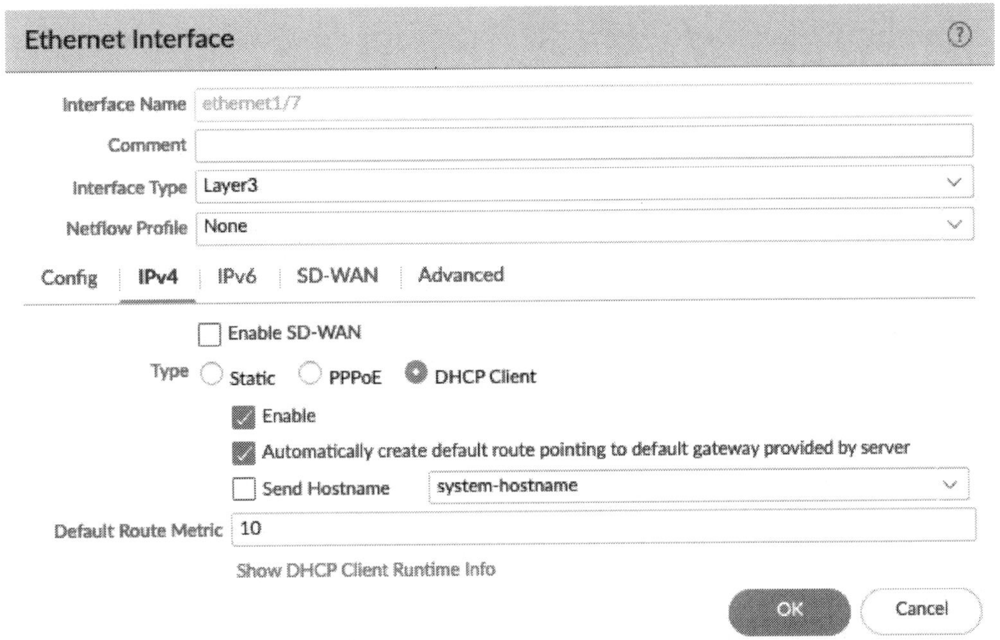

Figure 5.1 – Interface in DHCP Client mode

You can view the runtime info, renew, and release, once the change has been committed, in the interface configuration or the interface overview at **Network > Interfaces > Ethernet**.

Some useful CLI commands include the following:

```
> show dhcp client state all
> request dhcp client renew all
> request dhcp client release all
```

You are now able to configure the firewall as a DHCP client and receive an IP address on an interface.

Next, we can extend this service into the local zones, providing IP addresses to internal clients.

# DHCP server and relay

On the inside of your network, the firewall can function as a DHCP server and hand out IP addresses, DNS and **Network Time Protocol (NTP)** settings, and many other options. The DHCP server component needs to be attached to the interface that is in the same broadcast domain as the IP subnet or range it will be handing out. Do the following in **Network > DHCP > DHCP Server**:

1. Create a new DHCP server profile.

2. Select the interface your clients are connected to.

3. Select the appropriate mode:

    --**Auto** polls the network for another DHCP server and deactivates itself if one is found.

    --**Enabled** sets the DHCP server to always on; this could conflict with an existing DHCP server on the network.

    --**Disabled** sets the DHCP server as inactive.

4. Enabling **Ping IP when allocating new IP** makes the firewall ping an IP before assigning it to a new host. This prevents IP conflicts.

5. Choose **Unlimited** or **Timeout** lease time:

    --**Timeout** lease will time out and remove a lease after the set amount of time, forcing the client to renew its lease or lose it if the client is no longer online at the time the lease expires.

    --**Unlimited** lease time will keep the lease permanently. If the IP pool is depleted, the next new client will not be able to receive an IP.

6. Add the IP pool subnet or range, and add reservations as needed:

    --A reservation without a MAC entry will simply withhold the IP address from being assigned. The host using this IP needs to be configured manually.

    --A reservation with a MAC address will only assign the IP to the host with the matching MAC address on its interface.

7. In the options, you can inherit DHCP options from an upstream (ISP) DHCP server if you like. This could be useful to share the ISP DNS with your clients.

8. The gateway and subnet mask need to be set to the firewall interface IP and subnet mask.

9. DNS, NTP, and other options can be manually configured or set to the inheritance of the upstream DHCP server.

10. Custom options can be added in the range of *1-254*.

The following screenshot illustrates what the DHCP server configuration would look like:

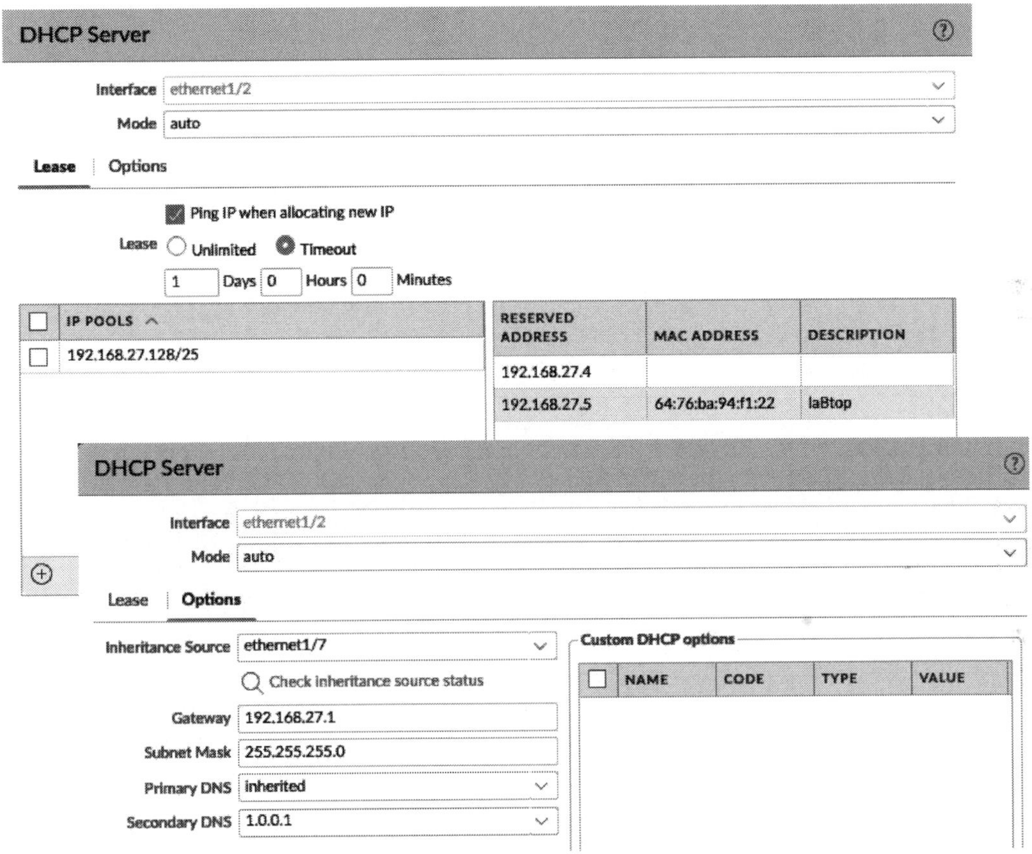

Figure 5.2 – DHCP server configuration

> **Important note**
> Don't forget to add an intrazone security rule that allows the application dhcp if a general drop rule has been configured to supersede the default intrazone allow rule.

As shown in the following screenshot, the DHCP relay only needs to be assigned to the interface the clients will be active in, and the IP where the DHCP requests need to be forwarded to. The firewall will listen for DHCP requests on the interface and forward all DHCP packets to the DHCP server that is located in a network that is connected to a different interface:

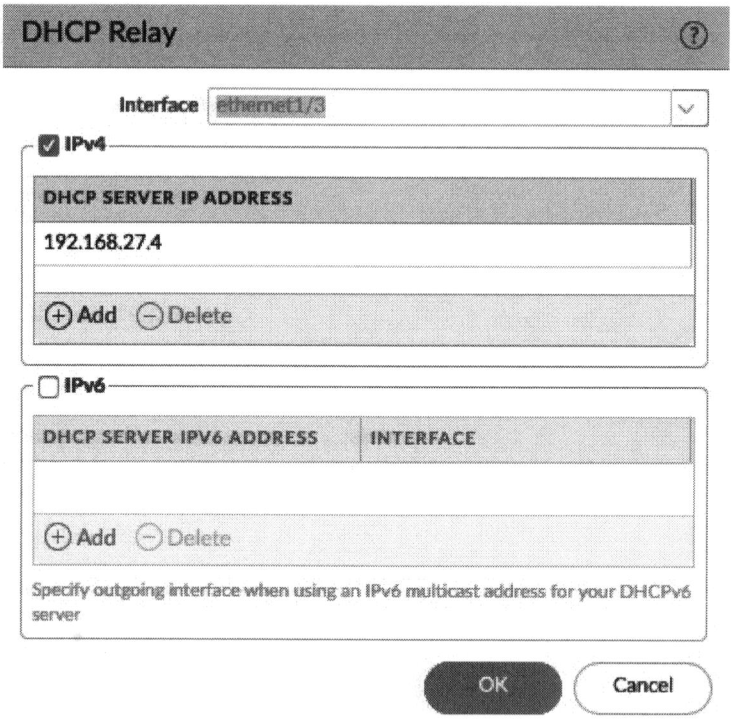

Figure 5.3 – DHCP Relay configuration

> **Important note**
> DHCP relay requires that the application dhcp is allowed from the client to the firewall interface, and also from the firewall interface to the DHCP server.

# Configuring a DNS proxy

A DNS proxy helps control how internal clients connect to DNS servers and where they get domain information from, or which information they receive.

> **Important note**
> Clients must be configured with the firewall's interface IP set as the DNS server. This can be forced via the DNS attribute in the DHCP server or may need to be set manually. The firewall may need a security rule that allows DNS connections to the firewall interface from the clients, and a second one that allows DNS from the firewall interface out to the internet.

Configure the DNS proxy by following these steps:

1. Create a new DNS proxy object in **Network > DNS Proxy**.

2. Add a name and, if you want to inherit DNS configuration from an upstream DHCP server (ISP), set the inheritance.

3. Set the primary and secondary DNS server for outgoing DNS requests to servers of your choice, or select **Inherit** if you want to use your ISP's DNS servers for generic lookups.

4. Add the interfaces the firewall will be accepting DNS queries on.

5. In the **DNS Proxy Rules** tab, add redirect rules. Requests for these **Fully Qualified Domain Names (FQDNs)** are redirected to different DNS servers, which can be internal DNS servers, serving up internal records with a private IP. This could be useful for internal clients to receive the private IP of internally hosted servers.

6. In the static entries, add the FQDNs that the firewall will reply to with the IPs you configure here. These queries will not be forwarded to any DNS server.

7. In the **Advanced** tab, you can configure the following:

   --The maximum concurrent pending TCP DNS requests (between 64 and 256).

   --The interval and maximum attempts for unanswered UDP queries.

   --Caching: The **Time To Live (TTL)** can be enabled to set the maximum time (between 60 and 86,400 seconds) a record can be cached before the firewall is forced to refresh the entry. By default, a record is not deleted until the firewall runs out of cache memory, or the record's own TTL expires.

   An extension mechanism for DNS can be cached if the option for EDNS is checked. This enables the caching of partial DNS responses that are greater than 512 bytes.

The following screenshot shows a fully configured DNS proxy object:

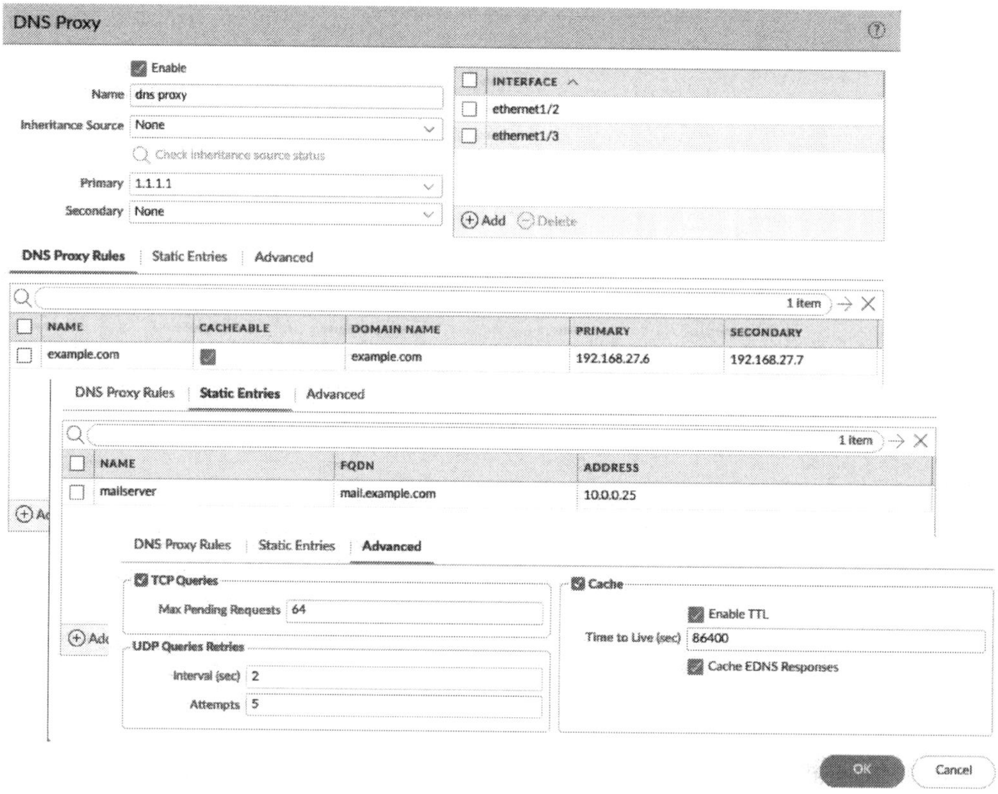

Figure 5.4 – DNS proxy object

You are now able to configure a DNS proxy object that can control which servers your clients are able to connect to and perform some rewriting where needed. In the next section, we'll learn how to set up clustering and redundancy.

# Setting up high availability

**High Availability (HA)** is a configuration where two identical (the same chassis or VM version) firewalls are connected to form a cluster. When clustering is enabled, both systems will form a single entity to the outside and will handle failover for certain problems, so the service remains available to users. These types of monitoring are or can be performed in a cluster member to ensure its own and its peers' health:

- **Link monitoring**: If an interface goes down, the member fails.

- **Path monitoring**: If an IP becomes unavailable, the member fails.

- **Heartbeat monitoring**: The peers periodically send heartbeat packages and hello messages to verify they are up and running.

- **Hardware monitoring**: The member continually performs packet path health monitoring on its own hardware and fails if a malfunction is detected.

When you enable HA, you need to select a **Group ID**. This ID needs to be identical on both members. The **Group ID** will also have an impact on the MAC addresses associated with each interface as they switch to a virtual MAC that both firewalls will be able to claim via gratuitous ARP in case one member fails.

As seen in the following screenshot, there is a check-box that allows you to disable **Enable Config Sync** between members. Use extreme caution if you disable this option as it will have far-reaching consequences (for one, each interface, zone, and object has a unique identifier that is normally synced between peers for session consistency; disabling this could prevent sessions from failing over). It should only be used in rare occasions where configuration must be different:

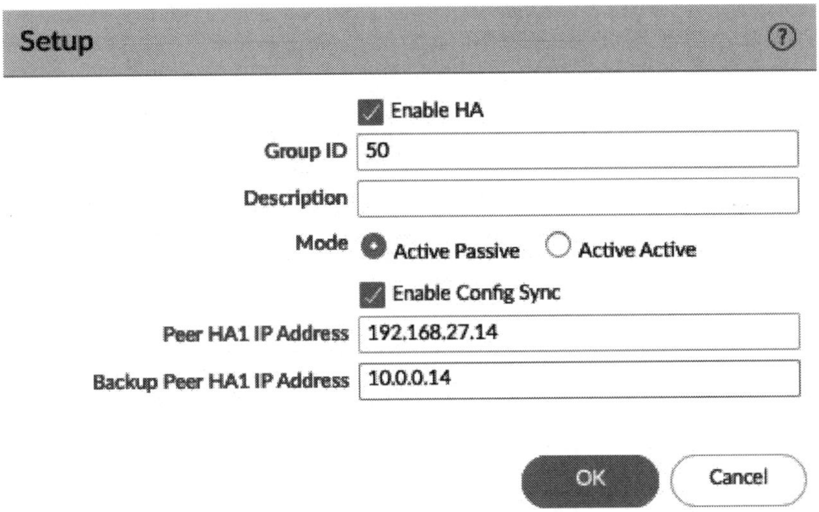

Figure 5.5 – Enabling HA

> **Important note**
>
> Any Layer 3 interface that is already active in the network will receive a new MAC address once HA is enabled (and committed), which could cause connectivity issues while switches and clients learn the new MAC associated with the firewall IPs. Some ARP tables may need to be cleared and static entries updated.

There are two modes in which the cluster can be configured, which will be covered in the following sections.

## Active/Passive mode

In Active/Passive mode, one member (the primary member) processes all traffic while the secondary peer does not participate.

By default, the passive device will have its interfaces in a shutdown state, meaning any connected devices will also see the link as being down. Depending on your environment, this could prevent other clusters from functioning properly, in which case you will need to set these to **Auto** (up but not accepting packets).

**Monitor Fail Hold Down Time** keeps the firewall in a failed state (non-functional, see the following **firewall states** topic) for the specified amount of time after an error was detected before setting the member to the passive state:

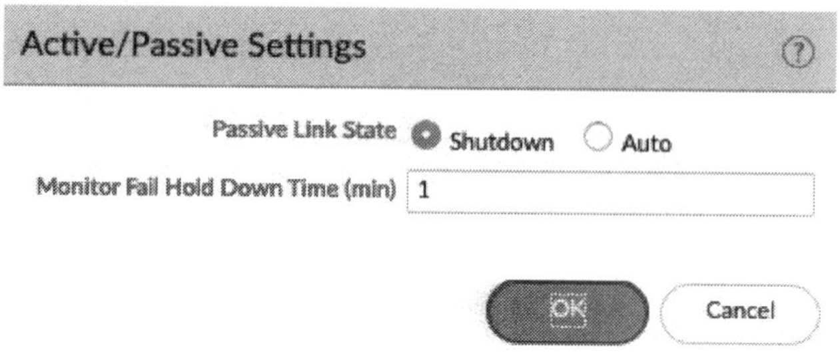

Figure 5.6 – Passive Link State

If you set **Passive Link State** to auto and you want even faster link negotiation, you can enable **Link Layer Discovery Protocol (LLDP)** and **Link Aggregation Control Protocol (LACP)** in passive mode by accessing the interface's **advanced** tab where these protocols have been enabled and checking **Enable in HA Passive State** as shown here:

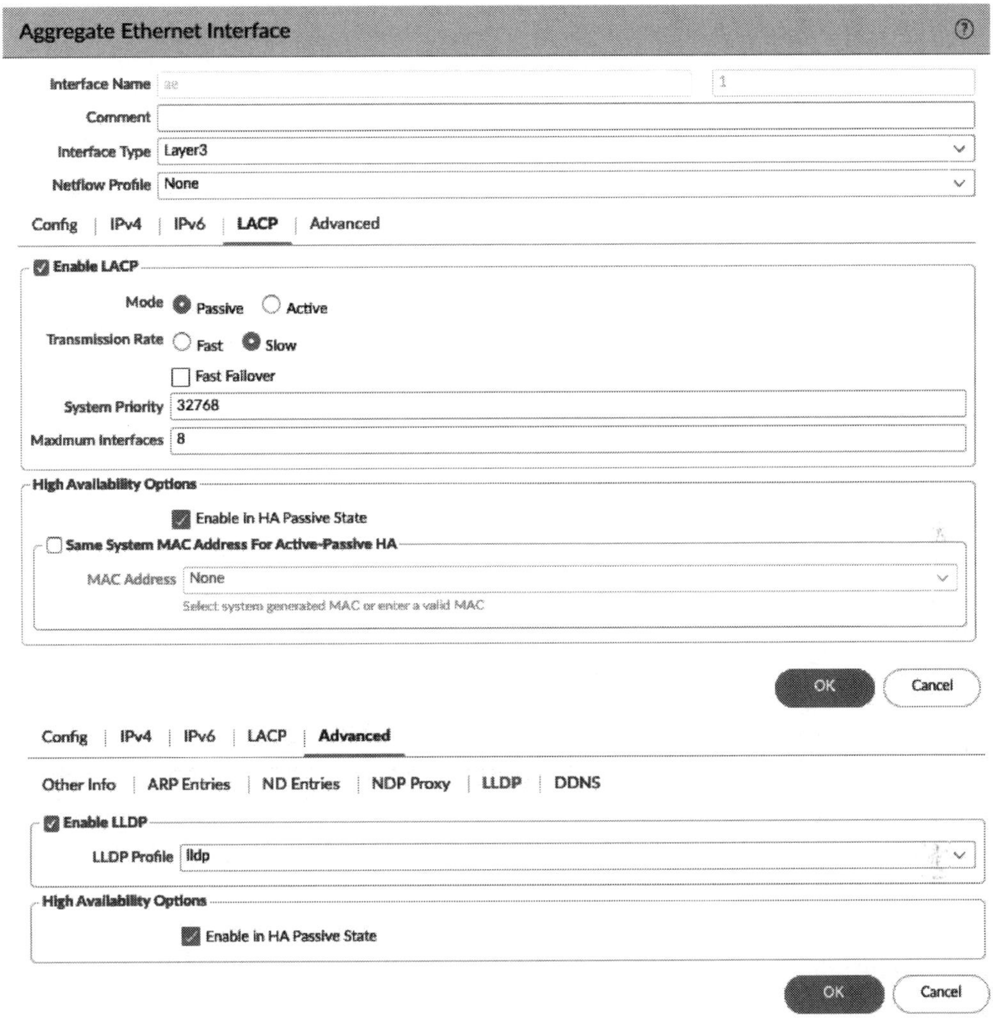

Figure 5.7 – LACP and LLDP in HA Passive state

The next clustering mode has both members participating in an active capacity.

## Active/Active mode

In Active/Active, both firewalls actively take sessions and maintain their own session table and perform scanning while synchronizing all their sessions and routing tables to their peer.

This mode only supports Layer 3 and Virtual Wire interfaces and can't run as a DHCP client, and only the Active-Primary member can act as a DHCP relay.

It is important to realize Active/Active is not a load-balancing configuration. The main issue Active/Active is intended to tackle is asymmetric flows or a requirement for faster failover. An Active/Active cluster will also be able to handle peak traffic bursts better than an Active/Passive cluster due to the availability of an additional active member, but the average load may be slightly higher for regular traffic as both peers will have more overhead synchronizing sessions.

Active/Active introduces far more complexity than Active/Passive so please consider the trade-off.

## Firewall states

The firewall can be in one of eight states while it is a cluster member:

- **Initial**: The firewall assumes this state after it boots up, at which time it will start looking for a peer. If none is found after the timeout expires, the firewall becomes active.

- **Active**: The firewall is accepting and processing packets.

- **Passive**: The firewall is in a standby state – it receives state table and runtime object updates from the primary while it monitors the active member with hello and heartbeat messages to ensure it does not need to take over.

- **Non-functional**: The firewall has encountered a failure condition, which could be a down interface or data plane error, but could also be caused by a configuration mismatch or PAN-OS mismatch (the member with the highest version of PAN-OS will go into a non-functional state).

- **Suspended**: The firewall still receives update information from the active member, but an administrator has temporarily made this device incapable of taking an active role. This could be useful for troubleshooting or during an upgrade.

- **Active-primary**: In Active/Active mode, DHCP servers, User-ID agents, NAT, and PBF rules can be assigned to one or both members.

- **Active-secondary**: All of the above, except that the active-secondary can't be a DHCP relay.

- **Tentative**: In Active/Active, if the firewall leaves the suspended or non-functional state, it will first become tentative while it synchronizes sessions. It will forward all received packets to its peer over the HA3 link for processing and then send them out over its egress interface until it leaves this state and starts processing packets itself.

To ensure both cluster members are able to synchronize configuration and share session tables, special interfaces are needed.

# High-availability interfaces

High availability requires several interfaces to perform certain tasks:

- **HA1**: This is the primary management link that is used to synchronize configuration and perform monitoring (hello messages) of the remote peer. HA1 can be enabled on the management interface, a dedicated interface (a visibly marked **HA1** interface on the chassis), or a data plane interface set to interface type **HA**.

-If the **HA1** link goes down, the passive member will assume the primary member is down and assume the **Active** state.

-**HA1** is a Layer 3 interface, so an IP address needs to be set for the local and remote **HA1** interface (see the following screenshot) and uses ports 28260 and 28769 for cleartext or 28 for encrypted communication.

-Due to the sensitivity of the information traversing **HA1**, the sessions can be encrypted: HA1 syncs all configuration except the management parameters (basically, everything under the **Device** tab is considered local). To allow encryption, both peers' HA keys need to be exported and imported on the other peer. You can find the export/import option in **Device | Certificate Management | Certificates**:

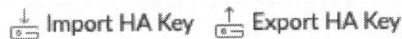

Figure 5.8 – Import and export of the HA key

HA1 synchronizes this runtime information:

--User to IP/group mapping

--DHCP lease

--IKE keys (phase2)

--**Forwarding Information Base (FIB)**

--URL cache

--PPPoE

--SSL VPN logged in users

- **HA1** backup: Because the **HA1** link is so crucial, it is recommended to have an **HA1** backup interface configured. If **HA1** is set on a dedicated interface, an **HA1** backup can be enabled on the management interface, a dedicated **HA1** backup interface, or a data plane interface set to interface type **HA**. An **HA1** backup uses ports 28260 and 28770:

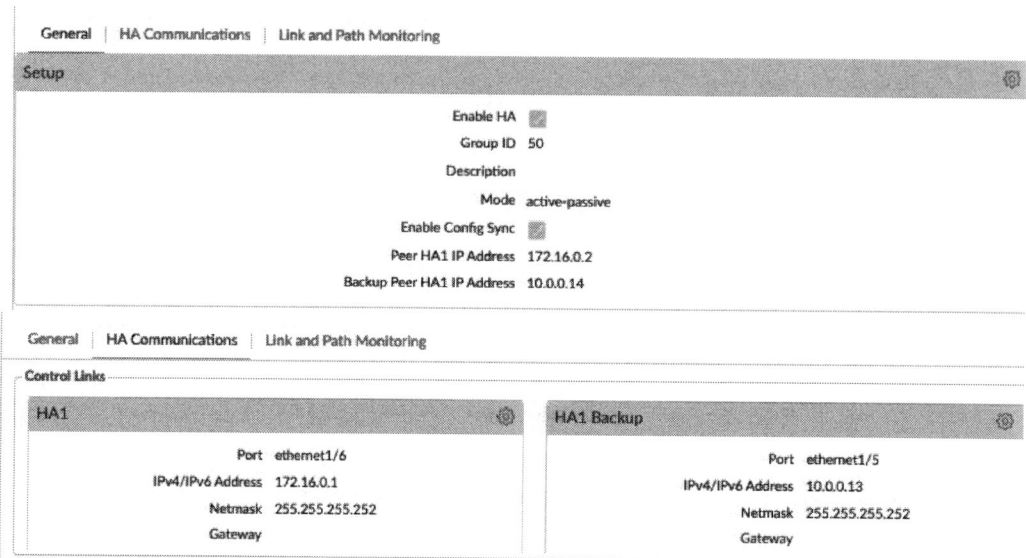

General | HA Communications | Link and Path Monitoring

**Setup**

| | |
|---|---|
| Enable HA | |
| Group ID | 50 |
| Description | |
| Mode | active-passive |
| Enable Config Sync | |
| Peer HA1 IP Address | 172.16.0.2 |
| Backup Peer HA1 IP Address | 10.0.0.14 |

General | HA Communications | Link and Path Monitoring

Control Links

**HA1**

| | |
|---|---|
| Port | ethernet1/6 |
| IPv4/IPv6 Address | 172.16.0.1 |
| Netmask | 255.255.255.252 |
| Gateway | |

**HA1 Backup**

| | |
|---|---|
| Port | ethernet1/5 |
| IPv4/IPv6 Address | 10.0.0.13 |
| Netmask | 255.255.255.252 |
| Gateway | |

Figure 5.9 – HA1 configuration

- **HA2** takes care of the session table being synced over to the peer. By default, the transport mode for **HA2** is **Ethernet (Ethertype 0x7261)**, which means it has a very low overhead as it doesn't use IP headers, which is ideal if both devices are directly connected. If some sort of transport is required, you can use the following:

-IP (IP protocol 99) mode, which uses very basic IP headers

-UDP (UDP port 29281) mode, which uses UDP to transport the session state information over a routed network

**HA2** keep-alive can be configured to monitor and maintain the **HA2** connection. A log will be written in the event of a failure, or in Active/Active mode the action can be set to **split datapath** to instruct both peers to keep processing traffic while only maintaining a local state table until **HA2** returns:

**Data Links**

| HA2 | ⚙ |
|---|---|
| Enable Session Synchronization | ☑ |
| Port | hsci |
| IPv4/IPv6 Address | |
| Netmask | |
| Gateway | |
| Transport | ethernet |
| Action | log-only |
| Threshold (ms) | 10000 |

| HA2 Backup | ⚙ |
|---|---|
| Port | |
| IPv4/IPv6 Address | |
| Netmask | |
| Gateway | |

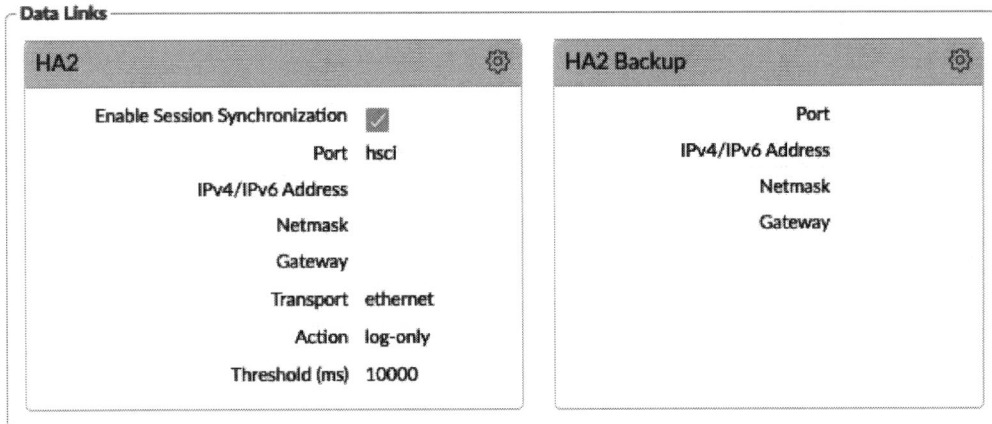

Figure 5.10 – HA2 configuration

**HA2** synchronizes this runtime information:

--Session table

--**Address Resolution Protocol** (**ARP**) table

--**Neighbor Discovery** (**ND**) table

--**Media Access Control** (**MAC**) table

--IPSec sequence number

--Virtual MAC

--**Stream Control Transmission Protocol** (**SCTP**) associations

- An **HA2** backup can be configured on a dedicated interface, or a data plane interface set to interface type **HA** to serve as a backup in case HA2 fails.

- **HA3** is used exclusively in Active/Active deployments and is used to forward (whole) packets to the peer for packet inspection. It uses MAC-in-MAC encapsulation to transmit packets between peers, with the entire packet as payload. The HA3 link therefore needs to support jumbo frames as frames will be larger than the data packets. This may be needed when the primary device is set as the session owner, when the session setup is IP modulo or IP hash and the remote peer is selected for session setup, or when asymmetric packets are received on the member that does not own the session. The packets are sent over for session completeness on the Session Owner device, and then returned to the recipient so it can egress the packet out of its data plane interface (asymmetry is maintained but the session is fully scanned by one session owner).

Now that you understand which HA modes are available, we can go ahead and set it up.

## Setting up Active/Passive mode

Follow these steps to configure Active/Passive mode, starting with the primary member:

1.  In **Device | High Availability | Setup**, enable **High Availability**.

2.  Pick a **Group Id**. Go with 50 if you don't have a clear preference.

3.  Leave the mode as **active-passive**.

4.  Make sure **Enable Config Sync is enabled**.

5.  Peer HA1 IP : Use a private IP (in a /30 subnet) that does not overlap with your existing internal subnets (for example, 172.16.0.2). If you have a smaller device without dedicated HA interfaces and need to use the management interface as the HA1 interface, set the peer's management IP.

6.  Backup peer HA1: If you are able to sacrifice a data plane interface as backup HA1 interface, add another non-overlapping private IP (for example, 172.16.1.2), or the peer's management IP if you intend to use the management interface as a backup HA1 link.

7.  Click **OK**.

If you need to change the passive link state interface's behavior, open **Active/Passive Settings** and change **Passive Link State** to **Auto** (this will set the interfaces electrically up when the device is in a passive state). **Monitor Fail Hold Down Time** is used to leave the device in a non-functional state for the specified amount of time after a monitor failure before it is allowed to transition to the passive state.

Next, open **Election Settings**:

1.  Set **Device Priority** to 50.

2.  Enable **Heartbeat Backup**. This will use the management interface to send a simple heartbeat to the remote peer.

3.  Don't set **Preemptive** unless you have a link that is *expected* to go down for a few seconds and self-recover (see HA timers in the next step).

4.  HA timers are set to **Recommended per platform**, but you can choose **Aggressive** for faster failover (but at a cost of overhead), or choose **Advanced** to manually change timers and counters. A few interesting counters:

-**Promotion Hold Time** is the amount of time the secondary will wait before becoming active after the connection with the primary has been lost.

-**Hello Interval** is the number of milliseconds between hello messages.

-**Heartbeat Interval** is the amount of time between ICMP heartbeat packets.

-**Flap max & Preemption Hold Time**: If you enable **Preemptive** the firewall will blindly *flap* back to the active state after the preemption hold timer expires. If the original error that caused it to fail still exists, it will fail again. The **flap max** counter will prevent the firewall from repeating this scenario more than the specified number of times, at which time the firewall will go into a *permanently* failed state that can only be recovered via manual intervention.

-**Monitor Fail Hold Up Time** is the amount of time the firewall will wait to fail over once a monitor (path, interface, and so on) has been detected, in the case of an extremely short interruption.

-**Additional Master Hold Time** is used to add even more hold time to **Monitor Fail Hold Up Time**.

5.  Click **OK**.

Next, we need to configure the HA links that enable both peers to communicate. First, open **Control Link**:

1.  Set the interface to the dedicated ha1-a link if possible, or the data plane interface you set to type **HA** to be used as the control link and fill in the IP address 172.16.0.1 and subnet mask 255.255.255.250. Add a gateway if needed, enable encryption (make sure you exported/imported the HA keys on both peers). Alternatively you can set the management interface instead of a dedicated or dataplane interface.

2.  **Monitor hold time** is the amount of time to wait before declaring a failure of the peer when **HA1** connectivity is lost. With heartbeat backup and **HA1** backup in place, this number can be lowered significantly. If neither backup options are available to you, do not lower this number as a short interruption could lead to a *split brain* where both peers become active, which is not fun for anyone.

3.  Repeat *step 1* for **HA1** backup, using the second dedicated interface, **ha1-b**, a second data plane interface, using the second IP range from *step 6* (172.16.1.1 to 255.255.255.250), or the management interface.

4.  Click **OK**.

Next up is the data link that will be used to synchronize the session state table:

1.  Open the **HA2** settings and enable session synchronization.

2.  If available, use the HSCI interface; otherwise, set a data plane interface (you can create an aggregate interface and set it to type HA, and use the aggregate here as well).

3.  If you are able to use the **ethernet** transport mode, there's no need for IP addresses. If you need to use the IP or UDP transport mode, use a third non-overlapping subnet (for example, 172.16.3.1 and subnet mask 255.255.255.250).

4.  Enable **HA2 Keep-alive** and leave it as **Log Only** (Split Datapath is an Active/Active feature).

5.  If you are able to sacrifice another data plane interface, you could add it as the HA2 backup interface. The **HA2** backup link is only used if the main **HA2** link goes down or if the keep-alive messages exceed the threshold.

Link state should be monitored to ensure the member fails over when an interface goes down. Path monitoring can be added in addition to ensure a remote router is available to pass traffic. Access the **Link and Path monitoring** tab:

1.  Enable link monitoring and create a **Link** group.

2.  In the link group, add all the interfaces that need to be monitored and set the fail condition to any. A group could be created where all interfaces need to be down for the chassis to fail, which could be helpful if you have redundant links and don't need a HA failover if just one or part of the links is down.

3.  If path monitoring needs to be enabled, create a path group: You can add a VWire, VLAN, or virtual router path monitor. For VWire and VLAN, you must specify a source IP the monitor will use to spoof its source. The monitored router must know a route back to the VWire or VLAN. For virtual router path monitoring, the source will be the egress interface closest to the monitored next-hop.

For the secondary member, repeat all of the preceding steps with the following differences:

1.  The peer's HA1 IP will be 172.16.0.1.

2.  The peer's HA1 backup IP will be 172.16.1.1.

3.  Set **Device Priority** to 100.

4.  Make sure that if preempt is enabled on the primary, it is also enabled on the secondary.

5. Also make sure the timers are identical: if you changed timers on the primary, set the timers to match on the secondary.

6. In the local control link (**HA1**), use the same interface as the primary, but set the IP to `172.16.0.2`.

7. For the **HA1** Backup, set the same configuration as the primary but set the IP to `172.16.1.2`.

8. For **HA2**, also use the same interface, and if you need to use an alternate transport mode, use `172.16.0.2`.

9. Make sure all other settings, including path and link monitoring, are identical to the primary member.

You are now able to configure an Active/Passive HA pair, the most common form of HA. The next HA mode is more complex but also a little more versatile.

## Setting up Active/Active

Before embarking on the wonderful journey that is Active/Active, make sure you're taking it for the appropriate reasons:

- "Fixing" asymmetric traffic flows

- A requirement to have (floating) IPs active on specific devices unless there is a failover situation (like having a double Active/Passive setup)

- Very low tolerance for dynamic routing renegotiation latency when a failure occurs (with both devices up, dynamic routing can renegotiate faster than when a passive device first needs to come online)

While Active/Active is better at handling burst traffic due to the availability of two firewalls, it should be considered as having a lower average throughput than an Active/Passive cluster due to the overhead introduced by remote inspection, where the local device needs to forward entire packets to the remote peer for inspection, rather than performing this operation locally.

To configure Active/Active, follow these steps:

1. In **Device | High Availability**, edit **Setup** and enable **HA**.

2. Set **Group ID**. The actual ID is only important if you need to avoid MAC address conflicts with other firewall clusters in the same broadcast domain.

3. Set the mode as **Active/Active**.

4. Select **Device ID** 0 or 1 (typically, **active-primary** is 0 and **active-secondary** is 1).

5. Enable **config sync**.

6. Set **Peer HA1 IP address** and **Backup peer A1 IP address** (you'll need two small subnets that do not overlap with any used internally, for example, 172.16.0.2 and 172.16.1.2 with subnets 255.255.255.250).

The election settings are similar to an Active/Passive cluster but serve to determine which member is the active-primary, rather than the Active:

1. In **Election settings**, set a device priority: **Active-primary** should have the lowest priority, so set it to 50.

2. Enable **preemptive** if you require floating IPs to be *sticky* to either cluster member. Keep it disabled to prevent floating IPs moving back and forth if a cluster member encounters issues.

3. Enable heartbeat backup unless **HA1** will be set up on the management interface (only recommended on smaller devices).

4. HA timers are set to **recommended per platform**, but you can choose **aggressive** for faster failover (but at a cost of overhead), or choose **advanced** to manually change timers and counters. A few interesting counters:

   -**Promotion hold time** is the amount of time the secondary will wait before becoming active after the connection with the primary has been lost.

   -**Hello interval** is the number of milliseconds between hello messages.

   -**Heartbeat interval** is the amount of time between ICMP heartbeat packets.

   -**Flap max & preemption hold timer**: If you enable **preempt**, the firewall will blindly *flap* back to the active state after the preemption hold timer expires. If the original error that caused it to fail still exists, it will fail again. The **flap max** counter will prevent the firewall from repeating this scenario more than the specified number of times, at which time the firewall will go into a "permanently" failed state that can only be recovered via manual intervention.

   -**Monitor Fail Hold Up Time** is the amount of time the firewall will wait to fail over once a monitor (path, interface, and so on) has been detected, in the case of an extremely short interruption.

   -**Additional master hold time** is used to add even more hold time to **Monitor Fail Hold Up Time**.

5. Click **OK**.

We need to configure the control link so the cluster is able to synchronize configuration and routing **FIB (Forwarding Information Base)**:

1. Set the interface to the dedicated **ha1-a** link if possible, or the data plane interface you set to type **HA** to be used as the control link and fill in IP address 172.16.0.1 and subnet mask 255.255.255.250. Add a gateway if needed, enable encryption (make sure you exported/imported the **HA** keys on both peers), or set the management interface.

2. **Monitor Hold Time** is the amount of time to wait before declaring a failure of the peer when **HA1** connectivity is lost. With heartbeat backup and **HA1** backup in place, this number can be lowered significantly. If neither backup options are available to you, do not lower this number as a short interruption could lead to a *split brain* where both peers become active, which is not fun for anyone.

3. Set the interface to **ha1-b**, a dedicated interface, and set IP address 172.16.1.K, or set the management interface if no alternative interfaces are available.

4. Click **OK**.

The data links need to be configured to synchronize the session, ARP, and MAC tables:

1. Open the **HA2** settings and enable session synchronization.

2. If available, use the HSCI interface; otherwise, set a data plane interface (you can create an aggregate interface and set it to type **HA**, and use the aggregate here as well).

3. If you are able to use the **ethernet** transport mode, there's no need for IP addresses. If you need to use the IP or UDP transport mode, use a third non-overlapping subnet (for example, 172.16.3.1 and subnet mask 255.255.255.250).

4. Enable HA keep-alive and set it as **split-datapath**. **Split-datapath** lets both peers take control of their local session and state table if the **HA2** link is disrupted, so they can keep processing local sessions.

5. If you are able to sacrifice another data plane interface, it is recommended to add it as the **HA2** backup interface. The **HA2** backup link is only used if the main **HA2** link goes down or if the keepalive messages exceed the threshold, and helps prevent **split-datapath** if the main **HA2** link is interrupted.

6. Click **OK**.

Link state should be monitored to ensure the member fails over when an interface goes down. Path monitoring can be added in addition to ensure a remote router is available to pass traffic.

Access the **Link and Path monitoring** tab:

1. Enable link monitoring and create a **Link** group.

2. In the link group, add all the interfaces that need to be monitored and set the fail condition to **any**. A group could be created where *all* interfaces need to be down for the chassis to fail, which could be helpful if you have redundant links and don't need a **HA** failover if just one or part of the links is down.

3. If path monitoring needs to be enabled, create a path group: You can add a VWire, VLAN, or virtual router path monitor. For VWire and VLAN, you must specify a source IP the monitor will use to spoof its source. The monitored router must know a route back to the VWire or VLAN. For virtual router path monitoring, the source will be the egress interface closest to the monitored next-hop.

In Active/Active mode, the **HA3** interface also needs to be enabled to pass along packets for session setup or session owner forwarding, and to synchronize the routing and QoS configuration:

1. Access the **Active/Active Configuration or HA Communications** tab.

2. In **Packet Forwarding**, select the HSCI interface if your chassis has one available. Otherwise, you'll want to set up an **AE (Aggregate Ethernet)** group of interfaces to carry the **HA3** sessions. The number of interfaces should be scaled to accommodate the expected amount of traffic flowing through a member where the remote peer is assigned the session owner role.

3. Check the boxes next to synchronize VR and QoS to ensure the routing table and QoS profile selection information is synced:

   --If you intend to run both peers as individual dynamic routing nodes (through dynamic routing such as OSPF or BGP), disable VR Sync.

   --If both peers have different bandwidth available, disable **QoS Sync** and set up individual QoS profiles per member.

4.  **Tentative hold time** is the time granted to the peer after it recovers from a failure for it to rebuild its dynamic routing table before assuming its normal active role. If no dynamic routing is used, you can disable this timer.

5.  **Session Owner Selection** will have an enormous impact on your device load depending on which type of deployment you choose:

    --If you intend to have the primary be the master device of all sessions and only need the secondary online for dynamic routing, or as an asymmetric routing solution, you can set the session owner to **Primary**: the primary device will perform all Layer 7 session scanning while the secondary will simply receive packets and hand them over to the primary for processing, and participate in dynamic routing.

    --If both members are intended to take an active role, select the first packet.

6.  With **Session Setup**, you can also select which member is responsible for all Layer 2 through Layer 4 (routing, NAT translation, and so on) operations by selecting **Primary Device**, **First Packet**, or a load balancing algorithm like **IP Modulo** or **IP Hash**.

    **IP Modulo** distributes the sessions based on the parity of the source IP address.

    **IP Hash** distributes the sessions based on a hash of the source IP address, or the source and destination IP addresses. A hash seed can be added to increase randomization.

7.  Click **OK**.

    You can add the Active/Active virtual addresses here too, and determine their behavior as you can see in the following screenshot:

    --A floating IP with a priority set to either member will stick to one member unless that member encounters a failure, at which time it will fail over, similar to the Active/Passive setup.

    --A floating IP that is bound to the active master also acts similarly to the Active/Passive configuration.

--ARP load sharing will leverage ARP in such a way that depending on the source IP (IP Modulo or IP Hash), a client will receive either ARP replies from member 0 or member 1 (see *step 4*) for a gateway IP, effectively load balancing sessions over both members. The firewall needs to be in the same broadcast domain as the client for this option to work (for example, a downstream router and hosts behind it will always talk to the same peer):

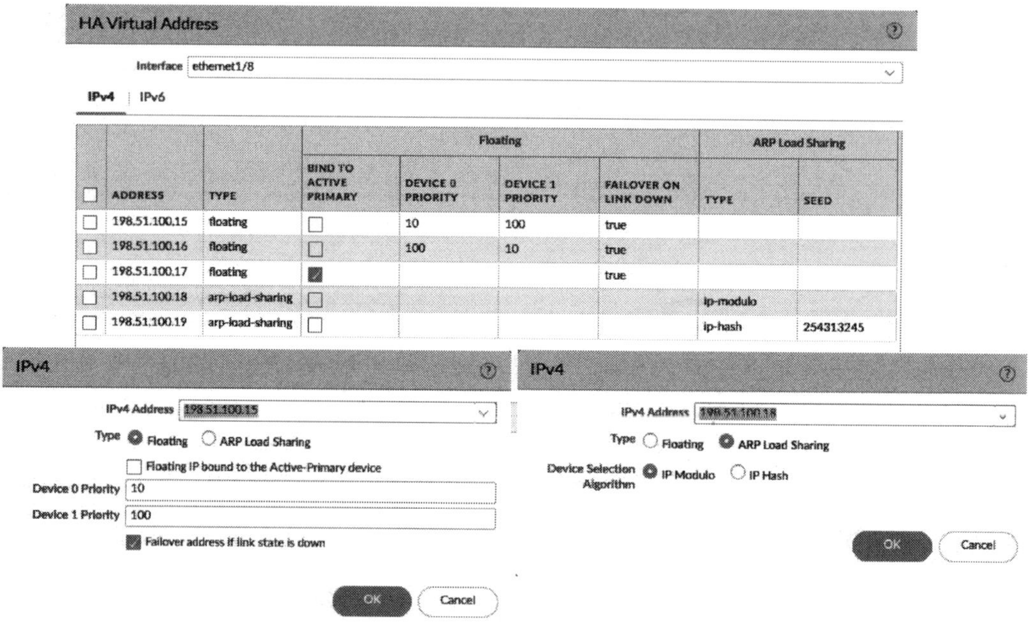

Figure 5.11 – Active/Active virtual addresses

NAT rules in Active/Active configuration have an additional tab where you need to decide which member a NAT policy sticks to, as you can see in the following screenshot. This needs to correspond to the virtual IP configuration in the HA configuration to ensure NAT is applied to the appropriate member that owns an IP address. The **primary** option is used when the primary member is chosen for the session setup. If either member has a lower priority for a certain IP, select that member's ID, or when using ARP load sharing, select both:

**NAT Policy Rule**    (?)

General    Original Packet    Translated Packet    **Active/Active HA Binding**

Active/Active HA Binding    primary    ⌄

primary

both

0

1

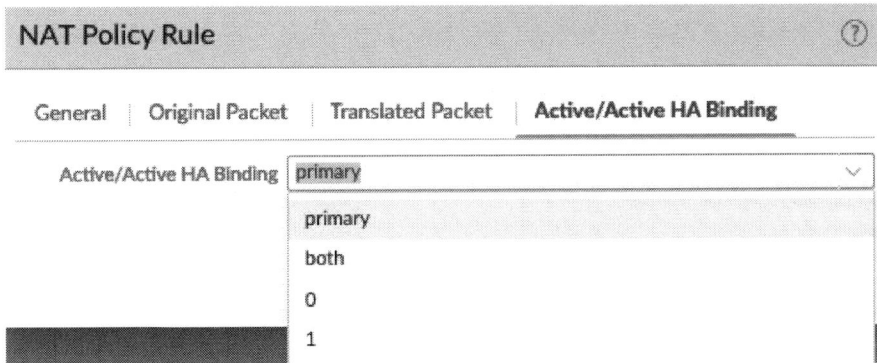

Figure 5.12 – NAT in an Active/Active configuration

You are now able to set up a cluster and decide whether you want a regular Active/Passive deployment or need the more complex Active/Active flavor. In the next section, you will learn how to set up virtual systems so you can segregate networks, or customers, into a logical firewall instance.

# Enabling virtual systems

Enabling **virtual systems (VSYSes)** on a firewall makes it into a multi-tenant system. Each VSYS represents a virtual firewall instance that can operate independently while sharing the resources available on the host system. The host system still retains control over all networking functions (interfaces and their configurations, routing tables, IPSec and GRE tunnels, DHCP, DNS proxy, and so on) and the management configuration. Each VSYS can be assigned its own (sub) interfaces and routing can either be taken care of at the system level or by creating virtual routers and assigning them to each VSYS.

> **Important note**
>
> By default, each firewall creates its objects in `vsys1`. This is the native VSYS even for devices that do not support multi-VSYS. Objects created in `vsys1` or any other VSYS will not be visible to other VSYSes unless its location is set as `shared`.

Only the larger physical platforms (PA-3220 and up as of time of writing) support multi-VSYS mode. The number of virtual systems supported also varies per device, with the largest platform supporting up to 225 virtual systems.

To enable multi-VSYS, you will first need to activate a VSYS license and import it onto the device. Then, in **Device | Setup | Management | General settings**, you can enable **Multi Virtual System Capability**. Enabling the option and clicking **OK** will pop up a warning that this action will cause the system to commit as shown here:

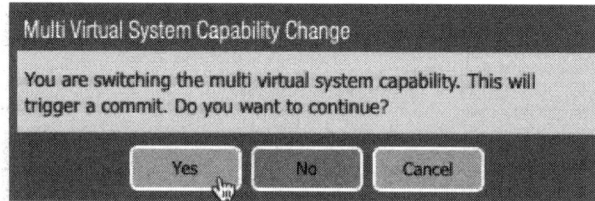

Figure 5.13 – Multi Virtual System Capability commit warning

Once the feature is enabled, two new menu items will appear under **Device**:

- **Virtual Systems**: Where you add a new VSYS.
- **Shared Gateways**: This is an aggregation zone in case multiple VSYSes need to use the same ISP uplink (commonly used in a shared services environment).

After enabling the capability, the first thing to do next is to create a new virtual system.

## Creating a new VSYS

When you create a new VSYS, there's not a lot you can configure yet as the interfaces, VLANs, VWire, and virtual routers will most likely still need to be created. You can already enable a "visible virtual system".

A **Visible Virtual System** allows you to select which virtual system can be reached by another VSYS. This can be useful if you need to segregate some network segments but need to allow some routing. Keeping visibility disabled will enforce segregation.

It is important to note that each VSYS can have several resources limited so it doesn't flood out other VSYSes by overconsuming the host's available resources. As seen in the next screenshot, the total amount of sessions can be limited, the number of VPN tunnels can be limited, and the number of rules each VSYS can hold can be limited. Each physical host has a finite number of rules and sessions it can maintain, so setting limitations helps maintain order when different administrators are put in charge of setting up their own rule bases:

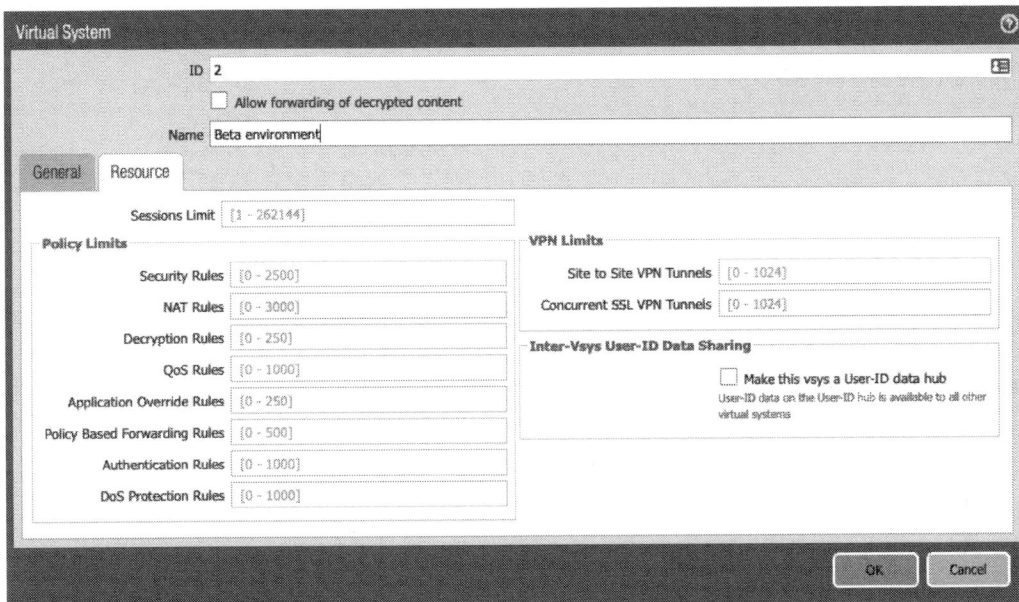

Figure 5.14 – VSYS resource limitation

Next up, you will need to configure all the interfaces, zones, and virtual router(s) as if setting up a factory-new device:

1. In **Network | Zone**, create new (internal, external, DMZ, and so on.) zones and set the new VSYS as **Location**.

2. In **Network | Virtual Router**, create a new VR and add the appropriate routing configuration you will be using in the new VSYS. Click **OK** and then add it to the appropriate VSYS by clicking the hyperlinked **none** next to the virtual system on the main page, as seen here:

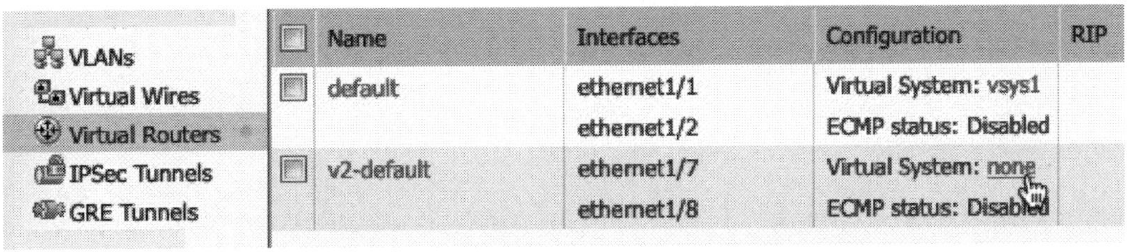

Figure 5.15 – Adding a new virtual router to a VSYS

3.  If you need a VWire in the new VSYS, create it already in **Network | Virtual Wires**.

4.  In **Network | Interfaces**, configure the interfaces you will add to the VSYS so they are themselves set to the proper VSYS and are using the VSYS VR and zones.

You should now have interfaces set similar to the following screenshot, with **ethernet1/1** and **1/2** set to **vsys1**, using the VR in **vsys1** and zones in **vsys1** while **ethernet1/7** and **1/8** are configured in the **vsys2** "Beta environment" with the VR and zones in **vsys2**:

| Interface | Interface Type | Link State | IP Address | Virtual Router | Tag | VLAN / Virtual-Wire | Virtual System | Security Zone |
|---|---|---|---|---|---|---|---|---|
| ethernet1/1 | Layer3 | | 198.51.100.2/24 | default | Untagged | none | vsys1 | L3-untrust-V1 |
| ethernet1/2 | Layer3 | | 10.0.0.0/24 | default | Untagged | none | vsys1 | L3-trust-V1 |
| ethernet1/7 | Layer3 | | 198.51.100.6/24 | v2-default | Untagged | none | Beta environment | L3-untrust-V2 |
| ethernet1/8 | Layer3 | | 10.1.0.0/24 | v2-default | Untagged | none | Beta environment | L3-trust-V2 |

Figure 5.16 – Interfaces configured on two different VSYSes

> **Important note**
>
> All VSYSes can have the same zone names as each system is segregated from the others, but this could lead to administrator confusion, so it is recommended to use a different naming convention for each VSYS. For a shared hosting environment where each customer only has access to their own VSYS, it could help to set every customer up with a `trust`, `untrust`, and `dmz` zone for ease of use.

When hosting multiple logical firewalls, there may also need to be administrators that only need access to a specific VSYS, rather than the whole system.

## Administrators in a multi-VSYS environment

With the activation of a multi-VSYS, new administrator types become available that are restricted to the confines of the virtual system – **Virtual System Administrator** and **Virtual System Administrator (read only)**:

- They are able to see but not edit all the device configuration, except anything that relates directly to other VSYSes.

- They can only see logs and ACC data related to their own VSYS.

- They can create, edit, and delete rules but only for their own VSYS.

- They are not able to see any interface-related configuration (interfaces, VWires, VRs, VLANs, and so on) except the zones attached to their VSYS and certain menu items are removed as shown in the following screenshot:

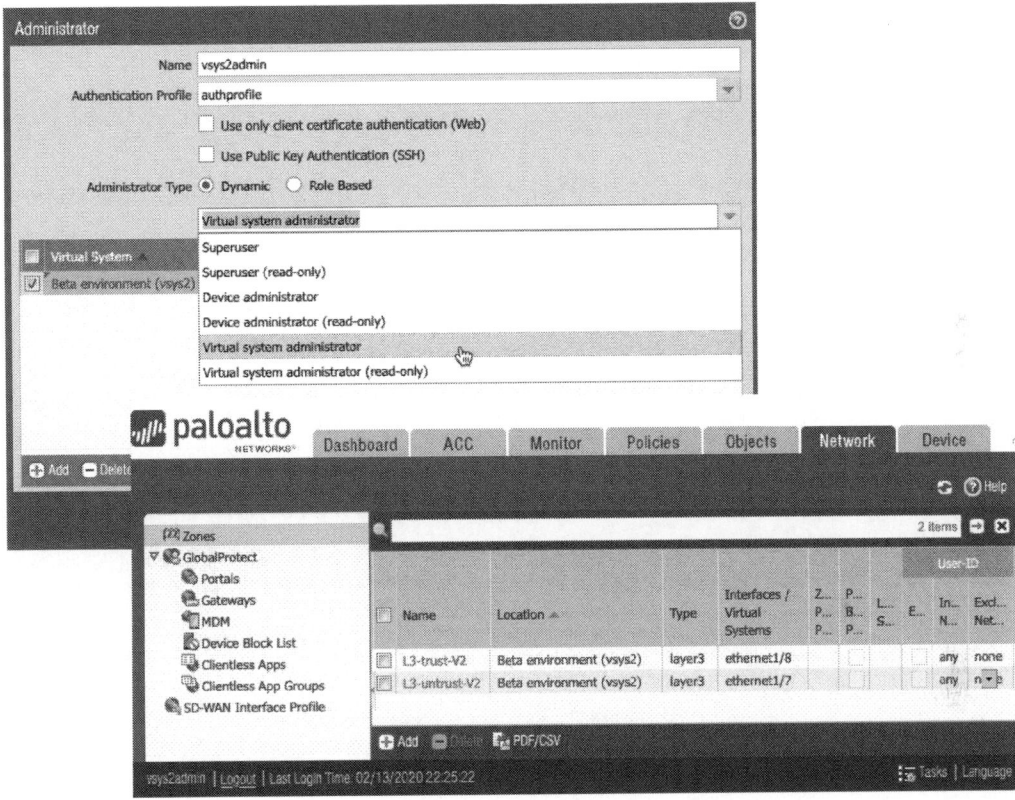

Figure 5.17 – Restricted view of a VSYS administrator

Access can be restricted even further by setting up a VSYS restricted admin role that limits the access of the administrator to the virtual system but can also remove tabs and menu items, and allow administrators read-only or edit privileges in individual menu options. In the following example, you can see the **Dashboard**, **ACC**, and **Device** tabs have been removed. The admin is unable to see logs because the log view is restricted to **vsys2** only:

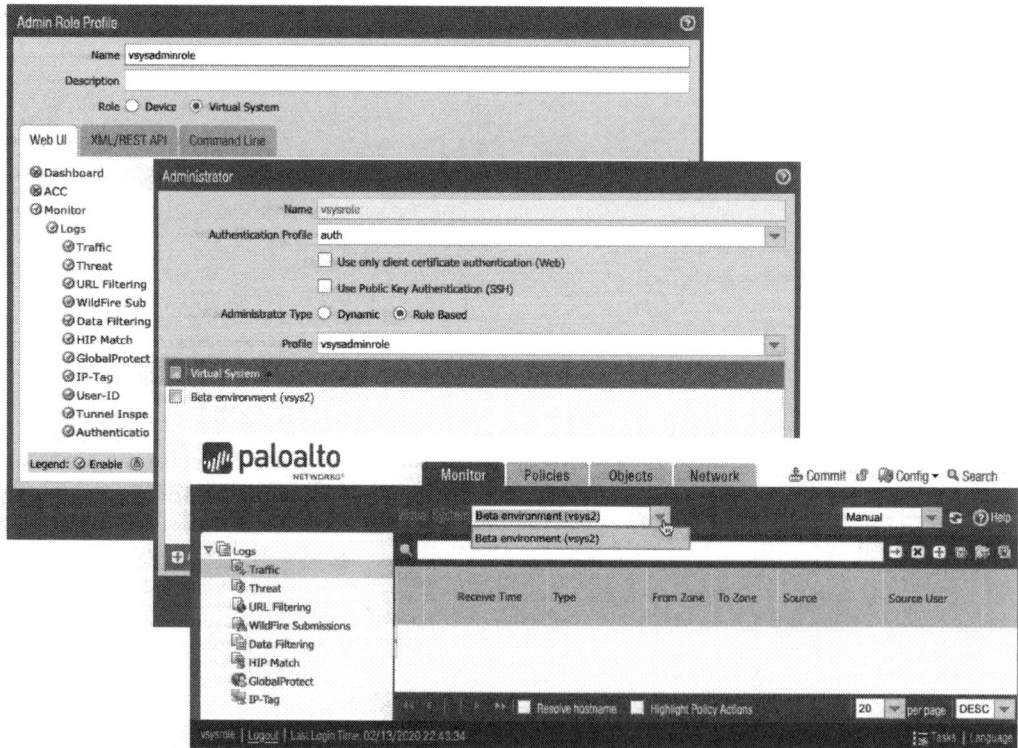

Figure 5.18 – Virtual System admin role

After you set up two or more fully segregated logical firewall instances, the need may arise to have certain hosts or subnets communicate with each other even though they belong to a different virtual system.

## Inter-VSYS routing

Because VSYSes are not aware of each other's existence, some steps are needed before sessions can be set up between VSYSes. Each VSYS will see the other VSYS as existing in the **External** zone, which is a special area for inter-VSYS routing:

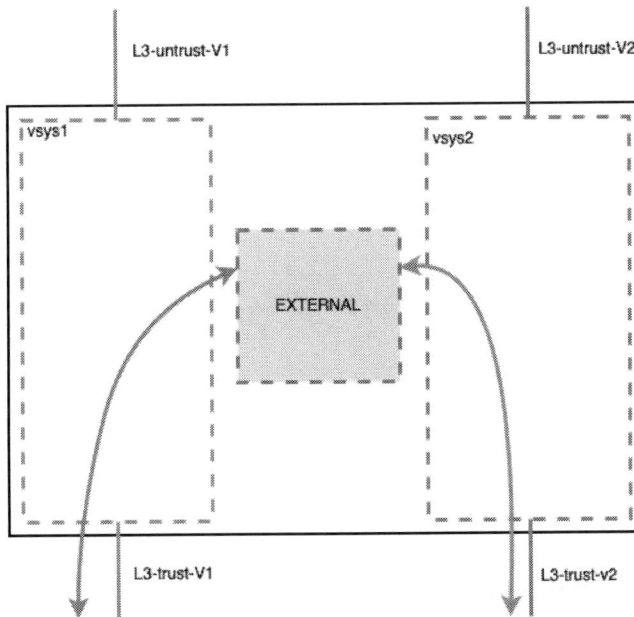

Figure 5.19 – Inter-VSYS routing

You need to follow these steps:

1.  Enable the visibility of the other VSYS in *each* VSYS profile.

2.  Create a new zone called out-to-vsys2:

    --Set it to location **vsys1**.

    --Set it to type **External**.

    --Add **vsys2** to the virtual system selection.

3.  Create a new zone called out-to-vsys1:

    --Set it to location **vsys2**.

    --Set it to type **External**.

    --Add **vsys1** to the virtual system selection.

4.  On the virtual router in **vsys1**, create a new static route:

    --Set the name to vsys2-subnet.

    --Add the destination subnet of **vsys2** (10.1.0.0/24).

    --Leave the interface as **none**.

--Set **Next Hop** to Next VR and assign the **VR** in **vsys2**.

--Click **Ok**.

5.  On the **VR** in **vsys2**, create a new static route:

    --Set the name to vsys1-subnet.

    --Add the destination subnet of **vsys1** (10.0.0.0/24).

    --Leave the interface as **none**.

    --Set **Next Hop** to Next VR and assign the **VR** in **vsys1**.

    --Click **Ok**.

6.  In **Policies > Security**, create a security rule for each direction and the applications that need to be able to be used in the session, plus security profiles.

    For sessions flowing from **vsys1** to **vsys2**, do the following:

    --In **vsys1**, create a security rule from **L3-trust-V1** to **out-to-vsys2**.

    --In **vsys2**, create a security rule from **out-to-vsys1** to **L3-trust-V2**.

    For sessions flowing from vsys2 to vsys1, do the following:

    --In **vsys2**, create a security rule from **L3-trust-V2** to **out-to-vsys1**.

    --In **vsys1**, create a security rule from **out-to-vsys2** to **L3-trust-V1**.

## Creating a shared gateway

Similar to inter-VSYS routing, a shared gateway is a VSYS that is intended to provide internet access to multiple VSYSes. This allows you to keep each VSYS separate while still using the same internet connection. Create a new shared gateway in **Device > Shared gateways**:

1.  Assign ID 1.
2.  Provide an easy to identify name.
3.  If a DNS proxy configuration is needed, set one.

Next, in **Network > Zones**, configure the **Zones** that will be used on the egress interface:

1.  Create a new zone and name it SG-untrust.
2.  Set it to type **layer3**.
3.  Set the location to **Shared gateway (sg1)**.

4. Create another zone and name it `SG-to-vsys1`.

5. Set it to type **External**.

6. Set the location as **Shared Gateways (sg1)**.

7. Add **vsys1** to the Virtual Systems.

8. Repeat *steps 4-7* for the additional VSYS.

9. In each **VSYS** also make a new zone set to type `External` that has **sg1 (SharedGW)** as the virtual system. Call this `to-SG-untrust`.

Then you will need a virtual router. Go to **Network | Virtual Routers**:

1. Create a new virtual router and call it `SharedVR`.

2. If you will use a static IP ISP link, create the static route for the default route (`0.0.0.0/0` out of the egress interface to the ISP router).

3. Add routes to the other VSYS by setting the destination subnet and setting the **Next Hop** to **Next VR** and assigning the appropriate VSYS virtual router (for example, `10.0.0.0/24` set to **Next VR** to `v1-default`).

4. Do *not* set the virtual system assignment; leave it as **none**.

5. In the other VSYS virtual routers, create a default route that points to the `SharedVR` (for example, `0.0.0.0/0` set to **Next VR** equal to `SharedVR`).

Then, configure the interface in **Network | Interfaces**:

1. Open the interface you will use for the shared gateway.

2. Set it to interface type **Layer3**.

3. Assign virtual system **SharedGW (sg1)**.

4. Assign zone **SG-untrust**.

5. Assign VR **SharedVR**.

6. Access the **Ipv4** tab and set the IP configuration (static IP or dynamic configuration).

The last step is to create policies:

7. Security policies are created on the individual VSYS and will look as follows:

L3-trust-V1 to to-SG-untrust with the desired applications, services set to application-default, and a security profile group.

NAT is set up on the shared gateway; you can use the individual SG-to_vsysX to create individual NAT rules if you want to assign each VSYS its own NAT address or put all the zones in the source of a single hide-NAT rule.

An inbound NAT will be configured as follows:

*From SG-untrust to SG-untrust, with the public IP as* **Destination**, *translate to the appropriate vsysX IP.* Routing will take care of delivery to the appropriate VSYS. On the VSYS, a security policy will need to be configured.

*From* '**to-SG-untrust**' *to* '**L3-dmz-V1**' *to the pre-NAT destination IP, allowing the appropriate applications, and using a security profile group.*

> **Important note**
> If an individual VSYS does not need its own routing table, you can run the entire system on a single VR that is set to none in the VSYS selection.

You are now able to create logical firewall instances and leverage a shared gateway to provide internet access via a single ISP uplink. In the next section, we'll learn about managing certificates on the firewall.

# Managing certificates

Certificates are used for all kinds of useful things when considering your firewall is the gateway through which most of your packets need to pass. When performing SSL decryption, the firewall needs to have access to a certificate the client will trust so it doesn't cause a certificate warning in the browser and it will also need to know which root certificate authorities are trustworthy and which ones *should* cause red flags to pop up. It will need to provide a valid certificate when a VPN client connects to the portal or gateway and the administrator should ideally also be greeted by a friendly lock in the address bar rather than a warning page. All these certificates can be managed from the **Device | Certificate management | Certificates** menu. As you can see from the following screenshot, certificates in a chain are automatically sorted so you have immediate visibility of what their relationship is. Several certificates also have a **usage**.

**A Trusted Root CA Certificate** is an imported or externally available root **certificate authority (CA)** that the firewall should treat as trusted. This could be, for example, an internal CA that is not an internet root CA that has signed internal server certificates that the firewall might encounter while performing forward decryption:

- **Forward Trust Certificate** is the certificate used in SSL decryption and will act as the intermediary for any website visited by the client.

- **Forward Untrust Certificate** is a faulty certificate on purpose (this one should *NOT* be installed on the clients as a trusted root CA) as it is intended to cause a certificate warning on the client side while still decrypting the session. This certificate is triggered whenever the visited site's root or intermediary CA is not in the Trusted Root CAs, has expired, or has some other defect that makes it untrustworthy.

- **Certificate for secure Syslog** can be used to secure syslog forwarding.

Other certificates may include GlobalProtect portal and gateway certificates, and web server certificates (with the Private Key) so the firewall can perform inbound SSL decryption, and a certificate for the firewall web interface:

| NAME | EXPIRES | SUBJECT | ISSUER | CA | K... | USAGE |
|---|---|---|---|---|---|---|
| ▼ root signing cert | Jan 20 20:50:19 2021 GMT | C = BE, O = example.com, CN = ro... | C = BE, O = example.co... | ☑ | ☑ | Trusted Root CA Certificate |
| decryption subordinate | Jan 20 20:52:59 2021 GMT | C = BE, O = example.com, CN = de... | C = BE, O = example.co... | ☑ | ☑ | Forward Trust Certificate |
| portal | Apr 16 21:10:19 2021 GMT | CN = portal.example.com | C = BE, O = example.co... | ☐ | ☑ | |
| captiveportal | May 1 23:24:32 2021 GMT | CN = captiveportal.pangurus.com | C = BE, O = example.co... | ☐ | ☑ | |
| gateway | Jun 24 22:35:47 2021 GMT | CN = gateway.example.com | C = BE, O = example.co... | ☐ | ☑ | |
| webserver | Jun 24 22:37:12 2021 GMT | C = BE, CN = www.example.com, e... | C = BE, O = example.co... | ☐ | ☑ | |
| firewall | Jun 24 22:37:35 2021 GMT | CN = firewall.example.com | C = BE, O = example.co... | ☐ | ☑ | |
| untrusted cert | Jan 20 20:57:29 2021 GMT | CN = DangerWillRobinson, emailA... | CN = DangerWillRobins... | ☑ | ☑ | Forward Untrust Certificate |

Figure 5.20 – Common certificates on a firewall

As part of User-ID and GlobalProtect, certificate profiles **Device | Certificate management | Certificates Profiles** can be leveraged to identify users. As you can see in the following screenshot, in the certificate profile, you can indicate which CA certificate should have been used to sign the received client certificates, which field to use to identify the user and the (NetBios) domain to map the user to, and whether **OCSP (Online Certificate Status Protocol** host) will be used and which host to poll, and if certain certificate conditions should lead to a block action:

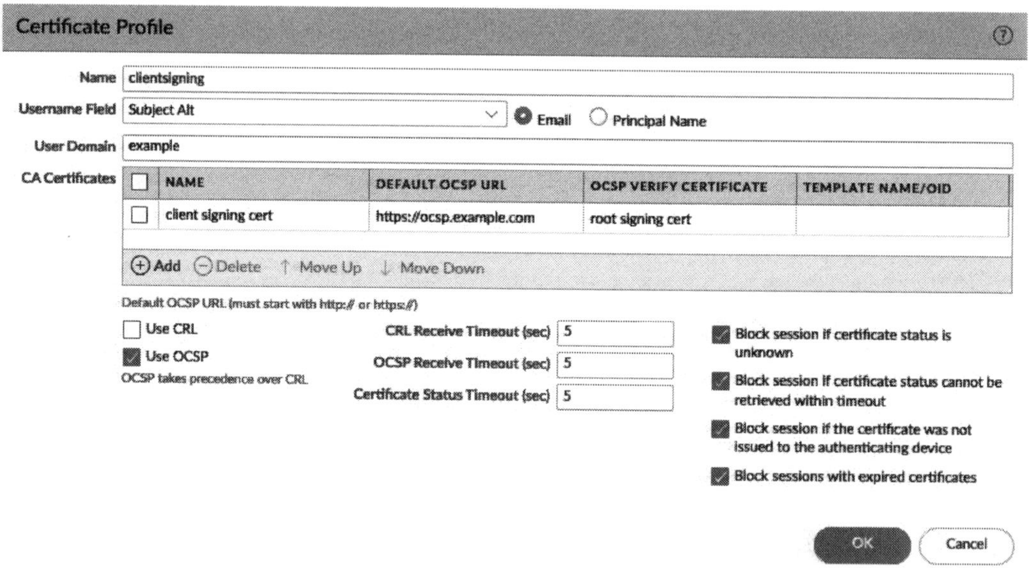

Figure 5.21 – Certificate Profile

The SSL/TLS service profile is used for all web interfaces (the GlobalProtect portal, gateway, and the firewall management interface) to set the minimum and maximum TLS version. As shown in the following example, always set **TLSv1.2** as the minimum version:

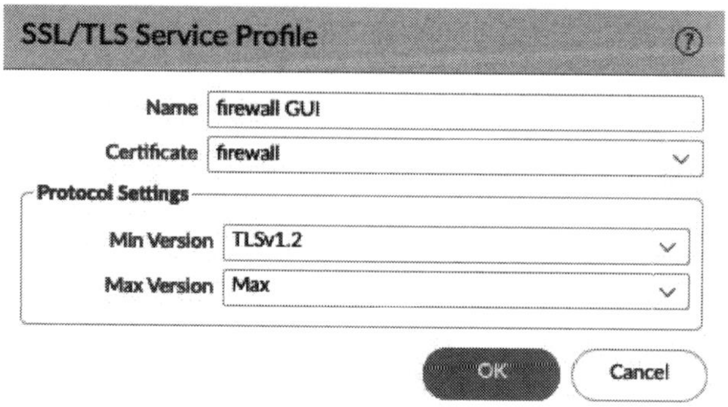

Figure 5.22 – SSL/TLS Service Profile

A **Simple Certificate Enrollment Protocol (SCEP)** profile can be created if your external CA supports SCEP. This makes generating new client, portal, and other certificates much easier as you simply create a new request for a certificate and the SCEP does all the work for you. The CA server will return a certificate with all the bells and whistles with little input from you:

- If your SCEP enrollment server requires it, you can select **fixed** for a simple password or **dynamic** for an OTP deployment (the OTP is handled between the firewall and CA and doesn't require interaction from you).

- You need to set the **Server URL**, **CA-IDENT Name**, and which type of certificate this SCEP profile will be used for. The variables are $USERNAME, $EMAILADDRESS, $HOSTID, and $UDID.

- Set the cryptographic preferences and the SSL authentication certificates if the CA is on HTTPS (not required if the CA is still on HTTP).

If you create a SCEP profile, it should look similar to this:

Figure 5.23 – SCEP profile and certificate generation using SCEP

To generate a **Certificate Signing Request (CSR)** to have a certificate signed by an external authority, simply generate a new certificate in **Device | Certificate Management | Certificates** and select `External Authority (CSR)` in the **Signed By** field as illustrated here:

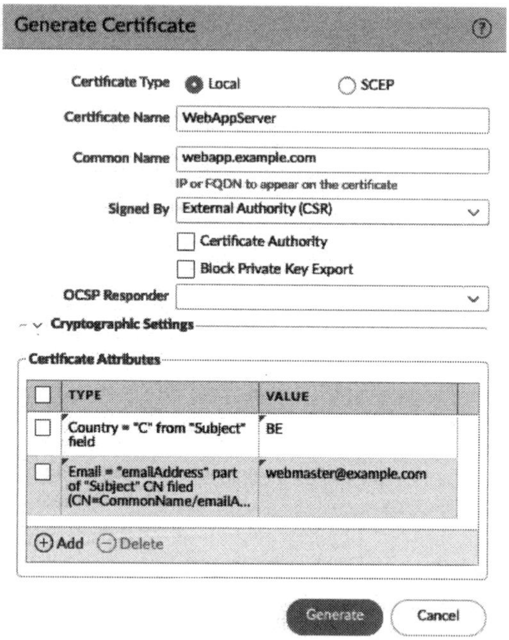

Figure 5.24 – Certificate Signing Request

Lastly, in the **certificate management** menu, you can also set **SSL Decryption Exclusions**, in case you want to manually prevent a specific website from being decrypted, or if a website is using an unsupported certificate that you need to bypass (for example, a partner that still needs to replace a legacy certificate).

# Summary

In this chapter, you learned how to configure the firewall so that it is able to work with a DHCP enabled ISP and how to serve IP addresses to clients on local networks or relay DHCP for an internal server. You also learned how to set the firewall as a DNS proxy and ensure internal hosts resolve domain names efficiently and securely. You are now able to set up HA, and form a functional cluster, and can maintain certificates.

In the next chapter, we'll take a closer look at the various methods to identify users and how group mapping can help build policies that enforce **Role-Based Access Control (RBAC)**.

# 6
# Identifying Users and Controlling Access

In this chapter, we will be learning about **User Identification (User-ID)** and the various ways in which we can intercept credentials or have users identify themselves. Once they're identified, their user-to-IP mapping can be leveraged to control which resources they can access. User-based reports can also be generated to keep track of users' habits or review incidents. In addition, we will link user-to-IP mappings to group membership so we can apply role-/group-based access control. This will help us to identify groups of users so they can access only the resources they need while roaming without the need for network segmentation or static IP addresses.

In this chapter, we're going to cover the following topics:

- User-ID basics
- Configuring group mapping
- Captive portals and authentication
- Using APIs for User-ID
- User credential phishing prevention

# Technical requirements

This chapter requires a working knowledge of Active Directory and **LDAP** (**Lightweight Directory Access Protocol**), as we will be collecting information from, and making changes in, Active Directory and setting up an LDAP connection to collect user group membership information.

# User-ID basics

In this section, we will learn how to set up the basics needed to identify users by preparing Active Directory and configuring the agent/agentless configuration to collect user-to-IP mappings. One universal truth is that for User-ID to work, the interface that receives connections from the users that need to be identified needs to have User-ID enabled in its zone, as you can see in the following screenshot. This setting needs to be active in local zones, or remote zones (such as VPNs) that receive user sessions, but should not be enabled for untrusted zones such as internet uplinks. In the include list, you can limit subnets to which User-ID is applied or exclude specific subnets by adding them to the exclude list:

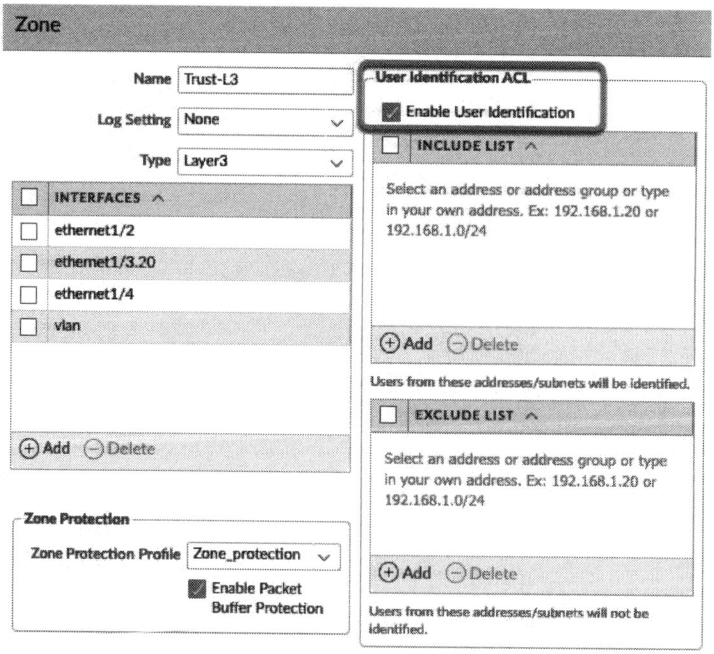

Figure 6.1 – User-ID in a zone

We first need to prepare Active Directory before we can start the firewall configuration.

# Preparing Active Directory and setting up the agents

One of the first steps we need to take is to enable audit logging in the **Active Directory** (**AD**) local security policy, as, by default, the logging we want to see is disabled. The User-ID agent (or the agentless deployment) needs to be able to capture at least one of four possible event IDs from AD: 4768 (Authentication Ticket Granted), 4769 (Service Ticket Granted), 4770 (Ticket Granted Renewed), and 4624 (Logon Success).

You will need to navigate to **Start** > **Windows Administrative Tools** > **Local Security Policy**. Then, in **Security Settings** > **Local Policy** > **Audit Policy**, set **Audit Logon Events** to **Success**, which will start logging all successful logon events that the User-ID agent can use to map the user to their workstation's IP.

You will also need to create a service account, which will be used to do the following:

- Run the service if an agent is being used
- Connect remotely if an agentless deployment is being used
- Be able to perform **WMI** (**Windows Management Instrumentation**) probing

If using an agent, do the following:

1.  Create a new user in **Active Directory Users and Computers | Managed Service Accounts**. In the **Member Of** tab, add **Event Log Reader**. In the **Dial In** tab, set **Deny access**.

2.  Then, in **Local Security Policy | Security Settings | Local Policy | User Rights Assignment**, add the service account to **Log on as a service**.

3.  For security, you'll also want to add the service to **Deny log on as a batch job**, **Deny log on locally**, and **Deny log on through Remote Desktop Services**.

4.  To add the user via **Group Policy Objects** (**GPO**), if you intend to install multiple agents, do so via **Group Policy Management | <domain> | Default Domain Policy** and then right-click **Edit**. Then, select **Computer Configuration | Policies | Windows Settings | Security Settings | Local Policies | User Rights Assignment** and add the service account to **Log on as a service**, and the three **Deny log on** policies mentioned in *step 3*.

If you're going agentless, just follow the same steps as those listed previously, but also add the role of **Server Operator** to the **Member Of** tab in the service account.

With these settings, you will be able to reactively map user logon events to the source IP that initiated the logon, but there is also a way to actively poll who is logged on to a system, which we'll look at next.

## WMI probes

One alternative method of collecting user information, or ensuring that a user is still logged on to their device, is having the agent send out periodical probes in the form of NetBIOS queries or WMI probes. NetBIOS does not require authentication and is a bit dated, making it less preferable than WMI. WMI uses authentication and is more secure (you may still need to allow it in the client firewall by adding **Windows Management Instrumentation** to Windows Firewall Exceptions). Let's look at what you need to do:

1. To enable WMI probing, add the **Distributed COM Users** role to the **Member Of** tab in the User-ID service account.

2. Next, you will need to set permissions for the service account to remotely probe systems: launch `smimgmt.msc` and right-click **WMI Control (local)** and open **Properties**.

3. In the **Security** tab, select **CIMV2**, click the **Security** button, add the User-ID service account, and check the **Allow** box next to **Enable Account** and **Remote Enable**.

> **Important note**
> If User-ID is not set up properly, probing could generate a large amount of network traffic, so be sure to enable probing only when everything else is set up and operational.

## User-ID agent

The next step is to download the agent from `https://support.paloaltonetworks.com` > **Updates | Software Updates** and install it on AD. Make sure to get `UaInstall*.msi` (`UaCredInstall.msi` is used for user credential detection, which we will cover in the final section, *User credential detection*).

> **Important note**
>
> If your AD is not an ideal location to run the agent, you can run it from a different server in the same domain and read the logs remotely. This will require the service account to be added to the **Server Operator** role. Reading event logs remotely will generate some load on the network, so make sure the server is close to your AD.

You will need to run the installer as administrator. If your Windows installer won't let you use the **Run as** option directly from right-clicking the file, a handy trick is to execute `command.exe` as administrator and execute the installer from the command line.

Once the agent is installed, you will first need to make two more adjustments:

1.  Right-click and open the properties of `C:\Program Files (x86)\Palo Alto Networks`, select **Security**, click **Edit**, and then add the User-ID service account and grant it full access to the directory.

2.  Open `regedit` and add the service account with full control permissions to the Palo Alto Networks key:

    `HKEY_LOCAL_MACHINE\SOFTWARE\WOW6432Node` (for 64-bit systems)

    `HKEY_LOCAL_MACHINE\SOFTWARE\Palo Alto Networks` (for 32-bit systems)

3.  From the **Start** menu (or from the `install` folder), run `UaController.exe` as administrator.

In **User Identification | Setup**, you can configure the agent. The access control list at the bottom lets you control which systems have access to the agent. You can restrict access to your management network or individual firewall IP addresses.

The configuration section at the top lets you set all the parameters in individual tabs:

1.  **Authentication** is where you need to fill in the service account used by the service and its password.

2.  In the **Server Monitor** tab, **Enable Security Log Monitor** is enabled by default and set to 1 second. This is the process that reads the AD event logs. In the following case, it connects each second and reads the logs that have been created since the last read. You can optionally enable **Server Session Read**, which is a process that keeps track of users who have mapped a drive or directory on the local system:

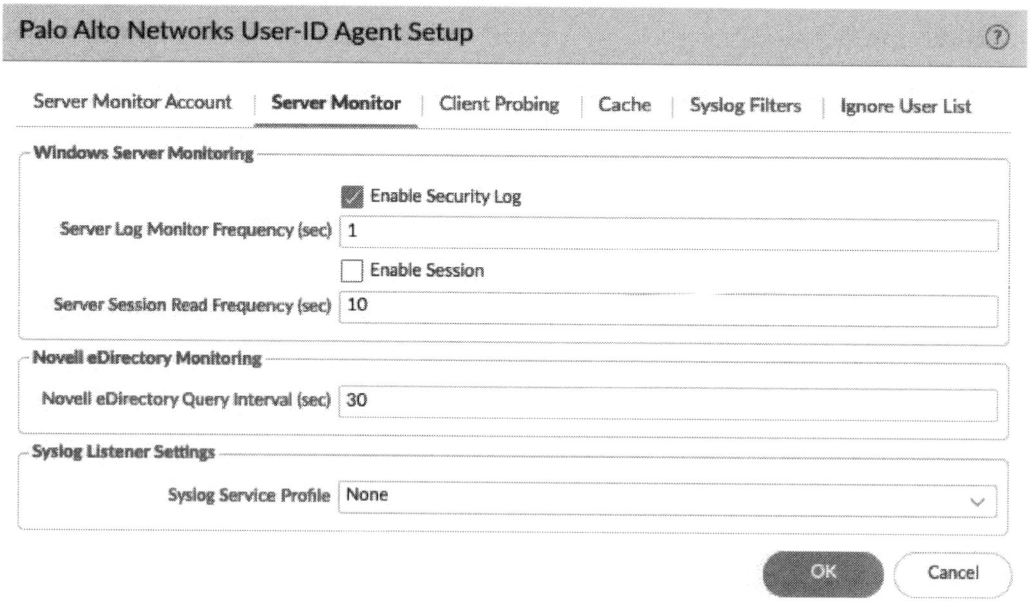

---

**Palo Alto Networks User-ID Agent Setup**                                                    (?)

Server Monitor Account  |  **Server Monitor**  |  Client Probing  |  Cache  |  Syslog Filters  |  Ignore User List

┌─ **Windows Server Monitoring** ──────────────────────────────────────────────────────────────
│                                              ☑ Enable Security Log
│   Server Log Monitor Frequency (sec)  │ 1                                                    │
│
│                                              ☐ Enable Session
│   Server Session Read Frequency (sec) │ 10                                                   │
└──────────────────────────────────────────────────────────────────────────────────────────

┌─ **Novell eDirectory Monitoring** ───────────────────────────────────────────────────────────
│   Novell eDirectory Query Interval (sec) │ 30                                                │
└──────────────────────────────────────────────────────────────────────────────────────────

┌─ **Syslog Listener Settings** ───────────────────────────────────────────────────────────────
│   Syslog Service Profile │ None                                                          ⌄  │
└──────────────────────────────────────────────────────────────────────────────────────────

                                                        ( OK )    ( Cancel )

---

Figure 6.2 – The Server Monitor tab

3.  In the **Client Probing** tab, you can select whether you want to use WMI and/or NetBIOS probing, and the frequency of the probes. Mind the caveats mentioned in the **WMI probing** section.

4.  In the **Cache** tab, you can control how long user credentials are cached. By default, this is enabled and set to 45 minutes. This timer is a hard timer, which means the user mapping is removed after the amount of time indicated and needs to be refreshed by a new logon or authentication event.

In a fairly static office environment, my recommendation is to set this timeout to 9 or 10 hours, which is the length of a normal workday (and the default length of a kerberos ticket is 600 minutes), as users tend to come in, log in, and then sit at their desk most of the day, possibly not generating any more logon or authentication events. Adjust the timeout to how dynamic you anticipate your environment will be.

5.  In the **Agent Service** tab, you can set the port that will be used by firewalls to connect; the default is 5007. You can also enable **User-ID XML API** (default port 5006) if you want to use the API to inject user mappings directly into the agent.

6.  In the **eDirectory** tab, you can poll a Novell eDirectory server for user information.

7.  In the **Syslog** tab, you can decide to receive syslogs from an external system, such as a Cisco ISE. You'll need to define filters using regexes to scrape the logs for relevant information. These filters will vary depending on your syslog forwarder:

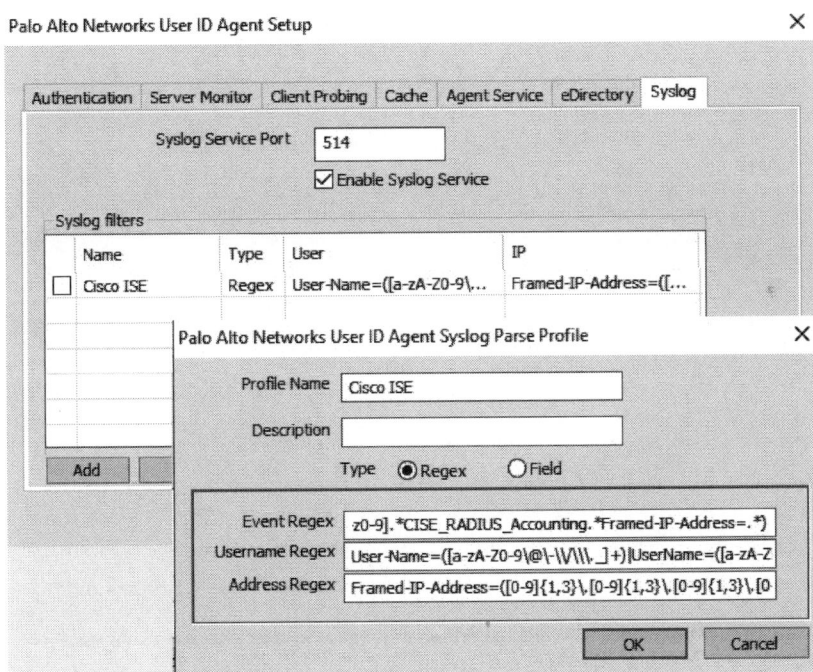

Figure 6.3 – User-ID Agent syslog service

Here's an example for Cisco ISE 2.2; your instance may vary, so some tuning may be required:

| Event Regex |
| --- |
| `([A-Za-z0-9].*CISE_Guest.*NADAddress=.*)|([A-Za-z0-9].*CISE_Guest.*GuestUserName=.*)` |
| **Username Regex** |
| `User-Name=([a-zA-Z0-9\@\-\\/\\\._]+)|UserName=([a-zA-Z0-9\@\-\\/\\\._]+)` |
| **Address Regex** |
| `NADAddresss=([0-9]{1,3}\.[0-9]{1,3}\.[0-9]{1,3}\.[0-9]{1,3})` |

Here's an example for Cisco ISE 1.3:

| Event Regex |
| --- |
| `([A-Za-z0-9].*CISE_Passed_Authentications.*Framed-IP-Address=.*)|([A-Za-z0-9].*CISE_RADIUS_Accounting.*Framed-IP-Address=.*)` |
| **Username Regex** |
| `User-Name=([a-zA-Z0-9\@\-\\/\\\._]+)|UserName=([a-zA-Z0-9\@\-\\/\\\._]+)` |
| **Address Regex** |
| `Framed-IP-Address=([0-9]{1,3}\.[0-9]{1,3}\.[0-9]{1,3}\.[0-9]{1,3})` |

8. Once you have completed the configuration, click **OK** to save the User-ID agent setup.

In the **User Identification | Discovery** menu, you can add the AD servers you want to poll. If the service account has been set up properly, AutoDiscover will discover and populate all of the AD servers associated with your forest (using the `_autodiscover._tcp SRV` record in your domain DNS). To remove servers, check the box and click **Delete**.

The include and exclude lists let you select which IP ranges are expected to contain known users and let you manually add exceptions. Typical exceptions include terminal servers where multiple users are logged on at the same time (see the upcoming *Terminal Server Agent* section).

> **Important note**
> If you add an exclusion, you must also add included subnets.

Add your user subnets and add any excluded servers, and then click **Save** and **Commit**. Return to the User-ID main page. If, at the top, it is indicated that the service is stopped, click **Start**. From this view, you will see which firewalls have made a successful connection to the User-ID agent and which AD servers are being connected to.

Once user events start being collected, new mappings will start appearing in **Monitoring**.

Now that you have configured the User-ID agent and it is collecting user information, the next step is to connect the firewall to the agent so it can benefit from the collected information and match users to security rules.

## Adding the User-ID agent in the firewall

In **Device | User Identification | User-ID Agents**, you can add a new entry for every User-ID agent you need to connect to.

As seen in the following screenshot, there are a few important settings:

- The **Serial Number** radio button can be used if you have a Panorama management server that is set up for User-ID redistribution. Panorama can be set up to collect information from individual User-ID agents and then function as a distribution point. Firewalls will connect to Panorama for user-to-IP mappings instead of User-ID agents.

- **Host and Port** lets you set an IP and port for an agent so the firewall connects directly to User-ID agents to collect user-to-IP mappings.

- The agent can be set up to function as an **LDAP proxy**, in case the firewall needs to perform LDAP authentication (for VPN users or administrators) but doesn't have direct access to an LDAP server.

- If NTLM authentication is configured in the captive portal, the firewall can proxy authentication requests via the User-ID agent (must also be enabled on the agent). If you can, use Kerberos instead of NTLM.

- **User-ID collector** information is used if the agent is another firewall configured in redistribution mode.

A normal User-ID agent configuration will look like what you can see in the following screenshot. Add NTLM or LDAP proxy functionality if needed, and add the User-ID collector name and the pre-shared key details if the agent is another firewall:

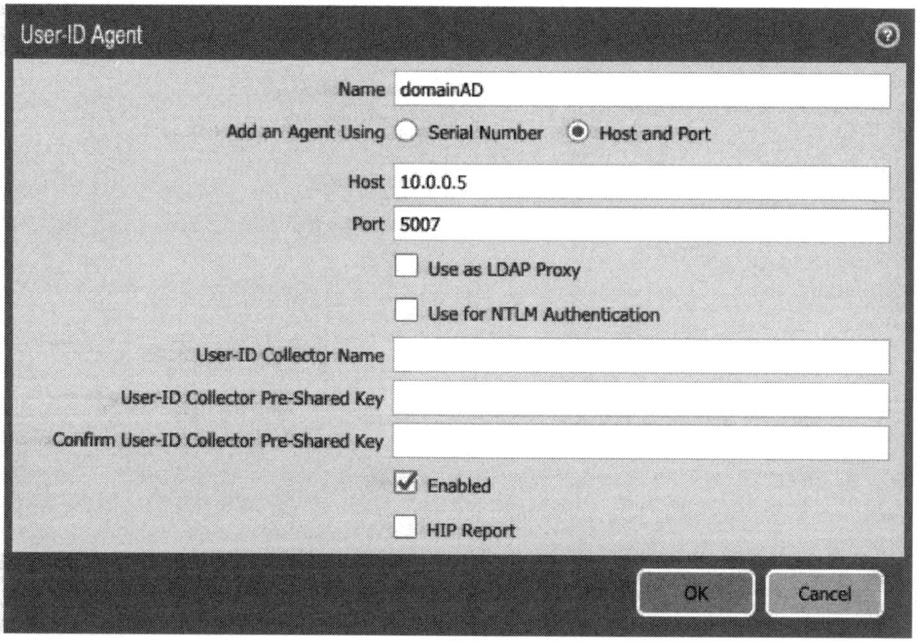

Figure 6.4 – Adding a User-ID agent on the firewall

> **Important note**
>
> When the User-ID agent is started, it will go and read the last 50,000 log entries in the event log to build a user-to-IP mapping database.
>
> When the User-ID agent is stopped, it will retain its database for 10 minutes, after which the database is purged.
>
> If you need to exclude specific users, such as service accounts, you can create a file in the User-ID agent `install` directory containing all the usernames, one per line. The file must be named `ignore_user_list.txt`.
>
> You can use a certificate for authentication: create a certificate on your corporate **Certificate Authority (CA)**, then import it into **Server Certificate** in the User-ID agent and create a certificate profile, and then add it to **Device | User Identification | Connection Security** on the firewall.

You are now able to set up a User-ID agent that is able to match a unique source IP to a username. Next, we will learn how we can set up a Terminal Server Agent for multiuser systems that host multiple unique users on the same source IP.

## Terminal Server Agent

The **Terminal Server (TS)** Agent is used to identify users who are all logged on to the same system. This means they will all have the same source IP, so to differentiate them, their source ports are adjusted to an assigned block of ports, so the firewall can identify which user is initiating a session just by looking at the source port of a session.

> **Important note**
> Some endpoint protection software will proxy sessions locally and randomize the source port, which interferes with TS Agent. You may need to configure the software to not touch the source port, or disable the proxy functionality altogether, for User-ID to work.

Install `TaInstall*.msi` as administrator; some environments may not let you open the executable as administrator directly. As a workaround, you can launch a command prompt by right-clicking it and choosing to **Run as administrator**, and then executing the installer from the command line.

Run `TaController.exe` as administrator once installation is complete and access the configuration.

On the TS Agent, you will see whether any devices are connected, and you can configure an access control list to limit which devices are allowed to connect.

As seen in the following screenshot, in the **Configure** menu, you will see **System Source Port Allocation Range** and **System Reserved Source Ports,** which show the ranges of ports that are used for non-user sessions. These ranges are called ephemeral ports and are controlled by the host operating system (Windows). You can change this port range if you need to by following this article: `https://support.microsoft.com/en-us/help/929851/the-default-dynamic-port-range-for-tcp-ip-has-changed-in-windows-vista`:

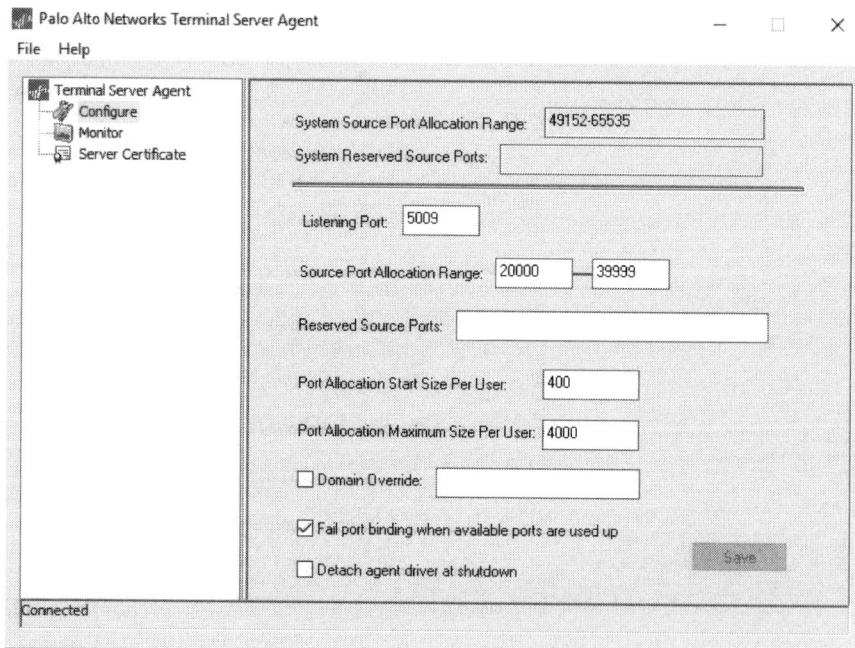

Figure 6.5 – TS Agent configuration

- **Listening Port** displays which port the firewall can use to receive source port information and associated usernames.

- The **Source Port Allocation Range** value determines the block of source ports that can be used by user sessions. This range can be increased as needed, as long as it doesn't overlap with the ephemeral ports.

- **Reserved Source Ports** lets you add an additional range of reserved source ports that the system can use exclusively.

- **Port Allocation Start Size Per User** is the range of ports a user can use for outgoing sessions. Once a user requires more source ports, a new block will be made available until the **Port Allocation Maximum Size Per User** value is reached or the total pool of available source ports is depleted.

- **Fail port binding when available ports are used up** prevents users from making any more connections once the available source ports are depleted. Disabling this option will allow users to still create sessions, but these sessions may no longer be identified.

- **Detach agent driver at shutdown** can be enabled in case the TS Agent becomes unresponsive when you try to shut it down.

There are a couple of cool windows registry keys that can be found in `Computer\HKEY_LOCAL_MACHINE\SOFTWARE\Palo Alto Networks\TS Agent\`:

- **Adv\HonorSrcPortRequest** (`0` or `1` – `0` by default) is used to allow applications to request a certain source port. This could prevent User-ID because the source port may fall outside of the source port range used by User-ID. This setting is disabled (`0`) by default.

- **Conf\EnableTws** (`0` or `1` – `0` by default) enables polling on ports in `TimeWaitState`. This can be useful if users use applications that spawn many sessions and then leave open connections, starving new sessions of available source ports.

As you can see in the following screenshot, the **Monitor** menu keeps track of connected users:

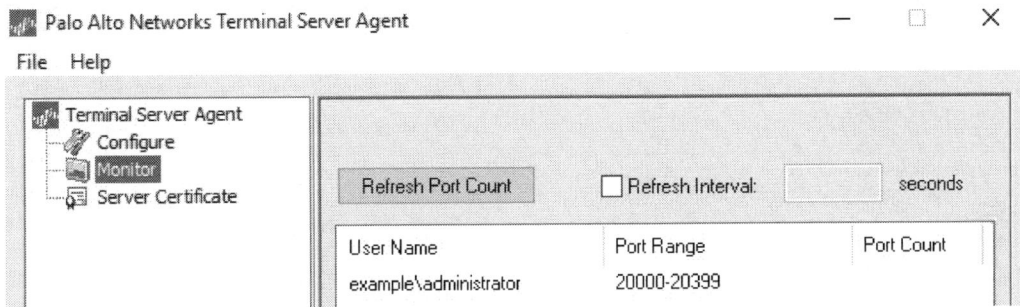

Figure 6.6 – A detected user and the assigned source port range

Now that you have configured the TS Agent, connect it to the firewall so users can start to get matched against security rules.

## Adding the TS Agent to the firewall

To add the TS Agent via **Device | User Identification | Terminal Server Agents**, do the following:

1. Set a name.

2. Set the main IP address or hostname.

3. Change the port if the default port was changed on the agent.

4. Add any additional IP addresses the server may have; this is optional of course.

The dialog box should look similar to the following screenshot:

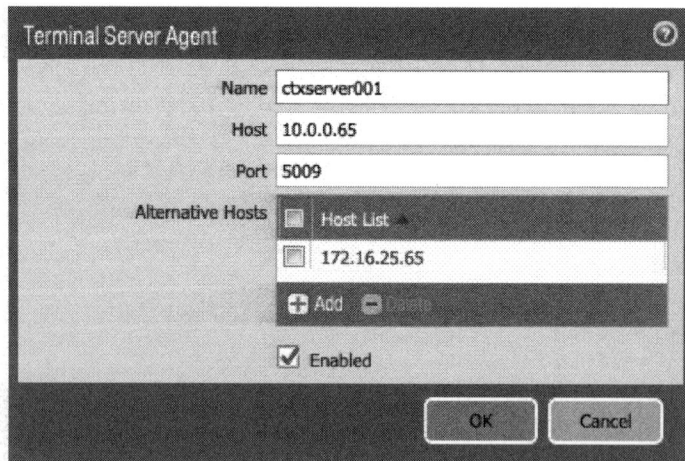

Figure 6.7 – Adding a TS Agent to the firewall

You are now able to configure both agents and connect them to the firewall, but the firewall can also function as an agent, which does not require the installation of a piece of software. In the next section, you'll learn how to set that up.

## Agentless User-ID

The firewall also supports a clientless version, where the firewall itself acts as the agent. In **Device | User Identification | User Mapping**, you can define four types of server that can be contacted to retrieve user information, as illustrated in the following screenshot:

- **AD**: Reads event logs over WMI, WinRM-HTTP, or WinRM-HTTPS

- **Exchange**: Monitors exchange connections over WMI, WinRM-HTTP, or WinRM-HTTPS

- **Novell eDirectory**: Accesses eDirectory user logins

- **Syslog sender**: Sets the firewall as a syslog receiver and sets a filter (including Aerohive, BlueCoat, Juniper, Cisco, Citrix, and Squid predefined filters over SSL or UDP):

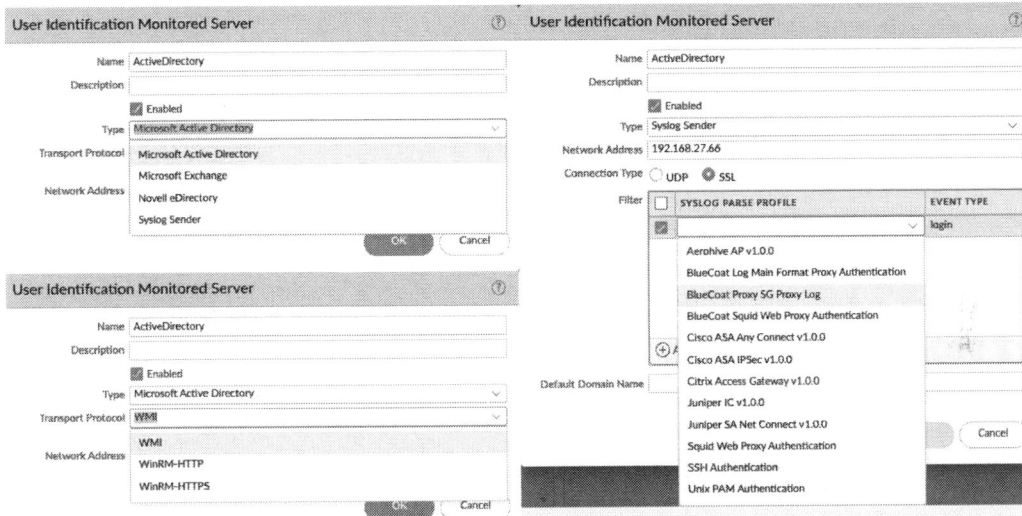

Figure 6.8 – Adding server monitoring servers

You can also autodiscover available servers by clicking **Discover** below **Server Monitoring**: make sure the firewall is configured to use the internal DNS servers (to pick up on the `_autodiscover._tcp` SRV record) and has the domain set in **Device | Setup**.

Add include/exclude networks to limit the scope to your actual user subnets and exclude servers that may need a TS Agent.

Configure the clientless agent and set the following settings:

1. As illustrated in the following screenshot, do the following:

   -In **Server Monitor Account**, add a service account.

   -Make sure that on the **ActiveDirectory** server, the account is set as a member of **Distributed COM Users** and **Event Log Readers**.

   -Enable the account for WMI probing.

   -Set the domain's full DNS name (`example.com`).

-If you want to use **Windows Remote Management (WinRM)** to connect to servers, you need to add a Kerberos server profile (make sure that the firewall is set up with internal DNS servers, has the domain in **Device | Setup | Management | General Settings**, and has the NTP servers set).

-To use WinRM-HTTPS, also add a User-ID certificate profile in **Device | User Identification | Connection Security**:

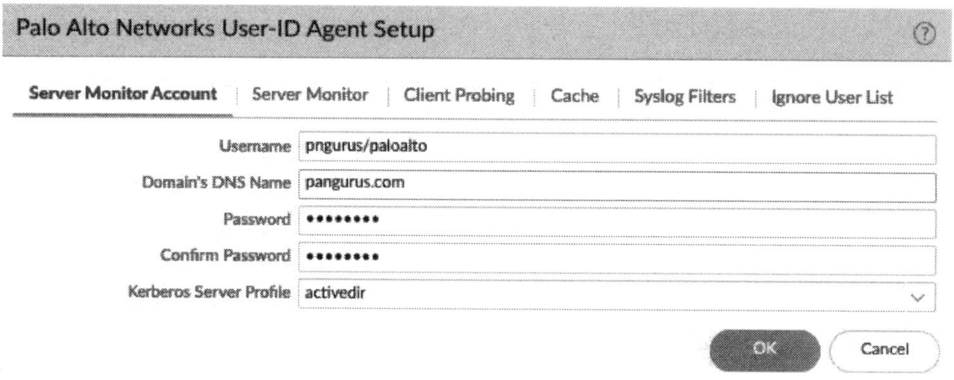

Figure 6.9 – The Server Monitor Account tab

2.  As seen in the following screenshot, in the **Server Monitor** tab, log reading is enabled by default, and server monitor can be enabled, giving you control over the poll frequency in seconds. If the agent should listen for syslogs, an SSL/TLS profile can be added here if the connection is set to use SSL instead of UDP:

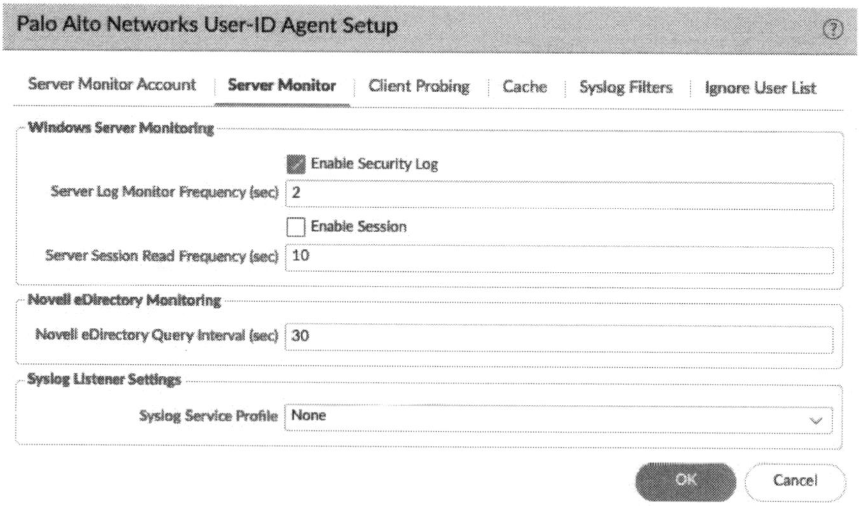

Figure 6.10 – Server Monitor

3. In **Client Probing**, WMI probes can be enabled and their frequency can be set in minutes. Unlike the client installed on a server, the clientless deployment does not support NetBIOS probing. If you intend to enable probing, make sure that the include and exclude networks have been set up so probes are not sent to inappropriate or high-security networks.

4. In **Cache**, you can choose whether user-to-IP mappings will live and how long they will live. Once the timeout expires, the mapping is removed and the user will need to create a new logon event before they can be identified again. For normal office environments, a timeout of 9 to 10 hours is usually appropriate. In a highly dynamic environment, a shorter period may be preferred. (In extremely static environments, a timeout may not be needed, although I would not recommend that.)

   If usernames are to be collected without domains, enable **Allow matching usernames without domain**.

5. If the captive portal needs to use NTLM, you can enable an NTLM proxy. Only one NTLM proxy can be set up per system, even if it is a multi-VSYS environment. If more are needed, agents will need to be deployed to serve as NTLM proxies per VSYS. Configure NTLM as follows:

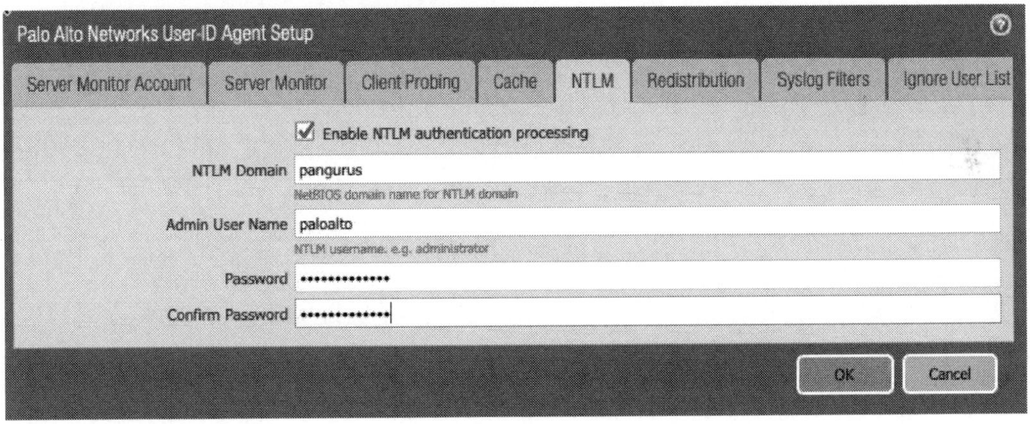

Figure 6.11 – NTLM configuration

---

**Important note**

In PAN-OS 10.0, NTLM has been retired in favor of Kerberos.

---

6. **Redistribution** enables the firewall as a User-ID agent for other firewalls: the firewall can only redistribute locally learned mappings (so not mappings it has learned from other firewalls or agents).

7. You can add additional syslog filters or check out the predefined ones for inspiration. As you can see in the following screenshot, many vendors have been preloaded, so you don't need to create regexes to interpret syslogs:

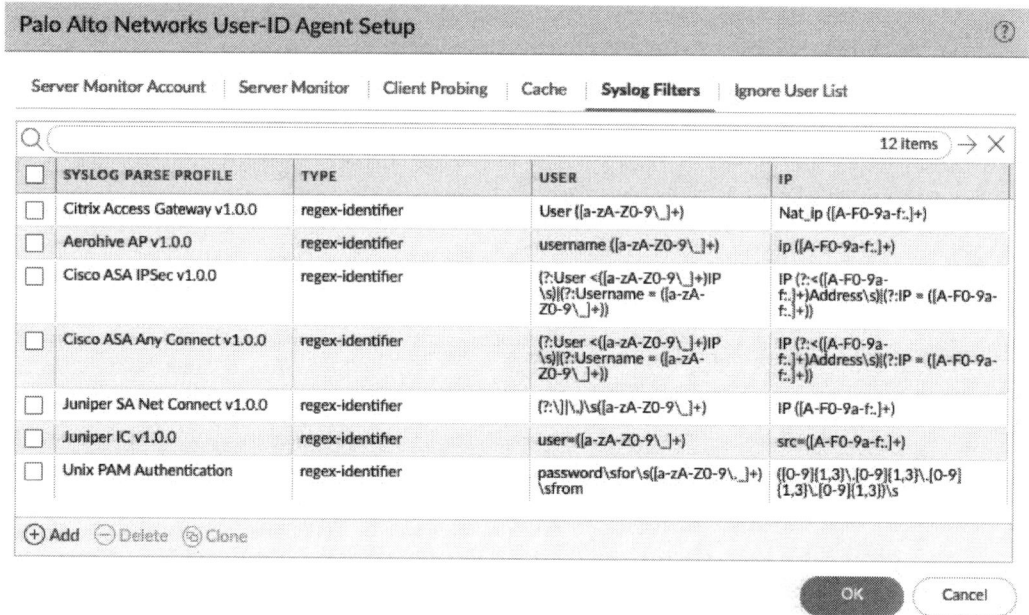

Figure 6.12 – Syslog filters for popular network vendors

8. If service accounts or specific user accounts need to be ignored, add them to **Ignore User List**.

You are now able to set up both the agents and the agentless User-ID to collect information from AD or probe the client for the logged-in user. In the next section, you will learn how to configure group mapping so that users can be identified by their LDAP/AD group memberships.

# Configuring group mapping

If you are able to identify users on your network, you are also able to create security rules to allow or limit their access to certain resources. **Role-Based Access Control (RBAC)** can easily be enforced by binding LDAP groups to security policies, granting members of a certain organization within your company exclusive and reliable access to the resources they need wherever they go.

To get started, we need to create an LDAP profile so we can fetch group information. Go to **Device | Server Profiles | LDAP** and create a new profile. You will need one LDAP profile per domain in a multidomain or forest configuration.

There needs to be at least one server, but there can be up to four for redundancy. Don't forget to change the port (389 by default) if you're going to use TLS encryption:

1. Add at least one server by IP or FQDN and set the appropriate port (389 unencrypted, 636 for TLS).

2. Set the type to active-directory unless you have a different deployment (sun, e-directory or 'other').

3. If you set the IP and port correctly, the base **Distinguished Name (DN)** will load automatically once you click the drop-down arrow. You can add **Organizational Units (OUs)** and **Common Names (CNs)** if needed.

4. Bind DN is the account that's used to read the directory structure and all members. A regular user-level account is sufficient; no special privileges are required unless you have hardened your LDAP environment.

5. Click **OK** and create additional profiles if there are more domains.

If all went well, your LDAP profile should look as follows:

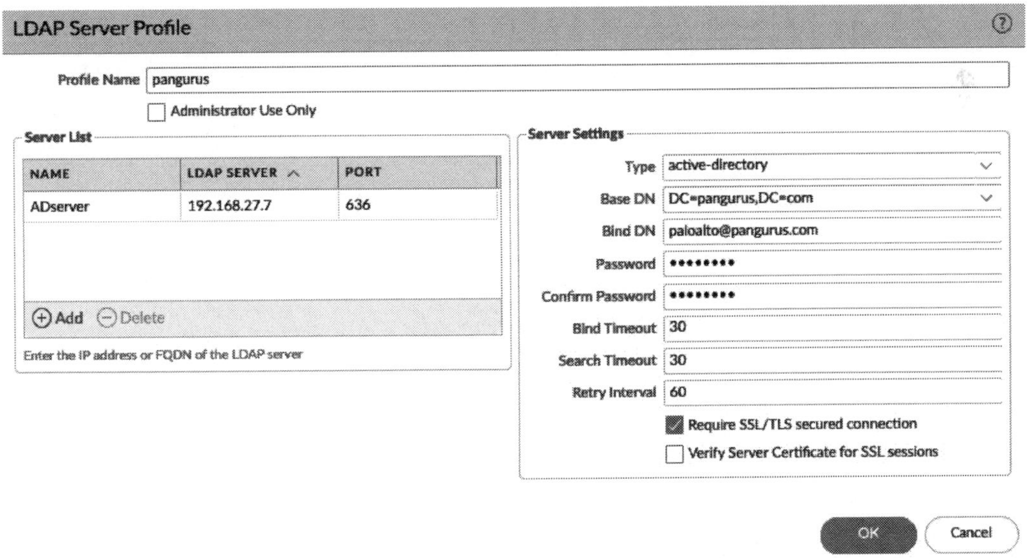

Figure 6.13 – The LDAP Server Profile window

If you have **Universal Groups**, do the following:

1. Create an LDAP server profile that connects to the root domain of the global catalog server on port 3268 or 3269 for SSL.

2. Create an LDAP server profile to connect to the root domain controllers on port 389 or 636 for SSL.

This will ensure that you are able to get information from all domains and subdomains.

The next step is to read the available domain tree and select which groups to monitor and keep user information on. Go to **Device | User Information | Group Mapping Settings** and create a new group mapping object:

1. Create a friendly name and set the LDAP profile you just created.

2. The update interval for the firewall to recheck user membership is 60 minutes, but it can be configured to be between 60s and 24h.

> **Important note**
>
> This interval means that when adding a new user to a group on AD, it may take up to an hour before the firewall is made aware of this change. Rather than setting the update interval really low, you can manually refresh the group memberships with one of the following commands:

```
> debug user-id refresh group-mapping group-mapping-name
<profilename>
```
```
> debug user-id refresh group-mapping all
```

3. In the **User Domain** field, you can optionally add a domain (NetBIOS, not FQDN) to override all user domains retrieved from the LDAP. This could be handy if User-ID picks up specific domains but LDAP has them listed differently. For a global catalog LDAP profile, leave this field empty as it would override all user domains.

4. There are also search filters available for group and user objects. (**sAMAccountName** or **userPrincipalName** (**UPN**) are useful filters for the user object.)

The **Server Profile** tab should look similar to the following screenshot:

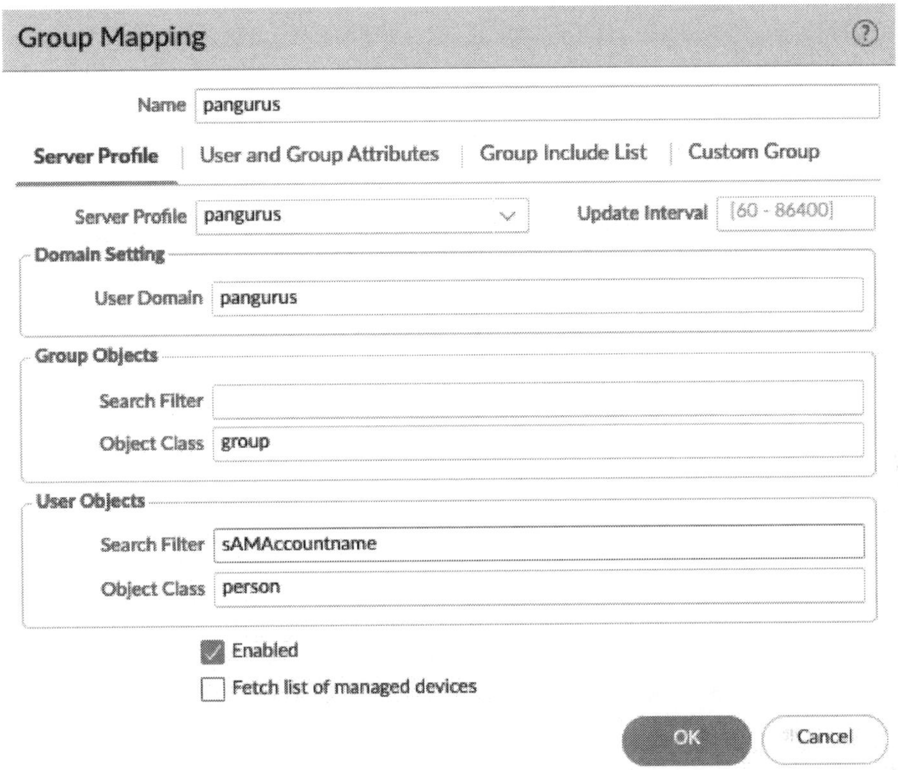

Figure 6.14 – Group mapping server profile

In the **User and Group Attributes** tab, you can fine-tune which attributes are included in the returned results. By default, sAMAccountName, email , and UPN are all set, with sAMAccountName set as the primary username. It is useful here to review which attribute is returned by your available User-ID sources and set that as the primary username (if the User-ID agent returns UPN usernames, set userPrincipalName as the primary username).

For Sun or e-directory type servers, the attribute will likely be uid.

In the **Group Include List** tab, you can add the groups you want to use in security rules. You can add all the groups you want to create specific rules for by expanding the base DN on the left-hand side and adding groups of interest to the right side, as shown in the following screenshot. There is no need to add groups that will not be used in security rules, nor the **cn=domain users** group. For rules that should apply to all users, the **known-user** user option is available in security rules to indicate any legitimately identified user:

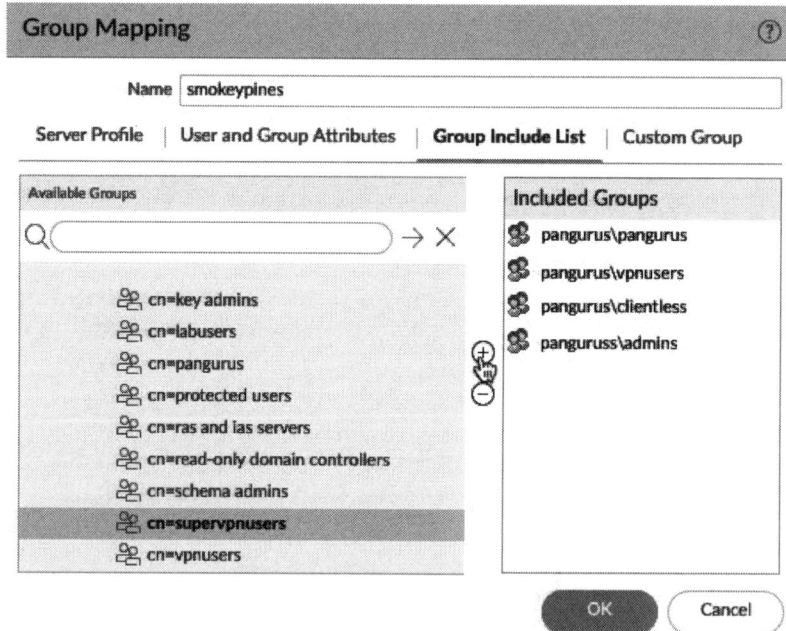

Figure 6.15 – Group Include List

If custom attributes are used within your organization, the **Custom Group** tab lets you set filters to identify and record usernames in these attributes. Make sure the attributes are indexed on the LDAP to expedite searches.

A useful command to verify which attributes are captured is show user user-attributes user all:

```
admin@firewall> show user user-attributes user all
Primary: example\tomfromit
Alt User Names:
1) example\tomfromit
```

```
2) tomfromit@example.com
Primary: example\jimfromhr
Alt User Names:
1) example\jimfromhr
2) jimfromhr@example.com
```

You can also list which users are in each group, to ensure that the data is being retrieved correctly. Retrieve a list for all available groups via show user group list. You can use both the DN and NetBIOS formats for the group via show user group name <groupname>:

```
admin@firewall> show user group name
cn=hr,cn=users,dc=example,dc=lab


short name:   example\hr
source type: proxy
source:       example.lab
[1      ] example\jimfromhr
```

> **Important note**
>
> The source type in the preceding code is set as **proxy**, because one of the User-ID agents is configured as an LDAP proxy. Without the User-ID acting as proxy, the source type would be as follows:
>
> source type: ldap

As you can see in the following screenshot, you can now build security rules where the source (or destination) **usergroup** can be selected to grant or deny a group of people access to a resource. The little icon next to the user object indicates whether the object is a group or a user. **known-users** indicates that the firewall will match any user, as long as they are identified:

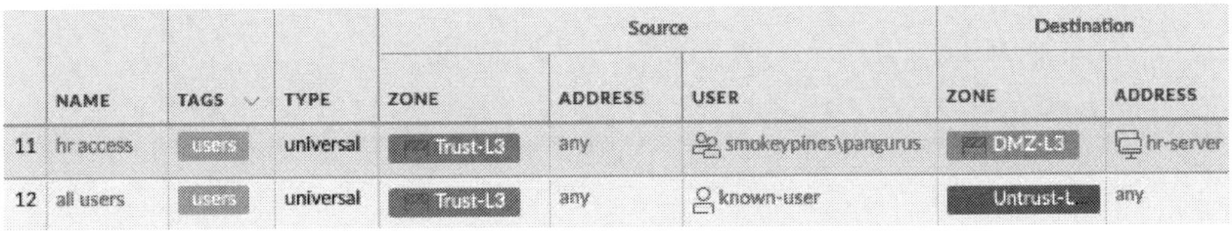

| | NAME | TAGS ⌄ | TYPE | Source | | | Destination | |
| | | | | ZONE | ADDRESS | USER | ZONE | ADDRESS |
|---|---|---|---|---|---|---|---|---|
| 11 | hr access | users | universal | Trust-L3 | any | smokeypines\pangurus | DMZ-L3 | hr-server |
| 12 | all users | users | universal | Trust-L3 | any | known-user | Untrust-L | any |

Figure 6.16 – Source user in security rules

You are now able to use group mapping to apply security rules to sets of users. In the next section, we'll take a look at captive portals, an alternative way to identify users that combines with authentication.

# Setting up a captive portal

A captive portal is a service that runs on the firewall and intercepts web sessions to have a user identify themselves. This can be a good addition to your user identification capabilities for unsupported operating systems that do not log on to the network, or guests that come into your network that you want to be able to identify.

It can also help pick up "strays"; for instance, a laptop may be used to roam a campus and hop SSIDs and Access Points, and it may be assigned a new IP address without generating a new logon event on Active Directory. At this moment, the user becomes unknown and a captive portal can be triggered to have the user log in manually.

To set up a captive portal, we will first need to be able to authenticate users, which we will cover in the next section.

## Authenticating users

To be able to authenticate users, we need to create an authentication profile that manages which protocol and server will be used. Create a new profile in **Device | Authentication Profile**:

1.  In the **Authentication** tab, set the desired type (**LDAP**, **local**, **RADIUS**, **TACACS**, **SAML**, or **Kerberos**).

2.  In **Server Profile**, select a matching server profile. You can create one from the drop-down by clicking the **New** link if you haven't created a profile yet. In most cases, this is just the IP and port of your server.

3.  By picking the type, all the common attributes for your preferred authentication method are prepopulated. Make changes if any are needed (for example, LDAP may need `userPrincipalName` instead of the default `sAMAccountName`).

4.  **Username Modifier** lets you change how the username is passed on to the authentication server. The default is `%USERINPUT%`, which passes along the user's exact input. `%USERDOMAIN%\%USERINPUT%` changes the user's input to `domain\username` and `%USERINPUT%@%USERDOMAIN%` changes it to `user@domain.ex`. This could be helpful if your users log on with all kinds of different usernames and your authentication server prefers a certain flavor.

5.  If your domain supports **Kerberos Single Sign-on**, enter the Kerberos domain and import the `kerberos` keytab so users are able to authenticate transparently. This URL can help you generate a keytab: `https://docs.microsoft.com/en-us/windows-server/administration/windows-commands/ktpass`.

For an LDAP profile, the **Authentication** tab should look similar to the following screenshot:

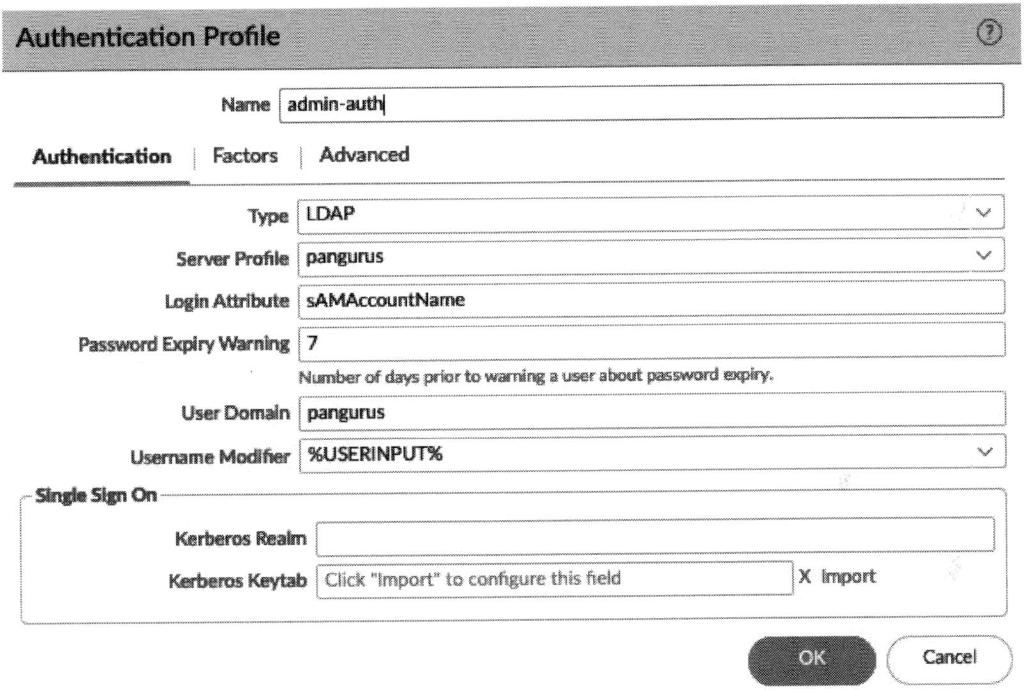

Figure 6.17 – Authentication Profile

6.  Optionally, you can enable MFA by checking **Enable Additional Authentication Factor** in the **Factors** tab and selecting which MFA provider to use.

7.  In the **Advanced** tab, you must select which users will be allowed to authenticate. If all users are allowed to authenticate, add an entry and set it to [**all**].

As per the following example, set **Account Lockout** to 4 failed attempts and set the lockout time to 30 to discourage brute-force attacks. A lockout time of 0 locks the account permanently until an administrator manually unlocks it. If **Failed Attempts** is 0, no lockout will occur:

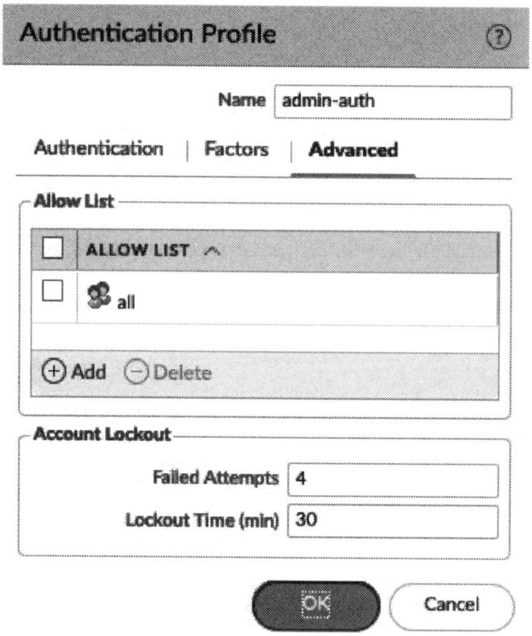

Figure 6.18 – Advanced Authentication Profile settings

We will also need to create an **SSL/TLS server profile** so that the captive portal landing page uses a trusted certificate.

You will first need to set up an appropriate certificate to use in the server profile:

1.  In **Device | Certificate Management | Certificates**, import a server certificate that's signed by your domain CA, or create a new self-signed server certificate that is signed by the self-signed root CA (the one we created for SSL decryption). This will ensure that the clients don't get a certificate error message if the root CA is properly trusted. *This certificate CN should be an FQDN* (cp.example.com) *that can be resolved on your internal DNS, or you should have the CN set to the IP address of the firewall interface* that will be used as the redirect destination. The generation page should look similar to the following screenshot:

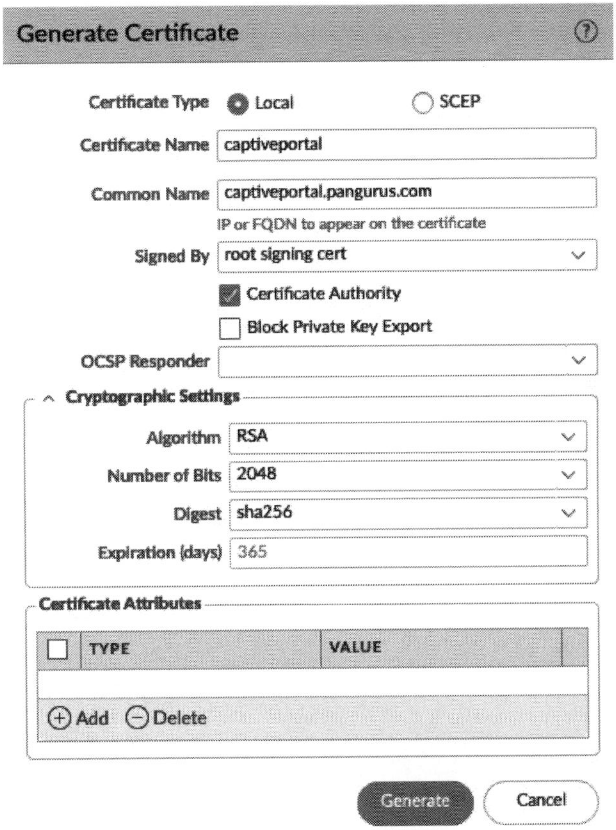

Figure 6.19 – Generating a server certificate for the captive portal

2.  In **Device | Certificate Management | SSL/TLS Service Profile**, create a new profile and name it captiveportal, add the captive portal certificate, and set **Min Version** to TLSv1.2, as you can see in the following screenshot:

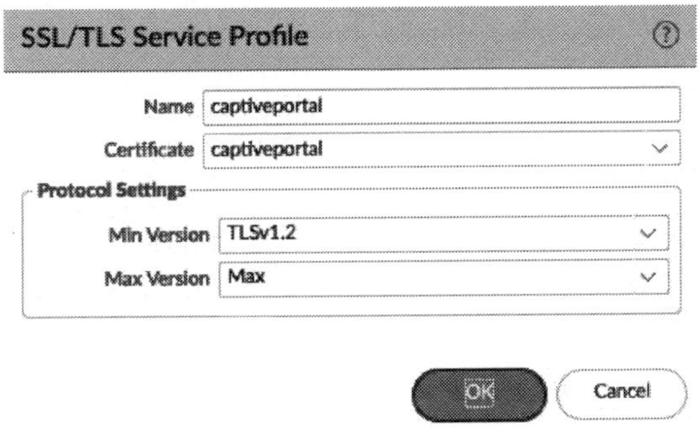

Figure 6.20 – Creating an SSL/TLS service profile

To accommodate a redirect page on the firewall interface, an **Interface Management Profile** needs to be created that has **Response Pages** enabled. Create one in **Network | Network Profiles | Interface Mgmt**:

3.  Set an identifiable name.

4.  Enable **Response Pages**.

5.  Enable **Ping** for troubleshooting.

The profile should look as follows:

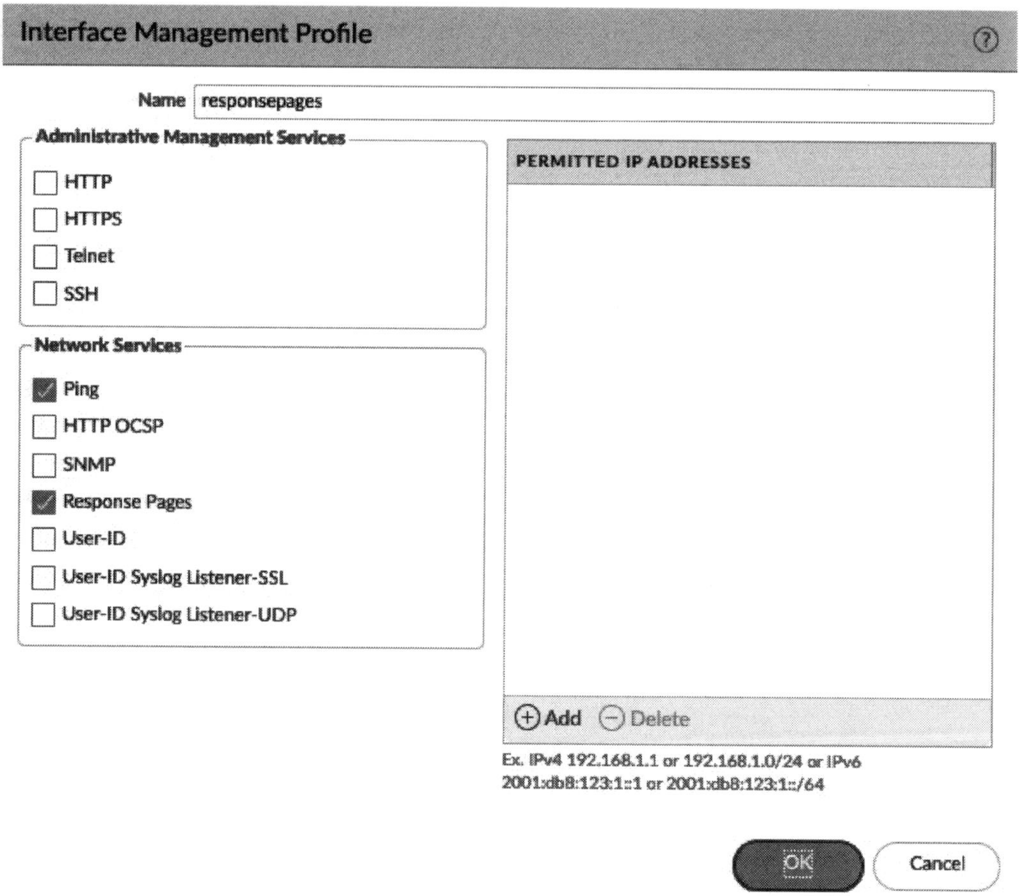

Figure 6.21 – Interface Management Profile

Attach the profile to the physical or loopback interfaces that will serve the captive portal by going into **Network | Interfaces | Interface | Advanced | Other Info | Management Profile** and adding the profile.

Lastly, **Enable User Identification** must be enabled in the zones associated with the interfaces that host user subnets. Go to **Network | Zones** and check the box in every zone that has users who need to be intercepted. Do **not** enable this on an external zone.

Now that all the preparations have been made, we can set up the captive portal.

## Configuring the captive portal

In **Device | User Identification | Captive Portal Settings**, edit the settings of the captive portal:

1. Make sure **Captive portal** is Enabled.

2. **Idle Timer** (the default is 15 minutes) indicates how long a user can remain idle before their session is expired, and **Timer** (with a 60-minute default) indicates how long a user session lasts before the user needs to reauthenticate.

3. The **GlobalProtect (GP)** port is used to help GP pop up an MFA authentication dialog if MFA is configured and the user has GP installed; the default port should not be changed.

4. Set the **SSL/TLS Service** profile.

5. Set the **Authentication** profile.

There are two modes to choose from, with **redirect** being the preferred one:

- **Transparent** mode intercepts the outbound session and impersonates the original destination URL while sending the user an HTTP 401 code to request authentication. Because the firewall is impersonating the remote site, the user may receive a certificate error.

- **Redirect** mode injects an HTTP 302 redirect message, prompting the browser to connect to the redirect host for further instructions. There, the user will be prompted for credentials or get authenticated transparently through NTLM or Kerberos. Redirect mode enhances user experience while roaming by supporting session cookies and enabling a longer session timer as the cookie travels with the user.

> **Important note**
> Both modes will also work with HTTPS sessions if you have SSL decryption enabled.

To set redirect mode, follow these steps:

1.  Select the **Redirect** radio button to Enable **Redirect** mode.

2.  Enable **Session Cookie** and **Roaming**.

3.  The default timeout of the session cookie is 1,440 minutes, which allows the user to roam for a day without needing to reauthenticate. Decrease this value if this is too long.

4.  Set the redirect host. This needs to match the certificate CN you created in the SSL/TLS service step, being either an FQDN that translates to the data plane interface or the IP of the interface.

Certificate authentication enables you to set a certificate profile with which to authenticate users. User browsers that are not able to present the appropriate client certificate will not be able to authenticate. This is recommended in a high-security network where only known hardware is allowed to authenticate.

NTLM authentication can be used as a fallback transparent authentication mechanism if one of the User-ID agents is set up as an NTLM proxy. It is recommended to use Kerberos as transparent authentication instead (by means of the Kerberos SSO keytab) because Kerberos is a more secure authentication protocol.

Both Kerberos SSO and NTLM depend on the browser supporting either authentication method. If the client browser doesn't support these methods, the user will be presented with a web form to authenticate.

Your captive portal configuration should look as follows:

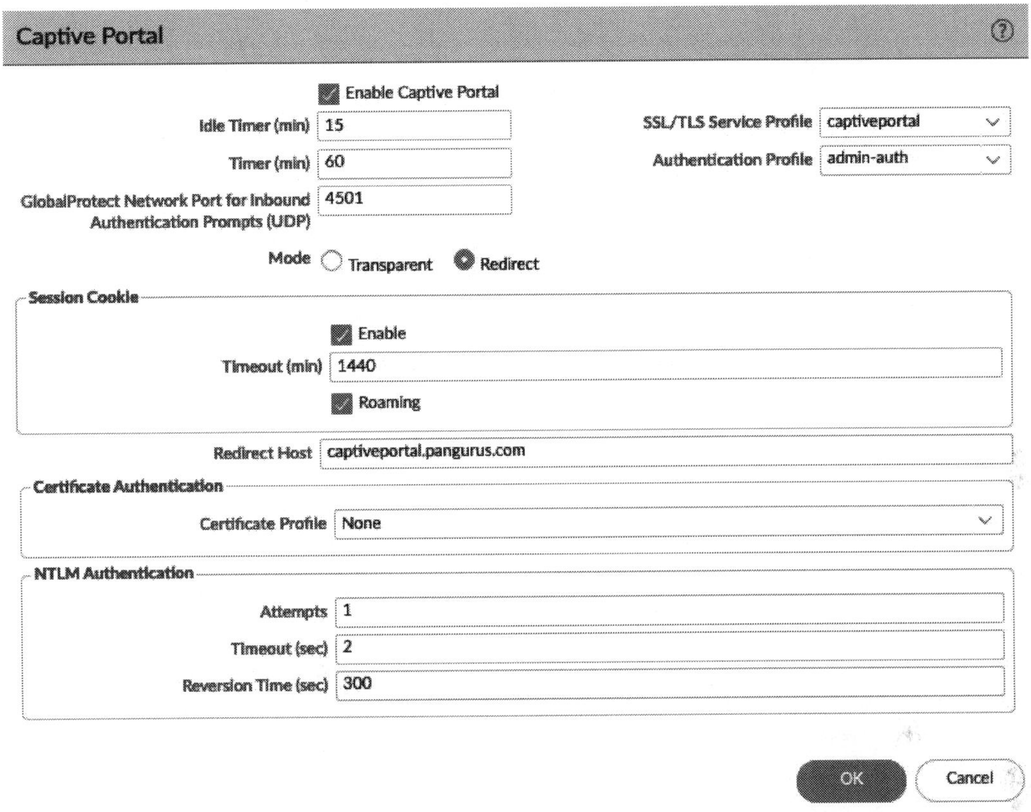

Figure 6.22 – Captive Portal configuration

The last step is to set up authentication rules in **Policies | Authentication**.

Rules are always evaluated from top to bottom, so the most specific rules should be at the top. If you want to allow users transparent authentication through NTLM or Kerberos, create the rule for this first:

1.  Set a friendly name and description.

2.  In the source, define the zones where users reside that could need captive portal authentication.

3. In the **User** field, you have several options. Select **Unknown**.

   **Any** includes all traffic to be intercepted, including already known users.

   **Pre-logon** includes remote users who are connected using the GlobalProtect pre-logon and have not logged in to their client system.

   **Known-users** includes traffic for which the firewall already has a user-to-IP mapping (this can add a factor of **authorization** to accessing a certain resource).

   **Unknown** includes traffic for which no user-to-IP mapping exists. *This is the main method to identify users who were not picked up by regular User-ID.*

   **Select** will only include traffic from specific users or groups (this could be used to specifically target guests while leaving employees alone).

4. In the **Service/URL** category, only the `http` service is included by default. Add `service-https`, if you have SSL decryption enabled, and any other ports that might be useful. The **URL** category can be added if User-ID is mandatory for only specific URL categories or if explicit authorization is required for a category.

5. In **Action**, set `default-browser-challenge`, which will use the Kerberos keytab if available in the authentication profile or will use NTLM via a User-ID agent.

   If needed, you can also create a new authentication enforcement profile with a different authentication profile. This overrides the authentication profile used in the captive portal.

   Your rule should look similar to the following screenshot:

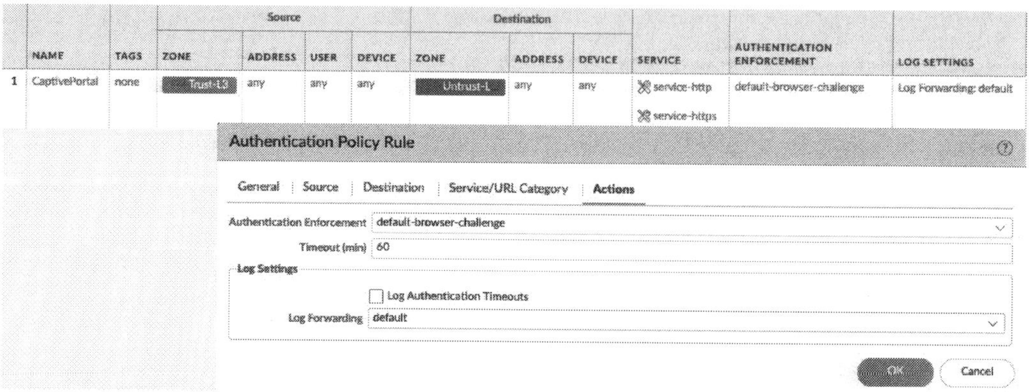

Figure 6.23 – Authentication policy rule

Next, repeat *steps 1* through *4* and set the authentication enforcement to `default-webform`, which will present the user with a landing page to enter credentials.

If any address or subnet does not trigger a captive portal intercept (this could be a remediation server or guest proxy), repeat *steps 1* through *4* and set the authentication enforcement to `default-no-captive-portal` and move it to the top of the rulebase.

Depending on which interface you associated the captive portal to, and which zone the users are connecting from, you may need to configure a security rule to allow these connections. You will find that the captive portal uses one of these ports:

- TCP `6080` is accessed by the client for NTLM authentication.
- TCP `6081`, if the captive portal was configured without an SSL/TLS service profile.
- TCP `6082`, when the captive portal is configured with a proper profile.

> **Important note**
> With a little creativity, the captive portal can be active on several interfaces: the certificate needs to be set to an FQDN, each individual interface has the management profile enabled for response pages, and clients in each subnet are served a different IP (by DNS) for the associated redirect host.

# Using an API for User-ID

We saw earlier that you can forward syslogs to the User-ID agent to extract user information, but for those cases where you can't get the desired information from syslogs, you can also use an API to automate user-to-IP mapping, or manually add and delete user mappings.

You will first need to get an authentication key. Make sure the administrator account you are going to use for these operations has API access.

To get a key, you can use this URL in a browser:

```
https://<YourFirewall>/
api/?type=keygen&user=<Username>&password=<Password>
```

Alternatively, you can use cURL at the command line:

```
curl -k -X GET 'https://<YourFirewall>/
api/?type=keygen&user=<username>&password=<password>
```

That would give you the following output:

```
<response status="success">
<result>
<key>
LUFRPT1TWFhUNWUk5N1Fjd3ZnMzh3MX1TOVJyb0kxSG5IWk5QTkdPNw==
</key>
</result>
</response>
```

You can now use this key in combination with any API command to change things on the firewall or request information. For example, you can request a list of users by using the following URL in your browser:

```
https://10.0.0.2//api/?type=op&cmd=<show><user><u
ser-ids><all></all></user-ids></user></show>&key=
LUFRPT1TWFhUNWUk5N1Fjd3ZnMzh3MX1TOVJyb0kxSG5IWk5QTkdPNw==
```

Alternatively, you can use cURL at the command line:

```
curl -k -X GET 'https://10.0.0.2//api/?type=op&cmd=<show>
<user><user-ids><all></all></user-ids></user></show>&key=
LUFRPT1TWFhUNWUk5N1Fjd3ZnMzh3MX1TOVJyb0kxSG5IWk5QTkdPNw=='
<response status="success"><result><![CDATA[
User Name                              Vsys    Groups
-----------------------------------------------------------------
----
example\tomfromit                      vsys1
cn=it,cn=users,dc=example,dc=com
example\jimfromhr                      vsys1
cn=hr,cn=users,dc=example,dc=com

Total: 3
* : Custom Group
```

> **Important note**
> You can browse through all the available API commands by logging in to your firewall and then replacing the URL with `https://<YourFirewall>/api`.

To add users, you can use the following command:

```
curl -F key=<APIkey> --form file=@<file>
"https://<YourFirewall>/api/?type=user-id"
```

For the file that will be used as the source, use the following syntax to add a user:

```
<uid-message>
<version>1.0</version>
<type>update</type>
<payload>
<login>
<entry user="domain\user" ip="x.x.x.x" timeout="60">
</login>
</payload>
</uid-message>
```

This is the syntax used to remove a user:

```
<uid-message>
<type>update</type>
<version>1.0</version>
<payload>
<logout>
<entry user="domain\user1" ip="x.x.x.x">
</logout>
</payload>
</uid-message>
```

You can add and remove users in the same update by simply adding `login` and `logout` syntax inside the payload.

You can add or remove multiple users at once by adding entries inside the login or logout elements:

```
<uid-message>
<type>update</type>
<version>1.0</version>
<payload>
<login>
```

```
<entry user="domain\user1" ip="x.x.x.x" timeout="60">
</login>
<logout>
<entry user="domain\user3" ip="y.y.y.y">
<entry user="domain\user3" ip="z.z.z.z">
</logout>
</payload>
</uid-message>
```

You can also add users to group(s):

```
<uid-message>
<version>1.0</version>
<type>update</type>
<payload>
<groups>
<entry name="groupA">
<members>
<entry name="user1"/>
</members>
</entry>
<entry name="groupB">
<members>
<entry name="user2"/>
</members>
</entry>
</groups>
</payload>
</uid-message>
```

In this section, you learned how to leverage APIs to control the creation and deletion of user-to-IP mapping entries and to add or remove users from groups.

# User credential detection

With phishing being a significant attack vector, user education is a very hot topic on many corporations' cybersecurity awareness programs. Being able to prevent users from sharing their credentials on an untrusted website is a good second line of defense in case a user does slip up.

As you can see in the following screenshot, in the URL filtering security profile, there is a column called **User Credential Submission**. Any categories set to `block` will not allow users to submit credentials.

A user will not be allowed to log on if a site is categorized as belonging to the `malware` category and if `malware` is set to `block` for USER CREDENTIAL SUBMISSION.

Any category set to `continue` will first warn the user that they are submitting credentials to a site and will require acknowledgment of their actions. Any category set to `alert` (with logging) or `allow` will let the user submit their credentials:

> **Important note**
> SSL decryption is required to be able to look inside a flow and intercept login credentials submitted by the user for inspection.

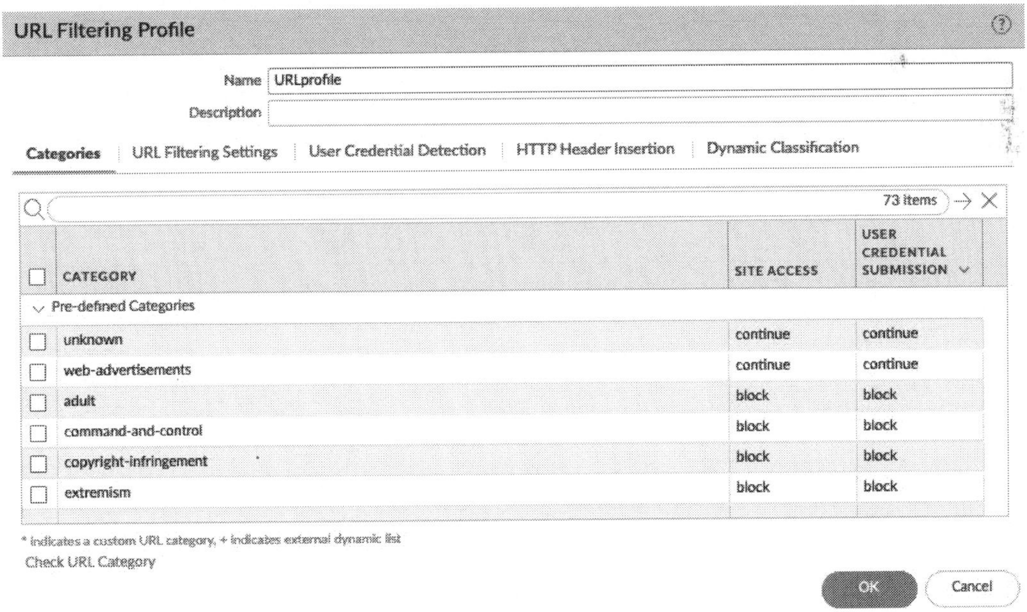

## URL Filtering Profile

Name | URLprofile
Description |

Categories | URL Filtering Settings | User Credential Detection | HTTP Header Insertion | Dynamic Classification

73 items

| | CATEGORY | SITE ACCESS | USER CREDENTIAL SUBMISSION ∨ |
|---|---|---|---|
| | ∨ Pre-defined Categories | | |
| ☐ | unknown | continue | continue |
| ☐ | web-advertisements | continue | continue |
| ☐ | adult | block | block |
| ☐ | command-and-control | block | block |
| ☐ | copyright-infringement | block | block |
| ☐ | extremism | block | block |

\* indicates a custom URL category, + indicates external dynamic list
Check URL Category

OK    Cancel

Figure 6.24 – The URL Filtering Profile page

Take this one step further and access the User Credential Detection tab to enable the detection of actual corporate user credentials. This will help distinguish between users logging on to Facebook with their private account and those doing so with their corporate emails, as well as helping to distinguish whether they are using the same password as they do in the corporate environment.

If the submitted credentials do not match the detection method result, the user will be allowed to log on, else the USER CREDENTIAL SUBMISSION action is applied.

There are three options available, and all methods require User-ID to be already set up on the firewall:

> **Important note**
> Verify that the user-to-IP mapping uses the same format as the primary username in LDAP (for example, if the primary username is UserPrincipalName, the user-to-IP mapping should also display UPN usernames).

- **Use IP User Mapping**: This lets the firewall compare the credential submitted to the website to the username in the user-to-IP mapping that it gets from User-ID. If a match is detected, the URL filtering profile will apply action defined in the USER CREDENTIAL SUBMISSION column.

- **Use Group Mapping**: The firewall uses User-ID group mapping to match the submitted username to a username known in the group mapping profile. This method only matches usernames against LDAP group membership.

- **Use Domain Credential Filter**: This enables the firewall to verify the username and password of a submitted credential and check whether they belong to the logged-in user. This method is the most thorough as it can also detect password matches, but it does require that a User-ID agent and a User-ID credential service add-on (UaCredInstall64-x.x.x-x.msi from the support portal software updates) are installed on a **Read-Only Domain Controller (RODC)**. Since you must install these agents on a separate domain controller, do not use the User-ID agent to collect user-to-IP mappings. The credential service add-on creates a bloom filter for all the usernames and passwords that the firewall can periodically fetch from the User-ID agent to then match credential submissions. Usernames and passwords are not saved on the firewall.

Each method allows you to set a log severity when a valid credential is detected. By default, URL filtering logs have a severity of `informational`; set the severity to `medium` or higher.

As shown in the following screenshot, the **Credential Detected** column can be enabled in the URL filtering log to reveal whether corporate credentials were matched in browsing sessions:

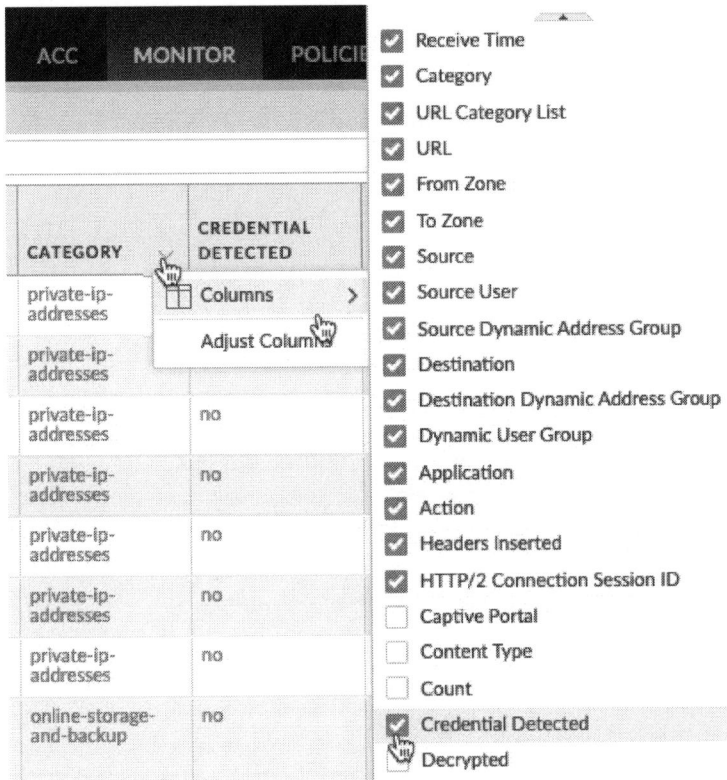

Figure 6.25 – Enabling the CREDENTIAL DETECTED column

Implementing this feature will ensure your users do not accidentally or deliberately share corporate credential information outside your network, and will discourage the use of corporate credentials for personal sites.

# Summary

In this chapter, you learned how to set up the User-ID agent and the TS Agent software agents on a server, and also how to properly configure the agentless configuration on a firewall. You also learned how LDAP groups can be leveraged to categorize users and apply security and which user attributes can be used to tailor the configuration to your needs. You also learned methods to prevent users from accidentally submitting corporate credentials to untrusted website categories

In the next chapter, we will learn how to manage and consolidate configuration for multiple firewalls using Panorama.

# 7
# Managing Firewalls through Panorama

In this chapter, we will learn about Panorama, a central management platform that enables an administrator to manage firewalls located in different locations or in the cloud in real time. You will learn how to create shared objects and policies, as well as use device groups to add some region- or purpose-based policies that can be deployed to multiple similar firewalls. You will also learn how to manage logs and push content updates from one single location and keep track of your **inventory**.

In this chapter, we're going to cover the following main topics:

- Setting up Panorama
- Device groups
- Setting up templates and template stacks
- Panorama management

# Technical requirements

For this chapter, you are expected to have a basic understanding of how to manage and maintain **Virtual Machines** (**VMs**) on any of the major hypervisor technologies (KVM, NSX, Hyper-V, ESX, and so on) or cloud providers (Azure or Amazon Web Services).

A copy of the Panorama configuration we touch on in this chapter can be found at https://github.com/PacktPublishing/Mastering-Palo-Alto-Networks.

# Setting up Panorama

Before you get started, you will first need to decide how you want to deploy Panorama as there are many options available that can influence your choices. Panorama can be deployed as a physical appliance or a VM image, both locally and in the cloud. All of these options have their advantages over the others. A physical appliance can either be deployed as a Panorama instance or as a log collector, which can be bundled and spread out to make it more resilient and bandwidth-efficient, while keeping physical control over logs. VMs are very easy to deploy and run on nearly all common hypervisors that are likely already available, so no hardware is needed to deploy them. Cloud-based Panorama allows the admin optimal access from any location for management and firewall access.

The first step is to configure Panorama so that it can manage firewalls.

## Initial Panorama configuration

Panorama can be deployed in a number of virtual environments, including KVM, NSX, Hyper-V, ESX, and cloud providers such as Amazon Web Services and Microsoft Azure. So, for example, you can simply download the Panorama **Open Virtual Appliance** (**OVA**) image from https://support.paloaltonetworks.com, in the **Software** section, and deploy it in a VMware ESXi environment, as in the following screenshots:

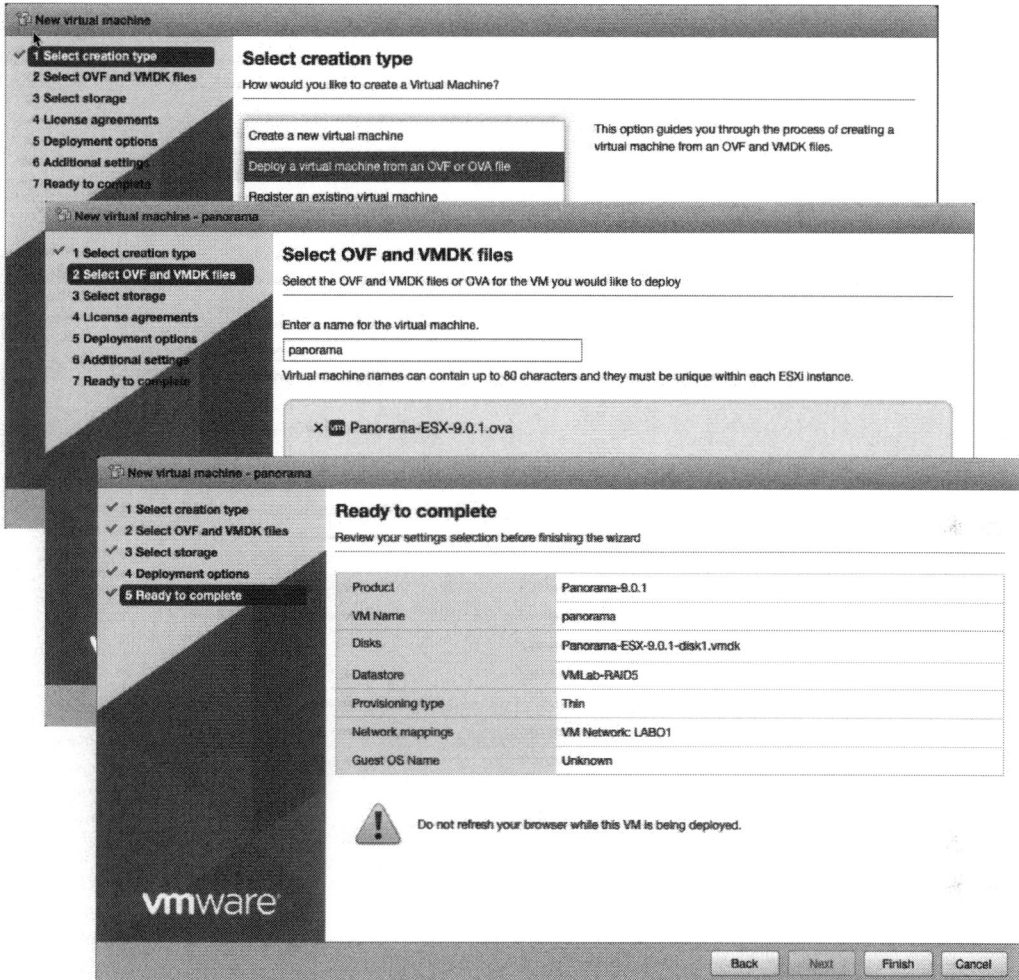

Figure 7.1 – Deploying a Panorama OVA in ESXi

Deploying one of the prepackaged VMs has the advantage that you don't need to choose the correct guest OS or select the correct number of CPUs or the amount of RAM; all these parameters are taken care of automatically.

Once the deployment is complete, start your virtual appliance and register Panorama in the support portal using the **UUID** and **CPUID**.

Here is a quick checklist of the things that you'll need to set so that Panorama is in good working condition:

1.  Go to **Panorama | Setup | Management** (shown in the following screenshot):

    --Set **Hostname**, **Domain** (`example.com`), and **Login Banner**.

    --Set **SSL/TLD Service Profile** with minimum version set to `TLS1.2`.

    --Ensure that the serial number you received after registration has been set properly:

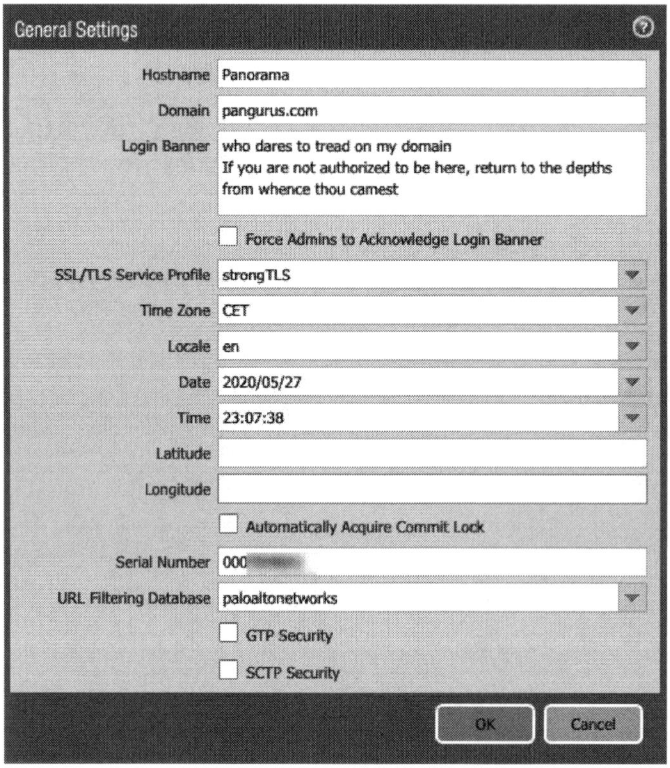

Figure 7.2 – The Management page's General Settings

2.  Review **Secure Communication Settings**. By enabling **Customize Secure Server Communication**, you can manually set **SSL/TLS Service Profile** and **Certificate Profile**, and then create a list of identifiers that can be used for communication between the firewalls and Panorama, as you can see in the following screenshot. This requires the firewalls and Panorama to be provisioned with an SSL/TLS service profile that uses certificates signed by the same root **Certificate Authority (CA)** so that they can establish trust. Currently, up to 25 identifiers can be added:

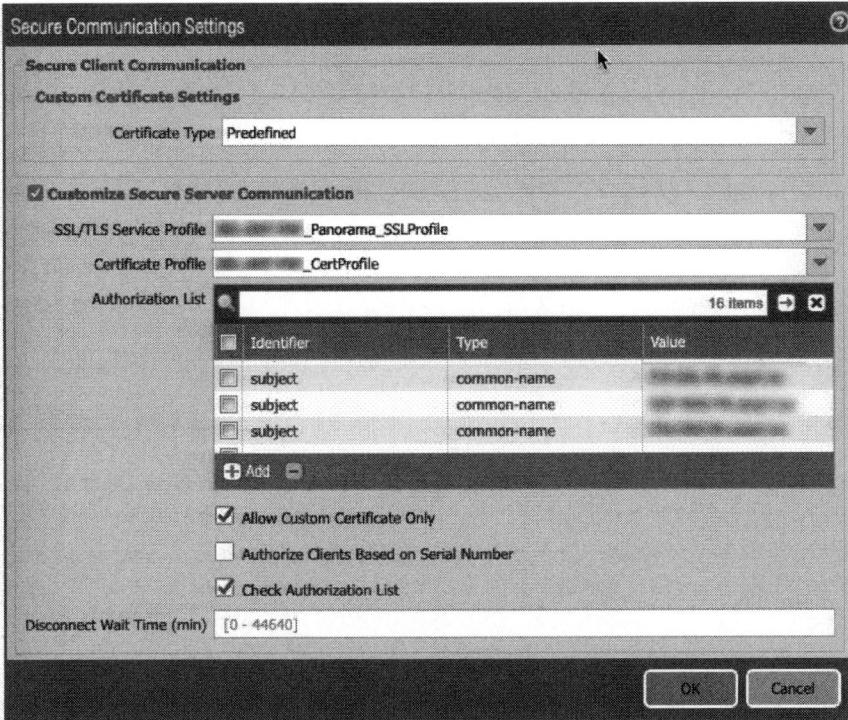

Figure 7.3 – Secure Communication Settings

The firewall side will look similar to the following screenshot:

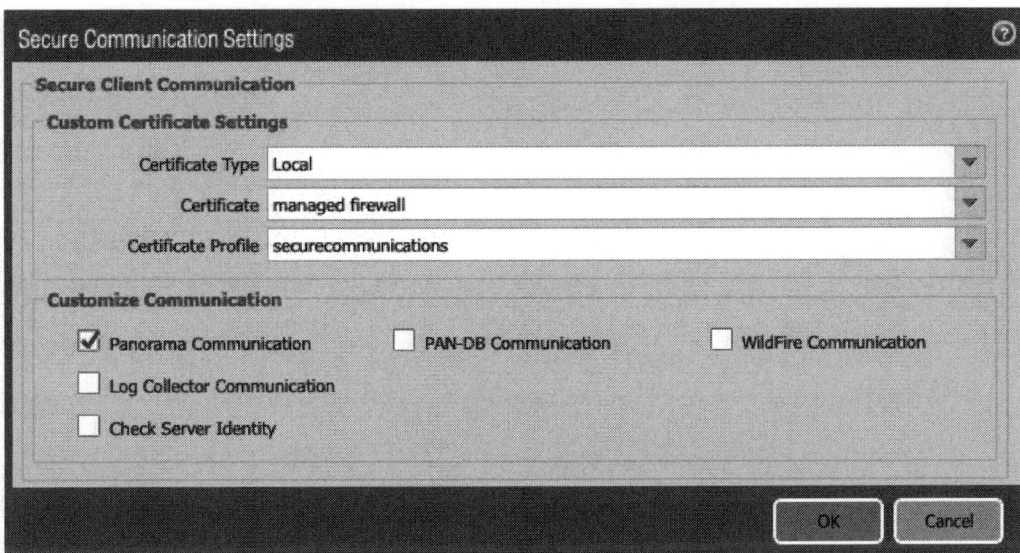

Figure 7.4 – Firewall secure communications

3.  Go to **Panorama | Setup | Services**, as in the following screenshot:

    --Set the DNS and NTP servers.

    --You can change the FQDN object refresh interval and set a timer to expire stale FQDN entries. By default, FQDN objects are refreshed every 1800 seconds and stale entries (entries that can't be updated) are not timed out:

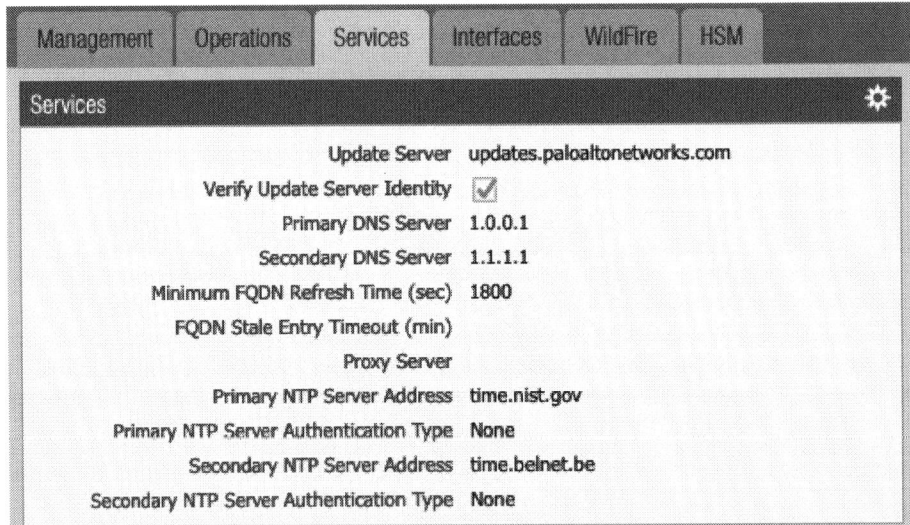

| Management | Operations | Services | Interfaces | WildFire | HSM |
|---|---|---|---|---|---|

| Services | ⚙ |
|---|---|
| Update Server | updates.paloaltonetworks.com |
| Verify Update Server Identity | ☑ |
| Primary DNS Server | 1.0.0.1 |
| Secondary DNS Server | 1.1.1.1 |
| Minimum FQDN Refresh Time (sec) | 1800 |
| FQDN Stale Entry Timeout (min) | |
| Proxy Server | |
| Primary NTP Server Address | time.nist.gov |
| Primary NTP Server Authentication Type | None |
| Secondary NTP Server Address | time.belnet.be |
| Secondary NTP Server Authentication Type | None |

Figure 7.5 – Panorama services

> **Important note**
> Beware of timing out stale entries if, for example, only one FQDN object exists in a security rule as the source or destination. If it goes stale, timing out may cause unexpected behavior as this would remove the object from the security rule at the data-plane level.

4.  Go to **Panorama | Setup | Interfaces**, as in the following screenshot:

    --In the **Management** interface, set **IP address**, **Netmask**, and **Default Gateway**.

    --If Panorama will also be reached over the internet, also add a **Public IP Address** value.

    --If Panorama will be used to redistribute User-to-IP mappings, you need to enable **User-ID** here.

    --**Permitted IP Addresses** determines which IP addresses are allowed to connect to the management interface. If you choose to set restrictions, make sure to add the firewall IP addresses here as well.

--Additional interfaces can be enabled and used to take some load off the management interface or provide an **Out-of-Band (OoB)** connection for certain services, such as **Device Management**, **Collector Group Communication**, and **Device Deployment** (pushing out software and updates to firewalls):

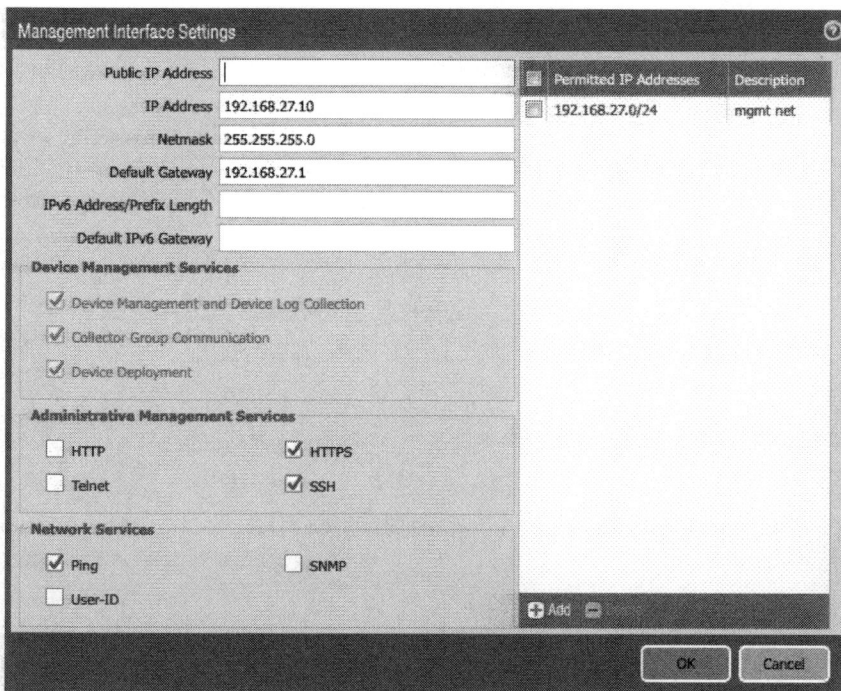

Figure 7.6 – Panorama interface

Now that Panorama is set up, the next step is to make sure it can receive logs from the firewalls.

# Panorama logging

Once deployed, Panorama can be configured to operate in one of two modes: **Panorama** mode and **management-only** mode.

By default, the VM is deployed in **management-only** mode. In this mode, the following conditions apply:

- In **management-only** mode, the appliance does not support receiving logs forwarded by firewalls directly.

- Either a log collector group using Panorama appliances (M-100 through M-600) needs to be configured or cloud logging (Cortex Data Lake) needs to be enabled.

The second operational mode, **Panorama** mode, has the advantage of being more scalable for medium environments:

- Panorama can have 1 to 12 partitions of 2 TB each, up to a total of 24 TB in RAID (10) configuration.

- Additional storage can be added by deploying logging appliances and configuring log collectors.

Panorama deployments that have been around for longer may still be in **Legacy** mode, which has been deprecated:

- Logs are stored in a single log partition that is part of the system disk (sda).

- The default log partition can be replaced by adding a second disk (sdb) of up to 8 TB (pre-ESXi 5.5, this capacity was limited to 2 TB).

> **Important note**
>
> **Legacy** mode was discontinued in PAN-OS 9.0 as a configurable mode and only exists on Panorama instances that were installed on PAN-OS 8.1 or earlier. Upgrading to PAN-OS 9.0 from **Legacy** mode will retain this mode, but once the system is changed to **Panorama** or **management-only** mode, it can no longer be reverted.

One drawback is that an existing log partition cannot be expanded, so if you initially add a 2 TB drive and later need a larger one, you will need to replace the 2 TB one with a larger one. **Legacy** mode also supports log collector configuration, using physical appliances as log collectors.

If you want to receive logs directly on a Panorama appliance, you will need to switch to **Panorama** mode. You can switch from any mode to **management-only** or **Panorama** mode, but you can't go back to **Legacy** mode once you have changed to either of the new modes:

```
> request system system-mode management-only
> request system system-mode Panorama
```

Once you execute this command to change the system mode, you will be prompted to confirm it by pressing *Y* if you are sure, after which Panorama will reboot to the new mode.

To be able to add disks, Panorama needs to be shut down. You can add one disk up to 8 TB for **Legacy** mode and any size larger than 2 TB for **Panorama** mode. A **Panorama** mode VM will automatically partition any disk into 2 TB partitions, so you can add a 24 TB (or smaller) disk at once and **Panorama** mode will automatically split it into 12 2 TB partitions. **management-only** mode will not take any actions with disks added to its virtual appliance.

There are three main methods for collecting logs:

- Using **Legacy** mode
- Using **Cortex Data Lake**
- Using log collectors

In **Legacy** mode, nothing needs to be set; Panorama will simply register logs to its local database.

**Cortex Data Lake** logs to the cloud. The advantage is that it is scalable, located virtually *near* your firewalls so that you don't need to deploy log collectors all over the place, and depending on your log volume, it may cost less than buying appliances or backhauling logs over expensive WAN links.

Enabling it is fairly simple:

1. Make sure Panorama is already registered and has a valid support license by going to https://support.paloaltonetworks.com and then clicking on **Assets**.
2. Acquire a cloud services auth code from your sales contact.
3. Activate the Cortex Data Lake service via **Assets | Cloud Services | Activate Cloud Service Auth Code**.
4. You will be asked for the Panorama Serial Number and logging region. Enter it.
5. Once you agree, the license will automatically be added to Panorama.
6. Next, click on **Generate OTP**.
7. Select **Panorama** and copy the **One Time Password (OTP)** to the clipboard (or to a text editor, as we will need it in a moment).
8. Access your Panorama instance and navigate to **Panorama | Licenses** to select **Retrieve license keys from license server**.

9.  Access **Panorama | Plugins** and click on **Check Now**. Download the latest **Cloud_ Service** plugin and then proceed to install it.

10. A new item will have appeared in the navigation to the left, just below **Plugins**, called **Cloud Services**. Access the **Status** submenu and paste the OTP, then click **Verify**.

You can check whether connectivity with Cortex Data Lake is successful by reviewing **Panorama | Cloud Services | Status**.

Lastly, log collectors need to be deployed before they can be added to Panorama. If Panorama was set to **Panorama** mode, it will also function as a log collector. You will need to add the local Panorama instance as a log collector before managed firewalls can forward logs to it. Additionally, you can add a Panorama HA peer and additional M appliances to increase the capacity and fault tolerance.

Before you can add an M appliance as a log collector, make sure to set it up beforehand:

> **Important note:**
> The M appliance does not have a web interface enabled unless it is configured in **Panorama** mode. Connect to its console via terminal emulation, TTY (9600-8-N-1), or use SSH on the **management port**.

1.  Configure the management interface. Set **DNS** and **NTP**.

2.  Register the device and add licenses.

3.  Set the system to logger mode:

```
> request system system-mode logger
```

4.  Build RAID pairs by adding A1, A2, B1, B2, and so on, depending on the number of disks in your system:

```
> request system raid add A1
> request system raid add A2
> show system raid detail
Disk Pair A       Available
Status            clean
```

5.  Add the Panorama IP. Add both IPs if you have a Panorama cluster, and click **commit**:

```
# set deviceconfig system Panorama-server <IP1> Panorama-
server-2 <IP2>
# commit
```

In **Panorama | Managed Collectors**, you can add all your Panorama and M- appliances:

1.  Enter the Panorama or log collector serial number and the IP address. If the Panorama instance is part of a cluster, add the HA peer's IP as `Panorama Server IP 2`. If you add the local Panorama serial number, Panorama will remove all the additional fields as it already has the details, as in the following screenshot:

Figure 7.7 – Local Panorama log collector

2.  If you are adding an external log collector, the dialog window will look similar to the following screenshot. Fill out the log collector details and the management properties that it should be configured with once it connects to Panorama. In the **Authentication** tab, set the admin password:

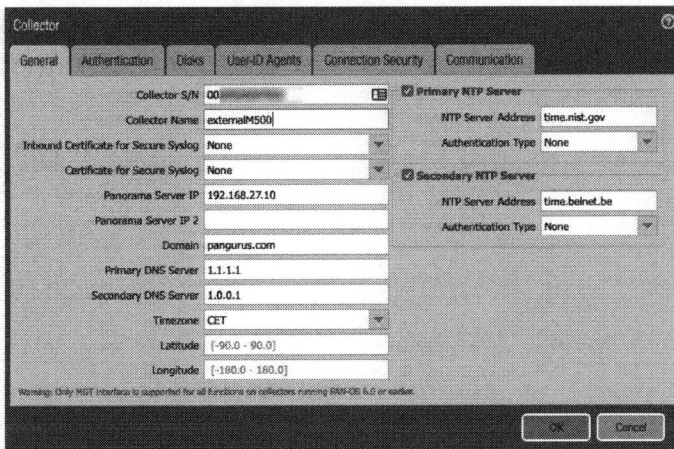

Figure 7.8 – External log collector

3.  You can add the DNS and NTP settings you want the device to use if these have not been configured yet.

4.  Click **OK** and then **Commit to Panorama** and **Push to Devices**. This will enable Panorama to retrieve the disk pairs.

5.  If you set up **Secure Communication** earlier, set up the *client* side of the log collector in the **Communication** tab.

6.  Reopen the collector and under the **Disks** tab, add all available disk pairs, as in the following screenshot. Some devices will only have a single disk, while larger platforms may have up to 12. Click **OK** and **Commit to Panorama**, then **Push to Devices**:

Figure 7.9 – Adding disks to the log collector

> **Important note**
>
> Panorama uses **Commit to Panorama**, which writes the configuration to Panorama's running config. The **Push to Devices** option will write configuration, such as templates and policy, to managed devices. **Commit and Push** does both actions is one job. I recommend doing both steps separately.

7.  Repeat this for all additional log collectors. If you add more than one log collector, bundle them by creating a new collector group in **Device | Collector Groups**.

8.  Add the log collector(s) to the new group, as in the following screenshot:

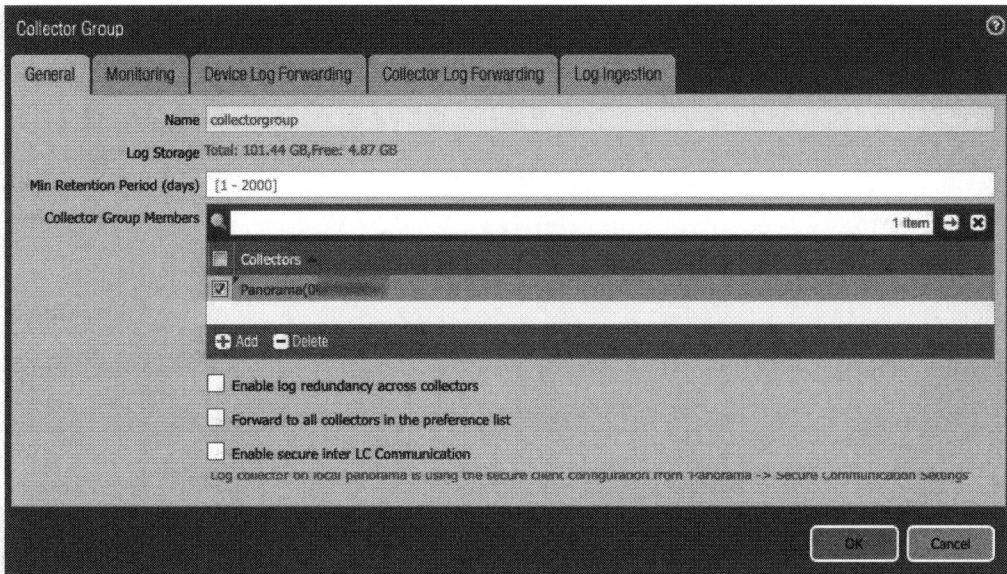

Figure 7.10 – Adding log collectors to a log collector group

9.    Click **OK** and then **Commit and Push**.

You have now learned the differences between the physical and virtual Panorama appliances and can start up Panorama from scratch. You can also choose which logging solution is best suited to your needs. In the next section, we will learn how to add managed firewalls and create rulebases for groups of firewalls and individual devices.

# Device groups

Before we can start managing devices, they first need to be connected to Panorama. On the Panorama side, the device is added by its serial number, and on the firewall side, the Panorama IP address needs to be added. This means the firewall always makes a connection out to the Panorama server. Any connections originating from Panorama are backchanneled over the **continuous** connection that a firewall has with its management station.

There are two TCP ports that are used for communication:

- TCP\3978 is a bidirectional connection initiated by the firewall and used for all communications between the firewall and Panorama or collectors. Panorama uses this connection to context switch to a firewall or push a configuration over while the firewall sends logs through the connection. Collectors also use it to connect to Panorama. (Log collectors communicate via TCP\28270 with collector group members.)

- TCP\28443 is used by managed devices to retrieve content and software updates from Panorama.

The first thing we'll need to do is add the managed devices to Panorama and set up groups to manage them.

# Adding managed devices

You can add any firewall that needs to be managed by Panorama by its serial number in **Panorama | Managed Devices | Summary**, as in the following screenshot. If you check the **Association** checkbox, you are taken to the next page, where you can assign the new firewall to a device group, template stack, collector group, or collector, as well as enable **Push on First Connect**, which automatically pushes out any configurations associated with it when the device connects to Panorama for the first time (be very careful with this last option as it could push an incomplete configuration).

For now, just skip the **Association** checkbox as we have not set up device groups or templates:

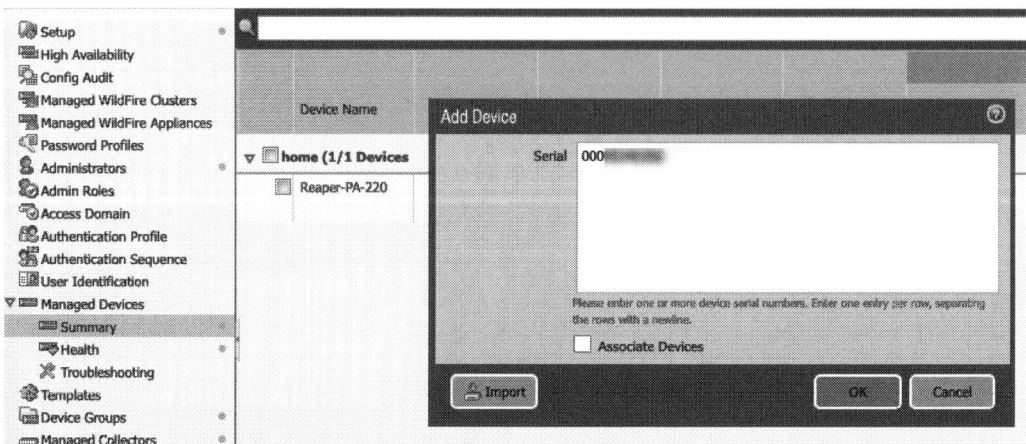

Figure 7.11 – Adding new managed devices

Then, in the individual firewalls, go to **Device | Setup | Management | Panorama Settings** and add the IP to your primary and secondary Panorama instances, as in the following screenshot (if you intend on having a Panorama cluster deployed). Be mindful of whether you use a public or private IP depending on how the firewall connects to Panorama:

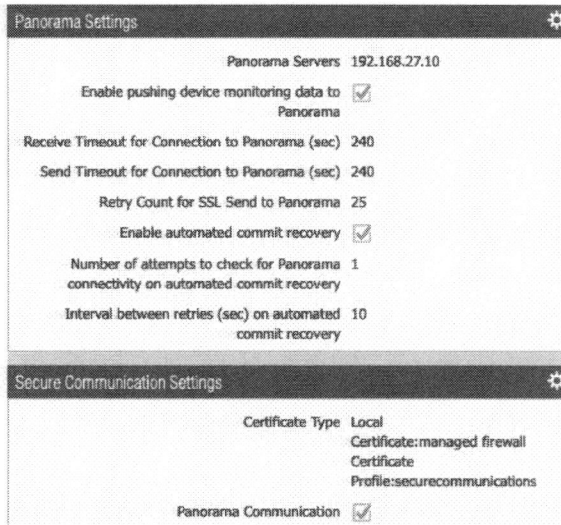

Figure 7.12 – Adding the Panorama configuration to the firewall

As you can see in the following screenshot, if you added managed devices that are in a HA cluster, Panorama can link them if you check the **Group HA Peers** checkbox. This will visually not only help identify HA pairs but also let you reassociate both peers at the same time, or push updates to both peer members simultaneously:

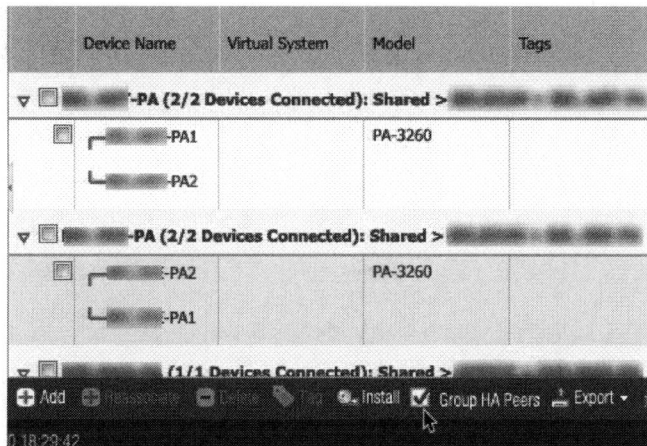

Figure 7.13 – Group HA Peers in managed devices

You can now add managed devices. The next thing we'll need to do is create the device groups.

# Preparing device groups

Next, we will create device groups that will contain firewalls by their characteristics or locations.

> **Important note**
>
> The main purpose of device groups is to bundle rule bases and policy objects so that all members of the same device group are configured to use them while not deploying them to other groups. It's important to keep device groups as simple as possible as there is inheritance to consider, which could overcomplicate your deployment if there is no real need to segregate your firewalls.

When you add a new device group in **Panorama | Device Groups**, you can provide a name and select which devices belong to it, but also, at the bottom, you can select the parent device group and the master device.

**Master Device** lets you pick one firewall in the group that will forward all its user ID information (user-to-IP mapping and group memberships), which can then be used in security rules.

**Parent Device Group** lets you nest device groups where the parent group shares all its objects and rules with the child group.

> **Important note**
>
> **Shared** is the *grandparent* device group, and any objects created in **Shared** will be made available on all managed devices, regardless of the device group they are in individually.

An example set of device groups can be seen in the following screenshot. In this scenario, the inheritance of rules and objects would work like this:

- Any objects or rules created in **EMEA** would only be visible to firewalls in the **EMEA** device group.

- Any objects or rules created in the **Field firewalls** device group would be visible to all firewalls in the **APAC**, **EMEA**, and **NAM** device groups, but not to **HQ firewalls**.

- Any objects or rules created in the **Shared** device group will be visible to all firewalls, regardless of which device group they are placed in:

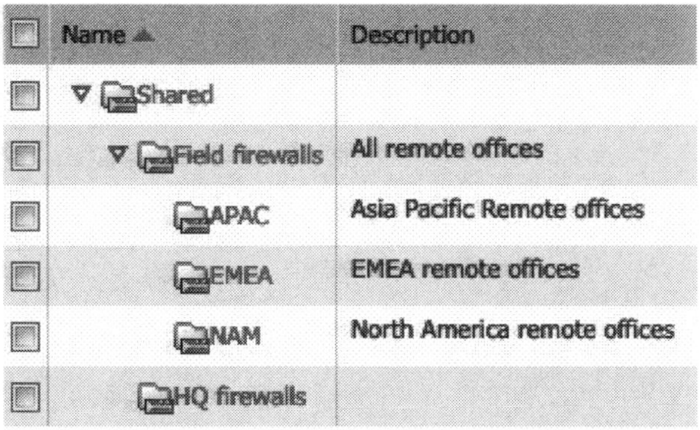

Figure 7.14 – Nested device groups

You have now learned how to add new managed devices and place them in device groups. In the next section, we will learn how to create policies for your device groups.

# Creating policies and objects

The goal of device group rules and objects is to manage everything from a central location and, where possible, end up with no local configuration on the firewalls.

While creating objects and rules, you always need to be mindful of the device group you are in while you create new objects. As the following screenshot illustrates, I am about to create a new address object while I am in the **EMEA** device group. If I do not check **Shared**, this object will only be usable by managed devices in the **EMEA** device group:

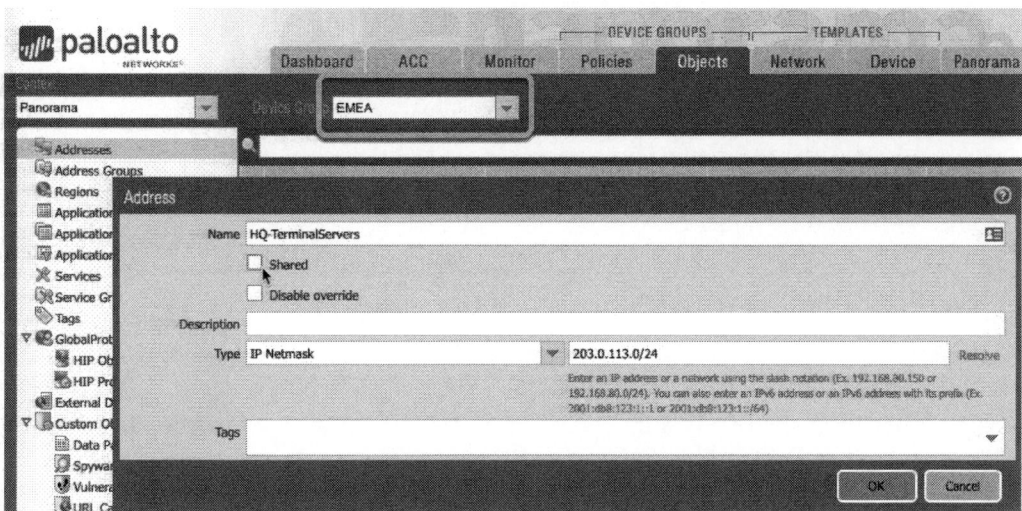

Figure 7.15 – Device group context

> **Important note**
>
> Objects that were created in a specific device group cannot be set to **Shared** afterward. They can, however, be *moved* to the **Shared** device group.

Most objects that are pushed from Panorama can be overridden by a local firewall admin. Address objects that are not shared can be set to **Disable Override** so that local admins are not able to change them locally.

Especially when using nested device groups, rule bases will be built in layers. A unique concept to Panorama is the use of **pre and post rules**. These are placed before and after local rules on the device. This enables administrators to set rules that override locally configured rules or make sure there are clean-up rules in place. The order of device groups' pre and post rules is illustrated in the following screenshot. Since rule bases are always evaluated from top to bottom, the **Shared** pre rules will always be hit first, and the **Shared** post rules last, just before the default rules:

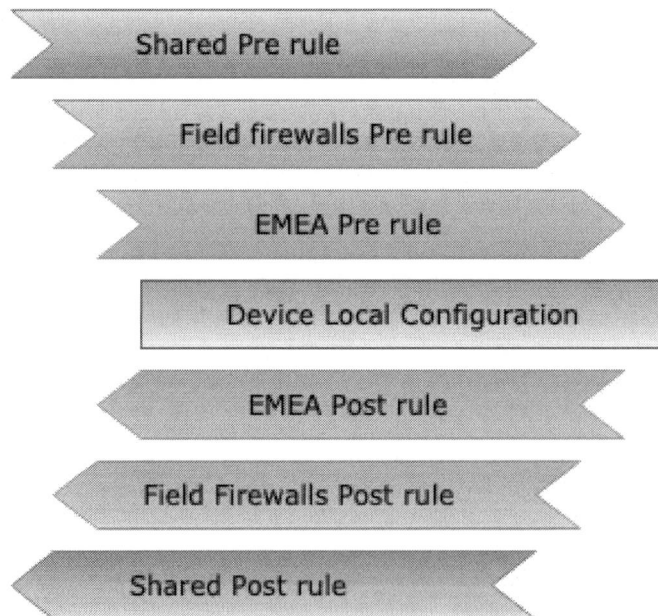

Figure 7.16 – The order of pre and post rules

Depending on the device context that you are currently in, some rules will be invisible, visible and editable, or visible and uneditable. Rules with an orange background belong to a higher-up device group, as you can see in the following screenshot. On the firewall, all Panorama rules will have an orange background and cannot be edited unless the local admin explicitly overrides it:

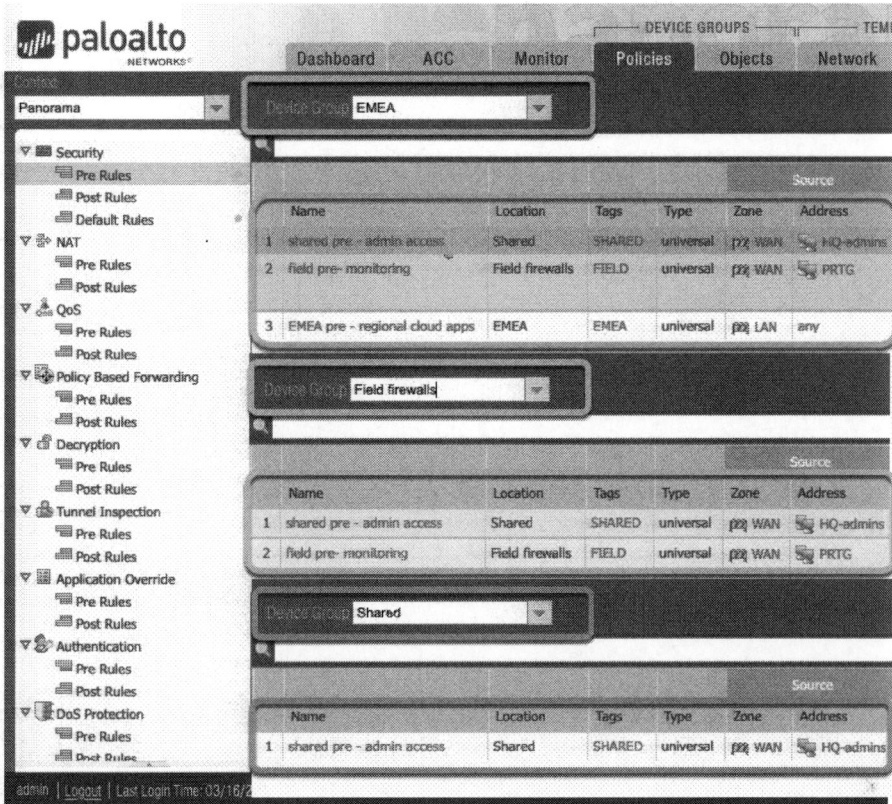

Figure 7.17 – Security rules in the device group context

On top of being able to control which rules are deployed to a certain group of firewalls, rules have an additional tab, **Targets**, which can be used to control, even more specifically, which firewalls a rule is applied to. This can help prevent the need for another nested device group if there are very few exceptions to the norm (for example, one firewall may need to be configured to allow access to a legacy server).

Now that you can create device groups, there's a couple of things you should do, or at least know about, to make your life easier.

## Important things to know when creating objects in device groups

When you first create rules, the zones will not be known by Panorama yet. When you create a rule, you will need to type the zone name as it is known on the firewall, or as you will set it in a template, and then click **OK**. After your first time typing in a zone, Panorama will learn the zone name and it will appear in the dropdown thereafter.

It is better to create objects in **Shared**, or as close to **Shared** as possible, to prevent duplicate objects in nested device groups.

Rules can be **cloned** to other device groups or **moved** to a different device group.

In **Objects | Log Forwarding**, create a **log forwarding** profile and call it `default`. Check the **Shared** box and add all the relevant log types that should be forwarded to Panorama by default (such as traffic, threats, URLs, WildFire, and so on). This will ensure that every security policy you create going forward has the log forwarding profile set and sends logs to Panorama. Your profile should look as in the following screenshot:

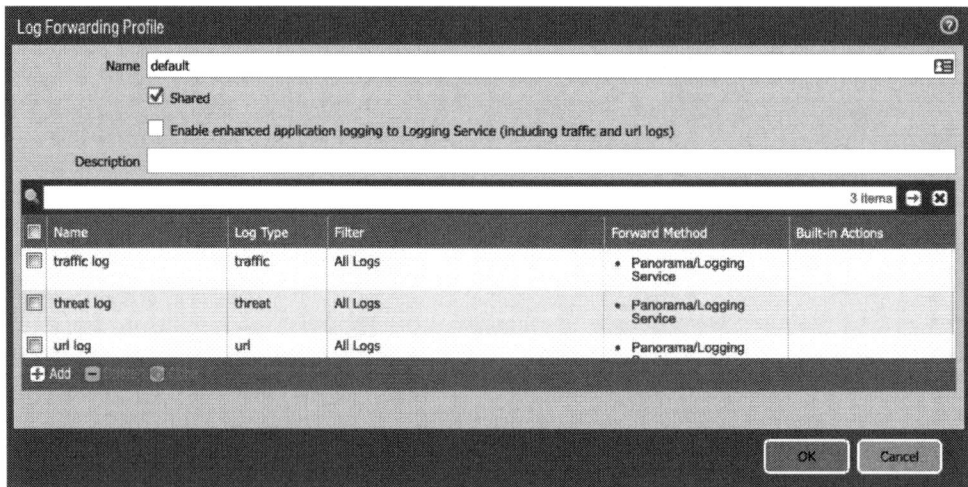

Figure 7.18 – The default log forwarding profile

In **Objects | Security Profiles**, create the security profiles, and in **Objects | Security Profile Groups**, create a new group, which you should call `default`. Set it to **Shared** and add all the security profiles you just created. This will ensure that every new security rule created automatically comes loaded with security profiles.

> **Important note**
> The intent of the preceding two **default** profiles is to create a baseline profile that will fit most cases, which is why they should be set to **Shared**. *Tuned* profiles can be created per device group if needed, and an admin can set a different profile in individual rules where appropriate.

You can now create device groups, and you understand what advantages and disadvantages are associated with nesting them. You can add managed devices and have learned how to create pre and post rules. In the next section, we will learn about templates and template, as well as how to aggregate common device configuration.

# Setting up templates and template stacks

Templates are a great way to deploy common device configuration across your managed devices. A template is a profile where you can set parameters in the **Network** and **Device** sections of the configuration for your managed devices. For example, you can set the same DNS servers, NTP servers, and domain name for all your firewalls.

To allow more flexibility, you can create **template stacks**. A stack is a container that holds several templates to combine their configurations into a tailored config bundle for a specific (set of) firewall(s).

Considering the previous example of three regions and an HQ location, we could create four template stacks – one for each firewall – in **Panorama | Templates**, and then add the associated firewalls to each **template stack**.

The next step is to create templates that contain broader configuration parameters:

1. Create templates that will be used to fulfill a certain task, as follows:

   --You could create an **admin template** containing all the security team admin accounts and authentication profiles, a standardized log-in banner, password complexity settings, and so on.

   --You could create a **network template** containing all the zones and basic interface configuration, as well as zone protection profiles.

   --You could create a **management template** containing the management interface DNS and NTP settings and update schedules.

   The possibilities are endless (until you reach 1,024 templates, which is the current limit).

2. Add template stacks as needed, usually one per firewall or firewall cluster, but these could also be deployed per region or by purpose. In each stack, you must add the firewalls that belong to the stack and the templates that will be added to the stack. Note the following:

   --Configuration made in the stack has priority over added templates.

   --Templates assign priority from top to bottom. A setting in the top template will overrule the same setting in consecutive templates.

The following diagram paints a simplified picture of the relationship between template stacks and templates:

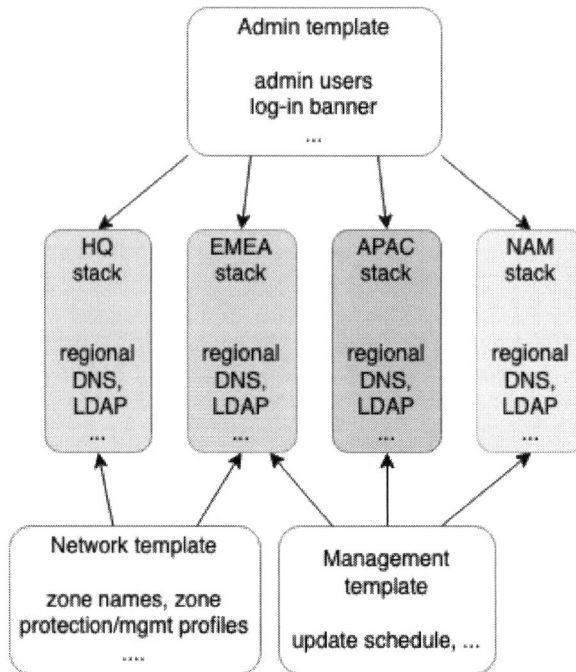

Figure 7.19 – Templates and template stacks

As the following screenshot shows, all you need to do to edit a template is select it from the template dropdown while in the section of the configuration where you want to add the configuration. An important caveat is that Panorama is not fully aware of some settings that could be active on your firewall. As shown by the **Mode** dropdown, the default assumption is that the firewall is a multi VSYS system, it is running in **Normal** mode, and that a VPN is enabled.

This will cause Panorama to show options that might not be available on the firewall (such as VSYSx on a configuration that is intended for a single VSYS system, weak encryption options on a FIPS enabled system, and so on). You can either set these options from the dropdown to remove unavailable config options or keep track of specific device limitations yourself:

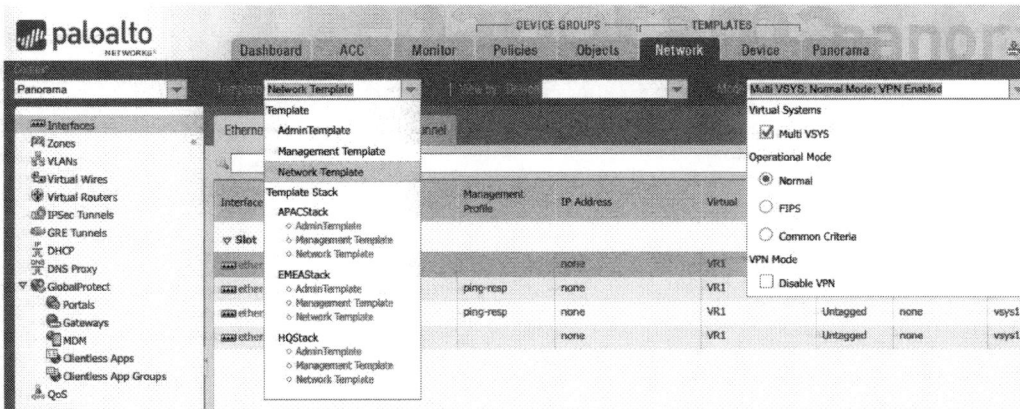

Figure 7.20 – Template selection and configuration mode

You have now learned how to plan out template stacks and how to leverage separate templates to ensure all your firewalls get the configuration they need while simplifying the configuration repository. In the next section, we are going to learn how Panorama can perform other tasks that simplify managing a diverse and geographically spread installation base.

# Panorama management

In this section, we will learn about the simple management tasks that you would normally need to perform on each firewall individually, which can be very time-consuming. The first task of an administrator is to make sure all firewalls have up-to-date signatures and content packages.

## Device deployment

Content updates can be managed through Panorama in two ways. A template can be created that sets a local update schedule on each firewall, which will require each firewall to connect to the update server individually and collect and install updates. A second method is setting an update schedule on Panorama and pushing out updates to all devices. This last method gives you a little more control over what is being pushed to the managed firewalls and when, but does increase bandwidth usage on the Panorama site or cloud provider.

To schedule updates from Panorama, do the following:

1. Go to **Panorama | Device Deployment | Dynamic Updates** and click on **Schedules** at the bottom.

2. Create a schedule for **Apps & Threats** and do the following:

   --Set **Recurrence** to `Every-30-Minutes` at `24` minutes past the half-hour to prevent conflicts with other update schedules.

   --Action **Download and Install**.

   --Select the devices that should receive these updates.

   --**Threshold** is intended to hold off on installing a package and rechecking after the specified amount of time in case there is a recall. Set this to `6` hours or more.

   --**Application threshold** waits to activate new applications for a specified amount of time so that the security team can review the possible impact on security policies.

3. If you have firewalls without a Threat Prevention license, create an app-only schedule with a recurrence of `Daily at 22:05`.

4. Create a schedule for **Antivirus**:

   --Set **Recurrence** to `hourly`.

   --Set **Minutes Past Hour** to a random number so that there is no conflict with the **Apps & Threats** updates.

   --Action **Download and Install**.

   --Select the devices that need to receive these updates.

   --Set **Threshold** to `3` hours.

5. Create a schedule for WildFire:

   --Set **Recurrence** to every minute (or `15` if bandwidth is an issue).

   --Action **Download and Install**.

   --Select the devices that will receive WildFire updates.

6. Create duplicate schedules in case there are firewalls in vastly different time zones.

7. In **Panorama | Dynamic Updates**, also set schedules for Panorama's own updates that mimic the preceding recurrence, but to a different minute past the hour to avoid conflicts.

A URL database update is only required if the target firewalls are not capable of performing cloud category lookups, as a URL database update will also purge and replace the local URL cache on the firewall.

Upgrading firewall OSes can be done from Panorama, as well through **Panorama | Device Deployment | Software**.

After clicking on **Check-Now**, every available PAN-OS version will be listed next to every available platform:

1. Download the PAN-OS version of the platform you want to upgrade.

2. Click **Install**. Panorama will then display all the matching managed devices that are eligible to be upgraded.

3. Select the devices that need to be upgraded and do the following:

   --Click **OK** to install the software **without rebooting** the target firewall.

   --Select **Upload only to device** to upload but not install the software image, then click **OK**.

   --Select **Reboot device after install** to also reboot the firewall after the installation completes, then click **OK**.

> **Important note**
>
> While upgrading a firewall is fairly straightforward, it is recommended and encouraged to plan accordingly and have someone standing by at the site of the upgrade in case something does go awry.

Plugins and GlobalProtect Client packages can be distributed in the same way.

In **Panorama | Device Deployment | Licenses**, you can review all the licenses deployed across all your devices and their expiration dates.

You can now manage all aspects of provisioning your firewalls with content updates and upgrading them from Panorama. In the next section, we will review how to import an existing firewall into Panorama.

# Migrating unmanaged to managed devices

Unmanaged devices that have already been fully configured may need to be integrated into Panorama, which can be challenging. Instead of trying to gradually replace local configuration with Panorama Templates and device group configuration, a firewall can be imported and its configuration converted into a template and a device group per VSYS:

1.  Add the firewall as a managed device (do *not* associate the device to device groups or template stacks at this time) and select **Commit to Panorama**.

2.  In **Panorama | Setup | Operations**, click on **Import device configuration to Panorama**.

3.  In the dialog, you can select the freshly added managed device:

    --You should name the template so that it is easily identifiable.

    --The default name for the device group is the firewall name. If there are multiple VSYS the device name will be the VSYS name, so add a prefix to easily identify the firewall in the device groups.

    --By default, all of the firewall's shared objects are imported as **Shared** objects for Panorama. If you do not want other firewalls to receive these objects, uncheck the option and all the objects will be imported as part of the new device group.

    --Select whether rules need to be imported into the pre or post rule base.

4.  Create a new stack, then add the device and its templates. If you do not want to add the Panorama shared templates yet, you can add them later once you've verified the device has been successfully integrated.

    You can now use the device group or template context switches to review whether the configuration has been imported properly.

5.  Click on **Commit to Panorama**.

6.  Select **Push to Devices** and **Edit Selections** from the dialog window.

7.  Select **Force Template Values** to overwrite the device's local configuration with the Panorama template of its configuration.

> **Important note**
>
> Replacing the device's local configuration with Panorama template configuration *will* cause connectivity issues as the entire configuration is replaced, which will cause some services to briefly restart loading the newly received configuration.

You have now learned how to manage and maintain devices in your Panorama instance. In the next section, we will learn how to set Panorama in **High Availability** mode so that it becomes more resilient to failure.

## Panorama HA

Compared to firewall HA, Panorama HA is much less complicated. The only conditions are the following:

- Both HA members must have the same device type, version, and mode (for example, both are M-600 and in **admin-only** mode).

- They should be on the same PAN-OS and have the same set of licenses for smooth operation.

To enable HA, follow these steps:

1. Go to **Panorama | High Availability** and do the following:

   --Enable **HA**.

   --Set **Peer IP**.

   --Enable **Encryption**.

2. In **Election settings**, do the following:

   --Set the priority for this Panorama instance to **Primary**. The primary Panorama instance will be responsible for pushing configuration to firewalls, but both members can be used for configuration, log queries, and reports.

   --**Preemptive** should be enabled in most cases so that the primary member always returns to its active status.

3. **Repeat** the preceding steps for the peer, replacing **Peer IP** with the first Panorama instance and setting the priority to **Secondary**.

Unlike firewalls, however, Panorama sticks to the primary and secondary roles throughout failures. **passive-secondary** will become **active-secondary** if the primary Panorama instance experiences an outage. There are two important considerations to keep in mind:

- The device assigned as **Secondary** cannot be used to deploy software or manage licenses.

- A device in the **Passive** state cannot manage a shared policy or deploy software and manage licenses.

Panorama uses TCP/28 for encrypted connections between MGT interfaces. If you do not enable **encryption**, connections are set up on TCP/28769 and TCP/28260.

In the last section, we're going to take a look at a couple of bits of information to keep in your pocket while working with Panorama.

## Tips and tricks

If a device ever needs to be **replaced**, be it due to a defect followed by an **RMA (Return Merchandise Authorization)** or an upgrade, rather than manually adding it to all the device groups and stacks, a simple replace command is available to switch the serial number of the old device with the new one so that the configuration is immediately set accordingly:

```
> replace device old xxxxxxxx new yyyyyyyyyy
```

Then, hit **Commit and Push**.

**Committing** a configuration on Panorama requires extra steps before it becomes a running configuration on a Firewall. In the top-right corner of the web interface, you have several options. **Configuration | Save** saves your candidate, while **Configuration | Revert** undoes any configuration changes since your last save or commit.

**Commit to Panorama** activates your changes as the running configuration for Panorama, but this configuration still needs to be sent out to the firewalls.

**Push to devices** sends the running configuration on Panorama out to the firewalls. If you click **Edit Selection**, you will open the dialog window shown in the following screenshot. From here, you can select **Preview Changes** to compare the Panorama running config to the firewall running config to see which configuration elements will be changed, added, or deleted.

**Merge with Device Candidate Config** is enabled by default, as shown in the following screenshot. If a local admin is making changes to the firewall, they may not be ready to have their changes committed, so you can disable this option to prevent mishaps. If you don't want to include template configuration, you can either disable the option at the bottom or uncheck all the devices under the **Templates** tab. **Force Template Values** can be used to overwrite any local configuration with template values:

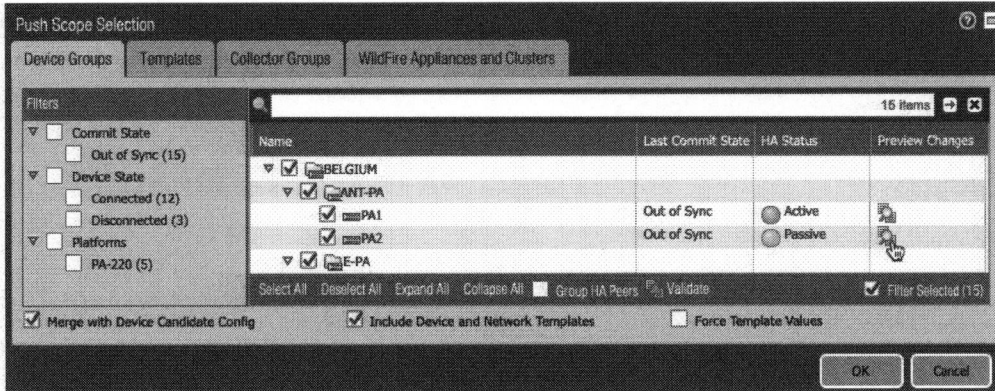

Figure 7.21 – Edit Selection in Push Scope Selection

**Commit and Push** does both of the preceding actions in one go. This is a great option if you only made a small change and want to push it out immediately

If you want to check what the state of the local firewall is (what configuration is in the candidate and the locally running config), you can use the device context switch to connect to the local web interface of your target device. This connection is backchanneled over the connection the firewall makes to Panorama. This can also be helpful if you lose direct access to a remote firewall that still has an active link to Panorama. As shown in the following screenshot, simply click on the **Context** dropdown and select the device you want to connect to:

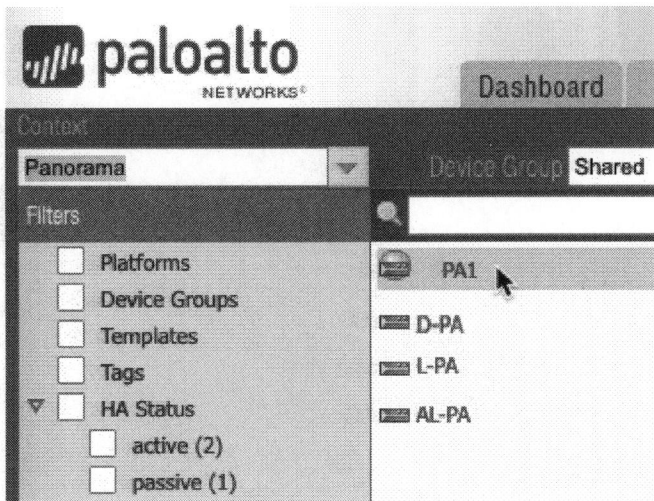

Figure 7.22 – The device context switch

If at one point you do need to temporarily **override** a configuration parameter pushed by Panorama, you can connect to the firewall and, as shown in the following screenshot, select the object that has a template value and click on **Override** at the bottom of the page. You can then change the parameters and commit to activate the new configuration. If you later want to revert to the Panorama template settings, you can select the object and click **Revert**:

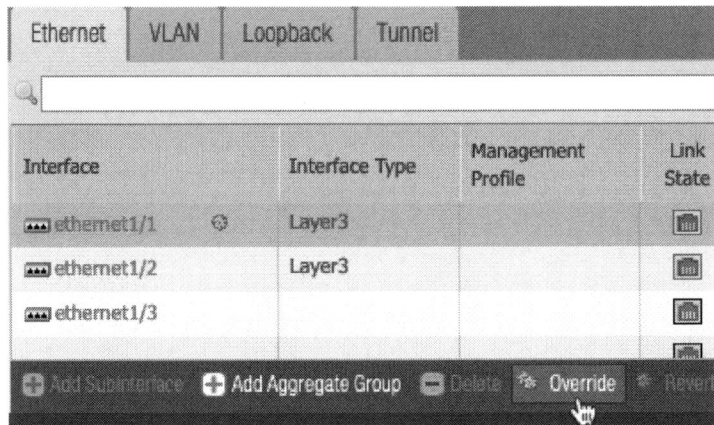

Figure 7.23 – Applying an override to a Panorama template configuration

Panorama can also function as a **user ID collector and redistribution center**.

If you add all your deployed user ID agents (server-installed user ID agents or firewall-sourced clientless user ID collectors) to **Panorama | User Identification | User-ID Agents**, Panorama will start to collect all the user-to-IP mapping from these agents and store them locally. Then, go to **Panorama | Setup | Interfaces | Management Interface** and enable **User-ID Services**. Panorama can then be targeted by firewalls as a user ID agent.

In your template (stack), go to **Device | User Identification | User-ID agents** and add a new user ID agent. Instead of **Host** and **Port**, use the serial number and put in the serial number of your Panorama instance. If Panorama is set up in HA mode, add another user ID agent and add the serial number of the **second** Panorama instance.

To back up configuration files, go to **Panorama | Scheduled Config Export** and create a backup profile:

1. Give the profile a friendly name and check the **Enable** box.

2. Set a convenient time, such as 22:30.

3. Select the protocol to use for transfer. SCP is preferred as it provides encryption.

4.  Set the hostname, port, path, username, and password.

5.  Select whether you want to use **PASV** mode if you selected FTP as the transfer protocol.

This scheduled backup will save a bundle containing all the Panorama configuration settings and the managed device local configuration so that you have a handy backup of all the configuration settings.

# Summary

In this chapter, you learned about the Panorama central management platform and how it can be leveraged to make managing groups, clusters, and geographically spread out firewalls, users and locations much less complex. You learned how device group configuration and templates can be used to simplify and make configuration consistent across all of your managed devices.

In the next chapter, we will review the best practices for upgrading firewalls and Panorama.

# Section 3: Maintenance and Troubleshooting

In this last section, you will learn how to perform routine maintenance operations and how to troubleshoot different issues using built-in tools and some tips and tricks.

This section comprises the following chapters:

# 8
# Upgrading Firewalls and Panorama

Just like any other operating system, bugs are sometimes found in PAN-OS, which could cause all kinds of issues. These bugs need to be fixed, and so update packages, called **maintenance releases**, that customers can install to improve the resilience and stability of their systems are made available. New features are also introduced through new major releases of the operating system.

In this chapter, we will learn how to upgrade firewalls, Panorama, and **High Availability (HA)** pairs. We will review what steps need to be taken to prepare for an upgrade and how to ensure continuity throughout the upgrade process, as well as any limitations that may apply, any issues that may arise, and the steps that need to be taken to upgrade.

In this chapter, we're going to cover the following main topics:

- Documenting the key aspects
- Preparing for the upgrade
- Upgrading standalone and HA firewalls and Panorama
- Upgrading log collectors
- Aftercare, emergency rollback, and downgrading

# Technical requirements

This chapter assumes that you have a working knowledge of testing system functionality, so you should be able to ascertain that everything is working nominally after an upgrade has taken place. If you are going to upgrade a cluster, you should first get comfortable with how it is configured before proceeding.

# Documenting the key aspects

Before you can start the upgrade procedure, you should first take some time to document the key aspects of the network surrounding the firewall or Panorama. This information will need to go into a test plan that you can execute immediately after you have performed the upgrade as you will need to quickly ascertain whether the device is up and running and passing traffic as expected. It is important to identify key production applications and if possible, identify personnel who can assist in testing application functionality post-upgrade.

It may be prudent to make an upgrade checklist so that you don't forget any important caveats, as well as a contingency plan in case something goes wrong, which includes at which point fallback is required. Set this point so that you have plenty of time to troubleshoot for minor oversights, but not so long that it impacts the business. Arrange for an appropriately sized maintenance window beforehand. Here's a checklist to help you get things organized:

- Map out key application data flows.
- Identify personnel that can assist in verifying application functionality.
- Document the upgrade plan beforehand.
- Document a contingency or rollback plan.
- Ensure out-of-band connectivity is available to the device.

Depending on the PAN-OS version that you start with, some steps in the upgrade path may require the installation of a minimum version content update, or there may be other considerations. Always check the release notes of every version you plan to upgrade to (`https://docs.paloaltonetworks.com/search.html#q=pan-os-release-notes`).

In the next section, we will take a look at some important considerations you need to be aware of before starting the upgrade process.

# Upgrade considerations

PAN-OS comes in a major version (**X.y.z**), a feature release (**x.Y.z**), and a maintenance release (**x.y.Z**). On average, a new major version is released every year, with a feature release following about half a year later, containing some new and updated features. Both versions get their own maintenance releases, which mostly contain bugfixes. Maintenance packages are usually released every 6 to 8 weeks, with an occasional hotfix version (**x.y.z-h\***) arriving sooner.

For the purposes of this chapter, *I will refer to both major releases and feature releases as "major"* if the intention is to upgrade or downgrade from one code train to the next.

Each major and feature release has a **base image**, which is the install medium for the whole release. This version always needs to be **downloaded** before later maintenance versions can be added. It does not usually need to be installed (see the *Special case for upgrading older hardware* section).

In most circumstances, a release can be considered **mature** when it reaches a minimum maintenance release version of x.y.5 or later. Carefully weigh the need to upgrade if x.y.5 or a later version is not available.

If your environment has Panorama, you should plan to upgrade it first, as Panorama is **backward-compatible** with almost any version of PAN-OS running on the firewall. However, it should not support firewalls that are more than two maintenance versions higher than itself (that is, Panorama should always be upgraded first and should be on the highest PAN-OS version of the entire installation base before considering any other upgrades).

When upgrading HA pairs, upgrading one member to anything higher than two major versions over its peer could cause session-sync issues during failovers. If you want to ensure as little disruption on the network as possible during the upgrade process, consider upgrading the firewalls **in lockstep**, rather than upgrading one member several versions up before starting on its peer.

When one peer is upgraded and the other is not in a HA cluster, the lowest PAN-OS version peer will naturally become the active member of the cluster, leaving the upgraded member in a non-functional state (faulty but participating in a forced passive capacity).

When upgrading to the latest maintenance release from an earlier maintenance version (for example, from 9.1.1 to 9.1.10), you do not need to install any intermediary maintenance versions unless explicitly indicated in the release notes.

When upgrading across multiple major versions, you must upgrade to the next major version before moving on to the one after it; you cannot skip a major version (for example, going from 8.1 to 9.0 to 9.1). It is wise to install the preferred maintenance release instead of the base, even for the "middle" major version, as this will prevent any bugs from making an appearance in the middle of an upgrade process.

In the next section, we'll take a closer look at the steps you should take before starting an upgrade.

# Preparing for the upgrade

Before we get started on the upgrade process, there are a few precautions we should take to ensure we are properly prepared and have everything set so that the upgrade process itself goes smoothly:

1.  Go to **Device | Setup | Operations** for the firewall or **Panorama | Setup | Operations** for Panorama, then click **Save named configuration snapshot** and name the configuration file for the device name, date, and time (for example, HQmember1-04052020-1005.xml).

2.  Next, click on **Export named configuration snapshot** and save the file somewhere where you can find it if you need it.

3.  You can also export running-config.xml so that you have the latest committed configuration, but remember to rename the file after downloading it.

    If you have Panorama, you should already have the scheduled backup configured under **Panorama | Scheduled Backup**, but it doesn't hurt to have a fresh backup just in case.

4.  Go to **Device | Dynamic Updates**, click on **Check Now**, and make sure the device has installed the latest content packages available to your system. Some PAN-OS versions require a minimum version of content packages to be installed before the OS can be installed. If a newer content package version is available, download and install it before the PAN-OS upgrade takes place.

    If the device is running in HA mode, verify that the peer has the same content version installed and upgrade it if necessary.

5.  For HA pairs that have **Device | High Availability | Election settings | Preemptive** enabled, disable it on the primary member. A pre-empt could cause unexpected automated failovers during the upgrade process, which you will want to prevent.

6. Determine which maintenance version you should reach by the end of the upgrade process by reviewing the security advisories at `https://security.paloaltonetworks.com/`. Take note of which versions are marked as **preferred** at `https://live.paloaltonetworks.com/t5/Customer-Resources/Support-PAN-OS-Software-Release-Guidance/ta-p/258304` as I will refer to these as the **preferred maintenance release**.

7. To save time, download all the required base images and *preferred* maintenance versions needed for the upgrade process to the device from the **Device | Software** or **Panorama | Software** pages, or to a local repository by going to `https://support.paloaltonetworks.com` then **Update | Software Updates**. If you intend to skip ahead by more than one major version, you may not be able to download the latest code train directly onto the device as the software manager may not be able to understand these software packages. You can download those versions on local storage or wait until after the first stage to then download them from the update server.

From the CLI, you can use the following commands to refresh the available software repository, download, and eventually install the PAN-OS images:

```
> request system software check
> request system software download version x.y.z
> request system software install version x.y.z
```

It is generally a good idea, if you are not already using the latest version of your current code train, to first install and reboot the latest version in your current PAN-OS environment before moving on to the next major release. Follow these steps to prepare yourself for the upgrade event:

1. Download the **preferred** version of the currently installed major or feature release.

2. Download the base image to the next major release you want to go to.

3. Download the preferred maintenance release version of the major release.

4. Prepare your maintenance window(s)—schedule to upgrade Panorama (the cluster) first and then schedule the firewalls in another maintenance window. This will give you more time to focus on a single objective and will make troubleshooting, should anything unexpected happen, easier since you will only need to focus on one area. Make sure you provision plenty of time for the upgrade to complete, check the connectivity, and troubleshoot and roll back if needed, even if the upgrade itself is not expected to take long.

5. After the install completes, you will need to reboot. After the reboot, it may take a few minutes for the management server to return to full functionality, at which time you may be able to reach a login prompt but it will appear as if your password is incorrect. If this is the case, your reboot may simply need a few more minutes to fully set up all of its services—**don't panic** and don't reboot.

6. Once you are logged in after the upgrade, the system will need to commit its configuration to the data plane and perform some post-upgrade jobs. These are performed during the `AutoCommit` process. Once the `AutoCommit` process completes, indicated as `FIN OK`, the system will be up and running. Track the progress with the following command:

```
> show jobs all

Enqueued Dequeued ID PositionInQ Type Status Result
Completed

-------------------------------------------------------------
-----

2020/05/10 23:01:33 23:01:33  1  AutoCom  FIN OK 23:02:04
```

Some devices may have two consecutive `AutoCommit` cycles; the first one is a regular `AutoCommit` and the second is used to synchronize the `idmgr` process between HA devices. idmgr maintains IDs on objects, network elements, and policies on the firewall. These IDs need to match for both members for the session failover to work flawlessly. You can verify whether idmgr is synced with the following command:

```
> debug device-server dump idmgr high-availability state
```

You can also verify whether the system is ready to process traffic with the following command:

```
> show chassis-ready
```

7. From the CLI, run the following command and take note of any deviating settings that need to be verified and potentially reset post-upgrade:

```
> show session info
```

8. Prepare a checklist of services to check post-upgrade. Refer to the upcoming *After the upgrade* section for a baseline and add additional or more-specific checks as needed for your environment.

Now that we have made all the preparations and the maintenance windows have been set, it is time to perform the upgrade.

# The upgrade process

When you start the upgrade process, quickly recheck each of the preceding eight steps and reach out to your stakeholders to let them know that the maintenance window is about to start and to wait for your signal to test whether all the applications and processes are running smoothly. Do this well in time so that they have time to shut down any processes that do not handle interruptions too well.

The first step is to upgrade Panorama.

## Upgrading a single Panorama instance

While upgrading Panorama introduces the least risks in terms of network impact as it doesn't process sessions, a standalone Panorama instance does require an appropriate amount of precaution as a failed upgrade could introduce some difficulties with managing the firewalls. Be extra sure that an up-to-date configuration save is stored in a secure location, then follow these steps:

1.  If any configuration changes have not been committed, review and save them, then collect a `running-config.xml` backup. Otherwise, discard the changes.

2.  Go to **Panorama | Software** to install the preferred maintenance version of the currently installed major release, or run the following command in the CLI:

    ```
    > request system software install version x.y.z
    ```

    Keep track of the installation process from the CLI by using the following command:

    ```
    > show jobs all
    ```

3.  When the upgrade completes, the dialog window will request you to reboot. Click **Yes** to do so. If this dialog does not appear, go to **Panorama | Setup | Operations** and click on **Reboot Device**, or to the CLI, add the following:

    ```
    > request restart system
    ```

    Press *Y* to confirm.

4.  After the reboot, make sure the next major release base image and maintenance release are both downloaded on Panorama. If not, download them now, starting with the base image.

5.  Install the preferred maintenance release package.

    When the installation is completed, click **OK** on the **reboot** dialog or manually initiate the reboot.

    If you need to upgrade to another major version, repeat *steps 4* through *6*. Download or manually upload them, starting with the base image.

6.  Install the maintenance release.

7.  Reboot Panorama.

If you have a Panorama HA cluster the procedure is a little different.

## Upgrading a Panorama HA cluster

In a Panorama cluster that is still set in legacy mode and has an NFS volume set for log storage, only the primary Panorama instance receives logs, so there may be an interruption in log reception when upgrading the primary member. Firewalls will retain logs and forward them when Panorama comes online again.

If your Panorama environment is still in legacy mode, consider transitioning to Panorama or Management-Only, which offloads the log reception responsibility to log collectors. You can check your Panorama instance's current mode with the following command:

```
> show system info | match system-mode
```

Follow these steps to upgrade the cluster:

1.  Verify that there is still uncommitted configuration. If there is, save and collect a fresh copy of `runing-config.xml`; otherwise, discard it.

2.  Start the upgrade process on the **Secondary-Passive** device first. Install the preferred maintenance version of the current code train.

3.  When the installation task completes, reboot the secondary device.

4.  Verify that Panorama is up and running.

5.  Suspend the **Primary-Active** member from the cluster by going to **Panorama | High Availability | Operational Commands** and clicking on **Suspend Local Device**. Alternatively, run the following command from the CLI:

```
> request high-availability state suspend
```

6. Verify that the peer is now set to **Secondary-Active** and is operating normally.

7. On the **Primary-Suspended** device, install the preferred maintenance release of the current code train.

8. Reboot the device after the installation process completes.

9. When the reboot completes and the device is up and running, unsuspend the device by going to **Panorama | High Availability | Operational Commands** and clicking on **Make Local Panorama Functional**, or by using the following CLI command:

```
> request high-availability state functional
```

Now that both members have been upgraded to the preferred maintenance version and we are certain that the cluster performs failovers as expected, we are ready for the major upgrade. Verify that the next major version base image and preferred maintenance release are present on both members. Download or manually upload them if needed:

1. On the secondary member, install the preferred maintenance release of the next major version.

2. Reboot the secondary device and wait for it to return to full functionality.

3. Suspend the **Primary-Active** member.

4. Verify that the **Secondary-Active** is working as expected.

5. Install the preferred next major version maintenance release.

6. Reboot **Primary-Suspended**.

7. Unsuspend the primary device.

8. If **Preemptive** was enabled previously, enable it again on the primary device.

9. On the primary device, save to Panorama and manually execute **sync to remote** via **Dashboard | High Availability Widget**, or by using the following CLI command:

```
> request high-availability sync-to-remote running-config
```

The next phase is to upgrade the firewalls.

# Upgrading a single firewall

Upgrading a standalone firewall will cause interruptions to the network as all connections are dropped while the firewall reboots. Make sure all the stakeholders are notified and any critical processes are halted before commencing with the reboot phase of the upgrade process:

1. Verify whether there are any uncommitted changes. Save and collect a fresh `running-config.xml` file; otherwise, discard it.

2. From **Device | Software**, install the latest maintenance release for the currently installed major version:

   ```
   > request system software install version x.y.z
   ```

3. Keep track of the installation process from the CLI with the following command:

   ```
   > show jobs all
   ```

4. When the upgrade completes, the dialog window will request you to reboot. Click **Yes** to do so. If this dialog does not appear, go to **Device | Setup | Operations** and click on **Reboot Device**; otherwise, run the following in the CLI:

   ```
   > request restart system
   ```

   Press *Y* to confirm.

5. After the reboot, the firewall will need to perform an `AutoCommit` process, which is a job that pushes the newly upgraded configuration down to the data plane. It may take longer than a regular `commit` process to complete:

   ```
   > show jobs all
   Enqueued Dequeued ID Type       Status Result Completed
   ------------------------------------------------------------
   23:22:18 23:22:18 1  AutoCom   ACT    PEND             5%
   ```

6. Verify that the next major base image and preferred maintenance release packages are present in **Device | Software**. Download or manually upload the software package if needed, starting with the base image:

   ```
   > request system software info
   ```

7. Install the preferred maintenance version.

8. Click **Yes** if the dialog window asks you to reboot, or otherwise, reboot the firewall manually.

9. Wait for `AutoCommit` to complete and then test the firewall functionality.

When upgrading a firewall HA cluster, take the following steps to ensure a smooth upgrade.

# Upgrading a firewall cluster

When upgrading a cluster, little to no sessions should be lost as the transition between peers is seamless. It is important to pace the process so that the firewalls have enough time to sync session states before the other member is suspended. Performing the following command on both members in between upgrades should result in nearly identical session counts:

```
> show session info
```

Follow these steps to start the upgrade:

1. Verify whether there are any uncommitted changes. Run `commit` and `sync` on the peer and collect a fresh `running-config.xml` file from both members; otherwise, discard the changes.

2. On the secondary device, in **Device | Software**, install the latest maintenance release for the currently installed major version, or run the following via the CLI:

```
> request system software install version x.y.z
```

3. Keep track of the installation process from the CLI with the following command:

```
> show jobs all
```

4. When the upgrade completes, the dialog window will request you to reboot. Click **Yes** to do so. If this dialog does not appear, go to **Device | Setup | Operations** and click **Reboot Device**, or run the following from the CLI:

```
> request restart system
```

Press *Y* to confirm.

5. After the reboot, the firewall will need to perform an `AutoCommit` process, which is a job that pushes the newly upgraded configuration down to the data plane. It may take longer than a regular `commit` process to complete:

```
> show jobs all

Enqueued Dequeued ID Type      Status Result Completed
------------------------------------------------------------
23:22:18 23:22:18 1  AutoCom   ACT    PEND          5%
```

6. Wait until the secondary device is in the `NonFunct` state. Check whether the session table is being synced:

```
> show session all
```

7. On the primary device, go to **Device | High Availability | Operational Commands** and click **Suspend local device**, or run the following on the CLI:

```
> request high-availability state suspend
```

8. On the primary device, install the *preferred* maintenance release of the current code train.

9. When the upgrade completes, reboot the firewall.

10. Wait for the `AutoCommit` process to complete and the firewall to go into a `Passive` state.

11. To return the primary device back to an `Active` state, run `suspend` and then `unsuspend` for the secondary device:

```
> request high-availability state suspend
> request high-availability state functional
```

12. Verify that the next major base image and preferred maintenance release packages are present in **Device | Software** on both devices. Download or manually upload the software package if needed, starting with the base image:

```
> request system software info
```

13. On the secondary device, install the preferred maintenance version of the next major release:

```
> request system software install version x.y.z
```

14. Click **Yes** if the installation dialog window asks to reboot, or reboot the firewall manually:

```
> request restart system
```

Press *Y* to confirm the reboot.

Wait for the AutoCommit process to complete and the secondary device to go into the NonFunct state.

15. Verify whether the state table is being synchronized:

```
> show session all
```

16. On the primary device, click on **Suspend local Device** in **Device | High Availability | Operational Commands**, or run the following in the CLI:

```
> request high-availability state suspend
```

17. In **Device | Software**, install the preferred maintenance release of the next major version, or run the following via the CLI:

```
> request system software install version x.y.z
```

18. When asked to reboot in the **Install** dialog, click **Yes**, or manually reboot via **Device | Setup | Operations**. Alternatively, run the following in the CLI:

```
> request restart system
```

Press *Y* to confirm rebooting the firewall.

Wait for the AutoCommit process to complete.

19. In the **Dashboard | High Availability** widget, verify that the configuration is in sync. If not, sync the configuration to the secondary device with the widget or through the CLI:

```
> request high-availability sync-to-remote running-config
```

20. Verify that the primary device is in a passive state. If it is still suspended, unsuspend it:

```
> request high-availability state functional
```

21. To return the primary device back to an active state, suspend and then unsuspend the secondary device:

```
> request high-availability state suspend
> request high-availability state functional
```

22. Re-enable **Preemptive** on the primary device if it was enabled before, and save the changes.

Log collectors also need to be upgraded, ideally right after Panorama is upgraded.

# Upgrading log collectors (or firewalls) through Panorama

All of the log collectors in a collector group need to be upgraded at the same time as they all need to be on the same operating system for them to successfully pair up. During the upgrade process, logs will not be forwarded to the collector group and firewalls will store logs locally until the collector group comes back online, at which point the backlog is uploaded to the collector group. Since multiple devices need to be upgraded at the same time, it is best to perform the upgrade from Panorama. Upgrade Panorama to the same or a newer version before you upgrade the log collectors, then follow these steps:

1. In **Panorama** | **Device Deployment** | **Dynamic Updates**, ensure that the latest content updates are installed on all members of the collector group.

   Click **Check Now**, then download and install the latest updates if needed.

2. In **Panorama** | **Device Deployment** | **Software**, click **Check Now** and download the *preferred* maintenance release of the currently installed major version.

3. After the download completes, click **Install** and select all the members of the collector group. Check the `Reboot device after install` checkbox and click **OK**.

4. Download the base image and the *preferred* maintenance release for the next major version.

5. Monitor **Panorama** | **Managed Collectors** for the log collectors to re-establish a connection to Panorama.

6. In **Panorama** | **Device Deployment** | **Software**, click **Install** next to the new base image, but select **Upload only to device (do not install)**.

7. Then, click **Install** next to the *preferred* maintenance release and select **Reboot device after install**.

8. Repeat *steps 4* through *7* until you reach the desired major and maintenance release.

When upgrading log collectors to a new major version, there may be changes to the log database that take a longer time to complete than a regular upgrade. To monitor the process, you can log on to the CLI of the log collector and check the progress:

```
> debug logdb show-es-upgrade-time
```

After the log migration has completed, you can check the cluster health by issuing the following command:

```
> show log-collector-es-cluster health
```

Once the upgrade has completed, there should be sufficient time for aftercare.

## After the upgrade

During the aftercare phase, you should go over your checklist to ensure all the applications are up and running and any other critical infrastructure or business processes are fully functional and not being blocked by the firewall. Use this list as a template, adding your own checks as needed:

- Reach out to your stakeholders to run tests and verify that everything is working as expected. Monitor their tests in the traffic log to verify that all the allowed sessions are allowed and blocked sessions are still being blocked.

- Verify whether any deviating session settings have been included in the upgrade and reset them if needed.

- For firewalls managed by Panorama or a Panorama upgrade, verify whether pushing configuration from Panorama works as expected.

- Check the VPN and GlobalProtect connections.

- Verify whether the dynamic routing protocols are picking up routes as expected.

- Check the system logs for unexpected error messages.

In the next section, we'll review what to do if the upgrade fails.

# The rollback procedure

If the upgrade causes unexpected issues and troubleshooting is unable to clarify why, the last resort is to roll back to the previous deployment.

If you find yourself in this situation, make sure you do the following:

- Write down all the symptoms.

- Note down which troubleshooting steps were taken.

- In **Device | Support**, create a `Techsupport` file as you may need to reach out to Palo Alto Networks support if you are unable to find what went wrong.

- Save any related files, the CLI output, troubleshooting files, packet captures, and so on in one location.

Once you've documented your troubleshooting efforts, the easiest way to roll back is to switch the `sysroot` boot partition. The firewall has two system volumes that contain a fully installed PAN-OS, of which only one partition is active. The inactive partition either contains the previously installed version, or the next version if you have just installed it but not rebooted yet.

From the CLI, you can query the status, which shows you which version is currently `RUNNING-ACTIVE` and which one is installed on the inactive partition, and can be reverted to the following:

```
> debug swm status


Partition          State             Version
-------------------------------------------------------------
sysroot0           REVERTABLE        9.1.0
sysroot1           RUNNING-ACTIVE    9.1.3
maint              EMPTY             None
```

To roll back after an upgrade, you can simply activate the previous partition by executing the following command:

```
> debug swm revert


Reverting from 9.1.3 (sysroot0) to 9.1.0 (sysroot1)
```

Then, reboot the system:

```
> request restart system
```

This will take you back to the previously installed PAN-OS.

If this procedure fails, reverse the steps of the installation procedure until you have installed the maintenance version that you started from:

1. If needed, download the base image of the previous major version, then download the preferred maintenance release or the maintenance release you were on when you started.

2. Install the maintenance release directly. The system will prompt whether you would like to choose a specific configuration file to download to. Pick your backup file. If you don't have a backup file, just pick `running-config.xml`.

3. Reboot.

4. If you need to go down another major version, download the base and maintenance release.

5. Install the maintenance release, pick the desired backup configuration file, and reboot.

6. After the device has rebooted to the desired release, if you did not have a device-loaded backup config file, go to **Device | Setup | Operations** and click **Import named configuration snapshot** to load your backup config.

7. Then, click on **Load named configuration snapshot**, pick your backup configuration file, and click **Commit**.

In the next section, we'll review a corner case when upgrading older hardware.

# Special case for upgrading older hardware

Some older hardware may not have sufficient space on the hard drive to accommodate upgrading directly from one major version to the next. This will become apparent if you first download the base image and then download and install the maintenance release as you will receive an error message saying that the **base image is missing**. This is caused by the system trying to load the maintenance image by deleting any images that are not in use at the time, which in this case is the base image. For these special cases, follow these steps to upgrade successfully:

1. Delete any non-essential software images.

2. Download the base image of the next major version, install, and reboot.

3. After the reboot, download the maintenance version, install, and reboot.

If you want to, you can also downgrade to a previous version.

# The downgrade procedure

There may be a time where you have upgraded to a newer version but feel you want to remain on the previous version for a while longer and need to downgrade.

If you want to follow a more structured approach than the rollback procedure, you can apply the upgrade process in reverse to graciously revert to an older version by following these steps:

1.  Verify that both the base image and preferred maintenance release versions have been downloaded on both members when downgrading a cluster. If the images were removed, download the base image first, then download the maintenance version.

2.  If you are downgrading a cluster, suspend and upgrade the primary device first.

    When you initiate the downgrade to a lower major version, the system will ask whether you want to load a configuration file that was saved just before the previous *upgrade*. This will ensure you revert to a configuration file that was used in the version you are downgrading to. Unless a lot of changes were implemented after the upgrade, it is a good idea to load the file, rather than relying on the conversion process of the current configuration to the lower major version.

3.  If the primary device is still in a suspended state after the reboot, set it to **functional**. This will cause the primary device to become active and start processing sessions, regardless of whether **preempt** is enabled. This is due to the higher priority that a lower version release has in a cluster:

    ```
    > request high-availability state functional
    ```

4.  Downgrade the secondary device, making sure you make the same choice regarding the configuration file. Load the previous version or rely on the downgrade conversion.

5.  After the downgrade completes on the secondary device, set it to the **functional** state.

6.  Sync the configuration from the primary to the secondary device:

    ```
    > request high-availability sync-to-remote running-config
    ```

Following these steps should bring you back safely to a previous version.

# Summary

In this chapter, you have learned how to upgrade the Panorama management system, log collectors, and firewalls. You are now able to upgrade a firewall cluster in such a way that it will cause no or minimal impact on your business, and can plan in advance which steps will need to be taken to ensure that the upgrade goes smoothly. You can also roll back in the event of failure, or gracefully downgrade if needed. You also know which precautions need to be taken when upgrading an older or smaller form factor device.

In the next chapter, we will learn how to set up log collectors and set them up redundantly, as well as how to create custom reports.

# 9
# Logging and Reporting

In this chapter, we will learn about how logs can be forwarded to log collectors or Syslog servers or be emailed. We'll learn how to select which logs are sent to a specific destination and what event triggers logs should be sent. We'll learn how to configure log collectors and how a log collector group can be created to ensure redundancy and increase log capacity. We'll also learn about built-in reports and how custom reports can be created.

In this chapter, we're going to cover the following main topics:

- Log storage and forwarding
- Configuring log collectors and log collector groups
- Using the logging service and syslog
- Configuring log forwarding profiles
- Creating custom reports
- Using the application command center
- Filtering logs

# Technical requirements

In this chapter, we will be forwarding logs via syslog and sending out alerts via email. If you do not have access to a syslog server and an email relay, set these up so that you can test the topics we discuss.

# Log storage and forwarding

In its standalone configuration, a firewall has somewhere between a few terabytes of storage on high-end devices and a few gigabytes on low-end devices for logs. This space then has to be split up among all the different log databases, such as `Traffic`, `Threat`, `WildFire`, and several others. This could cause a skewed perception of how much log storage is actually available and, combined with high traffic volume, this could lead to the system having only enough storage for a couple of days' worth of logs.

To review the current log capacity and what percentage of the capacity has been assigned to individual databases, check **Device | Setup | Management | Logging and Reporting Settings**. You can change how much space is reserved for each log database by changing the percentage next to each log database, as you can see in the following screenshot. Keep an eye on the total allocation near the bottom left of the screen:

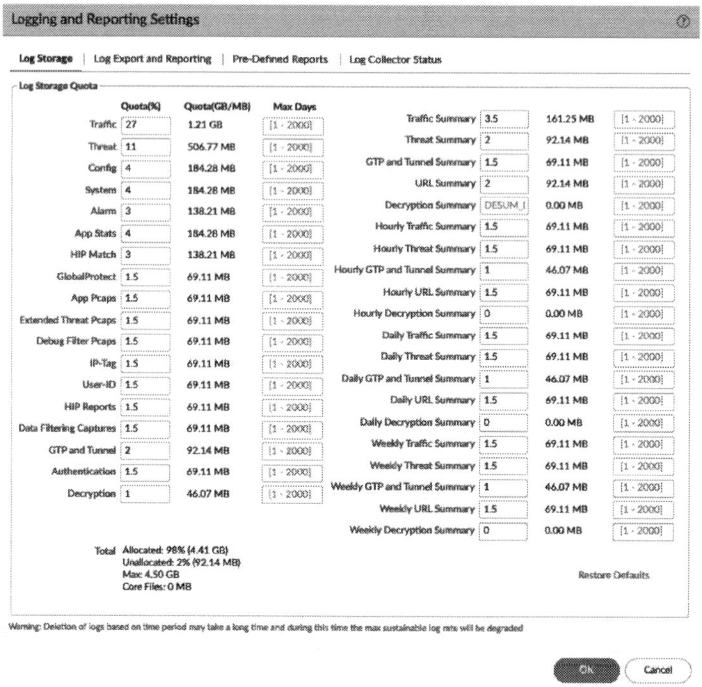

Figure 9.1 – Log storage percentage

> **Important note**
>
> Changing the percentage of the total space assigned to a log database requires the database to be recreated and will purge all existing logs.

The rule of thumb is that for an average log rate of 10 logs per second and a retention period of 30 days, you need around 60 gigabytes of storage. The average log rate on a midrange firewall is estimated at around 400 logs per second, which requires nearly 2.5 terabytes of storage to save for 30 days.

There is a calculator available at `https://apps.paloaltonetworks.com/cortex-sizing-calculator`.

> **Important note**
>
> On the local hard drive, logs are pruned on a *first-in-first-out* basis in accordance with their LogDB quota. If the `Traffic` database is full, the oldest logs from the this database will be pruned. Other databases are left alone.

Review the quota usage and retention estimate with the following command:

```
> show system logdb-quota
```

In the next section, we will learn how to set up log collectors and log collector groups.

# Configuring log collectors and log collector groups

To ensure that logs can be stored for an extended period of time, as you may need to comply with certain standards that require lengthy log storage (regulations such as SOX and HIPAA and standards such as ISO 27001 require several years' worth of logs to be stored), exporting them from the firewall and into a dedicated log management system is required.

You can create additional log collectors by setting up (and licensing) a second (to create a high availability cluster) Panorama **Virtual Machine** (**VM**) in Panorama mode, or add M (physical) appliances of panorama and configure them in logger mode.

You can do so from the CLI of the device you want to set to logger mode by executing the following command:

```
> request system system-mode logger
```

In Panorama, you can add multiple log collectors in **Panorama | Managed Collectors** and then add them to one or more groups in **Panorama | Collector Groups**.

To improve availability, you can select **Enable log redundancy across collectors** in the log collector group. This will create a second copy of every log entry, which is stored in a different log collector. This will ensure that logs are always available, even if a log collector is unreachable. This will consume additional disk space, so carefully weigh the need for availability over the retention period.

As you can see in the following screenshots, there are several different ways that log collectors can be deployed to best suit an organization's needs:

- To split managed devices up into groups and set a preferred log collector. The top collector is preferred, and the next collector will be used if the primary one fails or is unreachable:

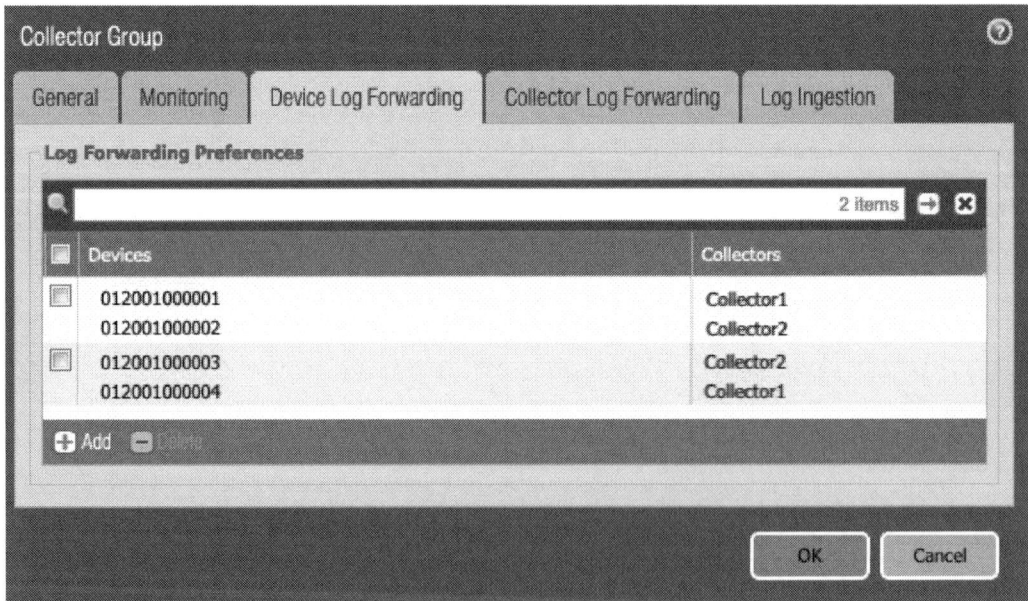

Figure 9.2 – Different collector groups

- To add all managed devices and collectors to one pool and have all devices send logs to the same collector:

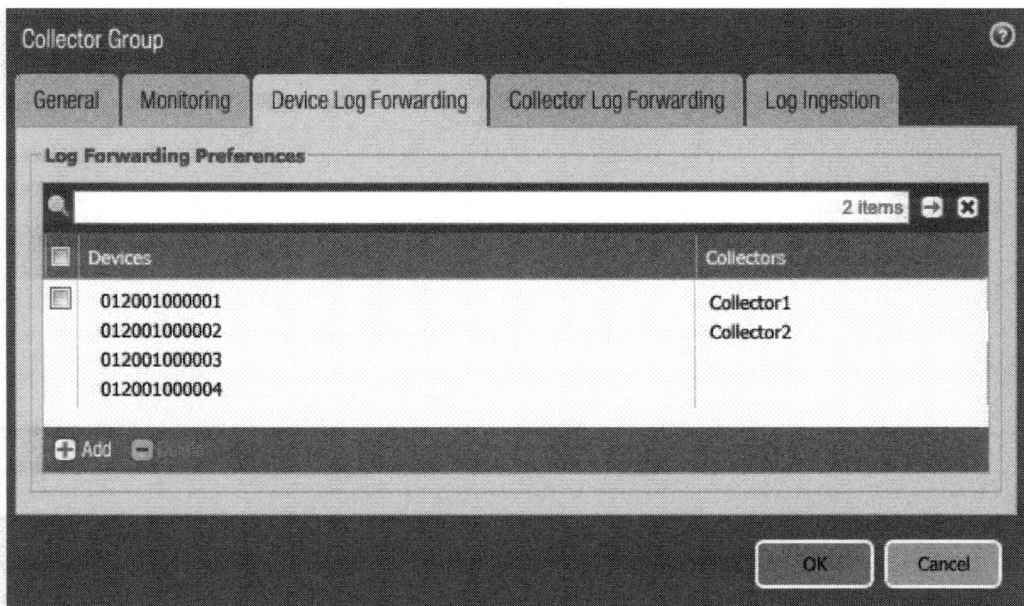

Figure 9.3 – A single collector group

- To limit the collectors available to managed devices. This could be helpful if devices and collectors are spread out geographically:

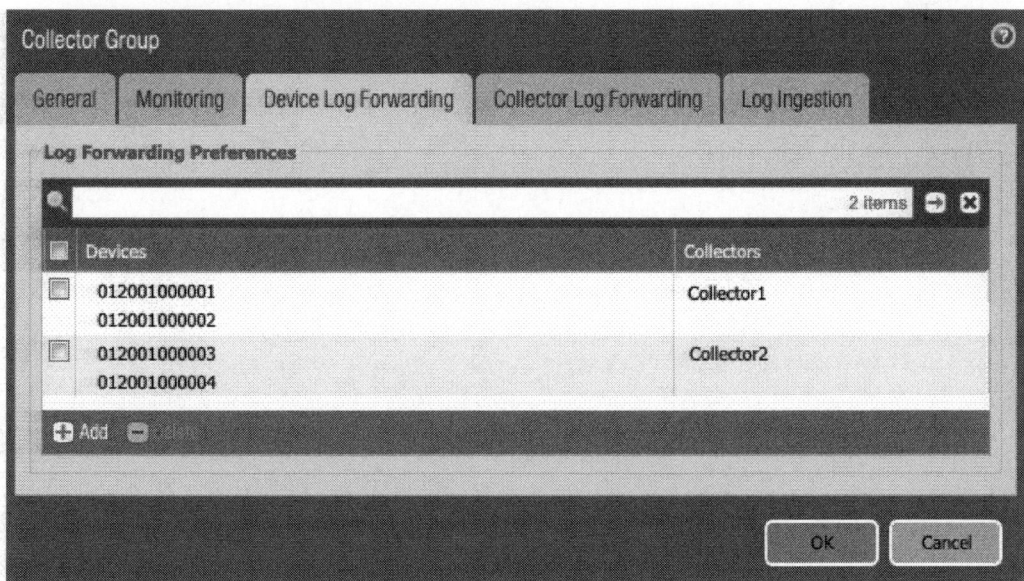

Figure 9.4 – Limited availability of log collectors to devices

> **Important note**
>
> Even though logs are forwarded to the preferred log collector device, the log collector group will evenly distribute logs among all members of the collector group as the collector group is considered one logical unit.

If the bandwidth between geographical locations is too limited for a collector group to efficiently distribute logs among its peers, consider making multiple groups.

Panorama will push these settings out to the managed devices so that they are made aware of which exact destinations they are expected to log to. In the firewall, you can verify the preference list by executing the following command:

```
> show log-collector preference-list
```

You can also verify whether logs are being forwarded properly:

```
> request log-collector-forwarding status
```

As an alternative to deployed physical log collectors, you can also log to the cloud, which we'll see in the next section.

# Logging Service

With **Logging Service**, currently called **Cortex Data Lake**, logs are no longer sent to Panorama or a collector group, but instead go up into the cloud through a secure connection. This is a licensed feature, so every firewall that should log to the cloud will need to be outfitted with a license. Once the licensing is in order and Data Lake is properly set up at `https://apps.paloaltonetworks.com/marketplace/cortex_data_lake`, you can configure each firewall locally or through a Panorama template.

From **Device | Setup | Management | Logging Service**, you can select **Enable Logging Service**. As the following screenshot shows, you can also use **Enable Duplicate Logging**, which writes logs to Panorama or the log collectors and sends a copy to Cortex Data Lake. PA-5200 and PA-7000 can have multiple (up to 20) simultaneous connections to Cortex Data Lake. **Enable Enhanced Application Logging** will increase information gathered about applications and sends this to Cortex Data Lake. These logs can only be consumed by cortex applications and will not be visible to you:

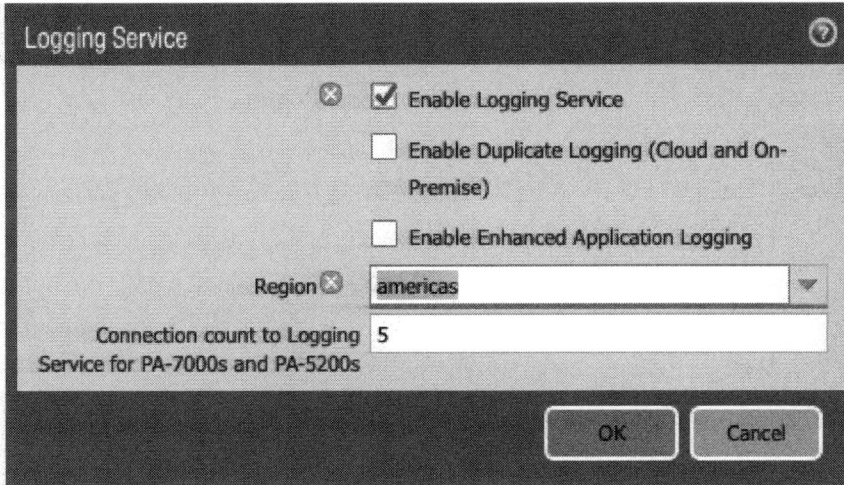

Figure 9.5 – Logging Service

Starting from PAN-OS 9.0.2, you can also connect firewalls that are not managed by Panorama to **Logging Service**. As you can see in the following screenshot, **Onboard without Panorama** has a **Connect** option, which lets you connect to **Logging Service** using a **Pre-Shared Key (PSK)**, which you first configure in the Cortex Data Lake portal:

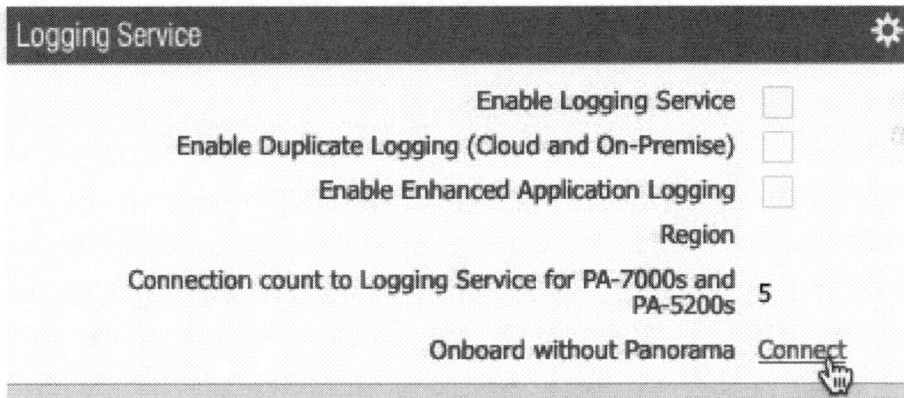

Figure 9.6 – Onboard without Panorama

You can check whether the firewall is connected to **Logging Service** by issuing the following command:

```
> request logging-service-forwarding status
```

You now have a good grasp of the advantages of leveraging cloud storage. In the next section, we'll review alternative options for sending logs out.

# External logging

As well as *native* logging to Palo Alto Network products, you can also forward logs to syslog servers, email them out, send SNMP traps, or forward to an HTTP server.

To be able to forward logs, we will first need to create server profiles that we can later use when we set up forwarding.

For SNMP, we can create a new profile in **Device | Server Profiles | SNMP Trap**. Here, we can choose V2c or V3 SNMP compatibility and provide connectivity details of the SNMP server. If **ENGINEID** is left blank, as in the following screenshot, the firewall will insert its serial number:

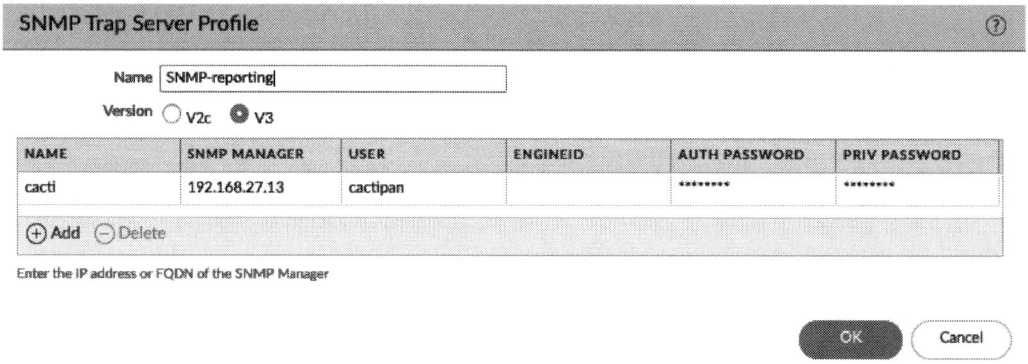

| NAME | SNMP MANAGER | USER | ENGINEID | AUTH PASSWORD | PRIV PASSWORD |
|------|--------------|------|----------|---------------|---------------|
| cacti | 192.168.27.13 | cactipan | | ******** | ******** |

**SNMP Trap Server Profile**

Name  SNMP-reporting
Version  ○ V2c  ● V3

⊕ Add  ⊖ Delete

Enter the IP address or FQDN of the SNMP Manager

OK    Cancel

Figure 9.7 – SNMP v3 server profile

For syslog, we can create a profile in **Device | Server Profiles | Syslog**. We have the option of forwarding over UDP, TCP, or SSL. If possible, select **SSL** as these logs should be considered highly sensitive, and forwarding them as plaintext can generally be considered a bad idea (it could lead to data leaks if intercepted in plaintext). In the **Custom Log Format** tab, you can change how outgoing syslog messages are formatted for each log type. This may be handy if your syslog server configuration has been tweaked to accept different log formatting.

For email, we can create a profile in **Device | Server Profiles | Email**. Here, you need to provide your email relay address, your from and to email addresses, and a friendly display name. You also have the option to customize the log format.

You have now learned which options are available to forward logs from your device and how to set them up. In the next section, we will learn how to configure log forwarding and review how we can select which logs are forwarded.

# Configuring log forwarding

The firewall will not automatically forward all logs to Panorama or **Logging Service**. Log forwarding needs to be configured and assigned to specific logs or log types before anything is sent out. There are two main types of logs that can be forwarded:

- System event logs
- Traffic flow-related logs

Device daemon-related logs are only stored locally.

> **Important note**
> Only logs that are being stored locally can be forwarded. Any rule, policy, or profile that is set to not log also cannot generate logs to be forwarded. Forwarded logs will also remain available locally (for as long as storage is available); they are not purged after being forwarded.

In the firewall, you can check whether log forwarding is available and working with the following commands:

```
> request log-collector-forwarding status
> request logging-service-forwarding status
```

Let's first take a look at the system logs

## System logs

In **Device | Log Settings**, you can set forwarding profiles for **System**, **Configuration**, **User-ID**, **HIP match**, **GlobalProtect**, and more. Simply add a new profile for the logs that need to be forwarded to be centrally available.

If you create a log forwarding profile for, say, a system log, you can check the box next to Panorama/Logging Service to forward logs to Panorama or the cloud, and/or you can set any of the other log forwarding preferences. You can also create multiple forwarding profiles. Each profile has a filter field at the top that has severity filters prepopulated, as well as a filter builder. You can create your own filter incorporating the AND or OR operators so that only specific events trigger this forwarding action.

For example, as depicted in the following screenshot, an email could be sent out to the security team, and a syslog event sent if a failed authentication event is detected for an administrator trying to log into the firewall, while all logs with a severity of **medium** or higher (the geq operator) are forwarded to Panorama or **Logging Service**:

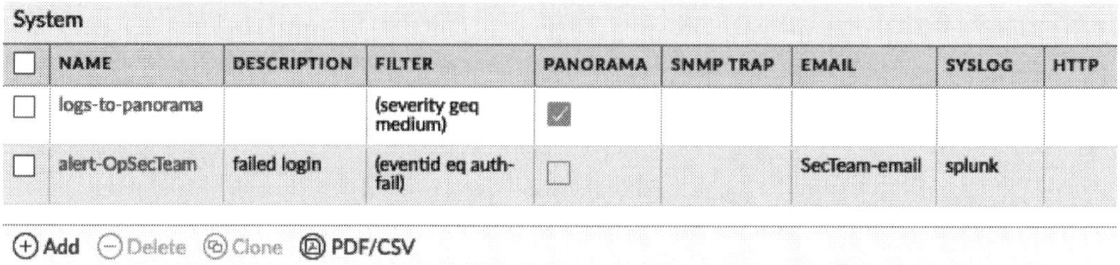

**System**

| | NAME | DESCRIPTION | FILTER | PANORAMA | SNMP TRAP | EMAIL | SYSLOG | HTTP |
|---|---|---|---|---|---|---|---|---|
| ☐ | logs-to-panorama | | (severity geq medium) | ☑ | | | | |
| ☐ | alert-OpSecTeam | failed login | (eventid eq auth-fail) | ☐ | | SecTeam-email | splunk | |

⊕ **Add**  ⊖ Delete  ⊙ Clone  ⊚ **PDF/CSV**

Figure 9.8 – The Log Forwarding filter for failed authentication and Panorama logs

When creating filters, you can use the built-in **Filter Builder** feature, as shown in the following screenshot. All of the available attributes are there, and in many cases, the values are also prepopulated. Simply select the attributes, operators, and values, then click **Add**, and the filter is created:

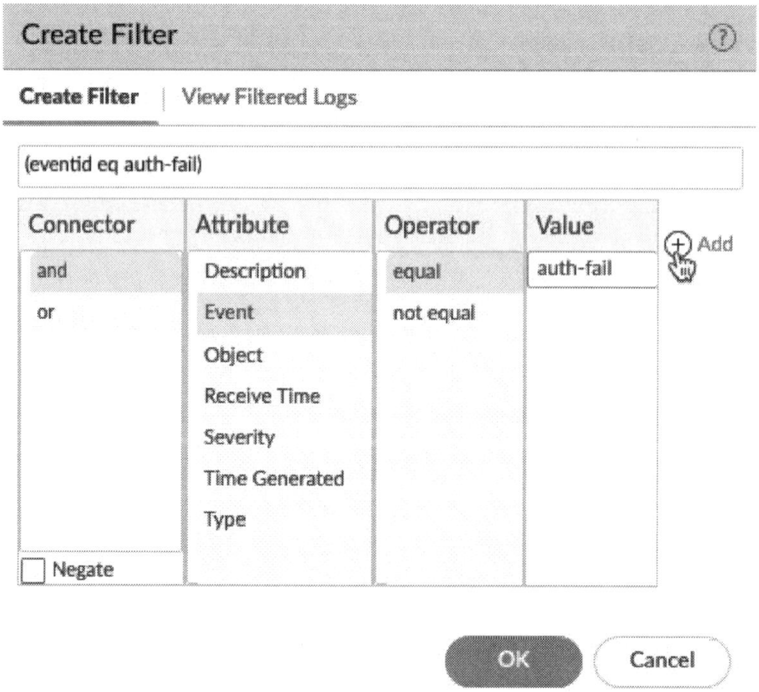

Figure 9.9 – Filter Builder

Next, let's take a look at all the logs that relate to packets flowing through the system.

## Session logs

For logs related to sessions handled by the firewall, a log forwarding profile needs to be created in **Objects | Log Forwarding**.

> **Important note**
>
> If you create a log forwarding profile and name it `default`, it will be automatically added to any new security rule that is created, thus ensuring log forwarding to Panorama or **Logging Service** is not forgotten.

For each log type (**traffic**, **threat**, **url**, **wildfire**, **auth**, **data**, and **tunnel**) that you want to forward, you can create a rule with instructions. You can also add more specific rules that perform a specific action if a certain event is encountered. In the following screenshot, you can see an example of this where a syslog and email will go if a brute-force attack of high or critical severity is detected:

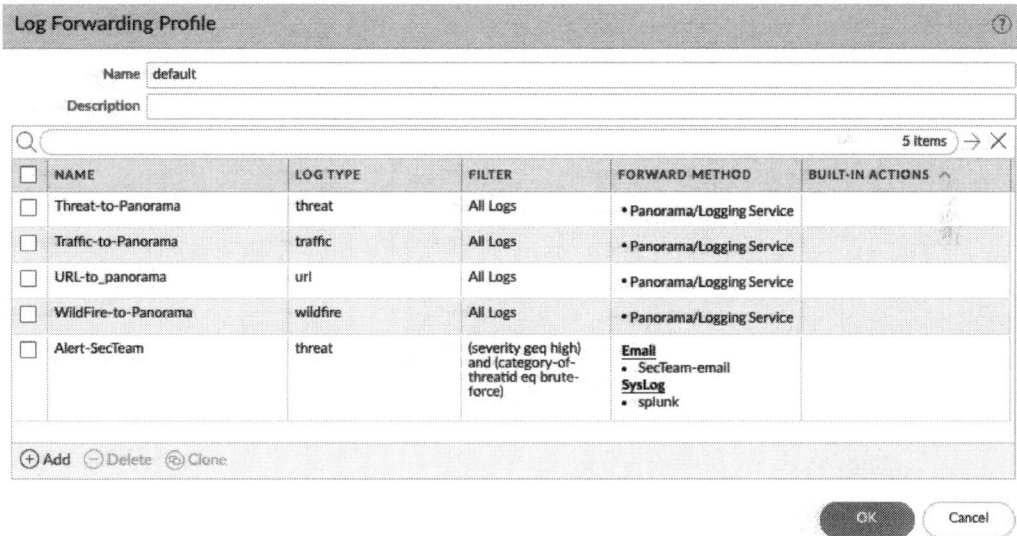

**Log Forwarding Profile**

Name: default
Description:

5 items

| | NAME | LOG TYPE | FILTER | FORWARD METHOD | BUILT-IN ACTIONS |
|---|---|---|---|---|---|
| ☐ | Threat-to-Panorama | threat | All Logs | • Panorama/Logging Service | |
| ☐ | Traffic-to-Panorama | traffic | All Logs | • Panorama/Logging Service | |
| ☐ | URL-to_panorama | url | All Logs | • Panorama/Logging Service | |
| ☐ | WildFire-to-Panorama | wildfire | All Logs | • Panorama/Logging Service | |
| ☐ | Alert-SecTeam | threat | (severity geq high) and (category-of-threatid eq brute-force) | **Email**<br>• SecTeam-email<br>**SysLog**<br>• splunk | |

⊕ Add   ⊖ Delete   ⊚ Clone

OK      Cancel

Figure 9.10 – Log Forwarding Profile

If you want to verify which kinds of logs are captured with the filter you created, you can review them in **View Filtered Logs**. As you can see in the following screenshot, the filter will be transported into a log view so that you can review the type of logs that will be forwarded:

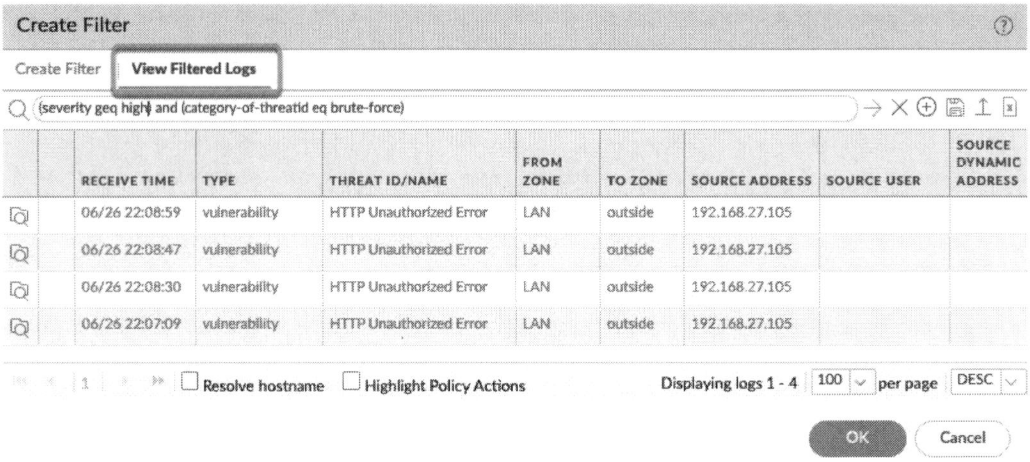

Figure 9.11 – The View Filtered Logs preview tab

If you want to build more-specific log forwarding rules, you can either add more rules to the log forwarding profile, or you can create more log forwarding profiles.

As an example, you may need to forward all critical severity events to an incident response team, but there may be a different team for different servers. You can create two log forwarding profiles, each with a rule that filters for all critical events and forwards them to a different email profile for each log forwarding profile. Then, attach these log forwarding profiles to two different rules.

> **Important note**
> While you can have many log forwarding profiles, only one profile can be attached to a security rule at a time.

Let's take a look at this with a practical example.

In **Objects | Log Forwarding**, we create two different log forwarding profiles. As you can see in the following screenshot, they both forward all logs to Panorama/**Logging Service**, but also have a filtered rule for threat logs of critical severity with a different email action set:

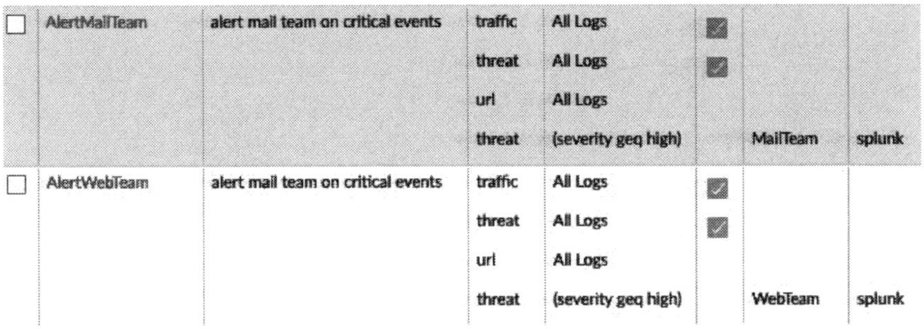

| | | | | | | | |
|---|---|---|---|---|---|---|---|
| ☐ | AlertMailTeam | alert mail team on critical events | traffic | All Logs | ☑ | | |
| | | | threat | All Logs | ☑ | | |
| | | | url | All Logs | | | |
| | | | threat | (severity geq high) | | MailTeam | splunk |
| ☐ | AlertWebTeam | alert mail team on critical events | traffic | All Logs | ☑ | | |
| | | | threat | All Logs | ☑ | | |
| | | | url | All Logs | | | |
| | | | threat | (severity geq high) | | WebTeam | splunk |

Figure 9.12 – Log forwarding profiles with a filter

In **Policies | Security**, we create two new rules – one for inbound connections to the web server farm and one for inbound connections to the mail server farm – and attach the log forwarding profiles, as in the following screenshot:

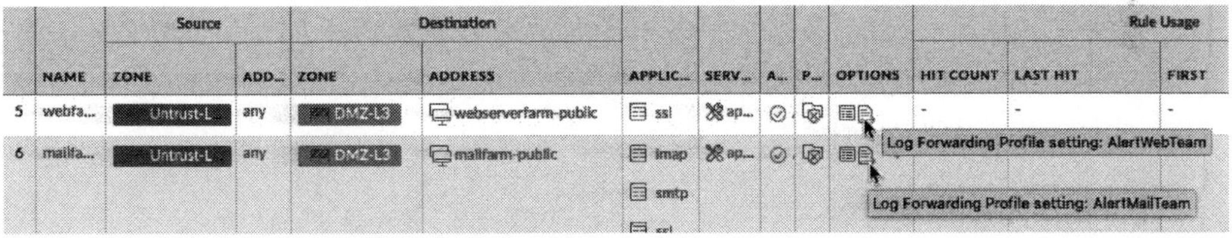

Figure 9.13 – Log forwarding profiles attached to security rules

While it is good practice to forward all logs to Panorama, some applications, such as DNS, may generate so many logs that it may be better not to log these sessions at all, not even on the local firewall. The result is that no traffic log is written for these sessions, but any threat actions triggered by a security profile will be logged in the threat log. For these cases, you would disable the **Log at Session End** and **Log at Session Start** options, but still set a log forwarding profile so that threat logs are forwarded to Panorama, as in the following screenshot:

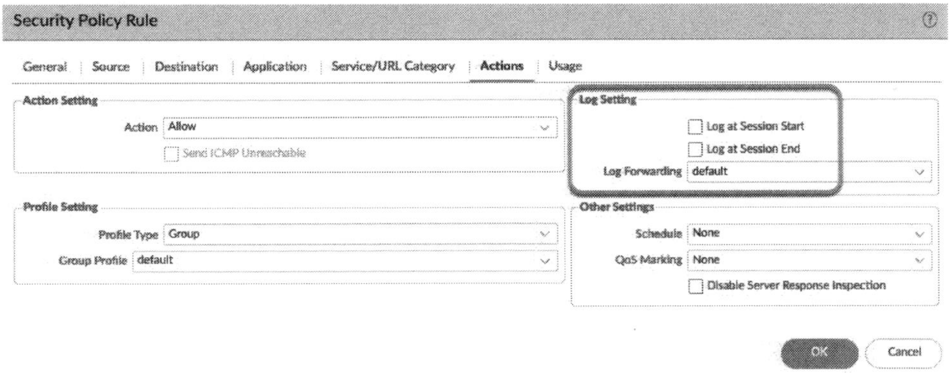

Figure 9.14 – Log settings for a chatty security rule

> **Important note**
> **Log at Session End** will write the log once the session is completed, including all the session details, in a single log file. **Log at Session Start** will create a log entry at the start of each session and each time the application of the session changes. This could mean there will be several start logs for a single session, so this will have an impact on the log volume.

In this section, you have learned how to set up log collection and how to forward logs from the firewall to a remote server. In the next section, we will look at reporting and how to create custom reports.

# Reporting

Reports can be generated on the firewall to provide an overview at a glance about which applications are most popular or how many threats were detected for a certain timeframe.

The firewall has a set of predefined reports that run overnight and provide the most common insights.

## Pre-defined reports

These reports provide a wide variety of information about the types of applications, threats, traffic, and URL filtering activity. They are set to run at 2 A.M., but if this is not a convenient time, you can change the start time in **Device | Setup | Management | Logging and Reporting Settings | Log Export** and reporting and change **Report Runtime**. As you can see in the following screenshot, you can also disable some reports in the **Pre-Defined Reports** tab by unchecking them and committing the change:

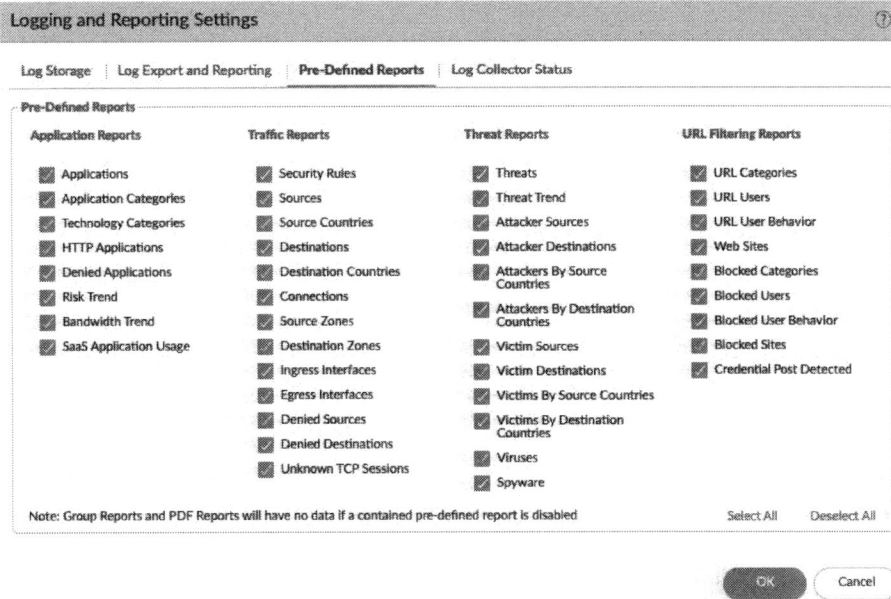

Figure 9.15 – Enabling or disabling pre-defined reports

You can find the reports in **Monitor | Reports**. On the right-hand side, you can select which report category you want to see, and then select one of the reports. As you can see in the following screenshot, once a report type is selected, you can use the calendar at the bottom to select which day you want to review, which will then load the corresponding report on the left-hand side. Entries seen in these reports can be clicked on to drill down into more detailed information, which will take you to the **Application Command Center (ACC)**:

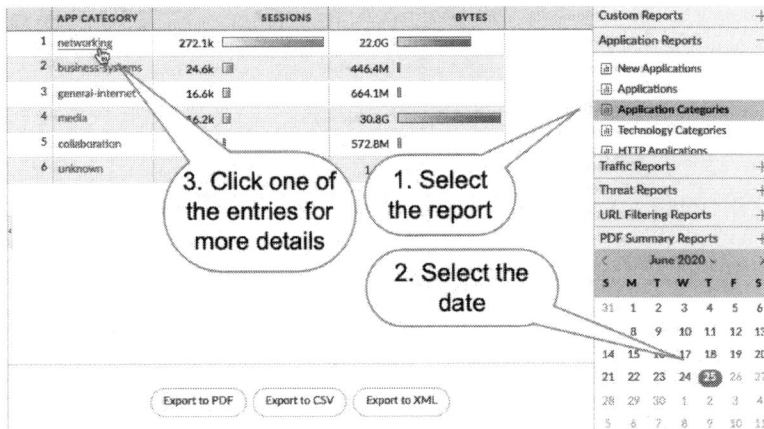

Figure 9.16 – Pre-defined reports

You can also build your own reports that contain the data most relevant to you.

## Custom reports

In **Monitor | Manage Custom Reports**, you can build custom reports. There are two major sources of information that can be used to generate reports: **Summary Databases** and **Detailed Logs**:

- Summary databases are comprised of pre-summarized statistics on applications, traffic, threats, and tunnels, which the data plane collects and stores. Reports created from these databases are faster to generate but may not have all the columns that a log has.

- Detailed log databases are the actual log files that are parsed and data extracted to generate the report. These reports take longer to generate and may see increased management plane CPU usage during generation, but can contain more information than the summary databases.

The pre-defined reports can be loaded as a template so that you can finetune a type of report if you like the original but want more granularity or, for example, an additional column.

If you want a custom report to run periodically, you must enable **Scheduled**.

Let's create an example report:

1. Add a new report and select **Load Template** to load Top-Destinations.

2. The template automatically loads the traffic summary database and loads the columns with **Destination Address**, **Destination User**, and **Bytes and Sessions**, as well as sets **Sort By** to **Sessions**.

3. Set **Scheduled**.

4. Set **Time Frame** to Last Calendar Week.

5. You can click **Run Now** to see what the report will look like. You'll see that the report simply shows which IPs are the most popular destinations based on the session count.

6. Now, add the Application column by selecting it from the available columns and clicking on the little + sign.

7. Now, click on **Run Now** again and compare the two reports. The new report still has the most popular destinations sorted by session count, but now, the destinations are split up based on **Application.**

8. Now, set **Group By** to **Application** for **10 Groups**.

Your custom report will now look as in the following screenshot:

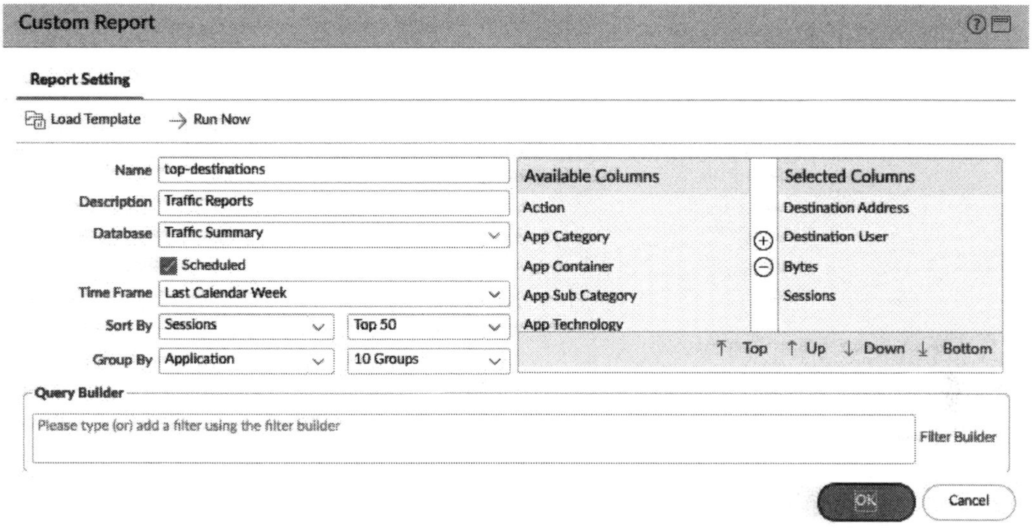

Figure 9.17 – Custom report from a template

9. If you hit **Run Now** again and compare the report, you will notice that the destinations are now sorted in groups per application, with the top destination for each application sorted by session count.

10. Click **OK**.

You can also add filters to get more-granular reports:

1. Add a new report and call it `Threats per Week`.

2. Select the **Threat Summary** database.

3. Set **Scheduled**.

4. Change **Time Frame** to **Last Calendar Week**.

5. From the columns, select **Count**, **Action**, **Severity**, **Threat/Content Name**, **Application**, **Source Address**, and **Source User**.

6. Sort by **Count** and **Top 10**.

7. Group by **Application** and **10 Groups**.

8. To prevent this report from getting filled to the brim with informational severity threats, click on the **Filter Builder** option in the bottom-right corner.

9. Set a **And Severity Greater than or Equal high** filter, then click on **Add** and then **Apply**.

Your custom report will look as in the following screenshot:

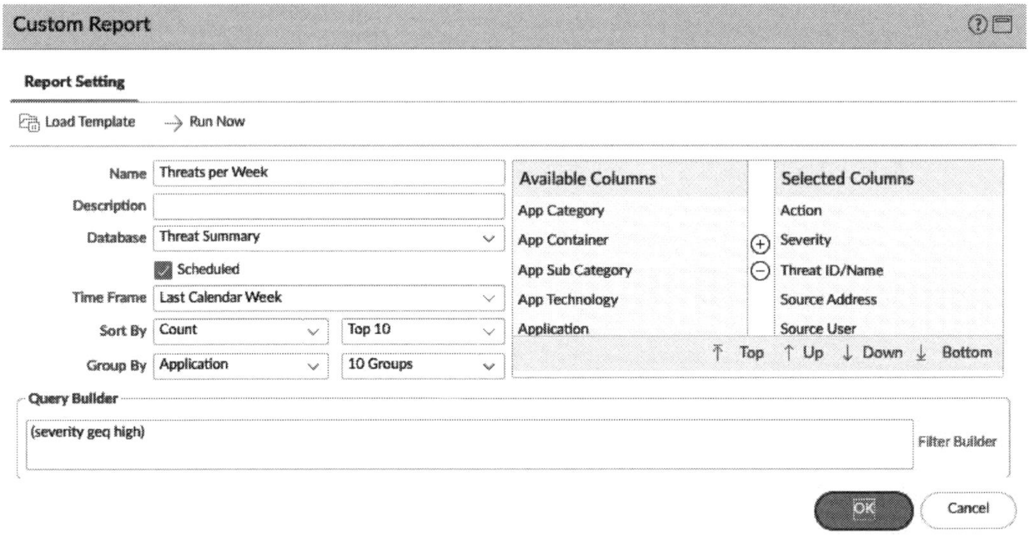

Figure 9.18 – Custom report with additional filters

10. Click **Run Now** to get a preview of the report. Only high or critical vulnerabilities will show up in the report.

11. Click **OK**.

> **Important note**
> Reports that are scheduled for a specified timeframe will only run once that timeframe has been reached. In the case of Last Calendar Week or Last Calendar Month, the report will run the first time a full Monday–Sunday week has passed since creating the report, or a full 1st to 30th/31st month has passed.

To be able to send out emailed reports, we still need to create a report group, or a PDF summary.

In **Monitor | PDF Reports | Manage PDF Summary**, you can create a new PDF summary. A new PDF summary will have all the threat reports selected and part of the **Application** reports. You can disable and add any predefined or custom reports, as well as trend reports, which are only available in PDF summaries. So, go ahead and create a new PDF summary:

1.  Remove all the predefined reports.

2.  Add all the trend reports.

3.  Name the report `Trends`.

4.  Click **OK**.

The PDF summary will look as in the following screenshot:

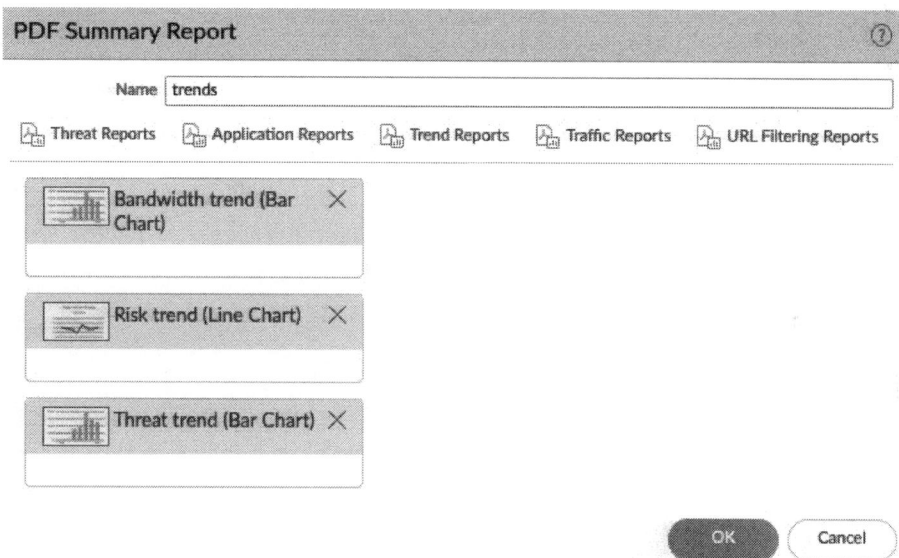

Figure 9.19 – PDF summary report creation

In the report groups, you can group predefined and custom reports, and you can also add summary PDFs:

1.  Add a new report group and call it `Weekly Report`.

2.  Select **Title Page** and set **Title** to `Weekly Report`.

3.  Add the PDF summary report.

4.  Add the two custom reports (make sure to select the reports listed under **Custom Report** and not the ones under **CSV**).

5.  Add any reports you'd like to get a weekly report on.

    The **Report Group** page will look similar to the following screenshot. Add additional reports as you wish:

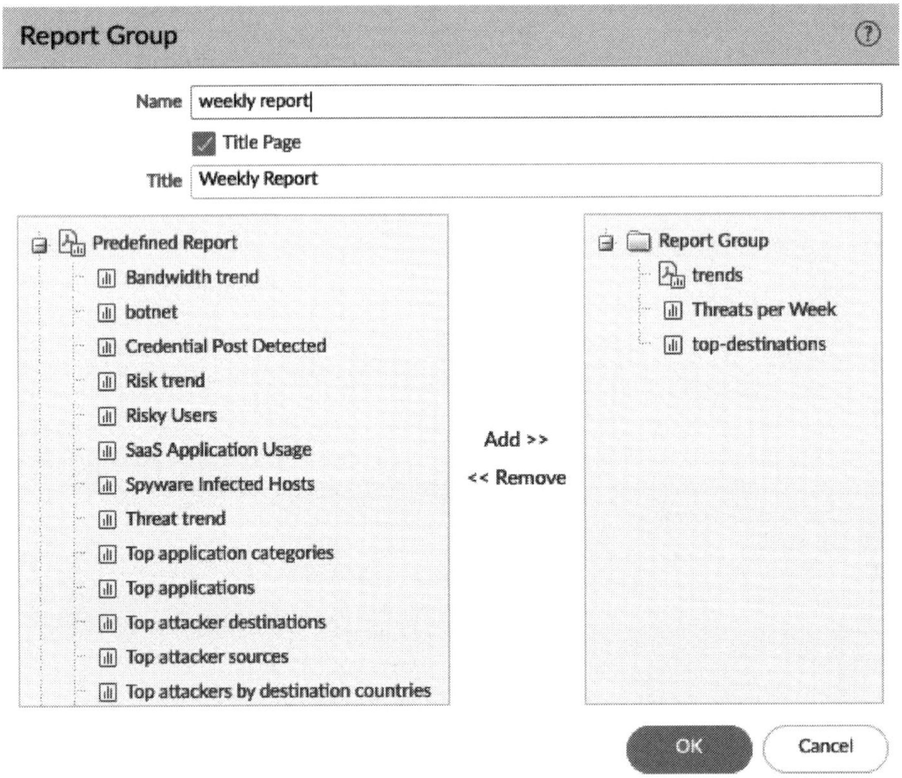

Figure 9.20 – Report Group

6.  Click **OK**.

The last step is to create an email scheduler in **Monitor | PDF Reports | Email Scheduler**:

1.  Set **Name** to Weekly Report.
2.  Select the Weekly Report report group.
3.  Select one of the email profiles you created earlier, or create a new one for these reports.
4.  Set **Recurrence** to Every Monday.

    The **Email Scheduler** page will look similar to the following screenshot:

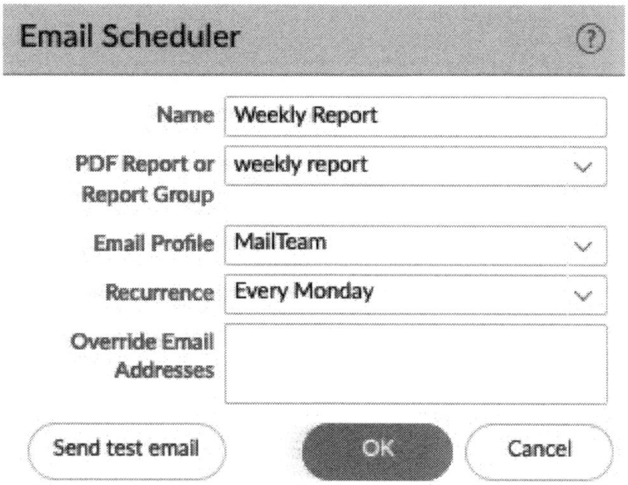

Figure 9.21 – Email Scheduler for reports

5.  Click **OK**.

6.  Commit the changes.

The system will now start collecting statistics to create custom reports and a summary PDF. The resulting output will be emailed every Monday. The first time that this report will be emailed and be complete could take more than a week as custom reports take a full Monday to Sunday week to create a full report (so, if today is Friday, then the first report containing statistics from the custom reports will arrive in 10 days).

There are also two *on-the-fly* reports intended to supply information about a user or SaaS applications:

- **User Activity Report** creates a report regarding a user or group activities. You only need to supply the username or group name and a timeframe for the report to be generated (and select whether you want to see detailed browsing information, which could be a privacy concern).

- **SaaS Application Usage** lets you run a report on the past several days for source users and zones, or only source zones on the usage of SaaS applications.

The **SaaS Application Usage** report will mention sanctioned and unsanctioned SaaS applications, as shown in the following screenshot. To mark applications as **Sanctioned**, open **Objects | Applications** and look for the applications you want to mark. In the **Applications** dialog, hit **edit** in the tags and then select **Sanctioned**, then click **OK**:

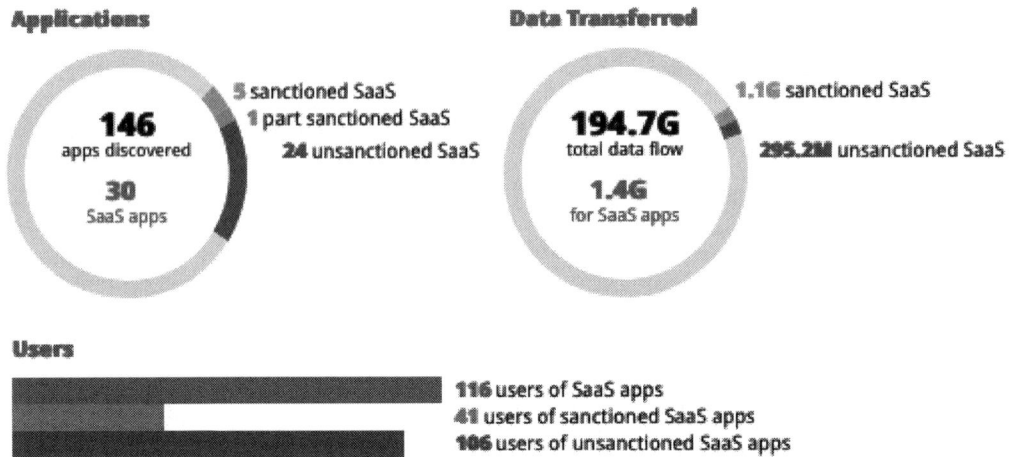

**Applications**

**146** apps discovered

**30** SaaS apps

5 sanctioned SaaS
1 part sanctioned SaaS
24 unsanctioned SaaS

**Data Transferred**

**194.7G** total data flow

**1.4G** for SaaS apps

1.1G sanctioned SaaS
295.2M unsanctioned SaaS

**Users**

116 users of SaaS apps
41 users of sanctioned SaaS apps
106 users of unsanctioned SaaS apps

Figure 9.22 – Sanctioned and unsanctioned applications in an SaaS report

You can now build and schedule your own reports. You may have noticed that you can drill down, or zoom into, the reports by clicking on addresses, applications, threats, or other details, which then redirects you to the **Application Command Center** (**ACC**).

# The Application Command Center

Next to reports that run on a daily basis, the ACC lets you get a quick look into what is happening in your network by using simple graphs that you can drill down into for more information. There are four default tabs:

- **Network Activity**, which gives you an overview of all the applications seen in the specified timeframe, their byte count, the session count, the threat count, and the number of users. If you scroll down, you will see more detailed source and destination graphs and which rules have been hit most.

- **Threat Activity** gives you a breakdown of all the types of threats and how many times they were seen.

- **Blocked Activity** shows which applications have been blocked due to threats, content, or URL actions

- **Tunnel Activity** is used to report on tunnel inspection for GRE, GPRS, and non-encrypted IPSec.

You can also add a tab and create a page with all the widgets you like in one single pane, which may be useful if you want to be able to keep tabs on something more specific. As shown in the following screenshot, when you are investigating an entry, you can either create global filters from the left-hand side filter creator, or you can click on the little arrow that appears when you hover over any item that can be filtered:

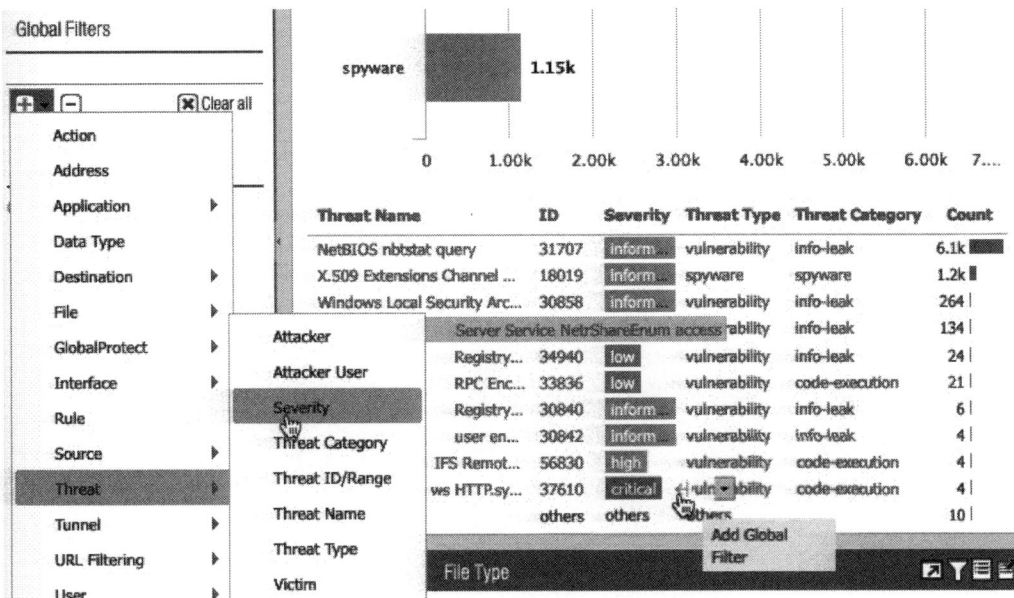

Figure 9.23 – Adding filters in the ACC

Once you've drilled down to the information you want to investigate and you want to access the associated logs, you can use the **Jump to Logs** quick link, which will take you to the log viewer with the appropriate filters already filled in, as you can see in the following screenshot:

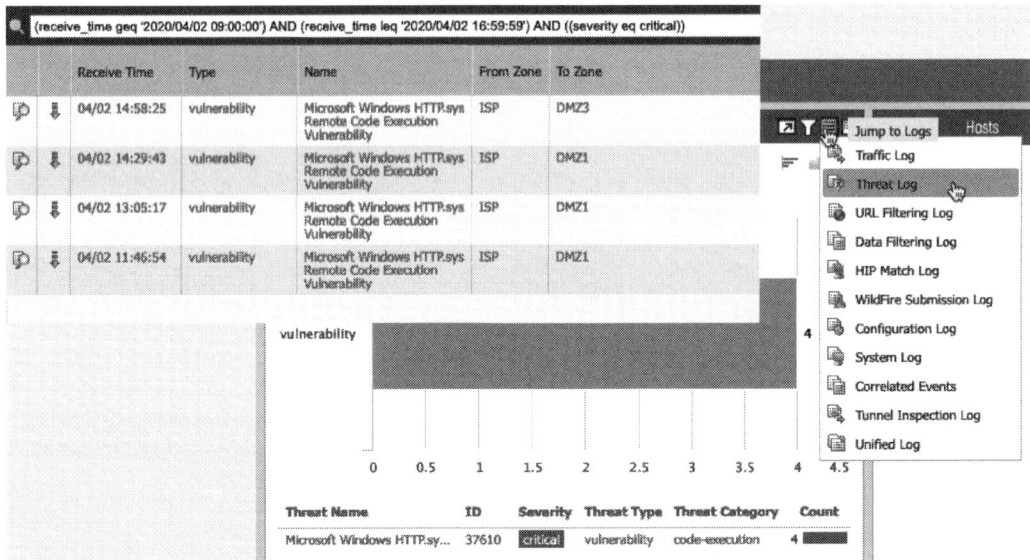

Figure 9.24 – The Jump to Logs link in the ACC

As another example, as you can see in the following screenshot, today I have had a peak in my network traffic in the outbound direction:

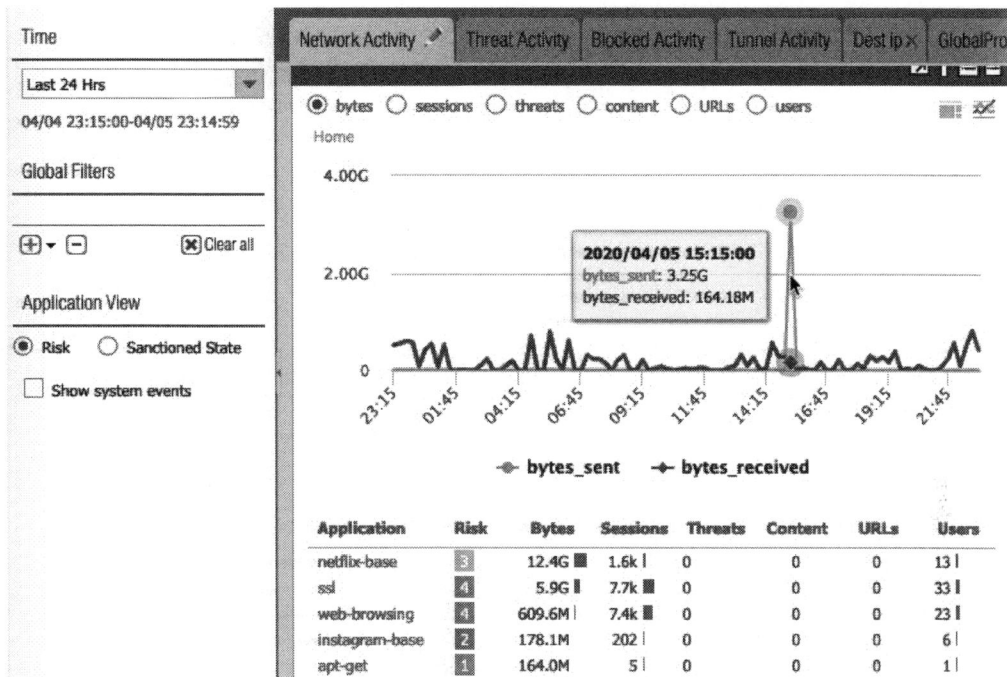

Figure 9.25 – Network Activity in the ACC

If I scroll down to the source and destination IP addresses widgets, I can see that there is a lot of traffic flowing to `192.168.27.5`, which is a VM server in my **DMZ** (**demilitarized zone**). So, as you can see in the following screenshot, I can click on the arrow to the right of the IP to add it as a filter:

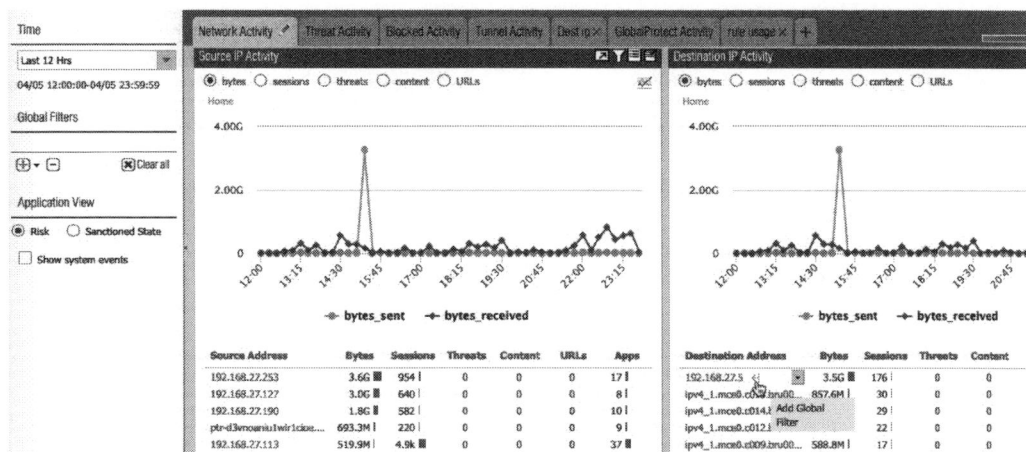

Figure 9.26 – Reviewing the source and destination IP in the ACC

After applying the filter, as you can see in the following screenshot, I can see that the application used to transmit this volume was `ssl` and the sender was `192.168.27.253`, which is my laptop:

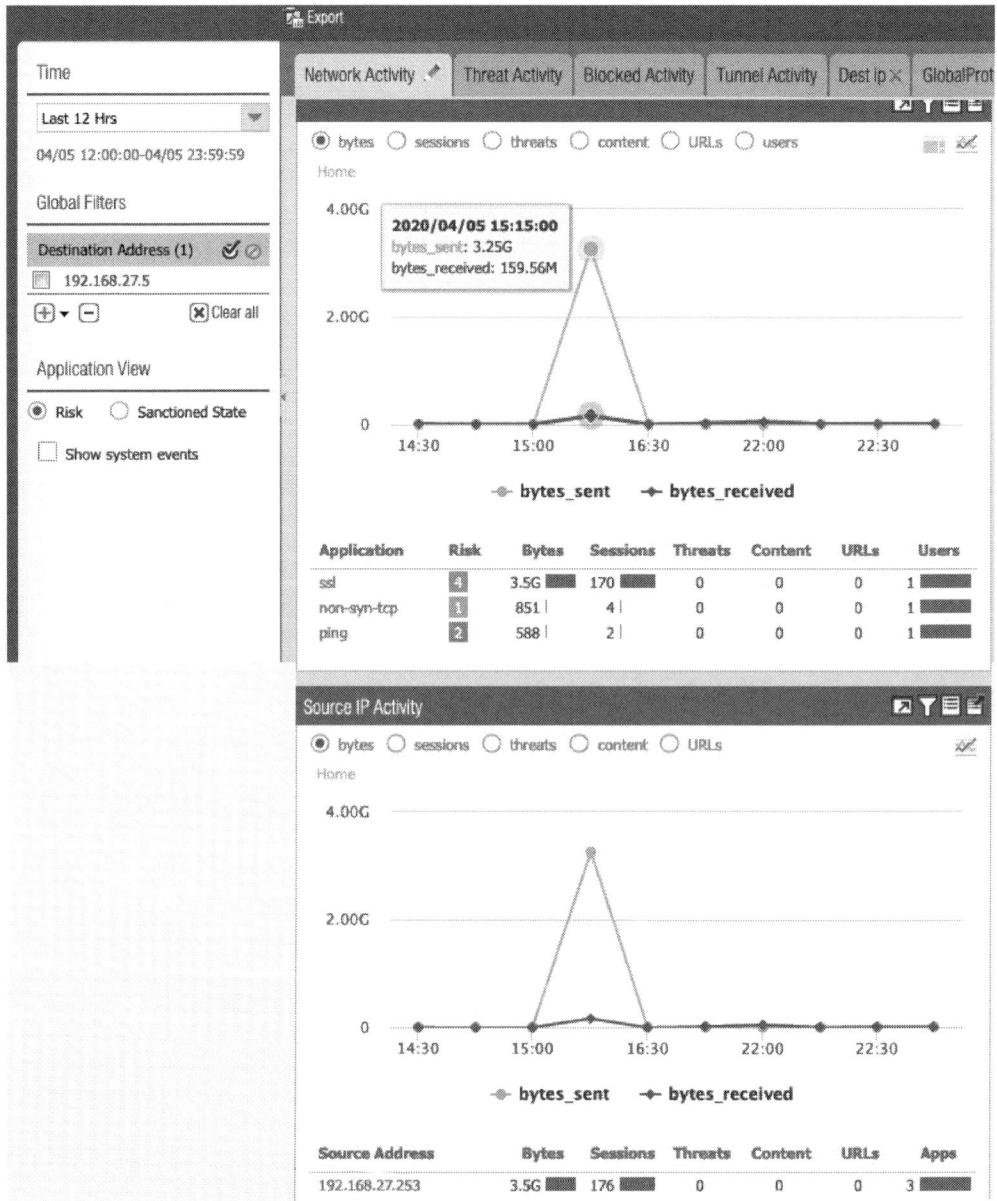

Figure 9.27 – Filtered view in the ACC

You can now use the ACC to gain an eagle-eye view of the things happening on your network. I do encourage you to create a custom tab and add widgets. One of my favorite combinations of widgets is using **Rule Usage**, **Rules Allowing Apps On Non Standard Ports**, and **Security Policies Blocking Activity** to keep track of my security policy and help me make tweaks where needed.

In the last section, we'll learn how logs can be filtered and how additional information and actions can be taken from logs.

# Filtering logs

When you access any of the logs in **Monitor | Logs**, the sheer volume of information can be overwhelming and difficult to navigate at first. Once you learn how to master log filters, you'll be able to get to the information you need quickly. Log filters are built by combining several statements via logical operators. Most fields in the log view are clickable and will automatically create a filter for you. You can then edit the filter and add more conditions to return the information you need.

For example, if you want to look at a 5 minute timeframe, you can click on any date in the log view twice and then edit both entries to look something like this:

```
( receive_time geq '2020/04/05 14:45:00' ) and ( receive_time
leq '2020/04/05 14:50:00' )
```

receive_time is the parameter for when a log was received

geq stands for **Greater or Equal**, while c means **Less than or Equal**. So, this filter restricts the log view to anything received after 2020/04/05 14:45, but before 14:50 of that same date.

> **Important note**
> Receive_time is the time the log is received ("written") by logreceiver. This entry will usually be written at the **session's end**, so the session could have started much earlier. There is an additional column that you can activate that is called generate_time, which is when log collection for a particular session is started at the **start of the session**.

You can add additional filters by clicking on and editing desired information, such as adding port 443 and sessions that have been allowed:

```
and ( port.dst eq 443 ) and ( action eq allow )
```

If you need to add a source, destination, or any IP or subnet, you can add any of the following variants:

```
and ( addr.src in 192.168.27.253 )
and ( addr.dst in 192.168.27.253 )
and ( addr in 192.168.27.253 )
and ( addr.src in 192.168.27.0/24 )
and ( addr.src notin 192.168.27.253 )
```

For addresses, you can use `.src` or `.dst` to denote a source or destination or leave the extension to `addr` blank to indicate *anywhere*. For addresses, you can also set subnets of any size or add `not` to the operator to negate the statement.

For the `eq` operator, you can use `neq` to **negate**, and as a negative connector, you can use AND NOT, which allows plenty of flexibility as both the following statements have the same outcome:

```
( port.dst eq 443 ) and not (app eq ssl)
( port.dst eq 443 ) and  ( app neq ssl )
```

You can also add round brackets to combine statements in an AND or OR statement, as follows:

```
( port.dst eq 443 ) and  (( app eq facebook-base ) or ( app eq
facebook-video ))
```

The preceding filters require port 443 to be used in the session, but their application can either be `facebook-base` or `facebook-video`.

Most filters use the eq, neq, leq, geq, in, and notin operators, but there are two exceptions:

- Some filters can have an `is present/is not present` statement by using (x neq '') or (y eq '') (double single quote marks).

  For example, `user.src neq ''` means a user must be present, and logs where there is no username will be filtered out.

- The Flags attribute uses has as it indicates whether the log entry has a flag set for a special condition – for example, PCAP, NAT, or SSL proxy – which is added to the log entry to indicate that a packet capture was stored for this session or threat and that the session was NATed or SSL-decrypted.

As you can see in the following screenshot, you can also use a filter builder by clicking on the green + sign to the right of the filter bar. To add a filter, do the following:

1. Select the connector.

2. Choose the attribute that you want to filter by.

3. Set the appropriate operator.

4. Select or fill out the value.

5. Click **Add**.

6. Click **Apply**.

7. Click **Close**:

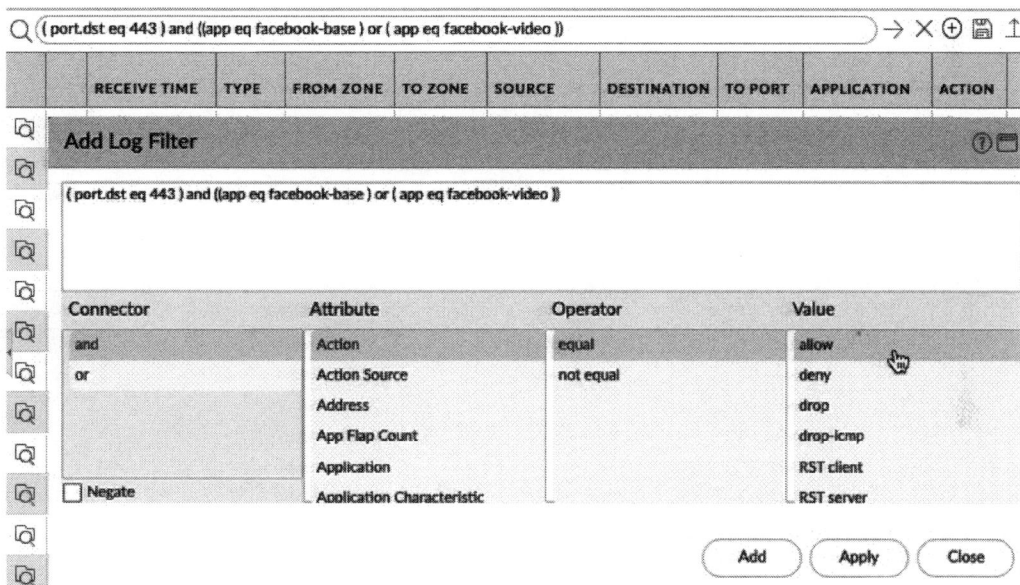

Figure 9.28 – Using the log filter builder

Once you have set up all the appropriate filters and found the log you are looking for, you can click on the little magnifying glass icon to the left-hand side of the log entry to drill down into the session details of the log. In the following screenshot, you can see that there is additional information about the session:

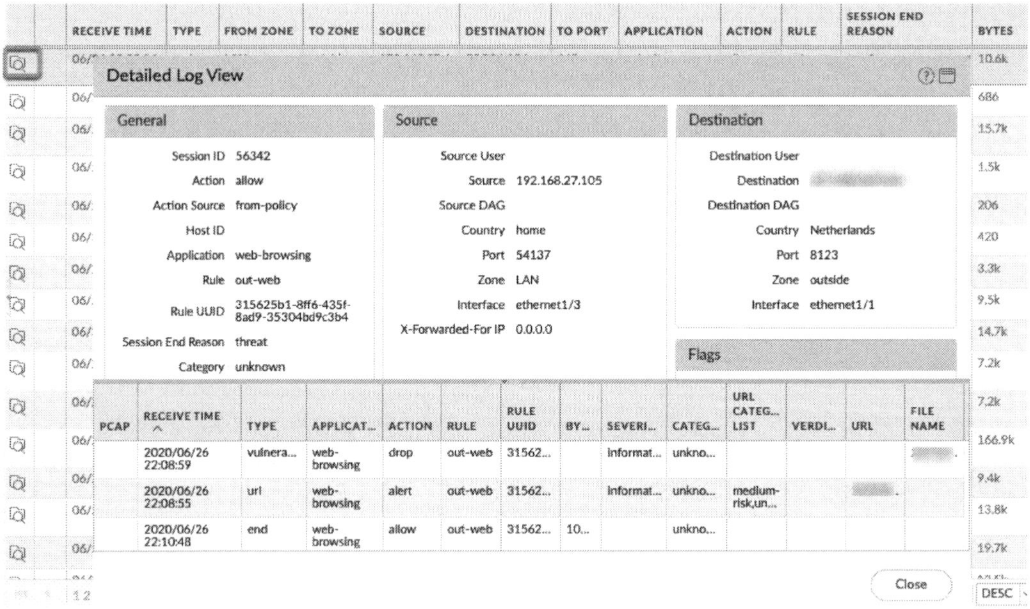

| | RECEIVE TIME | TYPE | FROM ZONE | TO ZONE | SOURCE | DESTINATION | TO PORT | APPLICATION | ACTION | RULE | SESSION END REASON | BYTES |
|---|---|---|---|---|---|---|---|---|---|---|---|---|
| | 06/ | | | | | | | | | | | 10.6k |

**Detailed Log View**

| General | | Source | | Destination | |
|---|---|---|---|---|---|
| Session ID | 56342 | Source User | | Destination User | |
| Action | allow | Source | 192.168.27.105 | Destination | |
| Action Source | from-policy | Source DAG | | Destination DAG | |
| Host ID | | Country | home | Country | Netherlands |
| Application | web-browsing | Port | 54137 | Port | 8123 |
| Rule | out-web | Zone | LAN | Zone | outside |
| Rule UUID | 315625b1-8ff6-435f-8ad9-35304bd9c3b4 | Interface | ethernet1/3 | Interface | ethernet1/1 |
| Session End Reason | threat | X-Forwarded-For IP | 0.0.0.0 | | |
| Category | unknown | | | **Flags** | |

| PCAP | RECEIVE TIME | TYPE | APPLICAT... | ACTION | RULE | RULE UUID | BY... | SEVERI... | CATEG... | URL CATEG... LIST | VERDI... | URL | FILE NAME |
|---|---|---|---|---|---|---|---|---|---|---|---|---|---|
| | 2020/06/26 22:08:59 | vulnera... | web-browsing | drop | out-web | 31562... | | informat... | unkno... | | | | |
| | 2020/06/26 22:08:55 | url | web-browsing | alert | out-web | 31562... | | informat... | unkno... | medium-risk,un... | | | |
| | 2020/06/26 22:10:48 | end | web-browsing | allow | out-web | 31562... | 10... | | unkno... | | | | |

Close

Figure 9.29 – Detailed log view

At the bottom of the detailed view, there are related log files. Clicking on these will bring up those logs' details, as you can see in the following screenshot. This allows you to review any related log files to learn more about what is happening with the session. In many cases, there will be a **traffic** log, a **url** log, and a **threat** log listed, so you can review all the details for each log from one window:

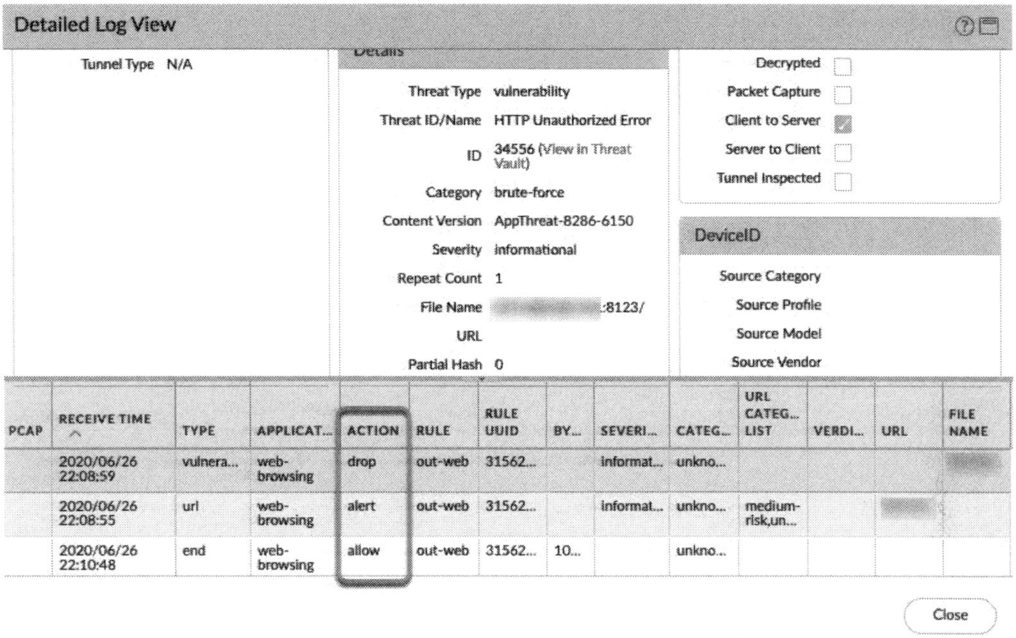

Figure 9.30 – Related log file details in the detailed log view

**Important note**

You may have noticed that the action on both logs is different. This is because the **traffic** log records what happened to the session at the network layer (in this case, the TCP session was ended naturally), while the **threat** log records what happened at the application layer, which may be that a file was discarded, the user was redirected to a block page, or other actions.

In some cases, threats may be expected for certain situations as they could simply be badly implemented services or intentionally changed protocols. For these situations, you can add exceptions by hovering over the threat name in the threat log and clicking on the arrow and then the **Exception** dialog. As you can see in the following screenshot, you can then select the security profile that you want to add an exception to, and the IP (source or destination) you want to set the exception for:

Figure 9.31 – Adding exceptions for threats

For the last step, you may want to go to the security profile in **Objects | Security Profiles** and change the exception action associated with the vulnerability to something else (you can use the exception to change the behavior to allow or block exempted IP addresses, depending on your needs). In the following screenshot, you can see how you can change the action of the exception. By default, an exception is set to the **allow** action, which stops the logging of these events as well. Depending on your needs, you may opt to set the exception to **Alert** so that logs are still created:

> **Important note**
>
> You may notice, in the following screenshot, that the default action of this threat is **default (allow)**, but it was being denied in the logs earlier. This means the security profile associated with the security rule that this session was hitting is configured to bypass default actions and apply different actions.

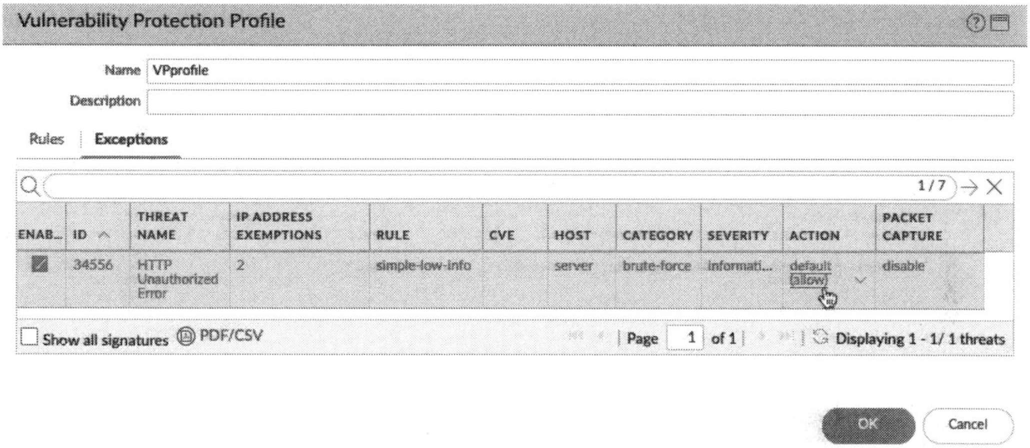

Figure 9.32 – Changing the action of an exception

With the information you just learned, you should now be able to find logs that are relevant to your needs quickly and drill down into the finer details of each session, as well as find associated logs and add exceptions to threats where needed.

# Summary

In this chapter, you learned all about how logging works and how to scale and set up the infrastructure to capture logs. You also learned some methods to send logs out to Palo Alto Networks logging appliances or cloud instances. You learned how to set up forwarding to syslog servers and send out emails on certain events. Finally, you learned how to leverage filters to drill down into detailed information so that you can quickly find what you need.

In the next chapter, we will be learning how to set up site-to-site and GlobalProtect VPN tunnels and how to create custom applications and threats.

# 10
# VPN and Advanced Protection

In this chapter, we will learn about advanced configuration features, such as site-to-site VPN and the challenges it poses when connecting to different vendors. We will learn how to set up a GlobalProtect VPN and verify whether hosts connecting remotely are in a permissible state to enter the network or need to be quarantined. We will create custom applications and custom threats and apply them to a policy, and we will review how zone protection and **Denial of Service (DoS)** protection can defend the network and individual resources from attackers.

In this chapter, we're going to cover the following main topics:

- Site-to-site VPN
- The GlobalProtect client and satellite VPN
- Custom applications and application override
- Custom threat signatures
- Zone protection and DoS protection

# Technical requirements

In this chapter, we will be covering remote connections and protection from inbound connections. If you have a lab environment where you can simulate setting up VPN connections to other devices or produce incoming connections from a client, this will help greatly in visualizing what is being explained.

# Setting up the VPN

There are several ways of connecting devices in a secure way. Palo Alto Networks firewalls currently support the following protocols:

- **Generic Routing Encapsulation** (**GRE**) is a fairly old protocol that is not very secure but can be useful if legacy devices need to be connected to the firewall to provide rudimentary security to the encapsulated packets.

- **Internet Protocol Security** (**IPSec**) is the de facto tunneling protocol between remote sites and can be used for very strong encryption.

- **Secure Socket Layer** (**SSL**), which is really **Transport Layer Security** (**TLS**), is used to connect endpoints over a *network-friendly* protocol.

To set up GRE tunnels, you can set up a connection in **Networks | GRE Tunnels**. All you need to configure is the following:

- Name
- Source interface
- Source IP
- Destination IP
- Tunnel interface
- TTL (default 64)
- Keepalive

Set up the same configurations on the remote end to get it going. Routing and security are handled in security policies and the virtual router.

In the next section, we will set up IPSec connections and learn about the different ways to implement the configuration.

# Configuring the IPSec site-to-site VPN

Before you can set up a VPN tunnel between two peers, you first need to agree on the cryptography settings that will need to be applied on both sides so that the tunnel can be negotiated. If the remote end is not under your control, you will need to reach out to your peer to agree on which configuration to use.

In the first phase (phase 1) of the negotiation, both peers authenticate one another through the **Internet Key Exchange** (**IKE**) process. Once the authentication has been established, an IPSec **Security Association** (**SA**) is created on both sides that contains all the parameters needed to set up the phase 2 IPSec VPN tunnel.

The phase 1 crypto profile can be created in **Network | Network Profiles | IKE Crypto**. As you can see in the following screenshot, there are three default profiles already present with the following settings:

| | NAME | ENCRYPTION | AUTHENTICATION | DH GROUP | KEY LIFETIME |
|---|---|---|---|---|---|
| ☐ | default | aes-128-cbc, 3des | sha1 | group2 | 8 hours |
| ☐ | Suite-B-GCM-128 | aes-128-cbc | sha256 | group19 | 8 hours |
| ☐ | Suite-B-GCM-256 | aes-256-cbc | sha384 | group20 | 8 hours |

Figure 10.1 – IKE crypto profiles

The default profile represents the most common cryptographic scheme and should not be used unless the remote peer does not know which cryptographic profile is configured, or if the remote end is a legacy appliance with limited cryptographic capabilities.

The **Suite-B** profiles (already superseded by the CNSA suite) are NSA-recommended cryptographic settings. The latest recommendations can be found at https://apps.nsa.gov/iaarchive/programs/iad-initiatives/cnsa-suite.cfm.

The **Suite-B** profiles contain good options and are **recommended** for most situations, but use your judgement and confer with the remote peer about which cryptographic options are best suited for phase 1.

If possible, use Suite-B-GCM-128 for small remote devices and Suite-B-GCM-256 for larger peers.

To add a new phase 1 profile, review the options in the following steps:

> **Important note**
> Ideally, review which settings are supported on both devices and pick a set that meets the highest possible security standards.

1. Click on **Add** and name the profile so that you can easily identify it.

2. Set **DH group**:

   --**DH Group 1**: `768-bit group`

   --**DH Group 2**: `1024-bit group`

   --**DH Group 5**: `1536-bit group`

   --**DH Group 14**: `2048-bit group`

   --**DH Group 19**: `256-bit elliptic curve group`

   --**DH Group 20**: `384-bit elliptic curve group`

3. Set **Authentication**:

   --**md5**

   --**sha1**

   --**sha256**

   --**sha384**

   --**sha512**

4. Set **Encryption**:

   --**des**

   --**3des**

   --**aes-128-cbc**

   --**aes-192-cbc**

   --**aes-256-cbc**

5. Set **Key Lifetime** in hours (8 is the industry default).

6. **IKEv2 Authentication Multiple** lets you set the number of IKEv2 re-keys that are allowed before the gateway is forced to start a fresh authentication. This will hinder snooping efforts.

7. Click **OK**.

> **Important note**
>
> Do not use **md5**, **sha1**, **des**, or **3des** unless you are required to connect to a legacy device that does not support more modern algorithms, as all of these options are easily defeated by modern cracking and decryption tools.

The phase 2 cryptographic profiles can be found in **Network | Network Profiles | IPSec Crypto**. As you can see, there are three pre-configured profiles that you can opt to use if they suit your needs:

| | NAME | ESP/AH | ENCRYPTION | AUTHENTICATION | DH GROUP | LIFETIME | LIFESIZE |
|---|---|---|---|---|---|---|---|
| ☐ | default | ESP | aes-128-cbc, 3des | sha1 | group2 | 1 hours | |
| ☐ | Suite-B-GCM-128 | ESP | aes-128-gcm | none | group19 | 1 hours | |
| ☐ | Suite-B-GCM-256 | ESP | aes-256-gcm | none | group20 | 1 hours | |

Figure 10.2 – IPSec crypto profiles

The **Encapsulating Security Payload** (**ESP**) protocol provides full encryption of the payload, while **Authentication Header** (**AH**) just adds headers and guarantees the integrity of the payload, but does not encrypt or otherwise obfuscate the payload by itself.

To add a new phase 1 ESP profile, *pick the strongest options available on both peers*. If possible, use `Suite-B-GCM-128` for small remote devices and `Suite-B-GCM-256` for larger peers, or create a new profile with the following steps:

1. Click on **Add** and name the profile so that you can easily identify it.

2. Set the IPSec protocol to **ESP** or **AH**.

3. Set **Encryption**:

   --**des**

   --**3des**

   --**aes-128-cbc**

   --**aes-192-cbc**

   --**aes-256-cbc**

   --**aes-128-ccm**

   --**aes-128-gcm**

   --**aes-256-gcm**

   --**Null**

4.  Set **Authentication**:

--**md5**

--**sha1**

--**sha256**

--**sha384**

--**sha512**

--**none**

5.  Set **DH group**:

--**DH Group 1: 768-bit group**

--**DH Group 2: 1024-bit group**

--**DH Group 5: 1536-bit group**

--**DH Group 14: 2048-bit group**

--**DH Group 19: 256-bit elliptic curve group**

--**DH Group 20:  384-bit elliptic curve group**

--**No pfs (Perfect Forward Secrecy)**

6.  Set **Lifetime** in hours (1 is the industry default).

7.  Optionally, enable **Lifesize,** which triggers a re-key if a certain amount of data has been transmitted.

8.  Click **OK**.

> Important note
>
> Do not use **des**, **3des**, **md5**, or **sha1** unless you need to connect to a legacy system that does not support stronger algorithms.

The next thing we need to set up is the IKE Gateway, which can be found in **Network | Network Profiles | IKE Gateways**. The IKE Gateway represents the settings needed during phase 1. IKE phase 1 is the authentication phase where the peers verify each other's authenticity before moving on to creating a secure tunnel in phase 2. Follow these steps to create the IKE Gateway:

1.  Click on **Add** and set a descriptive name for the peer you will be connecting to.

2.  Set **Version** to **IKEv2 only mode**, or **IKEv2 preferred mode** if you're not sure whether the remote end supports IKEv2.

If the remote end only supports IKEv1, leave the default of **IKEv1 only mode**, which will skip attempting to negotiate IKEv2.

3. Choose whether you'll set up a tunnel between **IPv4** or **IPv6 nodes**.

4. Select the physical interface that will be maintaining the connection to the remote end (this could be a loopback interface as well).

5. Set **Local IP Address**.

6. Select whether the peer has a static IP or a resolvable FQDN, or whether it is a dynamic IP host.

7. Set **Peer Address** by adding an IP or FQDN (if the peer is dynamic, this field disappears).

8. Select **Pre-Shared Key** or **Certificate** for **Authentication**.

9. Type in and confirm the **Pre-Shared Key** (**PSK**).

10. Optionally, you can agree with the peer to use FQDN, the IP address, the key ID, or the user FQDN (an email address) as an additional form of identification during the handshake.

The IKE Gateway should look similar to the following screenshot:

Figure 10.3 – IKE Gateway

11. Go to **Advanced Options**.

If you selected **Certificate** as the **Authentication** method, the last few steps are a little different:

1. Select **Local Certificate**. If it hasn't been uploaded or generated yet, you can do so from the dropdown.

2. You can optionally set **HTTP Certificate Exchange** to use the hash-and-URL exchange method to let the peer know where to fetch the certificate from.

3. Select **Distinguished Name, FQDN, IP**, or **User FQDN** for **Local and Peer Identification** and set a matching value for the **Local and remote peer**.

4. For **Peer ID Check**, set **Exact** if **Peer Identification** must exactly match the peer certificate and **Wildcard** if the identification is a subdomain or the certificate is a wildcard certificate.

5. Optionally, if the data used in the identification does not match that of the certificate, select **Permit peer identification and certificate payload identification mismatch**.

6. Add or create the certificate profile that supports the local certificate.

7. Go to **Advanced Options**.

> **Important note**
>
> The **Local** and **Peer** identification can be filled out with any information the remote admin and you agree on whether a PSK is used, but in the case of certificates, this data is matched against the certificates and could cause issues if there are mismatches.

In the **Advanced Options** tab, follow these steps:

1. Set **Enable Passive Mode** if the local device should only receive inbound connections and not attempt to connect to the remote peer. This can help preserve the bandwidth or prevent unsuccessful connection attempts if the remote peer goes offline regularly or has a dynamic IP that is prone to change.

2. Set **Enable NAT Traversal** if either side is behind a NAT device that is not itself.

3. Set **IKE Crypto Profile**.

4.  In the **IKEv2** tab, set the following:

    --Optionally, you can force the use of cookies by the initiator in IKE_SA_INIT by setting **Strict Cookie Validation**.

    --**Liveness Check** will send an empty informational packet if no IKEv2 packet has been received (idle) for the amount of time specified and will function as a keepalive. After 10 liveness packets have been sent with no reply, the tunnel is broken down and needs to be reinitiated.

5.  In **IKEv1**, if this tab is available, set the following:

    --Select the **main** mode if both sides use a static IP or **aggressive** if at least one side has a dynamic IP.

    --If fragmentation is expected, put a checkmark in the **Enable Fragmentation** box.

    --Review the parameters for **Dead Peer Detection**.

6.  Click **OK**.

7.  The **Advanced Options** settings should now look similar to the following screenshot:

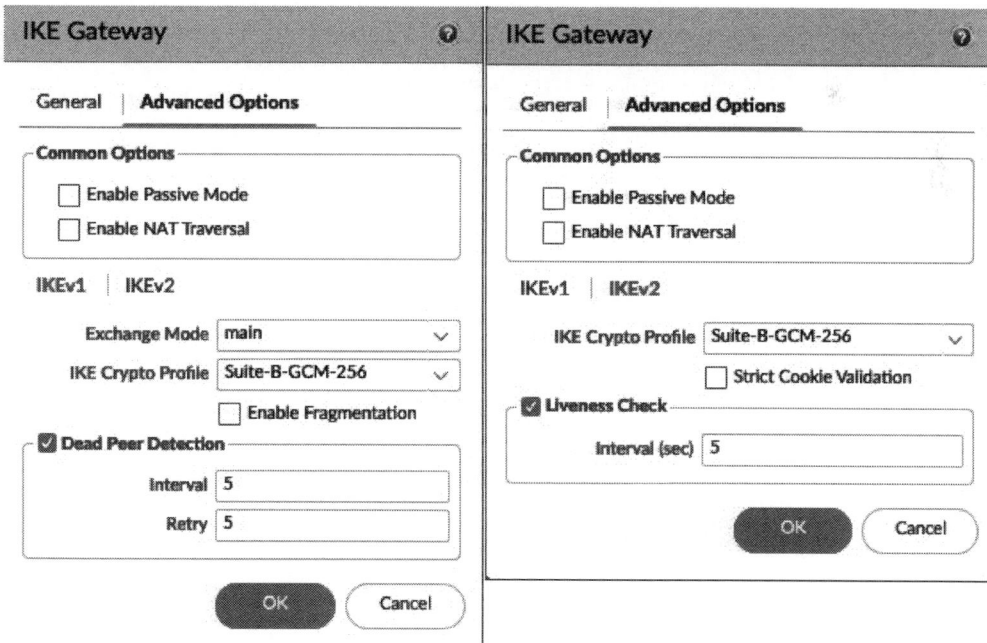

Figure 10.4 – The IKE Gateway advanced settings

Before we set up the actual tunnel, make sure you have a tunnel interface available in **Network | Interfaces | Tunnel**. If needed, create a new one and make sure to set it to a unique zone, such as **VPN**, and add it to your virtual router. If you need to set up tunnel monitoring, or if the remote end requires **numbered tunnel interfaces**, you can add an IP address, but this is not required if the tunnel is set up between two Palo Alto Networks devices. If you are going to use tunnel monitoring, also enable a management profile that allows ping, as follows:

| INTERFACE | MANAGEMENT PROFILE | IP ADDRESS | VIRTUAL ROUTER | SECURITY ZONE | FEATURES |
|-----------|--------------------|-----------|----------------|---------------|----------|
| tunnel | | none | default | vpn | 🔋 |
| tunnel.3 | ping | 172.31.0.1/30 | default | vpn | |

Figure 10.5 – Tunnel interface

As shown in the following diagram, phase 1 is established between the physical (or loopback) interfaces of both peers and serves to carry IPSec phase 2. IPSec is established between the tunnel interfaces on both ends. Tunnel interfaces are virtual interfaces and should be treated as if there is a physical interface with a network connected to it, as well as be configured with its own zone.

In the security policy, note the following points:

- Connections from the client will be established between the **trust zone** and the **VPN zone.**

- The IPSec tunnel will require a security rule that is established from the **Untrust zone** to the **Untrust zone** (from the external interface out to the internet):

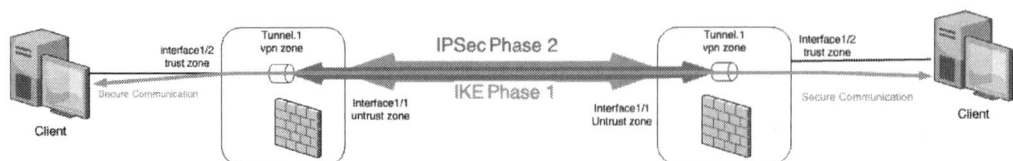

Figure 10.6 – A VPN tunnel from the firewall's perspective

To create the IPSec tunnel, go to **Network | IPSec Tunnels** and follow these steps:

1. Click on **Add** and provide a descriptive name.

2. Set the appropriate tunnel interface.

3. For **Type**, you can have the firewall create the SPI automatically, set it manually, or set the tunnel for GlobalProtect Satellite.

4.  If you select **Auto Key**, set the following:

--Set **IPv4** or **IPv6** for **Address Type**.

--Select the appropriate IKE Gateway.

--Select the IPSec crypto profile.

--Select **Show Advanced Options**.

--Select **Enable Replay Protection**.

--**Type of Service** (**ToS**) headers can be carried from the inner IP header to the outer IP header by enabling **Copy ToS Header**. You can transport a GRE tunnel inside the IPSec tunnel by selecting **Add GRE Encapsulation**, which will add a GRE header after the IPSec header.

--Enable **Tunnel Monitor** and set the remote tunnel interface IP for **Destination IP**. Add a monitoring profile to set an action if the tunnel fails – **wait-recover** will keep the tunnel interface up and will keep routing packets to it until the tunnel is restored. **fail-over** will bring the interface down and have routing take care of packets via an alternative route. Use **fail-over** if you set up a second tunnel; otherwise, use **wait-recover**.

Your tunnel configuration will look as in the following screenshot:

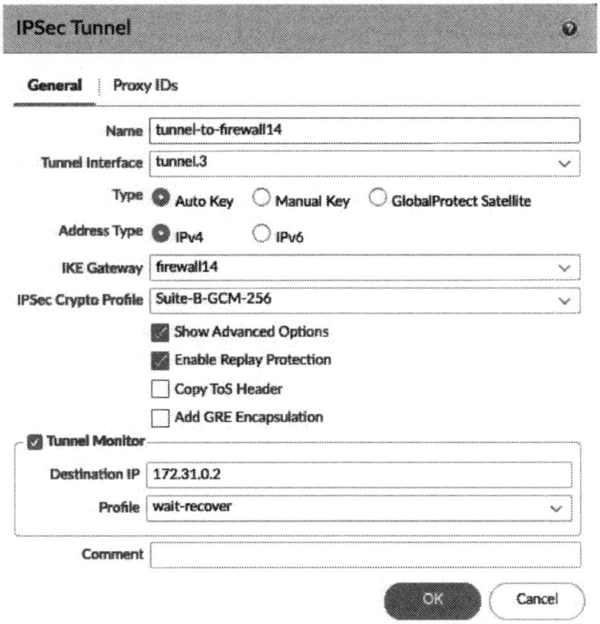

Figure 10.7 – IPSec tunnel configuration

--In the **Proxy IDs** tab, add local to remote subnet pairs if the remote peer is policy-based.

5.  In **Manual Key**, you get to set all the phase 1 and phase 2 parameters for a single IPSec tunnel. This works well with a route-based peer but could become troublesome with a policy-based peer as multiple manual IPSec tunnels will need to be created.

6.  In **GlobalProtect Satellite**, set the following:

    --Set (IP) **Portal Address**.

    --Select the external interface.

    --Set the local IPv4 or IPv6 address.

    --Open the **Advanced Options** tab.

    --Either select **Publish all static and connected routes to Gateway** to share the entire routing table to the GlobalProtect gateway or manually configure the subnets to publish to the gateway.

    --If you have an external device certificate for the firewall, select **External Certificate Authority** and set the certificate and matching certificate profile to authenticate against the gateway.

7.  Click **OK**.

> **Important note**
>
> A policy-based firewall will create an IPSec tunnel based on subnet pairs as defined in a policy (`subnet-A-local` gets access to `subnet-X-remote`), whereas a routing-based firewall will simply create a tunnel and then route packets into it. The Palo Alto Networks firewall is route-based, so it will default to using a single tunnel for all communications. Proxy IDs force splitting the single configuration into multiple IPSec tunnels. Pro-tip: while having a single tunnel simplifies configuration, it may suffer from performance degradation due to how sessions are handled on the data plane and a single tunnel will be processed by a single CPU. Creating multiple tunnels through proxy IDs will spread the load over more cores.

The last step is to add routes that forward any packets destined for the remote subnet into the tunnel. In **Network | Virtual Routers**, open the virtual router that holds the tunnel interface. In **Static Routes**, add a new route:

1. Give it a descriptive name.

2. Set the **Destination** subnet.

3. Select the tunnel interface for **Interface**.

4. **Next Hop** can either be **None** to simply route packets into the tunnel or the remote tunnel IP, which some systems may require.

5. Change **Admin Distance** and **Metric** if needed.

6. Click **OK**.

7. Commit your changes.

8. The route should look similar to the following screenshot:

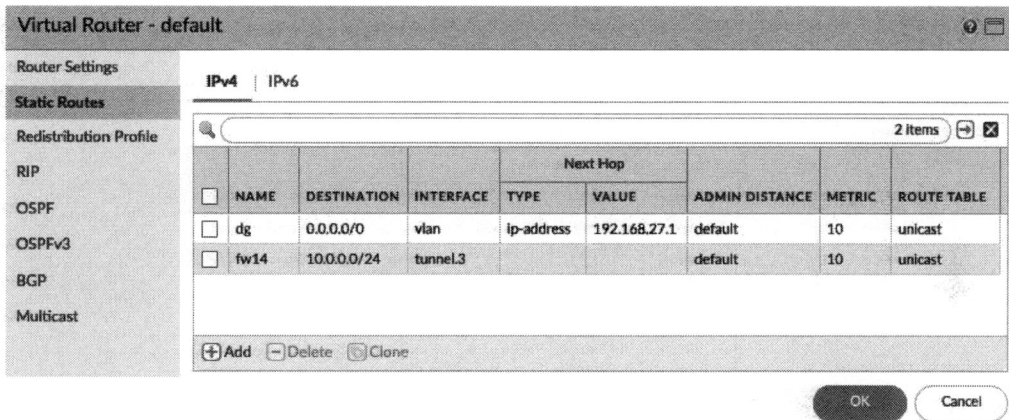

**Virtual Router - default**

| | | | | Next Hop | | | | |
|---|---|---|---|---|---|---|---|---|
| | NAME | DESTINATION | INTERFACE | TYPE | VALUE | ADMIN DISTANCE | METRIC | ROUTE TABLE |
| | dg | 0.0.0.0/0 | vlan | ip-address | 192.168.27.1 | default | 10 | unicast |
| | fw14 | 10.0.0.0/24 | tunnel.3 | | | default | 10 | unicast |

Figure 10.8 – A static route into a tunnel

To test connectivity and manually initiate the connection, you can use following commands to initiate phase 1 and phase 2, respectively:

```
> test vpn ike-sa gateway <IKEgateway>
> test vpn ipsec-sa tunnel <tunnel name>
```

The IKE SA first needs to succeed before the IPSec SA can be tested. You can follow the connection attempts through the system log while using the (subtype eq vpn) filter.

You can follow the actual process logs via the CLI to see how the tunnel is being negotiated and set up any errors or interesting information if the tunnel doesn't come up:

```
> tail follow yes mp-log ikemgr.log
> tail follow yes mp-log cryptod.log
```

Here is a checklist of the things you need to agree on with the remote peer:

- For phase 1, which encryption authentication, Diffie-Hellman group and key lifetime will be used.

- For phase 2, whether you will set up ESP or AH. If you choose ESP, which encryption algorithm will be used, and if you choose if AH, which authentication will be used, which Diffie-Hellman group, and how long should the lifetime be?

- Does the remote peer support IKEv2?

- What is the remote peer IP or FQDN, or is the host on a dynamic IP?

- Will you use a PSK or a certificate to establish phase 1 authentication?

- Is either host behind a NAT device?

- Does the remote end support replay protection?

Now that you have a firm understanding of how to set up a site-to-site VPN, we will move on to configuring GlobalProtect for a client VPN.

## Configuring GlobalProtect

Using a site-to-site VPN is a very robust and secure method of connecting two systems, which is less appropriate and much harder to configure for endpoints such as laptops or mobile phones. To accommodate many different OSes and easier configuration options, GlobalProtect is available to provide connectivity to employees, contractors, and guests.

GlobalProtect is an SSL VPN client that also supports IPSec, which means that the VPN connection can tunnel over HTTPS, so the client will likely be able to connect from most locations where traditional IPSec may be blocked by a firewall or other filtering device. IPSec can be enabled and set as the preferred connection method with a fallback to SSL if IPSec is blocked.

Most of the GlobalProtect functionality does not require an additional license, but there are a few features that do the following:

- Perform **Host Information Profile (HIP)** checks
- Support GlobalProtect on mobile endpoints (such as Android, iOS, Chrome OS, and Windows UWP) and Linux
- IPv6 support for external gateways
- Split tunnel based on destination domains, the client process, or the streaming application
- Clientless VPN

There are two main components that need to be configured when setting up GlobalProtect:

- **Portal**, which provides clients with a download portal to get the client package, provides configuration to the agents once installed, and provides a Clientless VPN.
- **Gateway**, which is the where the agent connects to establish a secure connection.

You can have one portal per GlobalProtect deployment and as many gateways as needed. Gateways can be spread over strategic locations, so users always have an optimal connection to the corporate "backbone." Gateways can be deployed on physical or virtual appliances on-premises or in the cloud (such as with Azure, AWS, GCS, and so on) or as part of Prisma Access. An internal gateway can also be set up to function as a User-ID and HIP enforcement point for internal users to be able to access sensitive resources on the network.

## Setting up the portal

To create a new **Portal** object, go to **Network | GlobalProtect | Portals** and follow these steps:

1. Click on **Add**.
2. In the **General** tab, set a name for the portal.

3.  Select the interface that the portal will be listening on:

    --If you have an IP to spare, I would recommend creating a loopback interface in the external/untrust zone.

    --Use the **Untrust** interface to make the portal available on the internet.

    --Use an internal interface to only provide portal services to internal or connected hosts (the latter means you will not be able to change critical information easily as users need to be logged in first before being able to get config updates when they are connected remotely).

    > **Important note**
    >
    > Setting the portal on a loopback interface makes any packets carrying an exploit targeting the portal IP go through full threat prevention before actually hitting the interface. This should be considered best practice.

4.  Select **IPv4**, **IPv6**, or **IPv4 and IPv6**.

5.  In the appearance dropdowns, you can choose to use the default page, upload a custom page, or disable the landing page entirely (when disabled, the agent will be able to fetch the configuration, but no page is displayed if someone connects using a browser).

6.  In **Log settings**, keep **Log Unsuccessful SSL Handshake** enabled.

Move on to the **Authentication** tab:

1.  You need to provide an SSL/TLS service profile that serves the certificate that will be used for the portal. Ensure the certificate matches the FQDN that is used for the portal (for example, `portal.example.com`) and has been imported in **Device | Certificate Management | Certificates**, then create a new service profile. Set **Min. version** to `TLSv1.2`

2.  Create a new client authentication:

    --Set a descriptive name.

    --You can select which client OS this authentication method will apply to. Set **Any** for everyone or set a specific OS if different OSes should log in using different profiles.

    --Choose the authentication profile that will be used to authenticate users. You can create a new one from the dropdown.

--By default, users need to provide a username and password. If these are enabled (see the next step), provide a client certificate. You can set **Allow Authentication with User Credentials OR Client Certificate** to `Yes` so that users can log in with either their username/password *or* a client certificate.

--Click **OK**.

3.  If you want clients to use a client certificate when connecting, create a certificate profile:

    --Set a profile name.

    --Set the **Username** field to `Subject` (common name) or `Subject Alt` (and select **Email** or **Principal Name**). Leave this as **None** if a generic (machine) certificate will be used, rather than a personalized one.

    --Set **NetBIOS Domain** in **Domain**.

    --Add the CA certificate that will sign the user certificates and add appropriate OCSP (**Online Certificate Status Protocol**) URLs.

    --Click **OK**.

In the **Portal Data Collection** tab, you can have GlobalProtect collect the Windows registry key or MAC Plist entries. These values can be used to select which configuration is sent to the client. Collection can be configured as follows:

1.  Set the certificate profile that will be used to match the machine certificate used by the GlobalProtect agent.

2.  Add the registry/Plist keys that need to be registered.

3.  In the **Agent** tab, you can control the configuration sent to the Agent so that it can establish a connection.

    -- In the **Trusted Root CA** box, you can add CA and intermediary certificates if the portal and Gateway certificates are self-signed so that the client trusts the certificates. An **SSL Decryption** certificate can also be installed in the client's trusted root certificates by checking **Install** in **Local Root Certificate Store**

    -- **Agent User Override Key** is the **master key** used in the ticketing process to allow users to disable an always-on GlobalProtect agent on their system. If left unchanged, the system will use the system's default key. You can choose to change this key for security reasons (the key used to sign tickets – administrators will not need to know the key).

Multiple agent configurations can be created for different users' types or client machines. The agent configs are processed **top to bottom** when a user connects, so make sure the more specific configs are placed at the top. Create a new profile as follows:

1. Click on **Add** to create a new config.

2. In the **Authentication** tab, set a descriptive name:

   --The client certificate can be used to push a certificate and its private key to the client. This certificate can be used to authenticate against the gateways.

   --The user credentials are saved by default in the GlobalProtect agent. Set this so that only the username can be saved, or so that the credentials can be saved if the user uses biometric authentication.

   --Select **Generate cookie for authentication override** so that a (unique) cookie is generated and sent to the client by the portal after the user first logs in to the portal.

   --Select **Accept cookie for authentication override** if the cookie will be used to authenticate, rather than the user credentials. Set an amount of time for which the cookie will be valid (maximum 365 days). Once the cookie expires, the user needs to provide credentials when logging into the portal and will receive a new cookie.

   --If cookies are used, set the certificate that will be used to encrypt them.

   --You can select which components (**Portal, internal-gateway**, the external gateways manual, or **Autodiscover**) will require **Multi-Factor Authentication (MFA)**.

3. In the **Config Selection Criteria** tab, you configure which user/user group or type of endpoint device this configuration will apply to:

   --In the **User/User Group** tab, a user or LDAP group and a client OS can be selected.

   --In the **Device Checks** tab, you can set an action to check whether a machine account with a device serial exists or a machine certificate has been installed.

   --In the **Custom Checks** tab, you can look for the registry key or Plist entries we set in the **Portal Data Collection** tab.

4. In the **Internal** tab, we can set **Internal Host Detection** for IPv4 and IPv6 and **Internal Gateways** for HIP checking:

   --Set the IPv4 and FQDN hostname of an internal resource to prevent internal hosts from setting up a VPN tunnel to the external gateways while inside the network (this can be any internal server or host or an internal gateway configured on the firewall).

   --Set **IPv6** and **IPv6 enabled FQDN** if IPv6 is used in the network.

   --Add internal gateways by their IP or FQDN (this value will need to match the certificate used on the internal gateway). **Source addresses** can be added to control which subnets will connect to a specific internal gateway.

5. In the **External** tab, external gateways can be added, as well as a third-party VPN.

   When multiple gateways exist, the GlobalProtect agent will poll (**through a TLS handshake**) all of them to see which ones provide the optimal connection speed. The **cut-off time** is the time allowed for a gateway to reply:

   --Add a gateway and give it a descriptive name. This name will be visible to the user, so it should help them understand where their connection is being made to.

   --Add the FQDN or IP the connection that will be made to. This should match the certificate that will be used on the **Gateway** object.

   --Add a source region. This can be **Any** or any country, subnet, or global region.

   --Set a priority: from lowest to highest or manual user selection only. The priority has an inferior value compared to the result of the responsiveness poll – the highest, high, and medium priority items will be polled and if none in that priority are available, the agent will move to the lower priority items.

   --Check the **Manual** box if the user is permitted to select this gateway as a preferred connection.

   --Click **OK**.

In the **App** tab, we can configure how the GlobalProtect agent will behave. On the right-hand side, you can do the following:

- Enable a welcome page that pops up every time a user connects.

- If users are normally *not* allowed to disable GlobalProtect but an exceptional event could require some users to disable their agent, a password can be set here to share with users.

- A password can also be set for users to be able to uninstall GlobalProtect.

- A **Mobile Device Manager** (**MDM**) can be set to enroll mobile devices connecting through GlobalProtect.

On the left-hand side, you can configure how the agent behaves. I'll highlight the options that may need to be changed from the default or that are of interest:

1. **Connect Mode** is set to **user-logon** (always on) by default and can be changed to **On-demand**, which lets the user decide when to connect, or **Pre-logon**, which establishes a connection using the machine certificate before the user logs on to their desktop environment

2. **Allow User to Disable GlobalProtect** is set to **Allow**. Change this to **Allow with Comment, Allow with Passcode**, or **Allow with Ticket** (or **Disallow** altogether). **Allow with Ticket** requires users to call in and get a challenge response by an admin that can run **Generate Ticket** in **Network | GlobalProtect | Portals**.

3. Windows users can be prevented from uninstalling GlobalProtect or required to enter a password before being able to uninstall.

4. **Allow User to Upgrade GlobalProtect App** will prompt the user by default. This can be set to **Disallow, Allow Manually, Allow Transparently**, or **Internal**. Both **Allow Transparently** and **Internal** will update the agent automatically, but **Internal** will only perform the upgrade when the user is on the corporate network.

5. Set **Allow users to Sign Out from GlobalProtect** to **No** if users are not permitted to disable GlobalProtect.

6. **Enforce GlobalProtect Connection for Network Access** disables all network access if GlobalProtect is not connected to an internal or external gateway (no exceptions need to be set for the gateway IPs or FQDNs):

   --If this option is set, also set **Captive Portal Exception Timeout** to allow users to authenticate to a captive portal if they are at a hotel or airport before network access is blocked.

   --Edit **Traffic Blocking Notification Message** so that users are made aware when traffic is being blocked due to GlobalProtect not being connected.

7. **Enable Advanced View** can be set to **No** if users should have a simplified experience.

8. **Allow user to change Portal Address** can be set to **No** if the user is not allowed the option to change the portal address, which could be used to enter portal information to a different organization. The drawback is that the portal address will need to be pushed (via **Global Policy Objects (GPO)**, for example) to the clients:

   `HKEY_LOCAL_MACHINE\SOFTWARE\PaloAlto Networks\` `GlobalProtect\PanSetup` with the **Portal** key.

   `/Library/Preferences/com.paloaltonetworks.GlobalProtect.` `pansetup.plist` with the **Portal** key

9. Set **Allow User to Continue with Invalid Portal Server Certificate** to **No**.

10. You can keep the tunnel connected for a specified amount of time by setting a timeout in **Preserver Tunnel on User Logoff**.

11. **Connect with SSL Only** forces the use of SSL for this agent configuration profile, even if IPSec is enabled on the gateway (leave this as **No**).

In the **HIP Data Collection** tab, you can select whether to collect HIP data or not. If a GlobalProtect license has been purchased, each GlobalProtect agent on Windows or macOS will send a HIP report about running processes, patch levels, and so on to the gateway when they connect, and periodically afterward. You can exclude several categories and vendor products from being collected, or add custom checks to Windows and macOS hosts for specific registry entries to be present or processes to be running.

Set the certificate profile to verify the machine certificate sent by the GlobalProtect agent.

Once you've reviewed HIP checks, click **OK** to complete the agent configuration.

In the **Clientless VPN** tab, you can create a portal interface that allows users to connect to a web page and have access to internal applications without needing to set up a full tunnel. It works by populating the **Portal** page with tiles that lead to application interfaces:

1. In **General**, enable Clientless VPN:

   --Set the FQDN or IP of the portal.

   --Set the security zone. This will be the source zone for outgoing proxied connections from the firewall to the application.

   --Select a **DNS Proxy** object. Create one if you don't have one yet; it does not need to be attached to an interface for it to work with Clientless VPN.

   --Change **Login Lifetime** and **Inactivity Timeout** if the defaults (3 hours and 30 minutes, respectively) are not suitable.

   --In **Max Users**, select the maximum number of concurrent users. The default is 10.

2. In the **Applications** tab, you can select the clientless applications that are available to users. You can either create these individually in **Network | GlobalProtect | Clientless Apps** and then create Clientless Apps groups in **Network | GlobalProtect | Clientless App Groups** or you can create apps directly with the following steps:

--Click on **Add** to create a new application-to-user mapping and give it a friendly name.

--**Display application URL address bar** lets a user to input custom URLs, which the Clientless VPN will proxy for them. Disable this option unless your users are allowed to browse the internet via Clientless VPN.

--If an application should only be visible to a specific user or user group, click on **Add** and select the users(s) or group(s) you want it to be visible to.

--In **Applications**, click on **Add** and select an application, or create a new clientless app:

   a) When creating a new clientless app, set a name so that the user will be able to identify the application.

   b) Set an appropriate URL for the application.

   c) Add a description with additional details.

   d) Optionally, upload an icon for the Clientless App tile.

   e) Click **OK**.

--Create additional applications as needed.

3. In the **Crypto Settings** tab, you can control the security of the outbound connections from the firewall to the applications:

--Set **Min Version** to `TLSv1.2`.

--Disable **SHA1** as this is no longer considered a secure algorithm. It should only be used if there is no alternative available to communicate with the remote peer.

--Enable all the server certificate verifications unless some internal certificates are known to be problematic.

4. In the **Proxy** tab, additional proxy servers can be configured if the outbound connections need to pass through a proxy server. Proxy rules can be configured for specific domains and processed from top to bottom, so put the most specific ones at the top:

--Click on **Add** and set a descriptive name.

--Add the domains that need/don't need to be proxied, one per line.

--Check or uncheck the **Use Proxy** box.

--Fill out the proxy IP or FQDN, port, and credentials details.

--Click **OK** and add additional proxy server settings as needed.

5.  In the **Advanced Settings**, you can add exclusions for any applications that have a sub-page that should not be accessed through the portal. Paths are not supported, however.

In the following screenshot, you can see what the GlobalProtect portal looks like with some clientless applications and the application URL enabled. The GlobalProtect agent can be downloaded from here as well:

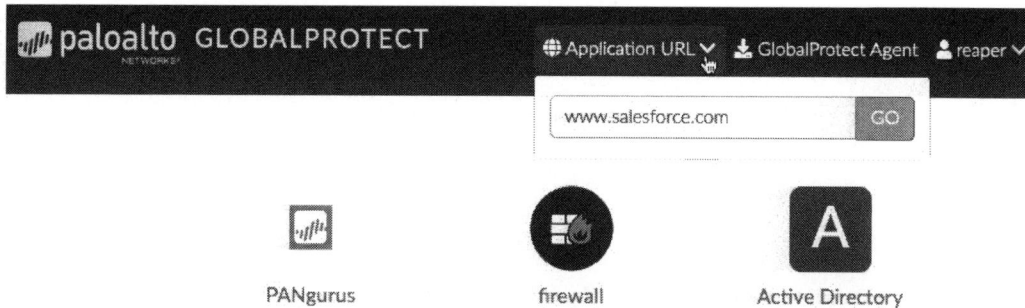

Figure 10.9 – Clientless VPN-enabled GlobalProtect portal

In the **Satellite** tab, you can configure firewall appliances that will use a simplified VPN to connect to the organization. This is an ideal solution if, for example, several smaller firewalls are being used to set up pop-up locations or operate a booth at conventions to quickly set up, and break down shortly after the VPN tunnels, so the remote team has access through an actual firewall for additional security over the GlobalProtect agent. Larger or static sites will benefit most from a traditional VPN connection. Follow these steps to create a satellite group:

1.  Click on **Add** to add a new satellite group.

    --In **General**, set a descriptive name and review **Config Refresh Interval**. This sets the cadence for how frequently satellites check whether there is a new connection configuration available.

    --In the **Devices** tab, add devices by their serial number and set a descriptive name for each device.

--In the **Enrollment User/User Group** tab, you can add users or groups of users that are allowed to manually enroll devices. If a new device is set up in the field and the serial number has not been communicated for it to auto-enroll, the admin will be prompted to manually enroll, at which time their username or group membership must match the one you set here.

--In the **Gateways** tab, configure which gateways the satellite will connect to and what their routing priority will be. As opposed to GlobalProtect agents, which connect to the fastest or highest priority gateway, satellites connect to all the gateways you configure and use routing priority to direct traffic.

--Click **OK**.

2.  Click **Ok** to complete the portal configuration.

Now that the portal is configured, you can start adding the internal and external gateways.

## Setting up the gateway

Gateways are where the connections that the agents connect to are. Each firewall can have multiple gateways, but they can't share an IP address, so if multiple gateways are needed, they will each require a unique IP. A portal and a gateway can share the same IP.

> **Important note**
> Gateways cannot coexist with an HTTPS-enabled management profile (*never* set a management profile that hosts services on an external or untrusted interface). In these cases, you should enable the management profile on a loopback interface and use port address translation; so, for example, port 4443 is translated to 443 on the loopback interface.

To create a new gateway, go to **Network | GlobalProtect | Gateways** and follow these steps:

1.  Click on **Add** and provide a descriptive name.

2.  Select the appropriate interface and select **IPv4**, **IPv6**, or **IPv4 and IPv6** and set the IP. Just like the portal part, it is good practice to set the gateway on a loopback interface.

3.  In the **Authentication** tab, set the following:

--Use the same SSL/TLS service profile as the portal if you reuse the same FQDN or have the certificate set to an IP. If you want to use a different FQDN, import or generate the appropriate certificate and create a new SSL/TLS service profile.

--To use client certificates, set **Certificate Profile**.

--Create a new client authentication profile, set a descriptive name, and select the appropriate authentication profile. You can use the same profile as the portal or create a new one that leverages MFA for added security. Review whether you need credentials and a client certificate, or credentials or client certificate.

In the **Agent** tab, several considerations can be made that will alter the user experience:

1.  In the **Tunnel Settings** tab, set the following:

--**Tunnel mode** must be enabled for external gateways. On an internal gateway, you can leave **Tunnel mode** disabled if you intend to use the gateway for HIP and authentication only. If **Tunnel mode** is enabled, the agent will set up a tunnel even when inside the network for added security.

--Select a tunnel interface. This interface can be created in **Network | Interfaces | Tunnel** and does not require an IP address, but it does need to be set in the appropriate virtual router and in a different security zone than the local network. Check the box next to **Enable User-ID** in the zone configuration.

--Leave **Max Users** empty to allow the maximum number that your platform supports.

--Unchecking **Enable IPSec** will force the use of SSL/TLS. If IPSec is checked but is unavailable from the agent's location, the fallback protocol is SSL/TLS.

--Create a new **GlobalProtect IPSec Crypto** profile from the dropdown that uses a GCM cipher (the default uses `aes-128-cbc`).

--The **Enable X-Auth support** option enables third-party VPN clients that support X-Auth to connect to a gateway. Enable this if you want to connect OpenVPN, for example. Set **Group Name** and **Group Password**. You can force the user to need to re-authenticate when the IPSec key expires by unchecking **Skip Auth on IKE Rekey**.

2.  In the **Client settings** tab, you can control how the gateway interacts with a subset of users, the host OS, or the region. **Skip this step if split tunneling is not required**:

--Click on **Add** and set a descriptive name.

--Select the source user, host OS, region, or source addresses that should apply to the intended users. Otherwise, leave this all as **Any** if all users should fall into this profile.

--In the **Authentication Override** tab, select whether an override cookie should be generated, whether it should be accepted, and the amount of time the cookie should be valid for, and then select the encrypt/decrypt certificate for the cookie. It should be signed by the trusted root certificate associated with the portal and gateway certificates.

--In the **IP Pools** tab, you can set regular IP pools, which will be assigned from top to bottom; or, you can enable **Retrieve Framed-IP-Address attribute from authentication server** if your authentication server supports the **Framed-IP-Address** attribute so that clients are assigned a static IP address when they log in. **Authentication Server IP Pool** needs to be large enough to support all users as these are static assignments that are not cleared after a user logs off.

--In the **Split Tunnels** tab, you can configure which route sessions should take. If left blank, all sessions will be sent over the tunnel. Direct access to the user's home network (or hotel, airport, coffee shop, and so on) can be disabled by checking **No direct access to local network**:

a) Subnets added to the **Include** field will cause the GlobalProtect agent to only route sessions destined for these subnets over the VPN tunnel.

b) Subnets added to the **Exclude** field will not be sent over the tunnel.

c) **Include** and **Exclude** domains and their associated ports can be used to control which FQDNs are or are not sent over the tunnel. This feature requires a license.

d) **Include and exclude Client Application Process Name** lets you control which running processes will be forced to send all their traffic over the tunnel or are disallowed from using the tunnel. This feature also requires a license.

In the **Network Services** tab, you can add DNS servers and DNS suffixes assigned to the clients.

3.  The **Client IP Pool** tab holds the global IP pool for all users connecting to the gateway. Multiple pools can be added, both IPv4 and IPv6. IP addresses are assigned from the top pool first; once this is depleted, the next pool will be used, and so on. **The IP pools will automatically be added to the virtual router that the tunnel interface belongs to**.

4.  In the **Network Services** tab, you can control which DNS and WINS servers the agent receives when a connection is established, and the DNS suffixes relevant to your organization. If a dynamic or DHCP client interface exists, this can be set as an inheritable source for DNS and WINS information to be passed along to GlobalProtect agents.

5.  In the **Connection Settings** tab, set the following:

    --**Login Lifetime** sets the maximum amount of time a user is allowed to be connected continuously.

    --**Inactivity Logout** disconnects the user after no HIP report is received for the set amount of time. If no HIP checks are enabled, this timer is ignored.

    --**Disconnect On Idle** interrupts the connection when no packets have been received over the VPN tunnel for the set amount of time.

    The **Disable Automatic Restoration of SSL VPN** option will prevent automatic reconnection after the connection is interrupted for any reason, requiring the user to manually reconnect. **This option will prevent always-on mode from working**.

    **Restrict Authentication Cookies** lets you set limitations to the authentication override by restricting the cookie  to only work on the original source IP or the subnet that the cookie was created for (if the user shifts to a different IP or subnet, the cookie will no longer work for authentication override and the user will need to reauthenticate).

6.  In the **Video Traffic** tab, you can force video applications to use the local internet breakout instead of the tunnel to conserve bandwidth. Any video streaming service that is not allowed should not be excluded and is instead blocked on the firewall by the security policy. This feature requires a license.

7.  In the **HIP Notifications** tab, you can create profiles containing HIP objects or HIP profiles and their **User Notification** settings:

    --Click on **Add** and select the HIP profile or the HIP profile to match (see the following bullet points).

    --If a **match** needs to be reported to the user, set **Enable Match Message** and set a system tray balloon or pop-up message and type the text that needs to be displayed to the user.

    --If a required check was not detected (not-match) and this event needs to be reported to the user, set **Enable Not Match Message** and set a system tray balloon or pop-up message and type the text that needs to be displayed to the user.

8.  In the **Satellite** tab, you can configure the tunnel settings for Satellite firewalls.

    In the **Tunnel Settings** tab, set **Enable Tunnel Configuration** and set a tunnel interface. Since these will be branch offices, you should use a different tunnel interface, with an IP assigned, and a different security zone than the one that the regular gateway is using. The tunnel monitoring settings are the IP addresses that the remote gateways will use to monitor connectivity and fail over to a different gateway if monitoring fails. Set this to the tunnel IP.

    In the **Network settings** tab, DNS settings and DNS suffixes can be set, or an inheritance source can be set. The IP pool will be used to assign an IP to the remote tunnel interface. Access routes let the remote peer set routes into the tunnel to reach the main site's network. Leave this blank to send everything into the tunnel.

    In the **Route Filter** tab, you can enable **Accept published routes** to install routes advertised by the satellites into the virtual router. To prevent overlaps with local subnets, you can add subnets that will be accepted this way into the **Permitted Subnets** field.

9.  Click **OK**.

You now have a fully functional gateway that your users can start connecting to. If you want to perform HIP checks, here's how to set those up.

## HIP objects and profiles

**HIP** checks verify whether the agent's host OS lives up to the standards set forth by your organization. Remember that a license is required to perform these checks on your hosts.

Before we begin, verify that the GlobalProtect fata file is being downloaded periodically in **Device | Dynamic Updates**. This will ensure that the firewall has current information on vendor patch levels and software versions.

You can create HIP objects in **Objects | GlobalProtect | HIP Objects**.

A HIP object would typically cover one type of device for manageability, as there may be managed Windows and macOS laptops, company-owned mobile devices, and BYOD devices. All of these will have different characteristics. Follow these steps to build a basic HIP object:

1.  Click on **Add** and set a descriptive name.

2.  In the **General** tab, provide all relevant host information, such as the OS version, the GlobalProtect client version, the domain, and for mobile devices, which WIFI network or carrier they are connected to.

3.  In the **Mobile Device** tab, you can enable this profile for mobile devices and set parameters for the types and models of the device, the phone number, and the IMEI number. You can have HIP verify whether the passcode is enabled, the mobile device is jailbroken, disk encryption is enabled, and whether certain applications are installed.

4.  In the **Patch Management** tab, you can set detection for missing patches by severity level and different vendors. These patch signatures are included in the Dynamic Updates package.

5.  In the **Firewall** tab, you can enable detection if the firewall software is installed and enabled.

6.  In the **Anti-Malware** tab, you can enable detection for installed antivirus or anti-malware software and see whether real-time scanning is enabled, check the minimum virus definitions and the product version, and see when the last scan took place.

7.  In the **Disk Backup** tab, you can enable detection for backup software and see when the last backup was run.

8.  In the **Disk Encryption** tab, you can enable detection for encryption software and see whether certain locations have been encrypted.

9.  In the **Data Loss Prevention** tab, you can enable detection for data loss software and see whether it is enabled.

10. In the **Certificate** tab, you can verify whether the certificates used by GlobalProtect have specific attributes set.

11. In the **Custom Checks** tab, you can add checks for running processes and registry or Plist keys.

In **HIP Profiles**, you can combine HIP objects through **AND, OR**, and **NOT** conditions, which allows you to build a set of conditions that apply to many devices. Once you add these conditions to GlobalProtect or the security policy security controls can be applied to users meeting, or failing, said checks.

A HIP profile could, for example, be set as follows:

```
("corp-laptop" or "corp-mobile") and not "byod"
```

This can be done to include all the corporate devices, but not the private ones.

To create security rules that leverage HIP profiles, do the following:

1. Create a new security rule and set a descriptive name.

2. In the **Source** tab, set the GlobalProtect security zone and create and set a user IP pool object.

3. In the **User** tab, set the user group and the HIP profiles to apply this rule to. Only devices matching the HIP objects in the profile will match this rule.

You can set the **HIP** dropdown to no-hip if this rule does not require HIP information to be available from the client, which allows third-party VPN clients to access resources, while **any** will allow any device. Create the rule as follows:

1. In the **Destination** tab, set an appropriate destination, such as to the DMZ servers or other internal resources.

2. Add appropriate applications in the **Application** tab.

3. Set services or the destination URL categories in the **Service/URL Category** tab.

4. Set the action, threat profiles, and logging settings in the **Actions** tab.

5. Click **OK**.

You can also set a HIP match for **Quarantine**, which will include any devices that the administrator has manually added to quarantine by adding the device through **Device | Device Quarantine** or by manually selecting it in a traffic or threat log, or any devices that were added to quarantine automatically by matching a security rule with a log forwarding profile that has a quarantine action set, as shown in the following screenshot:

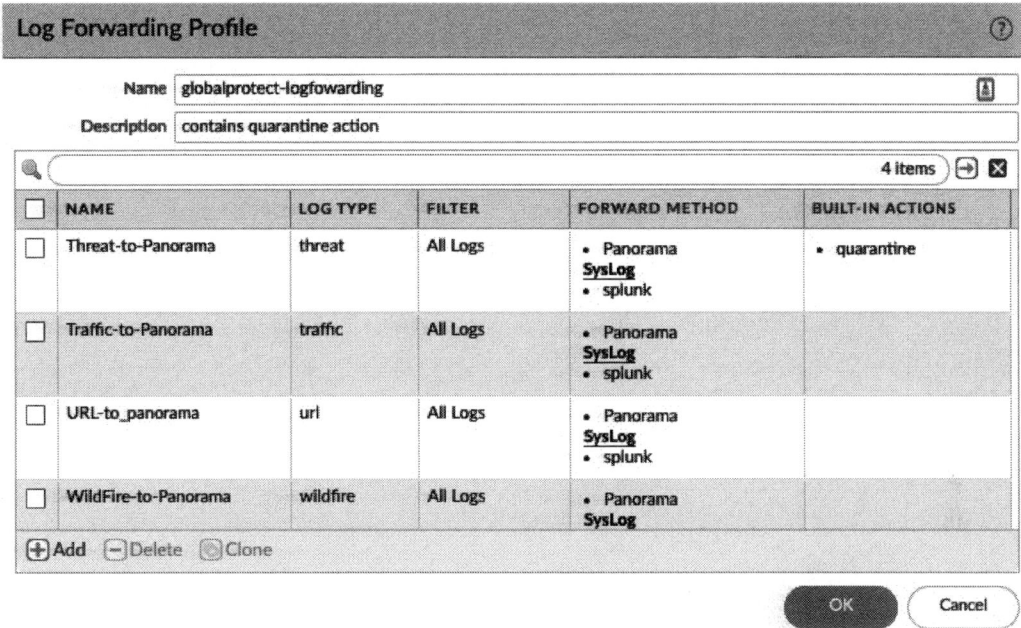

Figure 10.10 – Automated quarantine

A rule base for HIP-enabled clients could look something as in the following screenshot. Each rule is for the same zone, user, and IP pool, but the HIP matches are different for each rule, so they will apply to different source devices:

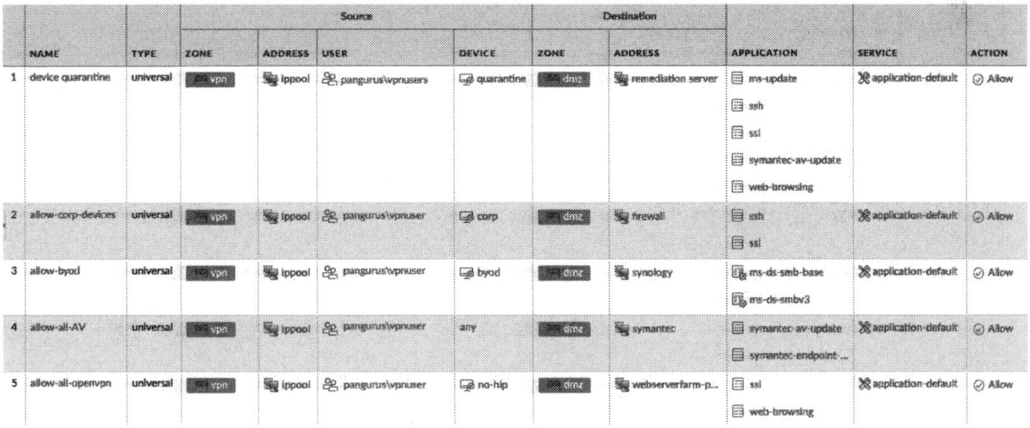

Figure 10.11 – HIP-enabled security rules

> **Important note**
> By default, agents send a HIP update every hour. This interval can only be changed from the CLI with the following commands:

```
> debug global-protect portal interval <60-86400>
> configure
# commit
# exit
> debug global-protect portal show
```

You are now able to set up a complex GlobalProtect environment. In the next section, we'll learn how to create custom applications.

# Custom applications and threats

Every once in a while, an application may not be known. This could be due to it being a new application that has not been used much in the wild or could be something a developer created in-house for which it is not reasonable to expect there to be signatures to identify the session. In these cases, it is possible to create custom applications that use custom signatures and can trigger an App-ID to positively identify the previously unknown application.

The need for a custom application usually starts with the discovery of an abnormality in the traffic log. In the following screenshot, I have discovered my solar power converter, and an IoT device is communicating with its home server over an **unknown-tcp** connection:

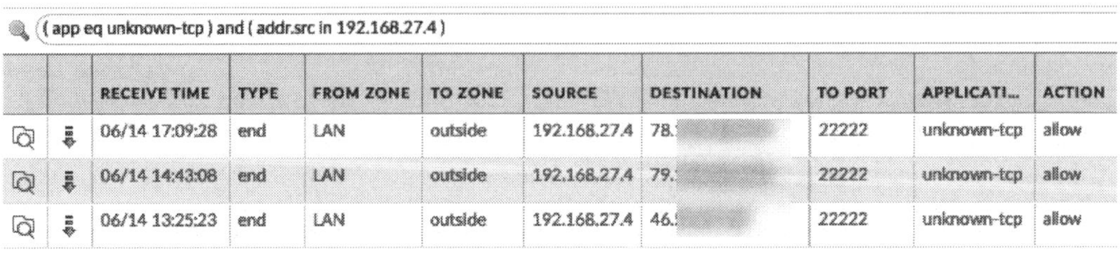

( app eq unknown-tcp ) and ( addr.src in 192.168.27.4 )

| | | RECEIVE TIME | TYPE | FROM ZONE | TO ZONE | SOURCE | DESTINATION | TO PORT | APPLICATI... | ACTION |
|---|---|---|---|---|---|---|---|---|---|---|
| | | 06/14 17:09:28 | end | LAN | outside | 192.168.27.4 | 78. | 22222 | unknown-tcp | allow |
| | | 06/14 14:43:08 | end | LAN | outside | 192.168.27.4 | 79. | 22222 | unknown-tcp | allow |
| | | 06/14 13:25:23 | end | LAN | outside | 192.168.27.4 | 46. | 22222 | unknown-tcp | allow |

Figure 10.12 – An unknown-tcp application in the traffic log

There are two ways to address this issue:

- Implement an **application override** that forcibly sets all these sessions to a specific application.

- Create a **custom application** using signatures to positively identify these sessions, and still perform security scans on the sessions.

Let's take a look at the easiest solution first.

## Application override

Implementing an app override is "quick and dirty;" it forcibly replaces the application identification process with a custom application. The advantage is that you simply set a few simple parameters and you are done. The drawback is that there is no granularity, there is room for mistakes, and most importantly, if you set a custom application, the security profiles will no longer apply to the sessions (packets will no longer be scanned for threats and malware).

> **Important note**
> Setting a predefined application could help "fix" an otherwise broken App-ID process if the data flow is somehow different than what would normally be expected from the application, causing the regular App-ID to fail. This will only work if the application flow exactly matches the application being set in the override, with the **rare** condition of some key packets being out of order. I wouldn't recommend this as a fix-all, but keep it in your pocket for a rainy day.

The first step is to create a custom app that will be used to identify the session. Create a new application in **Objects | Applications** as follows:

1. Click on **Add** and set a descriptive name for the new application. In this case, we will call the application Solar.

2. In the **Configuration** tab, set the **Properties** and **Characteristics** settings. For my solar converter, we'll set the following:

   --**Category**: **business-system**

   --**Subcategory**: **management**

   --**Technology**: **client-server**

   We'll leave all the characteristics blank as this is a friendly app, calling home to report on my solar gains.

3.  In the **Advanced** tab, you can select to use TCP and UDP ports by checking the **Port** radio button, or select an **IP Protocol**, **ICMP Type**, **ICMPv6 Type,** or **None**. In the Port settings you can add `tcp/` or `udp/` followed by a port number (such as `tcp/88`), port range (such as `udp/50-100`) or `dynamic` (such as `tcp/dynamic`) for dynamically assigned ports . We will set the following:

    --Set **Port** to `TCP/22221-22222`.

    --I'll leave all the **Timeouts** settings blank to indicate that I wish to use the system default timeouts for TCP.

    --There's an option for scanning **File Types**, **Viruses**, and **Data Patterns**, but this will only work if there is no override in place, so I will leave these blank for now as well.

4.  We do not need the **Signatures** tab right now, so we can click **OK**.

The application now looks as in the following screenshot:

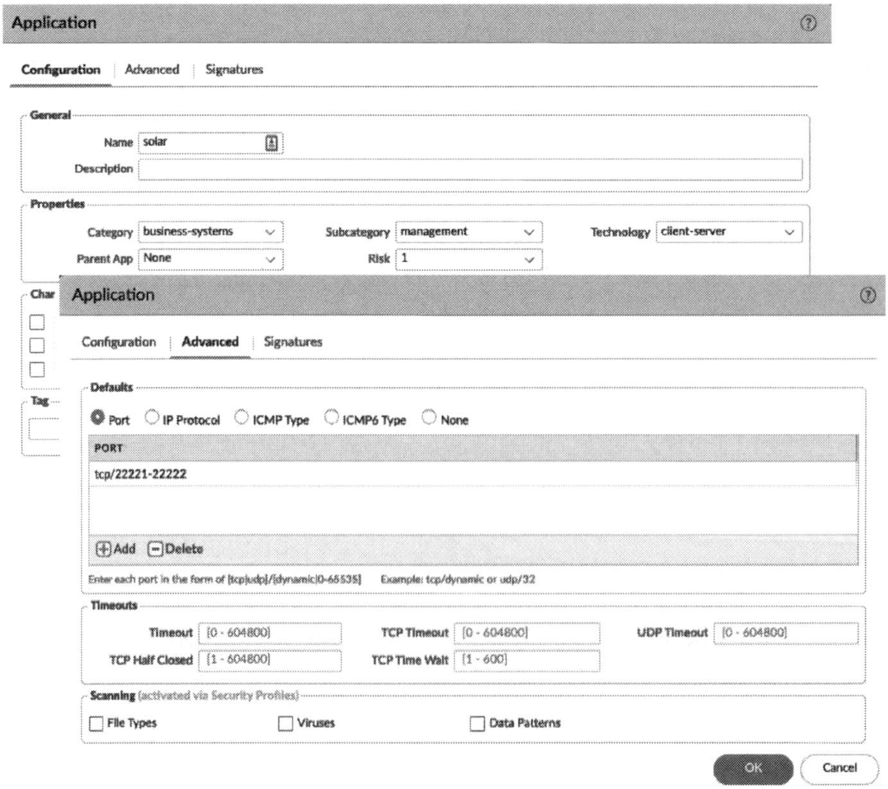

Figure 10.13 – A custom application

To create the override, go to **Policies | Application Override** and create a new override policy:

1. Click on **Add** and set a descriptive name.

2. In the **Source** tab, we'll set the source zone to LAN and the source IP to 192.168.27.113 for my solar converter.

3. In the **Destination** tab, we can set the destination zone to outside and the IP addresses associated with my converter's cloud interface.

4. In the **Protocol/Application** tab, set the destination ports to tcp 22221-22222 and the **solar** custom application that we created earlier.

5. Click **OK** and **Commit**.

The override rule will look as in the following screenshot:

| | NAME | TAGS | Source | | Destination | | PROTOC... | PORT | APPLICATI... |
| | | | ZONE | ADDRESS | ZONE | ADDRESS | | | |
|---|---|---|---|---|---|---|---|---|---|
| 1 | solar override | none | LAN | 192.168.27.4 | outside | | tcp | 22221-22222 | solar |

Figure 10.14 – Application override rule

Once the changes are committed, you should start seeing the sessions show up as a different application in your session table and traffic log, as you can see in the following screenshot:

| | | RECEIVE TIME | TYPE | FROM ZONE | TO ZONE | SOURCE | DESTINATION | TO PORT | APPLICATION | ACTION |
|---|---|---|---|---|---|---|---|---|---|---|
| | | 06/17 00:57:18 | end | LAN | outside | 192.168.27.2... | 80.239.175.38 | 22222 | solar | allow |
| | | 06/16 19:49:46 | end | LAN | outside | 192.168.27.2... | 80.239.175.38 | 22222 | solar | allow |
| | | 06/16 16:29:25 | end | LAN | outside | 192.168.27.2... | 185.121.71.38 | 22222 | solar | allow |

Figure 10.15 – The session identified as a custom application

While this is a great solution for simple applications, especially internal ones where you have control over the endpoints and can leverage host-based security to make up for the lack of scanning capabilities on the TCP flow, it is better to use signature-based identification and let the App-ID and Content-ID fully scan the flow.

Don't forget to disable the application override policy before moving on to the next section.

# Signature-based custom applications

Identifying applications based on a signature or signatures provides far more accuracy when identifying custom sessions. Any sessions that do not match the signatures you set to identify the traffic will still be identified as unknown, which should either be blocked or raise an alarm if you have accounted for all possible signatures.

We first need to do some research into the application we want to identify before we can create custom signatures. Packet captures provide the best information for this.

To set up a basic packet capture, go to **Monitor | Packet Capture** and click on **Manage Filters**.

In the Packet Capture Filters , you can add up to four lines that tell your system what you want to capture, based on **Ingress Interface**, **Source IP or Port**, **Destination IP**, or **Port and Protocol Number**. You can also opt to include, exclude or exclusively capture non-IP protocols, which is helpful if you're trying to capture DHCP. So, for example, in my case, we'd do the following:

1.  Click on **Add** and set the filter ID to 1.

2.  Select **Source** and set the IP of my solar converter, 192.168.27.113.

3.  Set the destination port to 22221.

4.  Click on **Add** and set the filter ID to 2.

5.  Select **Source** and set the IP of my solar converter, 192.168.27.113.

6.  Set the destination port to 22222.

7.  Click **OK**.

8.  Enable filtering by setting the **Filtering** toggle to **ON**.

9.  Then, configure capturing by doing the following:

10. Click on **Add**.

11. Set a capture stage:

    --**Receive** captures packets on the incoming interface.

    --**Transmit** captures packets on the outgoing interface.

    --**Drop** captures packets that are being discarded.

    --**Firewall** captures packets while they are being processed.

    For this exercise, we will use the **firewall** stage and call the file solar.pcap.

12. Click **OK**.

Enable capturing by switching the **Packet Capture** toggle to **ON**.

Once packets have been captured, the file will appear in **Captured Files**, where you can click on the file to download it. Wait a sufficient amount of time, and then if possible, restart the session. Once enough data is collected, click on the file and open it with Wireshark to start looking for signatures.

In my case, I discovered that my solar converter will always sign in using the same fingerprint, as you can see in the Data field of the fourth packet in the following screenshot:

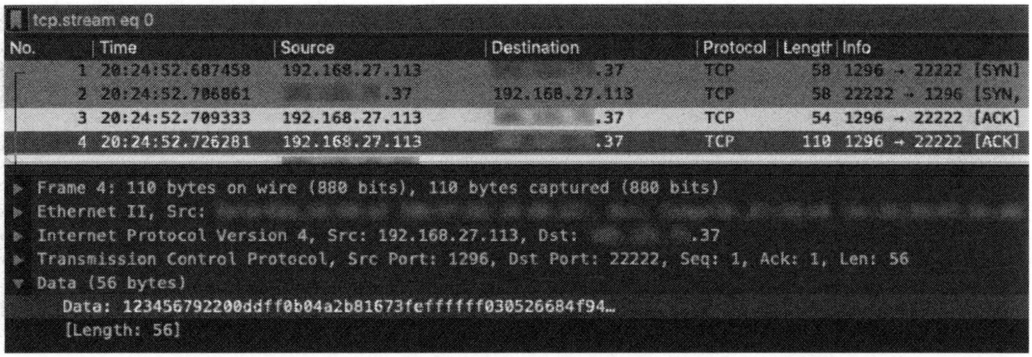

Figure 10.16 – Packet capture in Wireshark

We can now add this to the custom application we created earlier. Go to **Objects | Applications** and open the custom application (solar). In the **Signatures** tab, click on **Add**:

1.  Set a descriptive signature name.

2.  Set the scope. **Transaction** is used to match a signature in a single packet and **Session** is used to match signatures across multiple packets.

    I'll set my scope to **Transaction**, since the fingerprint identification happens in the fourth packet and we don't need the signature engine to keep analyzing after it identifies the fingerprint.

3.  **Ordered Condition Match** requires multiple conditions to be matched in order from top to bottom. With this option unchecked, they can be matched in any order. We'll keep it unchecked as there is only one signature.

4.  Add an OR condition:

    --Set **Operator** to Pattern Match.

    --The context for this signature is unknown-req-tcp-payload as there is no decoder that *claimed* this session (unknown-tcp). Many different contexts are available depending on the decoder that picks up on a session. If the custom app is a sub-application to web-browsing, for example, the context could be http-req-host-header.

    --Set the pattern. To match ASCII, just add the ASCII text in the field, and to match the hexadecimal value, you must enclose the hex between two \x tokens, which lets the signature engine know that this is a hexadecimal value.

    --We'll use \x123456792200dd\x to match the fingerprint, which meets the 7-byte minimum for a custom signature.

    --Some contexts can have **qualifiers** that filter where a string can be matched (for example, for http-req-host-header, you could add the http-method qualifier with the GET value).

5.  Click **OK** twice.

The custom application will now look as in the following screenshot:

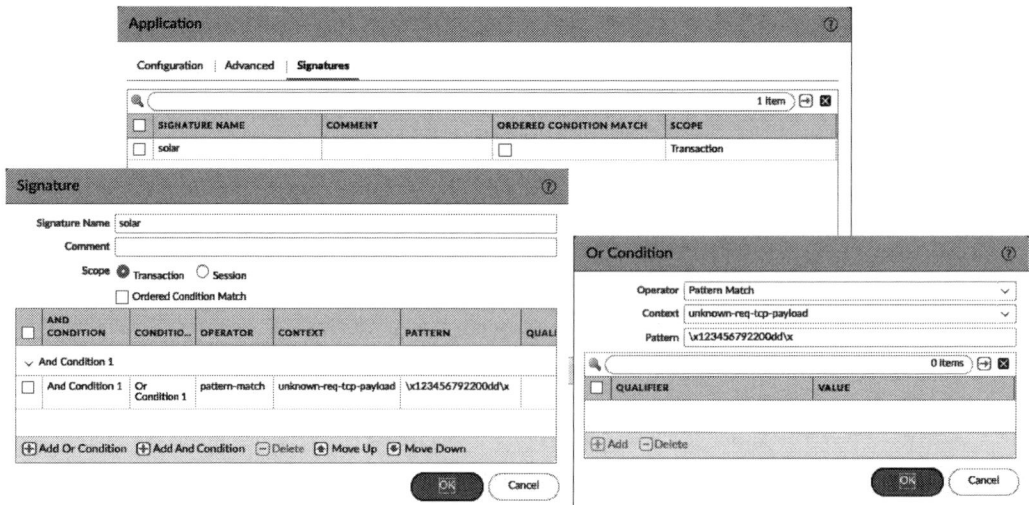

Figure 10.17 – Custom application with a signature

Once you commit this, you should start seeing the sessions being picked up as the custom application.

A few notes on creating signatures:

- A signature pattern must contain at least a 7-byte string with fixed values.

- Enclose hexadecimal strings in \x.

- Be mindful of upper- and lowercase letters in ASCII. You may need to include a signature for both if there could be instances where one is used versus the other (for example, GOOGLE.COM versus google.com).

- Outside of the 7-byte string, you can add **Regular Expressions** (**RegEx**) to match more complex patterns.

The following characters can be used as wildcards in a RegEx string:

| | | |
|---|---|---|
| . | 1.3 | matches a single character (e.g. 123, 133) |
| ? | dots? | matches string with or without last character (e.g. dot, dots) |
| * | dots* | matches string with or without last character, and multiple repeats of last character (e.g. dot, dots, dotsss) |
| + | dots+ | matches single or multiple repetitions of the preceding letter (e.g. dots, dotsss) |
| \| | ((exe)\|(msi)) | OR function to match multiple possible strings (e.g. dot.exe, dot.msi) |
| [ ] | x[abc] | matches preceding string followed by any character between squared brackets (e.g. xa, xb, xc) |
| - | x[a-z] | matches any character in a range (e.g. xa,xm) |
| ^ | x[^AB] | matches any character except the ones listed (e.g. xC, x5) |
| { } | x{1,3} | matches anything after x as long as it is 1 to 3 bytes in length (e.g. x1, x123) |
| \ | x\.y | Escape character to exactly match a special character (e.g. www\.pangurus\.com) |
| &amp | | used to match & in a string |

Figure 10.18 – RegEx wildcard characters

An outdated but still usable list of all contexts and qualifiers can be found at this Palo Alto Networks Knowledgebase document:

https://knowledgebase.paloaltonetworks.com/
KCSArticleDetail?id=kA10g000000ClOFCA0

You can now analyze packets to find identifiable patterns and apply them to signatures of custom applications. You can apply this same knowledge to custom threats!

# Custom threats

If you need to take a more complex approach to a certain data pattern than allowing or blocking through a simple App-ID-driven security rule, you can also create custom threats that can block or reset a client or server or both, or block the IP of an attacker if a specific pattern is detected in a session.

You can create either a custom vulnerability or custom spyware. Both profiles have the same options but fall into different security profiles and reporting categories.

We will build a custom vulnerability, but the process for creating custom spyware is identical.

In **Objects | Custom Objects | Vulnerability**, create a custom vulnerability by following these steps:

1. Click **Add**.

2. In the **Configuration** tab, you need to set a threat ID and a descriptive name. All threats are identified by their ID, and a window from 41000 to 45000 is reserved for custom threats (15000–18000 for custom spyware).

   Let's set an ID of 41000 and give it the name BlockBrowser.

3. Set the severity. If your vulnerability profile has a specific action other than **default** for the severity, that action will be applied unless you create an exception in the profile. Let's set **high**.

4. For **Direction**, you can set whether this vulnerability should only match if the packet is traveling in a specific direction – from client to server or from server to client – or if it can be detected in both directions. We will set **client2server**.

5. Define a default action. Set **Reset Client**.

6. **Affected System** is the only unique setting to vulnerabilities that is not also found in spyware; it indicates who is involved with a certain signature. As we're going to capture outgoing browsing sessions, we'll set this to **client**.

7. If there's any CVE, vendor bug ID, or Bugtraq information you'd like to add for completeness, there are fields available to add this information.

The **Configuration** tab should look as in the following screenshot:

Figure 10.19 – Custom Vulnerability Signature

In the **Signatures** tab, we can add the patterns as we did before with custom applications, but there are two signature types:

- **Standard** is the same type of pattern match as the custom application.

- **Combination** adds a timing attribute that lets you define a number of hits over a specified amount of time, and the aggregation criteria (hits from the source, destination, or the source to the destination are counted). This can help identify brute-force conditions where one or two signature matches in a timeframe could be normal, but five is suspicious. **Combination can only be applied to predefined vulnerability IDs**.

We've already covered how to identify the payload, so let's create a standard signature and block Firefox as a browser.

As shown in the following screenshot, if you packet capture a web-browsing session from a regular browser, it will advertise its User-Agent, which is the software used to retrieve the web page. We can use this information in a signature to prevent certain browsers from accessing web pages:

| No. | Time | Source | Destination | Protocol | Length | Info |
|---|---|---|---|---|---|---|
| 19 | 20:14:27.249912 | 192.168.27.7 | .29 | TCP | 66 | 62747 → 80 [SYN, ECN, CWR] Seq=0 |
| 20 | 20:14:27.272031 | .29 | 192.168.27.7 | TCP | 66 | 80 → 62747 [SYN, ACK] Seq=0 Ack=1 |
| 21 | 20:14:27.274027 | 192.168.27.7 | 29 | TCP | 54 | 62747 → 80 [ACK] Seq=1 Ack=1 Win= |
| 22 | 20:14:27.274728 | 192.168.27.7 | 29 | OCSP | 444 | Request |

```
Frame 22: 444 bytes on wire (3552 bits), 444 bytes captured (3552 bits)
Ethernet II, Src:
Internet Protocol Version 4, Src: 192.168.27.7, Dst:
Transmission Control Protocol, Src Port: 62747, Dst Port: 80, Seq: 1, Ack: 1, Len: 390
Hypertext Transfer Protocol
  POST / HTTP/1.1\r\n
  Host:              \r\n
  User-Agent: Mozilla/5.0 (Windows NT 10.0; Win64; x64; rv:75.0) Gecko/20100101 Firefox/75.0\r\n
  Accept: */*\r\n
  Accept-Language: nl,en-US;q=0.7,en;q=0.3\r\n
  Accept-Encoding: gzip, deflate\r\n
  Content-Type: application/ocsp-request\r\n
  Content-Length: 83\r\n
  Connection: keep-alive\r\n
  \r\n
```

Figure 10.20 – A packet capture web session from Firefox

Add the details learned from the packet capture to the custom threat:

1.  In the `BlockBrowser` custom threat's **Signature** tab, click on **Add** and set a name, `Firefox`.

2.  Set **Scope** to **Transaction**.

3.  Add an OR condition:

    --Set **Operator** to `Pattern Match`.

    --Set **Context** to `http-req-headers`.

    --Set **Pattern** to `Firefox/`.

    --Add a qualifier and set it to `http-method` with a value of POST.

4.  Click **OK**.

If you want to add multiple User-Agents, you can add more OR conditions, each matching a different browser type:

1.  Add an OR condition:

    --Set **Operator** to `Pattern Match`.

    --Set **Context** to `http-req-headers`.

    --Set **Pattern** to `Chrome/`.

    --Add a qualifier and set it to `http-method` with a value of POST.

2.  Click **OK** twice.

The **Signature** tab should look as follows:

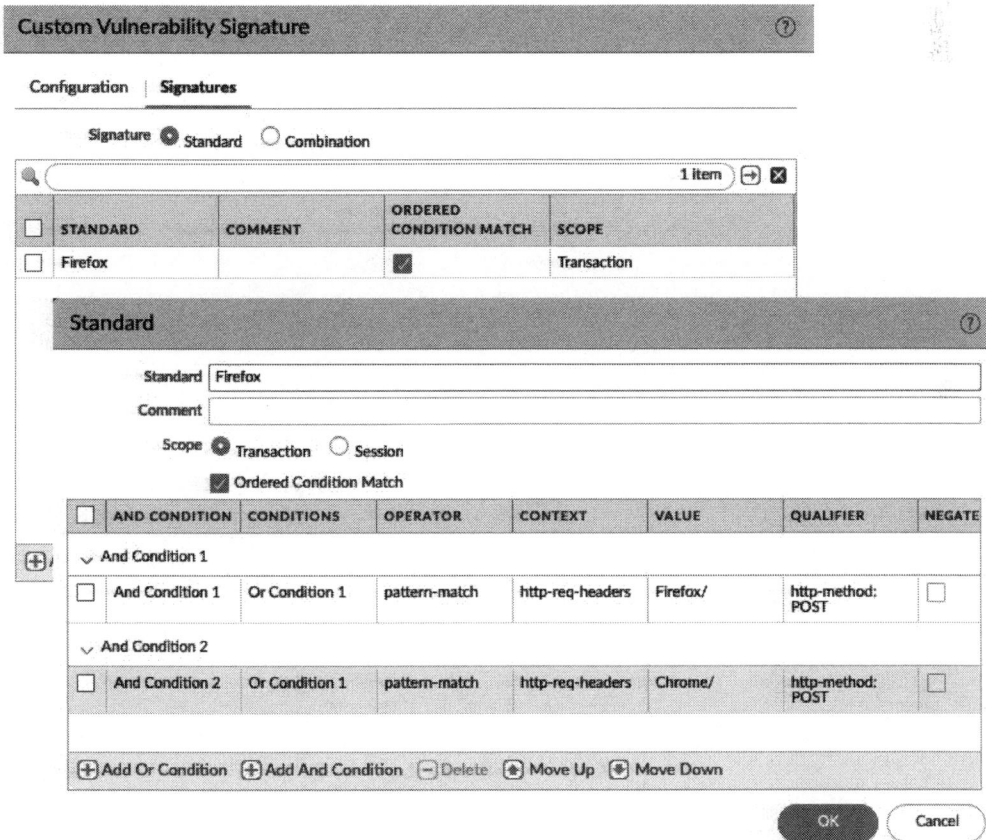

Figure 10.21 – Custom Vulnerability Signature

Once this new vulnerability is committed, you will start to see it show up in the threat logs once someone uses a Firefox browser.

> **Important note**
> SSL decryption needs to be enabled for patterns to be matched in encrypted payloads or headers.

Pay close attention to the action, as it may differ from the one we set in the custom vulnerability itself. This is because for high- and critical-severity threats, we usually set an action that replaces all the default actions. If the custom threat action differs from the **Security Profile** settings, add an exception, as shown in the following screenshot.

To add an exception, open the profile where the action needs to be changed:

1. In the **Exceptions** tab, type the threat ID into the search field.

2. Check the **Show All Signatures** box at the bottom.

3. Check the **Enable** box to activate the override for this signature.

4. Make sure the action is set to **default**:

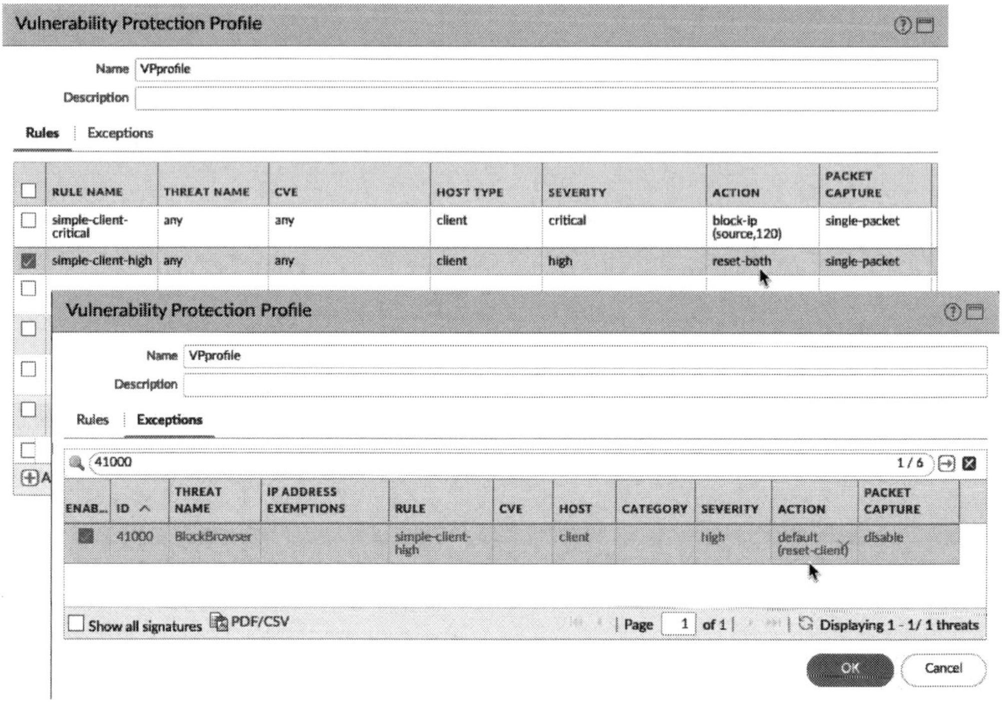

Figure 10.22 – Adding a custom vulnerability to the exceptions

You can now use the information you find in a packet capture to create custom applications or custom threats depending on your needs. In the next section, we're going to protect our network from floods and other low-level attacks.

# Zone protection and DoS protection

While layer 7 threats generally revolve around stealing data, blackmailing users through sophisticated phishing, or infecting hosts with complex and expensive zero-day vulnerabilities, protecting the network layer against **DoS** and other attacks is equally important. Protecting the system and the network is achieved in three different ways:

- System-wide settings that defend against maliciously crafted packets or attempts at evasion through manipulation
- Zone protection to protect the whole network against an onslaught of packets intended to bring the network to its knees
- DoS protection to more granularly protect resources from being overwhelmed

The system-wide settings are, unfortunately, not all neatly sorted in one place. I'll go over the most important ones.

## System protection settings

A good deal of the global session-related settings can be accessed through the **Device | Setup | Session** tab. In the **Session** settings, you can control several nice features such as Jumbo Frames, IPv6, and accelerated aging. An important setting here that should be enabled is **Packet Buffer Protection**. The firewall has buffers to process traffic while it is coming in and may need to rely on these buffers when CPU usage is high or a session requires extra attention. Attack methods exist that try to exploit such buffers and could cause DoS conditions if they manage to flood the buffer. **Packet Buffer Protection** will keep track of these sessions and discard them if their abuse threatens legitimate sessions:

- **Activate** is the level of buffer usage where the protection will start monitoring sessions that are heavily taxing the buffers and discard the session if needed.
- **Block Hold Time** is the amount of time a session is granted to *act abusively* in case it is expected behavior of passing nature.
- **Block Duration** is the amount of time the blocked IP will be blocked for if the behavior lasts longer than the block hold time.

Enable **Packet Buffer Protection** in each security zone individually.

From the CLI, you can check whether **Packet Buffer Protection** has been engaged:

```
> show session packet-buffer-protection
```

You can also check which zones have been enabled:

```
> show session packet-buffer-protection zones
```

In **TCP Settings**, all protections are enabled by default, but some may need to be disabled (temporarily) to fix an issue. Most commonly, **Asymmetric Path**, which refers to TCP packets arriving out of the window or containing out-of-sync ACK, is useful for troubleshooting. Packets dropped by this protection would show up as follows:

```
> show counter global filter category tcp | match out_of
tcp_out_of_sync      0 0 warn tcp  pktproc    can't continue tcp
reassembly because it is out of sync
tcp_drop_out_of_wnd 0 0 warn tcp   resource   out-of-window
packets dropped
```

The TCP settings can be verified by running the following command in the CLI:

```
> show running tcp state
```

In the following screenshot, you can see the default values, which in most cases should be sufficient:

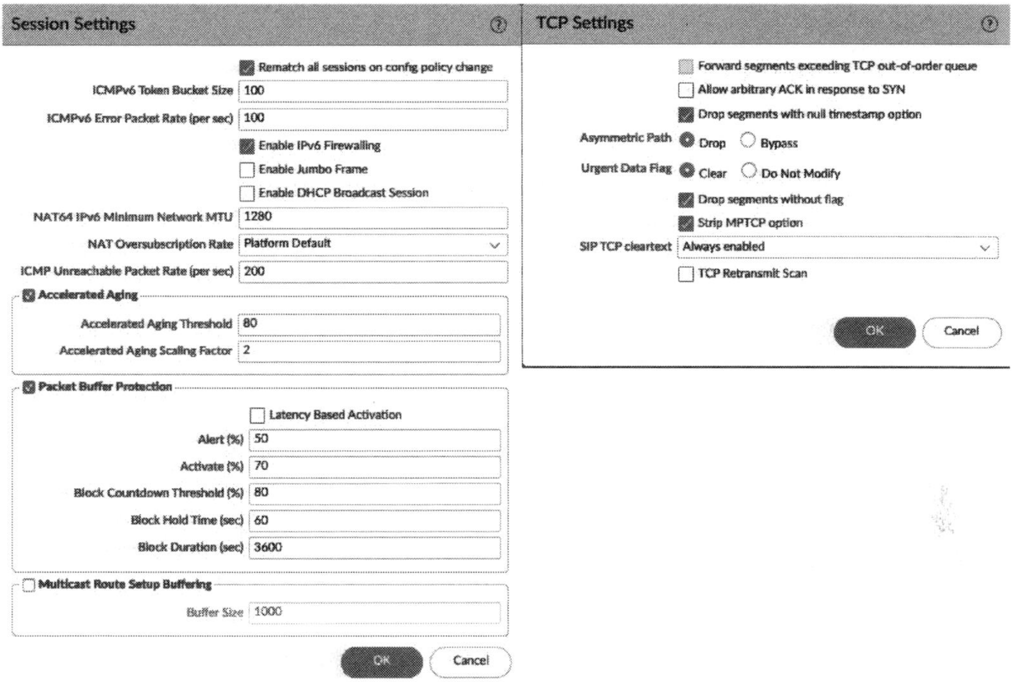

Figure 10.23 – The Session and TCP settings

The **Session Setup** configuration can only be checked and changed from the CLI:

```
> show session info

        -------------------------------------------------------

        Session setup
            TCP - reject non-SYN first packet:          True
            Hardware session offloading:                True
            Hardware UDP session offloading:            True
            IPv6 firewalling:                           True
            Strict TCP/IP checksum:                     True
            Strict TCP RST sequence:                    True
            Reject TCP small initial window:            False
            Reject TCP SYN with different seq/options:  True
            ICMP Unreachable Packet Rate:               200 pps

        -------------------------------------------------------
```

**TCP – reject non-SYN** prevents ACK packets from getting through without first having received an SYN packet to initiate a session.

There's an operational command and a configuration command to change this setting:

```
> set session tcp-reject-non-syn yes|no
# set deviceconfig setting session tcp-reject-non-syn yes|no
```

**Strict TCP/IP checksum** requires the checksum header to be accurate and unaltered; otherwise, a corrupted checksum will be discarded.

This setting can only be controlled through an operational command:

```
> set session strict-checksum yes|no
```

**Strict TCP RST sequence** will only accept an RST packet if it has a sequence number that matches the session's flow. RST packets with a mismatching sequence number will be discarded (this could be used to inject reset packets in an attempt to provoke a DoS). This protection can only be controlled through an operational command:

```
> set session tcp-strict-rst yes|no
```

**Reject TCP small initial window** is disabled by default, but lets you set a discard option for SYN packets where the *Window size value* in the TCP header is lower than the value you set:

```
> set session tcp-reject-small-initial-window-enable yes|no
> set session tcp-reject-small-initial-window-threshold
<0-1024>
```

**Reject TCP SYN with different seq/options** blocks duplicate SYN packets with different sequence numbers or options:

```
> set session tcp-reject-diff-syn yes|no
```

Now that we've covered the system settings, let's move on to protecting zones.

# Configuring zone protection

Zone protection does exactly what its name states: protects a zone. This means that each zone needs to be enabled individually and different settings may apply to different zones. It is important that you have a good understanding of what traffic volumes are to be expected and where the limits of your infrastructure lie for you to be able to set certain flood protections so that they function efficiently. You may want to perform an audit before enabling zone protection. You can create new zone protection profiles by going to **Network | Network Profiles | Zone Protection** and following these steps:

1.  Click on **Add** and set a descriptive name.

2.  In the **Flood Protection** tab, we can enable protection for **UDP**, **ICMP**, **ICMPv6**, and **Other IP**. There are three settings per protocol:

    --**Alarm rate** is when a log entry is created, alerting the admin that a threshold has been reached. This will be a critical log entry in the threat log, as we can see in the screenshot at the end of this list.

    --**Activate** is the rate at which **Random Early Drop** (**RED**) will start randomly discarding packets. This should ideally start happening at a higher rate than what is normal for your network in the appointed zone.

    --**Maximum** is the upper limit of the connections/seconds the system will accept. Anything over this limit will be discarded. The maximum is also used to calculate the progressive rate at which RED discards packets; the closer the connections/ seconds get to the limit, the more packets get discarded.

3.  **SYN** has one additional setting, called **Action**, where RED can be switched to SYN cookies instead. When SYN cookies are enabled, the firewall does not add SYN queue entries and it discards the SYN packet instead, but it does reply with an SYN/ACK containing a particular sequence number that allows it to reconstruct the original SYN if the client is able to reply with an appropriate ACK to the sequence number. This prevents the SYN queue from getting flooded (as no entries are added). When SYN cookies are used, it is fine to set **activate** at 0. When the maximum is reached, all excess SYN packets will still be dropped:

| | Receive Time | Type | Name | Direction | From Zone | To Zone | Source address | Destination address | To Port | Application | Action | Severity |
|---|---|---|---|---|---|---|---|---|---|---|---|---|
| 📄 | 04/29 00:12:21 | flood | UDP Flood | client-to-server | LAN | LAN | 0.0.0.0 | 0.0.0.0 | 0 | not-applicable | allow | critical |
| 📄 | 04/29 00:12:18 | flood | ICMP Flood | client-to-server | LAN | LAN | 0.0.0.0 | 0.0.0.0 | 0 | not-applicable | allow | critical |
| 📄 | 04/29 00:07:47 | flood | TCP Flood | client-to-server | LAN | LAN | 0.0.0.0 | 0.0.0.0 | 0 | not-applicable | syncookie-sent | critical |

Figure 10.24 – Flood alert logs

The **Flood Protection** tab should look as in the following screenshot. Make sure to baseline your network before applying aggressive protection. If no tools or services are available, try setting **Alarm Rate** fairly low and monitor your threat log. Gradually increase the alarm rate until you stop receiving alarms, which should be your peak. At this point, you can set your activate rate for RED and make an educated estimate of where the maximum should be:

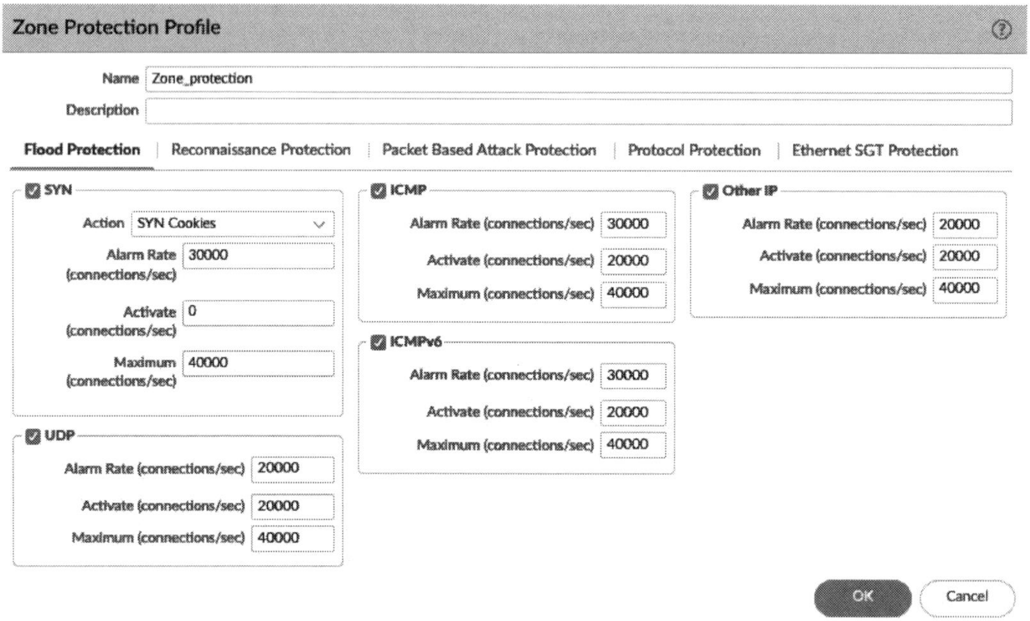

Figure 10.25 – Flood protection

In the **Reconnaissance Protection** tab, we can set protection against discovery scans directed at hosts to find out what services are running, or the entire network to map the environment. In the following screenshot, you can see the three types of scans that can be intercepted:

- **TCP Port Scan** detects TCP connections on many different ports to a single destination from a single source.

- **UDP Port Scan** detects UDP connections on many different ports to a single destination from a single source.

- **Host Sweep** detects whether a single source is making many connections to many destinations.

A source address exclusion can be set in case a known server, such as a PRTG or Nmap server, needs to be able to perform scans for legitimate reasons.

For all scans, the threshold and interval indicate the number of events detected in a certain amount of time, before the action is applied to the source. Actions include **allow**, which disables the scan protection, **alert**, which simply logs detected scans, **block**, which drops new packets that match the type of scan after the threshold was reached, and **block-ip**, which adds the IP to a block list and, depending on whether **Track By** is set to **source** or **source-and-destination**, will block packets from the source or all packets from the source to the destination, regardless of whether the packets are directly associated with the detected scan:

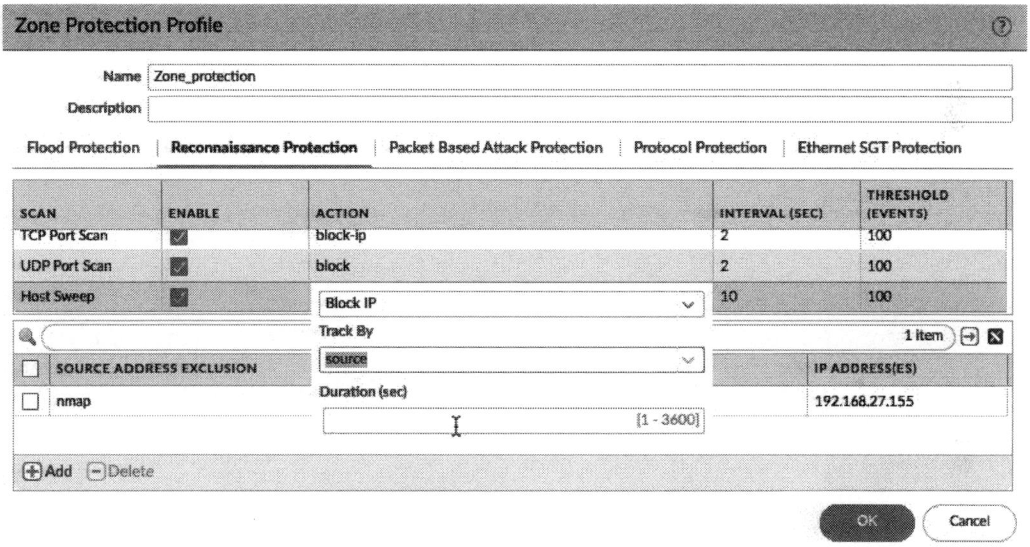

Figure 10.26 – Reconnaissance protection

In the **Packet Based Attack Protection** tab, we find several sub-tabs with a couple of important protection mechanisms. As the following screenshot shows, in the **IP Drop** tab, we will find the following options:

- **Spoofed IP address** will look up the routing table and will only accept packets that are ingressing on an interface that has a route associated with the source IP.

- **Strict IP Address Check** checks that an IP is not the broadcast IP of a subnet and the source IP is routable over the source interface.

- **Fragmented Traffic** lets you drop fragmented packets (handle this with care as some links may need fragmentation due to **MTU** (**Maximum Transmission Units**) restrictions).

- **Strict Source Routing** and **Loose Source Routing** are the datagram header options that allow the sender to set the route a packet should take.

- **Timestamp** prevents the sender from requesting timestamps from any machine processing the packet.

- **Record Route** is an IP header that lets the sender collect the IP from every host processing the packet.

- **Security** and **Stream ID**, with IP options 2 and 8, respectively, can also be blocked.

- **Unknown** is the packets that have an unknown class or number.

- **Malformed** is the packets with inconsistent combinations of their length, class, and number (based on RFCs 791, 1108, 1393, and 2113):

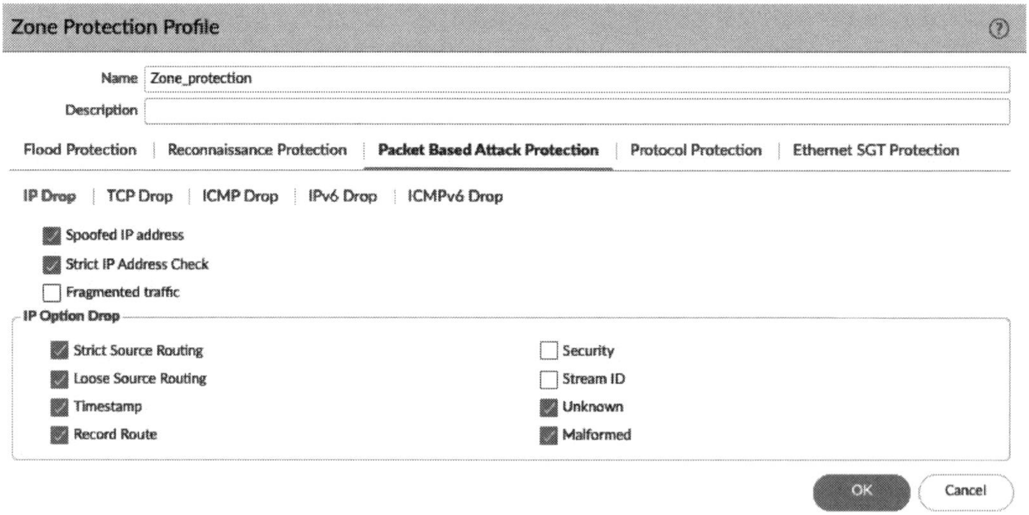

Figure 10.27 – IP drop packet-based attack protection

As you can see in the following screenshot, in the **TCP Drop** tab, we can protect against TCP-based malformations or irregularities that could be abused to gain access or exploit systems:

- **Mismatched overlapping TCP segment** blocks packets that are using an incorrect sequence number and could have been injected into a flow.

- **Split Handshake** prevents TCP handshakes that have been fragmented or split over more than three packets.

- **TCP SYN with Data** and **TCP SYNACK with Data** block SYN and SYNACK packets that contain data, since these packets should only be used to establish a handshake and not to transport data.

- **Reject Non-SYN TCP** and **Asymmetric Path** are normally set globally but can be set differently per zone to accommodate some zones needing either of these TCP anomalies without compromising the other zones by changing the global setting.

- The **TCP Timestamp** option should be stripped from the TCP header to prevent timestamp DoS attacks.

- The **TCP Fast Open** option can be stripped. If this check is left disabled (the default), SYN or SYNACK data will be allowed for the purpose of **TCP Fast Open**, even if **TCP SYN with Data** and **TCP SYNACK with Data** are set to blocking.

- **Multipath TCP (MPTCP Options)** can also be left as the global setting or controlled per zone to allow exceptions to the global setting as some zones may need to support multipath:

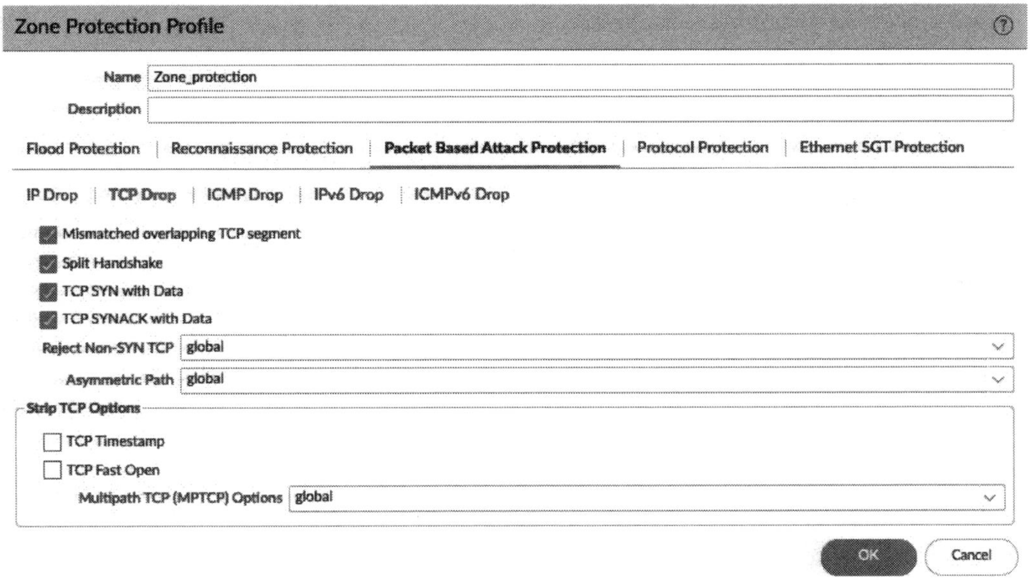

Figure 10.28 – TCP drop packet-based attack protection

As you can see in the following screenshot, all the **ICMP** and **ICMPv6** options are disabled by default. Because ICMP is commonly used for troubleshooting, most options may be desirable from a support perspective. ICMP settings can only be set to discard packets, while any options checked in ICMPv6 can be overruled by adding explicit security rules that allow the options:

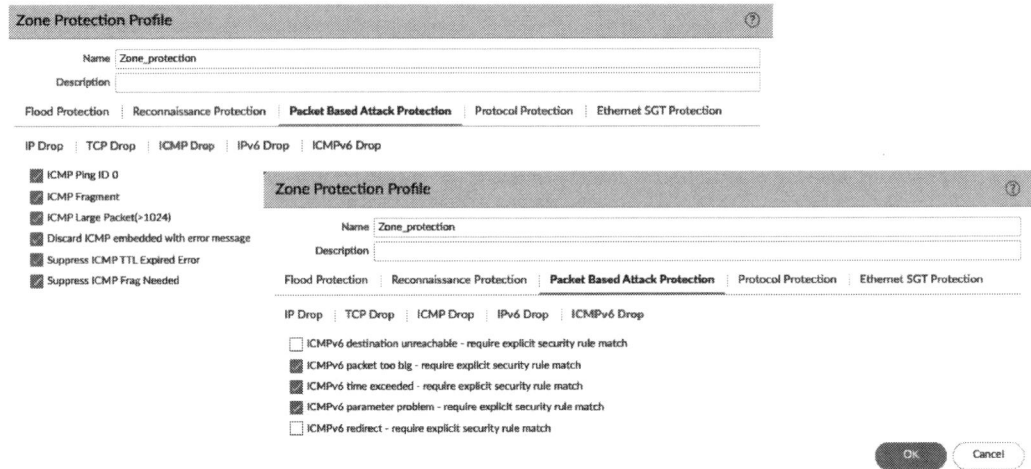

Figure 10.29 – Default ICMP drop settings

As you can see in the following screenshot, by default, all routing headers, except type 3, 253, and 254, are dropped in **IPv6 Drop**:

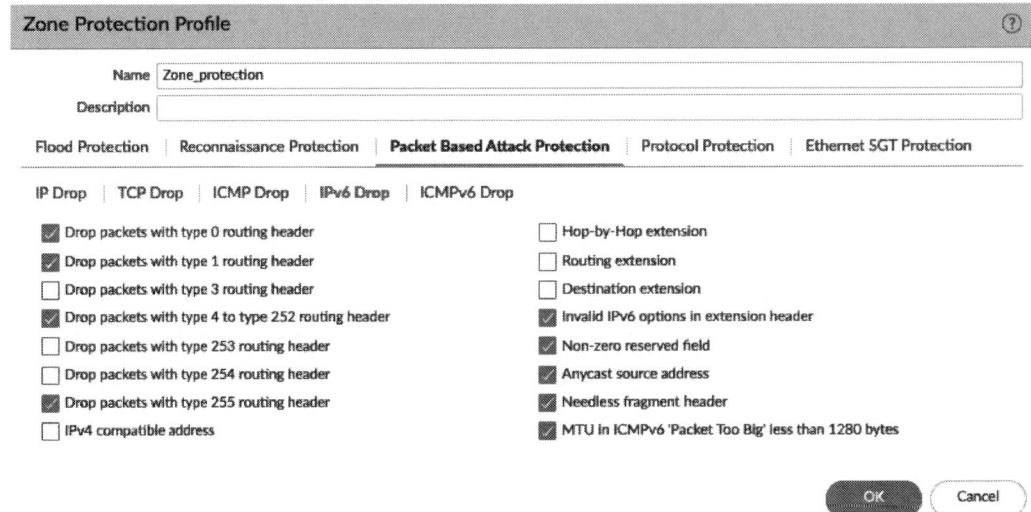

Figure 10.30 – IPv6 drop options

In the **Protocol Protection** tab, you can add other protocols outside of IPv4, IPv6, ARP, and VLAN-tagged frames by their hex ethertype value. You can find a list of protocols and their hex ethertype at `http://standards-oui.ieee.org/ethertype/eth.txt`.

As you can see in the following screenshot, this section is fairly straightforward; we can add several different protocols, but we need to choose whether we set this to be an include or exclude list:

- **Exclude List** will drop all the protocols listed. As the following screenshot shows, an ethertype of `0x890d` would be blocked while all the other protocols would be allowed.

- **Include List** allows only the protocols listed in addition to IPv4, IPv6, ARP, and VLAN-tagged frames. All other protocols will be dropped:

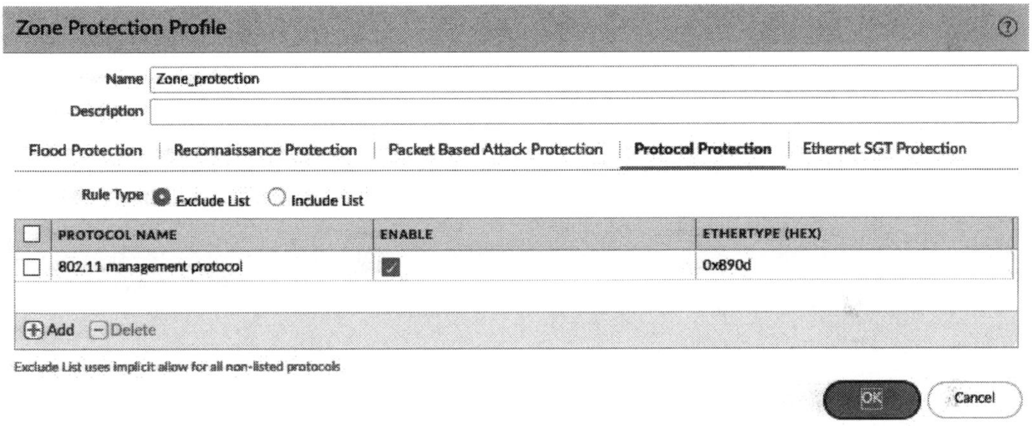

Figure 10.31 – Protocol Protection

In **Ethernet SGT Protection**, you can add Cisco TrustSec **Security Group Tags (SGTs)**. If an incoming packet has an `802.1Q` header that contains an SGT that matches one of the tags in the list, the packet will be dropped.

To enable zone protection, go to **Network | Zones** and add a zone protection profile to all the zones by selecting the appropriate one from the dropdown. Make sure to also enable **Packet Buffer Protection**.

Now that we've set up protection for our zones, we can add protection for specific resources by setting up DoS profiles and creating a DoS protection policy.

# Configuring DoS protection

A DoS protection profile is similar to zone protection, but it applies resource limitations at a smaller scale. A server may have limited resources and could be easily flooded by a focused attack leveraging a volume of traffic much lower than what the zone protection profile permits. New profiles can be created in **Objects | Security Profiles | DoS Protection**.

As you can see from the following screenshot, the DoS profiles are simpler than zone protection. There are two types:

- The **Aggregate** profiles count the total number of connections matching the rule and profile.

- The **Classified** profiles count individual sessions based on the source, the destination, or the source and destination.

There are only two tabs:

- **Flood Protection** contains all the same settings as the **Flood Protection** tab in the **Zone Protection** profile, but someone decided to break it up into smaller topical tabs. The only difference is the addition of **Block Duration**, which will be used in the DoS protection policy.

- **Resource Protection**, which can be enabled to limit the maximum number of concurrent sessions to a resource:

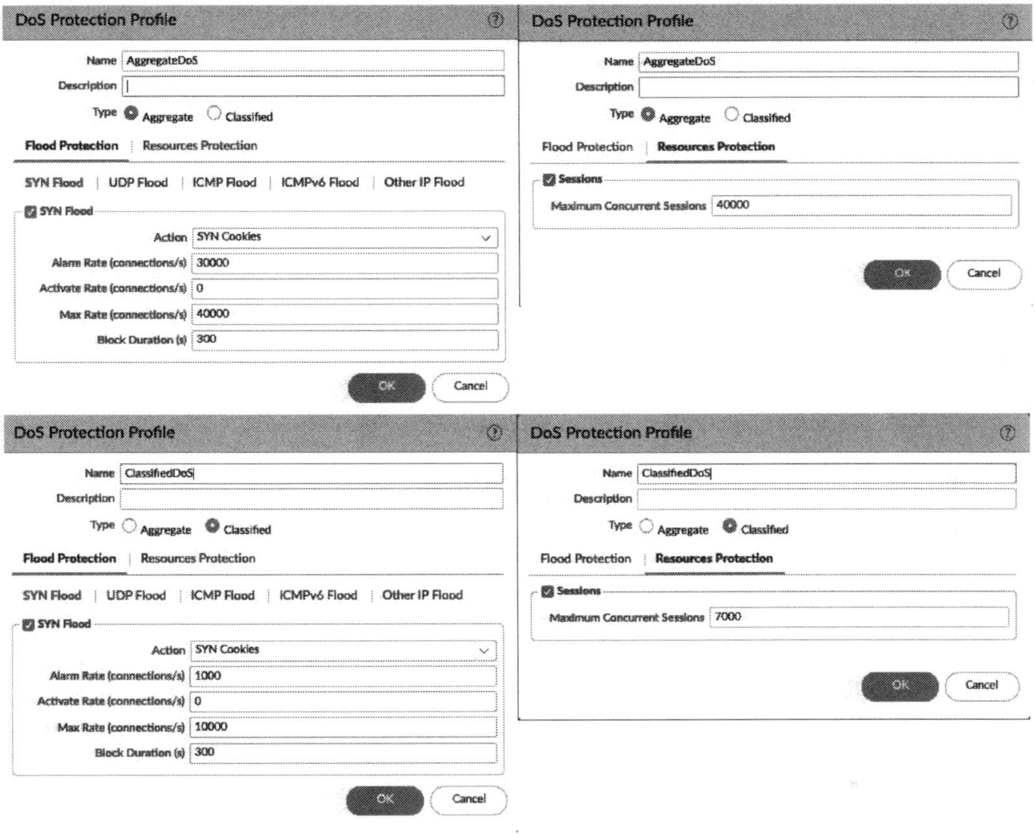

Figure 10.32 – The Aggregate and Classified DoS protection profiles

To apply these profiles to a resource, create a new rule in **Policies | DoS Protection**:

1. Click on **Add** and set a descriptive name.

2. In the **Source** tab, set **Type** to **Zone** or **Interface** and select the appropriate zone or interface. Add a source IP/subnet if needed.

3. In the **Destination** tab, set **Type** to **Zone** or **Interface** and add the destination zone or interface. Set the destination IP address(es) of the resource you are going to protect. Use the public IP address if the connection will come in from the internet and goes through the destination NAT.

4.  In the **Option/Protection** tab, do the following:

Add the service ports that need to be protected.

Select the action:

--**Deny** will block all sessions matching the rule.

--**Allow** will allow and not protect all sessions matching the rule.

--**Protect** will apply DoS profiles to all sessions matching the rule.

--**Deny** and **Allow** can be used to create exceptions above a more generic **Protect** rule.

--Set a schedule if the rule should only be active at certain moments.

--Set the appropriate **Log Forwarding** profile if alarm settings need to translate into an email being sent or a syslog sent out to a SIEM. If you created a `default` log forwarding profile, it will be added automatically.

--Select the appropriate **Aggregate** profile.

--If more granular protection is needed, check **Classified** and select the classified profile.

Set the **Address** classification as **source-ip-only**, **destination-ip-only**, or **src-dest-ip-both**.

> **Important note**
>
> Address classification takes up resources to keep track of sessions. You should be careful or defer using **source-ip-only** or **destination-ip-only** for internet facing protection rules.

Your rule should look similar to the following screenshot:

| | NAME | Source ZONE/INTERFA... | ADDRESS | Destination ZONE/INTE... | ADDRESS | SERVICE | ACTION | Protection AGGREGATE | CLASSIFIED | SCHEDULE |
|---|---|---|---|---|---|---|---|---|---|---|
| 1 | protect webserver | ethernet1/1 | any | dmz | webserverfarm-public | service-https | protect | AggregateDoS | profile: ClassifiedDoS src-dest-ip-both | none |

**DoS Rule**

General | Source | Destination | **Option/Protection**

☐ Any

☐ SERVICE ∧

☐ ⚔ service-https

⊕ Add  ⊖ Delete

| | |
|---|---|
| Action | Protect |
| Schedule | None |
| Log Forwarding | default |
| Aggregate | AggregateDoS |
| ☑ Classified | |
| Profile | ClassifiedDoS |
| Address | src-dest-ip-both |

OK    Cancel

Figure 10.33 – A DoS protection rule

With this information, you are now able to protect your network and individual servers from getting flooded. (Disclaimer: there's only so much a firewall can do. If the ISP uplink is physically flooded, only alternative paths can make resources available to the outside. The firewall's job is to contain the attack to one zone while all other zones can continue working.)

# Summary

In this chapter, you learned how to set up site-to-site VPN tunnels and a client-to-site VPN with GlobalProtect. You can now not only provide connectivity but also scan the client machine for compliancy and know how to control the user experience. We've also learned how to create custom applications and custom threats that will allow you to identify packets unique to your environment and take affirmative action, and we've learned how to set up zone and DoS protection to defend against all kinds of packet-based attacks.

In the next chapter, we will be getting our hands on some basic troubleshooting. We will learn about session details and how to interpret what is happening to a session.

# 11
# Troubleshooting Common Session Issues

In this chapter, we will learn how to read session output and how to troubleshoot basic session issues. We will learn how to use the tools available in the web interface to find problems and test policies. We will go over the steps to collect all the information you need to find out why a session may not be working as expected or predict how a new rule will react to certain sessions. We will also look at a powerful user tool called **Maintenance Mode** or the **Maintenance Recovery Tool** (**MRT**), which allows some very powerful system-level interactions with the firewall.

In this chapter, we're going to cover the following main topics:

- Using the tools available in the web interface
- Interpreting session details
- Using the troubleshooting tool
- Using Maintenance Mode to resolve and recover from system issues

# Technical requirements

Since we're going to be doing some troubleshooting, having a lab available so that you can reproduce some of the steps explained here will greatly help you to understand the materials we will cover.

# Using the tools at our disposal

Knowing your way around the web interface is a great start if you need to troubleshoot an issue. There are plenty of spaces where valuable information is stored, and knowing just where to look can be the difference between quickly checking and fixing an issue versus spending hours trying to figure out why something isn't working.

As we saw in *Chapter 9, Logging and Reporting*, the **Monitor** tab is such a place where knowing where to look can make a difference. Logs are maintained for just about any event, from sessions passing through or being blocked by the firewall or a security profile to things happening on the firewall itself. In most cases, the log files will be the first place to look if something unexpected happened.

## Log files

There are many different log databases that collect specific information. Knowing where to look is essential if you want to quickly find information relating to the issue you are investigating:

- **Traffic** holds all the logs related to sessions. This includes the source and destination IP, the port, the zones and users, the application (or lack thereof), bytes, packets sent and received, and the reason for an action applied by a security policy and session end. You can enable a column to indicate whether a session was decrypted or intercepted for captive portal authentication. For each session start or session end log action, an entry is created.

- **Threat** also logs the log source and destination IP, the port, the zones and users, and the application, but these logs are created as a result of a detected vulnerability or malware. A log will contain the name of the threat and the direction in which it was detected – client-to-server or server-to-client. The action listed is what the content engine performed in response to detecting a threat, so it may not correlate with the traffic log; a traffic log may indicate that a session was allowed because it hit a security rule that permitted the connection, but the threat response may have been to send an RST packet or simply create an alert log. In the case of an RST package being sent, the traffic log end reason would read `threat`.

  If packet captures were enabled in the security profiles, any threats that triggered a packet capture will have a little green arrow associated with the log entry, which can be clicked on to download the packet capture.

- **URL Filtering** holds a log of all the URL filtering profile actions, except `allow`. These logs contain the basic source and destination information and the URL and URL category accessed. Actions taken in URL filtering will not reflect at all in the traffic log, as the TCP session will simply have been allowed, but the content engine may have returned a `blocking` or `continue` page.

- **WildFire Submissions** contains a log entry for every file that was intercepted and forwarded to WildFire. The log will contain all the basic source and destination information, as well as a verdict. Grayware and benign verdicts can be enabled in **System | Setup | WildFire** if you want to keep track of all the files. It may take a while for the WildFire log to appear after a file is uploaded as the log is written when the verdict is learned. The full report can be accessed on the WildFire portal by clicking on the **Detailed log view** icon and clicking the WildFire Analysis Report.

- **Data Filtering** contains logs for any events that were triggered where keywords were detected in a data filtering profile. The log will contain the basic source and destination information, the filename, and/or the URL accessed.

- **HIP Match** maintains a log for all HIP profiles matched to users logging in through GlobalProtect.

- **GlobalProtect** keeps a record of every user logging in or retrieving a configuration and which portal or gateway they connected to.

- **IP-Tag** keeps a log each time a tag is assigned to a particular IP address.

- **User-ID** keeps track of all the user-to-IP mappings and the source the information was learned from.

- **Tunnel Inspection** writes a log for each inspected tunnel, the start and end time, the application used to tunnel, the session and tunnel ID, and the security and tunnel inspection rules matched for the session.

- **Configuration** contains all the configuration changes and information about the administrator that made the change, as well as the time and date and the source address that the admin was connecting from.

- **System** contains all the logs relating to events happening at the system level: any dynamic updates that were downloaded and installed, IPSec tunnels that were established or torn down, commit jobs, admin authentications, daemons reporting on commit outcome, syslog events, satellite connection events, high-availability events, hardware alarms, DoS alarms, and LACP and LLDP events.

- **Alarms** contains specific logs relating to alarms. Default alarms include fan speed/fan tray, temperature issues, and power supply issues. Additional alarms can be configured in **Device | Log Settings**. If you enable an alarm, set the log quotas higher as log pruning happens at around 95% of capacity.

- **Authentication** contains logs for users authenticating against an authentication (captive portal) rule in **Policies | Authentication**.

- **Unified** displays the **Traffic**, **Threat URL Filtering**, **WildFire**, and **Data Filtering** logs all in the same view. When proper filtering is applied, this log view supplies a great single-pane overview.

All logs have a little magnifying glass to the far left of each log entry that opens a detailed log view with a treasure trove of information, as you can see in the following screenshot. At the bottom is a clickable list of related log entries, which allows you to review **Traffic (start or end)**, **Vulnerability**, **URL**, and other related log types. Any associated packet captures are listed here as well. If, for example, a vulnerability was detected that matches a security profile that has  **packet captures** enabled, the packet capture will appear next to the **Vulnerability** log:

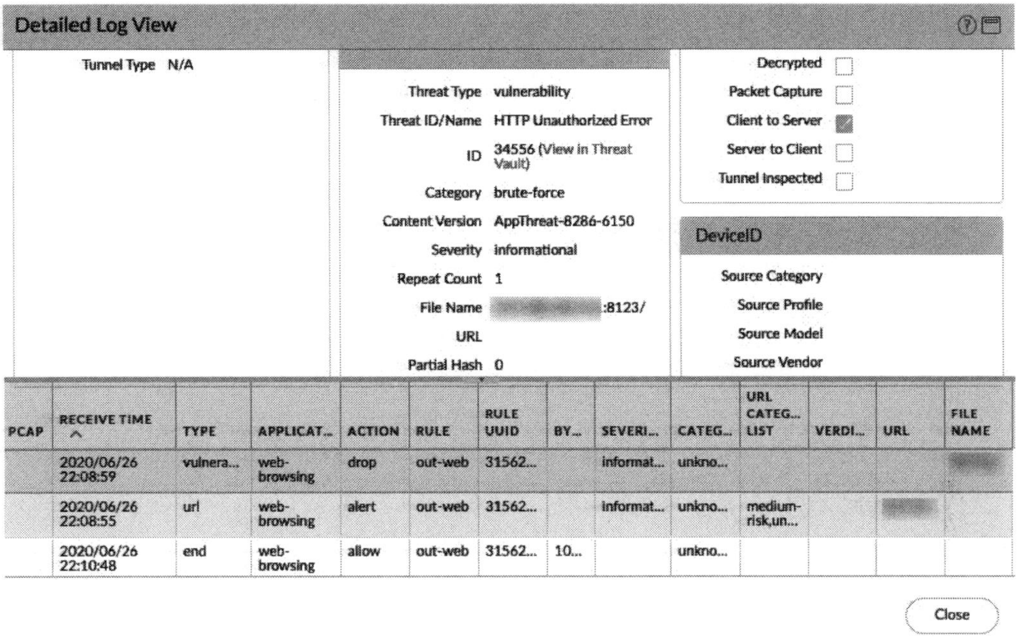

Figure 11.1 – Detailed log view

Logs provide an abundance of information, but for some troubleshooting sessions, more information will need to be collected and a deeper look at the actual packets will be required to find out what is going on. In the next section, we will learn how to capture packets.

# Packet captures

The real fun begins in **Monitor | Packet Capture**, as we can set up packet capturing for sessions crossing or bouncing off the data plane. Packet captures will intercept the actual packets flowing from the client to the server, and the other way around, and write them to a convenient `pcap` file, which you can load into a tool such as Wireshark to investigate everything that is happening at the packet level.

As you can see in the following screenshot, there are several areas that can be configured.

In the upper-left quadrant, you can configure filters by clicking on **Manage Filters** to add up to four filter rules. Each filter rule has several fields that can be used to narrow down the scope of the packet capture:

- **ID**: This is required and must be 1, 2, 3, or 4 – with no duplicate IDs.

- **Ingress Interface**: This can be set to only capture whether a matching packet is received on a specific interface.

- **Source**: This is the source IP of the packets being captured.

- **Destination**: This is the destination IP of the packets.

- **Src Port**: This is the source port of the packet that needs to be captured.

- **Dst Port**: This is the destination port to filter for.

- **Proto**: This is the IP protocol – commonly 1 for ICMP, 6 for TCP, and 17 for UDP. There's a handy list on the **Internet Assigned Numbers Authority (IANA)** website at `https://www.iana.org/assignments/protocol-numbers/protocol-numbers.xhtml`.

- **Non-IP**: This can be set to Exclude so that only IP protocol packets will be captured, Include to capture both IP and non-IP protocols, or Only to exclusively filter non-IP protocols. Non-IP protocols include, for example, NetBEUI, AppleTalk, IPX, and so on.

- **IPv6**: This must be checked to include IPv6 packets that match the filters.

> **Important note**
>
> The filters are session-aware, which means if you set a filter for one direction of traffic, return packets will also be captured. It is good practice, however, to also include a returning traffic filter in case the packets do not match the session (for example, if the sequence number is somehow completely wrong or the ports have changed somehow). Remember, when setting a filter for returning packets, the destination IP may be the NAT source of the outbound packet, and the original destination port will be the source port.
>
> Any field not filled in will count as a wildcard for that filter value.

To activate the filters, **Filtering** needs to be toggled to the **ON** position, as in the following screenshot:

---

**Important note**

**Pre-Parse Match** is an (advanced troubleshooting) toggle that captures packets before they reach the filtering stage. Some packets may not reach the filtering stage due to them being discarded beforehand. This could be due to a failed routing lookup for the packet. Enabling **Pre-Parse Match** will capture all packets coming into the firewall, essentially bypassing the set filters, so proceed with caution.

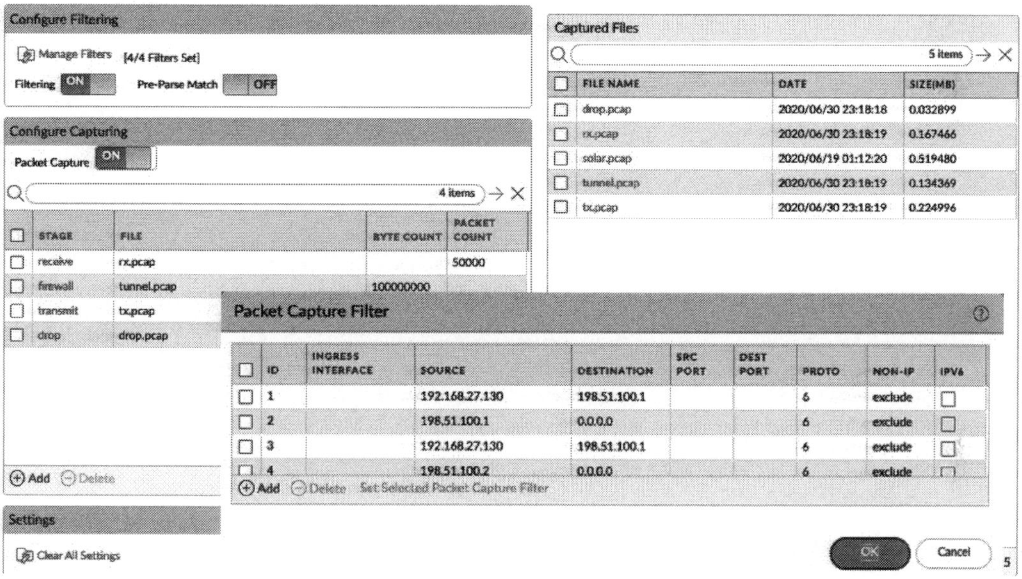

---

Figure 11.2 – Packet captures

In **Configure Capturing**, four stages can be designated to capture packets:

- Receive captured packets as they are received on the data plane processor.
- Transmit captured packets as they leave the data plane processor.
- Firewall captured packets while they are being matched to a session in the firewall process.
- Drop captured packets as they are being discarded by a policy action or an error.

Each stage can be set individually, and it is not necessary to set all stages. Each stage needs to have a unique filename set so that it can write to its own file. Each stage can be limited to how many bytes or packets can be captured; the capture will stop for each stage once the limit is reached.

> **Important note**
>
> The maximum size of a single packet capture file is 200 MB. Once that size is reached, the file is renamed with a .1 extension and a fresh file is started. Once the new file reaches 200 MB, the old .1 file is purged, the new file is renamed to have the .1 extension, and a fresh file is generated to continue the capture.

Once the capture stages have been set, you can enable capturing by setting the **Capturing** toggle to **ON**.

If you then hit the refresh button in the top-right corner, files will start appearing and increasing in size once matching packets are received.

A couple of important considerations when capturing packets should be made:

- **Sessions are marked by the filter**: The system knows which packets to capture and write to the file by the filters marking sessions to be captured by the processor when the packets reach the designated capture stage during processing. These markings are added to the session when it is created after the filter is made active, so when a packet capture is started, sessions that existed before the filter was activated will not be included in the capture.

    Existing sessions can be added to the marked sessions manually by using the following command:

    ```
    reaper@pa-220> debug dataplane packet-diag set filter-
    marked-session id <session ID>
    ```

    All the marked sessions can be reviewed using the following command:

    ```
    reaper@pa-220> debug dataplane packet-diag show filter-
    marked-session
    ```

If you are done capturing but need to start another capture for a different set of filters, previously marked sessions may inadvertently be captured as they are still marked. Before setting new filters and configuring capture stages, you can delete markings from existing sessions with the following commands:

```
reaper@pa-220> debug dataplane packet-diag clear filter-
marked-session id <session ID>
```

```
reaper@pa-220> debug dataplane packet-diag clear filter-
marked-session all
```

- **Offloaded sessions can't be captured**: On platforms that have hardware offloading (pa-3000, pa-3200, pa-5000, pa-5200, and PA-7000), packets will be put into a fast path once processing has completed, which bypasses data plane processing and puts the packets directly onto the networking chip. This will prevent further capturing as the captures happen on the data plane processors, rather than the physical interfaces. If a session needs to be captured that is being offloaded, offloading can be disabled; this could cause additional load on the data plane CPUs, so do not disable offloading when the load is high. You can check whether offloading is enabled with the following commands (the default is True):

```
reaper@pa-3220> show session info | match offload
            Hardware session offloading:
True
            Hardware UDP session offloading:
True
```

To disable offloading, issue the following command:

```
reaper@pa-3220> set session offload no
```

> **Important note**
> Packet capture on the management interface can only be performed from the CLI using the tcpdump command. Keep this in mind if you want to inspect sessions between the management interface and, for example, an LDAP server. The capture output file can be read and exported from the CLI.

To start a capture on the management interface, use the tcpdump command with following options. To end the capture, press *Ctrl+C*.

Setting `snaplen 0` ensures full packets are captured; without setting this option, the capture size per frame is limited to `96` bytes.

The filters that can be added are similar to the ones used by `tcpdump` in a Linux system. Some examples are `"src 192.168.27.2"` or `"net 192.168.27.0/24 and not port 22"`:

```
reaper@pa-220> tcpdump snaplen 0 filter "host 192.168.27.130
and not port 22"
Press Ctrl-C to stop capturing
tcpdump: listening on eth0, link-type EN10MB (Ethernet),
capture size 65535 bytes
30 packets captured
30 packets received by filter
0 packets dropped by kernel
```

To read the capture output from the CLI, use the following command:

```
reaper@pa-220> view-pcap mgmt-pcap mgmt.pcap
```

To export the file, use either TFTP or SCP to `localhost`:

```
reaper@pa-220> tftp export mgmt-pcap from mgmt.pcap to
192.168.27.7
```

In addition to using log files and packet captures to review information that you know, Botnet reports collect behavioral information that can help find suspicious hosts in the network.

## Botnet reports

In **Monitor | Botnet**, there is a log consolidation tool that will keep track of sessions that, when encountered by themselves, are not suspicious at all, but when seen combined with other events, may indicate something is going on that may need some extra attention. As you can see from the following screenshot, you can edit the configuration for the triggers by clicking on the **Configuration** link below the calendar. Detection is based on the repetition of certain events within a specified timeframe. You can tweak how many occurrences need to happen before something is reported in the Botnet report:

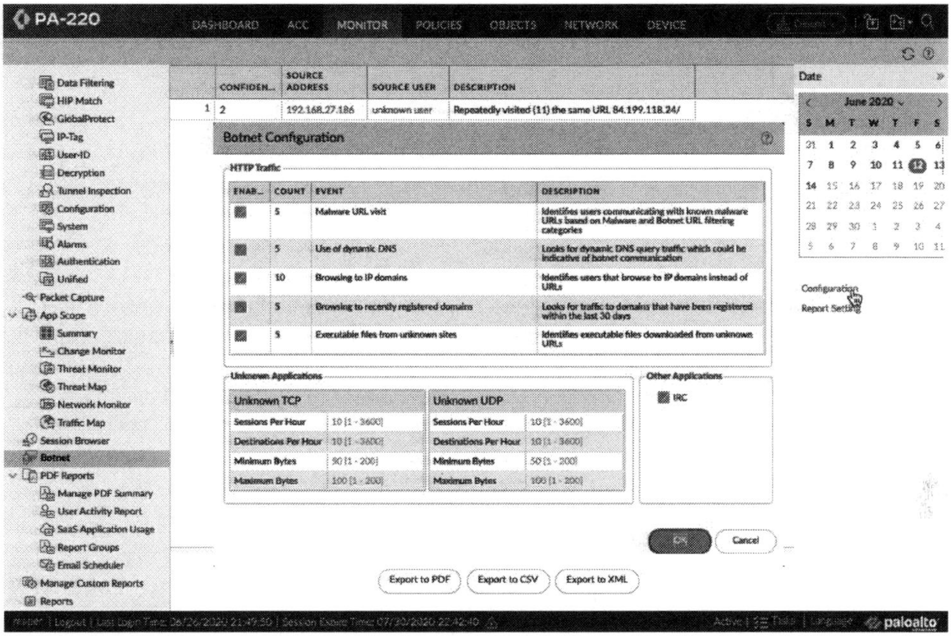

Figure 11.3 – Botnet report

Now that you have a good understanding of how to filter logs and capture traffic, we'll take a look at what a session is made up of.

# Interpreting session details

The log details tell you a lot about a session, but not everything. Sessions, while being processed, have several different parameters that only translate to how they are being processed at a particular moment in time.

The session table is made up of a finite number of session IDs, so session IDs end up getting reused after the available IDs have been cycled through. There are seven different states that a session can be in:

- **Initial or INIT**: A session that is ready and waiting to be used by a new flow is in the `INIT` state.

- **Opening**: This is a transient state in which a session ID is assigned to a flow while it is being evaluated to become a full session. This stage accounts for half-open TCP connections, so it has more aggressive timers that close the session if the handshake is not completed within due time.

- **Active**: This is the state in which everything happens – the flow is up and packets are being passed back and forth.

- **Closing**: This is a transient state. If a flow has reached its time-to-live or idle-timeout, this means the session is set to expire soon but has not been removed from the aging process or the session lookup table.

  During this stage, new packets will no longer be matched against this session and be queued to create a new session, or they are discarded because they are **ACK** packets that no longer match an active session (non-SYN TCP).

- **Discard**: Here, the flow is hitting a drop/deny rule or is hitting a threat set to block. All packets matching the session will be discarded for the duration of the discard phase.

- **Closed**: This is a transient state. The session has been removed from the aging process, but not from the session lookup table. No new packets can match this session, so they are either queued for a new session or are dropped.

- **Free**: This is a transient state. The session has been closed and removed from the session lookup table but still needs to be made available for a new flow.

  Once the Free state has completed, the session is returned to the INIT state.

Transient states are usually very short and could be hard to spot. INIT, ACTIVE, and DISCARD are stable states and will represent most of the sessions you would be able to see.

All the timers associated with session creation, time to live, and session teardown can be consulted with the following command:

```
reaper@pa-220> show session info
------snip------
Session timeout
TCP default timeout:                             3600 secs
TCP session timeout before SYN-ACK received:        5 secs
TCP session timeout before 3-way handshaking:      10 secs
TCP half-closed session timeout:                  120 secs
TCP session timeout in TIME_WAIT:                  15 secs
TCP session delayed ack timeout:                  250 millisecs
TCP session timeout for unverified RST:            30 secs
UDP default timeout:                               30 secs
ICMP default timeout:                               6 secs
SCTP default timeout:                            3600 secs
SCTP timeout before INIT-ACK received:              5 secs
SCTP timeout before COOKIE received:               60 secs
```

| SCTP timeout before SHUTDOWN received: | 30 secs |
|---|---|
| other IP default timeout: | 30 secs |
| Captive Portal session timeout: | 30 secs |
| Session timeout in discard state: | |
| TCP: 90 secs, UDP: 60 secs, SCTP: 60 secs, other IP protocols: 60 secs | |

All of these timers can also be changed to suit your environment through **Configuration**
Mode or in **Device | Setup | Session | Session Timeouts**:

```
reaper@pa-220# set deviceconfig setting session timeout-
```

| + timeout-captive-portal timeout value in seconds | set captive-portal session |
|---|---|
| + timeout-default value in seconds | set session default timeout |
| + timeout-discard-default session in discard state | set timeout of non-tcp/udp |
| + timeout-discard-tcp discard state | set timeout of tcp session in |
| + timeout-discard-udp discard state | set timeout of udp session in |
| + timeout-icmp seconds | set icmp timeout value in |
| + timeout-scan value in seconds | application trickling timeout |
| + timeout-tcp | set tcp timeout value in seconds |
| + timeout-tcp-half-closed timeout (after receiving first FIN/RST) value in seconds | set session tcp half close |
| + timeout-tcp-time-wait timeout (after receiving second FIN/RST) value in seconds | set session tcp time wait |
| + timeout-tcp-unverified-rst after receiving a RST with unverified sequence number in seconds | set session tcp timeout value |
| + timeout-tcphandshake timeout (before 3-way handshaking is completed) value in seconds | set tcp handshake session |
| + timeout-tcpinit (before SYN-ACK is received) value in seconds | set tcp initial session timeout |
| + timeout-udp | set udp timeout value in seconds |

There are also five session types:

- **FLOW**: These are all the regular sessions.

- **FORW**: (forward) This is used when a captive portal is used to intercept and redirect browsing sessions to a login page, or when policy-based forwarding is applied to a flow.

- **PRED** (Predict): **Application Layer Gateway** (**ALG**) protocols that require a return session be set up outside of the established session (SIP, FTP, and so on) will set up predict sessions to anticipate the inbound connection. If the return session is received, the `Predict` session will be transformed into a `Flow` session. `Predict` sessions are based on the control information detected in the outbound session.

- **Tunnel**: VPN connections will be set up in a `Tunnel` session.

- **VNI**: If VXLAN **Tunnel Content Inspection** (**TCI**) is enabled in **Policies | Tunnel Inspection**, VXLAN tunnels will be **vni**-type sessions.

The sessions can be displayed from **Monitor | Session Browser** and, as you can see from the following screenshot, there's a lot of information regarding the session that is not in the logs. There are a couple of interesting fields that can help you understand the state that a session is in:

- **Timeout** is the amount of time a session is allowed to exist.

- **Time To Live** is the amount of time left on the timeout.

Each session will have a timeout assigned, which can also tell you a lot about what is going on. An established TCP session may get a timeout of `3600` seconds, while a UDP session may only get `30` seconds. A `DISCARD` stage session will also only get a short timeout.

When troubleshooting sessions that go out to the internet, incorrectly configured NAT is often the root cause:

- The NAT source and destination are indicated by **True** or **False**.

- A NAT rule is used by the session.

- Flow 1 is the **Client-to-Server** (**c2s**) flow and shows the original source IP (`10.0.0.8`) and the port destined for the server.

- Flow 2 is the **Server-to-Client (s2c)** flow and shows the server's IP to the NAT's IP (`192.168.27.251`) that the client is translated behind, and the NAT's source port as the destination port (`44666`) for the returning flow.

Reviewing all of these things can help in spotting NAT issues early on.

Sessions can also be forcibly terminated by clicking on the **X** mark under the **Clear** column, as you can see in the following screenshot. This will set the session in the `INIT` state immediately. Any packets still arriving on the firewall will not have any sessions to match against, so will either be discarded as non-SYN TCP or evaluated for a new session to be created:

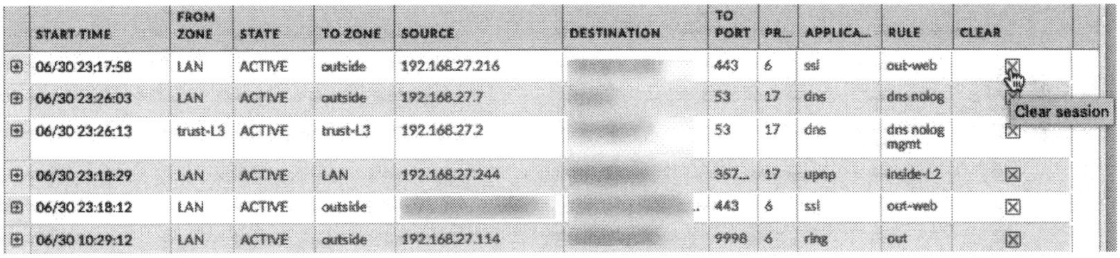

| | START TIME | FROM ZONE | STATE | TO ZONE | SOURCE | DESTINATION | TO PORT | PR... | APPLICA... | RULE | CLEAR |
|---|---|---|---|---|---|---|---|---|---|---|---|
| ⊕ | 06/30 23:17:58 | LAN | ACTIVE | outside | 192.168.27.216 | | 443 | 6 | ssl | out-web | ☒ |
| ⊕ | 06/30 23:26:03 | LAN | ACTIVE | outside | 192.168.27.7 | | 53 | 17 | dns | dns nolog | ☒ Clear session |
| ⊕ | 06/30 23:26:13 | trust-L3 | ACTIVE | trust-L3 | 192.168.27.2 | | 53 | 17 | dns | dns nolog mgmt | ☒ |
| ⊕ | 06/30 23:18:29 | LAN | ACTIVE | LAN | 192.168.27.244 | | 357... | 17 | upnp | inside-L2 | ☒ |
| ⊕ | 06/30 23:18:12 | LAN | ACTIVE | outside | | ... | 443 | 6 | ssl | out-web | ☒ |
| ⊕ | 06/30 10:29:12 | LAN | ACTIVE | outside | 192.168.27.114 | | 9998 | 6 | ring | out | ☒ |

Figure 11.4 – Session browser

Sessions can also be cleared from the CLI using the following command:

```
reaper@pa-220> clear session id <ID>
reaper@pa-220> clear session all
```

From the CLI, the same information can be collected using the following command. The CLI allows a more flexible use of filter options, so this will usually be the preferred way to review sessions:

```
reaper@PA-220> show session id 256


Session             256


        c2s flow:
                source:     10.0.0.8 [trust]
                dst:        204.79.197.222
                proto:      6
                sport:      49710               dport:      443
                state:      DISCARD             type:       FLOW
                src user:   unknown
```

```
                dst user:    unknown


s2c flow:
        source:      204.79.197.222 [untrust]
        dst:         192.168.27.251
        proto:       6
        sport:       443            dport:      44666
        state:       DISCARD        type:       FLOW
        src user:    unknown
        dst user:    unknown


    start time                        : Tue May 19
23:20:13 2020
    timeout                           : 90 sec
    time to live                      : 79 sec
    total byte count(c2s)             : 316
    total byte count(s2c)             : 66
    layer7 packet count(c2s)          : 3
    layer7 packet count(s2c)          : 1
    vsys                              : vsys1
    application                       : ssl
    rule                              : block push
    service timeout override(index)   : False
    session to be logged at end       : True
    session in session ager           : True
    session updated by HA peer        : False
    address/port translation          : source
    nat-rule                          : outbound
hide(vsys1)
    layer7 processing                 : enabled
    URL filtering enabled             : True
    URL category                      :
    session via syn-cookies           : False
    session terminated on host        : False
    session traverses tunnel          : False
    session terminate tunnel          : False
    captive portal session            : False
```

| | |
|---|---|
| ingress interface | : ethernet1/2 |
| egress interface | : ethernet1/1 |
| session QoS rule | : N/A (class 4) |
| tracker stage firewall | : appid policy |
| lookup deny | |
| end-reason | : policy-deny |

The CLI also shows **Tracker Stage Firewall**, which indicates why a session was closed. In the case of the preceding session, an application was detected that was denied by the security policy, and the session was put into the DISCARD state. Other tracker stages are as follows:

- **Aged out**: The session has reached its timeout.
- **TCP FIN**: FIN packet received to terminate the session.
- **TCP RST -client or – server**: The client or server has sent an RST packet.
- **Appid policy lookup deny**: Policy lookup sets an application to deny or drop.
- **Mitigation tdb**: Threat detected that terminates the session.
- **Resource limit**: Rollup of many errors that could happen in a flow (exceeded packets out of order in a flow, and so on).
- **Host service**: Sessions set up toward the firewall for a service that is not allowed from this source or not enabled on this interface.
- **L7 proc**: Processing of layer7 ongoing. In the case of a DISCARD session, this could be a child application that requires additional APP-ID effort to identify (as opposed to **Appid** policy **lookup deny**).
- **ctd decoder bypass**: A session has reached the end of its content inspection and was offloaded to hardware.
- **Session rematch**: This session was previously allowed, but new security has been pushed that now blocks this session.

Other session attributes can include the following. Some attributes that are not relevant to a session will not be displayed:

- **Layer7 processing**: If an application override is in place, or the protocol in the session does not have a decoder, **Layer7 processing** will be False.
- **Session via SYN-cookies**: This shows whether SYN-cookies were used when the session was set up (these are controlled from the zone protection profile).

- **To Host Session**: This is `true` when the session is connecting to a service running on the firewall, such as DNS Proxy or a management profile.

- **Session traverses tunnel**: These are sessions that are going into an IPSec, SSL, or GRE tunnel.

- **Session terminates tunnel**: These are sessions that terminate a tunnel on the firewall.

- **Session QoS rule**: This indicates whether a QoS (**Quality of Service**) rule is used for this session, and the class assigned to the session.

- **Captive Portal**: This is set to `true` if a session was created that intercepted and redirected a client session to the captive portal page. The s2c flow will indicate whether the original destination was replaced by a captive portal redirect, while the c2s flow has the captive portal as the destination:

```
reaper@PA-220> show session id 865


Session            865


    c2s flow:
            source:     10.0.0.8 [trust]
            dst:        10.0.0.1
            proto:      6
            sport:      50311               dport:      6081
            state:      INIT                type:       FLOW
            src user:   unknown
            dst user:   unknown


    s2c flow:
            source:     127.131.1.1 [captive-portal]
            dst:        10.0.0.8
            proto:      6
            sport:      6181                dport:      50311
            state:      INIT                type:       FLOW
            src user:   unknown
            dst user:   unknown
```

To get a list of all the active sessions, you can use the following command. There are many filters:

```
reaper@pa-220> show session all
```

From the following screenshot, you can see that there are several filters that you can add to narrow your search. The resulting output lists each session in two rows: the top row is the c2s flow and the bottom row is the s2c flow. `Flag` indicates whether the session is applying source NAT (NS), destination NAT (ND), or both (NB):

```
reaper@PA-VM> show session all filter protocol 6 nat source from trust type flow state active

------------------------------------------------------------------------------
ID            Application    State    Type Flag  Src[Sport]/Zone/Proto (translated IP[Port])
Vsys                                             Dst[Dport]/Zone (translated IP[Port])
------------------------------------------------------------------------------
261           ssl            ACTIVE   FLOW NS    10.0.0.8[49915]/trust/6   (192.168.27.251[35448])
vsys1                                            .122.2[443]/untrust   (        .122.2[443])
353           web-browsing   ACTIVE   FLOW NS    10.0.0.8[50011]/trust/6   (192.168.27.251[43839])
vsys1                                            .4.52[80]/untrust   (        .4.52[80])
356           web-browsing   ACTIVE   FLOW NS    10.0.0.8[50010]/trust/6   (192.168.27.251[54552])
vsys1                                            .4.52[80]/untrust   (        .4.52[80])
253           ssl            ACTIVE   FLOW NS    10.0.0.8[49918]/trust/6   (192.168.27.251[64354])
vsys1                                            .37.44[443]/untrust   (        .37.44[443])
267           ssl            ACTIVE   FLOW NS    10.0.0.8[49919]/trust/6   (192.168.27.251[3751])
vsys1                                            .38.49[443]/untrust   (        .38.49[443])
231           ssl            ACTIVE   FLOW NS    10.0.0.8[49917]/trust/6   (192.168.27.251[16008])
vsys1                                            .121.44[443]/untrust   (        .121.44[443])
```

Figure 11.5 – The output of the show session all command with a filter applied

> **Important note**
>
> By default, the system view in the command line is VSYS1. For most commands, this does not matter, but if you need to list sessions in VSYS2, you will first need to change the system perspective to VSYS2 so that the commands relate to the correct VSYS. Use the following command to switch to the VSYS perspective:

```
reaper@pa-3020> set system setting target-vsys ?
```

| none  | none |
| ----- | ---- |
| vsys1 | prod |
| vsys2 | beta |

You should now be able to find a session and correlate it against the expected behavior. You can see whether the session is being allowed or blocked and whether NAT, QoS, or PBF are being applied as expected. In the next section, we will review the troubleshooting tools that allow us to see how a session will behave before it has taken place.

# Using the troubleshooting tool

The web interface is a very convenient way to configure the firewall, but it also holds several tools that you can use to troubleshoot issues you might encounter. The troubleshooting tool, which you can find in **Device | Troubleshooting**, lets you run several tests past your configuration to see what the system is expected to do in the given situation.

Some of the available tests let you verify whether the system can connect to cloud services, as illustrated in the following screenshot.

Click on **Test Result** to see the **Result Detail** pane on the right-hand side:

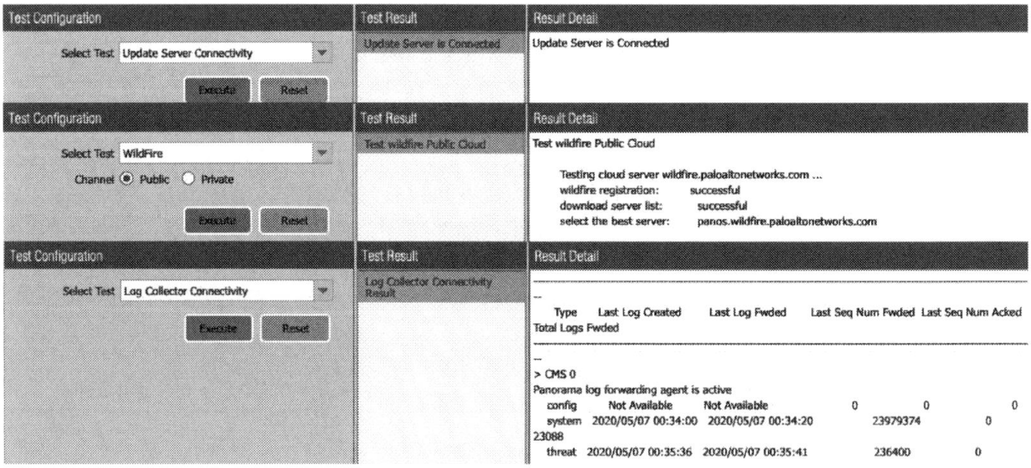

Figure 11.6 – A cloud connectivity test

The troubleshooting tool lets you test several policies to see whether they will behave as you expect. The following policies can be tested:

- Security policy match
- QoS policy match
- Authentication policy match
- Decryption/SSL policy match
- NAT policy match
- Policy-based forwarding policy match
- DoS policy match

The following screenshot shows a security policy match test; you can put in some parameters, such as `source IP`, `destination IP`, `destination port`, `protocol`, `application`, or `URL Category`. The system will match your set of parameters against the entire security rulebase to see which rule matches

> **Important note**
> The **URL Category** parameter in **Security Policy Match** only reflects rules that have a category set in the destination. This is not matched against **URL Filtering profiles**, as you can see in the following screenshot:

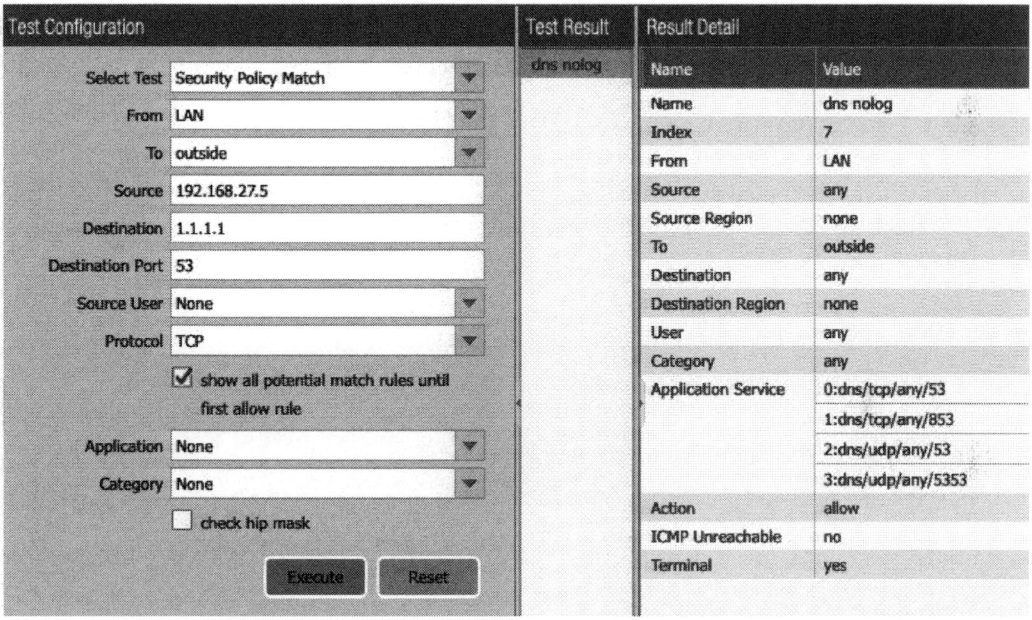

Figure 11.7 – Security Policy Match

The troubleshooting tool can also be used to test connectivity. The ping test lets you send ICMP echo requests to a host. You can define some typical parameters, such as the following:

- **Count**: The number of ping requests to send.
- **Interval**: The time between requests in seconds.
- **Source**: The data plane interface to send the packets from.
- **Host**: The destination to be pinged.

- **Size**: This lets you change the payload size of the ping packet. This can be useful to test whether larger packets take longer to return or get dropped along the route.

- **Tos**: This lets you set a **Type of Service (ToS)** IP option to verify whether upstream devices apply.

- **Ttl**: This is the maximum number of hops the packet can pass before being discarded. The default is 58.

As you can see in the following screenshot, there are also a couple of special features you can set:

- **Bypass routing table, use specific interface** lets you put packets directly into an interface instead of performing a routing lookup. This can be useful to test a redundant path.

- **Don't fragment echo request packets (IPv4)** lets you set the don't fragment bit in the IP header of ping packets, which is useful if you want to discover Path MTU by sending ever-increasing-sized ping packets. When you reach the size where the packets are dropped, you have found the maximum MTU that your path will allow, as packets that are too large and are not allowed to be fragmented must be discarded.

- **Pattern** lets you add a specific pattern to the payload, which can help identify the packet in an upstream device:

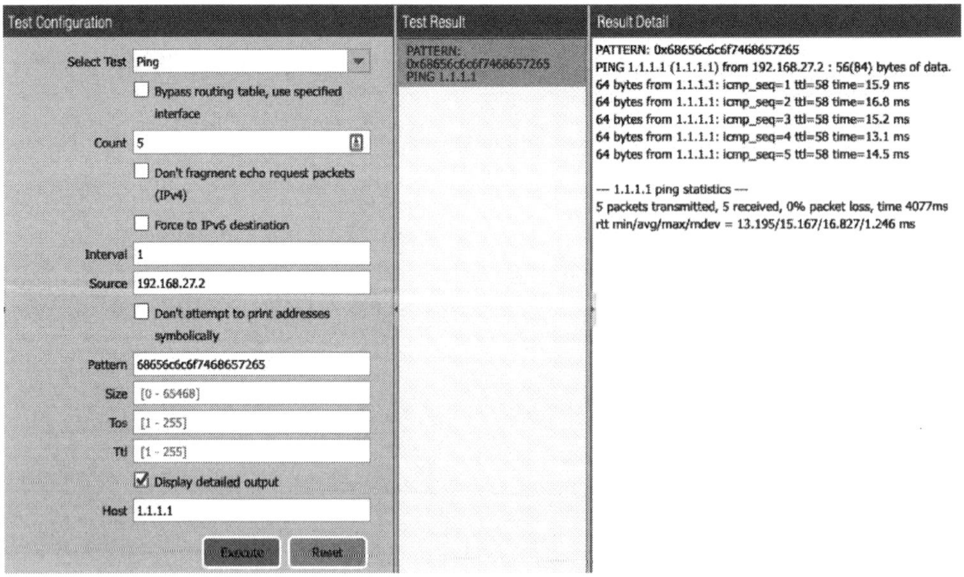

Figure 11.8 – The ping tool

All of these options are available from the CLI as well:

```
reaper@pa-220> ping
+ bypass-routing      Bypass routing table, use specified
interface
+ count               Number of requests to send (1..2000000000
packets)
+ do-not-fragment     Don't fragment echo request packets (IPv4)
+ inet6               Force to IPv6 destination
+ interval            Delay between requests (seconds)
+ no-resolve          Don't attempt to print addresses
symbolically
+ pattern             Hexadecimal fill pattern
+ size                Size of request packets (0..65468 bytes)
+ source              Source address of echo request
+ tos                 IP type-of-service value (0..255)
+ ttl                 IP time-to-live value (IPv6 hop-limit
value) (0..255 hops)
+ verbose             Display detailed output
* host                Hostname or IP address of remote host
```

The output should look similar to this:

```
reaper@pa-220> ping count 2 interval 1 source 192.168.27.2 host
1.1.1.1
PING 1.1.1.1 (1.1.1.1) from 192.168.27.2 : 56(84) bytes of
data.
64 bytes from 1.1.1.1: icmp_seq=1 ttl=58 time=10.9 ms
64 bytes from 1.1.1.1: icmp_seq=2 ttl=58 time=15.1 ms

--- 1.1.1.1 ping statistics ---
2 packets transmitted, 2 received, 0% packet loss, time 1017ms
rtt min/avg/max/mdev = 10.972/13.073/15.174/2.101 ms
```

Where there is ping, there is traceroute. Traceroute test lets you send UDP traceroute packets to identify hops along the path toward a remote host. This is a very practical tool to find routing issues; packets are sent out with an ever-increasing TTL value starting from 1, and each hop along the path is required to decrease the TTL counter by 1 before sending the packet to the next hop. If the counter reaches 0, the hop must discard the packet and send back an ICMP option 11 (time exceeded) packet to the sender. The sender will, theoretically, receive a notification from all the hosts along the path to the final destination, revealing the routing involved to get packets to the final destination.

As you can see from the following screenshot, there are plenty of options to make the test more thorough:

- Both IPv4 and IPv6 can be tested.
- **First Ttl** lets you set a starting TTL higher than 1, which could be useful if the first few hops are not to be included in the test or the resulting output.
- **Max Ttl** is the maximum number of hops taken before giving up.
- **Port** lets you set a static destination port used for the UDP packet. By default, a random high port is chosen at the start of the test, sequentially increasing with every packet sent.
- **Tos** lets you set the ToS IP option.
- **Wait** is the number of seconds that the firewall should wait for a reply message to arrive.
- **Pause** is the amount of time, in milliseconds, that the firewall should wait between probes.
- **Gateway** lets you set up to 8 **loose source routing** gateways.
- **Don't attempt to print addresses symbolically** prevents a reverse lookup of the IP against DNS.
- **Bypass routing tables and send directly to a host** puts the packets directly onto the wire.
- **Source** is the data plane interface to use as the source. By default, the management interface is used.
- **Host** is where the traceroute should try to reach:

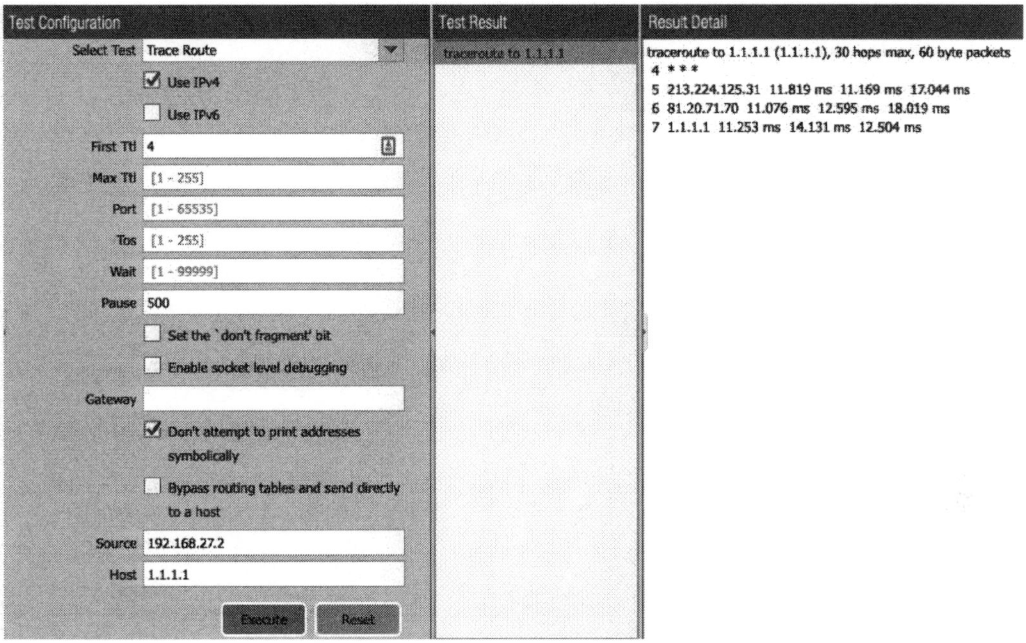

Figure 11.9 – A traceroute test

Traceroute can also be executed from CLI with all the same options:

```
reaper@pa-220> traceroute
+ bypass-routing      Bypass routing tables and send directly to
a host
+ debug-socket        Enable socket level debugging
+ do-not-fragment     Set the `don't fragment' bit
+ first-ttl           time-to-live used in the first outgoing
probe packet
+ gateway             Specify a loose source route gateway (8
maximum)
+ ipv4                Use IPv4
+ ipv6                Use IPv6
+ max-ttl             Set the max time-to-live (max number of
hops)
+ no-resolve          Don't attempt to print addresses
symbolically
+ pause               Set the time (in milliseconds) to pause
between probes
+ port                Set the base port number used in probes
```

```
(default udp/33434 tcp/80 icmp/1)
```

| | |
|---|---|
| + source probe packets | Use specified source address in outgoing |
| + tos | IP type-of-service value (0..255) |
| + wait response | Set number of seconds to wait for a |
| * host | Hostname or IP address of remote host |

The output for a traceroute test should look similar to this:

```
reaper@pa-220> traceroute first-ttl 4 ipv4 yes source
192.168.27.2 no-resolve yes host 1.1.1.1
traceroute to 1.1.1.1 (1.1.1.1), 30 hops max, 60 byte packets
 4  * * *
 5  213.224.125.31  20.784 ms   21.148 ms   20.968 ms
 6  81.20.71.70  20.383 ms   20.179 ms   21.393 ms
 7  1.1.1.1  19.391 ms * *
```

You can now determine whether the firewall has proper connectivity to its services and whether an expected session will hit all the appropriate policies.

# Using maintenance mode to resolve and recover from system issues

The MRT, also called **Maintenance Mode**, resides on a separate bootable partition and can be invoked if the system has an unexpected failure. If, for example, the system is unable to complete the auto-commit process, it will reboot to try and rectify what is causing the failure. If after three reboots the auto-commit is still failing, the system will boot into maintenance mode.

If the system failed, you can SSH into the device using the maint username and the serial number of the device as the password. If you connect to the console, you don't need a username and password.

You can force the system to boot into maintenance mode from the command line by executing the following command. The system will ask whether you want to reboot after you hit *Enter*:

```
> debug system maintenance-mode
```

You can also manually start **Maintenance Mode**. During the boot process, there is a short window where a dialog asks whether you want to interrupt the boot sequence by hitting any key. If you do, you have 5 seconds to take action.

If you type `maint`, you will be taken to the bootloader, where you can choose the maintenance partition, as displayed in the following screenshot:

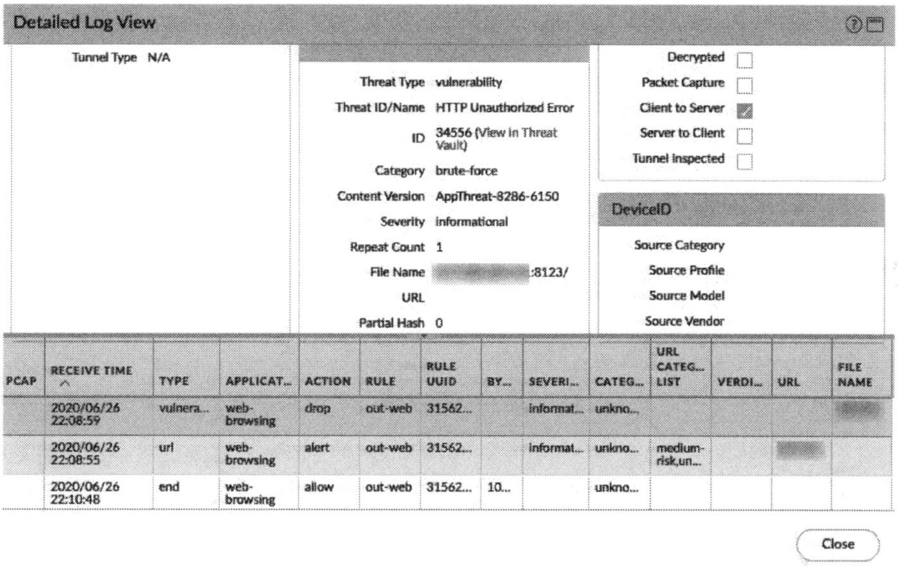

Figure 11.10 – The Maintenance Mode boot loader

You are taken to a welcome page that has details on getting support. Once you hit *Enter*, you will be taken to the main menu, as follows.

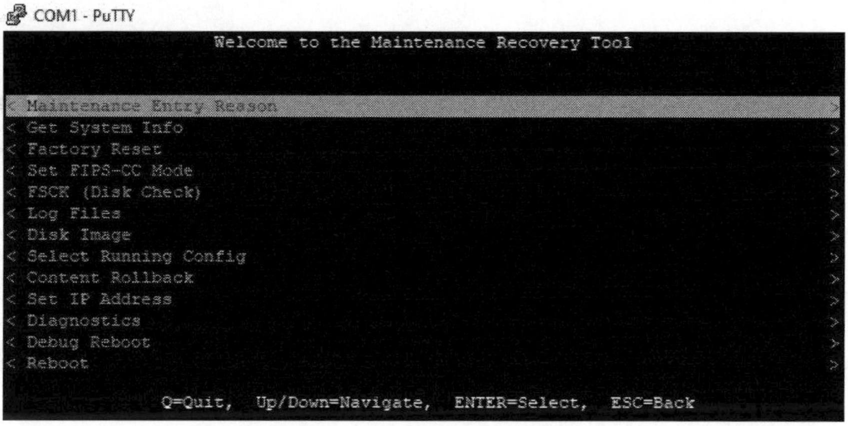

Figure 11.11 – Maintenance Mode

Any advanced features that require a password can be accessed using MA1NT as the password.

If **Maintenance Mode** was invoked by the system, there should be some additional information in **Maintenance Entry Reason**.

**Get System Info** returns an overview of all the system information, such as the serial number, installed OS, and content updates.

**Factory reset** lets you revert the system to clean factory settings. The configuration files are purged and reset to the default configuration and all logs and reports are wiped from the system. As you can see in the following screenshot, you can choose which PAN-OS version the system should be set to during the reset.

If you require the logs to be securely purged and not just deleted, you can opt to scrub the system. You can pick between the **NNSA** (overwrite all locations twice with pseudo-random pattern and once with a known pattern) and **DOD** (overwrite all addressable locations with a character, its complement, and then a random character) scrub.

In the **Advanced** menu option, you can choose an older PAN-OS version to install:

```
                         Factory Reset
WARNING: Performing a factory reset will remove all logs and configuration.

Using Image:
    (X) panos-9.0.0

WARNING: Scrubbing will iteratively write patterns on pancfg, panlogs, and any
extra disks to make retrieving the data more difficult.
NOTE: This could take up to 48 hours if selected.  Scrubbing is not recommended
unless explicitly required.

    [ ] Scrub

If scrubbing, select scrub type:
    (X) nnsa                       ( ) dod

< Factory Reset                                                              >

< Advanced                                                                   >

          Q=Quit,  Up/Down=Navigate,  ENTER=Select,  ESC=Back
```

Figure 11.12 – Factory reset

**Set FIPS-CC mode** converts the system into FIPS compliance; it will take the following actions:

- Disables all weak crypto ciphers.
- Disables the console port as CLI, only output.
- Sets the minimum password length to 6.

- Weak management protocols (such as `http`, `ftp`, and `telnet`) are disabled and no longer available.
- Encryption on **HA1** is mandatory.

**FSCK** can be used to scan all the partitions for issues and attempt to repair any bad sectors. You can scan the following partitions:

- **panlogs**
- **panrepo**
- **sysroot0**
- **sysroot1**
- **pancfg**

You can opt to automatically select *Y* to any question to fix a bad sector, and you can format the **panlogs** partition if the disk check fails for that partition.

**Log Files** lets you access all the system logs in case you need to review whether a process was able to write a critical error and copy the logs to an external location. You need to select **Set IP address** in the top menu before you can start the copy.

**Disk Image** lets you reinstall the currently installed PAN-OS version, without changing the running configuration, or revert to the previously installed version. In the **Advanced** options, you can do the following:

- Review the install history and current bootable partition status
- Revert to the previously installed PAN-OS version
- Verify the integrity of the currently installed image
- Purge older images from the disk
- Manually select which partition to set as the boot in the bootloader
- Manually boot into a PAN-OS version without changing the bootloader

**Select Running Config** lets you select previously saved configuration files and set them as the running config, which can come in quite handy if you lose your admin password, as there is no password recovery procedure other than performing a factory reset or loading a saved configuration.

---

**Important note**

Don't save a configuration file containing a default **admin/admin** account as that will allow a backdoor for anyone able to boot into **maintenance mode**.

---

**Content rollback** lets you revert to an older content version package if something goes dramatically wrong when installing a content update.

**Set IP address** lets you manually set an IP if the device does not load its management IP or is unable to get a DHCP IP.

**Diagnostics** runs a disk performance check.

**Debug reboot** reboots the system, but outputs all boot dialog in verbose mode, which will help if the system fails to boot.

With this knowledge, you will be able to recover from several highly critical failures, or at least collect sufficient information to perform a postmortem and find out what caused the situation in the first place.

# Summary

In this chapter, you learned where to find all the different types of log files and how aggregated information can lead to identifying a botnet. You can now perform a packet capture using filters to capture only what you need. You can interpret a session on the firewall and identify key attributes, such as the NAT direction, the end reason, and the timeout settings. You can verify whether the firewall has connectivity to all its cloud services and whether an anticipated flow will hit all the intended policies using the troubleshooting tool. You can also perform key tasks such as a factory reset or loading a different configuration file from **Maintenance Mode**.

In the next chapter, we will take what you have learned in this chapter to the next level by using the packet capture filters to analyze global counters and look at the actual flow as it goes through the firewall and is touched by different processes.

# 12
# A Deep Dive into Troubleshooting

In this chapter, we will learn how a session is formed and how flows traverse the firewall. We will learn how to interpret global counters and take things a step further to look at all the stages that a packet goes through between entering and leaving the firewall. We will see how sessions are set up and how packets are handled at every step.

In this chapter, we're going to cover the following main topics:

- Understanding global counters
- Analyzing session flows
- Debugging processes
- CLI troubleshooting commands cheat sheet

## Technical requirements

For this chapter, it is strongly recommended that you have a lab environment where you can emulate the steps we will be taking in this chapter to get a better feel for the commands and the output we will be reviewing. There is a cheat sheet with useful commands and a list of all the global counters, available at `https://github.com/PacktPublishing/Mastering-Palo-Alto-Networks`.

# Understanding global counters

When you are troubleshooting a connectivity issue, the log files and packet captures provide a wealth of information, but sometimes, they're not enough to figure out what is happening to a session. All sessions, whether they are traversing the firewall or getting dropped, are tracked by all the processes that touch them, and counters are incremented for each step that a packet takes and for each packet in a session. This can provide a wealth of information if something is not working as expected.

The global counters can be viewed by running the following command:

```
reaper@PA-VM> show counter global
```

This will output all of the global counters, which is not very useful. You can add a `delta` filter to only show global counters for the period between the last and the penultimate time that the command was issued. The duration will be indicated in the output:

```
reaper@PA-VM> show counter global filter delta yes
```

The output will look similar to the following:

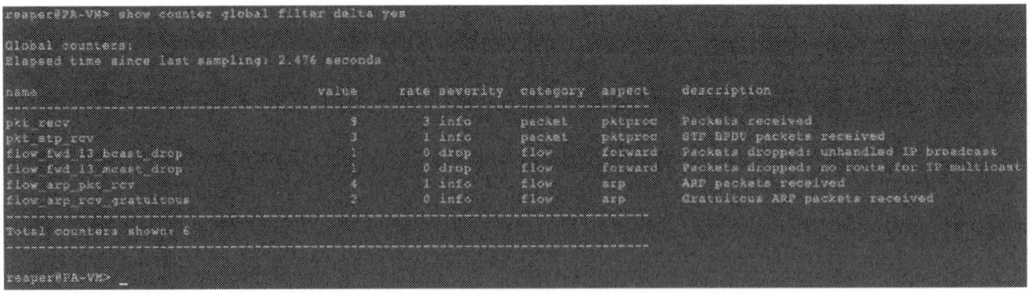

Figure 12.1 – The show counter global delta output

This is far easier to read than simply outputting all of the counters, but this is still not related to anything you might be interested in, as the counters are still system-wide.

Let's first take a look at the attributes of a global counter:

- **name**: Each counter has a name that usually tries to convey which process saw what. For example, `flow` is used for packet processing and `_fwd` is used to indicate packets that would need to be forwarded somewhere, while `_arp` is used for **ARP (Address resolution protocol)** packets that don't need to be routed and `_l3` indicates that they were received on a layer 3 (routing) interface.

- **value**: This is the total number of hits on that counter over the full duration of the delta.

- **rate**: This is an approximate progression of the hits per second over the specified duration as seen by the system. If you see a number in the `value` field but the rate is `0`, there hasn't been a hit on the counter for a while, depending on the length of the delta. This could indicate a cluster of hits at the beginning of the delta and none near the end.

- **severity**: There are four levels of severity:

    --**info** is the default severity for all counters.

    --**drop** is used to indicate something that was intentionally discarded. This could be due to a security policy, a threat profile, or an irregularity relating to where a packet is coming from or needs to go.

    --**error** indicates packets that are malformed and are discarded.

    --**warn** is used when something goes wrong at the system level or if there is an abnormality in received packets – for example, a failed reassembly of a fragmented packet or a split handshake.

- **category** : This indicates which process this counter is related to. A few interesting ones include the following:

    --**dfa** is the APP-ID algorithm engine. Counters indicate packets going into the engine.

    --**appid** is for the counters related to APP-ID processing.

    --**aho** is a threat- and data-filtering algorithm engine.

    --**ctd** is for content inspection events.

    --**dlp** is for data loss prevention events.

    --**fpga (field programmable gate array)** is the hardware offloading chip. This one is only included in `PA-3000` and higher hardware models.

    --**flow** is for packet processing.

    --**packet** is for packet buffering events.

    --**uid** is for user ID events.

    --**zip** triggers when `.zip` files are being unpacked.

    --**nat** is the **Network Address Translation (NAT)** actions.

    --**tcp** is TCP packet events.

--**mprelay** is triggered when sessions require interaction with the management plane routing process.

--**Proxy** is for proxy events, such as SSL decryption or DNS proxy.

* **aspect**: This adds more detail regarding which stage a packet was in when the counter was incremented. For example, parse, session, and forward are three stages of flow.

* **description: This** helps to identify counters more clearly.

You can use all of these attributes to filter the global counters for more meaningful output, as shown in the following screenshot:

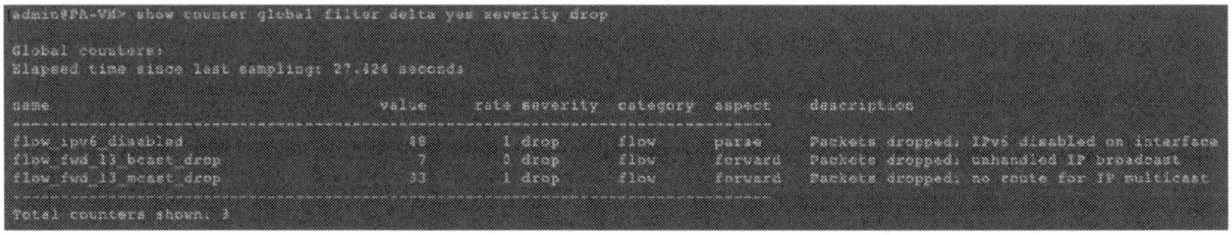

Figure 12.2 – Global counters with a severity filter

However, this still only reflects system-wide global counters. To narrow down the scope to just the sessions we want to know more about, we can leverage the same filters used for packet captures. I have set up a lab device that is pinging out to 194.7.1.4, which is an internet DNS server.

To filter global counters, we first need to set up the same packet-diag filters we would use to set up a packet capture.

First, clear any previously configured filters:

```
reaper@PA-VM> debug dataplane packet-diag clear all
```

Unmark any sessions that were marked by the previous filter:

```
reaper@PA-VM> debug dataplane packet-diag clear filter-marked-
session al
```

> **Important note**
>
> The `packet-diag` filters mark sessions, and any packets belonging to them, as part of the marked sessions. This marking is then used by different processes to keep tabs on packets and to make packet capture, global counter filtering, and flow analysis possible. Any sessions previously marked by a filter will maintain this "tag" for as long as the session is active. If several filter sessions follow one another, old sessions may show up in the debug session due to them still being tagged by the previously configured filters.

Next, add all the filters and turn them on. In the following example, we have one filter from the internal IP of the host to the DNS server for outbound packets, and a returning filter for the DNS server as the source with the NAT address as the source, while the filters are session-aware. This is good practice to catch any packets that somehow manage to escape the original session. One such example could be packets arriving with such latency that the session was already closed:

```
reaper@PA-VM> debug dataplane packet-diag set filter match
source 10.0.0.10 destination 194.7.1.4
```

```
reaper@PA-VM> debug dataplane packet-diag set filter match
source 194.7.1.4 destination 198.51.100.2
```

```
reaper@PA-VM> debug dataplane packet-diag set filter on
```

Your CLI session will look similar to the following:

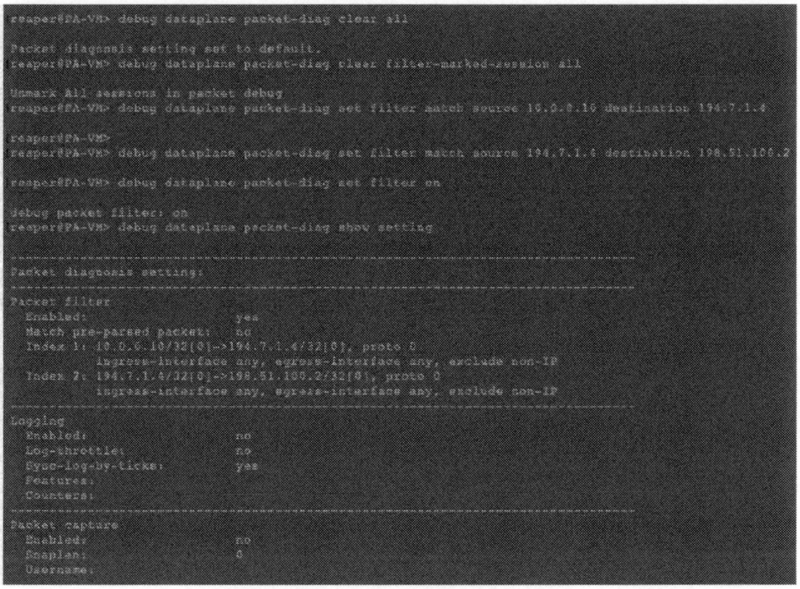

Figure 12.3 – Setting up filters

We can now start looking at global counters that only relate to our filters by adding packet-filter yes to the global counter filter:

```
reaper@PA-VM> show counter global filter delta yes packet-
filter yes
```

The output of the global counters should look similar to the following:

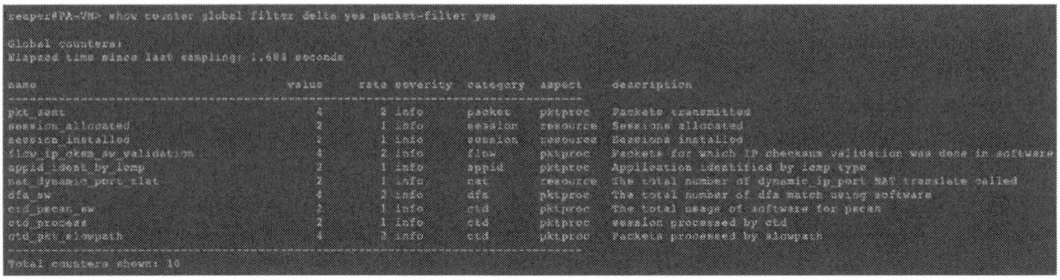

Figure 12.4 – Global counters for ping

The global counters extracted from the session will appear as follows:

- pkt_sent tells us four packets were sent in the delta timeframe.

- session_allocated means valid sessions were set up to handle the ping request (the opening state).

- session_installed means the session was accepted and set to the active state.

- flow_ip_chksm_sw_validation is the packets for which IP checksum was validated in the software.

- appid_ident_by_icmp means App-ID was able to identify these packets as pings immediately by their ICMP echo request signature.

- nat_dynamic_port_xlt indicates the packets were translated by a NAT rule set to use dynamic source ports for translation. A ping will be exempted to the dynamic nature of this type of NAT due to the need for these types of packets to retain the same source and destination port. This can be verified by looking at the sessions, as you can see in the following screenshot:

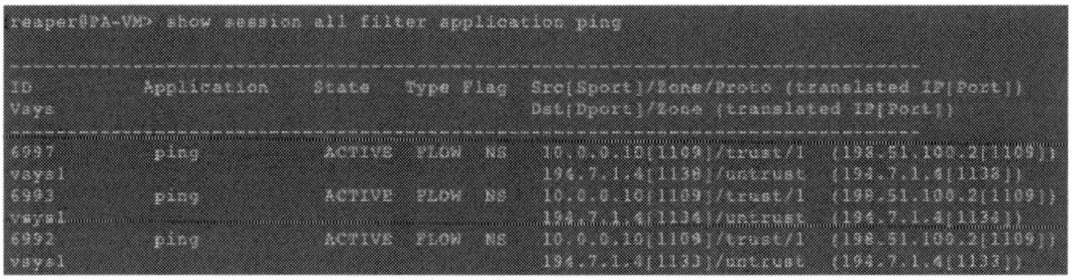

Figure 12.5 – The show session output

- `dfa_sw` are the packets identified by `App-ID` in the software.

- `ctd_process` is the number of sessions processed by `content-ID`.

- `ctd_pkt_slowpath` are the number of packets that went through slowpath.

> **Important note**
> Slowpath is the first stage of a session where packets need to be verified and matched against NAT and security rules before a session can be created. Once the session is set up, packets are processed in fastpath.

All of the preceding counters indicate that the session is progressing as expected.

To quickly spot that something is going on that could be causing issues, add a `severity` filter for dropped packets:

```
reaper@PA-VM> show counter global filter delta yes packet-
filter yes severity drop
```

There are several common counters:

- `flow_tcp_non_syn` is triggered when an ACK packet is received and no TCP handshake has been established that matches the packet tuples. This is commonly an indication of asymmetric flows where only one path of the client-to-server communication passes by the firewall.

- `flow_fw_zonechange` is another indication of asymmetric flows where returning packets are detected in a different zone, or a routing change has happened after the session was started and the destination zone is now on a different interface.

- `flow_policy_deny` is when the session hits a deny policy in the security rule base.

- `flow_fwd_l3_norarp` indicates that a packet can't be forwarded to the final destination because the firewall is unable to get an ARP address for the destination IP. You can review the ARP table using the following commands:

```
reaper@pa-220> show arp interface <interface e.g. ethernet1/1>
reaper@pa-220> show arp all
```

There are also plenty of counters that indicate whether something has happened that blocked or interrupted a session. A full list of all counters can be found at `https://github.com/PacktPublishing/Mastering-Palo-Alto-Networks`.

An example of a common configuration issue can be seen in the following screenshot. It is made abundantly clear when using global counters to troubleshoot why internal hosts are unable to reach a server in the DMZ:

```
reaper@PA-VM> show counter global filter delta yes packet-filter yes

Global counters:
Elapsed time since last sampling: 2.740 seconds

name                                    value     rate severity  category  aspect    description
--------------------------------------------------------------------------------
session_allocated                           1        0 info      session   resource  Sessions allocated
session_freed                               1        0 info      session   resource  Sessions freed
flow_policy_nat_land                        1        0 drop      flow      session   Session setup: source NAT IP allocation result in LAND attack
nat_dynamic_port_xlat                       1        0 info      nat       resource  The total number of dynamic_ip_port NAT translate called
nat_dynamic_port_release                    2        0 info      nat       resource  The total number of dynamic_ip_port NAT release called
--------------------------------------------------------------------------------
Total counters shown: 5
--------------------------------------------------------------------------------
```

Figure 12.6 – The packet dropped due to a LAND attack

This global counter output indicates that packets are being dropped and are ticking the `flow_policy_nat_land` counter. A LAND attack happens when the source and destination IP are identical, which could cause a loop in the system that receives these packets, causing it to reply to itself. In this case, it is caused by a misconfiguration in NAT causing the outbound packet to get translated by the Hide NAT rule, changing the source IP of the session to that of the firewall's external interface. This issue can be resolved by creating a U-Turn NAT rule above the generic Hide NAT rule, as illustrated in the following NAT rule:

| | | | Original Packet | | | | | | Translated Packet | |
|---|---|---|---|---|---|---|---|---|---|---|
| | NAME | TAGS | SOURCE ZONE | DESTINATION ZONE | DESTINATION INTERFACE | SOURCE ADDRESS | DESTINATION ADDRESS | SER... | SOURCE TRANSLATION | DESTINATION TRANSLATION |
| 1 | U-Turn | none | Trust-L3 | Untrust-L3 | ethernet1/1 | any | 198.51.100.2 | any | dynamic-ip-and-port<br>ethernet1/3<br>10.0.0.1/24 | destination-translation<br>address: 10.0.0.5<br>dns-rewrite: reverse |
| 2 | inbound SSH server | none | Untrust-L... | Untrust-L3 | ethernet1/1 | any | 109.51.100.2 | any | none | destination-translation<br>address: 10.0.0.5 |
| 3 | dynamic ip-port interface | none | Trust-L3 | Untrust-L3 | ethernet1/1 | dhcpsp... | any | any | dynamic-ip-and-port<br>ethernet1/1<br>198.51.100.2/24 | none |

Figure 12.7 – A U-Turn NAT rule to prevent a LAND condition

In this section, we learned how to interpret all kinds of global counters and how to go about applying filters so that the appropriate counters can be collected.

When the global counters indicate that there is an error in processing a packet, you may need to take a deep dive into the flow and look at how a session is being handled by the system. We will learn how to analyze session flows in the next section.

# Analyzing session flows

We've all been there; you've reviewed the logs, collected packet captures, and looked at the global counters, but you still can't find out what exactly is happening with a session. The last resort is to look at a session one packet at a time as it goes through the firewall and see what is happening to each packet at every stage and process:

> **Important note**
>
> Inspecting the flow is a very labor-intensive task for the data plane processor to do, so it is paramount that a very strict filter is set, which will also help prevent clutter, as well as ensure that the data plane is not already low on resources. To keep an eye on the data plane, use the following command while collecting the information to make sure you're not creating more issues by overloading the data plane.

```
reaper@PA-VM> show running resource-monitor second
```

Be vigilant in ensuring that the data plane cores do not hit 100% consistently and that the packet descriptors, which are on-chip buffers, remain below 85%.

We first need to determine which processes we need to capture. There are several options available:

```
reaper@PA-VM> debug dataplane packet-diag set log feature
> all        all
> appid      appid
> base       base
> cfg        cfg
> ctd        ctd
> flow       flow
> http2      http2
> misc       misc
> module     module
> pow        pow
> proxy      proxy
> ssl        ssl
```

| | |
|---|---|
| > tcp | tcp |
| > tdb | tdb |
| > tunnel | tunnel |
| > url_trie | url_trie |
| > zip | zip |

As you can see, there are many options available. Use the following list to find all the options needed to troubleshoot any issues. Do be careful about how many options you enable based on the filter you set. It may be wise to start small or capture individual logs in separate sessions so as not to overload your firewall:

- all will capture absolutely everything. This option should only be used in a lab (seriously, don't turn this on in a production environment).

- appid adds capturing for the App-ID process.

- base allows deeper logging for HA operations.

- cfg helps log config changes.

- ctd lets you log several content engine processes, including DNS, URL, and credentials.

- flow includes packet processing from ingress to egress.

- http2 can log how http2 sessions are processed.

- misc includes additional services, such as the clientless VPN portal.

- module is used to track core engines, such as aho, dfa, and URL.

- pow is the scheduling of work to cores. This could be useful if there appears to be an issue with how packets are distributed among cores.

- proxy is the proxy processes (outbound SSL decryption and DNS proxy).

- ssl is the inbound SSL decryption.

- tcp is any additional TCP actions, such as reassembly.

- tdb is for threat scanning.

- tunnel lets you look more closely at tunnel operations (such as flow and ager).

- url_trie is the URL-matching mechanism.

- zip is the unpacking process to scan inside compressed .zip files.

As you can see in the following screenshot, each feature has its own set of sub-features. These can range from child processes to overall log levels. In many cases, a good place to start is to use basic:

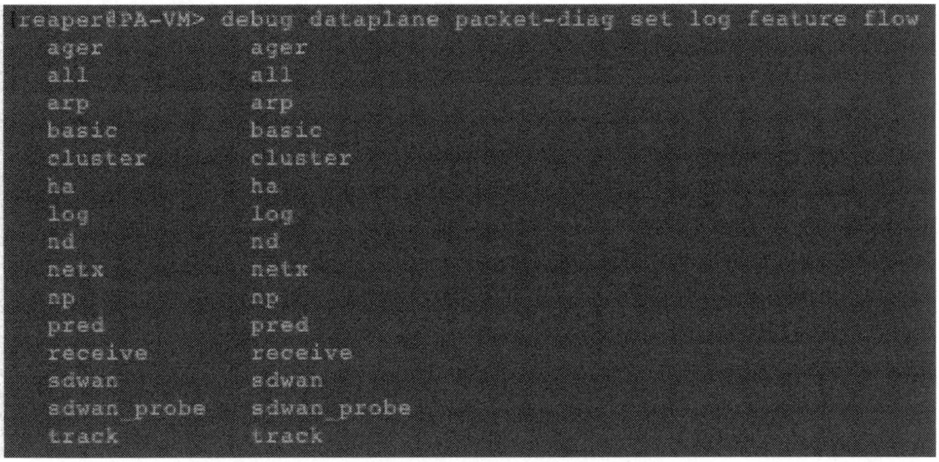

```
reaper@PA-VM> debug dataplane packet-diag set log feature flow
  ager          ager
  all           all
  arp           arp
  basic         basic
  cluster       cluster
  ha            ha
  log           log
  nd            nd
  netx          netx
  np            np
  pred          pred
  receive       receive
  sdwan         sdwan
  sdwan_probe   sdwan_probe
  track         track
```

Figure 12.8 – Flow features and sub-features

A good starting point to investigate connectivity issues is flow basic. Add more features if the output from flow basic indicates that packets are encountering an issue in a specific process.

Similar to the filter and packet capture diagnostics, log has an on and off toggle:

```
reaper@PA-VM> debug dataplane packet-diag set log feature flow
basic
```

```
reaper@PA-VM> debug dataplane packet-diag set log on
```

Once the on command is executed, the system starts logging at every stage that the packets matching the filter pass through, so keep an eye on the data plane CPU cores.

To run a successful log session, follow these steps.

## Preparation

To prepare for the execution stage of the data collection effort, follow these commands to prepare filters and ensure the stage is set:

1. debug dataplane packet-diag clear all

2. debug dataplane packet-diag clear filter-marked-session all

3. `debug dataplane packet-diag set filter match <filter settings>`

4. Add up to four filters.

5. `debug dataplane packet-diag set filter on`

6. `debug dataplane packet-diag set feature flow basic`

7. `set session offload no`

8. If there are any active sessions, it is best to clear them and hold off on creating new sessions until you are ready to start logging.

> **Important note**
>
> Hardware offloading bypasses the data plane processors. This means once a session is hardware offloading, we can no longer collect captures or logs for the session as all this data is captured on the data plane. This is why we should turn off offloading during troubleshooting if possible, but keep in mind that this will have an impact on the data plane core usage.

## Execution

It can be helpful to have multiple SSH sessions open so that you can run different commands in different windows so that you don't mix outputs:

1. To clear the global counter delta, run the following command:

```
Show counter global filter delta yes packet-filter yes
```

2. To ensure the data plane is in a healthy state before we enable logging, run the following command:

```
show running resource-monitor
```

Ensure the dataplane load is not dangerously high before continuing to the next step.

3. Execute the following command to start the log collection:

```
debug dataplane packet-diag set log on
```

4. Start the session that you are troubleshooting.

5. In separate SSH windows, periodically run the following command:

```
> show session all filter  <appropriate filters for the
sessions you are tracking>
```
```
> show counter global filter delta yes packet-filter yes
```
```
> show running resource-monitor
```

6. Once the session has ended or the issue you are trying to learn more about has occurred, wait for a few seconds to capture any "late" packets, and then turn the log off:

```
> debug dataplane packet-diag set log off
```

7. Enable offloading again:

```
Set session offload yes
```

Because sessions are assigned to a specific core for processing, and each core logs to its own file, the flow logs may be spread over multiple pan_task_*.log files, in dp-log for larger platforms, and mp-log for small and virtual platforms. These can be combined into a single pan_packet_diag.log file in the mp-log directory.

Once you execute the aggregation command, wait for a while for the logs to be merged:

```
reaper@PA-VM> debug dataplane packet-diag aggregate-logs
```
```
reaper@PA-VM> less mp-log pan_packet_diag.log
```

## Cleanup

You can export the pan_packet_diag.log file, along with all the other management plane log files, so that you can analyze it in your favorite text editor:

```
reaper@PA-VM> scp|tftp export log-file management-plane to
user@host:/path/
```

After you are done, you should delete the file from your system due to its potentially sensitive content:

```
reaper@PA-VM> debug dataplane packet-diag clear log log
```

## A practical example

Let's put this into practice. In the following screenshot, you can see the lab layout. There is a client on a private network with the IP address 10.0.0.10, connecting to the firewall as the default gateway on 10.0.0.1. Outbound connections are source-translated behind the firewall's external IP address of 198.51.100.2.

Session 1 tries to establish an SSH connection to IP address 198.51.100.2.

Session 2 establishes an SSH connection with upstream router 198.51.100.1:

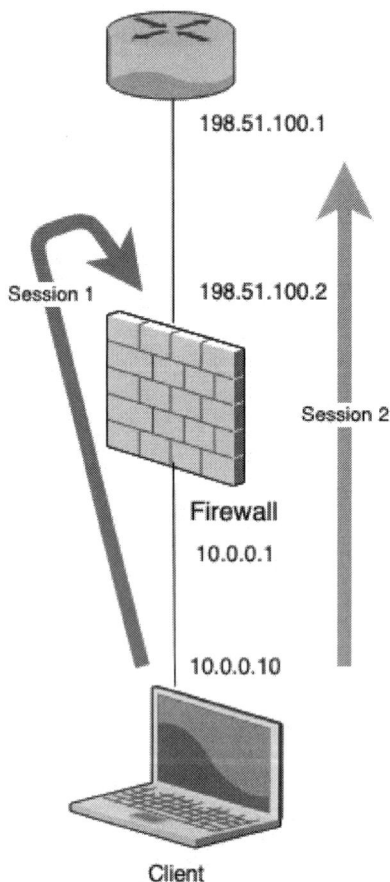

Figure 12.9 – Example scenario

We prepare the configuration by clearing out all the previous filters and ensuring no marked sessions remain by clearing all the markings. We then set up the filters, disable session offloading, and prepare the log feature:

```
reaper@PA-VM> debug dataplane packet-diag clear all

Packet diagnosis setting set to default.
reaper@PA-VM> debug dataplane packet-diag clear filter-marked-
session all

Unmark All sessions in packet debug
reaper@PA-VM> debug dataplane packet-diag set filter match
source 10.0.0.10 destination 198.51.100.2

reaper@PA-VM> debug dataplane packet-diag set filter match
source 10.0.0.10 destination 198.51.100.1

reaper@PA-VM> debug dataplane packet-diag set filter match
source 198.51.100.1 destination 198.51.100.2

reaper@PA-VM> debug dataplane packet-diag set filter match
destination 198.51.100.2

reaper@PA-VM> debug dataplane packet-diag set filter on

debug packet filter: on
reaper@PA-VM> show session all filter source 10.0.0.10

No Active Sessions
reaper@PA-VM> set session offload no

reaper@PA-VM> debug dataplane packet-diag set log feature flow
basic
```

Once we're ready to get the session going, open an additional SSH window so that we can keep an eye on the data plane resources. We could influence the outcome of the test and impact other network traffic, or even the system's stability, if we overload the data plane.

> **Important note**
> It is good practice to log all your SSH sessions while troubleshooting so that you can rebuild your timeline afterward. It helps to occasionally add visual time cues to the SSH output if the troubleshooting session takes an extended length of time. You can do that by using the following command:

```
reaper@PA-VM> show clock
Thu Jun  4 23:10:35 CEST 2020
```

Once we're all set to start the collection effort, enable the log option and clear the global counter delta:

```
reaper@PA-VM> debug dataplane packet-diag set log on

Packet log is enabled
reaper@PA-VM> show counter global filter delta yes packet-filter yes

Global counters:
Elapsed time since last sampling: 159.191 seconds
```

| name<br>category | aspect | description | value | rate | severity |
|---|---|---|---|---|---|
| pkt_recv<br>packet | pktproc | Packets received | 2 | 0 | info |
| pkt_sent<br>packet | pktproc | Packets transmitted | 14 | 0 | info |
| pkt_stp_rcv<br>packet | pktproc | STP BPDU packets received | 2 | 0 | info |
| flow_arp_pkt_rcv<br>flow | arp | ARP packets received | 2 | 0 | info |
| flow_arp_rcv_gratuitous<br>flow | arp | Gratuitous ARP packets received | 2 | 0 | info |

```
flow_ip_cksm_sw_validation                    9         0 info
flow      pktproc    Packets for which IP checksum validation
was done in software
log_pkt_diag_us                              82         0 info
log       system     Time (us) spent on writing packet-diag logs
--------------------------------------------------------------
-----------------
Total counters shown: 7
--------------------------------------------------------------
-----------------


reaper@PA-VM> show counter global filter delta yes packet-
filter yes


Global counters:
Elapsed time since last sampling: 5.588 seconds


    --------------------------------------------------------------
    -----------------
Total counters shown: 0
    --------------------------------------------------------------
    -----------------
```

Now that the global counter delta is cleared and logging is enabled, we can start the first session by launching an SSH session from the client at 10.0.0.10 to the firewall's external interface IP, 198.51.100.2. We can then check to see whether a session was created and what the output of the global counters is:

```
reaper@PA-VM> show counter global filter delta yes packet-
filter yes


Global counters:
Elapsed time since last sampling: 24.931 seconds


    --------------------------------------------------------------
    -----------------
Total counters shown: 0
    --------------------------------------------------------------
    -----------------
```

```
reaper@PA-VM> show session all filter source 10.0.0.10

No Active Sessions
reaper@PA-VM> show counter global filter delta yes packet-
filter yes

Global counters:
Elapsed time since last sampling: 13.132 seconds

name                                      value    rate severity
category   aspect     description
-----------------------------------------------------------------
-----------------
session_allocated                             4        0 info
session    resource   Sessions allocated
session_freed                                 4        0 info
session    resource   Sessions freed
flow_policy_nat_land                          4        0 drop
flow       session    Session setup: source NAT IP allocation
result in LAND attack
nat_dynamic_port_xlat                         4        0 info
nat        resource   The total number of dynamic_ip_port NAT
translate called
nat_dynamic_port_release                      8        0 info
nat        resource   The total number of dynamic_ip_port NAT
release called
log_pkt_diag_us                             262       19 info
log        system     Time (us) spent on writing packet-diag logs
-----------------------------------------------------------------
-----------------
Total counters shown: 6
-----------------------------------------------------------------
-----------------


reaper@PA-VM> show session all filter source 10.0.0.10

No Active Sessions
```

We can see that a session has not been created and the global counters indicate that the packets were dropped.

We can now start the second session by launching an SSH session from the client at `10.0.0.10` to the upstream router at `198.51.100.1`.

This time a session is created, and we can view the details in the command line:

```
reaper@PA-VM> show session all filter source 10.0.0.10


---------------------------------------------------------------
------------------
ID          Application    State    Type Flag  Src[Sport]/Zone/
Proto (translated IP[Port])
Vsys                                     Dst[Dport]/Zone
(translated IP[Port])
---------------------------------------------------------------
------------------
270          ssh           ACTIVE   FLOW  NS
10.0.0.10[49402]/trust/6   (198.51.100.2[12607])
vsys1
198.51.100.1[22]/untrust  (198.51.100.1[22])


reaper@PA-VM> show session id 270


Session                270

        c2s flow:
                source:      10.0.0.10 [trust]
                dst:         198.51.100.1
                proto:       6
                sport:       49402          dport:     22
                state:       ACTIVE         type:      FLOW
                src user:    unknown
                dst user:    unknown

        s2c flow:
                source:      198.51.100.1 [untrust]
                dst:         198.51.100.2
```

```
                proto:       6
                sport:       22              dport:       12607
                state:       ACTIVE         type:        FLOW
                src user:    unknown
                dst user:    unknown


        start time                          : Thu Jun  4
00:46:11 2020
        timeout                             : 3600 sec
        time to live                        : 3589 sec
        total byte count(c2s)               : 3961
        total byte count(s2c)               : 6143
        layer7 packet count(c2s)            : 22
        layer7 packet count(s2c)            : 27
        vsys                                : vsys1
        application                         : ssh
        rule                                : outbound
        service timeout override(index)     : False
        session to be logged at end         : True
        session in session ager             : True
        session updated by HA peer          : False
        address/port translation            : source
        nat-rule                            : outbound
hide(vsys1)
        layer7 processing                   : completed
        URL filtering enabled               : True
        URL category                        : any
        session via syn-cookies             : False
        session terminated on host          : False
        session traverses tunnel            : False
        session terminate tunnel            : False
        captive portal session              : False
        ingress interface                   : ethernet1/2
        egress interface                    : ethernet1/1
        session QoS rule                    : N/A (class 4).
```

```
                tracker stage l7proc            : ctd decoder done
                    end-reason                  : unknown
reaper@PA-VM>
```

We can see that the session is active and the outbound connection is being source-NATed behind the firewall external IP of 198.51.100.1. Packets are traveling in both directions.

We can now take a look at the global counters to verify whether everything is working as expected:

```
reaper@PA-VM> show counter global filter delta yes packet-
filter yes


Global counters:
Elapsed time since last sampling: 55.235 seconds


name                                    value      rate severity
category   aspect     description
-------------------------------------------------------------
----------------
pkt_recv                                   5         0 info
packet     pktproc    Packets received
pkt_sent                                  20         0 info
packet     pktproc    Packets transmitted
session_allocated                          1         0 info
session    resource   Sessions allocated
session_freed                              1         0 info
session    resource   Sessions freed
flow_policy_nat_land                       1         0 drop
flow       session    Session setup: source NAT IP allocation
result in LAND attack
flow_ip_cksm_sw_validation                27         0 info
flow       pktproc    Packets for which IP checksum validation
was done in software
nat_dynamic_port_xlat                      1         0 info
nat        resource   The total number of dynamic_ip_port NAT
translate called
```

```
nat_dynamic_port_release                      2        0 info
nat        resource  The total number of dynamic_ip_port NAT
release called

dfa_sw                                        4        0 info
dfa        pktproc   The total number of dfa match using
software

ctd_sml_exit_detector_i                       1        0 info
ctd        pktproc   The number of sessions with sml exit in
detector i

ctd_run_detector_i                            1        0 info
ctd        pktproc   run detector_i

ctd_sml_vm_run_impl_opcodeexit                1        0 info
ctd        pktproc   SML VM opcode exit

ctd_fwd_err_tcp_state                         1        0
info       ctd       pktproc   Forward to varrcvr error: TCP in
establishment when session went away

ctd_pscan_sw                                  4        0 info
ctd        pktproc   The total usage of software for pscan

ctd_pkt_slowpath                              4        0 info
ctd        pktproc   Packets processed by slowpath

log_pkt_diag_us                              303        5 info
log        system    Time (us) spent on writing packet-diag logs
--------------------------------------------------------------
-----------------

Total counters shown: 16
--------------------------------------------------------------
-----------------
```

Once the SSH session is ended on the client, we can verify whether the session still exists on the firewall. Once the session is closed, we can collect a last global counter output to ensure we have all the details, and then turn off the logging feature and re-enable session offloading:

```
reaper@PA-VM> show session all filter source 10.0.0.10

--------------------------------------------------------------
-----------------
ID          Application    State    Type Flag  Src[Sport]/Zone/
Proto (translated IP[Port])
```

```
Vsys                                      Dst[Dport]/Zone
(translated IP[Port])

-------------------------------------------------------------
-----------------
270          ssh           ACTIVE  FLOW  NS
10.0.0.10[49402]/trust/6   (198.51.100.2[12607])
vsys1
198.51.100.1[22]/untrust   (198.51.100.1[22])
reaper@PA-VM> show session all filter source 10.0.0.10


No Active Sessions
reaper@PA-VM> show counter global filter delta yes packet-
filter yes


Global counters:
Elapsed time since last sampling: 54.857 seconds


name                                  value     rate severity
category   aspect      description
-------------------------------------------------------------
-----------------
pkt_recv                                 3         0 info
packet     pktproc   Packets received
pkt_sent                                14         0 info
packet     pktproc   Packets transmitted
flow_ip_cksm_sw_validation               9         0 info
flow       pktproc   Packets for which IP checksum validation
was done in software
log_pkt_diag_us                        100         1 info
log        system    Time (us) spent on writing packet-diag logs
-------------------------------------------------------------
-----------------
Total counters shown: 4
-------------------------------------------------------------
-----------------
```

```
reaper@PA-VM> debug dataplane packet-diag set log off

Packet log is disabled
reaper@PA-VM> set session offload yes
```

The final step is to aggregate all the pan_task_*.log files into a single file:

```
reaper@PA-VM> debug dataplane packet-diag aggregate-logs
pan_packet_diag.log is aggregated
```

We should wait a minute to give the firewall time to compile the aggregated file. The time needed to accomplish this may vary depending on the size of the individual log files.

You can review the aggregated file on the firewall by using the less command:

```
reaper@PA-VM> less mp-log pan_packet_diag.log
```

Alternatively, you can export the log files so that you can read them in Notepad++ or another text editor:

```
reaper@PA-VM> scp export log-file management-plane to
reaper@192.168.27.16:/home/reaper/
```

In the resulting tar.gz file, pan_packet_diag.log is located in the /var/log/pan directory.

As you can see from the following screenshot, session 1 is over in just two log entries. The first paragraph shows the ingress stage where the SYN packet is first received and all of its attributes disseminated. You can use this first segment to review whether the initial SYN packet is coming in on the right interface and looks "normal." The ingress stage will also check whether the packet matches an existing session. In our case, this is a new session, so the packet is enqueued to create a new session:

```
== 2020-06-04 00:45:37.522 +0200 ==
Packet received at ingress stage, tag 0, type ORDERED
Packet info: len 74 port 17 interface 17 vsys 1
  wqe index 33521 packet 0x0xc0013b0900, HA: 0, IC: 0
Packet decoded dump:
L2:     00:0c:29:d7:40:22->00:0c:29:7e:38:e5, type 0x0800
IP:     10.0.0.10->198.51.100.2, protocol 6
        version 4, ihl 5, tos 0x00, len 60,
        id 41859, frag_off 0x4000, ttl 64, checksum 63842(0x62f9)
TCP:    sport 43100, dport 22, seq 3116136369, ack 0,
        reserved 0, offset 10, window 64240, checksum 24589,
        flags 0x02 ( SYN), urgent data 0, 14 data len 0
TCP option:
00000000: 02 04 05 b4 04 02 08 0a  69 3f 75 a2 00 00 00 00    ........ i?u.....
00000010: 01 03 03 07                                         ....
Flow lookup, key word0 0x600020016a85c word1 0  word2 0xa00000affff0000 word3 0x0 word4 0x26433c6ffff0000
* Dos Profile NULL (NO) Index (0/0) *
Session setup: vsys 1
No active flow found, enqueue to create session


== 2020-06-04 00:45:37.522 +0200 ==
Packet received at slowpath stage, tag 3223295891, type ATOMIC
Packet info: len 74 port 17 interface 17 vsys 1
  wqe index 33521 packet 0x0xc0013b0900, HA: 0, IC: 0
Packet decoded dump:
L2:     00:0c:29:d7:40:22->00:0c:29:7e:38:e5, type 0x0800
IP:     10.0.0.10->198.51.100.2, protocol 6
        version 4, ihl 5, tos 0x00, len 60,
        id 41859, frag_off 0x4000, ttl 64, checksum 63842(0x62f9)
TCP:    sport 43100, dport 22, seq 3116136369, ack 0,
        reserved 0, offset 10, window 64240, checksum 24589,
        flags 0x02 ( SYN), urgent data 0, 14 data len 0
TCP option:
00000000: 02 04 05 b4 04 02 08 0a  69 3f 75 a2 00 00 00 00    ........ i?u.....
00000010: 01 03 03 07                                         ....
Session setup: vsys 1
Session setup: ingress interface ethernet1/2 egress interface ethernet1/1 (zone 1)
NAT policy lookup, matched rule index 1
Policy lookup, matched rule index 0,
Allocated new session 265.
set exclude_video in session 265 0xe03cb10780 0 from work 0xe014f40f00 0
Rule: index=1 name=outbound hide, cfg_pool_idx=1 cfg_fallback_pool_idx=0
NAT Rule: name=outbound hide, cfg_pool_idx=1; Session: index=265, nat_pool_idx=1
Packet dropped, vsys 1 NAT rule index 2 result in LAND attack, same SA/DA 198.51.100.2
```

Figure 12.10 – Discarded syn packet in flow basic

Interface `17` is the ID of the `ethernet1/2` interface, which you can check by issuing the following command:

```
reaper@PA-VM> show interface all
```

Paragraph 2 is the slowpath stage. The packet will be matched against the forwarding table to determine the egress interface, so a NAT lookup can take place. The egress zone is determined to be zone 1. You can determine all the zone IDs by issuing the following command:

```
reaper@PA-VM> debug device-server dump idmgr type zone all
```

A session ID of 265 is assigned to this SYN packet as it is going to turn into a session. An exact NAT rule match is found and then the NAT logic is verified, and it is found that this NAT action will cause a LAND attack, so the packet is immediately discarded. This is why we couldn't see a session in the show session command because the session was terminated before it formed:

The second session shows a different story. In the ingress stage, we see a similar packet arriving on interface 17. A forwarding lookup is performed and the egress interface and zone is determined, followed by a NAT lookup. The NAT rule is matched and this time, there is no conflict, so the NAT action is prepared. A session ID of 941 is assigned to this flow and enqueued to be installed:

```
== 2020-06-05 00:16:22.030 +0200 ==
Packet received at ingress stage, tag 0, type ORDERED
Packet info: len 74 port 17 interface 17 vsys 1
  wqe index 23554 packet 0x0xc0013fdf40, HA: 0, IC: 0
Packet decoded dump:
L2:    00:0c:29:d7:40:22->00:0c:29:7e:38:e5, type 0x0800
IP:    10.0.0.10->198.51.100.1, protocol 6
       version 4, ihl 5, tos 0x00, len 60,
       id 29076, frag_off 0x4000, ttl 64, checksum 59796(0x94e9)
TCP:   sport 49404, dport 22, seq 4257280317, ack 0,
       reserved 0, offset 10, window 64240, checksum 17082,
       flags 0x02 ( SYN), urgent data 0, 14 data len 0
TCP option:
00000000: 02 04 05 b4 04 02 08 0a  3d 06 e8 fe 00 00 00 00    ........ =.......
00000010: 01 03 03 07                                         ....
Flow lookup, key word0 0x600020016c0fc word1 0  word2 0xa00000affff0000 word3 0x0 word4 0x16433c6ffff0000
* Dos Profile NULL (NO) Index (0/0) *
Session setup: vsys 1
No active flow found, enqueue to create session

== 2020-06-05 00:16:22.030 +0200 ==
Packet received at slowpath stage, tag 1688519813, type ATOMIC
Packet info: len 74 port 17 interface 17 vsys 1
  wqe index 23554 packet 0x0xc0013fdf40, HA: 0, IC: 0
Packet decoded dump:
L2:    00:0c:29:d7:40:22->00:0c:29:7e:38:e5, type 0x0800
IP:    10.0.0.10->198.51.100.1, protocol 6
       version 4, ihl 5, tos 0x00, len 60,
       id 29076, frag_off 0x4000, ttl 64, checksum 59796(0x94e9)
TCP:   sport 49404, dport 22, seq 4257280317, ack 0,
       reserved 0, offset 10, window 64240, checksum 17082,
       flags 0x02 ( SYN), urgent data 0, 14 data len 0
TCP option:
00000000: 02 04 05 b4 04 02 08 0a  3d 06 e8 fe 00 00 00 00    ........ =.......
00000010: 01 03 03 07                                         ....
Session setup: vsys 1
PBF lookup (vsys 1) with application none
Session setup: ingress interface ethernet1/2 egress interface ethernet1/1 (zone 1)
NAT policy lookup, matched rule index 1
Policy lookup, matched rule index 0,
TCI_INSPECT: Do TCI lookup policy - sppid 0
Allocated new session 941.
set exclude_video in session 941 0xe03cb3ab80 0 from work 0xe014cd2080 0
Rule: index=1 name=outbound hide, cfg_pool_idx=1 cfg_fallback_pool_idx=0
NAT Rule: name=outbound hide, cfg_pool_idx=1; Session: index=941, nat_pool_idx=1
Packet matched vsys 1 NAT rule 'outbound hide' (index 2),
source translation 10.0.0.10/49404 => 198.51.100.2/63571
Created session, enqueue to install. work 0xe014cd2080 exclude_video 0,session 941 0xe03cb3ab80 exclude_video 0
```

Figure 12.11 – Accepted session in flow basic

In the next screenshot, we can see the SYN packet enter the final stage, called `fastpath`, which means a session has been created; the packet can egress out and the firewall is ready to receive a reply packet. In the egress stage, DSCP tags are added if any are configured and NAT is applied.

We also see additional information about the `layer3` routing decisions, and finally, the packet being sent out of the `ethernet1/1` interface with ID `16`:

```
== 2020-06-05 00:16:22.030 +0200 ==
Packet received at fastpath stage, tag 941, type ATOMIC
Packet info: len 74 port 17 interface 17 vsys 1
  wqe index 23554 packet 0x0xc0013fdf40, HA: 0, IC: 0
Packet decoded dump:
L2:    00:0c:29:d7:40:22->00:0c:29:7e:38:e5, type 0x0800
IP:    10.0.0.10->198.51.100.1, protocol 6
       version 4, ihl 5, tos 0x00, len 60,
       id 29076, frag_off 0x4000, ttl 64, checksum 59796(0x94e9)
TCP:   sport 49404, dport 22, seq 4257280317, ack 0,
       reserved 0, offset 10, window 64240, checksum 17082,
       flags 0x02 ( SYN), urgent data 0, 14 data len 0
TCP option:
00000000: 02 04 05 b4 04 02 08 0a  3d 06 e8 fe 00 00 00 00    ........ =.......
00000010: 01 03 03 07                                         ....
Flow fastpath, session 941 c2s (set work 0xe014cd2080 exclude_video 0 from sp 0xe03cb3ab80 exclude_video 0)
IP checksum valid
* Dos Profile NULL (NO) Index (0/0) *
* Dos Profile NULL (NO) Index (0/0) *
2020-06-05 00:16:22.030 +0200  pan_flow_process_fastpath(src/pan_flow_proc.c:3928): SESSION-DSCP: set session DSCP: 0x00
NAT session, run address/port translation
Syn Cookie: pan_reass(Init statete): c2s:0 c2s:nxtseq 4257280318 c2s:startseq 4257280318 c2s:win 0 c2s:st 3 c2s:newsyn 0
0 plen 0
CP-DENY TCP non data packet getting through
Forwarding lookup, ingress interface 17
L3 mode, virtual-router 1
Route lookup in virtual-router 1, IP 198.51.100.1
Route found, interface ethernet1/1, zone 1
Resolve ARP for IP 198.51.100.1 on interface ethernet1/1
ARP entry found on interface 16
Transmit packet size 60 on port 16
```

Figure 12.12 – SYN packet going into fastpath

The next two log entries represent the returning SYN-ACK from the upstream server.

First, we see the ingress stage, which is similar to the original outbound SYN packet, with the exception that flow `1883` was found, which is the entry in the session table that was created when the SYN packet was accepted and a session was created. The SYN-ACK is immediately forwarded to fastpath.

The second log is the packet arriving in fastpath and a reverse forwarding lookup is taking place. Reverse NAT is applied and the ARP table is verified if the post-NAT destination can be found. The packet is then egressed back out to the client:

```
== 2020-06-05 00:16:22.032 +0200 ==
Packet received at ingress stage, tag 0, type ORDERED
Packet info: len 74 port 16 interface 16 vsys 1
  wqe index 23554 packet 0x0xc002c89380, HA: 0, IC: 0
Packet decoded dump:
L2:     00:0c:29:7a:5e:82->00:0c:29:7e:38:db, type 0x0800
IP:     198.51.100.1->198.51.100.2, protocol 6
        version 4, ihl 5, tos 0x00, len 60,
        id 0, frag_off 0x4000, ttl 64, checksum 20966(0xe651)
TCP:    sport 22, dport 63571, seq 671986244, ack 4257280318,
        reserved 0, offset 10, window 28960, checksum 36020,
        flags 0x12 ( SYN ACK), urgent data 0, 14 data len 0
TCP option:
00000000: 02 04 05 b4 04 02 08 0a  07 57 06 99 3d 06 e8 fe    ........ .W..=...
00000010: 01 03 03 07                                         ....
Flow lookup, key word0 0x60001f8530016 word1 0  word2 0x16433c6ffff0000 word3 0x0 word4 0x26433c6ffff0000
Flow 1883 found, state 2, HA 0
Active flow, enqueue to fastpath process, type 0

* Dos Profile NULL (NO) Index (0/0) *

== 2020-06-05 00:16:22.032 +0200 ==
Packet received at fastpath stage, tag 941, type ATOMIC
Packet info: len 74 port 16 interface 16 vsys 1
  wqe index 23554 packet 0x0xc002c89380, HA: 0, IC: 0
Packet decoded dump:
L2:     00:0c:29:7a:5e:82->00:0c:29:7e:38:db, type 0x0800
IP:     198.51.100.1->198.51.100.2, protocol 6
        version 4, ihl 5, tos 0x00, len 60,
        id 0, frag_off 0x4000, ttl 64, checksum 20966(0xe651)
TCP:    sport 22, dport 63571, seq 671986244, ack 4257280318,
        reserved 0, offset 10, window 28960, checksum 36020,
        flags 0x12 ( SYN ACK), urgent data 0, 14 data len 0
TCP option:
00000000: 02 04 05 b4 04 02 08 0a  07 57 06 99 3d 06 e8 fe    ........ .W..=...
00000010: 01 03 03 07                                         ....
Flow fastpath, session 941 s2c (set work 0xe014cd2080 exclude_video 0 from sp 0xe03cb3ab80 exclude_video 0)
IP checksum valid
* Dos Profile NULL (NO) Index (0/0) *
NAT session, run address/port translation
Syn Cookie: pan_reass(Init statete): c2s:1 c2s:nxtseq 4257280318 c2s:startseq 4257280318 c2s:win 28960 c2s:
s2c:newsyn 0 ack 4257280318 nosyn 0 plen 0
CP-DENY TCP non data packet getting through
Forwarding lookup, ingress interface 16
L3 mode, virtual-router 1
Route lookup in virtual-router 1, IP 10.0.0.10
Route found, interface ethernet1/2, zone 2
Resolve ARP for IP 10.0.0.10 on interface ethernet1/2
ARP entry found on interface 17
Transmit packet size 60 on port 17
```

Figure 12.13 – Returning SYN-ACK

You may have noticed that the ingress packets have the ORDERED type , while the slowpath/fastpath packets are of the ATOMIC type. The ORDERED type indicates that a session is randomly assigned to a data plane core, which is common for newly ingressing packets, while ATOMIC means the session is assigned to a single core, which is common for established sessions.

The next two log entries represent the final ACK packet, completing the handshake:

```
== 2020-06-05 00:16:22.032 +0200 ==
Packet received at ingress stage, tag 0, type ORDERED
Packet info: len 66 port 17 interface 17 vsys 1
  wqe index 23554 packet 0x0xc0013fe900, HA: 0, IC: 0
Packet decoded dump:
L2:     00:0c:29:d7:40:22->00:0c:29:7e:38:e5, type 0x0800
IP:     10.0.0.10->198.51.100.1, protocol 6
        version 4, ihl 5, tos 0x00, len 52,
        id 29077, frag_off 0x4000, ttl 64, checksum 61588(0x94f0)
TCP:    sport 49404, dport 22, seq 4257280318, ack 671986245,
        reserved 0, offset 8, window 502, checksum 33324,
        flags 0x10 ( ACK), urgent data 0, 14 data len 0
TCP option:
00000000: 01 01 08 0a 3d 06 e9 00  07 57 06 99              ....=... .W..
Flow lookup, key word0 0x600020016c0fc word1 0  word2 0xa00000affff0000 word3 0x0 word4 0x16433c6ffff0000
Flow 1882 found, state 2, HA 0
Active flow, enqueue to fastpath process, type 0

* Dos Profile NULL (NO) Index (0/0) *

== 2020-06-05 00:16:22.032 +0200 ==
Packet received at fastpath stage, tag 941, type ATOMIC
Packet info: len 66 port 17 interface 17 vsys 1
  wqe index 23554 packet 0x0xc0013fe900, HA: 0, IC: 0
Packet decoded dump:
L2:     00:0c:29:d7:40:22->00:0c:29:7e:38:e5, type 0x0800
IP:     10.0.0.10->198.51.100.1, protocol 6
        version 4, ihl 5, tos 0x00, len 52,
        id 29077, frag_off 0x4000, ttl 64, checksum 61588(0x94f0)
TCP:    sport 49404, dport 22, seq 4257280318, ack 671986245,
        reserved 0, offset 8, window 502, checksum 33324,
        flags 0x10 ( ACK), urgent data 0, 14 data len 0
TCP option:
00000000: 01 01 08 0a 3d 06 e9 00  07 57 06 99              ....=... .W..
Flow fastpath, session 941 c2s (set work 0xe014cd2080 exclude_video 0 from sp 0xe03cb3ab80 exclude_video 0)
IP checksum valid
NAT session, run address/port translation
CP-DENY TCP non data packet getting through
Forwarding lookup, ingress interface 17
L3 mode, virtual-router 1
Route lookup in virtual-router 1, IP 198.51.100.1
Route found, interface ethernet1/1, zone 1
Resolve ARP for IP 198.51.100.1 on interface ethernet1/1
ARP entry found on interface 16
Transmit packet size 52 on port 16
```

Figure 12.14 – Completed handshake

From this point forward, the session has been established and both sides can start exchanging their payload, as you can see in the next four log entries.

The PSH ACK packet is received at the ingress stage:

```
== 2020-06-05 00:16:22.032 +0200 ==
Packet received at ingress stage, tag 0, type ORDERED
Packet info: len 107 port 17 interface 17 vsys 1
  wqe index 23554 packet 0x0xc0013ff2c0, HA: 0, IC: 0
Packet decoded dump:
L2:    00:0c:29:d7:40:22->00:0c:29:7e:38:e5, type 0x0800
IP:    10.0.0.10->198.51.100.1, protocol 6
       version 4, ihl 5, tos 0x00, len 93,
       id 29078, frag_off 0x4000, ttl 64, checksum 50836(0x94c6)
TCP:   sport 49404, dport 22, seq 4257280318, ack 671986245,
       reserved 0, offset 8, window 502, checksum 63771,
       flags 0x18 ( ACK PSH), urgent data 0, 14 data len 41
TCP option:
00000000: 01 01 08 0a 3d 06 e9 01  07 57 06 99              ....=... .W..
Flow lookup, key word0 0x600020016c0fc word1 0  word2 0xa00000affff0000 word3 0x0 word4 0x16433c6ffff0000
Flow 1882 found, state 2, HA 0
Active flow, enqueue to fastpath process, type 0

* Dos Profile NULL (NO) Index (0/0) *
```

Figure 12.15 – The client PSH ACK at the ingress stage

The packet is processed through fastpath and sent out:

```
== 2020-06-05 00:16:22.032 +0200 ==
Packet received at fastpath stage, tag 941, type ATOMIC
Packet info: len 107 port 17 interface 17 vsys 1
  wqe index 23554 packet 0x0xc0013ff2c0, HA: 0, IC: 0
Packet decoded dump:
L2:    00:0c:29:d7:40:22->00:0c:29:7e:38:e5, type 0x0800
IP:    10.0.0.10->198.51.100.1, protocol 6
       version 4, ihl 5, tos 0x00, len 93,
       id 29078, frag_off 0x4000, ttl 64, checksum 50836(0x94c6)
TCP:   sport 49404, dport 22, seq 4257280318, ack 671986245,
       reserved 0, offset 8, window 502, checksum 63771,
       flags 0x18 ( ACK PSH), urgent data 0, 14 data len 41
TCP option:
00000000: 01 01 08 0a 3d 06 e9 01  07 57 06 99              ....=... .W..
Flow fastpath, session 941 c2s (set work 0xe014cd2080 exclude_video 0 from sp 0xe03cb3ab80 exclude_video 0)
IP checksum valid
NAT session, run address/port translation
session 941 packet sequeunce old 0 new 1
Forwarding lookup, ingress interface 17
L3 mode, virtual-router 1
Route lookup in virtual-router 1, IP 198.51.100.1
Route found, interface ethernet1/1, zone 1
Resolve ARP for IP 198.51.100.1 on interface ethernet1/1
ARP entry found on interface 16
Transmit packet size 93 on port 16
```

Figure 12.16 – The client PSH ACK at the egress stage

The server ACK is received at the ingress stage:

```
== 2020-06-05 00:16:22.034 +0200 ==
Packet received at ingress stage, tag 0, type ORDERED
Packet info: len 66 port 16 interface 16 vsys 1
  wqe index 23554 packet 0x0xc002c83bc0, HA: 0, IC: 0
Packet decoded dump:
L2:    00:0c:29:7a:5e:82->00:0c:29:7e:38:db, type 0x0800
IP:    198.51.100.1->198.51.100.2, protocol 6
       version 4, ihl 5, tos 0x00, len 52,
       id 46303, frag_off 0x4000, ttl 64, checksum 31281(0x317a)
TCP:   sport 22, dport 63571, seq 671986245, ack 4257280359,
       reserved 0, offset 8, window 227, checksum 11152,
       flags 0x10 ( ACK), urgent data 0, 14 data len 0
TCP option:
00000000: 01 01 08 0a 07 57 06 9b  3d 06 e9 01                .....W.. =...
Flow lookup, key word0 0x60001f8530016 word1 0  word2 0x16433c6ffff0000 word3 0x0 word4 0x26433c6ffff0000
Flow 1883 found, state 2, HA 0
Active flow, enqueue to fastpath process, type 0

* Dos Profile NULL (NO) Index (0/0) *
```

Figure 12.17 – The server ACK at the ingress stage

The server ACK packet is processed through fastpath and sent out:

```
== 2020-06-05 00:16:22.034 +0200 ==
Packet received at fastpath stage, tag 941, type ATOMIC
Packet info: len 66 port 16 interface 16 vsys 1
  wqe index 23554 packet 0x0xc002c83bc0, HA: 0, IC: 0
Packet decoded dump:
L2:    00:0c:29:7a:5e:82->00:0c:29:7e:38:db, type 0x0800
IP:    198.51.100.1->198.51.100.2, protocol 6
       version 4, ihl 5, tos 0x00, len 52,
       id 46303, frag_off 0x4000, ttl 64, checksum 31281(0x317a)
TCP:   sport 22, dport 63571, seq 671986245, ack 4257280359,
       reserved 0, offset 8, window 227, checksum 11152,
       flags 0x10 ( ACK), urgent data 0, 14 data len 0
TCP option:
00000000: 01 01 08 0a 07 57 06 9b  3d 06 e9 01                .....W.. =...
Flow fastpath, session 941 s2c (set work 0xe014cd2080 exclude_video 0 from sp 0xe03cb3ab80 exclude_video
IP checksum valid
NAT session, run address/port translation
CP-DENY TCP non data packet getting through
Forwarding lookup, ingress interface 16
L3 mode, virtual-router 1
Route lookup in virtual-router 1, IP 10.0.0.10
Route found, interface ethernet1/2, zone 2
Resolve ARP for IP 10.0.0.10 on interface ethernet1/2
ARP entry found on interface 17
Transmit packet size 52 on port 17
```

Figure 12.18 – The server ACK at the egress stage

You can take a look at the full `pan_packet_diag.log` log, as well as a transcript of the troubleshooting session and a handy list of the commands, at `https://github.com/PacktPublishing/Mastering-Palo-Alto-Networks`.

In this section, you learned how to collect and read logs from the data plane packet-processing processes. In the next section, we'll learn how to debug other processes.

# Debugging processes

Like all operating systems, both the firewall and Panorama systems have several processes that perform specific tasks. Each of these processes has a log file and a configurable logging level, also called a debug level. By default, most processes have a lowered debug level, so only the most important log entries are written to the log file, which conserves space and is better for retention. Debug levels can be increased, but this could lead to shorter retention, and in some cases, an increase in resource use. You can verify the current debug level of each process by issuing the following command:

```
reaper@pa-220> debug <process name> show
```

You can change the debug level by issuing the following command:

```
reaper@pa-220> debug <process name> on <debug level>
```

You can turn off debugging altogether by issuing the `off` attribute, but I would not recommend turning off logging. Instead, opt for the lowest level of debugging. The following debug levels can be set for most processes:

- `dump` writes everything to log.
- `debug` writes errors, warnings, and informational and debug logs.
- `info` writes errors, warnings, and informational logs. Some daemons use `normal` instead of `info`.
- `warn` writes warning and error logs.
- `error` only writes error messages to log.

> **Important note**
> When you change the debug level of a process, remember to return it to its original setting after you're done debugging.

Depending on the platform, some processes will run on the management plane, while others run on the data plane. Platforms that have multiple data planes have a copy of every data plane process on each data plane. Smaller chassis, such as the PA-800 and PA-220, and virtual systems, such as the PA-VM, only have a single plane, so all processes reside on the management plane. Panorama does not have a data plane and doesn't have data plane processes. Some of the very large platforms have an additional control plane that takes on some of the processes, such as `routed` and `mprelay`. The location of the processes also dictates where their respective logs are stored. To read logs, you can use the `grep`, `less`, or `tail` commands, followed by the log directory and the log file.

The management plane log directory is `mp-log`, the dataplane log directory is `dp-log` (`dp0-log`, `dp1-log`, and so on for systems that have multiple data planes), and `cp-log` is used for systems that have an additional control plane:

```
reaper@pa-220> less mp-log authd.log
reaper@pa-220> tail follow yes mp-log ms.log
reaper@pa-220> grep count yes mp-log authd.log pattern reaper
```

The following is a list of the most important management plane processes/daemons:

- `appweb3-sslvpn` is the GlobalProtect SSL web process.
- `authd` handles the authentication of users logging on to the device.
- `cryptod` takes care of encrypting and decrypting passwords and private keys for the system.
- `devsrvr` is responsible for communicating with the data plane and pushes the configuration to the data plane. It also handles URL filtering queries from the data plane.
- `ha-agent` verifies the HA status and synchronizes configuration to the HA peer.
- `ikemgr` is the ISAKMP daemon.
- `keymgr` is the IPSec key repository.
- `logrcvr` receives and writes logs forwarded by the data plane.
- `masterd` is the master process that ensures all the other processes are running. You can verify the status of all the processes with the following command:

```
reaper@pa-220> show system software status
```

- `management-server` is the management server, which takes care of reporting, configuration management, and distributing commits to all processes. Its log is called `ms.log`.

- `rasmgr` is the backend process for GlobalProtect.

- `routed` is the routing daemon and maintains the routing and forwarding tables and FQDN mapping. It also maintains communication with dynamic routing peers and updates the data plane network chip with routing changes.

- `satd` is the GlobalProtect process for connected satellite devices.

- `sslmgr` performs OCSP and CRL operations and maintains a repository.

- `sysd` manages communication between processes.

- `useridd` maintains communication with the user ID agents.

- `varrcvr` is used to receive PCAP files for threats from the data plane and for WildFire logs. It also processes log forwarding to Panorama and syslog.

The data plane processes are as follows:

- `brdagent` configures and monitors interfaces and networking chips.

- `pan_comm` is the data plane partner process to the device server. It receives `commit` jobs.

- `mprelay` communicates with `routed` (route daemon) to receive routing updates and perform tunnel monitoring. It maintains the forwarding table and brings tunnels up or down.

- `pan_dha` performs high-availability link/path monitoring.

- `Pan_task_*` are the packet forwarding daemons. Each packet processing CPU core runs a `pan_task` process.

> **Important note**
> `pan_task` is a pre-spun-up process, so it will show as using 100% CPU, even when the system is at minimum load.

- `Sysdagent` monitors the data plane and communicates with `sysd` on the management plane.

You can now troubleshoot sessions using global counters and you have learned how to increase the debug level and access log files for specific daemons. In the last section, we will go over some of the most useful CLI commands that can help troubleshoot issues to make your life a lot easier.

# CLI troubleshooting commands cheat sheet

There is plenty of information that you can get from reading logs, but there are many commands that will simplify the search for information by providing the required information directly. In the following table, I have tried to group some of the more interesting commands for you to manage your systems. Unless stated otherwise, all commands are in **Operational Mode**.

The first set of commands are generally useful commands:

| Command | Function |
| --- | --- |
| find command keyword <keyword> | Lets you find any command as long as you know what you're looking for. |
| \| match <value> | Filters the output of a command and only returns the line that has a positive match. |
| \| except <value> | Filters the output of a command and returns everything except the lines that match the value. |
| tcpdump snaplen 0 filter "not port 22" | Captures all sessions on the management interface except sessions on port 22. |
| view-pcap debug-pcap\|filter-pcap\|mgmt-pcap no-dns-lookup | Shows packet captures taken on daemons, via packet-diag or tcpdump. |
| show admins | Shows currently logged-in admins. |
| delete admin-sessions username <user> | Terminates an admin's session. |
| set system setting target-vsys <vsys> | Changes operational commends to a vsys perspective. |
| show authentication allowlist | Shows the allow list for all authentication profiles. |
| show system environmentals | Shows system core temperatures and power levels. |
| scp\|tftp export <thing> to user@destination:/path/ | Many things can be exported from the system, including log files, packet captures, or core files. |

Figure 12.19 – Generally useful commands

The next set provides basic information about the system:

| Basic system information | Function |
| --- | --- |
| show system info | Returns basic device information, such as serial, IP, installed content, and software versions. |
| show system software status | Shows whether all processes are running properly. |
| show system logdb-quota | Returns the LogDB usage. |
| show system disk-space | Returns disk volume information. |
| show jobs all/id | Returns the status of all commit, download, install, and qfdn jobs, and additional details on specific IDs. |
| show system files | Shows wehther any core dump files have been created due to a process crash. |
| request license fetch/info | Retrieves and shows currently active licenses. |
| show netstat all yes | Shows all listening and established connections on the management plane, per process. |
| show chassis-ready | Shows whether the dataplane is ready to process sessions. |
| show panorama-status | Verifies connectivity with panorama. |

Figure 12.20 – System information commands

With the following commands, you will be able to verify and control **HA** modes and make sure the cluster is operating optimally:

| High availability | Function |
|---|---|
| show high-availability state | Shows a quick rundown of the local peer's HA condition. |
| show high-availability all | Summary of all HA runtime. |
| show high-availability state-synchronization | Displays statistics about sent and received sync messages. |
| request high-availability sessions-reestablish force | Re-establishes HA1 link if link was lost; use 'force' if HA1 backup is not configured. |
| show high-availability session-reestablish-status | Shows when HA1 and HA1-backup links were last re-established. |
| request high-availability sync-to-remote running-config | Manually syncs running configuration to peer, in case automatic sync failed or if status is out-of-sync. |
| request high-availability state functional\|suspend | Suspends or activates local device. |
| request high-availability state peer functional\|suspend | Suspends or activates peer device. |
| show high-availability transitions | Indicates how many times a device has transitioned between HA states. |
| show high-availability flap statistics | Details about preemptions 'flaps' (preemption activates device, error encountered again, device non-funct, recovers, preempt activates, error encountered again, and so on). |
| show high-availability control-link statistics | Detailed information about HA1 messages. |

Figure 12.21 – High availability commands

The following commands will tell you more about how the system is performing:

| Performance information | Function |
|---|---|
| show system resources | Shows management plane resource usage, similar to top in linux. |
| show running resource-monitor | Shows data plane CPU core utilization and buffer usage. |
| debug dataplane pool statistics | Shows software buffer pool usage. |
| show session info | Shows number of active sessions, packets per second, thoughput, and other session-related parameters. |
| debug log-receiver statistics | Information on log volume per second and any errors while writing or forwarding log. |
| show system statistics application\|session | Shows live statistics about top applications, or system throughput. |
| show report jobs | Indicates whether reports are currently being generated (this could have an impact on management plane CPU usage). |

Figure 12.22 – Performance-related commands

The DNS proxy is responsible for a couple of important functions within the system. These commands help you check whether the DNS resolution is working as expected:

| DNS operations | Function |
|---|---|
| show system setting ssl-decrypt dns-cache | Shows SSL decryption DNS cache. |
| show dns-proxy cache all | Shows the DNS proxy cache. |
| show system setting ssl-decrypt memory | Shows SSL decryption memory usage. |
| show dns-proxy fqdn all | Shows all FQDN objects with their resolved IP addresses. |
| request system fqdn refresh | Refreshes all FQDN objects. |
| debug dataplane internal vif link | Returns statistics on the internal hardwre interfaces. |

Figure 12.23 – DNS proxy commands

The following commands will help you verify whether sessions are running into unexpected configurations or other issues:

| Packet flow | Function |
|---|---|
| show counter global filter delta yes | Shows global counters. |
| show session all filter <filters> | Shows active, discard, and predict sessions matching the filter (or 'all' sessions). |
| set session offload yes\|no | Enables and disables session offloading to hardware. |
| set session tcp-reject-non-syn yes\|no | Disables dropping TCP ACK packets coming in without a proper handshake. |
| # set deviceconfig setting tcp asymmetric-path bypass\|drop | Disables dropping packets that arrive out of window or out of sync. |

Figure 12.24 – Packet flow commands

The next set of commands lets you verify routing, routing protocol, and MAC and ARP information:

| Layers 2 and 3 | Function |
|---|---|
| show routing route | Outputs the routing table (Routing Information Base, or rib). |
| show routing fib | Shows the forwarding table (Forwarding Information Base). |
| show arp all | Shows the content of the ARP table (layer 3). |
| show mac all | Shows the content of the MAC table (layer 2). |
| show routing protocol ospf\|bgp\|rip summary | Returns a summary of the OSPF, BGP or RIP status. |
| show routing resource | Verifies the number of routes is not reaching the system limits. |
| debug routing pcap ospf\|bgp\|rip on\|off | Enables/disables packet captures on the routing engine for the routing protocol. Use for troubleshooting only. |

Figure 12.25 – Layer 2 and layer 3 information

NAT, QoS, and zone/DoS protection depend on memory pools. The following commands help you verify that the system isn't being oversubscribed:

| Policies | Function |
|---|---|
| show running nat-policy | Shows all active NAT rules. |
| show running nat-rule-ippool rule <rulename> | Shows memory usage, over-subscription ratio, and allocations per rule. |
| show running global-ippool | Shows runtime statistics for global dynamic source NAT. |
| show running ippool | Shows overall source NAT statistics. |
| show session all filter qos-class [1-8] | Displays all sessions that match a specific QoS class. |
| show qos interface <interface> counter | Shows general counter on QoS configured on an interface. |
| show qos interface <interface> throughput <Qid as seen in counters> | Returns actual throughput for a Qid on an interface. |
| show zone-protection zone <zone> | Shows zone protection statistics for the zone. |
| show dos-protection rule <rulename> statistics | Shows statistics for a dos-protection rule. |
| show dos-protection zone <zone> blocked source | Shows which IP addresses are currently being blocked due to DoS protection. |

Figure 12.26 – Memory pool used by rules

URL filtering uses a data plane cache to store the most popular and most recently visited URLs. The management plane holds a larger cache of the most popular URLs. Initially, the cloud seed file is used to populate the management plane cache with the most popular URLs per region, and over time, the cache will start to retain the URLs most commonly used within your organization. When a URL is accessed that is now known to the data plane cache, a lookup is performed on the management plane cache. If the management plane does not have an entry for the URL, a cloud lookup will be performed. The following commands help you manage and maintain these caches:

| URL filtering | Function |
|---|---|
| test url-info-cloud <url> | Shows the category for a URL via cloud lookup. |
| test url-info-host <url> | Shows the category for a URL in the management plane cache. |
| show running url | Shows the category for a URL in the dataplane cache. |
| request url-filtering update url <url> | Refreshes the management plane cache entry for a URL with a cloud lookup. |
| show running url-cache all | Outputs the URL cache to mp-log dp_url_DB.log. |
| show running url-cache statistics | Shows memory usage of the URL cache. |
| show url-cloud status | Returns connectivity information for URL lookup cloud connections. |
| clear url-cache all\|url <url> | Clears a single URL from cache, or the entire cache from the dataplane. |
| delete url-database all\|url | Clears a single URL from cache, or the entire cache from the management plane. |

Figure 12.27 – URL filtering commands

Panorama has a few unique commands that can assist in troubleshooting log forwarding from firewalls:

| Panorama | Function |
|---|---|
| show logging-status device <serial> | Returns log forwarding information for a device logging to Panorama. |
| debug log-collector log-collection-stats show incoming-logs | Shows incoming log statistics, including the current log rate. |
| show system raid detail | Shows RAID array information on an M appliance. |
| show system disk details | Shows disk status information on a VM appliance. |
| replace old <serial> new <serial> | Replaces a managed device's serial with a new one after an RMA. This loads all the configuration previously associated with one device with a new one without needing to go in and assign configuration to the new serial (it removes the old serial). |
| request log-fwd-ctrl action latest\|start-from-lastack device <serial> | Starts log forwarding from device from the last log\|last acked log. |
| request log-fwd-ctrl start\|stop latest device <serial> | Starts or stops log forwarding from a device to panorama with buffering. |
| request log-fwd-ctrl action live device <serial> | Starts log forwarding without buffering (this could cause a large flood of inbound logs). |

Figure 12.28 – Panorama commands

Here are a few commands that are useful when troubleshooting IPSec phase 1 and phase 2 issues:

| IPSec | Function |
|---|---|
| show running tunnel flow info | Shows basic statistics about all VPN tunnels. |
| test vpn ike-sa gateway <gateway> | Initiates an IKE negotiation with the designated gateway. |
| test vpn ipsec-sa tunnel <tunnel> | Initiates an IPSec negotiation for the designated tunnel. |
| clear vpn ike-sa gateway <gateway> | Clears the IKE SA for a given gateway. |
| clear vpn ipsec-sa tunnel <tunnel> | Clears the IPSec SA for a given tunnel. |
| show vpn ike-sa gateway <gateway> | Shows the IKE SA for a given gateway. |
| show vpn ipsec-sa tunnel <tunnel> | Shows the IPSec SA for a given tunnel. |
| show global-protect-gateway current-satellite | Shows currently connected satellites to GlobalProtect. |
| show global-protect-gateway current-user | Shows currently connected users to GlobalProtect. |

Figure 12.29 – IPSec troubleshooting commands

User identification has many facets, from user-to-IP mapping to group mapping. The following commands will help verify whether all the information is being collected properly:

| User-ID | Function |
|---|---|
| show user ip-user-mapping all\|ip | Shows all mapped users or the mapped user(s) for a specific IP on the dataplane. |
| show user ip-user-mapping-mp all\|ip | Shows all mapped users or the mapped user(s) for a specific IP on the management plane. |
| debug user-id refresh group-mapping all | Refreshes group-mapping memberships. |
| show user group list | Shows all groups used in group-mapping. |
| show user group name <group> | Shows all members of a group. |
| show user group-mapping state all | Shows the state of all group-mapping profiles. |
| show user group-mapping statistics | Shows last/next refresh of group mapping. |
| show user user-id-agent statistics \| state all | Shows user-ID agent state and statistics. |
| show user ts-agent statistics \|state all | Shows terminal server agent state and statistics. |
| show user server-monitor statistics\|state all | Shows the state of the agentless user-ID agent. |
| show user ip-port-user-mapping all | Shows user-to-port mapping for terminal server agents or a specific server IP. |

Figure 12.30 – User-ID troubleshooting commands

There are a few useful commands to verify whether WildFire is working as expected:

| WildFire | Function |
| --- | --- |
| show wildfire status | Shows connection status to the WildFire cloud. |
| show sildfire statistics | Shows file transfer statistics. |
| test wildfire registration | Tests connectivity to the WildFire cloud. |

Figure 12.31 – WildFire

The following are a few useful commands to take control of DHCP on the firewall:

| DHCP | Function |
| --- | --- |
| show dhcp server lease all | Shows all DHCP leases. |
| clear dhcp lease interface <interface> ip\|mac\|expiredonly <value> | Clears a lease for an IP or MAC address, or all the expired ones. |
| debug dhcpd pcap on\|off | Enables packet capture of DHCP transactions on the daemon. |
| show dhcp client state <interface> | Shows DHCP information for an interface that is a DHCP client. |
| request dhcp client release\|renew <interface> | Releases or renews DHCP client lease for a DHCP client interface. |

Figure 12.32 – DHCP commands

The following commands are extremely versatile and let you extract just about any details from the system. They help determine what limits the system has, the memory addresses, the temperatures, the fan speeds, all of the configuration elements, the interface states, and even what kind of fiber optic transceiver is installed:

| Device state | Function |
| --- | --- |
| show system state | This command returns the state of the entire device. |
| show system state filter env.* | Shows system core temperatures and power levels. |
| show system state \| match fan | Searches the system state for any line containing 'fan' to find fan speeds. |
| show system state \| match cfg.general.max | Returns the maximum number of configurable objects the system supports. |
| show system state filter-pretty sys.s1.* | Shows information about all the interfaces in slot 1. |

Figure 12.33 – Device state

All the preceding commands can also be accessed from
`https://github.com/PacktPublishing/Mastering-Palo-Alto-Networks/blob/master/chapter%2012%20-%20CLI%20cheat%20sheet`.

The CLI commands we learned about in this section will help troubleshoot and debug most issues you will encounter. Make sure you keep the cheat sheet close by, and when in doubt, remember to fall back on the *find command* keyword as this has saved me numerous times.

# Summary

In this chapter, you learned how to use global counters to find out what is happening to a session and how to interpret the output. You are now able to collect deep-dive logs for each process that touches a session and should be able to add additional logging to suit explicit scenarios. You should also be able to organize a troubleshooting session efficiently so that you can get to the root cause of an issue much more quickly than you would have done before. The cheat sheet of CLI commands provided here should come in handy to collect any additional information.

In the next chapter, we will look at some handy tools that will help to keep track of the system's health and help identify trends so that action can be taken before issues emerge.

# 13
# Supporting Tools

In this chapter, we will be taking a look at a few tools that can make managing your firewalls and keeping an eye on the overall health of your organization straightforward. Many organizations have monitoring tools, such as **Security Information and Event Management (SIEM)**, in place that already collect and aggregate information from many systems just to keep track of important incidents or to keep on top of change management. We will learn about a couple of handy add-ons that elevate an admin's visibility into the system health or network security. We will also look at an interesting and convenient (and free!) tool that aggregates and helps to enforce external threat intelligence feeds. Lastly, we will have a look at the **Application Programming Interface (API)**.

In this chapter, we're going to cover the following main topics:

- Integrating Palo Alto Networks with Splunk
- Monitoring with Pan(w)achrome
- Threat intelligence with MineMeld
- Exploring the API

# Technical requirements

This chapter will demonstrate several ways to connect the firewall to an external monitoring or management device. Access to a lab environment to install some of these tools can be helpful to gain an insight into what information can be extracted that is most useful to your organization. We will be running one of the tools in a Docker container.

You can find instructions on how to install Docker at their official page: `https://docs.docker.com/engine/install/`

# Integrating Palo Alto Networks with Splunk

Splunk is a popular log aggregator and analyzer that can collect logs from many different sources and return information gathered from those logs in a wide variety of dashboards and "single panes of glass." To connect a firewall to Splunk, you will first need to set up a `syslog-ng` server to receive syslog messages from the firewall. Take the following steps to prepare your Splunk instance.

Depending on your flavor of Linux, the following instructions may vary. I've included `yum` and `apt-get`:

1.  You may need to uninstall `rsyslog` as per Splunk's recommendations:

    ```
    sudo rpm -e --nodeps rsyslog
    sudo apt-get remove rsyslog
    ```

2.  Install `syslog-ng`:

    ```
    sudo yum-get install syslog-ng
    sudo apt-get install syslog-ng
    ```

3.  Once the installation is complete, start `syslog`:

    ```
    sudo systemctl start syslog-ng.service
    sudo systemctl enable syslog-ng.service
    ```

4.  Lastly, verify whether `syslog-ng` is running by fetching the process ID:

```
sudo pidof syslog-ng
```

Once you are logged in to the Splunk portal, from the main screen, click on **Add Data** and, in the next screen, search for `Palo Alto Networks` (or `Palo`, as you can see in the following screenshot), and then click on the **Configure now** link on the output:

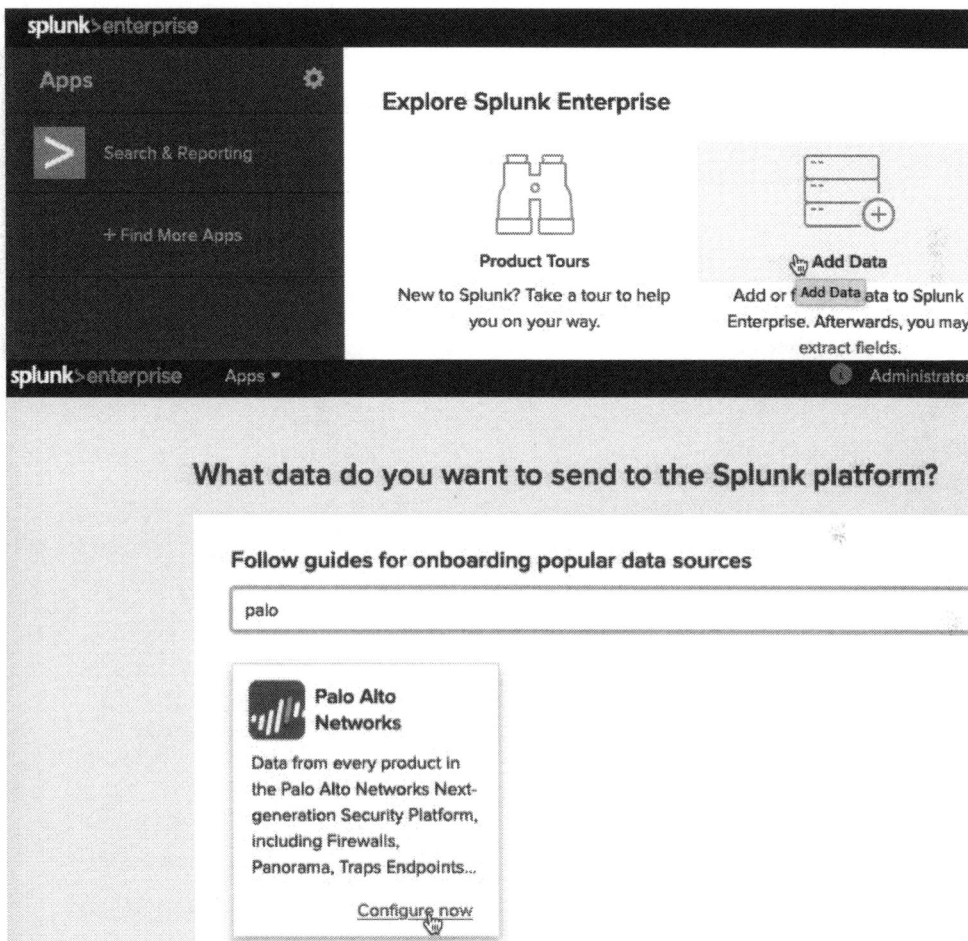

Figure 13.1 – Adding Splunk data

The next few steps, as shown in the following screenshot, guide you through the process and even give you step-by-step instructions on how to uninstall `rsyslogd` so that it can be replaced by `syslog-ng` on your Splunk server and so that you will be able to receive Palo Alto log files:

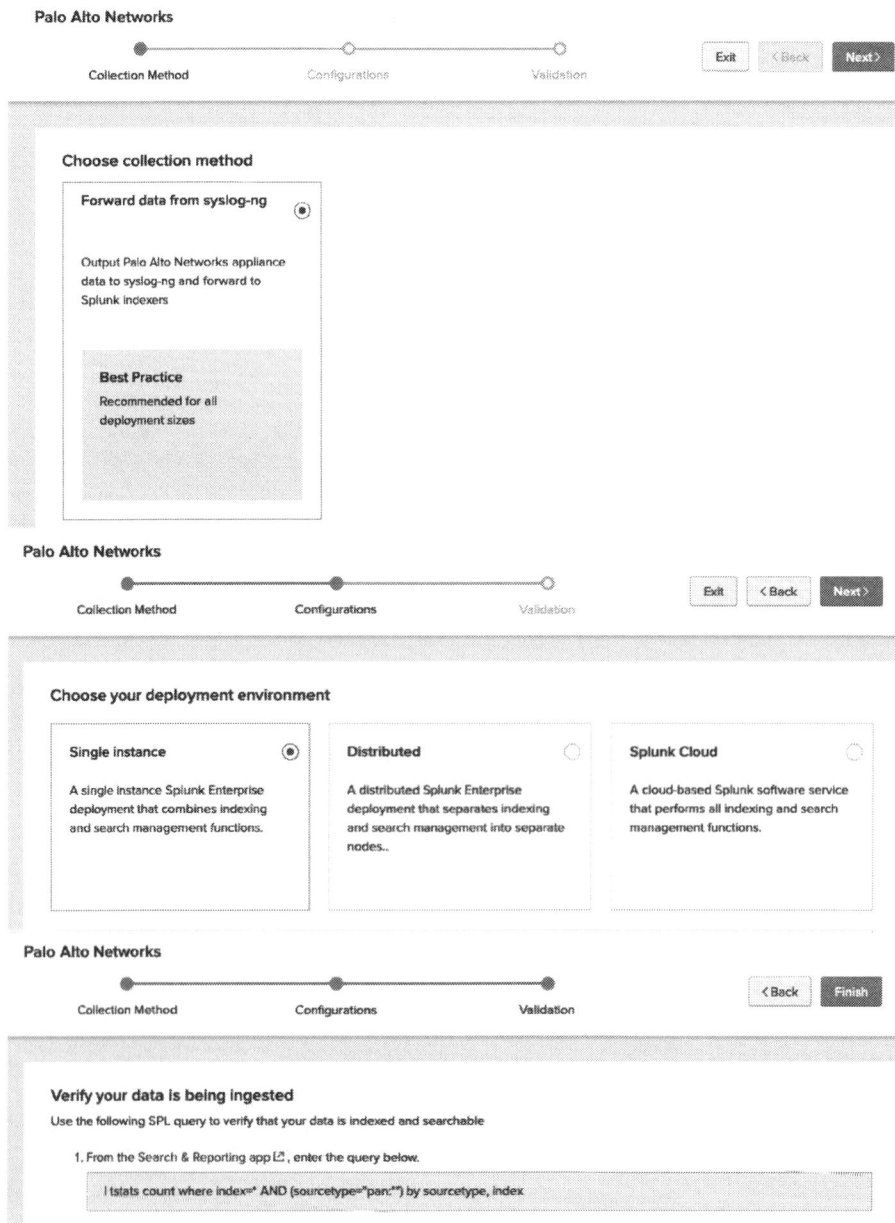

Figure 13.2 – Setting up data collection

The next step is to install the Palo Alto Networks applications by returning to the main page and clicking on + **Find More Apps**. In the application library, you can search for `Palo Alto`, which will return two applications:

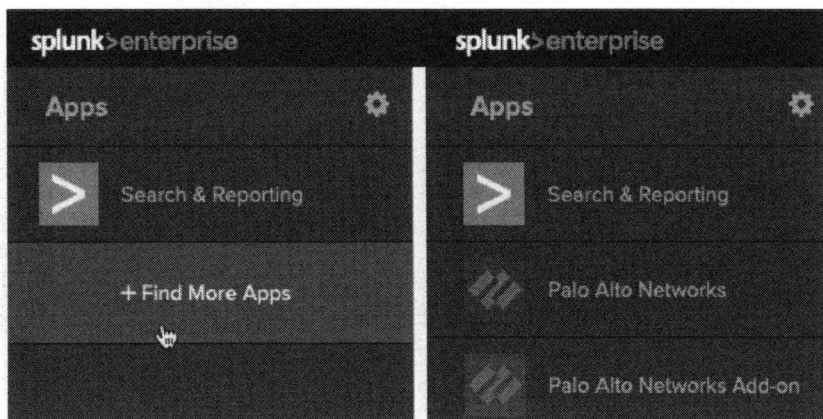

Figure 13.3 – Adding the Palo Alto applications

The first application provides log correlation for ingested logs and provides several dashboards with summary information, as you can see in the following screenshot. The second application can be used to correlate the MineMeld, Aperture, and Autofocus feeds:

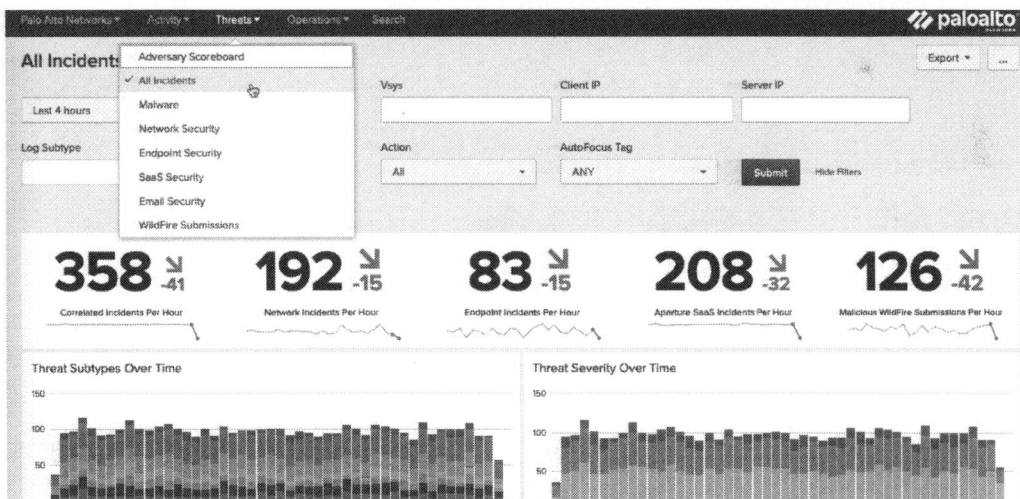

Figure 13.4 – Splunk threat dashboard

For all of this information to be made available to Splunk, you need to set up log forwarding on the firewall or Panorama.

In **Device | Server Profiles | Syslog**, or **Panorama | Server Profiles | Syslog**, create
a **Syslog** profile that points to the Splunk server:

1. Click on **Add** and name the profile `Splunk`.

2. Click on **Add** to create a new server and set the server hostname.

3. Set the IP of the Splunk server.

4. Set the protocol and port. The default is **UDP** on port `514`. Check your specific
   configuration as it may be configured differently.

5. Set the supported format to **BSD** or **IETF**.

6. Set the appropriate facility used by your syslog installation.

Then, for firewalls, in **Objects | Log Forwarding**, create or update the log forwarding
profile called `default` and add the **splunk** profile to **SysLog** for all log types, as shown in
the following screenshot.

Make sure the profile is also added to your security rules in **Policy | Security**:

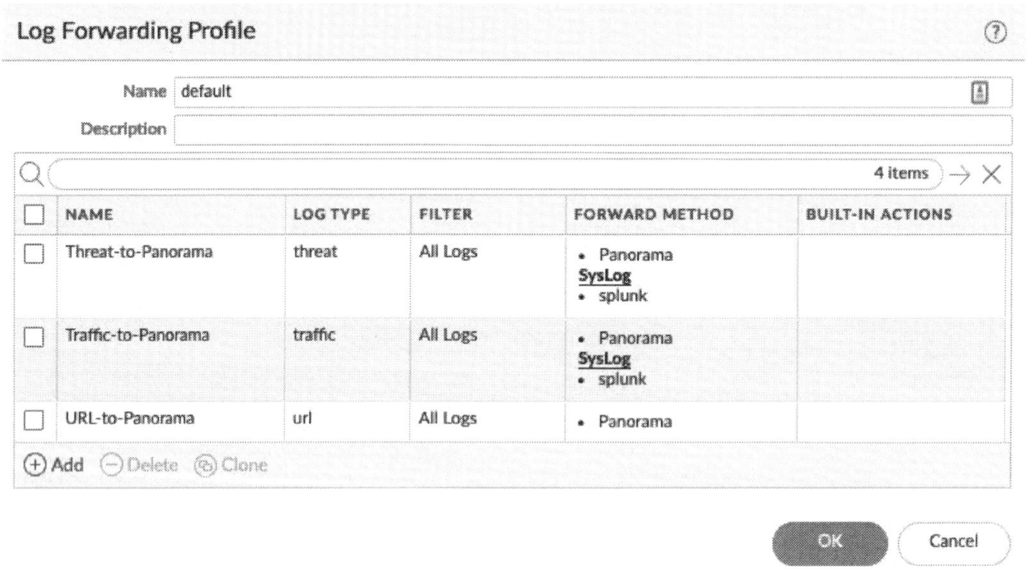

| Log Forwarding Profile | | | | | ⑦ |
|---|---|---|---|---|---|
| Name | default | | | | 🔋 |
| Description | | | | | |

| | NAME | LOG TYPE | FILTER | FORWARD METHOD | BUILT-IN ACTIONS |
|---|---|---|---|---|---|
| ☐ | Threat-to-Panorama | threat | All Logs | • Panorama<br>**SysLog**<br>• splunk | |
| ☐ | Traffic-to-Panorama | traffic | All Logs | • Panorama<br>**SysLog**<br>• splunk | |
| ☐ | URL-to-Panorama | url | All Logs | • Panorama | |

⊕ Add  ⊖ Delete  ⊛ Clone

OK      Cancel

Figure 13.5 – Default log forwarding profile

Next, add a log forwarding profile in **Device | Log Settings** for the **System**, **Configuration**, **User-ID**, **HIP Match**, and **GlobalProtect** logs, as illustrated in the following screenshot, for a firewall. Repeat the log forwarding on Panorama in **Panorama | Log Settings**. Splunk can correlate these events as well and provide a simplified dashboard for these logs:

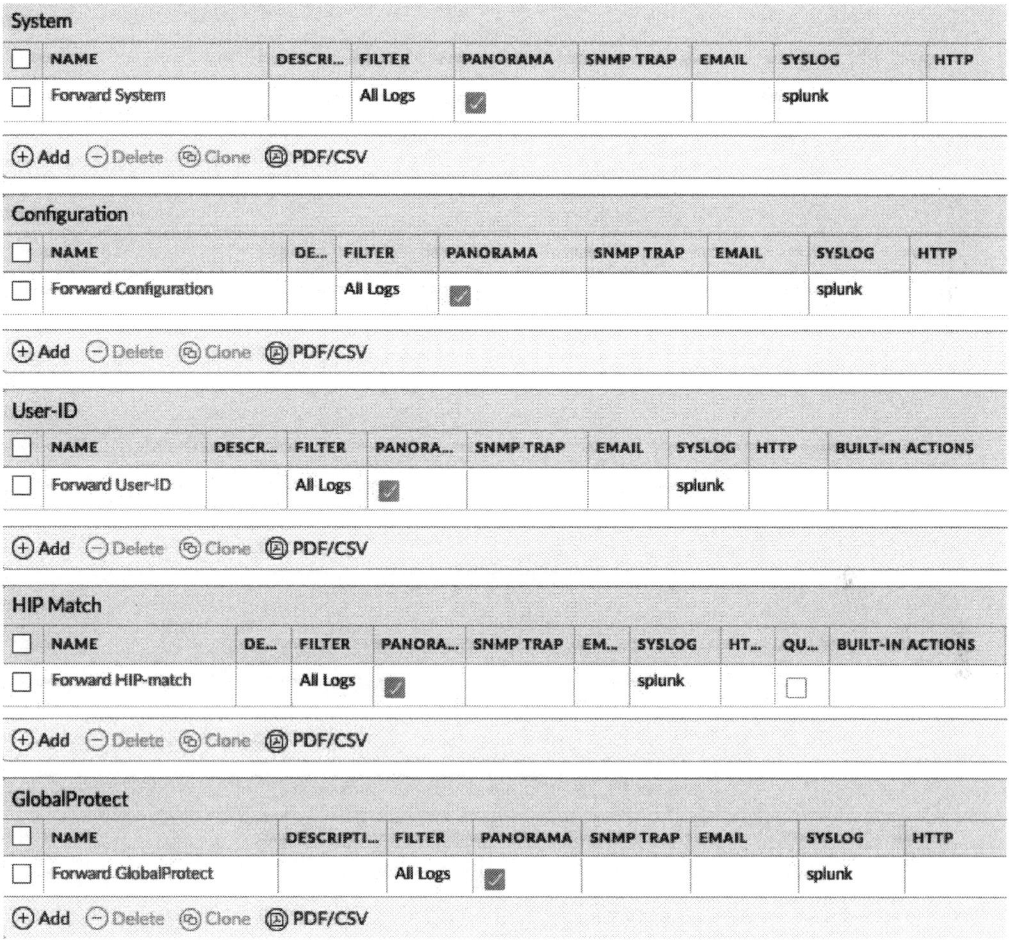

**System**

| | NAME | DESCRI... | FILTER | PANORAMA | SNMP TRAP | EMAIL | SYSLOG | HTTP |
|---|---|---|---|---|---|---|---|---|
| ☐ | Forward System | | All Logs | ☑ | | | splunk | |

⊕ Add  ⊖ Delete  ⊚ Clone  🄳 PDF/CSV

**Configuration**

| | NAME | DE... | FILTER | PANORAMA | SNMP TRAP | EMAIL | SYSLOG | HTTP |
|---|---|---|---|---|---|---|---|---|
| ☐ | Forward Configuration | | All Logs | ☑ | | | splunk | |

⊕ Add  ⊖ Delete  ⊚ Clone  🄳 PDF/CSV

**User-ID**

| | NAME | DESCR... | FILTER | PANORA... | SNMP TRAP | EMAIL | SYSLOG | HTTP | BUILT-IN ACTIONS |
|---|---|---|---|---|---|---|---|---|---|
| ☐ | Forward User-ID | | All Logs | ☑ | | | splunk | | |

⊕ Add  ⊖ Delete  ⊚ Clone  🄳 PDF/CSV

**HIP Match**

| | NAME | DE... | FILTER | PANORA... | SNMP TRAP | EM... | SYSLOG | HT... | QU... | BUILT-IN ACTIONS |
|---|---|---|---|---|---|---|---|---|---|---|
| ☐ | Forward HIP-match | | All Logs | ☑ | | | splunk | | ☐ | |

⊕ Add  ⊖ Delete  ⊚ Clone  🄳 PDF/CSV

**GlobalProtect**

| | NAME | DESCRIPTI... | FILTER | PANORAMA | SNMP TRAP | EMAIL | SYSLOG | HTTP |
|---|---|---|---|---|---|---|---|---|
| ☐ | Forward GlobalProtect | | All Logs | ☑ | | | splunk | |

⊕ Add  ⊖ Delete  ⊚ Clone  🄳 PDF/CSV

Figure 13.6 – Device log settings

Besides server-installed correlation engines, there are also lightweight browser plugins to keep an eye on your device's health, as we'll see in the next section.

# Monitoring with Pan(w)achrome

Some monitoring tools come in very simple packaging, such as the Chrome browser extension Pan(w)achrome (also known as **Panachrome**). You can install the extension right from the Chrome web store:

1. Open `https://chrome.google.com/webstore/category/extensions` in the Chrome browser.

2. Search for `pan(w)achrome`.

3. Click on **Add to Chrome**, as shown in the following screenshot:

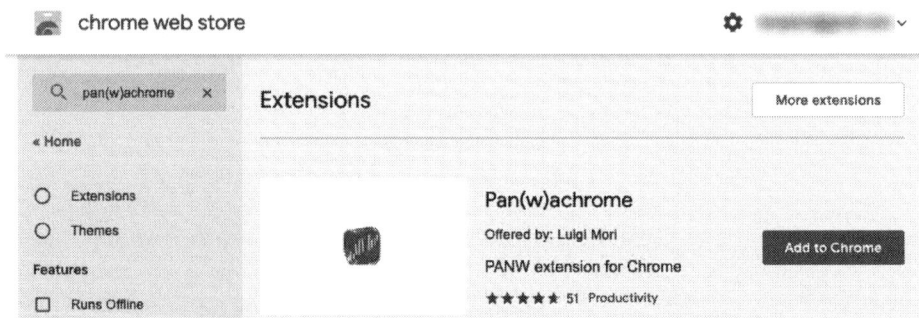

Figure 13.7 – Adding the Pan(w)achrome extension to Chrome

4. Once the extension is installed, the icon will appear in your extension quick launch.

5. Click on the icon to go to the landing page, where you can add new firewalls, as shown in the following screenshot:

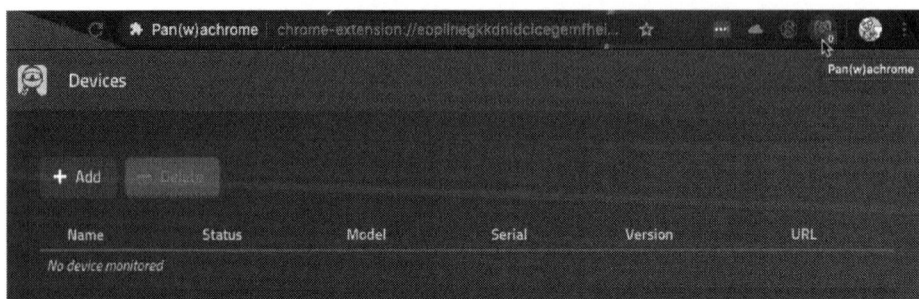

Figure 13.8 – Pan(w)achrome managed devices

6. Click on the **Add** button and add the firewall by its URL.

7. Select whether you want to authenticate using an API key or username and password.

The API key can be easily extracted from each firewall using the following command:

```
curl -k -X GET 'https://<firewall>/
api/?type=keygen&user=<username>&password=<password>'
```

Alternatively, use the following URL in a browser:

```
https://<firewall>/
api/?type=keygen&user=<username>&password=<password>
```

The output will look similar to the following. You will need to collect the string of text between the `<key>` and `</key>` tags without including the tags themselves:

```
<response status = 'success'><result>
<key>LUFRPT1OQ3JTZCM2Z4Yk91OE5EDSGF345YQ==</key> </
result></response>
```

8. You can now use the API key to add a new device, as in the following screenshot:

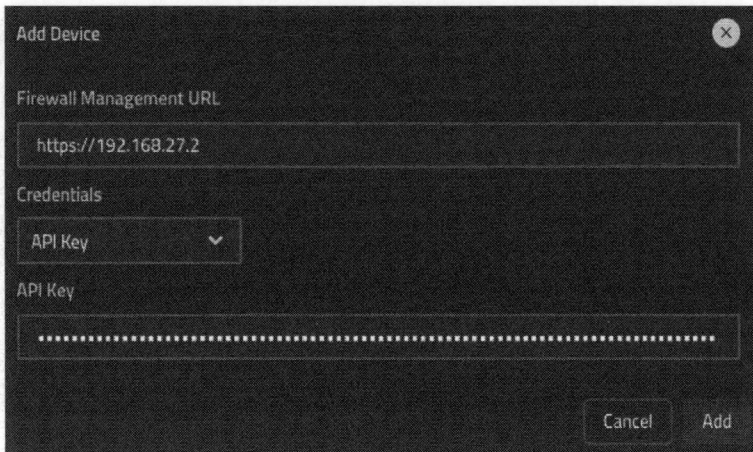

Figure 13.9 – Adding a new device

9.  Once the device is added, it will appear in the list of managed devices with some basic information, as you can see in the following screenshot:

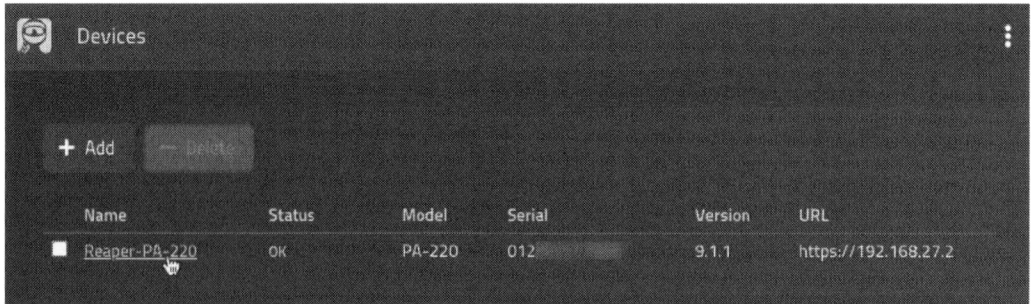

Figure 13.10 – Managed devices

The plugin is now installed and ready to go. You can now click on the device name to go to the dashboard, where you will see the following overview page, containing a live view of the current ingress, egress, active sessions, and connections per second:

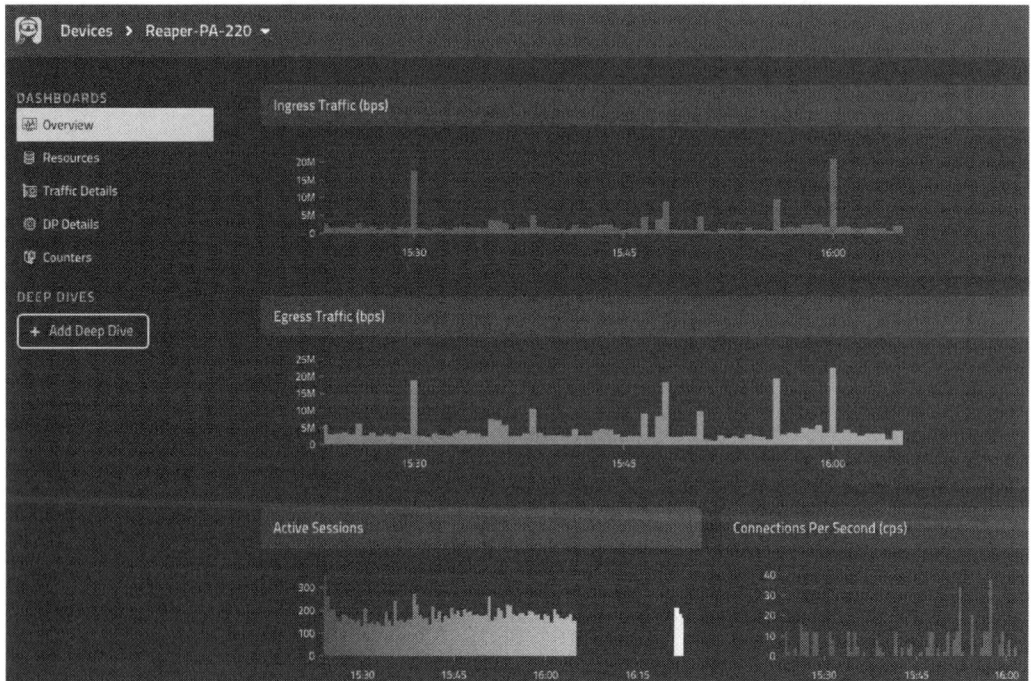

Figure 13.11 – Panachrome overview

> **Important note**
>
> The statistics will start to be collected once the gateway is added to the extension for as long as the browser is open. This is not a typical data collection tool as it does not keep a log and all the data is reset once Chrome is closed, including the connected gateways. A future version plans to contain gateway retention (you can keep track of updates via `https://www.pangurus.com/forum/panachrome`).

The other dashboards also provide valuable live output from your system. This is one of the traits Panachrome puts forward that none of the other tools are quite able to match :

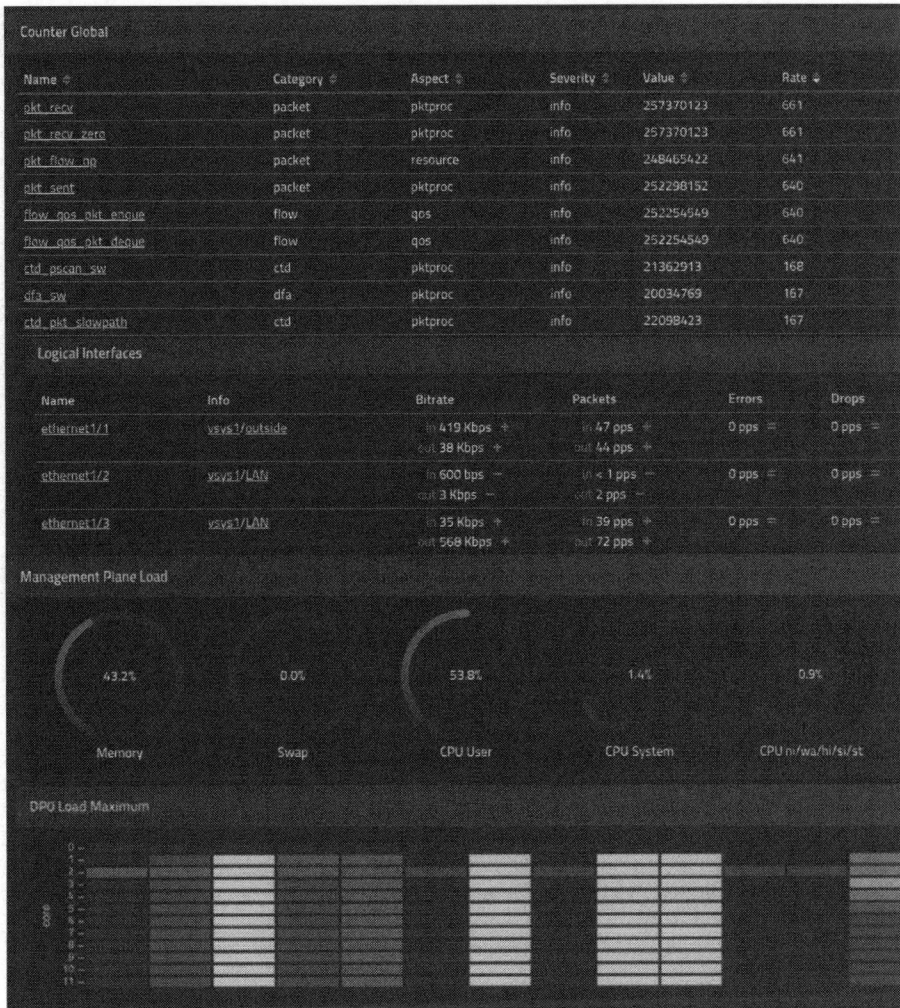

Figure 13.12 – The other default dashboards

Another cool feature is the ability to add deep-dive dashboards that contain more specific information (and where more options will become available in the future). You can add monitoring for GlobalProtect activity or SSL decryption, as well as add zone-specific dashboards. This can come in real handy when keeping a close eye on system health and user activity in times of heightened remote work:

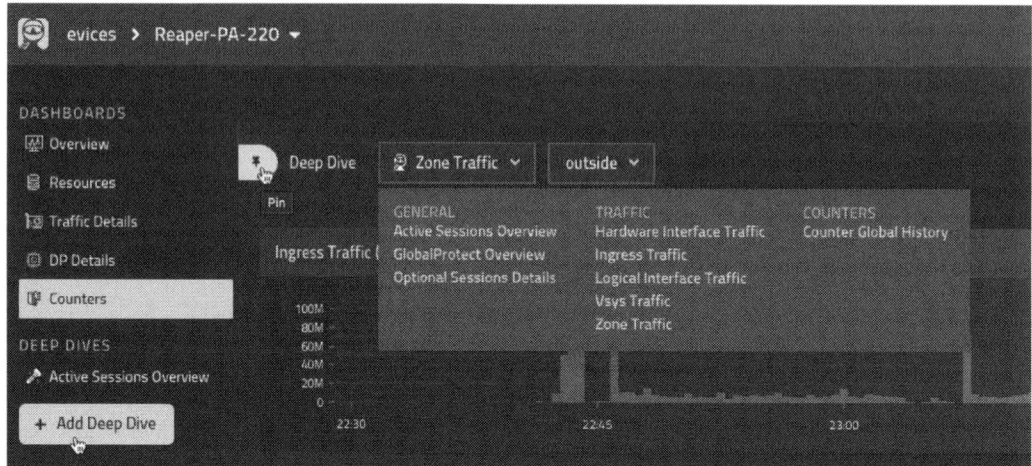

Figure 13.13 – Deep-dive dashboards

You can now leverage a simple but powerful browser plugin to keep an eye on the overall health of your firewalls without needing to go to a management or monitoring portal. In the next section, we'll learn how to consolidate freely available and powerful threat intelligence data.

# Threat intelligence with MineMeld

MineMeld is a tool provided by Palo Alto Networks and is an extensible threat intelligence processing framework. This means it is able to ingest several threat intelligence feeds and aggregate the information so that you can feed it into the firewall as an additional protection vector, which is pretty cool.

The installation is straightforward, and you can even run it in a Docker container:

```
sudo docker pull paloaltonetworks/minemeld
sudo docker volume create minemeld-logs
sudo docker volume create minemeld-local
sudo docker run -dit --name minemeld --restart unless-stopped
--tmpfs /run -v minemeld-local:/opt/minemeld/local -v minemeld-
```

```
logs:/opt/minemeld/log  -p 443:443 -p 80:80 paloaltonetworks/
minemeld
```

MineMeld can now be accessed via `https://<hostIP>`.

> **Important note**
> The `-p 443:443 -p 80:80` flags tell Docker which host ports to map
> to the container ports – in this case, ports `443` and `80` on the host are directly
> mapped to the same ports in the container. To change the ports that should be
> mapped to the host, change the first number – for example, `-p 8443:443`
> `-p 8080:80` would make the MineMeld instance available on ports `8443`
> and `8080` on the host IP or the `https://<HostIP>:8443` hostname.

By default, MineMeld will already take in information from `dshield` and `spamhaus`.
DShield is a project by the SANS internet storm center and Spamhaus is an international
non-profit organization. Both organizations track malicious activity on the internet and
maintain a live database of hosts that are involved in these activities.

When you log on to MineMeld, you are presented with the dashboard, as you can see in
the following screenshot. The dashboard provides an overview of the overall state of the
miners and outputs and the number of indicator updates that have taken place in the last
hour, 24 hours, 7 days, or 30 days:

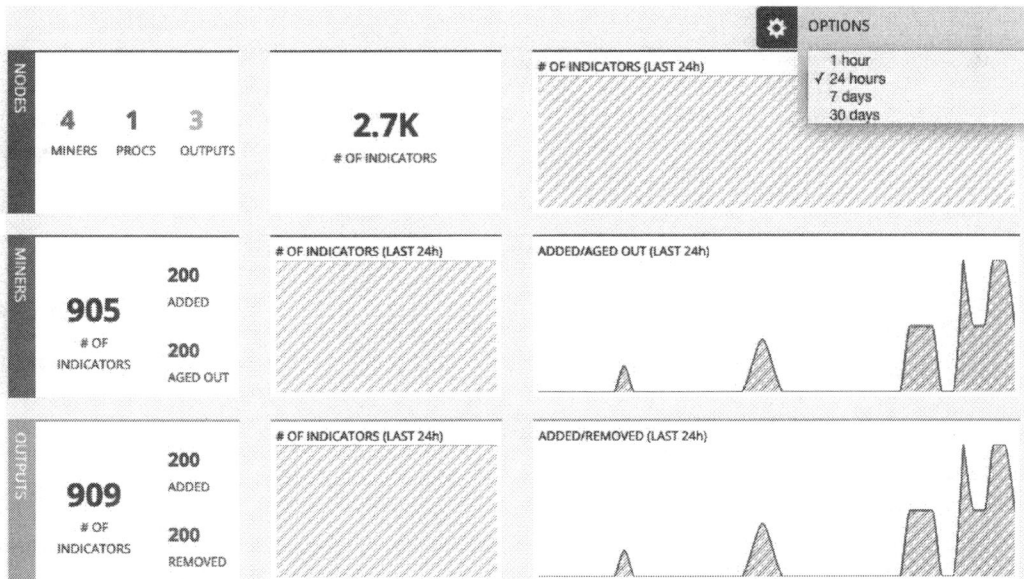

Figure 13.14 – The MineMeld dashboard

You can also create your own inputs from paid services or custom threat intelligence collectors inside your network.

In the following diagram, you can see how all the components are connected. The green input nodes, called **miners**, collect **indicators** from external services. The indicators are forwarded or removed to the red **processor**, which aggregates the data. The aggregated indicators are then forwarded to the yellow **output nodes**. The thickness of the gray line indicates the volume of updates that a certain miner has forwarded recently:

CONNECTION GRAPH

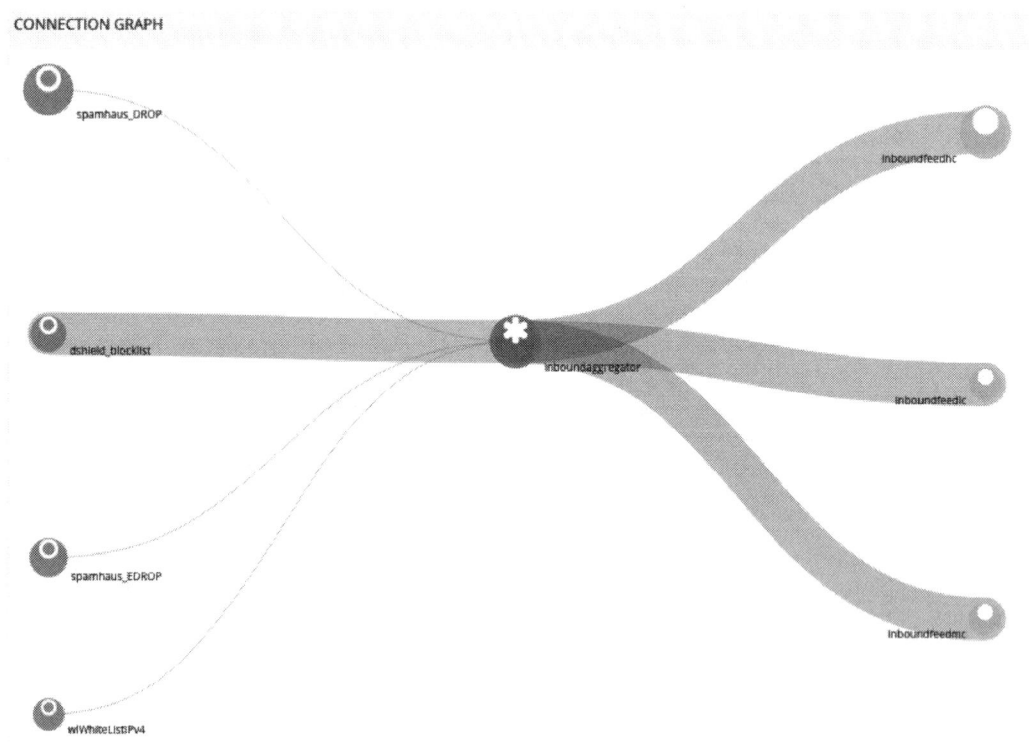

Figure 13.15 – MineMeld miners to output nodes

The default output nodes have been set so that they accept indicators depending on the confidence score assigned by the input node:

- `inboundfeedhc` only accepts a confidence score that is >75.

- `inboundfeedmc` accepts a confidence score that is >50 but <75.

- `inboundfeedlc` accepts a confidence score that is <50.

As you can see in the following screenshot, you can access all the existing nodes from the **NODES** menu. Clicking on each will bring up its status and statistics:

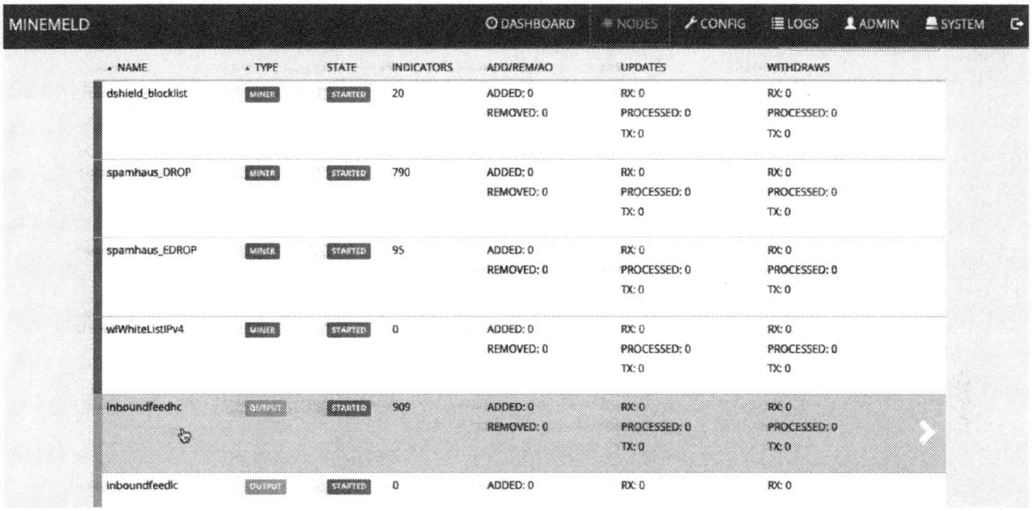

Figure 13.16 – MineMeld nodes

If you click one of the miners, you will get a new window showing its status and the prototype used for the miner, as in the following screenshot:

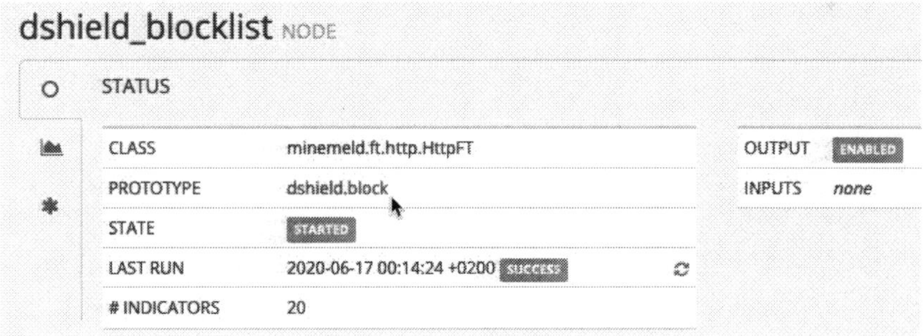

Figure 13.17 – Miner details

A prototype in MineMeld is basically the configuration that makes up a node. At the top, it indicates whether the prototype is a miner, a processor, or an output and whether it is stable or experimental. There is some basic information about where the node came from and who the author is, whether the indicators are IPv4, IPv6, and/or URLs, and the configuration associated with the node.

You can view many more prototypes by going to the **Config** page and clicking on **browse prototypes** in the bottom-right corner, as you can see in the following screenshot, or by manually browsing to `https://<minemeld>/#/prototypes`:

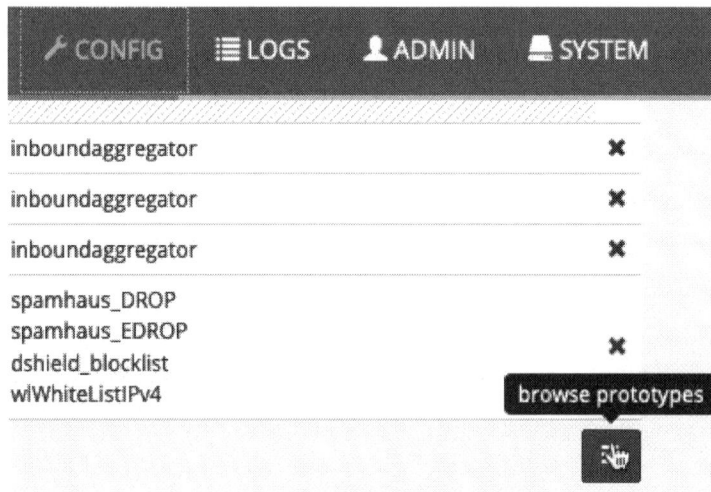

Figure 13.18 – browse prototypes

Once you find a prototype you like, you can either select to turn it into a node or create a new prototype using that node as a template, as you can see in the following screenshot:

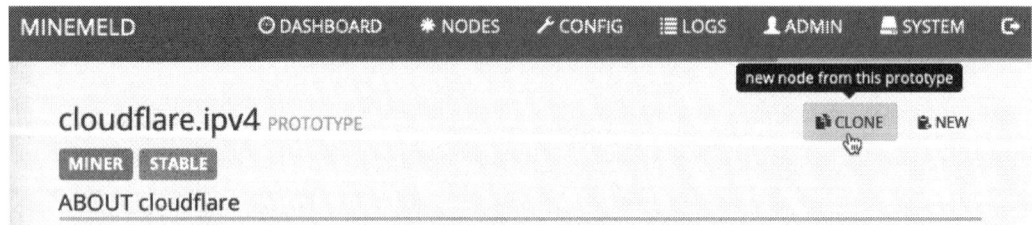

Figure 13.19 – Turning a prototype into a node

Once you select to create a new node from a template, you are asked to provide a name for the node and are then brought back to the **Config** page. Here, you should click on the **INPUTS** column of the processor and add the new miner, as follows. Lastly, you must click on **Commit** to activate the configuration and start the new miner:

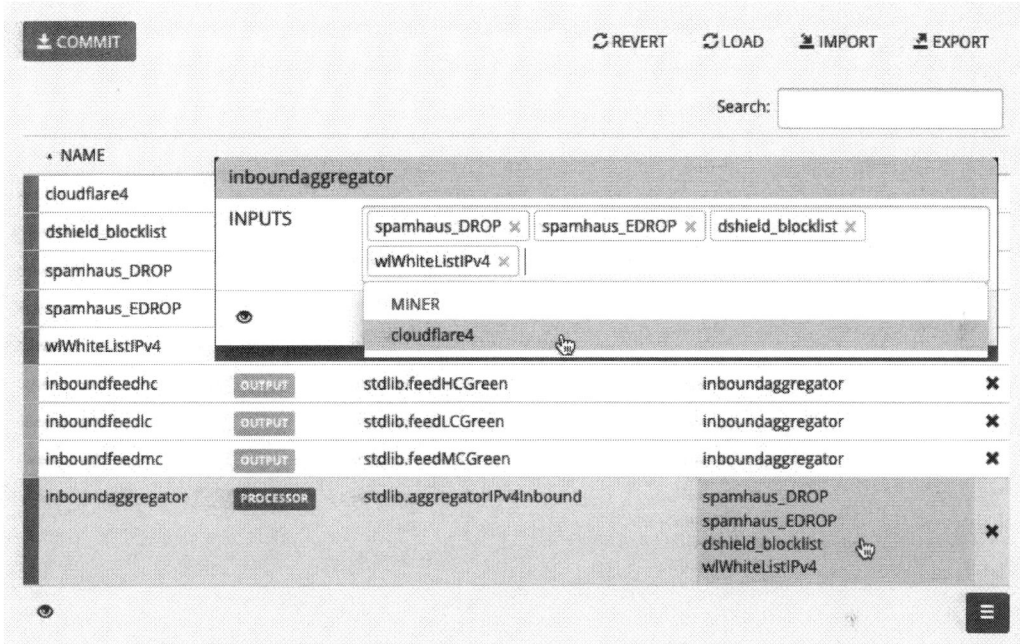

Figure 13.20 – Adding a miner to the processor

Now, go back to the **Nodes** page and click any of the output nodes. This will bring up the **FEED BASE URL** fields, as you can see in the following screenshot:

Figure 13.21 – inboundfeedhc details

Now, follow these steps to create an **External Dynamic List** (**EDL**) on the firewall:

1.  Copy the feed base URL (`https://<HostIP>/feeds/inboundfeedhc`).

2.  In the firewall, go to **Objects | External Dynamic List**.

3.  Create a new EDL and call it `Minemeld feed`.

4.  Set **Type** to **IP List**.

5.  Set **Source** to the feed base URL.

6.  Set the update interval (**Five Minute**, **Hourly**, **Daily**, **Weekly**, or **Monthly**).

7.  You can click on **Test Source URL** to make sure the firewall is able to fetch the IP list:

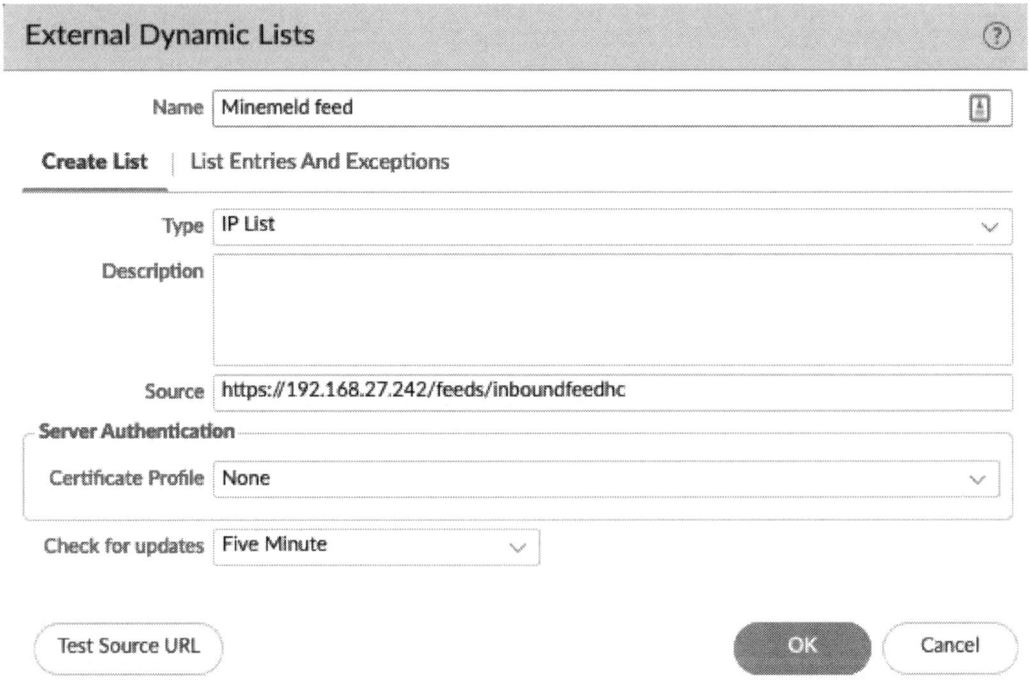

**External Dynamic Lists**                                                ⑦

Name | Minemeld feed

**Create List**   |   List Entries And Exceptions

Type | IP List
Description |

Source | https://192.168.27.242/feeds/inboundfeedhc

┌ Server Authentication ──────────────────────────────────
Certificate Profile | None
└────────────────────────────────────────────────────────

Check for updates | Five Minute

Test Source URL                                    OK          Cancel

Figure 13.22 – Firewall EDLs

Once you save the change to the firewall, it will start fetching the IP list and you can reopen the object to review the list and even make manual exceptions, as you can see in the following screenshot:

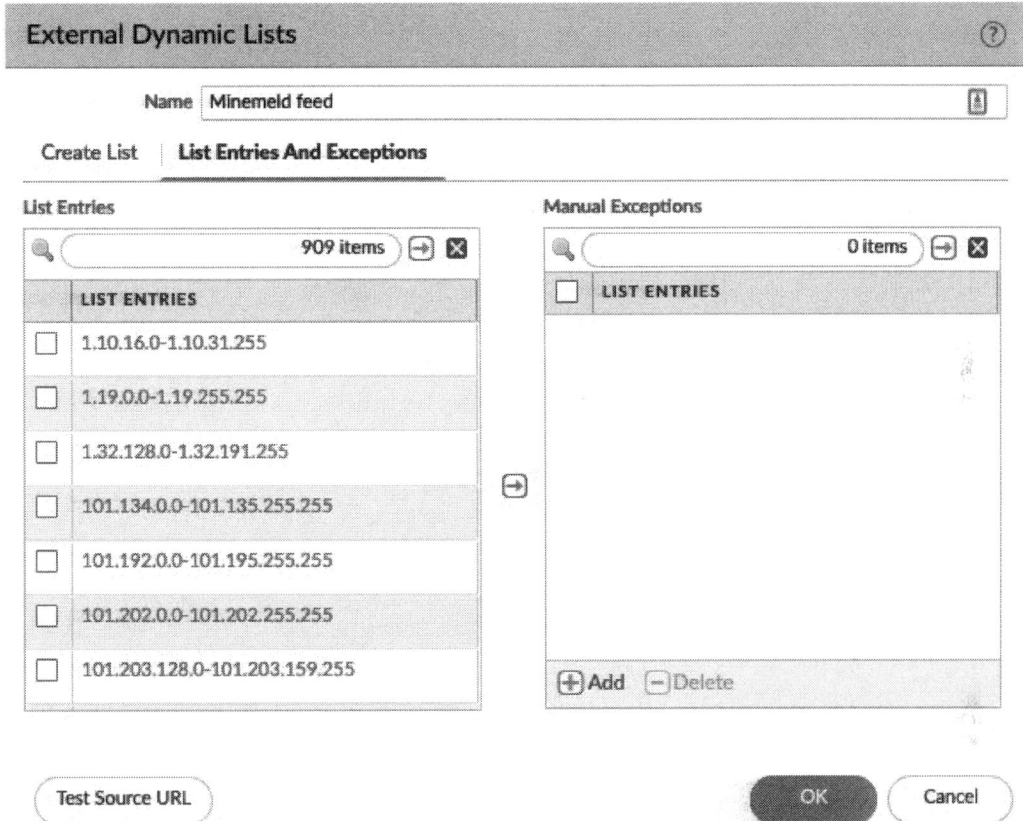

Figure 13.23 – Reviewing and adding exceptions to an EDL

You can also verify the state of the EDL from the command line with the following command:

```
reaper@PA-220request system external-list stats type ip name
"Minemeld feed"


vsys1/Minemeld feed:
        Next update at         : Tue Jun 16 23:57:27 2020
        Source                 : https://192.168.27.242/feeds/
inboundfeedhc
        Referenced             : Yes
        Valid                  : Yes
        Auth-Valid             : Yes
```

You can now set up MineMeld and collect threat intelligence feeds from external parties. You can add additional miners and bind them to a processor so that the information becomes available in an output feed. You can also create EDLs and apply them to security rules.

In the next section, we'll learn how to access configuration and operational commands through the API.

# Exploring the API

The API is a universally compatible way of accessing the firewall and executing all sorts of commands, from extracting information to adding and updating runtime information or configuration. If you have external monitoring, you could automate adding blacklisted IPs on the firewall when a security event is triggered, or if an access point supports sending out API commands, it could update user-to-IP mapping on the firewall when a user logs on or off.

To be able to use the API, however, you will always need an API key to authenticate any remote sources making a connection to the firewall. You can generate a key using the following command from the terminal or command line:

```
curl -k -X GET 'https://<firewall>/
 api/?type=keygen&user=<username>&password=<password>'
```

Alternatively, you can search the following URL in a browser:

```
https://<firewall>/
api/?type=keygen&user=<username>&password=<password>
```

The output will look similar to the following:

```
<response status="success">
  <result>
    <key>LUFRPT14MW5xOEo1R09KV1BZNnpnemh0VHRBOW16TGM9bXcwM3FGA
fDSF4564EWdGSet
    </key>
  </result>
</response>
```

You can use `curl` (both GET and POST) from any terminal, or you can simply access the firewall's web interface using the URL to execute the API commands.

Adding `&key=<key>` after API commands will now authenticate the connection.

This key represents an admin account, so keep it just as safe as you would the password to the user account. If the account used is a superuser account, API access will also be granted elevated status. It is advisable to create a unique account for API operations and assign it an admin role that restricts access to everything except the required API options, as you can see in the following screenshot:

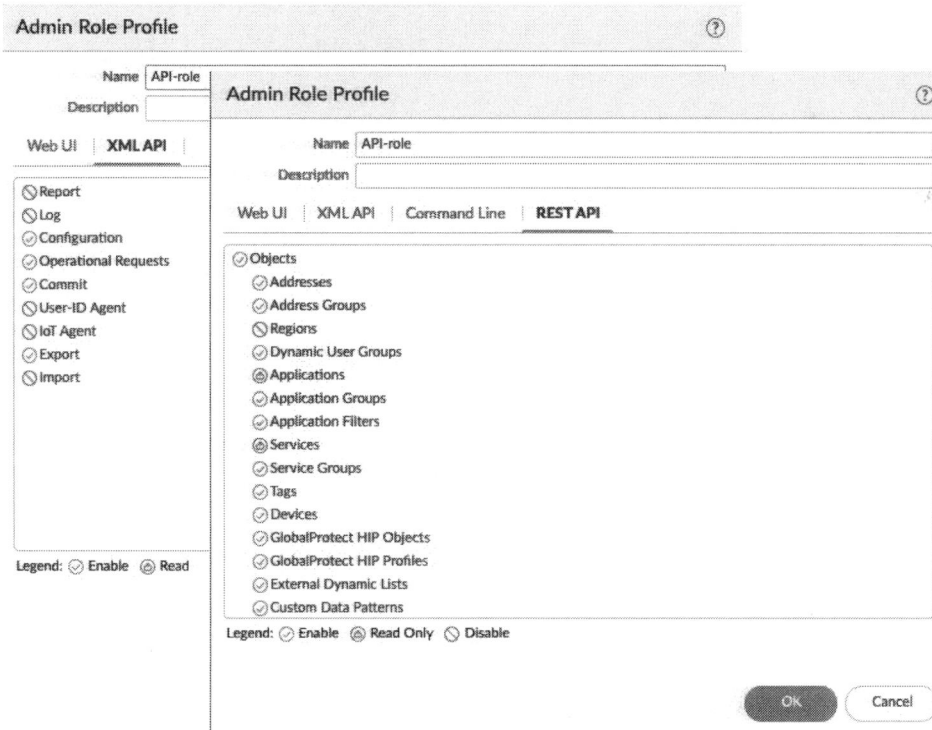

Figure 13.24 – API admin role

Here are a few common examples.

You can easily extract reports via the API so that you don't need to go in through the web interface:

```
https://192.168.27.2/api/?type=report&async=yes&reporttype=pred
efined&reportname=top-attacker-sources&key=LUFRPT14MW5xOEo1R09K
VlBZNnpnemh0VHRBOW16TGM9bXcwM3FGAfDSF4564EWdGSet
```

In the preceding command, I'm fetching a predefined report called `top-attacker-sources`. You can also retrieve custom reports.

You can also run a lot of CLI commands from the API, which lets you view a lot of the runtime statistics.

The following URLs, which you could also run via `curl` on the command line, will output CLI information directly in your browser, instead of needing to log on to the firewall.

You can view the logged-on administrators with the following API URL:

```
https://192.168.27.2/
api/?type=op&cmd=<show><admins></admins%></
show>&key=LUFRPT14MW5xOEo1R09KVlBZNnpnemh0VHRBOW16TGM9bXcwM3FGA
fDSF4564EWdGSet
```

Alternatively, you can review the currently known user-to-IP mappings:

```
https://192.168.27.2/api/?type=op&cmd=<show><user>
<user-ids><all></all></user-ids></user></show>&key=
LUFRPT14MW5xOEo1R09KVlBZNnpnemh0VHRBOW16TGM9bXcwM3FGAfDSF4564
EWdGSet
```

The following URL lets you see the logged-on GlobalProtect users:

```
https://192.168.27.2/api/?type=op&cmd=<show><global-protect-
gateway><current-user/></global-protect-gateway></show>&key=
LUFRPT14MW5xOEo1R09KVlBZNnpnemh0VHRBOW16TGM9bXcwM3
FGAfDSF4564EWdGSet
```

You can even disconnect GloblalProtect users using the following API URL:

```
https://192.168.27.2/api/?type=op&cmd=<request><global-protect
-gateway><client-logout><gateway>gateway</
gateway><user>reaper</user><reason>force-logout</reason<
```

```
/client-logout></global
-protect-gateway></request>&key=LUFRPT14MW5xOEo1R09KVlBZNnpnemh
0VHRBOW16TGM9bXcwM3FGAfDSF4564EWdGSet
```

From a monitoring perspective, you can quickly call up the current data plane load from an API call:

```
https://192.168.27.2/api/?type=op&cmd <show><running><resource-
monitor><minute></minute></resource-monitor></running></
show>&key=LUFRPT14MW5xOEo1R09KVlBZNnpnemh0VHRBOW16TGM9bXcwM3FGA
fDSF4564EWdGSet
```

If needed, you can collect the power supply, thermal, and board power stats:

```
https://192.168.27.2/api/?type=op&cmd=<show><system>
<environmentals></environmentals></system></
show>&key=LUFRPT14MW5xOEo1R09KVlBZNnpnemh0VHRBOW16TGM9bXcwM3FGA
fDSF4564EWdGSet
```

From a scripted operation perspective, a pretty cool trick is the following. If you have a second default route set with a higher metric, you can launch an API call to change the metric so that the backup route takes over when needed:

```
https://192.168.27.2/api?type=config&action=set&xpath=/
config/devices/entry[@name='localhost.localdomain']/network/
virtual-router/entry[@name='default']/routing-table/ip/static-
route/entry[@name=Second-Gateway']/metric&element=<metric>5</
metric>&key=LUFRPT14MW5xOEo1R09KVlBZNnpnemh0VHRBOW16TGM9bXcwM3
FGAfDSF4564EWdGSet
```

There are plenty of useful commands that can help set up remote monitoring or interact with configuration items. You can browse through the available API commands by navigating to the firewall (or Panorama) API interface at `https://<hostname>/api` and the REST API manual at `https://<hostname>/restapi-doc/`.

In this section, we learned about the API and a few simple tricks that can make life easier as you can use any browser or terminal that has `curl` installed to launch commands on a firewall.

# Summary

In this chapter, we reviewed a couple of handy tools that can be set up to augment an existing Syslog or SIEM solution. We looked at tools that provide an administrator with some quick and easy ways to perform and automate some management and monitoring tasks without needing to depend on cumbersome monitoring portals. You learned how to access the API section of the firewall and Panorama so that you can easily find the commands you need to set up automation. You are now also able to set up your very own threat intelligence server that can aggregate multiple data flows into easy-to-use security rule objects.

Congratulations, you made it to the end! I want to thank you for sticking with me all the way here. Hopefully, you've learned a lot and have been able to impress a few people left and right with your new skills. It is my sincere hope you thoroughly enjoyed reading this book and will keep it by your side as a trusted companion.

# Other Books You May Enjoy

If you enjoyed this book, you may be interested in these other books by Packt:

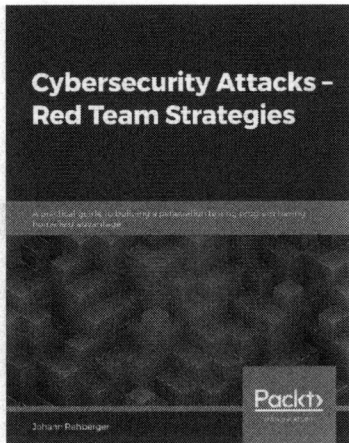

**Cybersecurity Attacks – Red Team Strategies**

Johann Rehberger

ISBN: 978-1-83882-886-8

- Understand the risks associated with security breaches
- Implement strategies for building an effective penetration testing team
- Map out the homefield using knowledge graphs
- Hunt credentials using indexing and other practical techniques
- Gain blue team tooling insights to enhance your red team skills
- Communicate results and influence decision makers with appropriate data

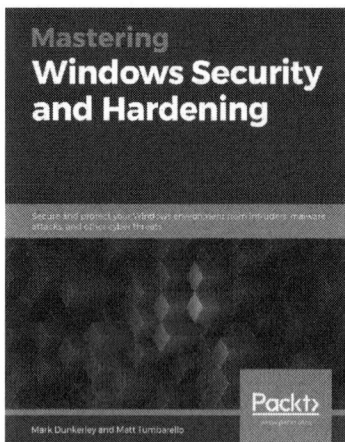

**Mastering Windows Security and Hardening**

Mark Dunkerley, Matt Tumbarello

ISBN: 978-1-83921-641-1

- Understand baselining and learn the best practices for building a baseline
- Get to grips with identity management and access management on Windows-based systems
- Delve into the device administration and remote management of Windows-based systems
- Explore security tips to harden your Windows server and keep clients secure
- Audit, assess, and test to ensure controls are successfully applied and enforced
- Monitor and report activities to stay on top of vulnerabilities

# Leave a review - let other readers know what you think

Please share your thoughts on this book with others by leaving a review on the site that you bought it from. If you purchased the book from Amazon, please leave us an honest review on this book's Amazon page. This is vital so that other potential readers can see and use your unbiased opinion to make purchasing decisions, we can understand what our customers think about our products, and our authors can see your feedback on the title that they have worked with Packt to create. It will only take a few minutes of your time, but is valuable to other potential customers, our authors, and Packt. Thank you!

# Index

# W

# X

# Z

Printed in Great Britain
by Amazon